Canadian Business Law

An Introduction to Business and Personal Law in Canada

ॐ **THIRD EDITION** ॐ

Canadian Business Law

An Introduction to Business and Personal Law in Canada

ᔭ THIRD EDITION ᓬ

Ernest Amirault, B.A., LL.B.

formerly Professor of Business Law, Ryerson Polytechnical Institute
Member of the Nova Scotia Bar

Maurice Archer, B.Sc. (Econ.), M.A.

Professor of Business Management, Ryerson Polytechnical Institute

With the collaboration of:

Gregory J. Sheehan, B.A., LL.B.
Professor of Business Law, Sheridan College of
Applied Arts and Technology
Member of the Ontario Bar

⬣ METHUEN

Toronto   New York   London   Sydney   Auckland

Canadian Cataloguing in Publication Data
    Amirault, Ernest J.
        Canadian business law

    Includes indexes.
    ISBN 0-458-99100-7

    1. Commercial law—Canada.   I. Archer,
    Maurice   II. Title.

KE919.A45 1986   346.71′07   C85-099949-9

Printed and bound in Canada by John Deyell Company
    2   3   4   5   91   90   89   88   87

Contents

Preface

This third edition of *Canadian Business Law* has retained the order and format of the previous edition. However, several of the longer chapters have been divided into self-contained units to make the study of the text material more manageable. Also, the complete text has been updated and, where appropriate, revised and simplified.

In Part 1 of the book, we begin with a discussion of the nature and origins of the law in Canada. This is followed with a review of the system of civil courts and the litigation procedure used therein; crime and the criminal courts; and finally the law of tort—the law that governs private wrongs such as physical injury or property damage committed by one person against another.

In Part 2 of the book, we examine the law of contract—the principles that govern agreements voluntarily entered into by ordinary people and business firms in the course of their daily activities.

In Part 3 of the book, we look at the legal forms of business ownership. Then, in Part 4, we examine the legal implications of buying, owning, mortgaging, and leasing real estate, for either business or personal use. The legal factors involved in employing other persons or working for someone else, and in employing an agent or working as one, are discussed in Part 5.

In Part 6, we consider, from both the producer's and the consumer's points of view, the laws that govern the marketing of goods and services, covering such topics as the sale of goods, product liability, restrictive trade practices, false or misleading advertising, and consumer protection. We also look at the law governing patents and trademarks and the law governing bailment—a contract in which the owner of a good temporarily entrusts it to someone else, for cleaning, repair, safekeeping, and so on.

Finally, in Part 7, we examine the laws that govern financial transactions in Canada—negotiable instruments, consumer credit, credit reporting and invasion of privacy, business and personal insurance, and bankruptcy.

The first edition of this book was published in 1976; since that time it has been widely used in Canada as an introductory law text at the first- and second-year college and university level—not only for business students but also for students in office and administrative studies, fashion, home economics, electrical and other technologies, and in various other non-law programs.

There appear to have been three reasons for the book's success. First, despite its title, it covers a broad spectrum of the law; hence the subtitle *An Introduction to Business and Personal Law in Canada.* Second, the book, although containing a generous amount of legal fact and opinion, is considered to be relatively easy to read and understand and, because of the variety of factual examples provided, able to capture and hold the reader's interest. Third, the abundance of review questions, problems, readings, and

synopses of key statutes at the end of chapters appears to have greatly facilitated the learning process.

As we said in the preface to the first edition, the study of law, even for those
not planning a legal career, has proven to be a valuable academic pursuit for
many generations of college and university students. This is because the
law, in its broadest sense, is an important part of our culture. And without
some knowledge of it, we cannot properly understand the society in which
we live, nor function effectively in our personal lives and in the careers that
we pursue. Also, since the ability to reason is an important goal of any type
of education, the study of law is an important means to this end; in fact, few
subjects are better suited for the sharpening of a person's wits.

This new edition of *Canadian Business Law* has benefited from the collaboration of Gregory Sheehan of Sheridan College who read the entire
manuscript and made numerous suggestions for its improvement—just as
the previous edition benefited from the collaboration of Ronald Flom and
Victoria Russell, both active members of the Ontario Bar. To them and all
the other lawyers, teachers, and students who have over the years made their
mark on this book, we gratefully extend our thanks.

ERNEST AMIRAULT
MAURICE ARCHER

To Pearl and Odette

1

Canada's Legal System

This first part of the book contains four chapters. In Chapter 1, we consider the nature and origins of our system of Canadian law. Next, in Chapter 2, we describe our system of civil courts and explain the procedure involved in making use of them. Then, in Chapter 3, we look at the principles of criminal law and the courts to which the offenders are brought. Finally, in Chapter 4, we examine the law of torts which governs civil wrongs committed by one person against another.

1

Nature and Origins of the Law

Unit 1.1
Different Types of Law

THE RULE OF LAW

A *law* is a rule or set of rules governing a person's conduct in society and is:
(a) enforced by the police or individuals themselves through the authority of
the courts of the land or, in certain cases, through specially appointed
administrative tribunals; and (b) accompanied by the imposition of a sanction on any person who fails to comply with it. The "sanction" imposed in
any particular case depends on the specific type of law that has been
violated. It may range from the imposition of a term of imprisonment or
other penalty in criminal cases, to a court order for the payment of damages
or the granting of some other remedy in civil lawsuits. This definition of
law excludes, therefore, such rules as those set by a business firm for the
conduct of its employees, or by a social club for its members.

The Legal System

A *legal system* consists of a body of law, which is interpreted and enforced by
the judicial system. The establishment and enforcement of laws are considered, by reasonable people, necessary for human beings to live harmoni-
ously together. In other words, a legal system is considered essential to the
existence of a stable society. The legal system performs a peacekeeping
function because laws are intended to be applied uniformly to all persons in
society regardless of such factors as social class or political affiliation.

If the legal system is to fulfil its purpose of helping to ensure both a stable
and a just society, there must be some mechanism or process whereby it can
be changed. This mechanism, in our type of society, has two parts. First,
judges interpreting the laws in the courts take into account, to some extent,
society's changing views—for example, views on what constitutes immoral
conduct. Second, and more important, the parliaments that are elected to
represent the people that make up society have the power to make written
laws, or *statutes*, that replace any existing common law. To the extent that
Parliament reflects the will of the people, the laws of a country can keep
pace with the needs of its inhabitants. If a society does not have a demo-
cratically elected system of government, then its legal system may soon be at
variance with the wishes and needs of its members and may even become an
instrument of oppression. In such a case, the only relief may be *revolution*—
the overthrow of the existing political system.

Purpose of the Law

Although the peacekeeping function has always been important, laws have been designed at one time or another for many other purposes—for example, the protection of people, property and goods; upholding public morals; maintaining the privileged position of a ruling, land-owning class; and promoting social justice. From the business point of view, laws have also been established to regulate business transactions and to facilitate the acquisition and ownership of property.

Law and Justice

Most laws are intended to coincide with our sense of public fairness or moral justice. In practice, this does not always turn out to be the case. Thus a judge who is bound to a strict interpretation of the law may, for example, uphold a creditor's rights even though they may have been established unfairly; or the court may, because of expropriation statutes, permit the government to seize a person's land.

A person who considers a law to be unjust may be tempted to break it, as evidenced throughout history. Why obey unjust laws—perhaps devised to oppress certain segments of the population—or laws that have not kept up with the times? One powerful argument for obeying the law is that if each person, as a matter of conscience, had the right to decide which laws to obey (for example, traffic laws) society would become chaotic. However, if a larger number of people feels that a law should not be obeyed because it is clearly unjust or impractical, then they reach the point where they must re-examine or alter the law. This does not mean that because a law is unpopular (for example, the Income Tax Act), it is also always unjust.

Underlying our western sense of justice is the notion of *natural law* as contrasted with human-made law. Natural law stems, according to one body of thought, from our religious beliefs, notably Judeo-Christian teachings. According to another view, its roots lie within people themselves, and their natural sense of reason. Whatever the origin, natural law is considered to embody human moral principles. Ideally, human-made law should reflect this natural law.

Business Law

The term *business law* refers to laws of special interest and concern to business firms. The most important of these laws is the *law of contract*—the rules that govern voluntary agreements between different persons or firms or between business firms and members of the public. Another important law affecting business is the *law of torts*—the rules that govern civil wrongs committed by one person against another—for example, injury caused to a consumer by the sale of a dangerous product by a business firm. In this country, there is also a whole range of laws passed by the federal and provincial governments to regulate the activities of business firms.

Business activity requires as a prerequisite the existence of "law and order" in society. In Canada we have a Criminal Code setting out the

various criminal offences and their punishments. We also have a system of
judges, courts, police forces and prisons to help ensure that the criminal law
is enforced.

THE COMMON LAW

After the Norman conquest of England in 1066, a system of touring judges
was gradually set up. These judges, or King's Justices, travelled the country-
side and held sittings, or *assizes*, to deal with all the civil and criminal
offences that had occurred in each area. These judges were instrumental in
establishing law and order, or what was called the *rule of law*, throughout
the Kingdom.

Rule of Precedent

After the King's Justices had dealt with a number of cases, their decisions or
"judgments" were followed in later, similar disputes. Eventually, any
previous judgments, called "precedents," became binding on judges of
equal or junior rank so long as the similarity of facts could be proved. This
principle was known as *stare decisis*—a Latin term meaning "to stand by
previous decisions."

The King's Justices learned of the precedents either by word of mouth or
by case reports which were written in those days by the law clerks or student
lawyers. This practice has continued down to the professional court reporting of today. Cases decided as far back as the thirteenth and fourteenth
centuries—and still in books in law libraries—have contributed to the legal
principles that guide our judges in making their decisions today. The
reports of the early trials were placed together in what were known as the
"yearbooks."

The role of the judge, it should be emphasized, is to follow precedent as
much as possible, not to make new law. Thus, as Justice Hogg in *R. v.
Morris*, [1942] O.W.N. 447 at p. 448, remarked:

> The trial judge disregarded the judgment of cases in point, as being
> obsolete and as not good law. It was hardly necessary to say that the
> function of the judge is not to make law. This is the function of the
> legislature, and the trial judge is, of course, bound by the decision in
> point, of a court of higher jurisdiction, and also of a court of co-
> ordinate jurisdiction except in the most special circumstances.

Common Law Defined

Common law, also called case law, is the body of legal principles, based on
the *rule of precedent* just discussed, set out in the thousands of court
decisions that have been reported in England and later in other common law
countries, including Canada, over the last 800 years. The use of the term
"common" derives from the fact that this law was common to the whole
country as compared with local or regional custom. The common law,
originating in England, was the one that the English colonial judges

applied in Canada, with the exception of Quebec where French private law was used.

Common law is also the basis of the present law in the United States, Australia, New Zealand, India, Pakistan, Hong Kong, and other countries that once formed part of the British Empire. As explained later, this common law is supplemented or replaced in parts by what is known as statute law, as the result of legislation passed by the various parliaments and legislatures.

Origins of the Common Law
The common law has various origins:

(a) *Tribal Customs*. Many ancient customs of the land were adopted by the English courts because these customs were traditionally respected and usually based on sound common sense. One example is the custom of allowing three days' delay in making payments of money owing. These days are called "days of grace."

(b) *Roman Influence*. After the Roman conquest of England in 55 B.C., Roman law prevailed until the fourth century A.D., and present common law in such areas as master and servant, adoption of children, trusteeship and bankruptcy still reflects the Roman influence.

(c) *Norman Influence*. This followed the Norman conquest in 1066 (e.g., the words "tort" meaning harm, and "assizes" meaning sittings of the judges).

(d) *Canon Law*. The Church developed its own set of laws affecting the people—clergy and non-clergy—within its jurisdiction. Important areas of later influence on the common law were the law of marriage, the law of wills, and the law of intestate succession. In the field of contracts, the Church made a substantial contribution to common law with the Christian concept of good faith. As many of the greatest fairs and their courts were controlled by the Church, there was every opportunity to enforce the Church's belief, for example, that a promise made by one person to another and received in good faith should be enforceable.

(e) *Law Merchant*. In the Middle Ages merchants, often travelling from town to town and country to country, usually could not afford to wait for the ordinary common law courts to settle a legal dispute. Also, the disputes in which the merchants were involved were of a predominantly commercial character. Consequently, they were usually accorded special treatment by the reigning monarchs of Europe, being granted their own separate system of courts which came to administer a recognized body of business law.

(f) *Law of Equity*. This is explain below.

Law of Equity
During the Middle Ages it became evident that the King's Justices, by slavishly following precedents in the common law courts, sometimes rendered harsh judgments. Consequently the King, and later his Chan-

cellor, while recognizing the authority of the common law courts, began to intervene to protect persons who might suffer particular hardship because of the inadequacies of the common law and its machinery of enforcement. This independent system of law, based on royal prerogative and administered by the King's Chancellor to "temper the harsh common law," came to be called *equity*. It was administered in a separate set of courts known as courts of equity (or courts of chancery).

The remedies available in these equity courts included: *specific performance*, which requires the defendant to sell or return a unique item where money compensation would not be satisfactory; *injunction*, which prohibits someone from doing something; *accounting*, which is an examination of the way in which funds have been used— and is sometimes ordered by the court in cases of funds administered by trustees, guardians, or partners where the beneficiary of a trust, a ward, or a partner, respectively, suspects some wrongdoing but lacks evidence; and *foreclosure of mortgage* whereby the court orders the transfer of the mortgaged property to the lender after many opportunities have been granted to the borrower to retrieve the property.

In the late nineteenth century, the common law courts and the equity courts were combined into one system. Consequently, judges now have the right to apply an equitable remedy if they feel a situation warrants it. Equity was developed to provide fairer remedies not available in the common law courts, where monetary compensation for injury suffered (*damages*) was regarded as the usual remedy for breach of contract.

Trial By Jury

During the Middle Ages, the principle that a person had the right to a trial by jury also became firmly established. A *jury* is a group of persons, theoretically unbiased in their views and unconnected with the Crown, who listen to the facts of a case and declare the accused innocent or guilty of the charges brought against him or her. This system is still used in many civil and criminal cases, depending on the gravity of the offence (or claim). Often the accused has a choice of being tried with or without a jury.

CIVIL LAW

At the same time that England was developing its system of common law, the countries of continental Europe were developing a system of their own. This *civil law*, as it came to be known, now applies throughout continental Europe, most of Scotland, many African countries, all of Central and South America, Mexico, Louisiana in the United States, and Quebec in Canada. The right to continue using French private law, a form of civil law, was guaranteed to the people of Quebec by the Quebec Act in 1774.

The main characteristic of the civil law is that a judge will settle a dispute according to the principles laid down in a country's code of law—a written statute specifying the legal rights and obligations of citizens. If the code does not specifically cover the point in dispute, the judge will try to apply the general principles of justice set out therein. A judge is not bound by earlier decisions in similar cases. However, for reasons of fairness, most judges operating under a system of civil law do try to be consistent in their decisions with those made previously.

The term civil law is also used, it should be noted, to refer to private law as compared with criminal law.

CODIFICATION

From time to time, the rulers of various countries have summarized in written form the existing body of law. The earliest known example of this codification is the Babylonian law that King Hammurabi had engraved about 2100 B.C. on a green basalt rock. A more recent example is Justinian's Code, a comprehensive summary of the laws of Rome, ordered by Justinian, the head of the Eastern Roman Empire, in the sixth century A.D. Another was the French Civil Code, or Code Napoleon, ordered to be drawn up by the French Emperor Napoleon in 1804.

Many common law countries have also adopted the idea of codification. Thus Parliaments in Canada and elsewhere have passed laws that embody not only newly made rules but also ones that have existed in the common law for many years. At the federal level, the Bills of Exchange Act, for example, consolidated all previous court decisions on negotiable instruments. At the provincial level, the Partnerships Act embodied all the existing law on partnerships; the Sale of Goods Act, all the law on the sale of goods.

REVIEW QUESTIONS

1. What is meant by the term "law"? How does a law differ from other types of regulation?
2. Why are laws usually obeyed?
3. Explain the nature and purpose of a "legal system." How does it keep up with the times?
4. What are the various purposes of the law?
5. What role should moral factors play in the formulation of laws?
6. Why obey laws that you may consider unjust? How can such laws be fully changed?
7. Does society have a duty to help prevent people from harming themselves (drug abuse, for example)?
8. What is meant by the term "business law"?
9. What is "common law"? Where is it in use?
10. What role does precedent play in common law?
11. What were the origins of the common law?
12. How did the Church influence the development of common law?
13. Explain the nature and use of the law merchant, which existed during the Middle Ages.

14. Explain the nature and purpose of the law of equity. What equitable remedies now exist?
15. Who were the King's Justices? How did they contribute to the development of the rule of law?
16. What is meant by "trial by jury"?
17. Explain and discuss the two different meanings of the term "civil law."
18. What is meant by "codification"? Give examples. What was its purpose?

APPENDIX 1-A: LEGAL CITATIONS

The purpose of this appendix is to explain briefly the system of abbreviations or "legal citations" that is used in law to refer to the large and ever-growing number of case reports in Canada and elsewhere. Such a system enables a judge, lawyer, or student of the law to locate fairly quickly in a law library the case that he or she is interested in reading more about.

The citation used for a case has a standard format as in the following example:

Walmsley v. Humenick, [1954] 2 D.L.R. 232

First comes Walmsley, the name of the *plaintiff*, the person who is bringing the lawsuit.

Second, the letter *v.*, standing for "versus," which indicates that a legal action is being brought against someone. If spoken aloud, one would say "and" or "against" rather than "versus," as in "Walmsley *and* Humenick."

Third, we have Humenick, the name of the *defendant*, the person being sued.

One *exception* to this standard format for case reports relates to the decisions of *appeal courts*, particularly in the United Kingdom. Usually, it is the party that brings the appeal, called the "appellant," who appears first. As this may be either the plaintiff or the defendant at the previous trial, the names may be reversed from those of the trial court report. Thus, if Humenick lost the case and went to the appeal court, its decision would be cited as *Humenick v. Walmsley*. In the appeal case, Walmsley would be known as the "respondent."

Another *exception* occurs where one party, instead of suing the other, is asking for some remedy other than monetary damages—for example, a petition to have a court order set aside. In such a case, only the one name appears, preceded by the term "Re"—for example, *Re Kendall* (1973), 9 D.L.R. (3d) 351.

The fourth thing to appear in the *Walmsley v. Humenick* citation is the year, 1954. If the brackets are round, as in (1954), then 1954 means the year in which the judge made the decision. If the brackets are square, as in this case, then 1954 means the year in which the volume of law reports containing the case was published. In addition, if the brackets are square, one must use the year as the reference to find the desired volume of the law report. Within that given year there will normally be more than one volume. One then chooses the volume desired. Normally, both years are the same. However, a differ-ence will arise if a case is decided towards the end of one year and not published until the next. The year in square brackets also indicates that knowing the year is necessary in order to find that particular volume, which may not be otherwise numbered. If the brackets are round, the book sought usually has an identifying volume number like "65."

The remainder of the citation denotes the number and edition of the volume, and page number, of the law reports in which the decision appears. In our example, this is Volume 2 of the [1954] Dominion Law Reports, beginning on page 232. Sometimes an indication of the series will appear after the volume citation; for example, (3d) means the third series.

The following is an alphabetical list of the abbreviations for well-used common law reports and various courts.

A.C.	Appeal Cases (England)
All E.R.	All England Reports
Alta. L.R.	Alberta Law Reports
B.C.R.	British Columbia Reports
B.L.R.	Business Law Reports (Canada)
C.B.R.	Canadian Bankruptcy Reports
Co. Ct.	County Court
C.C.C.	Canadian Criminal Cases
C.P.	Common Pleas
C.P.D.	Common Pleas Division
Ch.	Chancery
Ch.D.	Chancery Division
Ch.R.	Chancery Reports (England)
C.R.	Criminal Reports (Canada)
Dist. Ct.	District Court
D.L.R.	Dominion Law Reports (Canada)
E.R.	English Reports
E.L.R.	Eastern Law Reports (Canada)
Ex.	Exchequer
Ex. C.R.	Exchequer Court Reports (Canada)
F.C.	Federal Court; Federal Court Reports (Canada)
H.C.J.	High Court of Justice
H.L.	House of Lords
J.C.P.C.	Judicial Committee of the Privy Council
K.B.	King's Bench
L.Q.R.	Law Quarterly Review (England)
M.P.R.	Maritime Provinces Reports
N.B.R.	New Brunswick Reports
N.S.R.	Nova Scotia Reports
O.L.R.	Ontario Law Reports
O.R.	Ontario Reports
O.W.N.	Ontario Weekly Notes

Prov. Ct.	Provincial Court
Q.B.	Queen's Bench
Q.P.R.	Quebec Practice Reports
Rev.d.J.	La Revue de Jurisprudence (Quebec)
R.P.R.	Real Property Reports (Canada)
S.C.C.	Supreme Court of Canada
S.C.Q.	Supreme Court of Quebec
S.C.R.	Supreme Court Reports (Canada)
U.C.Q.B.	Upper Canada Queen's Bench
W.C.B.	Workers' Compensation Board
W.W.R.	Western Weekly Reports (Canada)
W.L.R.	Western Law Reporter (Canada); Weekly Law Reports (England)

Unit 1.2
Divisions of the Law

SUBSTANTIVE AND PROCEDURAL LAW

The law, as it exists today, can also be divided for convenience into two basic types: substantive law and procedural law. *Substantive law* comprises common law decisions and Parliamentary statutes that specify a person's rights and duties in society—for example, the right to vote, to own property, or to enter into contracts. *Procedural law* (also called *administrative law*) indicates how the rights set out in the substantive law are to be protected and the duties to be enforced. Thus, many Acts of Parliament are now accompanied by separate Rules and Regulations. The former is substantive law; the latter is procedural law.

PRIVATE LAW

The legal principles that comprise substantive law may in turn be divided into private law and public law.

The term *private law* (also called *civil law*) refers to laws that govern the relations between private individuals or groups of such individuals. One major type of private law is the *law of obligations*. This law is based on the fact that every person in society has obligations to fellow citizens. These obligations are of two types: those imposed by society and those which are assumed voluntarily. With the first type, for example, we are prohibited by the *law of torts* from trespassing on another person's land, from damaging another person's reputation, or otherwise injuring our fellow citizens. If we ignore such obligations, we are considered to have committed a *tort* (or "wrong" in French) and are liable to be sued for damages. With the second type we may voluntarily enter into an agreement or contract with other persons—for example, to rent a house or apartment. If we do not fulfil such an obligation, we are also liable to be sued, but under the law of contract. Another major type of private law is the *law of property*. Property, in the legal sense, comprises: (a) land and buildings—called real property or immovable property; and (b) goods—called personal property, movables, or chattels. The law of property provides for the settlement of disputes in a variety of matters related to property.

PUBLIC LAW

The term *public law* refers to laws that apply to the public as a whole or to certain segments of it. The main types of public law are briefly explained below.

Criminal Law. This is the law that permits the government to arrest and impose penalties on members of the public who intentionally commit illegal acts known as crimes. Canada's criminal law is now set out in a federal statute, the Criminal Code (although other federal and provincial statutes also provide criminal penalties).

Administrative Law. These are the regulations laid down with statutory authority by various government ministries and agencies and in many cases enforced by special government-appointed courts, or *administrative tribunals*.

Martial Law. These are the rules established in time of public emergency and administered by the military authorities. One example would be a curfew after dark; another, the prohibition of public meetings. Martial law applies when the military takes over the government, as in a *coup d'etat*.

Military Law. These are the rules imposed on members of the armed forces in addition to normal legal obligations.

Constitutional Law. These are the laws which govern our system of government.

International Law. These are the rules derived from international treaties, agreements, or customs that normally govern the relations between different countries in such matters as peace, war, and neutrality; territorial waters; fishing rights; air space; and extradition.

STATUTE LAW

The various laws passed by a Parliament (in Canada, the federal Parliament and the provincial legislatures) are together known as *statute law*. A statute may override the common law precedent concerning the matter. If there is a conflict between the two, the judge may ignore the statute if it does not specifically cover the matter in dispute. This is known as the "strict interpretation" of statute law.

In Canada, to bring a new federal statute (Act of Parliament) into being,

Figure 1.1: The Major Divisions of the Law

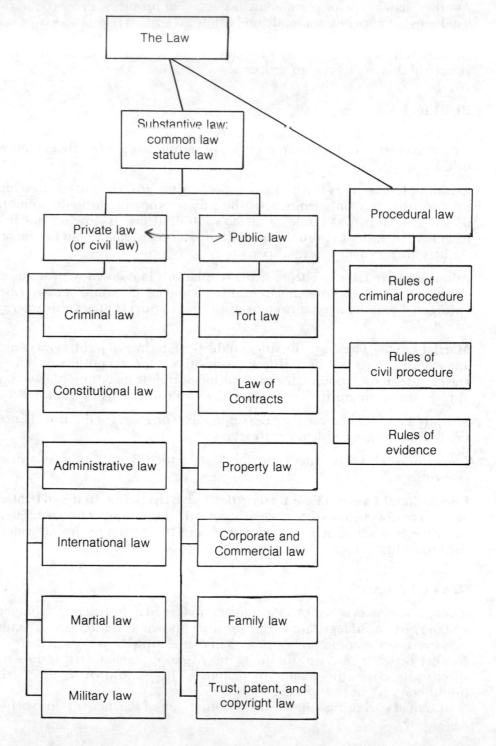

the federal government must first pass a bill through the House of Commons, then through the Senate, and finally have it signed by the Governor General, the Queen's representative. Provincial legislatures follow a similar procedure, with the Lieutenant Governor representing the Queen. Each provincial legislature delegates authority to the various municipal governments within the province to enact zoning, parking, health, and other bylaws. Although many statutes have been enacted, much of Canada's private law (particularly the law of contracts) still consists of common law. Usually, however, it is a mixture of both statute and common law.

Sections 91 and 92 of the Constitution Act, 1867 (previously called the British North America Act, 1867), allocate powers to pass laws between the federal Parliament on the one hand and the provincial legislatures on the other (see Appendix 1-B).

Primary and Subordinate Legislation

The term *primary legislation* is used to refer to the various Acts of the federal Parliament and provincial legislatures. However, these Acts confer powers on various specially created administrative bodies (like marketing boards) to establish rules and regulations that are necessary for implementation of the Act. These rules are known as *subordinate legislation.*

REVIEW QUESTIONS

1. Distinguish between substantive law and procedural law.
2. What are the various types of private law?
3. What are the various types of public law?
4. What is meant by statute law? How does it relate to common law?
5. Explain the term "strict interpretation."
6. How does a statute come into existence?
7. Distinguish between primary and subordinate legislation.

READING

Re Horan and Minister of Natural Resources (1974), 3 O.R. (2d) 533 (Div. Ct).

Facts: Mr. Horan, who was granted a licence on July 25, 1972, to open a quarry in Peel County, was given notice on February 9, 1973, of a proposal to revoke such licence on the following grounds:

(1) the licensee had not published notice of his application for a licence pursuant to the regulations;
(2) the applicant had been grossly inaccurate in his estimation of the volume of material being removed from the pit both preceding and following the application;
(3) unlicensed operators were permitted to remove material;

(4) operations were carried out too close to the CN railway line, contrary to regulations;

(5) although the application showed traffic to be proceeding to the west, it was in fact proceeding to the south.

When the case appeared before the Board on September 20, 1973, the Township of Caledon and seven ratepayers applied to be represented by counsel. The Board allowed this and was prepared to hear from any other parties on any other matter with respect to the issue. Counsel for the licensee objected that the only evidence which should be allowed must relate to the Minister's grounds for revocation. The Board ruled that any evidence pertinent to the issue would be admitted. At the request of counsel for the licensee, the matter was referred to the Divisional Court for a ruling as to whether, under a hearing pursuant to s. 9 of the Pits and Quarries Act, all evidence relating to the issues may be heard even if not relevant to the reasons set out in the Minister's notice re revocation of a licence.

Held: Section 6(1) of the Act provides that the Minister may refuse a licence under the Pits and Quarries Act where the plan does not comply with the Act or the regulations or if it is against the public interest on questions of environment, traffic density, effect on water table, nature of local land use, and character of nearby communities.

While the Board is ordered to hold a hearing as to whether a licence should be issued or revoked, s. 9 provides that all interested parties may be represented and there is no restriction on the matters that may be heard; thus the Board is not restricted to specific points set out by the Minister's revocation.

Section 9(4) provides that the Board merely acts as a fact-finding body and the Minister has thirty days after receiving the Board's report to give a decision to the licensee and such decision shall be final. Thus the entire problem in this case rests on the interpretation of the Act as to the scope of the hearing by the Board.

Comment: This case is included to point out the following facts:

1. That there is a tremendous number of regulations and rules which form part of a body of administrative law generally providing for the administration of many Acts.
2. That the Board, in this case, was required to act as a finder of fact; that is, were the Minister's reasons valid or was there any other detrimental environmental impact?
3. The Minister's decision under the Act is final.
4. All appeals in Ontario from administrative tribunals are taken to the Divisional Court.
5. The Divisional Court would undoubtedly interfere on a mistake of law but normally will not alter a finding of fact unless totally it is unsupported by the evidence.

Unit 1.3:
Canada's Constitution

THE CONSTITUTION ACT, 1982

In 1981, the federal Parliament passed a bill called the Canada Act that requested the British Parliament to approve a new constitution for Canada. The statute, passed by the British Parliament, was entitled the Constitution Act, 1982, and, in accordance with the status of Canada as an independent state, gave the Canadian Parliament rather than the British Parliament the sole right to amend the Canadian constitution in the future. It also provided for the recognition of various fundamental rights and freedoms, as incorporated in a Canadian Charter of Rights and Freedoms. Under the new Act, the British North America Act, 1867, was renamed the Constitution Act, 1867.

THE CONSTITUTION ACT, 1867

This statute forms the main part of Canada's political constitution—a confederation consisting of a federal Parliament and a number of provincial legislatures—with powers divided between them in a specified way.

Section 91 of that Act (see Appendix 1-B) lists the legislative powers given exclusively to Canada's federal Parliament. These include the regulation of trade and commerce, banking, bills of exchange and promissory notes, interest, bankruptcy and insolvency, and patents of invention and discovery. Section 92 lists the powers allotted to the provinces. These powers include the licensing of shops and other businesses, the incorporation of companies with provincial purposes, and property and civil rights in the province. Municipal governments, being established by provincial authority, are delegated powers by that government.

Other parts of Canada's constitution include other British statutes such as the Constitution Act, 1931 (previously called the Statute of Westminster, 1931) and certain fundamental Canadian Acts, such as those creating the provinces of Alberta, Manitoba, and Saskatchewan.

THE CANADIAN CHARTER OF RIGHTS AND FREEDOMS

In 1960, the federal Parliament, on the initiative of Prime Minister John Diefenbaker, passed an Act called the *Canadian Bill of Rights*, setting out in writing the fundamental human rights of persons resident in Canada. This was designed to overcome the glaring omission of such a guarantee in the British North America Act, 1867. However, the Constitution Act, 1982, went much further in guaranteeing fundamental human rights for persons resident in Canada by including in the Constitution a *Canadian Charter of Rights and Freedoms*.

Since the end of World War II and with the urging of the United Nations, Canada has been at the forefront of countries that desire to ensure basic freedoms and non-discrimination among its citizens. Because of the federal nature of the country, this has been more difficult to guarantee than would appear—for example, employment and accommodation, being local and private matters, are under provincial control and therefore require provincial laws. In fact, it took approximately twenty years between the time Canada started to implement the United Nations Charter of Rights until all the provinces had implemented legislation to protect persons from various types of discrimination.

Key features of the federally legislated Canadian Charter of Rights and Freedoms are as follows:

(a) rights and freedoms are guaranteed up to limits justified in a free and democratic society;

(b) Fundamental Freedoms include religion, conscience, thought, belief, opinion, expression, press, other media, free association, and peaceful assembly;

(c) citizens may move about anywhere in Canada subject to depressed areas being able to insist on a *residents-first* hiring policy;

(d) legal rights include the rights now guaranteed under criminal law, such as the right to be informed of reasons for arrest, to retain counsel, and to be tried without delay;

(e) at the federal level there must be no discrimination because of race, national or ethnic origin, colour, religion, sex, age, mental or physical disability;

(f) French and English are proclaimed the official languages with the right to be educated in either language where there is at least a 10% minority;

(g) rights of native peoples proclaimed in 1763 are protected;

(h) all governments in Canada must promote equal opportunities for all Canadians, endeavour to reduce economic disparity, and provide essential public services; and

(i) the Constitution may be amended only by a resolution of the House of Commons and the Senate and approved by two-thirds of the provinces containing at least 50% of the population of Canada.

REVIEW QUESTIONS

1. Explain the nature and purpose of the Constitution Act, 1982.
2. What is the Constitution Act, 1867? Why is it considered by some to be unsuitable for modern Canada?
3. Summarize the content and purpose of Section 91 of the above Act.
4. What did Section 92 of that Act state?
5. What other statutes form part of Canada's constitution?
6. What have been the main obstacles to constitutional reform in Canada?
7. What was the Canadian Bill of Rights?
8. What is the Canadian Charter of Rights and Freedoms? To whom does it apply?
9. What are the Fundamental Freedoms listed in the Charter?

10. What legal rights is a person guaranteed by the Charter?
11. How may Canada's constitution be amended, if necessary, in the future?
12. Discuss the amending formula found in the Canadian Charter of Rights, particularly its protecting effect on the Constitution.

PROBLEMS

1. A Canadian native Indian named Drybones was charged and convicted of being drunk in a public place, contrary to the provisions of the federal Indian Act. It was objected, during an appeal on his behalf, that the Indian Act made Indians subject to a different law from other Canadians who would have been charged under the appropriate Provincial Liquor Licence Acts for a similar infraction. Discuss this case in the light of your understanding of Canadian laws dealing with discrimination. Suppose Drybones had been refused employment because he was under 18 years of age: would this have been discrimination in your province?

2. In the 1980s, six employees of an Ontario manufacturing business brought complaints of harrassment against their foreman. These complaints involved requests for sexual favours, sexual touching, and threats of firing or non-attractive jobs unless such requests were granted. Under which Act or Acts should such complaints be proceeded with under our federal system of government? Which level of government should normally have jurisdiction? Give at least three examples involving the operations of the Human Rights Commission in your province.

3. One province passed legislation that provided that, if it was proven in Court that Communist literature was being distributed from a certain house or building, such premises could be closed completely for a period of one year. The owner of such a building who was convicted of distributing Communist literature appealed against his conviction under this Act on the grounds that it was a conviction for a criminal offence. Can you conceive of any jurisdictional grounds which would allow a Court of Appeal to overturn such conviction?

4. The Province of Ontario proposed to appoint a rentalsman or Provincial Official who would be empowered to deal with all complaints involving the rental of residential real property now deemed to be the exclusive prerogative of District Court Judges appointed by the federal government under the Constitution Act, 1867. To date, no further action has been taken to implement this law. Can you think of any reasons against the appointment and authority of such an official?

READINGS

Re Field Aviation Co. Ltd. and International Association of Machinists & Aerospace Workers, Local Lodge 1579 (1974), 49 D.L.R. (3d) 234 (Alta. C.A.).

Facts: Local Lodge 1579 applied to the Board of Industrial Relations of Alberta for certification as a bargaining agent for all non-managerial personnel of Field Aviation Company Limited. The Board certified the union. The Company appealed on the grounds that the company operations came under federal rather than provincial jurisdiction. The trial judge found that the labour relations of the company with its employees was a matter coming within the legislative authority of Canada and thus beyond the jurisdiction of the Board. The union appealed.

Held per Sinclair J.A.:

The basic approach to be taken . . . is that described by Ritchie J. . . . : "It has been accepted, at least since the case of *Toronto Electric Commissioners v. Snider*, [1925] 2 D.L.R. 5 that . . . legislation respecting employer and employee relations relates to property and civil rights and is therefore within the exclusive jurisdiction of the provincial legislature, but . . . it is not within the competency of a provincial legislature to legislate concerning industrial relations of persons employed in a work, business or undertaking coming within the exclusive jurisdiction of the Parliament of Canada."

. . . [T]he Canada Labour Code [that is, the successor Act of the Industrial Relations and Dispute Investigation Act, S.C. 1948, c.54] ". . . should not be construed to apply to employees who are employed at remote stages, but only to those whose work is intimately connected with the work, undertaking or business."

[There were 82 items of work carried on by the company outside of Alberta, including salvage, repairs, repair estimates, etc. Thus the Calgary based operations of the Company could not be said to come under s. 92(10)(a) of the British North America Act, 1867, ". . . other Works and Undertakings connecting the Province with any other or others of the Provinces or extending beyond the Limits of the Province," because of the limited amount of jobs done outside the province.]

. . . [I]n the words of Lord Reid in *C.P.R. v. A.G.B.C.*, [1950] 1 D.L.R. 721, [1950] A.C. 122. . . . at p. 730 D.L.R., p. 142 A.C.: "The latter part of the paragraph makes it clear that the object of the paragraph is to deal with matters of interprovincial communication."

. . . [S.]92(10)(a) has no application to the situation at hand.

. . . [What] effect, if any, [is] to be given to the Aeronautics Act, R.S.C. 1970, c.A-3, and to a number of Regulations and orders made thereunder[?]

In *Re Aerial Navigation; A.G. Can. v. A.G. Ont.*, [1932] 1 D.L.R. 58, the Privy Council decided that legislation with respect to aeronautics falls within the exclusive jurisdiction of the Parliament of Canada. . . .

[Mr. Justice Sinclair of the Alberta Supreme Court then considered an Ottawa letter dated September 28, 1971, which approved the Field Aviation Limited, Calgary, an Ontario incorporated company, registered in Alberta and carrying on its business from Calgary to exercise the privileges of an Aircraft Maintenance Engineer according to Air Navigation Order Series IV

No. 6 "A" and "B" category. The company approval number was 5-60. Many of the personnel whose names and qualifications were filed with and approved by the Department were members of the bargaining unit. Further, Air Regulations were also quoted which referred to the role of an aircraft maintenance engineer.]

After reading all of these Regulations and Orders, one is struck by the concern shown for ensuring proper standards of aircraft servicing, maintenance, inspection, modification, repair and overhaul. And one is impressed by the role played by aircraft maintenance engineers, a role linked to that played by flight crews and by air controllers, all of whom are involved in the safe operation of aircraft, and who are accordingly required to be licensed.

In my opinion the evidence discloses that the Calgary operations of Field Aviation Company Limited are so intimately connected with aeronautics as to constitute a work, business or undertaking coming within the exclusive jurisdiction of the Parliament of Canada. The services performed by the company, and accordingly by its employees, are an essential part of the field of aeronautics.

. . . [T]he appeal must be dismissed with costs.

Rocois Construction Inc. v. Quebec Ready Mix Inc. (F.C., December 4, 1979).

Facts: This was a test case on a 1976 amendment to the Combines Investigation Act, first legislated in 1889 against anticompetitive and unfair trade practices by making any such practices offences under the statute subject to criminal prosecution.

The 1976 amendment under s. 31.1 of the Combines Investigation Act allows someone who has suffered loss or damage as a result of conduct contrary to the Act to sue for and recover from the person who engaged in such unlawful conduct the loss or damaged proved to have been suffered.

The types of practices made illegal under the Act include price fixing, bid rigging, monopolies, price discrimination, misleading advertising, and resale price maintenance.

This case was the first challenge to the constitutional right to claim relief as provided in the 1976 amendment.

Held: The plaintiff and the Attorney General of Canada argued that the amendment to the legislation was validly enacted in that it was within the federal Parliament's powers either under the trade and commerce powers or the criminal law powers.

The defendants, Quebec Ready Mix Inc. and the Attorney General of Quebec, argued that the legislation was unconstitutional because it fell within the exclusive legislative authority reserved for the provinces either under property and civil rights or as a matter of merely local or private interest.

The court ruled in favour of the defendant, holding that the right contained in s. 31.1 to sue for loss or damage resulting from conduct contrary to the Combines Investigation Act was unconstitutional.

This decision has not been appealed.

APPENDIX 1-B: SECTIONS 91 AND 92 OF THE CONSTITUTION ACT, 1867

VI. DISTRIBUTION OF LEGISLATIVE POWERS

Powers of a Parliament

91. It shall be lawful for the Queen by and with the Advice and Consent of the Senate and the House of Commons, to make Laws for the Peace, Order and good Government of Canada, in relation to all matters not coming within the Classes of subjects by this Act assigned exclusively to the Legislatures of the Provinces: and for greater Certainty, but not so as to restrict the Generality of the foregoing Terms of this section, it is hereby declared that (notwithstanding anything in this Act) the exclusive Legislative Authority of the Parliament of Canada extends to all Matters coming within the Classes of Subjects next hereinafter enumerated: that is to say,—

1. The Public Debt and Property.
2. The Regulation of Trade and Commerce.
3. The raising of Money by any Mode or System of Taxation.
4. The borrowing of Money or the Public Credit.
5. Postal Service.
6. The Census and Statistics.
7. Militia, Military and Naval Service and Defence.
8. The fixing of and providing for the Salaries and Allowances of Civil and other Officers of the Government of Canada.
9. Beacons, Buoys, Lighthouses, and Sable Island.
10. Navigation and Shipping.
11. Quarantine and the Establishment and Maintenance of Marine Hospitals.
12. Sea Coast and Inland Fisheries.
13. Ferries between a Province and any British or Foreign Country or between Two Provinces.
14. Currency and Coinage.
15. Banking, Incorporation of Banks, and the Issue of Paper Money.
16. Savings Banks.
17. Weights and Measures.
18. Bills of Exchange and Promissory Notes.
19. Interest.
20. Legal Tender.
21. Bankruptcy and Insolvency.
22. Patents of Invention and Discovery.

23. Copyrights.

24. Indians and Lands reserved for the Indians.

25. Naturalization and Aliens.

26. Marriage and Divorce.

27. The Criminal Law except the Constitution of the Courts of Criminal Jurisdiction, but including the procedure in Criminal matters.

28. The Establishment, Maintenance and Management of Penitentiaries.

29. Such Classes of Subjects as are expressly excepted in the Enumeration of the Classes of Subjects by this Act assigned exclusively to the Legislatures of the Provinces.

And any matter coming within any of the Classes of Subjects enumerated in this Section shall not be deemed to come within the Class of Matters of a local or private Nature comprised in the Enumeration of the Classes of Subjects by this Act assigned exclusively to the Legislatures of the Provinces.

Exclusive Powers of Provincial Legislatures

92. In each Province the Legislature may exclusively make Laws in relation to Matters coming within the Classes of Subjects next hereinafter enumerated: that is to say,—

1. The Amendment from Time to Time, notwithstanding anything in this Act, the Constitution of the Province, except as regards the Office of the Lieutenant Governor.

2. Direct Taxation within the Province in order to the raising of a Revenue for Provincial Purposes.

3. The borrowing of Money on the sole Credit of the Province.

4. The Establishment and Tenure of Provincial Offices and the Appointment and Payment of Provincial Officers.

5. The Management and Sale of Public Lands belonging to the Province and the Timber and Wood thereon.

6. The Establishment, Maintenance and Management of Public and Reformatory Prisons in and for the Province.

7. The Establishment, Maintenance and Management of Hospitals, Asylums, Charities, and Eleemosynary Institutions in and for the Province, other than Marine Hospitals.

8. Municipal Institutions in the Province.

9. Shop, Saloon, Tavern, Auctioneer, and other Licenses in order to the raising of a Revenue for Provincial, Local or Municipal Purposes.

10. Local works and Undertakings other than such as are of the following classes:

(a) Lines of Steam or other Ships, Railways, Canals, Telegraphs, and other Works and Undertakings connecting the Province with any other of the Provinces, or extending beyond the Limits of the Province;

(b) Lines of Steam Ships between the Province and any British or Foreign Country; and

(c) Such Works, as, although situated within the Province, are before or after their Execution declared by the Parliament of Canada to be for the general advantage of Canada or for the Advantage of Two or more of the Provinces.

11. The incorporation of Companies with Provincial Objects.

12. The Solemnization of Marriage in the Province.

13. Property and Civil Rights in the Province.

14. The Administration of Justice in the Province, including the Constitution, Maintenance and Organization of Provincial Courts, both of Civil and of Criminal Jurisdiction, and including Procedure in Civil Matters in those Courts.

15. The Imposition of Punishment by Fine, Penalty, or Imprisonment for enforcing any Law of the Province made in relation to any Matter coming within any of the Classes of subjects enumerated in this Section.

16. Generally, all Matters of a merely local or private Nature in the Province.

APPENDIX 1-C: CANADIAN CHARTER OF RIGHTS AND FREEDOMS

BEING PART I OF THE CONSTITUTION ACT, 1982

Amended by the Constitution Amendment Proclamation, 1983, effective June 21, 1984

Whereas Canada is founded upon principles that recognize the supremacy of God and the rule of law:

Guarantee of Rights and Freedoms

RIGHTS AND FREEDOMS IN CANADA.

1. The *Canadian Charter of Rights and Freedoms* guarantees the rights and freedoms set out in it subject only to such reasonable limits prescribed by law as can be demonstrably justified in a free and democratic society.

Fundamental Freedoms

FUNDAMENTAL FREEDOMS.

2. Everyone has the following fundamental freedoms:

(a) freedom of conscience and religion;

(b) freedom of thought, belief, opinion and expression, including freedom of the press and other media of communication;

(c) freedom of peaceful assembly; and

(d) freedom of association.

Democratic Rights

DEMOCRATIC RIGHTS OF CITIZENS.

3. Every citizen of Canada has the Right to vote in an election of members of the House of Commons or of a legislative assembly and to be qualified for membership therein.

MAXIMUM DURATION OF LEGISLATIVE BODIES—Continuation in special circumstances.

4. (1) No House of Commons and no legislative assembly shall continue for longer than five years from the date fixed for the return of the writs at a general election of its members.

(2) In time of real or apprehended war, invasion or insurrection, a House of Commons may be continued by Parliament and a legislative assembly may be continued by the legislature beyond five years if such continuation is not opposed by the votes of more than one-third of the members of the House of Commons or the legislative assembly, as the case may be.

ANNUAL SITTING OF LEGISLATIVE BODIES.

5. There shall be a sitting of Parliament and of each legislature at least once every twelve months.

Mobility Rights

MOBILITY OF CITIZENS—Rights to move and gain livelihood—Limitation— Affirmative action programs.

6.(1) Every citizen of Canada has the right to enter, remain in and leave Canada.

(2) Every citizen of Canada and every person who has the status of a permanent resident of Canada has the right

(a) to move to and take up residence in any province; and

(b) to pursue the gaining of a livelihood in any province.

(3) The rights specified in subsection (2) are subject to

(a) any laws or practices of general application in force in a province other than those that discriminate among persons primarily on the basis of province of present or previous residence; and

(b) any laws providing for reasonable residency requirements as a qualification for the receipt of publicly provided social services.

(4) Subsections (2) and (3) do not preclude any law, program or activity that has as its object the amelioration in a province of conditions of

individuals in that province who are socially or economically disadvantaged if the rate of employment in that province is below the rate of employment in Canada.

Legal Rights

LIFE, LIBERTY AND SECURITY OF PERSON.

7. Everyone has the right to life, liberty and security of the person and the right not to be deprived thereof except in accordance with the principles of fundamental justice.

SEARCH OR SEIZURE.

8. Everyone has the right to be secure against unreasonable search or seizure.

DETENTION OR IMPRISONMENT.

9. Everyone has the right not to be arbitrarily detained or imprisoned.

ARREST OR DETENTION.

10. Everyone has the right on arrest or detention

- (*a*) to be informed promptly of the reasons therefor;
- (*b*) to retain and instruct counsel without delay and to be informed of that right; and
- (*c*) to have the validity of the detention determined by way of *habeas corpus* and to be released if the detention is not lawful.

PROCEEDINGS IN CRIMINAL AND PENAL MATTERS.

11. Any person charged with an offence has the right

- (*a*) to be informed without unreasonable delay of the specific offence;
- (*b*) to be tried within a reasonable time;
- (*c*) not to be compelled to be a witness in proceedings against that person in respect of the offence;
- (*d*) to be presumed innocent until proven guilty according to law in a fair and public hearing by an independent and impartial tribunal;
- (*e*) not to be denied reasonable bail without just cause;
- (*f*) except in the case of an offence under military law tried before a military tribunal, to the benefit of trial by jury where the maximum punishment for the offence is imprisonment for five years or a more severe punishment;
- (*g*) not to be found guilty on account of any act or omission unless, at the time of the act or omission, it constituted an offence under Canadian or international law or was criminal according to the general principles of law recognized by the community of nations;
- (*h*) if finally acquitted of the offence, not to be tried for it again and, if finally found guilty and punished for the offence, not to be tried or punished for it again; and

(*i*) if found guilty of the offence and if the punishment for the offence has been varied between the time of commission and the time of sentencing, to the benefit of the lesser punishment.

TREATMENT OR PUNISHMENT.

12. Everyone has the right not to be subjected to any cruel and unusual treatment or punishment.

SELF-CRIMINATION.

13. A witness who testifies in any proceedings has the right not to have any incriminating evidence so given used to incriminate that witness in any other proceedings, except in a prosecution for perjury or for the giving of contradictory evidence.

INTERPRETER.

14. A party or witness in any proceedings who does not understand or speak the language in which the proceedings are conducted or who is deaf has the right to the assistance of an interpreter.

Equality Rights

EQUALITY BEFORE AND UNDER LAW AND EQUAL PROTECTION AND BENEFIT OF LAW—Affirmative action programs.

15. (1) Every individual is equal before and under the law and has the right to the equal protection and equal benefit of the law without discrimination and, in particular, without discrimination based on race, national or ethnic origin, colour, religion, sex, age or mental or physical disability.

(2) Subsection (1) does not preclude any law, program or activity that has as its object the amelioration of conditions of disadvantaged individuals or groups including those that are disadvantaged because of race, national or ethnic origin, colour, religion, sex, age or mental or physical disability.

Official Languages of Canada

OFFICIAL LANGUAGES OF CANADA—Official languages of New Brunswick— Advancement of status and use.

16. (1) English and French are the official languages of Canada and have equality of status and equal rights and privileges as to their use in all institutions of the Parliament and government of Canada.

(2) English and French are the official languages of New Brunswick and have equality of status and equal rights and privileges as to their use in all institutions of the legislature and government of New Brunswick.

(3) Nothing in this Charter limits the authority of Parliament or a legislature to advance the equality of status or use of English and French.

PROCEEDINGS OF PARLIAMENT—Proceedings of New Brunswick legislature.

17. (1) Everyone has the right to use English or French in any debates and other proceedings of Parliament.

(2) Everyone has the right to use English or French in any debates and other proceedings of the legislature of New Brunswick.

PARLIAMENTARY STATUTES AND RECORDS—New Brunswick statutes and records.

(18). (1) The statutes, records and journals of Parliament shall be printed and published in English and French and both language versions are equally authoritative.

(2) The statutes, records and journals of the legislature of New Brunswick shall be printed and published in English and French and both language versions are equally authoritative.

PROCEEDINGS IN COURTS ESTABLISHED BY PARLIAMENT—Proceedings in New Brunswick courts.

19. (1) Either English or French may be used by any person in, or in any pleading in or process issuing from, any court established by Parliament.

(2) Either English or French may be used by any person in, or in any pleading in or process issuing from, any court of New Brunswick.

COMMUNICATIONS BY PUBLIC WITH FEDERAL INSTITUTIONS—Communications by public with New Brunswick institutions.

20. (1) Any member of the public in Canada has the right to communicate with, and to receive available services from, any head or central office of an institution of the Parliament or government of Canada in English or French, and has the same right with respect to any other office of any such institution where

(a) there is a significant demand for communications with and services from that office in such language; or

(b) due to the nature of the office, it is reasonable that communications with and services from that office be available in both English and French.

(2) Any member of the public in New Brunswick has the right to communicate with, and to receive available services from, any office of an institution of the legislature or government of New Brunswick in English or French.

CONTINUATION OF EXISTING CONSTITUTIONAL PROVISIONS.

21. Nothing in sections 16 to 20 abrogates or derogates from any right, privilege or obligation with respect to the English and French languages, or either of them, that exists or is continued by virtue of any other provision of the Constitution of Canada.

RIGHTS AND PRIVILEGES PRESERVED.

22. Nothing in sections 16 to 20 abrogates or derogates from any legal or customary right or privilege acquired or enjoyed either before or after the coming into force of this Charter with respect to any language that is not English or French.

Minority Language Educational Rights

LANGUAGE OF INSTRUCTION—Continuity of language instruction—Application where numbers warrant.

23. (1) Citizens of Canada

(a) whose first language learned and still understood is that of the English or French linguistic minority population of the province in which they reside, or

(b) who have received their primary school instruction in Canada in English or French and reside in a province where the language in which they received that instruction is the language of the English or French linguistic minority population of the province,

have the right to have their children receive primary and secondary school instruction in that language in that province.

(2) Citizens of Canada of whom any child has received or is receiving primary or secondary school instruction in English or French in Canada, have the right to have all their children receive primary and secondary school instruction in the same language.

(3) The right of citizens of Canada under subsections (1) and (2) to have their children receive primary and secondary school instruction in the language of the English or French linguistic minority population of a province

(a) applies wherever in the province the number of children of citizens who have such a right is sufficient to warrant the provision to them out of public funds of minority language instruction; and

(b) includes, where the number of those children so warrants, the right to have them receive that instruction in minority language educational facilities provided out of public funds.

Enforcement

ENFORCEMENT OF GUARANTEED RIGHTS AND FREEDOMS—Exclusion of evidence bringing administration of justice into disrepute.

24. (1) Anyone whose rights or freedoms, as guaranteed by this Charter, have been infringed or denied may apply to a court of competent jurisdiction to obtain such remedy as the court considers appropriate and just in the circumstances.

(2) Where, in proceedings under subsection (1), a court concludes that evidence was obtained in a manner that infringed or denied any rights or freedoms guaranteed by this Charter, the evidence shall be excluded if it is established that, having regard to all the circumstances, the admission of it in the proceedings would bring the administration of justice into disrepute.

General

ABORIGINAL RIGHTS AND FREEDOMS NOT AFFECTED BY CHARTER.

25. The guarantee in this Charter of certain rights and freedoms shall not be construed so as to abrogate or derogate from any aboriginal, treaty or other rights or freedoms that pertain to the aboriginal peoples of Canada including

(a) any rights or freedoms that have been recognized by the Royal Proclamation of October 7, 1763; and

(b) any rights or freedoms that now exist by way of land claims agreements or may be so acquired. [Amended by Constitution Amendment Proclamation, 1983, s. 1.]

OTHER RIGHTS AND FREEDOMS NOT AFFECTED BY CHARTER.

26. The guarantee in this Charter of certain rights and freedoms shall not be construed as denying the existence of any other rights or freedoms that exist in Canada.

MULTICULTURAL HERITAGE.

27. This Charter shall be interpreted in a manner consistent with the preservation and enhancement of the multicultural heritage of Canadians.

RIGHTS GUARANTEED EQUALLY TO BOTH SEXES.

28. Notwithstanding anything in this Charter, the rights and freedoms referred to in it are guaranteed equally to male and female persons.

RIGHTS RESPECTING CERTAIN SCHOOLS PRESERVED.

29. Nothing in this Charter abrogates or derogates from any rights or privileges guaranteed by or under the Constitution of Canada in respect of denominational, separate or dissentient schools.

APPLICATION TO TERRITORIES AND TERRITORIAL AUTHORITIES.

30. A reference in this Charter to a province or to the legislative assembly or legislature of a province shall be deemed to include a reference to the Yukon Territory and the Northwest Territories, or to the appropriate legislative authority thereof, as the case may be.

LEGISLATIVE POWERS NOT EXTENDED.

31. Nothing in this Charter extends the legislative powers of any body or authority.

Application of Charter

APPLICATION OF CHARTER—Exception.

32. (1) This Charter applies

   (*a*) to the Parliament and government of Canada in respect of all matters within the authority of Parliament including all matters relating to the Yukon Territory and Northwest Territories; and

   (*b*) to the legislature and government of each province in respect to all matters within the authority of the legislature of each province.

(2) Notwithstanding subsection (1), section 15 shall not have effect until three years after this section comes into force.

EXCEPTION WHERE EXPRESS DECLARATION—Operation of exception—Five year limitation—Re-enactment—Five year limitation.

33. (1) Parliament or the legislature of a province may expressly declare in an Act of Parliament or of the legislature, as the case may be, that the Act or a provision thereof shall operate notwithstanding a provision included in section 2 or sections 7 to 15 of this Charter.

(2) An Act or a provision of an Act in respect of which a declaration made under this section is in effect shall have such operation as it would have but for the provision of this Charter referred to in the declaration.

(3) A declaration made under subsection (1) shall cease to have effect five years after it comes into force or on such earlier date as may be specified in the declaration.

(4) Parliament or the legislature of a province may re-enact a declaration made under subsection (1).

(5) Subsection (3) applies in respect of a re-enactment made under subsection (4).

Citation

CITATION.

34. This Part may be cited as the *Canadian Charter of Rights and Freedoms*.

2

The Civil Courts
and Litigation Procedure

A person may suffer physical or financial loss through the intentional or negligent actions of another. However, he or she may not seek direct physical retribution or, in other words, "take the law into his own hands." Instead, he must take his claim for compensation, monetary or otherwise, to a civil court. Usually, this is in his own best interest—for the court can award damages in his favour in the event of breach of contract, can help him to recover or enforce his property rights, can award compensation for loss caused by another person's negligence or other tort, and make other awards.

JURISDICTION

The court chosen will depend on several factors. For example, a claim for under $1,000 in Ontario must be taken to the Provincial Court, Civil Division, commonly known as Small Claims Court. In the case of a contract, the place where the contract was made will normally have jurisdiction. In the case of a tort, the place where the tort occurred will normally determine the place of jurisdiction. The parties may even predetermine which court and which location is to have jurisdiction in case of a dispute. It is even left to the parties to a contract to agree not to sue each other in case of dispute or to decide to have disputes settled by an arbitrator, usually a lawyer, and to abide by the latter's decision. Other factors may also enter into the determination of the court's jurisdiction.

TRIAL COURTS

There are normally three different levels of provincial civil trial courts (or "courts of original jurisdiction"), each with varying financial jurisdiction.

Provincial Court (Civil Division). If the amount involved is relatively small (under $1,000, except Metro Toronto $3,000), the claimant (or plaintiff) must present the case to a Small Claims Court, which in Ontario is the Civil Division of the Provincial Court.

District Court. If the amount of a claim exceeds the maximum permitted in the small claims court, the case must be presented, depending on the province, to a county or district court. With the exception of Alberta, these courts have their own upper financial limits for jurisdiction. In Ontario, it is $25,000.

Provincial Supreme Court. Each province has a supreme Court that handles cases that exceed the financial jurisdiction of the lower courts. In Ontario, this is the High Court of Justice.

The Ontario Provincial Supreme Court includes a Divisional Court which deals mainly with appeals from administrative tribunals (such as the Workers' Compensation Board, Liquor Licence Board, and Labour Relations Board) of which there are a great many. While the Divisional Court will not normally interfere with findings of fact, it may alter the findings if the law has been misinterpreted or misapplied. The Divisional Court also hears appeals involving amounts up to $25,000.

Other Civil Courts

Surrogate Court (Probate Court)	Ontario court that deals with the administration of estates of deceased persons.
Youth Court	A criminal court that deals with young offenders (12-18 years).
Family Court	A division of the Provincial Court that deals with questions of support, and domestic issues.
Unified Family Court	Provincial Court that administers the Family Law Reform Act, together with the Divorce Act of Canada.
Bankruptcy Court	Provincial High Court Judge that administers Canadian Bankruptcy Act.

Federal Courts

Supreme Court of Canada	On the civil side, this court deals with appeals on constitutional matters and important questions of law.
Federal Court	Replaced the Exchequer Court, a branch of which sits in each capital, and deals primarily with claims by and against the federal Crown, such as customs, immigration matters, government contracts, accidents in government buildings, etc. This court has a trial and an appeal division. _Individual or corporation._
Tax Court	Deals with appeals by taxpayers from their income tax assessments as well as appeals by the Minister of National Revenue.

CIVIL COURT PROCEDURE

During the past two or three decades there has been much emphasis on the deformalization of civil court procedures and pleadings with the objective of making such proceedings more understandable to the non-lawyer. Efforts have also been made to "Canadianize" the language by replacing traditional Latin phrases with the equivalent in English.

To Sue or Not to Sue

Before a person decides to go to court, he or she should decide whether it is worth the effort, time, and expense involved. Perhaps an out-of-court settlement is more appropriate. The decision whether to proceed with a *lawsuit* (or legal action) will be influenced by the cost of the *litigation* (the legal proceedings), the legal complexities involved, the likelihood of winning the case, and the likely possible monetary award. Very often, a case is settled out of court before the trial date, by agreement between the two principal parties involved. This settlement usually occurs for two reasons: (a) the case is fairly clear-cut and the court decision can be anticipated and (b) the high legal fees that will have to be paid to the lawyers involved and that gradually mount up as legal proceedings drag on. Even successful parties will be awarded only part of their legal costs from the losing side because the fees are calculated according to a tariff rather than what the lawyer actually charges.

Court Proceedings

In the Small Claims (Provincial Court, Civil Division) Court, where each party may conduct his or her own case, the claimant initiates the claim which is served on the defendant who has a fixed period of time to file a defence. Pretrial proceedings have been instituted whereby a referee tries to settle the claim before trial. Failing settlement, a trial date is set and both parties may choose either to conduct their own case or proceed with a lawyer. Witnesses are heard on both sides. Witnesses may be questioned and then the judge gives his or her decision in the form of a judgment.

District and Supreme Court Proceedings

Until 1985 in Ontario all Court actions in these courts were formal and initiated by a Writ of Summons. Now all claims or court actions are initiated by a statement of claim or notice of action accompanid by a subsequent statement of claim which must be served on the defendant within six months after it is issued. This must be followed within 20 days by the defendant's statement of defence.

Any allegation made by the claimant which is not negated in the statement of defence will henceforth be taken to have been admitted. The statement of claim and the statement of defence must contain the information called pleadings on which each party bases his or her case. A cross-claim may be made against co-defendants.

Following the above proceedings, either party may resort to "discovery" or an examination to determine the evidence held by the other party. This discovery process may involve "any matter in issue in an action" by the following means: *discovery of documents, examination for discovery* (oral or written), *inspection of property*, and *medical examination* of a party.

FIGURE 2-1: THE CIVIL TRIAL COURT SYSTEM

Provincial Supreme Court—Court of Appeal

S. 17 • appeals from order of Divisional Court that are not fact alone;
- appeals from final order of Judge of High Court.

Provincial Supreme Court—High Court

S. 13 • appeals from local Judge of High Court;
- interlocutory orders;
- ordinary jurisdiction which is unlimited.

Provincial Supreme Court—Divisional Court

S. 15 • appeals involving any amount under $25,000.
- appeals from Provincial Court, Civil Division.

District Court of Ontario

S. 25 • replaces county courts or district courts of judicial districts;
- is a simple court of record having both civil and criminal jurisdiction;

S. 32 • has jurisdiction in civil matters where the sum claimed or property is valued at under $25,000.

Unified Family Court in and for the Judicial District of Hamilton-Wentworth

S. 39 • Experimental court which not only deals with questions of Divorce, but with all other matters such as division of property, support payments, custody of children, etc.

Provincial Court—Family Division

S. 75 • deals with custody of children and support payments; under the Family Law Reform Act, wardship proceedings under the Child Welfare Act and youth court proceedings under the Young Offenders Act.

Provincial Court—Civil Division

S. 78 • *jurisdiction:*
    (a) claim under $1,000 exclusive of interest;
    (b) property not exceeding $1,000;
    (c) Judicial District of York has maximum increased to $3,000.

S. 83 • appeal lies to Divisional Court in case of payment of money or property valued over $500.

The above is based on the Courts of Justice Act, 1984.

The foregoing may also be followed by: pretrial conferences, admissions, inspection of witnesses' reports, and financial statements. The case is then set down for trial. The new rules contain provisions that may be prejudicial to the party which unduly delays the trial beyond six months after the pleadings have been completed.

The trial itself is conducted in open court and witnesses give their evidence orally, subject to cross-examination. Each party must be represented by legal counsel. The new rules provides for an allocation of costs where an attempt to settle out of court has been made and the monetary judgment awarded is lower than the amount offered in settlement.

Judgment.   After hearing both sides, the judge gives his or her decision, or *judgment*. This may be: (a) *dismissal* of the claim; (b) *damages*—a sum of money awarded to the winning party; (c) *costs*—the court and other legal costs incurred by the winning party; (d) *specific performance*—a court order to do something, such as return property to the plaintiff; (e) an *injunction*— a court order to refrain from doing something, such as a certain type of conduct that is causing harm to the plaintiff; or (f) some combination of the foregoing. Sometimes the judge will reserve judgment until he or she has had extra time to study his or her notes and reference books.

Collection of Judgment.   If the losing party fails to pay the damages and costs awarded, the winning party may apply to the court for: (a) a *garnishee* order directed to the loser's employer to withhold part of the losing party's wages (a maximum of 20%, in Ontario except for claims for family support, which are 50%); or (b) a *writ of execution* directing the local sheriff to seize those of the losing party's goods not exempted from seizure by statute, to be sold at auction to satisfy the judgment. The winning party may also register a lien against any loser's real property, which may subsequently be sold in a court sale if the judgment is not satisfied beforehand. The losing party may be examined, if necessary, to determine what assets he or she has available to pay the amount owing, and may be committed for contempt for failing to attend such an examination or for failing or refusing to answer relevant questions. Once committed, payment of the judgment is not sufficient to obtain his or her release. Consent of the court is also required.

Appeals

The losing party in a civil lawsuit always has the right to appeal the judgment of the trial court judge. To hear such appeals, each province has a system of *appeal courts* (or courts of "appellate jurisdiction"). In Ontario, appeals against decisions of the Provincial Court Civil Division's judges are heard by the Divisional Court of the High Court of Justice; and appeals against the decisions of the District court judges are heard by the Ontario Court of Appeal, if the amount involved exceeds $25,000.

An appeal may be made on the grounds that (a) the judge made a mistake of law, (b) authority could not be based on the evidence of mixed law and fact or severity of the award, or (c) the "finding" was not supported by the evidence present. Normally, the appeal court's decision is based on a review of the "record," the written transcript, of the trial. Only in unusual circumstances are new witnesses examined or new evidence heard. If the court of appeal concludes that a miscarriage of justice has taken place, it may: (a) reverse the verdict; (b) alter the judgment (for example, the amount of damages awarded); or (c) order a new trial. The person bringing the appeal is known as the "appellant"; the other party is called the "respondent."

Figure 2.2: Appeal Courts of Ontario

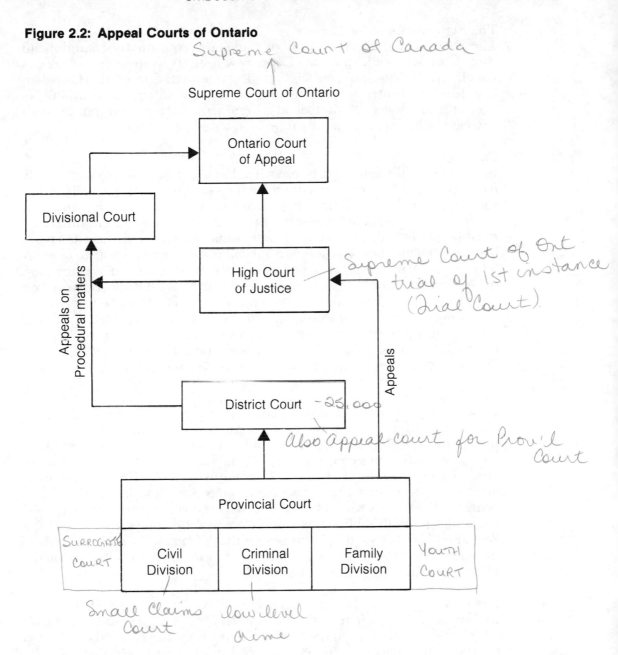

Supreme Court of Canada *(handwritten)*

Supreme Court of Ontario

Supreme Court of Ont trial of 1st instance (Trial Court) *(handwritten)*

Ontario Court of Appeal

Divisional Court

High Court of Justice

Appeals on Procedural matters

Appeals

District Court — 25,000 *(handwritten)*

Also appeal court for Prov'l Court *(handwritten)*

Provincial Court

| Surrogate Court *(handwritten)* | Civil Division | Criminal Division | Family Division | Youth Court *(handwritten)* |

Small Claims Court *(handwritten)*

low level crime *(handwritten)*

The Supreme Court of Canada

The role of the Supreme Court of Canada is continually changing. In connection with civil cases, the Court now restricts its jurisdiction to cases which involve questions of civil rights, interpretation of the Canadian Constitution, contentious principles of law, jurisdictional conflicts between the Provinces and the federal government, and certain important civil law cases when special permission is requested and granted.

Costs

In a civil case, the losing party, as well as having to pay damages, is usually required to pay the court and other legal costs of the winning party. Since such payment is usually in accordance with an official tariff, it may not cover the actual fees charged by the winning party's lawyer. The difference must be met by the client, even though he may have won the case. If a party believes that the lawyer's fees are exorbitant, he may appeal to a court official, called the taxing master, to have them reduced. There are, however, infrequent situations where a judge may order that the losing party pay legal costs at a higher scale of costs (known as "solicitor and client costs").

In some provinces (for example, Alberta), a lawyer is permitted to enter into a contingent fee arrangement whereby the fee will vary according to the results of the case. However, in Ontario, the foregoing practice, called "champerty", is prohibited as being against "public policy."

Court Officials

Each county, district, and supreme court has a *sheriff*, an appointed official whose duties include the serving of summonses, attendance at court sessions, and the enforcement of court orders by the seizure and sale of property. The small claims courts have an official called a *bailiff* to perform these tasks. There is also the *court clerk* who administers oaths, brings the court to order, announces that court has begun or recessed, and keeps a record of exhibits. The *court reporter* keeps a record of everything said at trial. In civil trials, the plaintiff's lawyer is called "counsel for the plaintiff" and the defendant is represented by "counsel for the defendant." In criminal trials, the lawyer representing the plaintiff and prosecuting on behalf of the Queen, is called the "Crown Attorney."

Lawyers

In Canada, lawyers often describe themselves as "barristers and solicitors." This is because they combine the functions performed in England by two separate types of lawyers. In that country, barristers are lawyers who appear in the courts to argue cases, or "briefs," given to them by solicitors. Solicitors, on the other hand, are lawyers who spend most of their time in the office rather than in court (although they do occasionally appear in the lower courts). The work performed in the office includes the provision of legal advice; the incorporation of companies; the drafting of deeds, contracts, and wills; arrangements for the adoption of children; the preparation of cases for trial; the drafting of pleadings; and the interviewing of witnesses. In Ontario a lawyer may also act as a *public notary* (a person who is authorized to witness signatures). However, a notary need not be a solicitor, but may have special authority to administer oaths and take affidavits under government regulations. In Ontario, every lawyer, by virtue of being a lawyer, is also a commissioner of oaths and thereby authorized to validate oaths that are to be used as evidence in Ontario; whereas a notary public is required to administer the oath if the evidence (document) is to be used outside Ontario. In Quebec, lawyers still comprise two distinct groups: advocates (or barristers) and notaries (solicitors). In the United States, no such distinction exists: all lawyers are known as attorneys. In Canada, by provincial statute, the lawyers in each province must belong to that province's "bar" (barristers society) and conform to its rules if they wish to practise law.

Appointment of Judges

Provincial court judges (or magistrates) are appointed by the provincial government. County court or supreme court judges, on the other hand, are appointed by the federal government. Before a person can be appointed to "the bench," as county or supreme court judges are said to be, he or she must be a qualified lawyer. A judge, once appointed, holds the position until the compulsory retirement age, normally 75.

Proper Law of the Contract

This term is used to describe the law that must be applied by a judge when hearing a case which involves more than one legal jurisdiction. This problem may arise in the case of a contract involving a manufacturer in one province selling to a customer in another province. When trying a case involving more than one legal jurisdiction, the court must choose the proper law. This is the law which, taking into consideration the facts of the case, is the one most closely related to the case. This assumes that the parties have not specified in their contract the law to be used in interpreting it, should any dispute arise. For example, "This warranty shall be construed under the laws of the Province of Ontario, Canada."

Prerogative Writs

Prerogative writs are orders occasionally issued by High Court judges to provide a remedy where process by the ordinary course of law would be inadequate.

Habeas Corpus.   This is a writ directed to an individual ordering the production of the body of any person whom the court has reason to believe is imprisoned or confined by such individual, in order that the court may enquire into the legality of such imprisonment or confinement.

Certiorari.   This writ orders a case to be transferred from an inferior court (including, for example, an administrative tribunal) to a superior one so that justice may be done.

Mandamus. This writ orders an inferior court, a person, or other body to perform any public duty the person or body may be liable to perform.

Prohibition. This writ orders an inferior court to discontinue the proceedings specified in the writ because of their illegality.

REVIEW QUESTIONS

1. How does the law assist a person in pursuing a small claim?
2. What factors affect the choice of the court?
3. Why would a person wish to settle "out of court"?
4. Outline the system of civil courts of original jurisdiction in your province.
5. On what grounds may an appeal be made in a civil case to the provincial court of appeal? What actions may the court take?
6. What cases may be heard in the Federal Court?
7. What is the role of the Supreme Court of Canada?
8. Explain the following legal terms:
    (a) statement of claim;
    (b) statement of defence;
    (c) pleadings;
    (d) judgment by default.
9. Explain the following terms:
    (a) writ of execution in a civil case;
    (b) garnishee order;
    (c) registering a judgment;
    (d) examination for discovery.
10. Explain how a civil trial is conducted. Why is the term "adversary system" sometimes used?
11. Who pays the cost of a civil trial? Should "champerty" be allowed?
12. What is a sheriff? What are the sheriff's duties? Distinguish between a sheriff and a bailiff. What is the origin of these terms?
13. In Canada, lawyers often describe themselves as "barristers and solicitors." Explain this phrase.
14. How are judges appointed?
15. What is meant by the term "the proper law of the contract"? When does it become important?
16. Which courts or tribunals would exercise jurisdiction in the following situations:
    (a) an unpaid bill for the purchase of a car valued at $3,000?
    (b) a land claim for under $400?
    (c) a claim for $1,000 for an accidental injury incurred at the post office?
    (d) the final court of appeal in the previous situation?
17. If the defendant loses his case when the plaintiff is suing him for $500, which of the following may be correct:
    (a) the plaintiff may personally seize the defendant's car to pay the claim;

(b) the defendant may be jailed until he pays;

(c) if the defendant does not pay voluntarily, nothing can be done;

(d) the plaintiff may proceed by obtaining an order to garnishee the defendant's salary;

(e) after a six months' delay, the court will arrange for satisfaction.

18. Would a successful party in a lawsuit always recover his or her legal costs?

19. Judges sitting in the district court and above in Ontario are appointed by:

(a) the Queen;

(b) the provincial government;

(c) the Lieutenant Governor;

(d) the federal government;

(e) the Bar Society.

3

Crime and the Criminal Courts

Unit 3.1
Criminal Offences

A *crime* is an act committed in violation of a law that forbids the act. However, it may also be the omission of an act commanded by law. Whoever is alleged to have committed a crime may be arrested, tried, and, if found guilty, punished by the state. The crime may vary in seriousness from taking another person's life to stealing a loaf of bread.

CRIMINAL JURISDICTION

The Criminal Code. Section 91 of the Constitution Act, 1867, gave Canada's Parliament the responsibility for criminal law in this country. Accordingly, a federal statute, the *Criminal Code*, was passed in 1892 to specify all the various criminal offences and the maximum penalties involved. Before the enactment of this Code, criminal cases had been tried, as in Britain, according to the English common law. The Criminal Code adopted by Canada was mainly a compilation of existing common law crimes and punishments. However, it is constantly amended to take into account the needs of the times. Recent changes relate to abortions, homosexuality, prostitution, pari-mutual betting, "hate literature," and bail.

Other Canadian statutes that specify criminal offences and punishments include the Official Secrets Act, the Food and Drugs Act, the Combines Investigation Act, the Customs Act, the Excise Act, the Income Tax Act, the National Defence Act, the Narcotics Control Act, the Weights and Measures Act, the Hazardous Products Act, and many new consumer-oriented statutes.

Quasi-Criminal Matters. Since, under s. 92 of the Constitution Act, 1867, the provincial legislatures were given authority to pass various types of laws, they were also by implication authorized to impose some penalty if these laws were broken. Accordingly, under the authority of s. 92(15) of the Constitution Act, the provincial legislatures have imposed such penalties. As a rule, they are administered under the summary conviction procedure, with the maximum penalty normally prescribed for an individual being a $2,000 fine or one year's imprisonment, or both; and for a corporation, a $25,000 fine. Municipal authorities, using powers delegated by the provincial legislature, also pass laws called *bylaws*, which carry a penalty for non-compliance.

Abroad. In Britain, there has traditionally been no criminal code or other comprehensive statute specifying the various types of crimes and punishments. In the United States, where there is also no national criminal code, the criminal law varies from state to state. However, the U.S. federal government has jurisdiction in crimes such as treasury offences and interstate commerce violations.

TYPES OF CRIME

In the English common law, crimes are classified as treasons, felonies, and misdemeanours. *Treason*, the most serious, is any crime against the security of the state, such as divulging official secrets. *Felonies* are other serious crimes such as murder, rape, or armed robbery. *Misdemeanours* are relatively minor crimes such as driving at an excessive rate of speed.

In the Criminal Code, by contrast, all crimes are divided into two main categories: summary conviction (or non-indictable) offences; and indictable offences. The Crown can also prosecute some offences summarily or by indictment.

Summary conviction offences. These are offences of a less serious nature such as common assault, being found in a gaming or bawdy house, theft under $200, or harrassing telephone calls. A person accused of such an offence is tried by a provincial court judge (or magistrate in some provinces) without a jury, usually with the minimum of delay—hence the term "summary."

Indictable offences. These are crimes of a more serious nature. If a person is believed to have committed such a crime, the Crown Prosecutor must lay what is called an "indictment," which is a formal method of instituting a charge against the accused.

Some sections of the Criminal Code provide for trial either by summary conviction or by indictment, and the Crown Prosecutor must choose which procedure to follow. According to their seriousness, some indictable offences must be tried by a provincial court judge or magistrate; others (at the choice of the accused) by a provincial judge, a district court judge, or a district court judge and jury; and others by a provincial supreme court judge and jury. Part XII of the Criminal Code deals with the jurisdiction of the various courts.

CRIMINAL INTENT

Originally, because of canon law influence, a crime was regarded as a sin which had been committed intentionally. Consequently, under common law, it was impossible to convict a person unless intent to commit a crime was proved. During the course of time, this requirement of "intent" has been eroded, although it still appears in some sections. Thus, for example, s. 283(1) of the Criminal Code states:

> Every one commits theft who ... converts to his use or to the use of another person, anything ... *with intent,* (a) to deprive, temporarily or absolutely, the owner of it or a person who has a special property or interest in it, of the thing or of his property or interest in it, ...

Although many sections of the Criminal Code may not specify the requirement of intent, every section of the Code is interpreted by our courts to require the element of intent unless the particular section provides otherwise. In fact an established principle of Canadian criminal law is that both "mens rea" (the criminal intent) and "actus reus" (the criminal act) must be proved by the Crown beyond a reasonable doubt before a conviction may properly be registered.

The Criminal Code also specifies that the element of intent is presumed in situations where a hit-and-run driver has left the scene of an accident; that is, it is presumed that the accused intended to avoid civil or criminal responsibility. A presumption applies to a person requested to take the breathalyzer test: the person who occupies the driver's seat is deemed to have had control of the vehicle. It is, of course, much easier to prove an offence if it is not necessary to prove intention, or if a statutory presumption of intent arises from the accused's own conduct. However, the presumption of intention may be rebutted by sufficient evidence that the accused did not have the intention required.

BUSINESS CRIMES

Examples of the types of crime which businesspeople are sometimes known to commit are examined in the following pages. However, this is by no means an all-inclusive list.

Disorderly Houses, Gaming and Betting.   Part V of the Canadian Criminal Code deals with disorderly houses, gaming and betting. Under s. 179, a *common gaming house* is a house that is kept for gain, or a house in which a bank is kept by one or more but not all the players. A *common bawdy house* is a place kept for the purpose of prostitution or indecency. A *common betting house* is a place where bets are received by the keeper.

Section 185(1) provides that a person who keeps a common gaming house or common betting house may be guilty of an indictable offence and liable to imprisonment for up to two years. The "found-in," on the other hand, is punishable on summary conviction. The same provisions apply under section 193 to the keeper of a common bawdy house and to any "found-ins." The Criminal Code was recently amended (s. 190) to permit the holding of lotteries under federal and provincial regulations.

Criminal Negligence.   Under s. 202 of the Canadian Criminal Code, *causing death by criminal negligence* is an indictable offence and may incur imprisonment for life. Causing bodily harm by criminal negligence is punishable by imprisonment for up to ten years. A separate offence for criminal negligence while driving is being created.

Theft. Part VII of the Canadian Criminal Code deals with *offences against the "rights of property."*

Section 292 deal with the *misappropriation of money held under direction*, for example, where property is given to a person to be held for a specific purpose such as the reservation deposit for a charter flight and is not used for that purpose.

Under s. 294, everyone who commits *theft* is guilty of an indictable offence and is liable (a) to imprisonment for ten years, where the property stolen is a testamentary instrument or where the value of the item stolen exceeds $200, or (b) to imprisonment for two years, where the value of the item stolen does not exceed $200.

An example of a theft conviction (name disguised) is as follows:

> Henry Smith, 43, a disbarred Toronto lawyer, yesterday was sentenced to five years by Judge F. J. MacCrae for theft of $525,000 in securities, cheques and money from 40 clients between 1966 and 1977.
>
> Smith, a father of three children, pleaded guilty.
>
> Detective Thomas Johnson of the Metro police fraud squad said those who lost money included widows, Italian immigrants and some of Smith's neighbours and relatives.
>
> Johnson said police received complaints about Smith through the Law Society of Upper Canada, governing body of Ontario's 7,500 lawyers. The Society has a compensation fund which pays a maximum of $15,000 to a victim of dishonesty with a maximum of $50,000 paid out on behalf of any one lawyer.
>
> Crown counsel Patrick LeSage told the court that forged mortgages and forged discharges of mortgages accounted for the $525,000.

Other Property Offences. Under s. 296, a *criminal breach of trust* occurs where a person holding property for a public or charitable purpose, with intent to defraud, uses such property for some other purpose; in this case, the punishment is up to fourteen years' imprisonment.

Section 300, dealing with the *destruction of documents of title*, is punishable as an indictable offence by imprisonment for up to ten years.

Under s. 312, a person *having possession of goods obtained through the commission of an offence* is liable, if the property exceeds $200, to imprisonment for ten years.

Under s. 319, *false pretences* (which is a representation made knowing that it is false with intent to induce another person to act on it) may be punished by imprisonment for up to ten years where the sum involved exceeds $200.

Under s. 324, *forgery* (which is making a false document with intention to have somebody act on it to their prejudice) is treated as an indictable offence, and may incur punishment of imprisonment for up to fourteen years.

Under s. 326, *uttering a forged document* (which is using or negotiating a document knowing it to be false) incurs punishment of imprisonment for up to fourteen years.

Fraudulent Transactions. Part VIII of the Criminal Code deals with "fraudulent transactions relating to trade and contracts."

Section 338 concerns *fraud*—that is, employing deceit or a falsehood to defraud the public of property, money or valuable security. It is an indictable offence, punishable by imprisonment for up to ten years.

Under s. 339, *using the mails to defraud* is punishable by imprisonment for up to two years. Fraudulent manipulation of stock exchange transactions, gaming in stocks or merchandise, reducing of stock by a broker selling his own account, are all liable to imprisonment for up to five years under s. 340.

Under s. 345, *fraudulent sale of property* is punishable by imprisonment for up to two years.

Under s. 354, *adding anything to mines*, such as "salting" a mine (that is, putting minerals into the earth to give the impression of valuable deposits), is an indictable offence and may incur imprisonment for ten years.

Under s. 358, a *false prospectus* is treated as an indictable offence and may make the offender liable to imprisonment for ten years.

Under s. 364, *forging a trademark, passing off*, etc., may be treated either as indictable offences with a punishment of up to two years, or as summary conviction offences.

Under s. 380, a *breach of contract which may endanger life, cause serious bodily harm*, or *expose valuable property to destruction*, is punishable as an indictable offence by imprisonment for up to five years.

An example of an allegedly fraudulent transaction is as follows:

> Five men charged with fraud in connection with the manipulation of shares in a mining company went on trial in Ontario Supreme Court yesterday.... In his opening remarks to the jury, prosecutor Rod McLeod said the crown alleges the accused men gained control of primary stock of Santack Mines Ltd., and proceeded to buy and sell shares between themselves and their associates, creating "a false impression of heavy active public trading."
>
> McLeod said, in outlining the crown's case, that the accused men "manipulated" the price of the shares from $1.20 up to $5 per share. They did this with the intent of ultimately getting out and dumping on the public shares of that value ($5) which the crown contends were not worth that much.
>
> All five men are charged with conspiring to defraud the public of money and other valuable securities through the promotion, purchase and sale of shares in Santack Mines Ltd. They are further charged with conspiring together to affect the market price of the shares.

Arson. Under s. 389 of the Criminal Code, *arson* (that is, wilfully setting fire to a building or other structure) incurs punishment of imprisonment for up to fourteen years. It has been estimated that up to 90% of business fires may be preset, but due to destruction of evidence very few cases are proved. *Fraudulently burning personal property* may incur punishment of imprisonment for up to five years.

Attempts, Conspiracies, and Accessories. Under s. 422, a person attempting, counselling, or who is an accessory after the fact, is liable to one-half of the punishment which might be awarded to the person committing the actual offence.

Section 423 deals with *conspiracy*. If the conspiracy involves murder, the punishment is imprisonment for up to fourteen years.

Income Tax Evasion. Under the Income Tax Act, a person may be charged with various criminal offences—for example, failing to declare income and thereby evading the payment of income taxes or conspiring to avoid payment of income tax.

An example (name disguised) is as follows:

> A Mississauga drain and concrete contractor was fined almost $24,000 in provincial court yesterday for failing to disclose business and investment income of $81,930 in his income tax returns for 1978 to 1983. Goeffrey Owen, 45, who has operated his contracting business since 1969, pleaded guilty to six charges of evading payment of federal taxes totalling $23,376.18. An investigation revealed he had declared less than half his actual net income in his tax returns. He was given a year to pay the fine and the back taxes with interest.

Restrictive Trade Practices. Under the Combines Investigation Act, a businessman may be held guilty of a crime if he engages in restrictive trade practices—for example, price-fixing agreements, monopolies, restraint of trade, discriminatory discounts, misleading advertisements, or resale price maintenance. In fact, the most serious convictions for business crimes during recent years have been offences under the Combines Investigation Act. For example, several presidents and senior officials of dredging companies were convicted of having conspired together to prearrange bids for government dredging contracts, thus eliminating competitive bids to the detriment of the Canadian public. The perpetrators were convicted, received personal sentences of imprisonment, and their companies were fined millions of dollars.

Usury. Most provinces have usury laws that forbid the lending of money at exorbitant rates of interest. In Ontario, the Unconscionable Transactions Relief Act applies. An example (names disguised) from Quebec is as follows:

> Two men who pleaded guilty to 41 charges of lending money at illegal interest rates were each fined $12,300 in sessions court.
>
> Jean-Paul LaPlante and Pierre Chevalier were also given suspended

sentences on an additional charge of operating a money-lending business without a permit.

The men were ordered to pay the fines within six months or spend a month in jail on each count.

The men, both members of the Interprovincial Brotherhood of Electrical Workers, admitted last December before a hearing of the Cliche commission inquiry into construction union freedoms that they ran a loan-sharking operation from an east-end tavern for three years.

According to evidence at the inquiry, headed by provincial court Judge Robert Cliche, the operation had annual interest rates ranging from 97 to 1,040% and once netted a return of $1,060 on $150 loaned for two years.

The men also admitted at the inquiry that they collected $360 from the 71-year-old mother of one of their clients who could not repay a loan.

The Criminal Code of Canada makes a charge of interest over 60% per annum a criminal offence.

Misuse of Clients' Funds. Officers of financial concerns have been involved in the illegal manipulation of clients' funds. In a major case in Ontario, mortgage money was advanced against insufficient security, resulting in the insolvency of the lending firm, causing many Canadians to lose their life savings. In a more recent case, trust companies were manipulated in deals that resulted in financing being increased threefold on some 10,000 rental units, thus driving up the value of these units and the rental charges necessary to pay off the increased finance charges, while the businessmen concerned attempted to maximize their profits at the lessees' expense. To prevent further resales of rental property for this purpose, Ontario law now prohibits the charging of more than 5% of the increased finance charges yearly.

Stock Fraud.   Provincial securities regulations now require the continual updating of company prospectuses relating to the sale of company stocks and bonds, so that potential investors have full knowledge of company business, financial statements, and prospects.

Unscrupulous Business Practices.   Each province, as well as the federal government, has passed laws to help protect Canadians who could possibly suffer monetary losses from unscrupulous business practices. These situations are reviewed in this book in Chapters 27 and 28 dealing with consumer protection. One example is to alert consumers as to the actual rate of interest being charged for credit purchases and to protect individuals who are required to make deposits pending completion of purchases—for example, deposits related to arrangements for travel and purchases of residences or condominiums.

Fraudulent Use of the Mails.   Use of the mails to defraud unsuspecting individuals is prohibited under the Criminal Code. An example of this would be an advertisement that advises interested persons to reply, sending $5 for information on "ways to earn easy money." In reply, the advertiser would advise to put in an advertisement like his, or to seek out a paper route, or to seek a position stuffing envelopes.

Savings. Savings of customers with banks, and other financial institutions, are now protected by government insurance up to a maximum of $60,000. per individual account, in case of insolvency.

Cheque Forgery, Counterfeiting, and "Con" Games. It is a criminal offence to forge cheques, to counterfeit (to pass off imitation money as real money), or to defraud people. In the last case, an example would be where an unsuspecting person is advised by a person posing as a police officer to draw out his or her life savings for investment in a "fly-by-night" operation.

Directors. Under the various federal and provincial Business Corporations Acts, company directors are now liable for up to six months' unpaid back wages to employees if their firms become insolvent. They must also make up any losses incurred by creditors if shares have been repurchased out of capital and it subsequently transpires that the company assets no longer cover creditor claims. Finally, directors may also be liable to creditors if it can be proved that business decisions rendering the corporation insolvent were not made with the discretion of "ordinary prudent businessmen."

Embezzlement. Accountants with banks and other financial institutions have occasionally "siphoned off" depositors' funds by setting up "fictitious accounts" or by other means. One Ontario banker cum gambler was convicted for having defrauded a major bank of over $8 million, solely used during weekend and holiday trips to major Atlantic City gambling resorts.

Computer Crimes. In the future, there are expected to be more business crimes involving computers, whereby stored business information may be stolen for competitive purposes, or fraudulent accounts may be instituted as a form of theft. Most nations are still exploring what type of laws are required to cope with these new types of crimes.

INGREDIENTS OF A CRIME

Each section of the Criminal Code specifies the ingredients of the particular crime. These ingredients, often as many as five or six points, must be proved by the prosecutor to obtain a conviction under that particular section. Thus, for example, s. 233(2), the hit-and-run offence section, states:

> Everyone who, having the care, charge or control of a vehicle that is involved in an accident with a person, vehicle, or cattle in charge of a person, with intent to escape civil or criminal liability fails to stop his vehicle, give his name and address and where any person has been injured, offer assistance, is guilty of

(a) an indictable offence and liable to imprisonment for two years; or

(b) an offence punishable on summary conviction.

Thus, in addition to proving the *who, what, where,* and *when* of the crime, the prosecutor would have to prove that the accused:

1. had the care, charge, or control of a vehicle in the first instance;
2. was involved in an accident with his vehicle;
3. involved another person, vehicle, or cattle in charge of a person, in an accident;
4. had intent to escape civil or criminal liability;
5. failed to stop the vehicle;
6. failed to give his or her name and address; and
7. failed to offer assistance where a person had been injured.

If after the presentation of the Crown's case any one of these points is not proven by the prosecutor, the defence may move for a directed verdict—that is, that no offence has been proven under this section.

LESSER INCLUDED OFFENCES

When a person is tried for a serious offence such as murder and the prosecutor fails to prove the charge, the judge may decide that a lesser charge of a similar nature has been proved. Where these offences are related they are called *lesser included offences.* Thus, in relation to murder, a lesser included offence would be manslaughter. In relation to robbery, lesser included offences would be breaking, entering and theft.

ATTEMPTS

Under s. 24(1) of the Criminal Code, a person is guilty of an attempt to commit a crime if he or she undertakes all the steps that are necessary to commit such a crime except that, through some incident beyond that person's control, the actual commission of the offence is frustrated. Thus, for example, a person who attempts to steal money from someone who, in fact, has none is guilty of an attempt to commit a crime (*R. v. Scott,* [1964] 2 C.C.C. 257).

Usually an attempt is punishable by a lesser penalty than the actual offence.

Many interesting cases have come before the courts where the facts support a conclusion that the accused has "prepared" for the crime (which is not a criminal offence) but has not gone so far as to "attempt" the crime. For example, is the purchase of a gun sufficient to support a conviction of attempted murder? Is pointing the gun sufficient to support the conviction? Does the trigger have to be pulled? What if the gun is not loaded?

CONSPIRACIES

While one cannot conspire with oneself, the moment that one conspires with another person (except one's spouse) to commit a crime, the offence of conspiracy is committed, even if no crime is actually carried out. For example, under s. 423(1) of the Criminal Code, conspiracy with anyone to commit murder, whether in Canada or not, is punishable by imprisonment for up to fourteen years; while conspiracy to induce, by false representations, a woman to commit adultery or fornication is punishable by imprisonment for up to two years. Here again, the punishment for conspiracy is generally less than for the commission of the actual offence itself.

ALIBIS AND OTHER DEFENCES

An accused person's usual line of defence when accused of a crime is to attempt to prove an *alibi*. This consists of evidence that the accused either was not where the crime was committed or did not have the ability to commit the offence and therefore could not have committed it. It is also possible for the defence to stay "mute," which means that the accused and the defence lawyer do or say nothing, except to appear at the place of trial. In such a case it is up to the judge to enter a plea of "not guilty," since our law proceeds from the assumption that the accused is not guilty until proven guilty. Other *general defences* are infancy and insanity.

Infancy
The Criminal Code provides in s. 12 that a child under seven years of age cannot commit a crime. This is what is called statutory "inability," an "irrebuttable presumption of law." See Appendix 3-B for a summary of the federal Young Offenders' Act, which details the procedure for handling criminal offences committed by youths 12 and over, but under 18 years old.

Insanity
Our criminal law is still governed by the *McNaughton* case. In England, in 1843, McNaughton shot and killed a Mr. Drummond, the Prime Minister's secretary, in the belief, as the jury found, that Drummond was the Prime Minister and that he, McNaughton, had a divine mission to kill him. The court came to the conclusion "that a person accused of a crime could not be acquitted on the grounds of insanity unless his delusion were proved to be such that it prevented him from *knowing the nature of the act which he did,* or, if he did know it, *that he did not know that what he did was wrong.*"

Not so long ago, in the province of Saskatchewan, a young man was charged with having killed all the members of one family, except one child, by shooting them. As the trial progressed, it was learned that the accused had been in and out of mental institutions and that, while at home, he had been observed standing in the fields apparently listening to voices, and crying out in mental anguish. It appeared that he heard a voice from heaven telling him that people residing at a certain house were in fact "pigs." When he carried out his crime, the accused thought he was "killing pigs," which is an example of that portion of the rule "that he did not appreciate the nature of his act." The accused was found "not guilty by reason of insanity" and was placed in a mental institution.

It should be pointed out that the plea of insanity is not used as frequently today as it was in the past. The reason is that the Criminal Code has been changed so that the punishment of death by hanging has been eliminated. Consequently, a defence counsel may advise his client to defend the case without pleading insanity and take the chance that the maximum punishment will be life imprisonment whereby the prisoner, after serving in a well-behaved manner, is virtually assured of being released in twenty years. On the other hand, where an offender is found "not guilty by reason of insanity," confinement to a mental institution is at the Lieutenant Governor's pleasure and, in such cases, the offender may never be released because of fear that he might commit the same type of offence again.

The effect of drinking or drugs in negating responsibility for crimes requiring *specific intent* seems to be accepted, providing the accused did not form the intent to commit the crime beforehand, then get drunk or drugged to carry out the crime. The accused, however, may be convicted of a lesser included offence not requiring intent.

In addition to the general defences discussed above, there are certain *limited defences*.

Provocation

It has been held that, in the case of murder, the provocation of the accused will serve to lessen or to negate "intention," one of the necessary ingredients of all common law crimes. Thus, if a person, charged with the offence of first-degree murder, can prove that he was provoked and temporarily lost his reasoning powers, or suffered what is called "temporary insanity" as a result of the provocation he received, this would be a mitigating factor. An example would be a husband who attacks and kills another man found molesting his wife. It could be argued that the husband was so provoked that he temporarily lost his reasoning powers, providing such act followed immediately after the provocation.

It should be noted that, in all other crimes not requiring "intent," provocation will be taken into consideration only in deciding on the severity of a sentence; it has no bearing on the guilt or the innocence of the accused.

The case of *R. v. Cunningham*, [1958] 3 All E.R. 711, which illustrates this point, dealt with an individual who was riding in a bus when he was accosted by another individual who whispered several words to him. The first man immediately proceeded to beat up the person who had spoken to him. When the first man was charged and later appeared in court, he stated in evidence that the second individual had asked him to engage in a homosexual act. Thus he had been provoked into taking the action he did, namely beating up the other man. The court ruled that while provocation might serve to negate intent in a murder trial, it was only to be taken into consideration in other cases in determining the severity of the sentence.

Coercion
Sometimes a person will argue that he was forced by someone else to commit a crime. However, it is possible to plead *coercion* as a defence only if one is forced by a third person to commit a crime against some other person's belongings. One cannot plead coercion as a defence if one was forced by a third person to commit a crime of violence against the person of any other party. An example of this would occur where a taxi driver is forced to drive would-be robbers to a bank. If he stays in front of the bank as the get-away driver under the threat of injury and the bank is robbed and the manager shot, it is no longer possible to plead coercion as a defence.

Under s. 17 of the Criminal Code, compulsion by threats is not a defence in the offences of treason, murder, piracy, attempted murder, assisting in rape, forcible abduction, robbery, causing bodily harm, or arson.

Self-Defence
Under ss. 34 and 35 of the Criminal Code, the principle of self-defence operates as a technical defence whenever an individual or that person's family is threatened with violence by another person. The first individual is allowed by law to take whatever steps are necessary to protect against the threat involved. This may vary from pushing the offender away to actually killing him, if there is no other way to avoid the threatening advances. Those who use self-defence must convince the court that, in their opinion, they used only sufficient force to ensure that the molesting influence was arrested and prevented from injuring anyone. A case illustrating this necessity is as follows:

R. v. Jacquot and Owen dealt with the situation in which the foreman of a wood-cutting operation drove to a work site and informed certain workmen that they were being discharged. One of these men became objectionable and jumped onto the cab of the truck when the foreman tried to drive away, and attempted to strike him. The foreman succeeded in dislodging him and could have driven away. However, he stopped and with a companion dismounted from the truck. Armed with axe handles, they then proceeded to assault the woodsman. Later, the foreman and his companion were tried in court. They stated that this was the only way that they could protect themselves against the assault being inflicted by the woodsman, and that they were *acting in self-defence*. The court found that this was not a case of self-defence since the aggravating act had ceased and that they could have continued on their way and lodged a charge of assault against the offender. Instead, they took the law into their own hands and were convicted accordingly.

Closely related to self-defence is the action of a police officer who is required to use force when arresting an offender, or a soldier who must shoot the enemy to avoid being killed himself. For example, in the case of *Goyer v. Gordon*, [1964] Que. Q.B. 558, the defendant police officer, after firing some shots over the head of the plaintiff who was fleeing from arrest, stumbled, causing his revolver to fire accidentally, injuring the plaintiff. The police officer was exonerated.

Automatism

This is the defence that the person who committed a crime was not conscious of what he or she was doing or, in other words, engaged in *unconscious, involuntary behaviour*. Thus, in *R. v. Sproule* (1972), 19 C.R.N.S. 384, Mr. Justice Lerner of the Ontario Supreme Court stated:

> Automatism is the state of a person who, though capable of action, is not conscious of what he is doing. In other words, it means an unconscious, involuntary act when the mind does not go with what is being done. An act is not to be regarded as involuntary because the doer of same does not remember doing it or remember the act itself . . . so long as the person doing it was conscious all the time.
>
> This is not to be confused with emotional or hysterical amnesia . . . in which the mind blocks out the memory of an incident because it is too painful to remember.

Entrapment

Another possible defence in a criminal case is that the alleged offence was instigated by police action which constituted entrapment. Thus, in *Connor v. People* (1893), 36 Am. St. R. 292 at p. 300, the court said:

> When in their zeal, or under a mistaken sense of duty, detectives suggest the commission of a crime or instigate others to take part in its commission in order to arrest them while in the act, although the purpose may be the capture of old offenders, their conduct is not only reprehensible, but criminal and ought to be rebuked rather than encouraged by the courts.

However, in *R. v. Timar*, [1969] 2 O.R. 90, the judge stated:

> Our laws have long recognized the necessity to employ agents provocateurs for the protection of society. This is primarily due to the existence of types of offences, the detection of which would, without such "police traps," as they have been called, be virtually impossible, and these special methods need to be employed if these crimes are to be controlled.
>
> It falls upon the courts to see that no abuse results in its operation. Each case of course must be dealt with on its own facts.

In one Canadian case in which two liquor inspectors ordered and were served beer after closing hours in a hotel, then charged the manager and the steward for this offence under the Liquor Licence Act, the court held that entrapment was not a defence. However, in Toronto a policewoman posed as a prostitute and charged with soliciting anyone who approached her with offers to pay for sexual favours. The magistrate refused to accept her evidence as a basis for conviction.

PROTECTION OF ACCUSED PERSONS

All citizens are aware of the legal principle "every accused is innocent until proven guilty," which was enshrined in the common law and is included in the Canadian Criminal Code. The Judges' Rules dealing with confessions contain measures which ensure that no "confession" made by the accused may be admitted before a court of law until it is proved to the satisfaction of the judge to have been made freely and voluntarily without any promise of reward or fear of any threat.

Since the 1960 Diefenbaker Bill of Rights, which was replaced by the 1982 Canadian Charter of Rights and Freedoms, the following additional safeguards for criminal proceedings are also enshrined in Canadian law:

1. No accused may be detained in custody without being made aware of the offence involved;
2. Every accused has the right to a legal counsellor and an interpreter if required;
3. Every accused may apply for a writ of "Habeas Corpus" requiring the jailer to explain why the accused is being detained;
4. Every accused is entitled to have a trial without delay.

Canadian law does not go as far as American criminal law in allowing a witness to refuse to answer a self-incriminating question or to exclude evidence obtained while searching for something else—for example, finding stolen goods while searching under a warrant for drugs. In Canada the witness must answer the question while pleading the Canada Evidence Act so that *this evidence may not be used* in a subsequent proceeding against that witness. Also, if any goods whatsoever involved in a criminal offence are found while the Canadian police are searching, the offenders may always be prosecuted for possession.

Up to now, the RCMP have been allowed to enter private dwellings at all times under a permanent *Writ of Assistance*. It is proposed, at present, to discontinue Writs of Assistance and proceed only by "search warrants" obtained for each separate search. These warrants are to be obtained by telephone from a justice of the peace, a procedure that will dispense with unnecessary delay.

REVIEW QUESTIONS

1. What is a crime? How does it differ from a civil offence?
2. Distinguish between federal and provincial criminal jurisdiction.
3. How do summary conviction offences and indictable offences differ?
4. What is meant by "criminal intent"? Why is it important?
5. Distinguish among a "common gaming house," a "common bawdy house," and a "common betting house."
6. Explain the concept of criminal negligence. Give a possible business example.
7. Give three examples of business theft. What is the possible punishment under the Criminal Code?

8. What are the other possible property offences?
9. Explain, with an example, how the mails may be used to defraud the public.
10. What is the "salting of mines"? Why is it a possible criminal offence?
11. What is "arson"? Why do people sometimes set fire to their own businesses?
12. Give some business examples of income tax evasion. What are the possible penalties for this criminal offence?
13. What are the various types of restrictive trade practices?
14. What is "usury"? Why is it a criminal offence?
15. What are the essential ingredients of a crime?
16. What is meant by the term "lesser included offences"?
17. Distinguish between an "attempt" and a crime.
18. If I plan with a friend to rob a bank but do not proceed, can I be charged with a criminal offence?
19. What is an "alibi"? Give an example.
20. How might infancy be a defence in a criminal case?
21. What was the rule, with regard to insanity as a defence, in the McNaughton case?
22. To what extent is provocation a defence in a criminal trial?
23. If forced to commit a crime, will I be sent to prison if caught?
24. Can a person be legally justified in injuring someone else? Explain.
25. A woman, while sleepwalking, robbed her neighbour's house. Could she be convicted of a crime, if caught?
26. Distinguish entrapment as a possible defence.

PROBLEMS

1. A person dressed as a trapper asked a taxi driver at a taxi stand in Yellowknife if he could get him a bottle of liquor, namely whiskey. After some discussion the trapper gave the taxi driver $15 and some fifteen minutes later a twenty-five ounce bottle of whiskey (sealed with the government excise tax label intact) was delivered to the trapper's motel room. It turned out that the trapper was an RCMP constable dressed as an undercover agent. The taxi driver was charged with bootlegging. Comment on the following:
   (a) that the accused should be considered as an agent in purchasing liquor for the purchaser, there being no evidence as to the source of the liquor;
   (b) there was no sale by the accused;
   (c) that the accused acted without "mens rea" (intention to commit a crime), having been induced by an officer in the course of duty;
   (d) that the accused was entitled to enjoy the same "de facto" immunity from the prosecution as the officer who induced him to do what was charged as an offence;
   (e) that proceedings should be stayed as an abuse of process as the

alleged offence was instigated by police action which constituted entrapment.

Refer to *R. v. Pratt* (1971), 19 C.R.N.S. 273.

2. A young man was arrested during a robbery attempt. He pleaded as his defence that he only committed this crime while he was under the influence of drugs. To escape liability for a crime through drunkenness or drug use the accused may possibly prove *lack of intent* if it can be established that the accused could bring himself under the McNaughton rules of insanity, i.e., either *that the accused could not distinguish between right and wrong or that the accused did not appreciate the nature and quality of his act.*

   Should this young man escape liability for his act because of drug use causing lack of intent? What would determine whether he should be convicted on such a charge? Give reasons for and against.

3. A taxi driver who had just picked up three male passengers was suddenly ordered to drive to a local bank. Once there, he was told to wait outside and leave the taxi's engine running. He was also told that one of the men would be stationed outside the bank entrance ready to shoot him if he tried to leave while the others, armed with guns, were inside robbing the bank. The taxi driver did as he was told. During the robbery the bank manager was seriously injured by a revolver bullet. The three men escaped in the taxi and ordered the driver, under the threat of death, not to reveal that he had been involved. After forty-eight hours, the police discovered his identity and charged him with having participated in the armed robbery.

   What defence could the taxi driver plead? How effective would this argument be? Discuss.

4. A farmer seeking revenge on a neighbour was seen on his neighbour's farm, kneeling by a haystack alongside the barn with a gasoline container and an open book of matches in his hands. He was then observed striking a match which was extinguished by a strong gust of wind before the haystack could catch fire. Has this farmer committed an offence?

   Compare this with the following situation: In a crowded subway, my pockets are empty but I catch another person's hand part-way into my pocket.

5. Two liquor inspectors registered at a hotel and, after the bar had closed, ordered a case of beer brought to their room. When the beer was delivered, the liquor inspectors revealed their identity and told the waiter that he and the owner of the hotel would be charged under the provincial Liquor Licence Act.

   Discuss the pros and cons of this charge. Can you see any difference between this case and one in which a policewoman poses as a prostitute and arrests any man who offers to pay for her sexual favours?

READING

Regina v. Dunn, 1 C.C.C. (3d)

Held by McIntyre J.:

In this appeal the Crown seeks to have the court consider and overrule a judgment of the Court of Appeal of British Columbia in *R. v. Parnell* (1978), 51 C.C.C. (2d) 413, and that the Court of Appeal for Alberta in *R. v. Cartier* (1980), 54 C.C.C. (2d) 32, 13 Alta. L.R. (2d) 164, 22 A.R. 257. These cases held that mere possession of the substance known as psilocybin, as an integral part of the plant in which it is found in nature, cannot support a conviction for possession of a restricted drug contrary to s. 41(1) of the *Food and Drugs Act*, R.S.C. 1970, c. F-27. The British Columbia Court of Appeal in reaching its conclusion in *Parnell,* accepted the reasoning of Lord Diplock in *Director of Public Prosecutions v. Goodchild,* [1978] 2 All E.R. 161, a case involving charges of possession of various hallucinogenic substances known as cannabinol derivatives in parts of the *cannabis* plant in the form in which the substance appears in nature.

The facts may be simply stated. The respondent was charged with trafficking in a restricted drug, pursuant to s. 42(1) of the *Food and Drugs Act,* in Courtenay, British Columbia, to two undercover R.C.M.P. officers in November 22, 1980. The information was in these terms:

> . . . on or about the 22nd day of November, 1980, at or near the City of Courtenay, in the County of Nanaimo, in the Province of British Columbia did unlawfully traffic in a restricted drug, to wit: 3-[2-(Dimethylamino)ethyl]-4-Phosphoryloxindole (Psilocybin), contrary to the form of the statute in such case made and provided.

The Crown proceeded summarily. The evidence revealed that Dunn met the police officers by a previous arrangement in the parking-lot of a hotel. There the respondent produced a one-pound bag of mushrooms, which it was later shown contained the drug psilocybin, and it was agreed that it would be sold to the undercover officers for $3,000. A conversation took place from which it was clear that the vendor was selling and that the purchaser was buying psilocybin. This conversation between the respondent and the undercover police officers included these comments:

> Respondent: This is a pound. We weighed it out with the scales.
> Lefler: You're sure of that, eh?
> Respondent: Yeah.
> Constable Lefler then examined the bag of mushrooms.
> Lefler: So this is the Psilocybin shit, eh?
> Respondent: Yeah, that's the stuff. Why don't you try a chew.
> Lefler: No thank you. I don't do that, it makes me sick. I'm only in this for the money. Dennis may want to.
> Constable Lefler then handed the bag to Constable Boissonnault who examined it.

Boissonnault: (to Lefler) Well, Russ, you'd better get the money.

Boissonnault: (to the Respondent) You're sure this is good stuff.

Respondent: Why don't you chew on a few, five or six. That's for $3,000.00

The money was produced and at that moment other police officers arrived on the scene and the respondent was arrested.

Throughout these proceedings it had been agreed by all parties that psilocybin is a restricted drug listed in Sch. H to the *Food and Drugs Act*, that it appears in nature in some types of mushrooms, several of which grow wild in British Columbia and that the mushrooms offered for sale in the case at bar did contain the drug psilocybin. At trial the respondent at the conclusion of the Crown's case moved for a dismissal of the charge on the basis that no evidence had been adduced to support the charge. The provincial court judge, following the *Parnell* case, *supra*, allowed the motion and acquitted the respondent. An appeal to the county court was dismissed on the same basis as was a further appeal to the British Columbia Court of Appeal. The matter comes before us and the Crown asks us to review and overrule *Parnell* and *Cartier*.

Because of the way the matter was disposed of in the courts below, there are few findings of fact for the assistance of the court. There was evidence from an expert that the mushrooms contained psilocybin which could be extracted from the mushrooms in a somewhat complicated process. As I understand it, the expert evidence on this question was that the drug is found in the mushrooms in its free form. In argument before this court counsel for the respondent agreed that this was so. I therefore concluded that the actual compound known as psilocybin, not merely the constituent elements from which it could be chemically produced, exists in the mushrooms, and that its hallucinogenic effects may be obtained by chewing or eating the mushrooms.

Part IV of the *Food and Drugs Act* deals with restricted drugs. Section 40 of the Act, the first section in Part IV, provides:

40. In this Part

"possession" means possession as defined in the *Criminal Code*.

"regulations" means regulations made as provided for by or under section 45;

"restricted drug" means any drug or other substance included in Schedule H;

"traffic" means to manufacture, sell, export from or import into Canada, transport or deliver, otherwise than under the authority of this Part or the regulations.

Schedule H appended to the Act lists the restricted drugs and includes: "3-[2-(Dimethylamino)ethyl]-4-phosphoryloxyindole (Psilocybin) or any salt thereof."

In *Parnell* Nemetz C.J.B.C., speaking for the court (Nemetz C.J.B.C.,

Aikins and Lambert JJ.A.), considered a case where a charge of possession resulted from the finding of a mushroom-like substance containing psilocybin in the accused's residence. He reached the conclusion that the simple possession of mushrooms containing the restricted drug as it occurs in nature would not support a conviction for possession. At p. 414 of the report he said:

> There is no doubt that the mushrooms found in the possession of the respondent contained psilocybin, though there was no evidence of what quantity of the drug was present in the mushrooms. Counsel for the respondent submitted, first, that the mere possession of the substance psilocybin as an integral part of the natural plant cannot support a conviction for possession of a restricted drug, and, second, that in enacting s. 41(1) and Sch. (H), Parliament intended to prohibit only the possession of the separated crystalline chemical substance. After anxious reflection, and after considering the circumstances of this case, as outlined above, I conclude that the first submission is correct insofar as psilocybin is concerned. It is not necessary for me to decide to what extent the second submission is correct.

He found support in the reasoning of Lord Diplock in *D.P.P. v. Goodchild, supra,* a case based on different English legislation, but expressing the same principle. He referred to the words of Lord Diplock at p. 166, where he said:

> . . . the offence of unlawful possession of any controlled drug described in Sch. 2 by its scientific name is not established by proof of possession of naturally occuring [*sic*] material of which the described drug is one of the constituents unseparated from the others.

He also found support in a comparison with the provisions of the *Narcotic Control Act* noting that in that Act where Parliament intended to prohibit possession of the plant as well as the drug it made specific provision for that result by naming the plant. He also expressed the view that the position adopted by the Crown, that is, that mere possession of the plant containing the naturally occurring drug was sufficient to support a conviction for possession, would lead to an absurd result opening the door to prosecution of farmers and others who merely by an accident of nature might have growing upon their land the nefarious "magic mushrooms".

Shortly thereafter the same question was presented to the Alberta Court of Appeal in *R. v. Cartier, supra.* McGillivray C.J.A. (McGillivray C.J.A., McDermid and Laycraft JJ.A.) reached the same conclusion that Nemetz C.J.B.C. expressed in *Parnell,* relying as well on the approach taken by Diplock L.J. in *Goodchild, supra,* and noting as well with apparent approval the remarks of the Chief Justice of British Columbia regarding the absurd result which could follow from the acceptance of the Crown's submission.

There have been other cases referring to the question raised in this appeal from trial courts but the two appellate decisions, *Parnell* and *Cartier*, are the leading cases on the subject. The *Parnell* case in particular is sought to be overturned by the appellant.

The Crown's contention is that to follow the *Parnell* and *Cartier* cases would be to render the *Food and Drugs Act* nugatory in this connection. It does not rely upon the concept of trafficking by holding out a substance to be a restricted drug but argues that the words of the Act and Sch. H are broad enough in themselves to include as a restricted drug mushrooms containing in their natural state the specifically restricted drug psilocybin. The position taken by the respondent is essentially to support the *Parnell* and *Cartier* cases and to stress the fact that mushrooms containing psilocybin are not mentioned as such in Sch. H and, therefore, cannot be classified as a restricted drug.

In approaching the construction of the relevant provisions of the *Food and Drugs Act* I must observe that the words employed are clear and unambiguous and in this case there seems to be no real difficulty in statutory interpretation. Section 40 provides in unmistakable language that possession means possession as defined in the *Criminal Code*. Reference to s. 3(4) of the *Criminal Code* describes the elements which must be shown to find possession. Section 40 also describes a restricted drug as "any drug or other substance included in Schedule H" and Sch. H specifically includes psilocybin. Section 41 prohibits possession of a restricted drug and s. 42, which is the relevant section in this case, prohibits trafficking in a restricted drug.

In reaching his conclusion on the "no evidence" motion the trial judge followed *Parnell* and decided that there was no evidence before him because psilocybin contained in a mushroom is not listed in Sch. H as a restricted drug. The question which faced him, however, was not whether psilocybin naturally occurring in a mushroom is listed in Sch. H but whether there was evidence before him upon which a properly instructed trier of fact could have found the respondent guilty of trafficking in psilocybin, which clearly is.

In the face of the evidence given at trial and the concession made by counsel for the respondent that psilocybin, not merely the constituents from which it could be made, existed in the mushrooms, it could not be said that there was not some evidence of trafficking in psilocybin. The mushrooms contained the drug. There was evidence that the respondent knew it and that he assured his prospective purchasers that it was "good stuff", that he invited them to try it and that he had offered a pound for sale for $3,000, which would tend to exclude the possibility that the mushrooms were to be sold for their value as food. In my opinion, it is impossible to come to any other conclusion than that there was evidence before the trial judge upon which a properly instructed trier of fact could have convicted the respondent of trafficking in psilocybin and that the trial judge was in error in allowing the motion of no evidence.

While this disposes of the case at bar, it does not deal with the question raised by the cases of *Parnell* and *Cartier*. As indicated above, the case at bar was not seriously considered in the courts below on the merits because all the judges dealing with it considered that the *Parnell* case was decisive on the matter and that the considerations involved in the charge of trafficking did not differ from those involved in a possession charge. It will be apparent from what I have said that, in my opinion, the fact that psilocybin may be contained within a mushroom does not destroy its character as a restricted drug under Sch. H of the *Food and Drugs Act*. It could therefore, in my view, be as much the subject of a conviction for possession as it could be for trafficking. If the *Parnell* case and the *Cartier* case go so far as to deny that proposition, then in my view, with the greatest respect for the learned judges involved in those decisions, I consider the cases were wrongly decided. I am not overlooking the absurdity argument which impressed the courts, but I would point out that what is prohibited with respect to possession is unlawful possession, not mere physical possession. To be unlawful there must be present a knowledge of the nature of the substance possessed. The farmer who unknowingly has "magic mushrooms" growing on his land is not guilty of unlawful possession. It would seem to me that reason and common sense on the part of the authorities would protect him if on discovery of the nature of the mushrooms he took the necessary steps to have them destroyed. In any event we are not here concerned with a possession case. Our case is that of an accused charged with trafficking in psilocybin in respect of whom evidence was placed before the trial judge that he had acquired the mushrooms, dried them and offered to sell them at $3,000 a pound. As I have said before, there was evidence of trafficking before the learned judge and it was error to allow the motion of no evidence. I would therefore allow the Crown's appeal and remit the matter to the trial court for the completion of the trial.

Appeal allowed.

APPENDIX 3-A: SUMMARY OF THE PROVINCIAL OFFENCES ACT, R.S.O. 1979, c. 400

This statute was enacted in the Province of Ontario in 1979 with the following objectives:

1. to simplify previous practices;
2. to eliminate unnecessary technicalities;
3. to enhance basic rights and protection;
4. to remove the obstacle of delay from the conduct of legal proceedings; and
5. to reduce the court costs involving minor offences.

Until this Act was passed, all offences, whether federal or provincial, were heard in the first instance in the Provincial Judge's (or Magistrate's) Court under the procedure set out in the Criminal Code. This procedure did not properly discriminate between a breach of a provincial statute, such as unlawful stopping or parking and a breach of the Criminal Code—for example, a thief who was being tried for his tenth offence of stealing; both appeared in the same court and entered the same pleas.

The new Act sets out a simpler procedure with the offender normally appearing in a Provincial Offences Court which has been established under Part IIA of the Provincial Courts Act.

This Act provides three different procedures for dealing with offences under provincial statutes:

1. proceedings under Part I of the Act, commenced by filing a certificate of offence, which is usual when the maximum punishment is $300 or less;
2. proceedings under Part II, commenced by filing a certificate of parking infraction; and
3. proceedings under Part III, commenced by laying an information before a justice of the peace.

Under Part I, a provincial offences officer (generally any police officer or provincial law enforcement official) may start proceedings under this part either by serving an *offence notice* or a *summons* within thirty days and also filing a certificate of offence. The offender may deal with such notice or summons in 3 ways:

1. if admitting "guilt," he or she can simply sign the document and return it with the fine enclosed;
2. endorse it "not guilty" and return the notice and a date will be fixed for trial;
3. appear on the trial date merely to dispute the amount of the fine or the method of payment. This choice is equivalent to pleading "guilty."

This Act adopts the default procedure of the civil court, and if the alleged offender does nothing, a conviction may be entered in his absence based on the evidence and the absentee will be notified when and how to pay his fine.

It should be noted that no convictions for imprisonment will be entered under Part I.

Demerit points may be entered for driving infractions, and goods seized— for example, a gun if a person is caught hunting without a licence.

Finally, an offender convicted *in absentia* may re-open the case if it can be proved that within thirty days of the alleged offence, the offender was not served with either the notice of offence or the summons, despite attempts to serve the offender under s. 3.

Part II provides a procedure which is similar to the foregoing for offences related to *parking* offences such as unlawful parking, standing, or stopping of a motor vehicle. However, for two years from the date of promulgation of the Act, this procedure does not apply to parking infractions in Ontario municipalities unless requested by such municipalities and approved by the Lieutenant Governor in Council.

Part III provides a procedure for dealing with serious provincial offences, whereby an information must be laid before a justice of the peace who after hearing the allegations of the informant, either a provincial offences officer or an individual, may decide either to proceed with a *summons* or deny any further action (s. 25).

This part also provides that it is merely sufficient that the allegation of the offence serve to acquaint the alleged offender with the ingredients or nature of the charge, and the Provincial Offences Judge is allowed to make corrections to the summons if justified and required. The summons containing particulars of the offence and informing the offender of the date, time, and place of trial must be served either personally or at the last known address and left with a person over sixteen years of age.

Normally the court where the offence occurred has jurisdiction. Section 46 states that the defendant will be informed of the charge and then asked to make a "plea." The judge may accept a plea of guilty on a lesser charge. The defendant may appear either personally, or by counsel or by an agent (s. 51).

Under s. 55 if the defendant does not appear at the place and time stated, the judge may proceed "ex parte" (without the defendant) and determine the guilt or innocence of the accused or may adjourn and issue a summons or a warrant.

The Provincial Offences Judge has the authority to amend the summons, order witnesses to attend subject to contempt charges, insist on the presentation of necessary evidence or documents, hear evidence under oath, request expert or medical evidence, exclude the public from the hearing, and dismiss the charge if the prosecutor does not appear. This Court may even be presided over by a Provincial Court Judge or Magistrate in the event of a serious offence.

Sentencing under the Act is covered by ss. 57-75. Generally, sentencing is flexible in that the judge is not bound by any minimum sentence and may even withhold a conviction and substitute probation or relieve a convicted offender from the burden of paying a fine—for example, a senior citizen on a fixed income.

If a fine is in default, the clerk of the court may file a certificate in a court of competent jurisdiction which will have the effect of making it an order of that court enforceable by a garnishee or by execution—that is, by seizing and selling personal possessions. Failure to pay a fine, without excuse, may result in imprisonment for four days for each $25 of fine in default up to a maximum of ninety days or half of the maximum punishment, whichever is the greater.

Procedures will be instituted allowing credits for work performed such as cleaning in public parks instead of fines.

Proceedings will be limited to the period prescribed in each provincial Act or six months if no limitation is prescribed.

Part VI of the Act provides for appeals. Appeals under procedures I and II, dealing with certificates of offences and parking offences respectively, may be taken to the Provincial Court (Criminal Division) which shall be conducted on the record, subject to hearing new evidence. This Court may alter, reverse, vary a decision, or order a new trial.

An appeal under Part III will be either from a justice of the peace to the

Provincial Court (Criminal Division) or from a provincial judge to the County or District Court. Such Court may, in case of a conviction, allow the appeal on grounds of lack of evidence, mistake of law or miscarriage justice, and either direct a new finding or order a new trial. In case of mental inability to conduct a defence, a new trial will be ordered. If the appeal is from an acquittal, the appeal court may either dismiss the appeal, order a new trial, or substitute a new verdict.

The provisions for bail and arrest parallel those found in the Criminal Code, except that an arrested person who resides outside of the province may be requested to provide cash bail of $300 if proceedings are commenced by certificate and $500 if commenced by an information.

A justice of the peace is authorized to issue search warrants which must be executed between 6 a.m. and 9 p.m. any day within fifteen days of issue.

This act is now in force in Ontario.

APPENDIX 3-B: SUMMARY OF YOUNG OFFENDERS' ACT

S. 2(1) Young person includes youths twelve and over and under eighteen years of age.

S. 5(1) Youth Court Judge has jurisdiction and powers of a Summary Conviction Court.

S. 7(3) Young offenders must be detained separately from adults.

S. 8 Only a Youth Court Judge may release a young offender from custody.

S. 9(1) Young offender's parents or, if they are not known, a friend of the youth must be notified of detention and hearings. The parent may be required to attend Court proceedings under penalty of contempt of Court [s. (3)].

S. 11(1) Any arrested young offender must be advised of rights to counsel and, if none is selected, the judge may order appointment of a counsel.

S. 11(7) If no counsel is selected, an adult may be allowed to assist a young offender.

S. 12(1) A young person appearing before the Court must be read the information or charge.
The Youth Court Judge may request medical and psychological reports, which may be given to the young person and his or her counsel.

S. 14(1) The court may require a predisposition report.

S. 16(1) A case involving a youth over fourteen may be transferred to ordinary court if in the interests of society and the needs of the offender.

S. 19(1) The youth may plead "guilty" to charge, or "not guilty," in which case the trial is proceeded with.

S. 20 Disposition by Youth Court Judge: after considering predisposition report, representations of parents, and so on, the judge may:

(a) order an absolute discharge;

(b) impose a fine of up to $1,000;

(c) order compensation to be made;

(d) order restitution;

(e) order the offender to compensate the innocent purchaser who has bought goods which were the subject matter of a crime;

(f) order personal compensation or community service;

(g) make an order of prohibition, seizure, or forfeiture;

(h) order probation;

(j) commit the offender for up to two years in jail or, if the offence provides for life imprisonment, up to three years.

(k) any other conditions deemed advisable.

S. 41   The Commissioner of the RCMP will designate a registry for the registration of files on young persons found "guilty." Police forces may keep records of any young persons alleged to have committed an offence.

Unit 3.2:
Criminal Courts and Procedure

CRIMINAL LAW COURTS

Each province has its own set of criminal law courts. These are divided, except in Quebec, into three levels of criminal jurisdiction. At the lowest level there is the provincial court, called in some provinces the magistrate's court, which strictly speaking is the criminal division of the provincial or magistrate's court. The other division of the court, the family court, hears family-related cases. Special youth courts hear cases involving children 12 to 18 years of age who are alleged to have committed offences specified in the federal Young Offenders Act.

At the intermediate level, there is a court called the District Court in Alberta, Saskatchewan, Newfoundland, and Ontario. And at the highest level, there is the supreme court. Each province also has a court of appeal.

Quebec has two levels of criminal courts: the Cour des Sessions de la paix being the lower and the Cour supérieure, the higher. There is also a provincial court of appeal, the Cour d'appel.

Federally, there is the Supreme Court of Canada, which hears criminal as well as civil appeals from the decisions of the provincial courts of appeal.

Provincial (or Magistrate's) Court
In the case of a summary conviction offence, the accused, after being arrested or summoned to provincial (or magistrate's) court, is tried by a provincial judge (or magistrate) without jury. In the case of an indictable offence, the accused is first brought before a provincial judge where the charge will be

read to him. This is known as an "arraignment." If the person is accused of the least serious type of indictable offence, the provincial judge may try him or her as a person accused of a summary conviction offence. Both these types of criminal cases fall within what is termed the provincial judge's *absolute jurisdiction*.

A second situation is one in which the person is accused of a more serious indictable offence—one that permits the accused a choice of being tried either by a provincial judge, a district court judge, or a district court judge and jury. If the accused chooses to be tried by a provincial judge, the trial is carried out forthwith. This is called the provincial judge's *consent jurisdiction*.

If the accused chooses to be tried by a district court judge alone or by a district court judge and jury, the provincial judge must then hold a *preliminary hearing*. The purpose of this is to determine whether there is sufficient evidence to commit the accused for trial. In most provinces, "judge alone" means a county court judge; in some, a county court or supreme court judge; and in Quebec, a judge of the Sessions de la paix. If the evidence is sufficient, the provincial judge will arrange for the accused to be tried at the next sitting of the higher court. If the evidence is insufficient, he will dismiss the charge.

A third situation is one in which the accused is charged with the most serious type of indictable offence, as listed in s. 427 of the Criminal Code. Such cases are reserved to a superior court of criminal jurisdiction. Here, the provincial judge also holds a preliminary hearing to review the evidence. If satisfied, he will commit the accused for trial at the provincial supreme court's next sitting.

In most cases, the accused remains at liberty while awaiting trial, except if he may injure himself, if the crime is very serious, or if there is reason to believe that the accused may not appear for the trial. Even if the accused person has been arrested (rather than attending court in response to a summons), he may be released on his signing a *recognizance*—a document whereby he promises to attend court on a certain date. Also, a person may be released on *bail*—that is, he or someone acting on his behalf assigns a sum of money or other property to the court as assurance that he will attend the court on the date set for the trial. Under the new bail laws, it is generally unnecessary for a person to put up money in order to obtain his release.

Bail. Bail is the privilege that an accused person has of being set free pending trial on the security, either of the accused's personal promise or of a sum of money. Bail was previously granted by a judge or magistrate and was usually fixed by him or her, on the recommendation of the police, at a high amount if it was desired that the alleged offender should not be released. However, under the federal Bail Reform Act, the rule has now been changed so that the police sergeant on duty can fix bail, acting on the principle that bail will not be refused unless: the offence is of a serious nature such as murder; the alleged offender needs protection from others; or there is no other way that the alleged offender's presence can be guaranteed at the trial.

It is now argued that many serious offenders are being too easily released on bail.

County (or District) Court

The judges in the county (or district) courts have criminal jurisdiction over a large range of indictable offences. They also hear appeals from certain decisions of the provincial judges in summary conviction cases. A further appeal may then be made, if desired, to the provincial court of appeal.

Superior Court of Criminal Jurisdiction

Each province has a supreme court, one of whose functions is to try persons accused of major criminal offences. Thus s. 429.1 of the Criminal Code states that an accused charged with an indictable offence under ss. 109, 144, 145, 203, 219, or 331(1)(a) must be tried by a judge of a superior court of criminal jurisdiction and a jury. These are offences such as murder which are beyond the jurisdiction of the provincial and county courts. In Alberta, Manitoba, and Saskatchewan, these superior courts are called the Court of Queen's Bench. In Ontario, the High Court of Justice (a division of the Supreme Court of Ontario) handles major criminal cases.

Provincial Court of Appeal

In New Brunswick, Nova Scotia, and Prince Edward Island, the provincial supreme court has an appeal division to hear appeals from all the trial courts in that particular province. In Alberta, British Columbia, Manitoba, Ontario, Quebec, and Saskatchewan, there is a separate provincial court of appeal. In Newfoundland, the Supreme Court of Judicature hears appeals. Whatever the province, a panel of three or more judges comprises the court, listens to an appeal, and accepts or rejects it by majority vote. Appeals may be made directly to the provincial court of appeal with regard to indictable offences that have been tried in the county court or provincial supreme court. It is unusual, at the appeal, for any new witness to be heard or new evidence examined. If the court concludes that an error has been made by the lower court judge, it may declare the convicted person not guilty, alter the judgment (for example, by imposing a lighter or heavier sentence), or order a new trial. The court may also dismiss the appeal, even if the trial judge has erred in law, so long as there has been no substantial wrong or miscarriage of justice. A further appeal may be made, if desired, to the Supreme Court of Canada. Generally, criminal convictions may be appealed on grounds of mistake of law, mistake of fact, mistake of both law and fact, or severity of sentence.

Supreme Court of Canada

The Supreme Court of Canada is a federal court that hears appeals from provincial supreme court criminal trials. Appeal is automatically permitted if the crime is a serious one, if a point of law is involved, or if the accused has been sentenced to death. Otherwise, special permission must be obtained.

CRIMINAL TRIAL PROCEDURE

When a person accused of a crime appears before a judge, the judge asks how the accused wishes to plead. If the plea is "guilty," there is no need for a trial. However, before passing sentence, the judge will require the prosecutor to produce evidence so as to ensure that the charge is justified. The judge will also try to ascertain that the accused has not pleaded guilty out of fear or ignorance.

If the accused pleads "not guilty," the crown prosecutor is asked to present the evidence against him or her. In turn, the defendant (or lawyer) may present evidence attempting to disprove the crown prosecutor's case. Eventually, after this adversary system of presenting evidence by the prosecution and defence, the judge or jury will be required to reach a verdict on the guilt of the accused. Finally, the accused will be sentenced by the judge or set free.

In the case of minor criminal offences, the provincial judge will reach a verdict on his or her own. However, in the case of more serious offences, the accused has the right to trial by chosen jury. A jury is a specially chosen group of lay citizens assembled to hear the evidence in a trial and reach a verdict for or against the accused. Once chosen, a person is called a *juror*. In the case of the most serious offences, notably murder, the accused must be tried by a jury selected from a list of persons drawn from the voters' lists by the county sheriff's office. In a criminal case, there must be twelve jurors to form a jury—"twelve good men [and women] and true"—and their verdict must be unanimous. If the jurors cannot agree, the jury is said to be a "hung jury." This means that a new jury must be formed and the case retried. The trial judge directs the jury as to the principles of law involved in the case. The jury are triers of the facts involved. A judge hearing a case without a jury is both the trier of the facts and interpreter of the law.) A *petit jury* consists of only six jurors and is permitted only in the Northwest Territories and the Yukon, where the population is small and the distances to travel to court are great.

INNOCENT UNTIL PROVEN GUILTY

One of the most important provisions in the Criminal Code is the declaration in s. 5(1)(a) that "a person shall be deemed not to be guilty of that offence until he is convicted thereof" or in layman's language, "a person is innocent until proven guilty." This declaration is known as a rebuttable presumption. Of course, during the course of a trial, evidence submitted by the prosecutor acting on behalf of the Crown may clearly prove that the accused committed the offence. In our criminal law, the burden of proving the accused guilty always remains with the prosecutor. As was stated in *Woolmington v. D.P.P.*, [1935] A.C. 462 at page 481, "Throughout the web of the English criminal law, one golden thread is always to be seen: that it is the duty of the prosecutor to prove the prisoner's guilt."

During the trial, the defence may also present its side of the case—although there is no obligation on the defence or the accused to give any evidence, or even to identify him- or herself. If the prosecutor fails to prove the accused guilty "beyond a reasonable doubt," the magistrate or judge has no alternative but to release the accused. Even if the prosecutor succeeds in convincing the magistrate or judge that there is a case, it is still possible for the defence, by establishing a believable defence, to put some doubt in the judge's mind as to the alleged offender's guilt. If this is the case, then the judge or magistrate has no alternative but to release the accused.

DOUBLE JEOPARDY

A person may have appeared in court and have been tried and been either "acquitted" or "convicted" of the charge. Under s. 535 of the Criminal Code, if the accused has to appear in court again on the same charge arising out of the same facts, he or she is entitled under our law to plead that this case has already been adjudicated and that, therefore, he has been placed in double jeopardy. If the judge finds this to be the case, he has no alternative but to let the person go. A person who has been found "not guilty" in the first trial cannot be retried, even though further evidence may have been uncovered which unquestionably points to him or her as the offender. The terms "autrefois acquit" and "autrefois convict" are sometimes used instead of double jeopardy.

EXTRADITION

Sometimes, a person who has committed a criminal offence will flee to another country in an attempt to escape punishment. However, if the country to which he has fled has an extradition treaty with Canada, he may, with the aid of the foreign police and legal authorities, be extradited—that is, forcibly returned to Canada to face trial. Not all countries, it should be noted, have extradition treaties with Canada. Furthermore, extradition applies only to some criminal offences, and not to political ones.

GRAND JURY PROCEEDINGS

Some provinces (Nova Scotia, Prince Edward Island, and Newfoundland) still have Grand Jury proceedings whereby an accused committed for trial to the Supreme Court for a serious criminal offence, following a preliminary hearing, must first appear before a specially constituted jury which again reviews the evidence. This jury consists of a number of carefully selected jurors, ranging up to twenty-three in Newfoundland. If the evidence is strong enough to warrant trial, a *true bill* verdict is brought in, meaning the case must proceed to trial. If the evidence is insufficient or unconvincing, a *no bill* verdict is given and the accused is discharged. The Grand Jury has been abolished in most provinces because its work is considered to duplicate that of the provincial judge in the preliminary hearing.

EVIDENCE

The trial courts are termed courts of first instance, where all the witnesses' evidence is heard "viva voce"—that is, spoken aloud. In addition to the personal or direct evidence given by the witnesses, other forms of evidence such as documentary evidence and real evidence (for example, a weapon) may also be tendered, but these forms of evidence must always be presented by a witness who is familiar with them. All the evidence received in these courts of first instance must be recorded.

PUNISHMENTS

A judge, in sentencing a person found guilty of a crime, may not award more than the maximum punishment set out in the Criminal Code or other relevant statute. Thus the maximum punishment for summary conviction offences is six months' imprisonment, a fine of $500, or both. A judge may, however, award a lighter sentence.

The various forms of punishment for a criminal offence are as follows:

Fine. This is a sum of money that must be paid by the offender. Usually the judge awards a period of imprisonment as an alternative punishment. If the offender needs time to raise the money required for the fine, the judge may allow a certain number of days to do so. Failure to pay means serving the term of imprisonment.

Imprisonment. A term of imprisonment is awarded for more serious crimes. If the term is less than three months, the prisoner will be sent to a local or county jail. If it is more than three months but less than two years, he or she will be sent to a provincial reformatory. And if it is two years or over, the offender will be sent to a federal penitentiary. After serving a third of the sentence, either in a reformatory or penitentiary, a prisoner is eligible for *parole*, or early release. To be eligible, the prisoner must have shown good behaviour in prison.

Hanging. Before 1977, a person could be sentenced to be hanged if found guilty of murdering a police officer or prison guard on duty, or if found guilty of treason. However, hanging as a punishment for murder was abolished in 1977.

Suspended Sentence. A judge may decide, in the case of a first offender or young offender, to suspend the passing of sentence until a later date. In the meantime, the offender is placed on *probation*. This means that he will have to report regularly to a probation officer, a court-appointed official, and follow the rules of conduct laid down by him. An offender who misbehaves during this period may be brought back to court and be sentenced for the original offence; otherwise, no further penalty is imposed.

Suspension of Privileges. In the case of driving offences, the judge may suspend a person's driving privileges for a certain period of time, usually prescribed by statute.

Confiscation.   This is automatic under certain statutes—for example, confiscation of guns when hunting out of season, or confiscation of goods and vehicles for customs offences or boats for fishing offences.

Restitution.   In theft and fraud cases, the judge may order the convicted person to return the goods or money to their rightful owner.

Community Service.   As a minor form of punishment, the judge may now make community service orders—for instance, requiring a convicted person to clean up a public park. These orders may be carried out (or "served"), at the judge's discretion, only on weekends.

CRIMINAL RECORD

It should be noted that a judge now has the power with regard to certain offences such as a first conviction for possession of marijuana to order that the accused receive a conditional or absolute discharge, which in effect enables the accused to avoid having a criminal record.

As discussed earlier, a person already found guilty may subsequently apply for a "pardon" to have his or her criminal record struck out. In fact, the record is still kept but it is permanently sealed.

COSTS

Normally no costs are payable by the accused in a criminal case, whether acquitted or convicted. However, in minor traffic offences and breaches of bylaws, witnesses' fees may be charged to a convicted defendant.

COMPENSATION

The federal government is considering reimbursement of the defence fees incurred by an accused on a criminal charge if eventually acquitted. In Ontario, if a person suffers physical injuries as the result of a crime either as a victim, witness, or bystander, the government may provide compensation if damages cannot be recovered from the criminals. The Criminal Injuries Compensation Act covers these situations.

PARDON

At the present time any person convicted by the courts may petition the Queen for "mercy" or a "pardon" under s. 683 of the Criminal Code so as to remove the criminal record. In such a case, the Queen receives a petition from the Governor General and returns it to the Canadian Cabinet. The Cabinet studies the case and makes a recommendation to the Queen who transmits the decision to the criminal through the office of the Governor General. A convicted person may make the application for a pardon after two years for a summary conviction and after five years for an indictable offence.

REVIEW QUESTIONS

1. Outline the system of criminal courts in your province.
2. Distinguish between a provincial judge's absolute jurisdiction and his or her consent jurisdiction.
3. Explain the nature and purpose of the "preliminary hearing."
4. Distinguish between "recognizance" and "bail." Is bail granted too easily?
5. Explain the role, including jurisdiction, of the provincial Supreme Court.
6. On what grounds may a criminal conviction be appealed?
7. What is the appeal procedure for criminal convictions?
8. What appeals are heard by the Supreme Court of Canada?
9. What happens in Criminal Court if the accused pleads "guilty"?
10. What happens in Criminal Court if the accused pleads "not guilty"?
11. When does the accused have the right to trial by jury?
12. Explain the role of the jury in criminal trials.
13. In criminal law, it is a rebuttable presumption that "a person is innocent until proven guilty." Explain.
14. Explain, with reference to a hit-and-run offence, the points that a prosecutor would have to prove to secure a conviction.
15. Can a person receive a pardon for a criminal offence? How and when?
16. Explain the principle of "double jeopardy."
17. If I commit a crime and run away to another country, can the Canadian authorities bring me back for trial?
18. Explain the nature and purpose of Grand Jury proceedings.
19. What kinds of evidence are permissible in criminal court?
20. What are the various possible types of punishment that a judge may hand out to a person convicted of a criminal offence?
21. What different points must be proved by the prosecutor in a case of theft?
22. Give your understanding of the following principles, "innocent until proven guilty" and "reasonable doubt."
23. Make up an example of a hit-and-run situation. Do you agree that "intent" to avoid civil and criminal responsibility should be presumed in these cases?
24. Discuss lesser included offences, also called cognate offences. Give an example of "other similar offences."
25. Why are conspiracies normally difficult to prove?
26. Criminal courts will admit the evidence of young children as witnesses only if the judge believes they understand the difference between "right and wrong." Drawing on your own experience, do you think children make reliable witnesses?
27. Should modern-day psychology and psychiatry overrule the McNaughton rules regarding insanity in criminal cases?
28. Show how provocation might have an effect on the punishment awarded for an offence of "causing bodily harm."

4

Law of Torts

Unit 4.1
Different Types of Tort

A *tort* is a private wrong committed intentionally or unintentionally by one person against another person or against another person's property. Examples, in the business field, include the sale by a firm of a defective electrical appliance which later causes physical injury to the purchaser, or the collision of a firm's delivery vehicle with a person's private car. In contrast, a crime is a public wrong for which society (by means of the police and courts) prosecutes the offender. The victim of a tort seeks redress by suing the person who committed the tort (the "tortfeasor") in the appropriate civil court.

The *law of torts* is the set of rules that has been established by the courts to apportion blame for such private wrongs and to determine the amount of compensation that should be paid by the person who has committed the wrong to the injured party. The word "tort" comes from the Norman French, in which it meant a "wrong." The French word itself derives from the Latin *tortus,* meaning "twisted."

Purpose. The law of torts is more concerned with securing compensation for the victim of a tort than with imposing punishment on the person who committed it. It is considered to be the responsibility of the criminal courts to punish a person who wilfully injures another. Thus, when a person commits a wrongful action that is both a tort and a crime (for example, assault and battery), he or she may be sued for damages in the civil courts by the victim and prosecuted in the criminal courts by the Crown. The primary purpose of the criminal prosecution is to secure a penalty for the offender that will serve, in some measure, as retribution for the crime committed. This penalty will in turn serve as a deterrent to other possible offenders and thereby help protect society as a whole. In addition there is the theory that punishment is also designed to rehabilitate the offender. In the case of a criminal offence such as theft, the tort liability exists mainly to compensate the person injured by compelling the wrongdoer to pay compensation for depriving the owner of possession of his or her goods.

The following reviews the most common types of tort.

Trespass to Land
In everyday conversation, trespass refers to the tort of trespass to land. Whenever a person enters and crosses another person's land (including

buildings) without permission, an act of trespass is committed. Under provincial statutes, this is also a criminal offence.

According to common law, a person owns the air above his property up to space and below it to the centre of the earth. However, the right to use air space for peaceful purposes is recognized. Also, some provincial legislatures have passed laws reserving oil and mineral rights for the province. Nevertheless, the owner of the land is entitled to royalties and rent for the use of the subsoil.

Necessity. Sometimes a person is considered to be justified, because of necessity, in doing something that might otherwise be held to be tortious. For example, in *Proof v. Putnam* (1908), 81 V1.471, the owner of a sailing boat moored his vessel to the defendant's dock during a storm to prevent the vessel's destruction. The defendant (landowner) cast it adrift, thereby causing it to be destroyed and the passengers injured. The court held the defendant liable.

The law also confers a complete privilege on a stranger who, acting only from a motive of saving the property of others, takes steps to save property from flood or other dangers (*Proudman v. Allen*, [1954] S.A.S.R. 336).

Nuisance

Nuisance is the act of wrongfully allowing or causing the escape of harmful or obnoxious things onto another person's land—for example, water, smoke, smell, fumes, gas, noise, heat, vibrations, and electricity that are capable of harming or destroying a person's health or property.

An example of a case involving nuisance is *Russell Transport Ltd. v. Ontario Malleable Iron Co.*, [1952] O.R. 621. In this case, Russell Transport Ltd., the plaintiff, alleged that the paint finish of trucks parked in their lot was damaged by deposits emanating from the defendant's nearby foundry, which had been operating since 1907. In giving his judgment, Chief Justice McRuer stated:

> If a man lives in a street where there are numerous shops and a shop is opened next door to him, he has no grounds for complaint because to himself individually there may arise some discomfort from the trade carried on in that shop. But when an occupation is carried on by one person in the neighbourhood of another and the result of that trade or occupation or business is a material injury to property, there unquestionably arises a very different consideration . . . the evidence shows that . . . the emissions from the cupola are responsible for the injury to the plaintiff and I think that they are in large measure responsible for the injury complained of, the defendant has adopted no method of modern smoke or fume control.

Accordingly, the judge granted an injunction ordering a halt to the nuisance and monetary damages as compensation for the harm done in the past.

Closely linked with nuisances are: (a) the right to support; that is, land cannot be excavated by a neighbour to the extent that it causes the other person's land to fall in; and (b) the right to water, the normal rule being that water may be taken by a person within whose land the water flows, but it should be returned to the river or stream from which it was taken, undiminished in quantity and quality except for that required for personal use.

Trespass to Goods

This is injury done to a neighbour's goods without consent. This occurs, for example, when the offence of theft is committed or when funds are misappropriated. These are cases where the tort was committed intentionally. However, as previously mentioned, intention is not required. Thus when a car accident occurs, however unintentional, any property damage caused to the other party comes under this classification of trespass to goods, and compensation may be required in the form of money damages.

Trespass to Person

Another type of trespass is that of trespass to the person, or "assault and battery". *Assault* is a threat to inflict unlawful force by causing another person to believe that intentional physical contact is imminent. The plaintiff must show that the defendant intended to commit a battery, had the ability to carry it out, and that the plaintiff's fear or apprehension was reasonable in the circumstances. *Battery* is the intentional application of force to another person, such as a man kissing a woman without her consent, giving rise to a possible additional award of exemplary (punitive) damages.

Strictly speaking, therefore, assault means the threat of violence, and battery, the actual attack. Assault is a crime, whereas battery may be both a crime and a tort—for example, a person injured by a burglar or thief. However, as the attacker usually has few assets, the victim will probably not bother to sue for damages. In resisting an attacker or other trespasser, a person who uses more than reasonable force may in turn be sued.

In Ontario, it should be noted, a victim of a crime may also bring an application for damages before the Criminal Injuries Compensation Board if there is no hope of collecting damages from the offender by court action. The claim may arise from: a crime of violence under the Criminal Code (except offences involving the use of an automobile); a lawful arrest or attempted arrest for an offence against a person or property other than the applicant or the applicant's dependants; assisting a police officer in his or her duties; or preventing or trying to prevent an offence or a suspected offence against a person or property. Benefits may be paid to the victim; to persons responsible for the maintenance of the victim; to the victim's dependants (if the victim died); or to the person responsible for the maintenance of a child born as a result of rape. The Board determines the amount of compensation, making sure that benefits from other sources (e.g., U.I.C., Workers' Compensation, etc.) are not duplicated. Claims must be made within one year. Relief is an alternative to suing in civil court. In Alberta, as another provincial example, the victim may apply to the Crimes Compensation Board whether or not damages or other compensation have been collected. However, such compensation may be deducted from the Board's own damages figure.

Mental Injury.   Trespass to the person may be mental rather than physical. Thus in 1896, in the case of *Wilkinson v. Dounton*, [1897] 2 Q.B. 57, in which the defendant falsely informed the plaintiff by way of a practical joke that her husband had been severely injured in an accident, the Court held that:

> Where a person wilfully does an act calculated to cause harm to another and thereby to infringe his legal right to personal safety, and in consequence causes physical harm through the infliction of mental disturbance, a cause of action arises in the absence of legal justification for the act.

One can imagine the difficult task facing the trial judge or jury (if there is one) in determining whether one person has caused mental harm to another. However, the plaintiff should not be denied the right to recover damages merely because the harm and the quantum of damages are difficult to assess. Consider, for example, the mental anguish of a bride who later discovers that her wedding photographer neglected to put film in the camera. One could reasonably argue that this situation calls for some sort of compensation.

Husband and Wife.   The courts have always considered a husband and wife to be one person with regard to torts. Thus a wife may not sue her husband for injuries received in a domestic quarrel, and vice versa. However, in Ontario since July 1975, a wife may sue her husband for tort. The same applies to most provinces.

False Imprisonment

This is the act of preventing a person from going in the direction in which he or she wants to go. It constitutes, in the eyes of the law, a trespass to the person. An example is the detention of a customer in a store, until the arrival of the police, on grounds of theft. If this is later disproved, the customer can then sue the store for the tort of false imprisonment. Thus in the case of *Chaytor v. London, New York and Paris Associates of Fashion Ltd. and Price* (1961), 30 D.L.R. (2d) 527, the plaintiffs (who were employed by a competitor) were seen examining materials and prices in a ladies fashion clothing store. They were questioned by the manager, a Mr. Price, and a heated discussion arose. The manager ordered the store detective to watch them while he telephoned the local police to come and evict "two loiterers." The plaintiffs believed that they would be detained by the store detective if they tried to leave. After the police arrived, they went voluntarily to the police station but were not held. The Newfoundland Supreme Court found that, in this case, the manager had exceeded his rights in that there was a great display of anger, and some show of force, since the store detective was openly told to watch them; also, telephoning for the police on an open telephone in the shop in the presence of the plaintiffs amounted to a threat. Judgment was given for the plaintiffs because they were forcibly detained.

Arrest.   A person who is arrested by the police may sue the police officers for trespass to the person. The police officers' defence would be that there were reasonable and probable grounds under the Criminal Code for arresting that person. Thus in the late 1970s when two constables in Toronto arrested a civil rights lawyer who happened to be in the neighbourhood where an offence was believed to have been committed, the court found that there was no justification for the arrest and awarded damages against the arresting police officers.

With respect to the commission of minor offences, the right to arrest is restricted to situations where: (a) it is believed that the accused will not appear in court; (b) the accused continues to commit the crime; or (c) the accused refuses to provide personal identification.

Discipline
According to s. 43 of the Criminal Code, parents and school teachers may inflict such punishment as is required to discipline children. This would serve as a defence by a teacher against a court action by an irate parent. Similarly, s. 44 of the Code gives a ship's captain the right to use necessary personal force to maintain discipline on board the ship.

TRESPASS TO REPUTATION (LIBEL AND SLANDER)

A *defamatory statement* is one which injures the reputation of the person to whom it refers; or, as one judge put it, "lowers him in the estimation of right-thinking members of society generally, and in particular, causes him to be regarded with feelings of hatred, contempt, ridicule, fear, dislike, or dis-esteem." *Libel* refers to a written or printed statement, including a cartoon, radio broadcast, telecast, film, and so on, while *slander* refers to verbal comments. For libel and slander to occur, the statement must not only be defamatory, it must also be false and be published—that is, spread to other persons by the defendant and not by the plaintiff.

Privilege.   Some people may not be sued even though they make defamatory statements. Thus, for example, judges, lawyers, witnesses, members of Parliament, and teachers are required to make statements that may be defamatory; but these individuals are protected if doing so in the course of their calling or occupation. There is also the theatre critic who criticizes the performers in a musical or dramatic production, or the employer who is asked to give a character reference for a former employee. So long as these statements are made in a spirit of fair comment and are expected as part of one's job (as in a teacher's comments about a student's work) no action can succeed against the person making them. However, if such statements are made purely out of spite or malice, the person whose reputation is injured may be successful in instituting a criminal action for defamation of character.

Of course the media are protected against libel or slander as long as the reporting is done in a spirit of fair comment or factual reporting of events.

Innuendo.   Sometimes libel or slander is not apparent in the words that are spoken or printed, but may be inferred from the characterization that is presented. Thus in the case of *Tulley v. Fry*, [1931] A.C. 333, an amateur golf champion recovered damages because the defendants, a firm of chocolate manufacturers, had published a caricature of him with a packet of their chocolate protruding from his pocket as an advertisement of their goods. The *innuendo* was, in effect, that he had consented to the use of his portrait as an advertisement for reward and had prostituted his reputation as an amateur golfer thereby.

INVASION OF PRIVACY

At present, Canadian courts recognize only libel, slander, and physical acts—such as threats or assault, false imprisonment, and trespass—as invasions of privacy. However, American courts have recently recognized "mental anguish" as an actionable tort resulting from the invasion of one's privacy. This remedy has so far been granted in cases involving the use, without permission, of a picture of a person for advertising purposes, wire tapping, and public disclosure of private facts. One Canadian case showed the back of a professional athlete in an advertisement. However, the court ruled that, although this athlete could possibly be identified by his number and the colour of his uniform, no right of recovery existed in Canada for the use of this picture of a football team lined up facing their opponents. This was because the theme represented in the advertisement was one of strength or force and did not single out any individual.

So far there have not been many cases in Canada involving these situations. This is possibly because present advertising laws require clearance and payment before any use may be made of pictures involving individuals. Of course, newspapers are permitted to reveal private facts, so long as such information is published in a spirit of fair comment.

The Canadian Criminal Code, makes it illegal to set up wire tapping, except on the express order of a judge of the superior court of criminal jurisdiction of the province or of the District or County Court. In addition every individual whose telephone conversations are tapped must be advised of such procedure at the expiration of 90 days.

Malicious Prosecution.   This occurs when one person brings a criminal action against another person knowing full well that there is no basis for it. It is a criminal offence as well as a tort.

Inducing a Breach of Contract.   This occurs when one person induces another to commit a breach of contract. Thus if a football club persuades a player already under contract to another club to break that contract, the club which suffers injury may sue the other for tort.

Deceit

The tort of deceit (also known as wilful or fraudulent misrepresentation) arises when a person wilfully makes false statements with the intent that another shall act in reliance on them and thereby suffer harm. An example is a sales rep making a false claim about a product.

Passing Off. This tort occurs when a person sells goods under the pretence that they are manufactured by someone else—for example, using a false name or other trademark.

Slander of Title. This type of tort may occur when one business person maligns a neighbouring store owner by saying the latter's goods are inferior.

Infringement of Copyright. This is the tort of using someone else's printed work without the copyright owner's permission.

REMEDIES FOR TORT

The main reason for instituting an action in tort is to claim money damages to compensate the victim in some measure for the injury which he has suffered. There are two main types of damages: special damages and general damages.

Special Damages are those for which a bill or receipt may be produced— for example, a receipt for car repairs, for medical expenses, or an account showing the wage or salary which has been lost due to absence from work following an illness caused by the use of a particular product. The purpose of special damages is to restore the plaintiff to the position he or she would have been in up to the date of trial if no tort had been committed.

General Damages are those which cannot be easily assessed and which require the judge's (or jury's) discretion in fixing a suitable monetary amount to compensate the plaintiff for the loss suffered.

Generally speaking, the purpose of general damages is to compensate the victim for pain and suffering and future loss of opportunities after the date of the trial. In 1980, for example, in an out-of-court settlement, a former engineer with Environment Canada who suffered irreparable brain damage in the crash of an Air Canada DC-9 in 1978 at Toronto International Airport was awarded $1,159,969 for damages, costs, pain, and suffering. The settlement was endorsed by Mr. Justice R. E. Holland of the Ontario Supreme Court.

By way of further illustration, suppose that a woman has lost her husband as the result of an airplane crash on a domestic flight. The aim of the court, if it finds that her husband's death was due to someone's negligence, is to put the wife and her children in roughly the same position financially as they would have been had the husband survived. Consequently, the wife of the president of a large manufacturing company would be awarded considerably more money in damages than the wife of an unemployed office clerk. The actual amount would be set by the court.

Nominal Damages. A judge who favours the claim of the plaintiff but does not believe that he or she has suffered any significant harm may award *nominal damages*—for example, one dollar—indicating a judgment in the plaintiff's favour, but little monetary compensation.

Punitive or Exemplary Damages may also be awarded by a judge who desires to punish the defendant as well as award compensation to the plaintiff. This may occur, for example, if the defendant persists in repeating a slander or libel by giving the same false testimony in court that he or she did previously elsewhere. Such damages can also be awarded where a published libel was committed wilfully or maliciously.

Injunction. A judge may issue a court order called an *interim* or *final injunction*, which prohibits a person or a company from doing something— for example, continuing to send unsolicited magazines or records. Similarly, a judge may issue a *mandatory injunction* requiring the defendant to do a positive act.

In all claims, the claimant may be required to show that he or she minimized or *mitigated* the loss; for example, protecting a wrecked automobile from further deterioration or disposing of perishable goods where refrigeration was negligently interrupted.

Consequential Damages. This is monetary compensation for losses closely connected, foreseeable or, as was expressed in a leading tort case, "arising naturally" from the incident which gives rise to the claim in tort.

Consequential damages may be claimed for physical pain, unaccompanied by any bodily lesion, and even for mental suffering, such as a narrow escape from sudden death or the helpless witnessing by a mother of the accidental death of her children. Over recent years, the courts have become more willing to recognize such claims for mental distress, notwithstanding the difficulty in assessing such consequential damages.

FATAL ACCIDENTS

According to the common law, if a person died as the result of someone else's negligence, the right to recover damages died with him or her. This rule resulted in obvious hardships to the widowed spouse and other dependants of the deceased, if the deceased person happened to be the breadwinner. Governments have realized this and over a hundred years ago the English Parliament passed what was first known as Lord Campbell's Act. This Act provided that, if a person died as the result of the negligence of another person which would have permitted him to sue for damages under the law of torts if he had lived, the executors or administrators of his estate may sue on his behalf for the benefit of his dependants. Later, this principle was incorporated in the Fatal Accidents Act of each Canadian province. In

Ontario, this Act has now been repealed and the fatal accidents principle has been included in the Family Law Reform Act.

Joint Tort Feasors

Ontario has a Negligence Act, which allows recovery against two or more negligent persons. For example, in one construction case where the statute of limitations excused the contractor but not the designer and supervising engineer, the court held the latter liable to the plaintiff in negligence and awarded damages. Thus, although the contractor was not liable to the plaintiff, the court nevertheless ordered the contractor to share the damages with the designer and supervisory engineer as a *joint tort feasor.*

LIMITATION OF ACTIONS

Limitation periods are for the most part under provincial jurisdiction and can therefore vary from province to province. In case of libel by newspapers or radio and television broadcasts, the limitation period is three months after such libel has come to the attention of the person defamed. For example, two sons of a former premier of British Columbia were defamed in a Vancouver newspaper, which published an article alleging that their office-supply firm was receiving privileged supply contracts from the B.C. government because of their father's influence. This was proven to be false and defamatory and their lawsuit was successful.

Section 226 of the Ontario Insurance Act provides that no action shall be brought against an insurer under the section dealing with the application of insurance money under a motor vehicle liability policy after the expiration of one year from the final determination of the action against the insured, including appeals, if any.

Section 238 of this Act also provides that every action or proceeding against an insurer under a contract in respect of uninsured automobile coverage, medical and rehabilitation benefits and accident benefits shall be commenced within the limitation period specified in the contract. In no event shall the limitation period be less than one year after the happening of the event.

Section 45 of the Ontario Limitations Act provides that an action for trespass is limited to six years, while civil actions for assault, battery, and wounding are limited to four years.

Claims against a hospital must be made within one year. Claims against most professions (engineers, architects, medical doctors) must also be made within one year. Claims against municipalities (for example, if a car hits a pothole and cracks an axle) may be limited to as little as six months. Special attention should be addressed to claims against a municipality as there is often a statutory requirement to notify the municipality of the injury within a short specified period of time before commencing court action.

The attitude of the courts to the observation of time limits is inflexible; therefore it is not uncommon for legitimate claims to be defeated by virtue of the lapse of the limitation period.

The institution of time limitations is designed to encourage persons to bring their causes to court before witnesses die or forget what transpired. In addition "real evidence" may tend to become lost or mislaid.

REVIEW QUESTIONS

1. What is a tort? Give three examples involving business firms.
2. What is the main purpose of the law of torts? What are the basic premises on which this law is based? How does this differ from criminal law?
3. Give two examples, involving business firms, of trespass to land.
4. What happens legally if a person is forced, out of necessity, to trespass on another's land?
5. What is meant by the legal term "nuisance"? Explain with a business example.
6. What is meant by: (a) right to support; (b) right to water?
7. Give two examples, involving business firms, of trespass to goods.
8. Distinguish between "assault" and "battery."
9. Trespass to a person may be mental rather than physical. Explain.
10. Can a husband sue his wife for tort, and vice versa? Explain, with an example.
11. Explain, with two business examples, the tort of false imprisonment.
12. Can a person, if arrested, sue the police for false imprisonment? Explain.
13. Distinguish, with examples, between libel and slander. Which persons are granted special privilege in this regard?
14. Give an example of tort by "innuendo."
15. What is a "malicious prosecution"? Give an example. What could be the motive?
16. Explain, with examples, the following torts: (a) inducing a breach of contract; (b) deceit.
17. Explain, with an example, the following torts: (a) passing off; (b) infringement of copyright.
18. What are the court remedies available to a person against whom a tort has been committed?
19. Distinguish between "special damages" and "general damages."
20. When would a judge award: (a) nominal damages and (b) punitive damages?
21. Explain the nature and purpose of an "injunction."
22. What are "consequential damages"? When may they be claimed?
23. If a person dies as the result of someone else's negligence, does his or her family have the right to sue the person responsible? If so, for what?
24. What is a "joint tort feasor"? Give an example.
25. What is meant by "limitation of actions"?
26. Within what time period must a tort action be instituted? Explain.

PROBLEMS

1. A landlord decides to try out his new fire-alarm bell without informing the tenants of his six-storey building. One of the tenants, hearing the bell, jumps out of a window twenty feet from the ground and breaks his leg. Has this tenant any claim against the landlord, particularly since there was no real danger? Explain.

2. What liability, if any, attaches to the employer of workmen who leave an open manhole along a sidewalk, thereby causing a preoccupied business-man to fall into it and injure himself? Are the workmen personally liable? Is the businessman in any way to blame for his injuries?

3. A young girl visited a department store on her way home from her music lesson. She had a brief case, containing her music books, and a box of popcorn. She looked at some books in the store and then put her box of popcorn in her briefcase. At that moment she was requested by a member of the sales staff, who had been watching her, to accompany that person to the security office where she was forced to submit to a search by a female security officer. She was allowed to leave when nothing was found. What are this young lady's rights?

4. A newspaper printed a libellous story about a fictitious college professor. Unbeknown to the newspaper publishers, a college professor of the same name actually lived at the same town given in the newspaper story and his friends believed the article related to him. Can the newspaper publishers be successfully sued, even though the article was fictitious?

5. While you were in a singles bar last night, one of the patrons started to get obstreperous and act completely out of hand. It was obvious that he had had too much to drink and yet you knew that he was sober when you entered the restaurant. Eventually he was ejected by the bouncers, but his head struck the door as he was being ejected, knocking him unconscious. Discuss the liability of the patron, of the bouncers, and of the management and whether it would have made any difference if the patron had slipped off the curb and struck his head after being evicted. Would it make any difference if it was proved that Ontario law makes the operators of taverns liable if a patron, who becomes intoxicated in a tavern or lounge, either dies of injuries on his way home or causes damage or injuries to another party?

6. Two young adults were drinking in a local tavern in celebration of the younger man's birthday. The tavern staff watched them leave, realizing that they were going to drive away in their own car and that both were in an intoxicated condition. They were subsequently involved in a single motor vehicle accident which resulted in one of the young men becoming a quadraplegic, requiring continual care for the remainder of his life. Ignoring the Ontario Liquor Licence Act, which may impose statutory liability in such a case as this, would you say that any liability arises in such a situation at common law? Discuss this situation from your own appreciation of everyday similar situations. Would contributory negligence or consent affect the rights of the claimants in this case? How would

damages, if any, be calculated? What action, if any, could the tavern owner or employees have taken to prevent this occurrence?

Unit 4.2
Negligence

Often, one person will cause injury or financial loss to another because of *negligence* rather than intention. In the eyes of the law, this lack of intention is no excuse. Everyone, as we will discuss later, has a duty to take care that his or her actions do not cause harm to other persons or their property. If a person fails to take proper care (acts negligently) and does cause harm, then he or she may be successfully sued for damages. In fact, negligence is the most common form of tort.

Tort law, as it relates to negligence is based on two fundamental premises: first, that a person is held to the standard of the reasonable person in the conduct of ordinary human affairs; and second, a person will be held responsible for any harm directly caused to others by falling below this standard.

ESSENTIAL ELEMENTS OF A NEGLIGENCE CLAIM

To succeed in a negligence claim, it must be proved to the satisfaction of the court that the party that committed the tort (a) had a duty to take care; (b) failed in this duty; and (c) caused foreseeable personal injury, property damage, or financial loss thereby.

Duty of Care
The need for a person to take reasonable care in his or her actions was stressed by Lord Atkin in the case of *Donoghue v. Stevenson*, [1932] A.C. 580, as follows:

> You must take *reasonable care* to avoid acts or omissions which you can *reasonably foresee* would be likely to injure your neighbour. Who, then, in law is my neighbour? The answer seems to be—persons who are so closely and directly affected by my act that I ought reasonably to have them in contemplation as being so affected when I am directing my mind to the acts or omissions which are called in question.

The amount of care required is that employed by a reasonable person, or, in other words, "an ordinarily prudent person" or "the average ordinary person, who goes about his business doing his best to ensure that he comes to no harm and that he causes no harm to others." Thus a person who does not care for the safety and wellbeing of others may, if he or she causes harm to them, be liable for the injury caused. On the other hand, if a person takes reasonable care, the courts may declare that no liability exists for harm which results from that person's actions.

An example of the standard of care considered reasonable is provided by the case of *Challand v. Bell* (1959), 18 D.L.R. (2d) 150.

A farmer fell in his barn one Sunday morning and fractured his arm, which left him with a bone sticking out of his flesh. He went immediately to his local country doctor for emergency treatment. The wound was then closed, the fracture set, and a plaster cast applied over the entire lower part of the arm. However, within twenty-four hours, the farmer suffered considerable pain in his arm and returned to the doctor to have the cast removed. It was then noticed that the wound was infected. At the hospital it was determined that gangrene had set in and the arm was amputated. The farmer then sued the doctor for negligence.

The court heard all the evidence, including that of several doctors who testified as to the way in which they would have treated a similar case. They said that, if they had received a patient suffering from the same injuries, they would have treated him in exactly the same way as did the defendant. A specialist even testified that in his elaborately equipped office he would have proceeded in the same manner. As a result, the judge found that the doctor had acted in a reasonable manner and attached no liability for the suit of the plaintiff, who therefore lost his case.

Foreseeability Rule.   To be successful in a tort action, the plaintiff must also be able to show that the injury suffered was foreseeable (that is, it could have been reasonably anticipated) by the defendant.

Handicapped Persons.   The standard of care required relates to normal situations. Thus a blind or deaf person who crosses a busy street cannot legally complain if he is knocked down or injured by a driver exercising the standard of care necessary under normal circumstances. In such a situation, the driver cannot usually know of and be expected to guard against the pedestrian's infirmity without some sort of warning. Also, for example, a manufacturer of bath salts has no special duty of care to a person with a certain type of skin allergy who suffers injury from using the salts when they are not injurious to the average person. This same reasoning applies to protection of property. However, if there is a duty to take care, and greater damages are suffered by an abnormal person (for instance, a person with a very thin skull) this person may recover greater damages because of greater injury. This is because injury has been caused through the defendant's negligence, and he or she is therefore fully liable. Thus a Canadian aircraft passing over a mink ranch was held to have no special duty of care, because it could not be foreseen that, in the breeding season, such an incident would cause the adult minks to panic and devour their young—*Nova Mink Ltd. v. T.C.A.*, [1951] 2 D.L.R. 241. In other words, the duty is to take reasonable care against foreseeable harm. If the harm is not reasonably foreseeable, there is no liability.

NEGLIGENT MISREPRESENTATION

Sometimes, out of negligence, a person will make a statement that is false—for example, a credit agency's report about an individual that contains inaccurate information. Another person, relying on the false statement, may then incur financial loss—for example, a retail store extending credit to a high-risk customer. In such a case, the party making the false statement may be successfully sued for negligence. To avoid this, the party making the statement should have issued an accompanying statement disclaiming responsibility for any loss incurred as a result of reliance on the previous statement—for example, as in an investment newsletter or the financial advice column of a newspaper. In this way they can contract out of liability.

In the case of *Derry v. Peek* (1889), 14 App. Cas. 337, the judge decided that an action for deceit would lie only for wilfully false misrepresentations. In this case, the directors of a tramway company had issued a prospectus stating that they were empowered by statute to use steam-powered cars. In fact, this authorization was conditional on government consent, which the directors honestly believed would be given as a matter of course. It was withheld, however, and in consequence the company went into liquidation. The plaintiff, who had become a shareholder on the basis of the prospectus, instituted an action against the directors for deceit. He won initially, but the decision was reversed on the ground that a false statement, honestly believed to be true, could not qualify as fraud, even if made carelessly and without reasonable grounds to support it.

As late as 1951, the English courts held that, in the absence of a contractual or fiduciary relationship between the parties, there existed no duty in the preparation of accounts or statements.

This view is no longer upheld. Today the Canadian courts hold that a person preparing financial statements negligently may be held liable to anyone who it is reasonable to believe might rely on such statements. This follows from the famous English decision of *Hedley Byrne & Company v. Heller & Partners Limited*, [1964] A.C. 465.

PROFESSIONAL NEGLIGENCE

Tort law has undergone considerable development during the past two or three decades particularly in relation to professional misconduct or negligence.

The question of medical procedures or surgical operations is considered on page 94, where it is mentioned that a surgeon is required to inform the patient of the risks of possible surgical procedures that may be required to alleviate a medical condition—for example, a 2% death rate in connection with open-heart surgery. This is the so-called informed consent. Failure to reveal this information could give rise to possible legal action if a fatality occurs.

Of course, there is no doubt about the existence of medical malpractice where a surgical clamp or cotton swab is left inside a surgical incision. The difficulty seems to be in assessing the degree of fault to be attributed to the surgeon, a self-employed professional, and to his or her assistants, the operating room nurses, who are employed by the hospital, thereby making their employer "vicariously liable."

The liability for professional misconduct has now been extended to all classes of professionals. This is illustrated by an Ontario case involving a nursery operated by a Mr. Fine (*Fine's Flowers Ltd v. General Accident Insur. et al (1974) 49 D.L.R. (3rd) 64*). This businessman used the same insurance broker or agent for over 20 years, repeatedly telling this agent that he (the nursery owner) depended on his knowledge and expertise to keep his business covered against any possible risk of loss.

One winter day the temperature dropped so low that one of the pumps bringing heat to a greenhouse, which had over $25,000 worth of flowers and plants, froze and a total loss resulted.

The insurance company refused to pay compensation for this loss, alleging that no coverage had been taken out against the possibility of the pumps freezing and thereby causing lack of heat circulation. However, this risk had been pointed out beforehand to Fine's insurance broker, who had ignored it.

Fine sued both his broker-agent and the insurers. Since the broker technically received his commission based on the premium paid to the insurers, then his duty as an agent in contract was owed to the insurers. The insurance contract was also with the insurers, not the broker-cum-agent. So Fine's claim could only be in tort against the agent for failing to advise and insure against the risk of loss from freezing pumps—that is, an act of professional negligence.

The court found, indeed, that the broker-cum-agent had failed in his duty to protect Fine against all possible loss, particularly because of the long period during which Fine had relied on the former's knowledge and expertise as a professional insurance agent to protect his firm from every insurable loss.

Today we can visualize many instances where third parties with no contractual relationship still rely on advice which is given by various classes of professionals. Such risk of reliance occurs, for example, in the auditing of business accounts, in financial statements, in connection with credit reports by banks, in cases of legal advice that may involve third party rights, and in medical specialists' reports to general practitioners. There exist a possibility that other persons may rely on such information or advice. Furthermore, if such information or advice is not up to professional standard, it may cause financial, business, or health risks to such other persons. In such cases the obvious procedure is to sue in tort for the losses incurred as a result of such negligence by professionals.

One of the first cases in which liability in tort towards third parties occurred was the case of *Hedley Byrne v. Heller & Partners [1964] A.C. 465*, where a company was led to extend credit on the basis of a favourable credit report obtained through its own bank from the proposed client's bank. When the client proved insolvent, the court found that, as the client's bank had been negligent in preparing this credit report, this institution owed a duty towards Hedley Byrne, a customer of the bank that requested this information. However, in this particular case, a disclaimer of liability included with the information absolved them from liability.

The principle of liability towards third parties espoused in the *Hedley Byrne case* has received widespread acceptance. Thus most professional societies have now included an obligation on their members to maintain the highest standards of professionalism in dealing with all clients so as to avoid instances where parties with no contractual relationship may nevertheless come to rely on such information and thus be able to recover damages for the tort of professional negligence.

Rescue Cases.   Despite English cases which attempted to preclude a rescuer from recovery of expenses incurred because of voluntary assumption of risk, contributory negligence, or remoteness of the loss sustained by the rescuer, it is now held, as expressed by Judge Cardozo in an American case, *Wagner v. International R.R.* (1921), 232 N.Y. 176, that the person rescued owes a duty of care towards the rescuer. Therefore, although a person may not have foreseen the possibility of being rescued, that person is accountable as if he or she had. And the foregoing principle applies not only to the rescue of persons but also to a lesser degree to the protection of property—for example, someone recovering a car after an accident.

OCCUPIER OF PREMISES

A special area of negligence law, in which the duty of care has been clearly established, is that relating to the duty of care of an owner or occupier of real estate. Under common law, the duty of care varied according to whether the person who had come on the premises was considered to be a trespasser, a licensee, or an invitee. The trespasser, who by definition was not invited on to the premises, merited the least care; and the invitee (for example, a customer, tradesperson, or municipal assessor) who came on business the most. In between came the licensee (for example, a social guest), who came onto the property for social or domestic purposes. Most provinces have now passed statutes that supersede the common law and impose one duty towards all lawful entrants. Nevertheless, a knowledge of the common law situation helps us to understand better the statutory position.

Trespassers.   These are persons who come onto someone else's property without express or implied permission. They are afforded no real protection under common law. However, while the owner is permitted to put up what are called "deterrent traps" such as fences and signs, he or she is not permitted to resort to "retributive traps" such as jagged glass, vicious dogs, or dangerously electrified fences. Thus, it is illegal, for example, for a householder to set a dog on an unwelcome door-to-door salesperson.

The child trespasser is in a different legal position from the adult trespasser. It has been recognized by the courts that children are attracted by

such things as swimming pools, haystacks, lumber piles, dirt piles, garbage disposal containers, and so on. These attractions are termed "attractive nuisances." The child is said to be invited to the occupier's premises, inasmuch as these attractions beckon or invite the child, and is considered to be a "licencee." Accordingly, the child must be treated as such. A frequently cited case in this respect is *Commissioner for Railways (N.S.W.) v. Cardy* (1960), 104 C.L.R. 278. A child returned after three years to play on railway yard slag heap. He broke through the crust and burned his foot. It was held that the Commissioner must have been aware of the slag heap's attraction to boys and should have warned of the danger concealed under the surface of the slag.

Licensees.   These are persons who come onto the premises with the occupier's permission but for their own advantage rather than that of the occupier. Persons who fall into this category include social guests, canvassers, and child trespassers. The occupier has a duty to inform these persons of *any unusual dangers* which are known to him. Thus they should be informed, for example, of a hidden well or a dangerous step.

A classic case in this regard is *Fairman v. Perpetual Investment Building Society*, [1923] A.C. 74. The plaintiff, who lived with her brother who was a tenant in one of defendant's flats, was seriously injured when her heel was caught in a depression while descending the main stairway. It was held that since the defendants maintained control of the stairway, they were liable to the brother, per the lease, as an invitee. In the present case, the plaintiff was a licensee and knew of the danger. The only obligation of the defendants was to warn of a known but concealed danger.

Invitees.   The third and greatest type of responsibility under common law relates to persons known as invitees—for example, the customer in a store, or the tradesperson who comes to repair the plumbing or electrical appliances. The occupier or owner must inform the invitee of any unusual dangers which are either known or which should be known to him or her—for example, a slippery floor. The essential basis for invitee status is the contractual relationship—for example, a customer in a store, a tenant in an apartment, or a student at a school, college or university.

In *Indermaur v. Dames* (1866), L.R. 1 C.P. 274, a gasfitter's servant fell through an open shaft while repairing a gas regulator. It was held that an occupier who invites a person onto premises (as customer or tradesperson) must give protection from unusual dangers either known or which should be known; on the other hand, the user must take reasonable care.

An invitee should not be confused with a social guest who, though invited, has the status of a licensee.

Occupiers' Liability Act

In Ontario, according to s. 3(1) of the Occupiers' Liability Act, an occupier of premises owes a duty to take care, as in all circumstances of the case is reasonable, to see that persons entering on the premises and the property brought onto the premises by those persons are reasonably safe while on the premises.

Subsection (2) applies whether the premises themselves or an activity on the premises may cause the danger.

Subsection (3) provides that the foregoing applies unless the occupier is free to and has restricted or modified his liability, but under s. 5 such restriction must be brought to the attention of the users.

Under s. 6 an occupier is not normally responsible for damage caused by the negligence of an independent contractor, providing action is taken to ensure that the contractor is competent and the work properly done.

The duty of care stipulated in this Act does not apply to a person who assumes a voluntary risk, who is committing a criminal offence, or is entering rural premises, closed golf courses, private roads and recreational trails.

Under s. 8, the landlord who is responsible for the maintenance and repair of premises owes a duty of care to both the tenants and any persons brought on the premises by such tenants.

The Trespass to Property Act provides that everyone who enters premises where entry is prohibited or engages in a prohibited activity on premises is guilty of an offence punishable by a fine of not more than $1,000.

Entry is prohibited without notice to a garden or field under cultivation or an enclosed area.

Allowing a certain activity (like snowmobiling) automatically prohibits other activities (such as skiing).

Notices of allowance or prohibition may be given, orally, in writing, by signs, or a marking system—namely, red for prohibited activities, yellow for allowed activities.

Signs may depict allowed or prohibited activities graphically as in the case of road signs.

Police officers may arrest offenders. So also may the occupier of the premises, subject to turning them over to the police.

The judge hearing a case where damage has been caused may award the claimant up to $1,000 plus costs, which may be in addition to any fine imposed.

DANGEROUS POSSESSIONS

In certain circumstances, a person has a special duty of care. Thus, by law, any person who keeps a potentially dangerous thing (for example, dynamite or wild animals) on his or her land may be held liable for any damage caused thereby to another person or his property.

The rule in this matter was clearly stated in the case of *Rylands v. Fletcher* (1868), L.R. 3 H.L. 330, as follows:

> We think that the true rule of law is, that the person who for his own purposes brings on his land and collects and keeps there anything

likely to do mischief if it escapes, must keep it at his peril, and, if he does not do so, is prima facie answerable for all the damage which is the natural consequence of its escape.

This rule resulted in the modern doctrine of *strict liability* for the escape of dangerous substances. In this case, the plaintiff operated a mine on land adjoining the defendant's reservoir. However, there were mine shafts under the plaintiff's land and under the defendant's adjoining land, and these mine shafts were joined by connecting corridors. Through no fault of the defendant, the reservoir leaked and the water went down through the shafts on his land, crossed to the plaintiff's land through the connecting corridors, and disrupted some mining which was being done there. The plaintiff brought an action for damages against the defendant. The courts held in this case that no responsibility attached to the fact that the defendant had erected a reservoir on his land but in doing this the defendant became responsible for any danger or damage which might result from the escape of a potentially dangerous item; that is, the water held in the reservoir. Thus the defendant was liable for the damage caused.

To attract the rule expressed in *Rylands v. Fletcher*, there must both be an extraordinary user of the land and the object must in the circumstances be classified as dangerous.

The category of *Rylands v. Fletcher* objects overlaps that of inherently dangerous things which attract a very stringent standard of care. Such things have included water, electricity, gas, oil, fire, explosives, poisonous trees, a flag pole, a chimney stack, and the roof of a house.

In at least one case it was held that there must be an escape of the dangerous substance from land under the control of the defendant to a place outside of his occupation. But this view has not prevailed. For example, a pleasure seeker in Hyde Park, London, was able to sue an ambulance brigade when he was injured by a falling flag pole previously erected by the brigade.

The defences most often accepted by the courts in the strict liability application of *Rylands v. Fletcher* include consent, default of the plaintiff, act of God, act of a stranger, and statutory exceptions.

If injury from fire does not come under the category of *Rylands v. Fletcher* situations, the plaintiff can only recover damages if he can prove the defendant's negligence. However, in Ontario, the Accidental Fires Act, R.S.O. 1980, c. 4, provides that "no action shall be brought against any person in whose house or building or on whose land any fire accidentally begins." (But this does not apply to an agreement made between landlord and tenant.)

ANIMALS

These are divided into two classes: animals *ferae naturae*, such as lions and monkeys, which are normally dangerous; and animals *mansuetae naturae*, such as cows and dogs, which are normally harmless. If an animal of the first type causes injury to a person, the owner of the animal will normally be required to pay damages. This is similar to the principle in *Rylands v. Fletcher*—that is, the escape of dangerous possessions. An example would be a tiger escaping from a zoo and biting a passerby. If there is contributory negligence (for example, a man visiting the zoo and getting too close to the tiger's cage), the damages will be reduced accordingly.

Domestic animals such as dogs and cats, not ordinarily being considered of a dangerous nature, fall into the second category. To successfully sue the owner of such an animal, a person bitten or otherwise injured by it must be able to prove *scienter*, or the defendant's knowledge of the animal's viciousness. In other words, has there been a similar, previous case involving the animal? This merely reflects the rule of negligence derived from the case *Donohue v. Stevenson* discussed below. Hence the saying: "every dog is entitled to one bite." In practice, local bylaws may require a dog to be put down after the first evidence of viciousness.

In some provinces (for example, Ontario), the Dog Owner's Liability Act makes the owner of a dog legally responsible for any harm caused by it to another person.

CAUSATION

As discussed earlier, one of the essential facts to be proved by the plaintiff when suing in tort is that the act or omission by the defendant caused harm to the plaintiff. Normally, there is a direct relationship between one party's failure to take care and the resultant injury to the other party—for example, a motorcyclist knocking down a pedestrian.

Intervening Forces
Sometimes, there may be tort liability even though the injury is caused only indirectly. One can imagine a series of occurrences whereby the defendant starts a chain reaction of events which results in harm to the plaintiff even though it was not the defendant's own hand that caused the injury. For example the "Squib" case, *Scott v. Shepherd* (1773), 2 Wm. Bl. 892, explains how the concept of "intervening forces" may serve to help the plaintiff succeed in the claim. In this case the defendant threw a lighted firework into a market which, landing on X's stall, was thrown by X onto Y's stall, who in turn threw it away to save his wares. Unfortunately, it struck the plaintiff and exploded, causing him to lose an eye. It was held that the defendant (the person who first threw the firework) was liable for the injury in trespass, because "all that was done subsequent to the original throwing was a continuation of the first force and first act and continued till the squib was spent by bursting."

Similarly, the defendant may initiate a course of conduct which is interrupted or set off in another direction by an intervening force ("novus actus interveniens") which actually causes the harm. In this latter situation the defendant would be exonerated or in some circumstances bear part of the responsibility.

Agony of the Moment

Another type of indirect causation is when, as a result of the prior negligence of another party, a person is put into a position of having to make a split-second decision that unfortunately results in injury to that person. The classic case illustrating this point is an old English one, *Jones v. Boyce* (1816), 1 Stark. 493, which involved a double-decker bus during the horse-drawn transportation days. A passenger riding on the upper deck suddenly became aware that the bus, while rounding a curve, was in danger of toppling over. In that split second, believing himself to be in immediate danger, he decided that the best course was to jump off the bus. However, as a result of doing so, he broke his leg. He later sued the bus company but the company stated quite accurately that if he had stayed on the bus, he would have suffered no injury because the bus righted itself. When the case went to trial, the judge stated that it was "not in the mouth of the person who placed another person in a position where such person must make a decision between one course of action and another, and in so doing, chooses the course of action which the injury was incurred, to say that such claimant caused his own injury." Accordingly, damages were awarded against the bus company, as the bus driver had created a situation called "agony of the moment" and the plaintiff had acted, in the circumstances, as any reasonable person might have.

This case also illustrates the principle that the defendant need not come into direct physical contact with the plaintiff to be held liable for damages caused by the defendant's conduct.

Vicarious Liability

Vicarious liability refers to the legal principle that one person may be held responsible in law for the torts of another. For example, an employer becomes liable for employees' torts or injuries caused to third persons while acting in the course of their employment. Suppose, for example, that a person is employed as a delivery driver for a large department store. In the cab of the van a sign states that all store drivers must make right hand turns only and the company will not be liable for any accidents incurred when the employee is not observing the company's instructions. It so happens that there is a shortcut so, instead of making a right turn, the employee makes a left turn and is involved in an accident that causes damage to a third person's car. In this particular case, because the driver is going about the employer's business, the employer is liable vicariously to compensate the injured party, even though the driver was expressly breaking one of the company rules.

On the other hand, had the accident occurred some ten or fifteen miles away from the delivery area while the employee was on a personal trip or, as the courts say, "on a frolic of his own" (for example, to visit a friend or to go to the races), then the employee would be solely responsible for the accident and the damage or injury caused, and the employer would have no liability whatsoever.

A business firm may also be liable, in the same way, for torts caused to third persons by an agent while working on the principal's behalf. An example would be a salesperson who is paid a straight commission (and is therefore considered to be an agent) and who, while driving a company car on business, knocks down and injures a pedestrian. The company car identifies the salesperson as working for a definite principal and is not an independent agent such as a broker.

Unauthorized Delegation of Authority

According to the legal maxim of *delegatus non potest delegare*, an employee (who is thereby a delegate) may not delegate his authority. Consequently, if an employee has delegated duties to a third person and such third person is involved in an accident, the employer is not liable since he or she had not consented to this subsequent delegation of authority.

This principle of law is also frequently applied in the area of administrative law where a statute confers power on a particular official—for example, the Registrar of Motor Vehicles—who may delegate to others some of the powers conferred on him or her.

Res Ipsa Loquitur

This principle, which translates from the Latin as "the thing speaks for itself," has wide application in the law of negligence. For example, a person who puts a table with four legs into a warehouse for storage may use it to force the warehouser to disprove negligence if only three legs are left on the table when the plaintiff collects it. In such a situation the defendant will win the case only if it can be proved that the damage occured as a result of third party negligence. This is a particularly useful legal principle in claims arising from aircraft accidents where the operating companies often do not know what caused the accident.

To plead "res ipsa loquitur," the accident must have been of a kind which does not ordinarily happen without negligence on the part of *those in control* of whatever produced the harm. For example, a stone is not ordinarily found in a bun; a barrel of flour does not normally drop out of a building. See *Byrne v. Boodle* (1863), 2 H.&C. 722.

In summary, for the principle of res ipsa loquitur to assist the plaintiff in proving his or her case the plaintiff must show that: (a) the defendant was in control of the situation when injury occurred; and (b) the defendant is in a better position to explain how the accident occurred.

The effect of the application of res ipsa loquitur is to shift the burden of proof from the plaintiff to the defendant. This means that the defendant will have to explain the cause of the accident to show he or she was not negligent; otherwise the defendant will lose the case.

POSSIBLE TORT DEFENCES

A person sued for tort can try to prove that there was no duty of care towards the plaintiff; or that, if there were, the defendant had not failed in this duty; or that the personal injury or financial loss suffered was not foreseeable; or that there was no causal relationship between the lack of duty to take care and the subsequent personal injury or financial loss.

Consent

According to this principle, also known as the "voluntary acceptance of risk" or, in Latin, as "volenti non fit injuria," a person who voluntarily participates in a sport or in a hazardous occupation is deemed to accept the normal hazards that are part of that sport or occupation. Thus a person whose leg is injured while playing soccer or some other team sport cannot normally succeed in suing the other player for damages, to the extent that such injury may be expected in the sport or occupation. However, injury resulting from other than expected behaviour may well be cause for a negligence suit.

Consent is also normally a valid defence in the case of "hospital operations," so long as the surgeon takes reasonable care. An example of a case in which the defence of "consent" failed is *Haluska v. University of Saskatchewan* (1965), 53 **D.L.R.** (2d) 436. A young undergraduate at the University of Saskatchewan desired to obtain employment during the summer holidays. He approached the placement officer and was informed that the only job available was in medical research, acting as a "guinea pig" for a hospital laboratory. He accepted and was advised that the remuneration would be $50 for a morning's work. He reported to the laboratory and was advised that he would be undergoing a test involving a new anaesthetic. It was explained that, after he had been given the anaesthetic, doctors would insert a tube through a vein in his left arm and down into one of the valves of his heart to measure his reaction to the drug. He then signed a form consenting to this procedure.

After the anaesthetic had been administered and the tube had been inserted, it was observed that his heart had stopped beating. The doctors immediately cut open his chest and gave him open-heart massage as a result of which he recovered, remaining in hospital for a recuperation period. On leaving the hospital a few months later he was given the prearranged fee of $50.

He then decided to sue the hospital and the doctors. The court, after hearing all the evidence, decided that, despite the fact that he had consented to undergo a test involving a new anaesthetic, the doctors had failed to advise him that this new drug was in the testing stage and the results unknown. Therefore the judge held that the consent was not effective in negating his right to sue for damages and accordingly awarded the student some $22,000. In other words, the defence of "consent" is only available to the defendant, if the plaintiff has given his "informed consent," that is, he is fully aware of the possible consequences of his giving consent.

In *Fairman v. Perpetual Investment Building Society*, [1923] A.C. 74, a person classified as a licensee injured her ankle when the heel of her shoe caught in the crack of the stairs she was using to reach her brother's apartment. In this case, the court held that she could not recover damages, as she was aware of the defects in the stairs and under the "reasonable person theory" should have been more careful.

Act of God
A person who is being sued for a tort may be able to plead in defence that the plaintiff's injury or other loss is the result of an "act of God," or *force majeure*—for example, a person who is struck by lightning while crossing a farmer's field, or a person who misses an airplane flight because of fog at the airport. Usually, fog is considered to be an act of God only in an area which has never previously had fog. Similarly, a hurricane would be an act of God in Canada but not in the southern United States or the Caribbean.

Lack of Foreseeability
A classic case with regard to lack of foreseeability is *Bourhill v. Young*, [1943] A.C. 92, judged by the British House of Lords. The facts of the case were as follows. The plaintiff had alighted from a bus and was engaged in removing her fish-basket from the driver's platform, when a speeding motorcyclist passed on the other side of the bus and collided with a motorcar at an intersection forty-five to fifty feet ahead of the bus. The plaintiff heard a crash and said she "just got in a pack of nerves." She saw and heard nothing until the noise of the impact. Later, after the cyclist's dead body had been removed, the plaintiff saw the blood left in the roadway. As a result of the shock, the plaintiff claimed to have sustained a wrenched back and about a month later her child was stillborn, which she attributed to shock and reaction to the event. Plaintiff sued the cyclist's executor.

The plaintiff's claim was rejected by the House of Lords. According to Lord Macmillan:

> It is no longer necessary to consider whether the infliction of what is called mental shock may constitute an actionable wrong. The crude view that the law should take cognizance only of physical injury resulting from actual impact has been discarded, and it is now well recognized that an action will lie for injury by shock sustained through the medium of the eye or the ear without direct contact. . . . But in the case of mental shock there are elements of greater subtlety than in the case of an ordinary physical injury and these elements may give rise to debate as to the precise scope of legal liability. . . .
>
> In the present instance the late John Young was clearly negligent in a question with the occupants of the motor-car with which his cycle collided. He was driving at an excessive speed in a public thoroughfare and he ought to have foreseen that he might consequently collide with any vehicle which he might meet in his course, for such an occurrence may reasonably and probably be expected to ensue from driving at a

high speed in a street. But can it be said that he ought further to have foreseen that his excessive speed, involving the possibility of collision with another vehicle, might cause injury by shock to the appellant? The appellant was not within his line of vision, for she was on the other side of a tramcar which was standing between him and her when he passed and it was not until he had proceeded some distance beyond her that he collided with the motor-car. The appellant did not see the accident and she expressly admits that her "terror did not involve any element of reasonable fear of immediate bodily injury to herself." She was not so placed that there was any reasonable likelihood of her being affected by the cyclist's careless driving. In these circumstances I am of opinion with the majority of the learned Judges of the Second Division that the late John Young was under no duty to the appellant to foresee that his negligence in driving at an excessive speed and consequently colliding with a motor-car might result in injury to her, for such a result could not reasonably and probably be anticipated. He was, therefore, not guilty of negligence in a question with the appellant.

There have, however, been cases in which the plaintiff suffered shock and obtained damages even though the injury may not have been foreseeable. Thus in the case of *Hambrook v. Stokes*, [1925] 1 K.B. 14, a mother died as the result of nervous shock from seeing a runaway truck rush down a hill and fearing for the safety of her children whom she had just left on their way to school. According to the judgment:

> No consideration was given as to whether she was herself within the area of probable danger, be it of shock or physical impact, but it was taken for granted that the defendant, having failed to secure his vehicle, was in breach of duty to all road-users and consequently responsible for any pain directly flowing from such breach.

Today it would appear that to succeed in such a tort action, nervous shock must have been induced by apprehension of personal danger or seeing a casualty through one's own senses, and at least fairly close to the time of the incident. Also, there must have been some personal relationship involved—as in, for example, a Peterborough, Ontario, case where a father arrived home only to find it blown to bits by an explosion caused by a ruptured gas line and his children lying dead in the rubble.

Children

The liability of children for torts is covered in *Walmsley v. Humenick*, [1954] 2 D.L.R. 232. In this case, a Canadian court dismissed an action against a five-year-old boy who accidentally put out the eye of a playmate while shooting with bow and arrows. This was because he had neither intended the injury, nor been capable of negligence in accordance with the standard of care which is applied to infants of tender years—namely, that which can be expected of a child of similar age, intelligence, and experience.

Contributory Negligence

A great many cases resulting in tort actions involve negligence on the part of both the plaintiff and the defendant. This is particularly true of automobile accidents. Many jurisdictions have already introduced a no-fault rule on the basis that it is difficult if not impossible to distinguish between the degrees of fault in most vehicle accidents. At one time, the common law provided that if the plaintiff was partly, however little, negligent, the claimant forfeited all right of compensation. This was the "all or nothing rule," which recognized contributory negligence as a complete defence. A classic case in this regard is *Butterfield v. Forrester* (1809), 11 East 60, where although the defendant wrongfully obstructed traffic by placing a pole across the highway, the plaintiff failed to recover damages for his injuries when he failed to keep a proper lookout, collided with the pole, and was thrown from his horse.

The "last opportunity rule" was applied in the famous donkey case of *Davies v. Mann* (1984), 10 M.&W. 546. In this case the plaintiff was probably somewhat negligent in hobbling the forefeet of his donkey and then leaving it to graze by the side of the road where it was knocked down and killed by the defendant's wagon proceeding at a fast pace. The jury found that the accident might have been avoided by the exercise of ordinary care on the part of the defendant, and the plaintiff was allowed to recover damages despite his own negligence.

The foregoing rule may still apply to those cases in which, despite the plaintiff's negligence, the defendant has failed to take proper evasive action despite the existence of ample time to do so.

In many cases, the "all or nothing rule" worked considerable hardship, and the courts gradually realized that some other remedy was required. Accordingly, they adopted the rule that applies in admiralty law; namely, that if two ships are approaching each other and are involved in a collision, the court attempts to determine the degree of fault on the part of both captains. If it is not possible to decide which captain caused the accident, the admiralty rule is that both parties share equally in the loss. The admiralty rule about the apportionment of fault has now been incorporated in the various provincial Contributory Negligence Acts (for example Ontario's Negligence Act, R.S.O. 1980, c. 315) and a court decides the degree of fault of each party and awards a judgment accordingly.

REVIEW QUESTIONS

1. What are the three essential elements of a negligence claim?
2. What is meant by a person's "duty to take care"?
3. What test do the courts apply to assess liability for negligence in a tort action?
4. What is the "foreseeability rule" in tort claims?
5. What duty of care do people have towards handicapped persons?
6. Suppose a person is injured while voluntarily rescuing another. Does he

or she have the basis for a tort claim if the injury was caused by the person being rescued?

7. What duty of care does an owner or occupier of premises owe towards: (a) trespassers? (b) licensees? (c) invitees? Explain, with examples, each category of person.

8. How has statute law affected the liability of an owner or occupier of premises for injuries sustained by a person entering the premises?

9. Explain, with an example, the concept of "negligent misrepresentation." What liability, if any, does the person responsible for it have?

10. What is meant by "dangerous possessions"? Give examples. What liability exists if they cause injury to some one? Explain, in this regard, the legal principle in the case of *Rylands v. Fletcher*.

11. What is a person's liability in tort for the actions of pet animals, such as cats, dogs, snakes, and tigers?

12. Is a person liable in tort if his or her action causes injury to another only indirectly. Explain, with reference to the case of *Scott v. Shepherd*.

13. Explain the legal principle referred to by the term "agony of the moment."

14. What is meant by the term "vicarious liability"? What significance does it have in the law of torts?

15. Is an employer at all liable if an employee, while making sales calls, lets his son drive the company car and causes injury to another driver? Explain.

16. Explain, with an example, the legal principle of *"res ipsa loquitur."*

17. When does the rule of *"volenti non fit injuria"* apply in a tort case?

18. When might a person successfully plead "Act of God" as a tort defence? Give an example.

19. How can "lack of foreseeability" be successfully used as a defence in a tort claim? Explain.

20. Are children liable in tort for their actions? Discuss.

21. What is meant by "contributory negligence"? How might it affect the outcome of a tort case?

PROBLEMS

1. A is a customer in a large department store. He notices that one section of the floor is being swept by a maintenance worker, and observes bits of glass on the floor. Being anxious to pick up a special purchase, A hurries by. Suddenly he slips and, as he falls, cuts his knee on the glass lying on the floor. A then has to take a taxi to the emergency ward of the local hospital. Does he have any claim for his injury, and against whom?

2. A woman drove to the nearest plaza in the middle of a Canadian winter and parked in the vicinity of her favourite supermarket. After getting out of her car she was walking across the parking lot in the dusk, when she tripped in a hole in the asphalt paving and twisted her ankle. Not only did she require medical attention, and incur loss of wages while away from work totalling $200, but she missed a chance to appear for a ballet

audition which might have earned her a contract at a yearly salary of $30,000. Discuss this case in terms of liability, assuming the parking lot is owned by the supermarket chain and also leased to some twenty independent merchants. Give arguments for and against.

3. One day a former Canadian Olympic skier decided to ski at a new ski run operated by the Blue Sky Lodge. He picked the hardest run and started on his way down. Part of the run led through bushy areas and through a ravine. He misjudged a bad area in the ravine, tripped and fell in some rocks. He was badly injured and eventually sued. It was proven at the trial that his ticket stated that each skier attempted the course at his own risk. It was also proven that the course hazards had been marked out by crossed branches which were partly obscured. Discuss the merits of the arguments for the defence and prosecution in this case.

4. One of your friends was entering a main branch of a large Canadian bank during the winter when she slipped on some water which had collected on the marble flooring. She was badly injured, missed work and her total claim came to $1,000. Has she any claim against the bank? What arguments could be used against her? Would it make any difference if a bank employee was mopping up the water every fifteen minutes, and she was injured just as he was about to recommence his duty? How would it affect her case if the bank paid $500 into court and she continued with her suit, but the judge only awarded her $450?

5. You are passing a private lodging house and are struck by a piece of debris which has fallen out of one of the upstairs windows. You sue the owner of the lodging house, and the judge dealing with this case is confronted by two legal precedents, one dealing with a brewery involving a beer barrel which rolled out onto the street injuring a passerby where the judge ruled that the owners of the brewery were liable because such an incident could not happen without somebody's negligence. The other case was *Rylands v. Fletcher* where water escaped from a large reservoir on A's land, leaked down through mine shafts, and damaged mine workings beneath B's adjacent land. In this case A was held responsible for the escape of a dangerous thing from his land causing damage to an adjacent property. What do you understand by the Rule of Law? If you were the judge which precedent would you apply in this case? Does this seem socially correct to you?

READINGS

Lawrie v. Woodward Stores (Oakridge) Ltd. (1966), 56 W.W.R. 557 (B.C.S.C.).

Facts: The plaintiff was injured when a revolving stand displaying children's books (approximately sixty-two inches high on a cast iron base some eighteen inches in diameter resting on casters) fell against her while she was standing at the tobacco counter of the defendant's department store waiting to buy cigarettes. Two witnesses testified that the stand could not topple without aggravated circumstances such as a small child trying to climb on it. No one saw the bookstand topple, but the defendant submitted that a small child, present with its mother, climbed on the stand causing it to fall.

Held per MacDonald J. at p. 560:

The plaintiff invokes the doctrine of *res ipsa loquitur*. . . . "Most frequently it is applied where the principle stated in *Scott v. London and St. Katherine Docks Co.* (1865), 3 H. & C. 596 at 601 comes into play . . .: 'There must be reasonable evidence of negligence. But where the thing is shown to be under the management of the defendant or his servants, and the accident is such as in the ordinary course of things does not happen if those who have the management use proper care, it affords reasonable evidence, in the explanation by the defendant, that the accident arose from want of care. . . .'"

In the case at bar it is clear that the book stand which inflicted the damage was under the sole management and control of the defendant. . . .

Therefore, this question arises: Was the accident which befell Mrs. Lawrie such as in the ordinary course of things does not happen if those who have the management use proper care? . . .

[The defendant objected that the plaintiff had failed to establish one of the conditions of "res ipsa loquitur," namely that "the occurrence is such that it would not have happened without negligence."]

". . . Schultz J. A. . . . in *Kullberg's Furniture Ltd. v. Flin Flon Hotel Co.* (1958), 26 W.W.R. 721, at p. 723 . . . said: 'The rule of evidence, *res ipsa loquitur*, does not give rise to a legal presumption of negligence but merely justifies an inference of negligence on the part of the defendant and casts on him the onus of going forward with the evidence.'"

". . . In *Sisters of St. Joseph v. Fleming*, [1938] S.C.R. 172. . . . "the plaintiff commences with an onus of establishing negligence on the part of the defendant resting upon him. If he proves, to the satisfaction of the tribunal, facts which bring the maxim into operation, then unless the defendant produces an explanation "equally consistent with negligence and no negligence" . . . the plaintiff will succeed. . . .'"

It is my view that the explanation of the defendant [that the casters on this did not render it any more liable to fall and that the stand probably toppled because some unseen child climbed on it, causing it to fall] . . . is "not sufficient weight either to overturn or to neutralize the force of the inference arising from the facts proved. . . ."

I find the defendant liable for the injuries and loss suffered by the plaintiff [assessed as special damages (i.e., the doctor's bill) at $62 and general damages (i.e., limping for three weeks) at $400; total judgment against the defendant, $462].

Wilson v. Blue Mountain Resorts Ltd. (1974), 4 O.R. (2d) 713 (H.C.)

Facts: On December 25, 1970, while skiing with his daughter and friends, Wilson suffered serious injuries to his leg when he skied on an access trail of a ski run which ended at the brow of a gully facing a steep drop of rough ground into a stream. Wilson at the time was 60 years old. He was also a former member of a Canadian Olympic Ski Team. His damages were assessed at $20,000 including special and general damages. The defendants alleged that the dangerous area had been marked off with crossed sticks indicating a hazardous area.

Held per Holland J.:

[While the area] was marked to some extent with branches and sticks . . . in order to adequately warn of the gully some continuous form of marking would be required, such as a string of red flags. . . .

. . . Part of the history was that Wilson swerved to miss another skier. . . . [N]o other skier was in the immediate area when the accident occurred.

. . . [Blue Mountain alleged] it was an express term of such contract and use that in so doing he [Wilson] agreed to assume all risk of personal injury. . . . Blue Mountain relies on the wording of the tow tickets. . . .

I accept the evidence of Wilson that he did not read the small print. . . . [N]o evidence to show that the wording on the back of the tow tickets had been brought to his attention. . . . I cannot find that the defendant successfully contracted out of liability. . . .

It was further pleaded . . . that Wilson knew and appreciated the condition of the area where he fell and assumed the risk of skiing there. . . . Skiing is . . . a dangerous sport . . . anyone taking part in some such sport must . . . accept certain dangers which are inherent in such sport in so far as such dangers are obvious or necessary. . . . Wilson, without knowledge of the existence of the gully across his path cannot be taken to have accepted the risk of injury by falling into the gully. . . .

. . . A common business interest existed between Wilson . . . and Blue Mountain. . . . As such, apart from contract, the duty that existed was set out in the classic statement of Willis J. in *Indermaur v. Dames* (1866), L.R. 1 C.P. 274 at p. 288: ". . . the occupier shall on his part use reasonable care to prevent damages from unusual danger, which he knows or ought to know . . . evidence of neglect, the question whether such reasonable care has been taken . . . must be determined by a jury as a matter of fact."

. . . It was urged . . . in argument that . . . the ski runs, and in particular the access run . . . were was safe as reasonable care and skill could make them. . . . In my view, the gully running as it did across part of the access hill constituted a hidden and unusual danger. . . . [T]here therefore existed an obligation on the occupier who knew of the dangerous situation to warn skiers of the danger. . . . [T]he warning given as of the day of the accident was quite inadequate.

. . . [T]here remains the question of contributory negligence on the part of Wilson. . . . [W]hen skiing down what to him [Wilson] was a new slope he had an obligation of keeping an especially good look-out. He failed in this obligation and . . . contributed to the accident. . . . I find the defendant Blue Mountain 75% to blame . . . and the plaintiff 25% to blame.

. . . [J]udgement against the defendant for the sum of $15,000, together with costs.

Pajot v. Commonwealth Holiday Inns of Canada Ltd.

Held per Boland J.:

This action concerns a claim for damages arising out of injuries sustained by the plaintiff, Ronald Pajot, hereinafter called Pajot, on February 12, 1972, when he fell through a glass door in a Holiday Inn owned by the defendant. Pajot suffered serious injury to his lower right leg, ankle and foot. The issues to be determined are liability and the quantum of damages.

At the time of the accident, Pajot was 34 years of age, married with two small children and was employed as sales representative for R. L. Crane and Company, Don Mills, Ontario. In response to a newspaper advertisement for a winter holiday with swimming and snowmobiling, the plaintiff, his wife and four friends were enjoying a week-end as paying guests at the defendant's Inn. This was their first visit to the Holiday Inn at Peterborough, Ontario. Saturday morning the group of six had breakfast, went snowmobiling and then decided to have a swim before luncheon. They changed in their rooms and were advised by the hotel staff that the entrance to the swimming pool was through room 116. Pajot and his friends proceeded down the dimly lit hallway to a door marked "116" and "pool" which they entered.

Room 116 is a regular guest-room situate on the ground floor. It is approximately 12 ft. by 20 ft. and there is a glass door consisting of two clear panels of glass. Each panel is approximately seven feet wide. One panel is permanent and the other opens into a temporary plastic-covered tunnel leading to the pool. According to the evidence, the pool was designed as an outdoor pool. During the winter months, the pool was enclosed with plastic, the furniture was removed from room 116 and guests of the Inn walked through the room and down the tunnel to the enclosed pool. The pool was not visible from the entrance to the tunnel. The sliding door and the tunnel are shown in the photographs filed as exs. 6 and 7.

Pajot testified that he was the last of his group to enter room 116 and the tunnel. He expected to see the pool on the other side of the hall door and was surprised to find himself in a dark, empty room. He followed his friends across the room and stated that he saw a doorway but no door. He proceeded through the doorway and down a cold tunnel five feet in width to the pool. He noted there was water and melting snow on the rough ground in the tunnel. Pajot spent five to 10 minutes in the cool pool and decided to have a sauna which was located just across the hall. He saw one person leave the pool and a few minutes later he got out of the water, picked up his towel and shoes and jogged briskly up the cold tunnel. He testified that he was cold and was watching where he was going. As he approached the dark opening to the room, he suddenly saw his reflection and realized there was a glass door directly in front of him. According to his evidence, he saw only his reflection and put his arms out and hit the glass with the flat part of his arms. Pajot further explained how the glass collapsed inward throwing him off balance and he fell through the glass and landed in a push-up position on the rug. His thighs were in the tunnel. According to his evidence, he was not stunned by the impact. He sensed that his thigh was injured and that there was a lot of broken glass around him. He started to back out the doorway and had taken three or four steps backwards when he realized his lower right leg was badly injured. He tied a towel around his leg. Shortly afterwards an ambulance was called and he was taken to the Peterborough Civic Hospital.

Having considered all the evidence and relying specifically on the evidence of Pajot and Patricia Ann Montgomery, I find that room 116 was dark at the time of the accident and that the tunnel leading to the pool was poorly lit. I also accept their evidence that Pajot was following Montgomery and that he was the last of the group of six to enter room 116 and the tunnel. Both witnesses testified they did not see a glass door when they initially entered the tunnel and I find that they did not see the glass door because it was open.

I find that at the time of the accident the sliding glass door was not properly marked as there were no visible markings on the glass that could be seen by someone coming up the tunnel to enter room 116. This in my judgment constituted negligence on the part of the defendant. In reaching this conclusion I rely on the evidence of Pajot and Montgomery.

The white paper sign marked "Please Keep This Door Closed," which is filed as ex. 8, was posted on the inside of the glass and could not be seen from the room if the glass door was open and could not be seen from the tunnel if the door was open or closed. Such a marking was completely inadequate to warn guests of the existence of the glass door. In my view, in order to adequately warn of the glass door some more permanent form of marking would be required such as wide strips of black and white tape on the outside and inside of the glass door.

I do not accept the evidence of the maintenance supervisor, John Bernard King, and the innkeeper, William Spencer Brown, that two strips of three-quarter-inch black tape had been affixed to the glass to warn guests of the danger of walking through the glass door. In light of the evidence that an insurance adjuster had examined the black tape purported to have been placed across the width of the sliding glass panel, it is curious that neither the adjuster nor the tape were available for the trial.

There is also evidence which I accept that the glass door was not intended to be opened from the outside. It was designed for a patio and not for a throughway. I also believe the evidence of Pajot that the first time he was aware of the existence of the glass door dividing room 116 and the tunnel was when he saw his reflection in the glass. At this point he was wet and cold and was jogging along at a brisk pace and I find that it was impossible for him to slow down and prevent the accident which resulted in his serious injuries.

Having considered all the evidence, I have no difficulty deciding that the relationship of the plaintiff and the defendant was that of invitor and invitee. The standard of care owed by an invitor to an invitee stated in *Indermaur v. Dames* (1866), L.R. 1 C.P. 274, applies. Apart from the duty of the invitee to take reasonable care for his own safety, there is a duty upon the invitor to use reasonable care to prevent injury to the invitee from unusual danger of which the occupier is or ought to be aware. In this case when determining whether or not there was an unusual danger, one must take into consideration the combination of special factors which led to the accident in question. One must consider the entrance through the dark and empty room, the sliding glass door with no visible marking, the temporary plastic tunnel which was cold and poorly lit and finally the cold pool itself. I find the combination of these miserable conditions concocted by the defendant's employees, to lure guests to the Inn during the winter months, constituted an unusual danger which directly resulted in the injuries suffered by the plaintiff. I find that the defendant knew or ought to have known of this danger. In view of the conditions, the fact that Pajot was running because he was cold, was looking where he was going and understandably thought the sliding glass was an open doorway, I can find no want of care or lack of prudence on his part and, therefore, find that there was no contributory negligence.

Furthermore, apart from tort liability, the defendant is also liable on the grounds of breach of contract. The plaintiff was a paying guest and he entered into a contract with the defendant to enjoy the privileges offered by the Inn, provided he exercise prudence himself. There was an implied warranty that the premises were as safe as reasonable care and skill could make them. In my respectful view, the defendant did not discharge its obligation to see that the glass door was properly marked. The failure to properly mark the door in view of the particular circumstances of this case, created a "hazard" for the plaintiff when he was entering room 116 through the sliding glass door. As I have already said, I can find no want of care or lack of prudence on the part of the plaintiff and, therefore, find the defendant in breach of contract and liable to the plaintiff for the damages resulting from such breach.

The next issue to be determined is quantum of damages. Counsel are agreed on special damages in the amount of $342.30 and I have only been asked to assess the general damages.

Pajot is now 39 years of age. He is married and has three young children, two boys and a girl. He is working in an administrative capacity with R.L. Crane and Company. The plaintiff gave his evidence in a straightforward manner and appeared as a sincere, energetic man who thoroughly enjoys his work and enjoys raising his children. Prior to the accident he was involved in athletics such as squash, tennis, golf, hunting, skating and skiing.

The evidence is clear that Pajot suffered nasty and significant injuries and that the major injury involved the lower right leg, ankle and foot. According to the hospital records, the medical report of Dr. Silverstein filed as ex. 10 and the evidence of Dr. Laurence Green, an expert in the field of orthopaedics, he sustained lacerations to his right hand, left forearm, left knee, ankle, foot and toes, right knee and a large laceration penetrating the quadriceps tendon in the right lateral thigh. There was a compounded laceration of the right tibial area which divided all the extensor mechanism to his foot as well as a compound penetrating injury of the right ankle which divided the lateral ligament of the ankle joint. These injuries involved considerable discomfort and pain.

He received operative treatment for his injuries at the Peterborough Civic Hospital where he remained for a week. He was home in bed with a knee cast for a further five weeks and he suffered considerable discomfort. After the cast was removed, he spent a further six weeks on crutches and having physiotherapy. The lacerations on his forearm, thigh and left foot healed without consequence except for minor scarring. There are a number of pronounced scars on his right leg and ankle. The residual problems lie in the right foot and ankle which still swell and ache and stiffen from time to time. He also experiences difficulty raising this foot.

The medical evidence substantiates that Pajot has reached a plateau of recovery. He will have permanent disability as a result of the limited dorsiflection of his ankle and foot and there will always be a muscle weakness and a loss of sensation and numbness in his right foot and ankle. This will interfere with his participation in athletic activities. He will suffer discomfort wearing ski boots and skates. He will have trouble with sports such as squash and tennis which involve running, pivoting and moving quickly. He will be able to hunt and play golf but will tire easily. In the future, he will not be able to fully participate in family activities and this will be a continuing frustration for this particular plaintiff. Having considered all the evidence, I am assessing the general damages for pain and suffering and loss of pleasures of life since the accident and in the future in the amount of $17,000.

The plaintiff Pajot will, therefore, have judgment against the defendant for the sum of $17,342.30, together with costs.

Judgment for plaintiff.

2

PRINCIPLES OF CONTRACT LAW

We have just considered some of the most important obligations that society imposes on its members—not to commit criminal acts, or "public wrongs," and not to commit torts, or "private wrongs," against other members of society or their property. Now we consider obligations that a person assumes voluntarily by means of a *contract*. This is an agreement between two or more persons whereby each agrees to perform a certain act (for example, to supply a certain type of equipment), or to refrain from performing a certain act (for example, in the case of an agent, not to handle the goods of firms competing with the agent's principal). However, for a contract to be legally enforceable, it must fulfil certain criteria that have been established over the centuries by the courts. There must have been:

1. a valid offer and acceptance;
2. an intention to create a legally enforceable contract;
3. consideration (that is, something of value passing from each party to the other);
4. legally competent parties involved;
5. a voluntary undertaking by all parties;
6. a legal purpose.
7. the requirement of writing (in certain intances).

   In this second part of the book, we examine in some detail these criteria relating to the formation of a contract. We also consider the statutory requirement that some contracts be in writing to be legally enforceable; the interpretation of a contract; the nature and consequences of completion, cancellation, and breach of a contract; and the possible involvement of third persons in a contract. With this knowledge, a person will be much better able to safeguard his or her interest when entering into a contract.

5

Offer and Acceptance

The first basic requirement of a legally binding contract is the existence of an agreement between the parties involved. This is considered to have occurred when there has been an offer by one party and an acceptance of it by the other. At this point, each party has agreed to the other's terms and consent has been reached.

At one time, this process of offer and acceptance was referred to as a "meeting of the minds" or, in Latin, *consensus ad idem*. However, for many years now, common law judges have declined to attempt to peer into men's minds to determine what they really intended. Instead, they rely on each party's stated intentions, as expressed orally, in writing, or by his or her actions. Thus, for example, when a person wishes to travel by train, he or she goes to the ticket counter and offers money for the ticket; the railway company then accepts the offer by giving that person a ticket valid for transportation from one point to another.

What constitutes a valid offer and a valid acceptance is discussed in the following pages.

Unit 5.1
Valid Offer

An offer is a tentative promise by a person, called the offeror, to do something—for example, to sell or buy a house. It is tentative because the offeror may make the offer subject to acceptance by the other party, usually by a certain date and time and will only be bound by the promise if the other party, the offeree, does something in return—namely, paying or agreeing to pay the price asked by a certain date.

The courts have held that an offer may be made in any form whatsoever, providing it can be interpreted as an offer. It may be written, it may be oral, or it may consist of a nod of the head, or it may be the act of sitting down in a restaurant, or entering a barber shop or beauty salon. The courts have often been called on to decide whether in fact an offer was made and by whom.

WORDING OF THE OFFER

Occasionally the courts have set aside an offer on the grounds that its wording is too vague or imprecise to be considered a valid offer. Thus, in the case of *Arnold Nemetz Engineering Ltd. v. Tobien Steel*, [1971] 4 W.W.R. 373, Judge McFarlane stated, "I am impelled to the conclusion that the contract is so vague and uncertain as to essential matters that it must be held unenforceable for want of mutuality."

Usually, a judge will also take into account local custom or trade practice in attempting to determine the offeror's intended meaning. Obviously, a person entering into a contract should make sure that the wording of the offer is as precise and unambiguous as possible. After all, it is the very essence of a contract that each party understand, with enough certainty, the content of the bargain.

It is acceptable for the parties to leave certain points in their contract unsettled, providing they agree as to how these points are later to be resolved—for example, the selling price of a house that has been expropriated to be determined later by an independent appraiser.

Incomplete Agreements. In the case of *Turney and Turney v. Zhilka* (1959), 18 D.L.R. (2d) 447 (S.C.C.) an agreement was made to sell and buy a piece of property *providing it was annexed to the adjacent municipality*. It was never annexed, and the buyer stated he was prepared to waive this provision. The court held that, since the agreement was subject to action by a third party (the municipality) which was never completed, there was an incomplete agreement. By proper drafting of the contract, this could have been avoided.

It has also been held that an agreement that includes vague terms, or lack of precision, also results in an incomplete agreement, and that even if one party is ready to rectify such inomplete agreement, there is no obligation on the other party to acquiesce. As there has been no "meeting of the minds," there is no legally binding offer and acceptance.

INVITATION VERSUS OFFER

As a general rule, the courts have interpreted signs in windows, advertisements in newspapers and other media, and items displayed on counters, as invitations to do business (that is to make an offer) rather than as legally binding offers in themselves. Consequently, a customer makes an offer by coming in, picking up the item, and indicating to the salesperson that he or she wishes to buy it. The salesperson accepts, as the company's agent, by wrapping up the item, giving it to the customer, and taking the money. Together, the offer by the customer and the acceptance by the salesperson, acting on behalf of the employer, meet this requirement for a valid contract. Of course, the salesperson may quite legally refuse the offer—or may refuse to sell the item at the price shown on it. However, it would be poor business practice to refuse a sale, and in certain cases may amount to a criminal offence of misleading advertising. (See Chapter 27.) Nevertheless, no legal liability in contract would be incurred because without acceptance there is no contract.

An example of an invitation to do business involving goods on display is the case of *Pharmaceutical Society of Great Britain v. Boots Cash Chemists (Southern) Ltd.*, [1952] 2 All E.R. 456.

In this case, a customer entered a self-service store and picked out two bottles of patent medicine. These contained a slight amount of some drugs included in the Poisons List, but not in sufficient amount to be covered by the Poisons Rules. The Pharmacy and Poisons Act of England required that all sale of poisons be carried out under the supervision of a pharmacist. If the goods displayed on the supermarket shelves were, in fact, an offer and the purchaser accepted this offer by taking the goods from the shelf, then there was a possibility that the contract was not completed under the supervision of the pharmacist. On the other hand, if the display on the supermarket shelf was merely an invitation to buy and the customer by taking the goods from the shelf to the cashier was making an offer, and the cashier by accepting the money was making an acceptance, then this transaction could have been said to have been carried out under the supervision of the pharmacist who stood nearby.

The judgment of the court included the following comments:

> The mere fact that a shopkeeper exposes goods which indicate to the public that he is willing to treat does not amount to an offer to sell. I do not think I ought to hold that there has been here a complete reversal of that principle merely because a self-service scheme is in operation. In my opinion, what was done here came to no more than that the customer was informed that he could pick up the article and bring it to the shopkeeper, a contract for sale being completed if the shopkeeper accepted the customer's offer to buy. The offer is an offer to buy, not to sell.
>
> ... Books are displayed in a bookshop and customers are invited to pick them up and look at them even if they do not actually buy them. There is no offer of the shopkeeper to sell before the customer has taken the book to the shopkeeper ... and said that he wants to buy it and the shopkeeper has said "yes". This would not prevent the shopkeeper from saying, "I am sorry I cannot let you have that book ... I have already promised it to another customer."

In this case, the judge found that the sale was carried out under the supervision of a pharmacist and gave judgment for the defendants.

Offer to The World at Large

One exception to the general rule that an advertisement in a newspaper is an invitation to do business rather than an offer is illustrated by the case of *Carlill v. Carbolic Smokeball Co.*, [1893] 1 Q.B. 269.

In this case, a company desiring to promote its product advertised in a daily newspaper that if any person took their product, a pill, three times daily for a period of two weeks, and still contracted influenza, it would pay a reward. To show good faith, the firm deposited a sum of money in one of the local banks. A Mrs. Carlill took the pill faithfully, caught influenza, then wrote to the company demanding the reward. They replied that their advertisement was merely an invitation to do business and that she should therefore have contacted them to offer to take the pills, and then following their acceptance, an agreement would have been formed.

The dispute went to court and the judge, looking at all the circumstances, ruled that this was more than a simple offer; it was an offer to the world at large. His conclusion was based on the fact that by placing reward money in the hands of a bank as trustee, the company must have intended that their advertisement was capable of being accepted by performance (conduct). The judge held that in these circumstances anybody who makes a rash offer is to be held accountable for the acceptance of such an offer without direct communication.

The Canadian case of *Goldthorpe v. Logan*, [1943] 2 D.L.R. 519, also illustrates an offer to the world at large.

This case arose out of the acceptance by the customer of an advertisement reading, "Hairs . . . removed safely and permanently by electrolysis . . . no marks, no scars, results guaranteed." The customer accepted this advertisement and attended for treatment but the results showed no improvement. The customer sued for a refund of her money. The judgment in this case contained the following quotation taken from Justice Hawkins in the case of *Carlill v. Carbolic Smokeball Co.*:

> Such advertisements do not appeal so much to the wise and thoughtful as to the credulous and weak portions of the community; and if the vendor of an article, whether it be medicine, smoke, or anything else, with a view to increasing its sale and use, thinks fit publicly to promise to all who buy or use it, that, to those who shall not find it as surely efficacious as it is represented by him to be, he will pay a substantial sum of money, he must not be surprised if occasionally he is held to his promises.

The customer was awarded a refund of her money.

An offer to the world at large should not be confused with the "satisfaction or money refunded" policy of large department stores. Such a policy is gratuitous and not based on legal liability. However, one may argue that such large department stores make "representations" which induce members of the public to enter into purchase contracts and that such promises are part of the contract as a contract may be partly written and partly oral.

In this category of advertisements which may be construed as offers to the world at large, should be included the reward offers, which are capable of acceptance only by the party who qualifies for the reward.

COMMUNICATION OF AN OFFER

Another general rule with regard to offers is that an offer must be communicated to a person before he can accept it. Suppose, for example, a person finds a lost item and returns it today, but tomorrow sees a reward offered in the newspaper for its return. Legally, the finder cannot claim the reward as no contract was formed. His (or her) return of the lost item was a gratuitous act. It cannot be considered an acceptance of the offer since he was unaware that the offer existed.

The problem of determining just what constitutes communication is illustrated by the case of *Olley v. Marlborough Court Ltd.*, [1949] All E.R. 127.

In this case, a lady seeking accommodation in a hotel signed the guest register. However, when she reached her room she noticed that there was a sign reading: "The proprietors will not hold themselves liable or responsible for articles lost or stolen, unless handed to the manageress for safe custody. Valuables should be deposited for safe custody. . . ." During the guest's stay, some items were taken from her room and she sued the hotel proprietors for damages. The court, in dealing with this case, reviewed the possible ways by which a guest could be said to have accepted such a provision. The best way, it was held, would be by *a written document signed by the guest*; a second way would be by a *written notice specifying certain terms* that would be included in the contract; and a third way would be by a *prominent public notice*. In this case, although there was a sign, the plaintiff did not see it until after she had been accepted as a guest. Consequently, the court decided that the guest could not be bound by this sign unless the defendants could show that she had agreed to be bound by the provision.

It should be noted that, in Ontario and many of the other common law provinces, a hotel-keeper, in order to limit his liability, must post a sign exactly as set out in the Innkeepers' Act—that is, not only in the bedroom but also at the front desk and in a public place.

STANDARD-FORM CONTRACTS

Nowadays many offers made by members of the public, when purchasing goods or services, take the form of detailed, printed documents. These are provided by the seller and must be used by the customer to make his or her offer—for example, to buy life insurance or a new car. Very often, the offeror has neither the time nor the legal ability to understand the full significance of the offer being made. Nevertheless, because of the customary nature of such documents and the common policy adopted by the companies concerned, the customer usually has no choice but to use the standard form. Hence the term "one-sided" contracts.

In the eyes of the law, a person who makes such an offer is legally bound by all its terms. However, as some small measure of protection, the courts have evolved the principle that, if the offeree can show that he or she was unaware of a particular term in the contract, the offeror must show that reasonable steps were taken to bring the term to the attention of the offeree.

Governments are becoming increasingly aware of the problems caused by standard-form contracts which are heavily "one-sided." Although generally there is respect for the sanctity of contracts that are freely entered into, there has been consumer protection legislation passed by various provincial governments to equalize the bargaining position of the parties involved—for example, in rental contracts between landlord and tenant. This takes the form of statutory clauses which must be included in the lease binding on either the landlord, tenant, or both—for example, that a landlord must provide rented premises which are furnished in a state fit for habitation throughout the term of the lease. It also takes the form of compulsory "non-exclusionary" clauses—for example, that the sellers of consumer goods may not disclaim or exculpate their contracts from the implied conditions and warranties of the Sale of Goods Act for that province.

In addition to the above, there may be provincial legislation such as Ontario's Business Practices Act (see Chapter 28) which has twenty-three different provisions relating to contracts. One provision, for example, states that if one party has exaggerated the benefits resulting from the contract, thus misleading the other party, the misled party may void the contract.

With the exception of the foregoing, persons who enter into standard-form contracts will normally be bound by them. However, in cases of doubt as to the meaning of words used in, for example, exclusionary clauses in an insurance contract, the courts will tend to favour the person who has been required to sign the standard-form contract. Specifically, the courts will apply the *contra proferentum* rule, whereby the interpretation given by the courts to a printed contract is the one least favourable to the person who has drawn it up.

It should also be noted that if one party commits a breach of a fundamental condition of a contract, the court may order the contract to be rescinded (abolished) and award damages to the injured party. This is so whether or not the printed contract used (for example, a bill of sale) specifically excludes the seller from liability. (See *Lightburn v. Belmont Sales Ltd.* on p. 238 of this book.)

DURATION OF AN OFFER

An offer does not remain in force indefinitely. It will in fact lapse as soon as one of the following circumstances occurs:

The offeree refuses to accept the offer. Suppose a grain merchant offers a supply of grain at a certain price to a customer. If the customer refuses the offer, he cannot later change his mind and demand to buy it. Unfortunately for him, the offer no longer exists.

The offeree does not accept within the stipulated time. If, for example, a person offers to sell her house to another person and gives her three days in which to accept, the offer will lapse at the end of those three days.

Sometimes an offeror is given something of value by the offeree for agreeing to hold an offer open for a certain period of time. Under such a contract, called an *option*, the offeror also agrees to permit only the offeree to accept the offer. This is a second exception to the general rule that an offeror can revoke his offer at any time before acceptance.

Options are commonly used in connection with land purchases when one party is trying to acquire a certain area of land that is owned by a number of different persons. Rather than buy one piece of land at a time, the purchaser makes an option to purchase with each of the different parties until he or she is sure that he can buy from all the land owners and so acquire the complete area. During the period specified in the option it is impossible for the offerors (the present owners of the land) to withdraw or revoke their offers to sell, without committing a breach of contract

Where no time limit is stipulated but the offeree fails to accept within a reasonable time.   If a person who is in the business of selling perishable fruit offers a load of strawberries to a retail store and fails to receive an acceptance within a few hours, he can treat the offer as having lapsed. Or if a bond dealer offers some bonds for sale at a certain price and the offer is not accepted within minutes, he or she can go ahead and sell them to someone else. However, if a person offers to sell gravel, the offer may be considered to last for several days or weeks. What is a "reasonable time" will have to be decided by a judge in a court of law, should the matter come into dispute.

In the case of *Shatford v. B.C. Wine Growers Ltd.*, [1927] 2 D.L.R. 759 (B.C. S.C.), the defendants, wine growers, sent a mailed offer to purchase loganberries from the plaintiff which was received by the latest on April 24, but the plaintiff did not mail his acceptance until April 30. Mr. Justice Murphy, in his decision that there was no contract formed, stated:

> The plaintiff's action must fail because he did not accept this offer within a reasonable time. . . . [O]rdinarily a proposal sent by mail calls for an acceptance, if not by return of post, at least during business hours of the day on which such offer was received. Here, having regard to the commodity being bargained for, the time of year of the offer, and the necessity, under the circumstances, as shown by the evidence of prompt decision, as to whether the offer would be accepted or not . . . the plaintiff did not accept the defendant's offer within a reasonable time. . . . Action dismissed.

The offeror or offeree dies, becomes insane, or becomes bankrupt before the offer is accepted.   The courts have held, reasonably enough, that if a person is dead, insane, or bankrupt, he or she is in no condition to enter into a legally binding agreement.

The offeree, instead of accepting the offer, makes a counter offer.   A counter offer may be a completely new offer. However, a qualified acceptance of the original offer is also considered to be a counter offer. An illustration of a counter offer is provided by the case of *Parkette Apartments Ltd. v. Masternak* (1965), 50 D.L.R. (2d) 581.

Here the plaintiffs offered to buy an apartment building for $64,000. The defendant changed the date for acceptance and made other amendments and returned the offer. The plaintiff's president initialled the alterations and amendments but made further alterations stating that the building "must be delivered free of tenants." The altered document reached the defendant after she had already accepted a new offer of $70,000. The plaintiffs then sued for specific performance (the equitable remedy which allows a person to ask the court for the specific item to be handed over). Mr. Justice Ferguson, of the Ontario Supreme Court, in giving his judgment said:

> The defendant [vendor] was making a counter offer by changing the date for acceptance; and the delivery of the document by the purchaser to his agent after initialling the changes did not constitute the required communication of acceptance to the vendor; and failure to communicate acceptance to him within the specified time was fatal to a claim of a concluded contract; and, in any event, the purchaser's further alteration of the document by striking out a clause respecting acceptance of a tenant in possession was in turn a counter offer to the vendor which required his acceptance and none was given.

A counter offer may be accepted by the original offeror who then becomes an offeree; in other words, the offeror's role has been changed.

The concept of offer and counter offer is illustrated by the following example. A offers to sell a house for $40,000, and B counter-offers with $35,000. Then if A says "no," this cancels B's counter-offer of $35,000. However, suppose A replies, "I cannot reduce my price." The courts have held that this means A is re-offering at $40,000. Thus B can validly accept the offer at $40,000.

The offeree realizes, before acceptance of the offer, that the offeror can no longer fulfil his or her promise. This legal principle is illustrated by the case of *Dickinson v. Dodds* (1876), 2 Ch.D. 463.

In this case, Dodds signed an agreement offering to sell a property for 800 pounds sterling on June 10, allowing Dickinson until 9 a.m. on June 12 to accept. The next day Dodds sold to Thomas Allen. Dickinson, learning of the sale through a third party, took steps before June 12 to serve Dodds with three separate Memoranda of Acceptance. Dickinson then sued for specific performance and this was granted by the trial court. When the case was heard on appeal, Lord Justice Mellish, in his judgment, made the following statement:

> The question which arises is this . . . if an offer has been made for the sale of property and before the offer is accepted, the person who has made the offer enters into a binding agreement to sell the property to someone else, and the person to whom the offer was made receives notice in some way that the property has been sold to another person, can he, after that, make a binding contract by the acceptance of the offer?
>
> If . . . in order to make a contract, the two minds must be in agreement at some one time, that is, at the time of acceptance, how is it possible

that when the person to whom the offer has been made knows that the person who has made the offer has sold the property to someone else and that, in fact, he has not remained in the same mind to sell it to him, he can be at liberty to accept the offer and thereby make a binding contract?

I am clearly of the opinion that just as when a man who has made an offer dies before it is accepted, it is impossible that it can then be accepted, so when once the person, to whom the offer was made, knows that the property has been sold to someone else, it is too late for him to accept the offer, and on that ground I am clearly of the opinion that there was no binding contract for the sale of this property by Dodds to Dickinson.

The offeror, or the offeree as the case may be, fails to fulfil a particular condition.   Thus a person may make an offer to purchase a house subject to being able to arrange a specified mortgage loan within a certain period of time. Failure to arrange that loan as specified would cause the offer to lapse.

REVOCATION OF AN OFFER

An offeror normally has the right to withdraw or revoke an offer at any time before its acceptance by the offeree. This is true even if the offeror has gratuitously agreed to keep the offer open for a given period. However, the offeror must communicate or attempt to communicate revocation to the offeree. Once an offer is accepted, it is too late to revoke it.

One exception to the general rule that an offeror can revoke the offer at any time before acceptance is the situation in which an offer, containing a time period for acceptance, has been made under "seal" or under an option.

REVIEW QUESTIONS

1. What is an "offer"? Distinguish between "offeror" and "offeree."
2. What are the various ways in which an offer may legally be made?
3. When is it permissible for the parties to leave certain points in their contract unsettled?
4. Distinguish, with examples, between a legally binding offer and an "invitation to do business."
5. Explain the legal principle involved in *Carlill v. Carbolic Smokeball Co.*
6. "An offer must be communicated to a person before he can accept it." Explain, with an example, the significance of this legal principle.
7. What is meant by a "standard-form" contract"? What protection do the courts give to the public with regard to such contracts?
8. To what extent can a business firm exclude liability for negligence in a contract?
9. What circumstances will cause an offer to lapse?

10. Does a person have the right to withdraw an offer: (a) once it has been made? (b) once it has been accepted?

11. Explain, with an example, the nature and purpose of an "option."

12. Can an oral or written notice or sign ever become part of an oral contract—for example, ticket conditions, disclaimers of liability, or exculpatory signs at parking lots?

PROBLEMS

1. A major Canadian university sent out applications for tenders on the construction of a new library, with extensive specifications. The conditions of the tender required the submission of tenders which were irrevocable and as a condition required the deposit of $50,000. Among the companies which tendered, the "A" Company tender was prepared by the company president who, in a last-minute hurry to submit a tender, neglected to include an escalation clause for unforeseen cost increases, although his covering letter referred to an escalation clause at page 2.

   When the mistake was realized, the President of "A" Company wrote a letter revoking his company's tender and requesting the return of the $50,000 deposit. The university officials, on opening the tenders and discovering that "A" Company's tender was the lowest, forwarded a completed contract to the "A" Company president for acceptance. "A" Company returned the contract unsigned and sued for the return of the $50,000 deposit.

   Discuss the merits of the claims of the university and "A" Company respectively, from the offer and acceptance point of view. Who should win? Why?

2. A municipality which desired to construct a new dam engaged a consulting company to run tests to determine the soil conditions at the location chosen for the dam site. Specifications were sent out and tenders were requested, advising at the same time that while tendering companies could use the consultants' soil test results, that each tenderer was responsible for its own tests. The company that submitted the lowest bid, W.E. Doit Co. was awarded the contract, but the water table proved so high that some $100,000 extra costs were incurred. The W.E. Doit Co. took advantage of an arbitration clause in the contract which awarded it half of the extra costs, or $50,000. The municipality appealed against this to the courts.

   Who should win this case and why? Give the reasons pro and con.

3. One of Canada's leading retail stores published an advertisement in a large circulation daily, reading "19" colour TVs for sale, $250." A newspaper employee had misread the advertisement and put in the selling price as $250 whereas the major retailer's ad had read $450. Some fifty people tried to buy these 19" colour TV sets before the advertisement could be retracted through the newspaper and radio. How many TV sets, if any, would the major retailer have to sell at the wrongly advertised

price? What is the offer and acceptance situation in this case? Is there any criminal liability involved? If so, indicate how this might be dealt with.

4. Negotiations were being carried on regarding the purchase of a block of apartments between the seller, an individual owner, and the corporate buyer. The buyers answered an advertisement in a newspaper, and after inspecting the property decided to put in an offer at $500,000. The seller signed the offer back to the would-be purchasing corporation at $525,000. The purchasers re-offered at $510,000. The seller re-offered at $515,000. The president of the corporate buyer then decided to accept at that figure and, after making a few minor alterations regarding payment terms and date of closing, signed and sealed the acceptance.

   Discuss the legal implications of the negotiations in this case and indicate when an enforceable contract was formed.

5. A, the owner of three farms, Blackacre, Whiteacre, and Greenacre, writes to B as follows: "I will sell you one of my farms for $50,000." B replies in writing, "I accept." Discuss the implications of this situation.

6. John, who operates a bus service, advertised a tour to Florida at Christmas, "leaving December 20, returning January 10 — please notify your acceptance by enclosing $200 fare." Dorothy sent her certified cheque for $200. John refused to accept it, claiming no contract. Discuss.

7. Mr. Johns was a coal broker whose business had gone downhill since the 1950s. When the energy crisis developed, he sought out the general manager of Dominion Coal Co. in Nova Scotia and persuaded the latter to give him a letter which contained the phrase *"Please be advised that this company is prepared to give you an option for 10,000 tons of coal per month at $50 per ton for the next 36 months dated 3 Dec. 80."* During the next four months, while travelling through the United States, Mr. Johns succeeded in obtaining orders for 9,000 tons of coal a month for 3 years. He then contacted the Dominion Coal Co. and ordered sufficient tons of coal to fulfil his orders, to start immediately, at the same time forwarding a letter confirming his credit of $450,000 per month from the Canadian Imperial Bank of Commerce. Dominion Coal refused to deliver, claiming that its existing orders were now taking up its full capacity.

   Give the pros and cons in this case.

8. Mr. Kahn owned several parcels of land, some of them in conjunction with his brother, who had authorized him to sell them if he wanted to. Mr. Smith, a younger man, had been leasing and farming these parcels and in 1973 succeeded in getting Mr. Kahn to agree to sell him some 441 acres of cultivated land and 214 acres of grass meadowland at $48 per cultivated acre and $24 per grassland acre, total price $26,304 with $1,500 paid on deposit. The agreement which was prepared by Mr. Smith and signed by Mr. Kahn provided among other terms "half the purchase price to be cash on possession of clear titles, the balance to be half the crop with no interest charged, on balance owing."

   The defendant Mr. Kahn returned the $1,500 deposit cheque and refused to carry out the sale, objecting that he was intoxicated at the time the agreement was made; that the agreement did not contain a provision as agreed; that he should be allowed to live in a house on the premises as he had been doing while Mr. Smith had been farming the land; that there was no provision as to when the cash was to be paid; and that there appeared to be no provision as to what would constitute the crop portion of the payment (for example, what proportion of the land was to be cultivated yearly).

In *Bocalter v. Hazle*, [1925] 4 D.L.R. 579, the judge stated: "How can the law fix the number of acres to be put in crop each year, the number of acres to be broken or summer fallowed? . . . Without an agreement as to them, no prudent vendor will sell on the crop payment plan."

The purchaser, Smith, who was suing for specific performance, agreed to waive any of these conditions as to payment and to pay the full amount in cash.

Give the arguments for the seller and purchaser, respectively. Discuss the probable outcome of the case. Refer to *Phibbs v. Choo* (1976), 69 D.L.R. (3d) 756.

READINGS

Turney and Turney v. Zhilka (1950), 18 D.L.R. (2d) 447 (S.C.C.)

Facts: A contract was made between the seller and the buyer to sell a piece of property, being part of west ½ lot 5, Con. 5 west, with the following condition: "providing the property can be annexed to the Village of Streetsville and the plan is approved by the Village Council for subdivision." It was later realized that the property in question measured only 62.37 acres and not the 65 acres which the seller believed. Also, the property was not annexed by the municipality. However, the plaintiff (purchaser) sued for specific performance—namely, the conveyance of the land in question (which had gone up in value) but lost. On appeal, the defendant (seller) objected "lack of certainty of description, and . . . no agreement either on quantity or description of land."

Held per Judson J.:

The date for the completion of the sale [was] fixed [at] . . ." 60 days after plans are approved". . . .

[The condition "that the sale and purchase should be dependent upon the annexation by the Village of Streetsville" was one introduced for the sole benefit of the purchaser—the plaintiff was willing to waive annexation.]

But here there is no right to be waived. The obligations under the contract, on both sides, depend upon a future uncertain event, the happening of which depends entirely on the will of a third party—the village council. *This is a true condition precedent—an external condition upon which the existence of the obligation depends.* Until the event occurs there is no right to performance on either side. . . . The purchaser now seeks to make the vendor liable on his promise to convey [the property] in spite of the non-performance of the condition and this to suit his own convenience only. This is not a case of renunciation or relinquishment of a right but rather an attempt by one party, without the consent of the other, to write a new contract.

Byrne & Co. v. Leon Van Tienhoven & Co. (1880), 5 C.P.D. 344 (Eng.)

Facts: On October 1, 1879, the defendants offered in writing to the plaintiffs 1,000 boxes of tin plates for 15s.6d. per box. On October 11, 1879, the plaintiffs accepted the offer by cable and followed this up on the same day by a letter confirming the cabled acceptance. The defendants had already written on October 8 cancelling their original offer because a large demand had caused prices to rise. This letter was received on October 20.

Held per Lindley J.:

It was agreed at the trial that . . . damages . . . should be 375 pounds [if the plaintiffs won]. . . .
    There is no doubt that an offer can be withdrawn before it is accepted. . . . For the decision of the present case, however, it is necessary to consider two other questions, viz.: 1. Whether a withdrawal of an offer has an effect until it is communicated to the person to whom the offer has been sent? 2. Whether posting a letter of withdrawal is a communication to the person to whom the letter is sent?
    . . . [S]ome . . . writers . . . are of opinion that there can be no contract if an offer is withdrawn before it is accepted. . . . The reason . . . is that there is not in fact any such consent by both parties as is essential to constitute a contract between them. Against this view . . . [there is the view] that a state of mind not notified cannot be regarded in dealings; . . . that an uncommunicated revocation is for all practical purposes and in point of law no revocation at all [Pollock, *Principles of Contract Law* (2nd ed.), p. 10)] . . . [N]ext question viz., whether posting the letter of revocation was a sufficient communication of it to the plaintiff. . . . It may be taken as now settled that where an offer is made and accepted by letters sent through the post, the contract is completed the moment the letter accepting the offer is posted . . . based on the principle that the writer of the offer has expressly or impliedly assented to treat an answer to him by a letter duly posted as a sufficient acceptance and notification to himself, or, in other words, he has made the post office his agent to receive the acceptance of the notification of it. But this principle appears to me to be inapplicable to the case of the withdrawal of an offer. . . . In my opinion the withdrawal by the defendants on the 8th of October of their offer of the 1st was inoperative; and a complete contract binding on both parties was entered into on the 11th of October, when the plaintiffs accepted the offer of the 1st, which they had no reason to suppose had been withdrawn. . . . [B]oth legal principles, and practical convenience require that a person who has accepted an offer not known to him to have been revoked, shall be in a position safely to act upon the footing that the offer and acceptance constitute a contract binding on both parties.

Unit 5.2
Valid Acceptance

If there is to be a legally enforceable contract, an offer (that is, a tentative promise) must be accepted.

If an offeror has stipulated that the offer must be accepted in a certain manner then it must be accepted in that way, or the acceptance at most amounts to a counter-offer.

The only exception to this rule would be if the third party were the agent of one of the other two parties. Thus, if B has appointed C as agent, then C may accept an offer from A on B's behalf—unless A has specifically stated that B must accept it in person.

As we saw earlier, anything short of an unconditional acceptance (one that complies exactly with the terms of the offer) is regarded as a counter-offer rather than an acceptance. Sometimes, it is necessary to determine whether the offeree has made an *inquiry* rather than a counter offer. The effect of an inquiry is merely to suspend the offer until such time as the details of the offer have been clarified.

An offer made by one party to another may not be accepted by a third party. Thus if A makes an offer to B, and C accepts, A is under no legal obligations to C. This is because the offer has not been made, or communicated, to C. Thus there is no *privity of contract* between A and C.

ACCEPTANCE BY PROMISE

In many contracts, acceptance takes the form of a promise by the offeree. As a result, there is a promise by the offeror (as contained in the offer) and a promise by the offeree (as contained in the acceptance). Thus, for example, in hiring someone for a job, the employer promises to pay a wage or salary and the employee promises to work for the employer. Or, as another example, the purchase of a good on credit that requires later delivery to the purchaser's home involves a promise by the customer to pay and a promise by the merchant to deliver the goods. Each party is in effect both a promisor and a promisee.

ACCEPTANCE BY PERFORMANCE

In other contracts, acceptance takes the form of an act rather than a promise. For example, a dog owner may offer a reward for information leading to the return of a missing dog. Acceptance would be the provision of the required information. Or, as another example, a person may offer to purchase a newspaper on a home delivery basis, promising to pay later. The publisher accepts by delivering the newspaper.

In other contracts, both offer and acceptance take the form of acts rather than promises. Thus a person shopping in a supermarket will take the desired goods and pay cash in exchange. Or, on public transportation, a person will pay the cash and receive a ride in exchange.

The courts have emphasized that some *positive action* is required to constitute acceptance. One example of this is the insurance company sending a notice stating that an insurance policy will automatically be renewed unless the insured notifies the company that he or she wishes to cancel the insurance. Another example is a record club sending out an album stating that if the addressee does not like it he should return it; otherwise he will be billed for it. With regard to such offers, the courts have consistently held that the offeree cannot be forced into a position of acceptance by *inaction*—in other words, "silence is not acceptance of an offer." Most provinces have now included such a provision in their consumer protection statutes. The Consumer Protection Act of Ontario, for example, specifically states that the recipient of unsolicited goods may not be charged in court for payment, despite "use, misuse, loss, damage or theft." Similarly, the recipient of a credit card that has not been requested or accepted has no legal obligation in respect of its use or disposal [s. 36(4)]. Of course, established business practice or express agreement may change this rule between business persons.

WITHDRAWAL OF ACCEPTANCE

The rule in law is that acceptance may be withdrawn up to the moment a legal agreement is formed—that is, when the offeror is advised that his offer has been accepted.

In normal circumstances, there is no problem because the contract is formed only when the offeror is informed, orally or by performance, that his offer has been accepted. A problem arises, however, when communication is by an agent. If, say, the offeror lives in Vancouver and the offeree in Halifax and the normal method of communication is by air mail, there may be a lapse of several days (including postal delays) between the time the offeror sends the offer and the offeree accepts it. Several more days may lapse before the offeror receives the written acceptance. However, we have seen that if the offeree accepts by the same manner as the offer was communicated to him or her, the contract is formed as soon as the offeree drops the acceptance into the mailbox. In these circumstances, the acceptance cannot be withdrawn because a legal agreement has already been made.

Interesting legal questions arise in the event of a mail strike. For example, an acceptance by mail pursuant to an offer by mail may well create a legally binding contract unless the offer clearly states that acceptance will not be valid unless it is acutally received by the offeror. Some businesses, as in the construction industry, operate almost exclusively on the basis of firm offers (or "tenders") when offering their goods or services for sale. By custom, in a particular industry, such a tender may not be withdrawn until the other party has had a reasonable time within which to accept or reject it. However, the only penalty for early withdrawal is loss of reputation. This is because, from the strictly legal point of view, the party making the tender may withdraw it at any time before acceptance. The only exceptions occur when the tender has been made under seal or when some consideration (discussed in the next chapter) has been given by the other party to obtain an "option." Once the offer has been accepted, the firm supplying the good or service is bound by the offer.

In one court case, a firm unintentionally omitted a page numbered "2," that included a price escalation clause, from a ten-page tender. The judge held that the acceptor must have been aware of this omission. Therefore, it could not hold the offeror to the contract containing the other nine pages because, as a result of the unintentional mistake, there had been no true meeting of minds, which is one of the requirements for a legally binding contract.

WHEN IS A CONTRACT MADE?

In some court cases, it is of the utmost importance to determine exactly when acceptance takes place and a contract is formed. Normally this is easy to determine when the parties are dealing face to face or when they spell out the terms of their contract in writing. Sometimes, however, the time at which a contract comes into being is not clear and may be the cause of contention between the parties. To help prevent such disputes, the Sale of Goods Act in each province (see Chapter 24) sets out certain rules as to when title in goods passes from the seller to the buyer, if this point is not agreed upon by the parties.

Court cases that involve the question of the timing of acceptance often arise in connection with the submission of tenders in connection with major construction or manufacturing contracts. Usually it is requested that tenders be accompanied by large deposits to ensure that the bids are realistic. Many business persons regard these firm bids, or tenders as they are called, to be irrevocable and binding until accepted or rejected by the party calling for the tenders. However, the law indicates clearly that a bid or tender is merely an offer which is capable of withdrawal or revocation up to the very moment that it is accepted. Some judges have even held that when the party calling for tenders becomes aware that the tenderer is trying to reach him to announce the withdrawal of his offer, it is already too late to accept the tender (see *Dickinson v. Dodds.* (1876), 2 Ch.D. 463).

Once a bid or tender has been accepted, a more formalized contract is customarily prepared. However, if the formal contract does not agree in all respects with the bid already submitted and accepted, the tenderer will be able successfully to withdraw from the agreement on the basis that the acceptance is really a counter-offer, again capable of acceptance or rejection by the successful bidder.

In *Johnston Brothers v. Rogers Brothers* (1899), 30 O.R. 150 (Div. Ct.), the defendants contacted the plaintiff bakers by letter, on April 26, 1898, offering to save them money by quoting prices for two types of flour, pointing out that prices were advancing and suggesting that they should order by "wire." On April 27, the bakers wired that they would take two car loads of the most expensive flour at the price quoted. On the same day, the defendants wired that prices had advanced by "30." The next day the plaintiffs, through their solicitors, requested fulfillment of the offer made by the defendants on April 26 and accepted by them on April 27. The plaintiffs won at trial and, on appeal by the defendants, the judge said:

> The real crux of the matter is whether there is a contract. . . .
>
> . . . In the *American and English Encyclopedia of Law*, 2nd ed., vol. 7, p. 138, the law is stated to be: "A quotation of prices is not an offer to sell, in the sense that a complete contract will arise out of the mere acceptance of the rate offered, or the giving of an order for merchandise in accordance with the proposed terms. It requires the acceptance by the one naming the price, of the order so made, to complete the transaction. Until thus completed there is no mutuality of obligation. . . .
>
> . . . [I]f we write in the equivalent phrase into the letter, "We give you the current or market price F.O.B. your station, of Hungarian Patent 3-40"; can it be for a moment contended that it is an offer which needs only an acceptance in terms to constitute a contract? . . . Appeal allowed.

TRANSACTIONS AT A DISTANCE

Many business transactions are carried out by parties located some distance from each other. If these transactions are carried out by telex or telephone, the communication is instantaneous and the normal rules of an offer by one party and an acceptance by the other party apply—that is, communication of the offer and the acceptance is essential. However, in the case of contracts that are required by the Statute of Frauds (see Chapter 10) to be in writing, although offer and acceptance by telephone might create a valid contract, such a contract will not be enforceable in a court of law.

In the past, much more than today, manufacturers and merchants transacted most of their business by mail or telegram. Legal precedents established the general principle that if the offeree used the same agent of communication as the offeror, the contract was formed when the reply was given into the hands of the agency of communication: that is, if by letter, to the post office; if by telegram, to the telegraph office.

If a different agency of communication were used, such as telegraphing an acceptance to a mailed offer, the principle of law established by precedent was that, because a different agency was used, no contract would be formed until the acceptance reached the offeror. However, if the offeror specifically stated the desired acceptance to be made, these instructions would have to be complied with; otherwise no contract would be formed.

An example illustrating this principle, in connection with an attempted cancellation of an offer, is the case of *Henthorn v. Fraser*, [1892] 2 Ch. 27. In this case, the plaintiff, following negotiations, was given an option for consideration to purchase certain houses in Birkenhead, England. The next day the vendors (defendants) accepted a second offer subject to being able to cancel the option given to the plaintiff. The letter of cancellation reached the original offeree after he had already despatched a letter of acceptance through his solicitor. The plaintiff lost his case for specific performance at the first trial. However, on appeal, the decision was reversed, Lord Herschell including in his judgment the following comments:

> I think that a person who has made an offer must be considered as continuously making it until he has brought to the knowledge of the person to whom it was made that it is withdrawn. . . .
> . . . Where the circumstances are such that it must have been in the contemplation of the parties, that, according to the ordinary usages of mankind, the post might be used as a means of communicating the acceptance of an offer, the acceptance is complete as soon as it is posted.
> . . . [D]ecree for specific performance made.

If an offeree communicates his acceptance by means of an agent other than the one specified by the offeror, the contract is formed only when the agent actually delivers the acceptance of the offeror. An example is the case of *Entores Ltd. v. Miles Far East Corporation*, [1955] 2 Q.B. 327. The following is an extract from the judgement:

> Although where a contract is made by post, acceptance is complete as soon as the letter of acceptance is put into the post box, where a contract is made by instantaneous communication, for example, by telephone, the contract is complete only when the acceptance is received by the offeror (the plaintiff) since generally an acceptance must be notified to the offeror to make a binding contract.

Some other illustrations of this principle are as follows: First, suppose that A mails an offer to B to sell a horse for $200. The offer is received by B, who sends her acceptance by telegram. Having changed his mind, A telephones B before A receives the telegram and tells her that the offer is withdrawn. In this case, no contract has been formed and the withdrawal of the offer by A is effective because the contract would not have been formed until the different agent had transmitted the acceptance to A.

Second, suppose again that A mails his offer to B to sell a horse for $200. B receives the offer but feels that $200 is too much. However, B replies by mail, stating that she agrees to buy the horse for $190. No contract is formed because the counter-offer caused the original offer to lapse. We now have a new offer in the amount of $190.

Third, suppose that A mails an offer to B to sell a horse for $200, asking her to accept by telegram. B immediately accepts in this way. The question arises as to when the legal agreement was formed. Because B has answered in the way that A stipulated—namely, by sending her reply by telegram—she has communicated to A by the agent chosen by A. By law, the contract is formed as soon as the message is delivered to the telegraph company.

These rules are significant because an offeror does sometimes reconsider the offer and wishes not to be bound by an acceptance. It will then be important to decide if and when a legal agreement was formed. As long as the offeror can communicate with the offeree and revoke the offer before acceptance has been made, no legally binding agreement has been made.

CROSS-OFFERS

Conceivably, two parties may send each other an identical offer. For example, imagine a situation in which A sends B an offer to sell a particular item and B, at the same time, sends A an offer to buy the same item. Until A and B receive each other's offer and accept it, according to the general rule about communication of an offer, there is no agreement—only two offers. However, some legal authorities (such as Cheshire and Fifoot, *The Law of Contract*, 7th ed., 1969, p. 47) do argue that agreement or consent in the matter has in fact been reached by the parties.

REVIEW QUESTIONS

1. What are the various ways in which an offer may be accepted?
2. How must an offer be accepted, if the offeror has not specified any particular way?
3. If A makes an offer to B, can C accept on his or her own behalf? Explain.
4. In many contracts, acceptance takes the form of a promise by the offeree. Explain, with an example.
5. If a person receives an unsolicited book or record in the mail and fails to return it within the specified time, what is this person's legal position?
6. What is the rule with regard to the offeree's withdrawal of acceptance?
7. When acceptance of an offer is being made by mail, when is the contract actually formed? What happens if a mail strike occurs?
8. What was the legal principle involved in *Entores Ltd. v. Miles Far East Corp.*?
9. What is a "cross-offer"? When is a contract formed?

PROBLEMS

1. A offered by mail to sell his sole farm to B for $175,000. A sent his letter on October 1 and it was received by B on October 4.
   (a) Assume that B took a week to locate sufficient money and mailed his reply, accepting the offer, on October 11. Discuss the legality of this situation.
   (b) Could a contract be validly formed if B had sent his acceptance by telegram on October 5? Discuss the offer and acceptance situation.
   (c) Suppose that B desired to hold A to his offer but also desired two weeks to consider the offer. Discuss how this could be done, if at all.
   (d) What might be B's legal position if B had learned, not from A but from friends, that C had bought the farm from A on October 6?
   (e) Suppose B mailed his acceptance on October 6, and A died of a heart-

attack unknown to B on October 5. Discuss B's legal position. Would it be different if A had died on October 7 after B had mailed his acceptance?

(f) Suppose B had wired A asking him if $175,000 was his "lowest price" and, on receiving an affirmative reply, accepted A's offer. Which of these communications, if any, amounts to an acceptance?

(g) Suppose A, intending to mail B the offer for the sale of his farm for $175,000 on October 1, had written the letter but lost it on the way to the post office. A good samaritan, finding the letter, delivered it by hand to B on November 1. Discuss the situation if B had accepted at once. Would it have made any difference if the lost letter had been delivered on October 2 and accepted immediately?

2. Frank offered in writing to sell his house to Jack for $150,000. This offer was received on January 20. A written acceptance was mailed by Jack on January 21, at 3:30 p.m. At 3:33 p.m. on the same date, before he received Jack's letter of acceptance, Frank telephoned to revoke his offer. Has a contract been formed?

3. Atlas, a company which manufactures physical exercise equipment, advertised that "anyone who uses this arm and leg stretcher for six months will never have rheumatism." John used this equipment faithfully for a year and then developed rheumatism. He sued to recover the $1,000 he had paid Atlas for the physical conditioning equipment. How would the court decide this case?

4. Marie, 65 years of age, continued to cohabit with John, 70 years of age, after hearing that he was already married. He told her in vague terms that his property would be hers and made a will to that effect, which he later revoked. After he died, Marie claimed the land and said there was an intention on the part of them both to enter into a binding legal contract.

(a) What would the court decide and why? Refer to *Lazarenko v. Borowsky*, [1966] S.C.R. 556, 57 D.L.R. (2d) 577.

(b) How would your answer be affected, in Ontario, by the existence of the Family Law Reform Act, which provides that cohabitation may entitle an unmarried spouse to financial support?

READINGS

Smith & Osberg Ltd. v. Hollenbeck (1938), 53 B.C.R. 296 (S.C.).

Facts: Smith & Osberg Ltd. in Vancouver was given by hand on July 13, 1938 by Hollenbeck in Seattle, U.S.A. a thirty-day option to purchase shares in an American Company. On August 12, Smith & Osberg Ltd. wired Hollenbeck accepting the option. This was an application to have the service taken out of the jurisdiction obtained by the plaintiff. The application was discharged, there being no evidence that the telegram of acceptance was received.

Held per Manson J.:

In *Charlebois v. Baril*, [1928] S.C.R. 88, it was held . . . that where an acceptance of a contract is made by mail, the post office only becomes the agent of the offeror where the offer was originally sent by mail but not where the offer was communicated in some other way. In the latter case an acceptor by mail who desires to enforce the contract must prove actual receipt of the letter of acceptance by the offeror.

I have not been referred to any authority . . . that the telegraph office becomes the agent of the offeror unless the offer has been made by telegram and an acceptance by telegram thereby impliedly authorized or unless the circumstances are such as to warrant the conclusion that an acceptance by telegram was impliedly authorized as in [*Bruner v. Moore*, [1904] 1 Ch. 305]. . . .

Had it been established that the defendant received the plaintiff's telegram, the acceptance would have been effective on its receipt and the contract would have been one concluded out of the jurisdiction.

Adams v. Lindsell (1818), 1 B. & Ald. 681 (Eng. K.B.).

Facts: The defendants, dealers in wool, wrote to the plaintiffs, woollen manufacturers residing in Bromsgrove, Worcestershire, on September 2, 1817, "We now offer you eight hundred tods of wether fleeces. . . ." The letter was mistakenly addressed "Bromsgrove, Leicestershire," and was not readdressed and received by the plaintiffs till September 5. The plaintiffs accepted immediately but the reply was only received by the defendants after they had sold this wool on the previous day. The plaintiffs sued for breach of contract and won. The defendants appealed.

Held:

The defendants . . . [argued that sinced they had] proposed by letter to sell this wool [they were] not to be held liable. . . . Till the plaintiffs' answer was actually received, there could be no binding contract between the parties. . . .

. . . [I]f that were so, no contract could ever be completed by the post. For if the defendants were not bound by their offer when accepted by the plaintiffs till the answer was received, the plaintiffs ought not to be bound till after they had received the notification that the defendants had received their answer and assented to it. And so it might go on ad infinitum. The defendants must be considered in law as making, during every instant of the time their letter was travelling, the same identical offer to the plaintiffs; and then the contract [was] completed by the acceptance of it by the latter. Then as to the delay in notifying the acceptance, that [arose] entirely from the mistake of the defendants, and it therefore must be taken as against them, that the plaintiffs' answer was received in course of post.

Unit 5.3
Intention to Form a Legally Enforceable Contract

The second essential element of a legally binding contract is intention. Sometimes an offer and acceptance will be made even though there is no intention to form a legally enforceable contract. This situation is clearly apparent in the case of a person who extends a dinner invitation to others. Even though the host may have incurred considerable financial expense as well as personal inconvenience in his or her preparations, he or she cannot sue the intended guest for breach of contract if they fail to attend. The same reasoning applies to most social engagements, particularly between relatives and friends.

Situations do occur, however, in which one party only pretends intention to form a legally binding contract. Thus if, for example, A, momentarily upset at his daughter's extravagant tastes, exclaims at a party, "I'll give five thousand dollars to anyone who'll take her off my hands," he may be taken seriously by one of his daughter's suitors, even though that was not the father's intention. Similarly, in *Carlill v. Carbolic Smokeball Co.*, mentioned previously, the person who read the newspaper advertisement and acted on its instructions believed that she was accepting the company's offer in a legally binding way, even though, as the company later alleged, its offer had not been meant seriously. In such cases, the court will have to decide whether there is a legally enforceable contract or not.

As a rule, a judge will start by presuming that both parties to a contract intended to be legally bound by their promises. It will then be up to the party who disagrees to disprove this presumption. This will be easier to accomplish if: (a) the agreement was between friends or relatives than between complete strangers; (b) the agreement was of a social rather than business nature; (c) the terms of the agreement were clearly unreasonable (for example, the offer of a $100 reward for the recovery of a $10 item with no sentimental value); or (d) the agreement was between husband and wife—see *Balfour v. Balfour*, [1919] 2 K.B. 571, a case in which a contract of support made between a husband and wife before they actually separated or divorced was held to be against public policy and therefore illegal. In Ontario, it should be noted, the Family Law Reform Act now permits some forms of premarital contracts concerning the allocation of individually owned property, except the matrimonial home, and the support, education, and custody of their children in the event of marriage breakdown.

Occasionally, though rarely, the parties to a business contract may expressly state therein that neither will sue the other should a breach of the contract occur. This was the situation in *Rose and Frank v. Compton*, [1925] A.C. 445, relating to business partners who agreed not to sue each other in the event of a breach of contract. A judge would uphold the clause should one party later change his mind and try to sue the other. More often, nowadays, the parties to a contract include an arbitration clause whereby any dispute is adjudicated privately by an outside party. Both parties agree, in the arbitration clause, to accept as legally binding the decision of the arbitrator.

In summary, the intention to create a legally binding relationship may be considered to be the second essential element of a contract.

REVIEW QUESTIONS

1. Sometimes one person will make an offer and another person accept it, without their intending to enter into a legally binding contract. Explain, with examples.
2. Suppose that B claims that he intended to enter into a legally binding agreement when he accepted an offer. However, A, who made the offer, claims that he, A, did not intend to create a legally binding contract. How would a judge go about resolving such a dispute?
3. How can two parties to a contract resolve an alleged breach other than by using the courts? Explain, with an example.

6

Consideration

CONSIDERATION DEFINED

Another essential requirement of a contract is the existence of "consideration." This has been defined by one judge as "some right, interest, profit, or benefit accruing to one party, or some forbearance, detriment, loss or responsibility given, suffered, or undertaken by the other" (*Currie v. Misa* (1875), L.R. 10 Ex. 62). It is "something done by each party at the request of the other." It may be the payment of a sum of money or the performance of a service. Or it may take the form of a promise to do something or even to refrain from doing something (for example, not to pursue a lawsuit even though a person may be entitled to do so).

The courts act on the principle, in matters of contract, that no one does anything for nothing. Therefore, they will not enforce a contract unless it can be shown that there is "consideration" (or something of value) given by each party to the other. Thus when a person dines out, the restaurant, on the one hand, serves the meal, and the customer, on the other hand, agrees either verbally or by his action to pay the price charged.

In the case of *Rann v. Hughes* (1778), 7 T.R. 356, a Mrs. Hughes, the administrator of an estate, promised in writing to pay to the plaintiff, out of her own pocket money, which was due from the estate. She later refused to pay on the grounds that she had received no consideration for her promise. However, the plaintiff contended that as she had complied with the Statute of Frauds by putting her promise in writing, no consideration was necessary. The court disagreed: "All contracts are by the law of England divided into agreements by specialty [under seal] and agreements by parol. . . . [I]f they be merely written and not specialties, they are parol and a consideration must be proved."

An agreement without consideration is said to be *nudum pactum* (a naked contract). This is derived from the Latin phrase: "Ex nudo pacto non oritur actio," meaning "from a naked contract no (legal) action can arise."

EXCEPTIONS TO THE REQUIREMENT OF CONSIDERATION

One exception is a document under seal; another is in connection with negotiable instruments.

Documents under Seal

Many years ago, when most people were illiterate, it was customary for persons requiring a deed or a document of any sort to go to the educated men of those times, such as the clergymen, lawyers, doctors, and teachers. These individuals, versed in the preparation of formal documents, wrote them in legalistic terms, and authenticated them with an official seal (either a wax imprint or a paper seal, usually red). Where people go to the trouble of having such a formal document prepared, the courts have ruled that they obviously intend to be bound by it. Accordingly, in these types of documents, the court does not look for consideration, but assumes that it must exist.

Contrary to popular belief, a seal need not be red or round. A postage stamp or other mark may constitute a seal if the parties intend it to be. In fact, some judges have held that the words "signed, sealed and delivered" normally printed on standard forms is sufficient to signify the existence of a seal even though no seal is in fact affixed.

Negotiable Instruments

Except in the case of a holder in due course, where consideration must exist, the law merchant and the common law courts did not require consideration to exist between parties to allow the holder to sue, for example, the acceptor in the case of a draft. This has been incorporated into Canadian law in the federal Bills of Exchange Act.

SUFFICIENT (OR "VALUABLE") CONSIDERATION

The law does not require that the consideration moving from each party be equivalent in value to the obligations assumed. However, it must be "sufficient" to satisfy the court. A small sum of money (for example, a dollar) is normally considered sufficient consideration, even for a contract involving thousands of dollars. Emotions such as love, honour, respect, undying gratitude are not considered to be sufficient consideration for a contract. These sentiments are classified as "good consideration" but not "*valuable* consideration."

A case which illustrates the principle of "valuable consideration" is *Thomas v. Thomas*, [1924] 2 Q.B. 851. In this case, John Thomas, on his death bed, called two witnesses and told them he wanted to leave his house to the plaintiff for life or so long as she should remain a widow and unmarried. Later, the defendants, John Thomas's executors, signed an agreement in which they agreed to prepare a conveyance or deed letting the plaintiff have the house for one pound yearly ground rent. Later yet, one of the defendants refused to execute the deed, and after the plaintiff had been in possession for four years, had her evicted. The judges in their decision stated, "Consideration means something which is valued in the law, moving from the plaintiff: *it may be of some benefit to the plaintiff, or some detriment to the defendant*, but in all events, it must be moving from the plaintiff."

"As to the suggestion of this being a voluntary conveyance, my impression [Coleridge J.] is that this payment of one pound annually is more than good consideration, it is *valuable 'consideration'.*" Thus although one pound sterling was in no way equivalent to the value of the house, the court found that it was sufficient to support a contract requiring the executors to execute the deed transferring title.

A second case illustrating the meaning of sufficient consideration is *Sumner v. Sapkos*, [1955] 5 D.L.R. 103. Here, the defendant, a partner in a hotel business, signed an exclusive listing with a real estate broker. The listing specified that the real estate broker was to be paid a commission regardless of how the hotel was sold. Eventually the hotel was sold by the other partner without the assistance of the real estate broker. The Saskatchewan Court of Appeal held, as far as the consideration was concerned, that the plaintiff had incurred some expense by advertising the hotel for sale and writing letters, and went on to say, "the court cannot set aside the contract entered into by Sapkos on account of the inadequacy of the consideration." Adequacy of consideration was a matter for the parties to consider when they were entering into the contract. It was not something for the court to consider when the contract was being enforced.

In *Cole v. Trecothick* (1804), 9 Ves. Jun. 246, Lord Eldon, speaking of mere inadequacy of consideration, stated, "Unless it is so gross as to shock the conscience an amount . . . is not of itself a ground on which specific performance of a contract will be refused."

PAST, PRESENT, AND FUTURE CONSIDERATION

Consideration must take place in the present or in the future—that is, it may be an act taking place at the present time, or the promise of an act to be done in the future. An act done in the past is not acceptable consideration to support a contract.

An illustration of this is the situation which concerned the parties in *Eastwood v. Kenyon* (1840), 113 E.R. 482. Here the plaintiff, the executor of his deceased friend's estate, borrowed and used his own money to finance the education of the deceased friend's daughter. She later promised to repay him. When she married, her husband repeated the promise and agreed that he would repay the executor. Neither husband nor wife repaid the loan. Following court action by the plaintiff, the judge held:

> Taking then the promise of the defendant, as stated on the record, to have been an express promise, we find that the consideration for it was past and executed long before, and yet it is not laid to have been at the request of the defendant, nor even of his wife while sole . . . and the declaration really discloses nothing but a benefit voluntarily conferred by the plaintiff and received by the defendant, with an express promise by the defendant to pay money. . . . In holding this declaration bad because it states no consideration but a past benefit not conferred at the request of the defendant, we conceive that we are justified by the old common law of England.

EXISTING OBLIGATION

Another rule relating to consideration is that an existing obligation on the part of one of the parties to a contract may not be used as satisfactory consideration for a new contract with the other party involved. Suppose, for example, a builder has contracted to build you a house for a stated price. Halfway through construction, he states that the price of his materials has gone up and insists that you pay him an extra $10,000, otherwise he will stop work. As you have to move out of your old house within a month, you agree. Are you legally bound by your promise? The answer is "no." This is because the builder was already obliged to build you the house. However, if you had asked for an additional bedroom for the extra money, the result would have been different. The additional bedroom would have been sufficient consideration. The logic behind the rule concerning an existing obligation not being satisfactory consideration is that it is considered extortionate for one party to a contract to take advantage of the circumstances (for instance, the need to move into the new house within a certain period of time) to force the other party to pay extra for what he is already entitled to.

A case that is sometimes cited in this regard is *Turner v. Owen* (1862), 176 E.R. 79. In this case, the defendants had signed on nineteen hands to take a ship with a cargo of coal from England and return with a cargo of guano from the Churchill Islands. On the return voyage, as the ship was leaking, it put in for temporary repairs. The crew refused to proceed until the captain agreed to pay each man five pounds extra for the return voyage, which he did in a signed agreement. The court held that once a seaman has signed articles, he cannot claim extra remuneration for the same services as are contained in the articles. On the other hand, when he signs articles, it is implied on the part of the owner, that the ship is reasonably fit for navigation. If before his ship sets out, the seaman discovers that it is one in which he cannot safely embark, he can refuse to do so and enter into a new contract. The question seems therefore to turn upon the facts. Was the ship seaworthy or not when the captain made the contract? The court went on to say that the ship was seaworthy and therefore the plaintiffs were not entitled to any claim because of their existing obligation.

In *Glasbrook Brothers v. Glamorgan County Council*, [1925] A.C. 270, a mining company fearing trouble during a strike requested police protection for its equipment. The police were provided as requested. When the danger had ceased, the company refused to pay for the extra police wages involved, claiming that the police were only doing their duty. The court held that the claim for compensation was valid because the police were in fact performing extra duties.

A more recent case illustrating this principle is *Gilbert Steel Ltd. v. University Construction Ltd.* (1976), 12 O.R. (2d) 19 (C.A.). In this case, Gilbert Steel Ltd., the plaintiff had entered into a written contract to deliver to University Construction Ltd., the defendant, at certain prices per ton, fabricated steel for apartment buildings to be erected at three separate sites. Deliveries for the first two projects were completed and paid for at the agreed-upon prices. However, the steel mill from which Gilbert Steel obtained its supplies then raised its price and gave warning of a further increase later. The plaintiff and defendant entered into a new contract for the supply of steel for the first building at the third site, at a new, higher price. While the building was under construction, the steel mill raised its price again and the plaintiff and defendant, after some discussion, orally agreed on another new, higher price. However, when the plaintiff submitted to the defendant a new written contract with two new clauses as well as the increased prices, the defendant refused to sign. The trial judge found that there had been an oral agreement as to the new prices but held it unenforceable for lack of consideration. Counsel for the plaintiff argued that the consideration for the oral agreement was the mutual agreement to abandon the earlier written contract and assume obligations under the new oral one. However, the appeal court found that this was not a new contract but an attempted variation of the existing one. The appeal was therefore dismissed on the grounds that the plaintiff was already obliged to deliver the steel and no new consideration had been forthcoming.

UNLAWFUL OR IMPOSSIBLE CONSIDERATION

Consideration, if it is to be valid, must not be unlawful. If, for example, A offered B a share of some stolen meat if B would repair A's truck, a court would not uphold such an agreement. Although the purpose of the contract is legal, the consideration is not.

Also, consideration must not be impossible. Thus a contract to pay a large sum of money in exchange for a trip to the centre of the earth would be void because of the impossibility of the consideration promised by one of the parties.

FORGIVENESS OF PART OF A DEBT

Sometimes a person who is owed money may decide to excuse the debtor from repaying part of the debt. However, such an agreement has for many years been held to be legally invalid because of the absence of consideration. Therefore the creditor who has a change of mind can insist on payment of the balance of the debt.

The classic English case dealing with partial payment is *Foakes v. Beer* (1884), 9 App. Cas. 605. Foakes, the defendant, owed Mrs. Beer some 2,000 pounds sterling plus interest. As the debt was overdue he asked her for extra time to make repayments. She signed an agreement whereby, if repayments of principal were made promptly and regularly until the debt was satisfied, she would not take any action. After the debt was paid she claimed interest and when Foakes refused to pay, she sued him. The court stated that:

> Payment of a lesser sum on the day in satisfaction of a greater cannot be any satisfaction for the whole, because it appears to the judges that by no possibility can a lesser sum be satisfaction for the greater sum: but

the gift of a horse, hawk, or robe, etc., in satisfaction is good, for it shall be intended that a horse, a hawk . . . might be more beneficial to the plaintiff than money.

. . . If the question be (as, in the actual state of the law, I think it is) where the consideration is, or is not, given in the case of this kind, by the debtor who pays down part of the debt presently due from him, being promised by the creditor to relinquish, after certain further payments on account, the residue of the debt, I cannot say that I think consideration is given, in the sense in which I have always understood that word to be used in our law.

EQUITABLE (OR PROMISSORY) ESTOPPEL

The common law rule in *Foakes v. Beer* has now been overcome by appeal to the doctrine of *equitable estoppel* (also known as *promissory estoppel*, and, in the United States, as *injurious reliance*). According to this equitable remedy, designed to relieve the harshness of the common law, a promise (for example, to forgive all or part of a loan) may be held binding if the promissor could reasonably expect that it would cause the promisee to take some major action, or refrain from taking such action, and if failure to enforce the promise would cause injustice to the promisee.

The doctrine of *equitable estoppel* was formally enunciated in the case of *Central London Property Trust Ltd. v. High Trees House Ltd.*, [1947] K.B. 130, some 63 years after *Foakes v. Beer*. The facts of this case were that during World War II, the landlord of a block of flats decided to reduce the ground rents of his flats by half while the flats were only partly let, in order to ensure occupancy. At the end of the war, when the flats were fully let, the landlord increased the ground rents, and sued not only for the increased rent, but also to collect the unpaid portion of the rents which had not been collected during the war years, a total of 7,916 pounds. It was held by Lord Denning at p. 130:

The lease under which it was payable was a lease under seal which, according to the old common law, could not be varied by an agreement by parol (whether in writing or not), but only by deed. Equity, however, stepped in, and said that if there has been a variation of a deed by a simple contract (which in the case of a lease required to be in writing would have to be evidenced by writing), the courts may give effect to it. . . . It was a representation, in effect, as to the future, namely that payment of the rent would not be enforced at the full rate but only at the reduced rate. . . .

. . . [There] are cases in which a promise was made which was intended to create legal relations, and which to the knowledge of the person making the promise, was going to be acted on by the person to whom it was made, and which was in fact so acted on. In such cases the courts have said that the promise must be honoured [i.e., promissory estoppel]. . . . In each case the court held the promise to be binding on the party making it, even though under the old common law it might be difficult to find any consideration for it. The courts have not gone so far as to give a cause of action in damages for the breach of such a promise, but they have refused to allow the party making it to act inconsistently with it. It is in that sense, and that sense only, that such a promise gives rise to an estoppel. . . . the time has now come for the validity of such a promise to be recognized. The logical consequence, no doubt is that a promise to accept a smaller sum in discharge of a larger sum, if acted upon, is binding notwithstanding the absence of consideration. . . .

. . . [T]he only question remaining for my consideration is the scope of the promise in the present case. I am satisfied on all the evidence that the promise here was that the ground rent should be reduced to 1,250 pounds a year as a temporary expedient while the block of flats was not fully, or substantially fully let, owing to the conditions prevailing . . . [which] had completely passed away by the early months of 1945. . . . and [the promise] did not extend any further than that.

STATUTORY CHANGES

Because the common law was unsatisfactory in the matter of forgiveness of debt, most provinces have by statute set their own rules in this regard. Under these statutes a creditor is bound by the promise to accept part performance in settlement of a debt once the lesser sum has been paid and accepted. The law is still not clear as to whether the creditor may renege on the promise before payment of the smaller sum is made. For example, according to Ontario's Mercantile Law Amendment Act, "Part performance of an obligation, either before or after a breach thereof, when expressly accepted by the creditor in satisfaction or rendered in pursuance of an agreement for that purpose, though without any new consideration, shall be held to extinguish the obligation."

PROMISES TO CHARITY

A promise by a person to donate money as a gift is not normally enforceable by the intended recipient unless the promise is made under seal, in which case the courts do not need to look for consideration. With regard to promises to donate to charities, however, the courts have looked for valuable consideration moving from the beneficiary to the pledgor. Examples of such consideration, based on past court decisions, include excavation work undertaken, construction of a building started, a particular position named after the pledgor, and advertisements placed in newspapers to the effect that a certain individual has pledged a large amount of money. Only if such consideration exists would the contract be enforceable.

However, as illustrated by the case of the *Governors of Dalhousie College v. Boutlier*, [1934] 3 D.L.R. 593, the pledgor must be shown to have made a personal commitment additional to making the pledge to give money.

In 1920 a Mr. Boutlier signed a pledge agreeing to subscribe $5,000 to Dalhousie College for the purpose of enabling the College to maintain and improve the efficiency of its teaching, to construct new buildings, and otherwise keep pace. Unfortunately, Mr. Boutlier, although he renewed his pledge several times, came under difficult financial circumstances and had not honoured the pledge when he died. The authorities of Dalhousie College sued the estate. The court held:

> As to finding the consideration for the subscription outside the subscription itself . . . the earlier Ontario cases relied upon . . . show that there was either a direct interest on the part of the subscriber in a particular project undertaken or some personal participation in the action of the promisee, as a result of which the expenditure or liability was incurred. . . . To hold otherwise (that there was a valuable consideration here) would be to hold that a naked voluntary promise may be converted into a binding legal contract by the subsequent action of the promisee alone without the consent, express or implied, of the promissor. There is no evidence here which in any way involves the deceased in the carrying out of the work for which the promised subscription was made, other than the signing of the subscription paper itself.

TORT LIABILITY

It should be noted that while there may be no contractual liability, because of the absence of consideration, tort liability may still arise. For example, if A repairs B's damaged roof while B is away, A cannot sue B if B does not pay. A could only recover from B in the case of necessity—that is, where A was acting to preserve B's property in an emergency. However, this doctrine has only a very limited application. Nevertheless, if A, the "Good Samaritan," accidentally caused some damage while making the repairs, B could successfully sue for tort. Rescue situations are discussed in Chapter 4.

Another example involves a firm of auditors who undertook gratuitously to keep the accounts of a charitable organization. After some time it was discovered that the books had been wrongly kept and that the charity had lost money rather than made a surplus. The charitable organization consequently sued the auditors who had failed to note and reveal this fact. The court held that, although the auditors were not bound in contract because there was no consideration to enforce a contract, it was still possible for them to be sued in court in a tort action for their negligence.

This principle has even been extended to provide protection for third parties who, it was reasonable to expect, were likely to rely on the negligently prepared statements of account.

REVIEW QUESTIONS

1. What is meant by the term "valuable consideration"? Why is it necessary in a contract?
2. Distinguish, with examples, between good consideration and valuable consideration.
3. Distinguish, with examples, between present and future consideration.
4. What legal principle is illustrated by *Eastwood v. Kenyon*?
5. Can an existing obligation be regarded as satisfactory consideration for a contract? Explain the facts in *Turner v. Owen*.
6. Give two examples of each of: (a) impossible consideration; (b) unlawful consideration.
7. What is a partial payment? How does the question of consideration arise?
8. Explain the legal principle established in *Foakes v. Beer*.
9. What is meant by "promissory estoppel"? How did the decision of *Central London Property Trust Limited v. High Trees House Ltd.* affect the principle established in *Foakes v. Beer*?
10. What is a "specialty"? What are the requirements for consideration that exist with regard to such documents?
11. Is consideration required for: (a) a promise to donate money as a gift to a relative? (b) a promise to donate money as a gift to a charity? If yes, give examples of satisfactory consideration.
12. What legal principle, with regard to promises to charity, was established in the case of the *Governors of Dalhousie College v. Boutlier*?
13. Explain, with an example, the statement, "while there may be no contractual liability, because of the absence of consideration, a tort liability may still arise."

PROBLEMS

1. G, who is regularly employed by a large department store, and does a satisfactory job, sues his employer because he is paid only his regular salary without the Christmas bonus gratuitously given by the company to all its other employees. Has G any legal claim?
2. One day, while sitting in the lobby of a major hotel, A heard cries for help coming from the direction of the swimming pool. As an expert swimmer, A jumped in and rescued an elderly man who was in trouble. This gentleman was so grateful, he asked A to come back the following day for a reward. However, the next day, he refused to pay. Are there any legal grounds on which to hold this person to his promise?
3. On January 2 of this year, G made arrangements to have a sail boat built to be ready for transportation to his nearby lake on June 30. The agreed price was $10,000 to be paid on delivery. On June 1, G, noticing that the work was behind, offered a further $1,000 in writing before witnesses if the builder would complete on time. On June 30, the boat was finished and

loaded on a truck transporter for delivery. What amount is G legally obliged to pay to the builder?

4. A stock brokerage company owner believed so strongly in private enterprise that he was against any form of private company pension plans for his employees. However, on the retirement of the company comptroller, who had not sold stocks but managed the office and accounts, he gave him a letter recognizing his years of valuable service and agreed to give him $200 a week for the rest of his life. The money was paid without fail for five years until the owner sold the business and retired, at which time the new owner cut off any further payments.

  (a) If the former comptroller sued to have his pension payments restored, on what grounds should he base his claim?

  (b) Would the pensioner have a better claim if the original owner still operated the company when his pension was cut off?

  (c) Suppose the pensioner could produce a letter, bearing the company seal, recognizing his valuable service. Would his claim be legally justified?

  (d) Is there any way that a claim such as this could be made legally enforceable after forty years of service?

5. An accountant by the name of Worrell was hired to keep the books of a young but progressive company for a yearly retainer of $2,000. As a result of the accountant's recommendations in simplifying purchasing and billing procedures, the company earned $20,000 more than the previous year, largely attributable to these innovations.

  (a) The accountant stated that he had based his fee on 10% of the previous years' earnings and since the earning had doubled, largely as a result of his efforts, he submitted his bill for an extra 10%—that is, $2,000 more. Discuss the probable legal result.

  (b) Suppose he was able to show that he had devoted twice as much of his efforts to this company than to any of his other clients. Would his claim be stronger in law?

  (c) Suppose, in appreciation, the company president had sent him a letter acknowledging that his work for the company was certainly worth twice as much as he had agreed to work for, but the Company could not offer to pay him an extra 10%. Discuss Worrell's chances of recovery in this case.

READING

Royal Bank of Canada v. Kiska (1967), 63 D.L.R. (2d) 582 (Ont. C.A.).

Facts: A young man who was in business was persuaded by his older brother to sign a $3,000 *unsealed* guarantee agreement at the plaintiff's bank covering his older brother's debts which totalled $6,000. The brother's debts were partially secured. Later his brother declared bankruptcy and the assets pledged as security were sold, leaving a balance owing of more than $3,000.

The plaintiff bank then called in the younger brother to hold him to his guarantee. Oddly enough the young guarantor tore from the written guarantee both his signature and that of a witness and then ate them in the belief that he could not be sued without this evidence. When advised that he could, and in the presence of the police, he executed a new guarantee agreement, this time under seal. The trial was dismissed on the ground that the original guarantee was not made under seal and there was no valuable consideration. This is an appeal to the Supreme Court of Ontario, Appeal Division.

Held per Kelly J.A.:

The defendant [admits] that the first guarantee was unlawfully destroyed by him; that such destruction did not constitute a cancellation or rescession of his obligation; that his rights are to be determined as if the destroyed document was still in existence: and that . . . the second guarantee . . . sets out the exact terms. . . .

. . . [W]hen he to whom the voluntary expression of willingness to be bound is conveyed, performs some act or forbears from some act, the performance of, or forbearance from, which was what the party making the proposal sought to accomplish, there is the required mutuality which converts the promise offered gratuitously into an enforceable obligation. . . .

The denial of consideration for the promise is twofold. First, that the plaintiff gave no promise nor did any act which could be qualified as consideration—second, . . . that consideration did not pass from the plaintiff to the defendant but to the defendant's brother. . . .

. . . [T]he first guarantee was signed . . . it was an expression of what the defendant was prepared to do in order to induce the plaintiff to accord some benefit to the brother or to incur some detriment to itself relative to the brother's indebtedness.

. . . [For over 6 months] the plaintiff refrained from instituting action to recover from the brother the money due to it. It is obvious that some forbearance did occur after the offer was made.

. . . Jessel M. R., in *Re Barker's Estate* (1875), 44 L.J. Ch. 187 at p. 490: ". . . the lender gives time and forbearance, or he gives some other advantage to the person giving the further security, and that is valuable consideration. . . and upon that ground it is that the courts have refused to disturb voluntary deeds where consideration was given for them.". . .

. . . [T]he House of Lords [stated] in *Fullerton v. Provincial Bank of Ireland* [1903] A.C. 309 . . . at p. 313-4: . . . "it is not necessary that there should be an arrangement for forbearance for any definite or particular time . . . you can infer from the surrounding circumstances that there was an implied request for forbearance for a time.". . .

. . . [I]n *Morley v. Boothby* (1825), 3 Bing. 107, 130 E.R. 455, . . . a case of guarantee, Best C.J., said: "No court of common law has ever said that there should be a consideration directly between the persons giving and receiving the guaranty. It is enough if the person for whom the guarantor becomes surety has benefit, or the person for whom the guaranty is given suffer inconvenience, as an inducement to the surety to become guaranty for the principal debtor.''. . .

. . . Even though the first guarantee be not executed under seal either one satisfies the requirements of s. 4 of the Statute of Frauds, R.S.O. 1960, c. 381.

Appeal Allowed.

7

Capacity to Contract

There are some people in Canada who, for various reasons, are limited in their freedom to enter into a contract. These people include: persons under the age of eighteen (legally described as *minors* or *infants*); persons who are confined in mental institutions; persons who, although not confined in mental institutions, are considered for contract purposes mentally incompetent; persons whose mental capacity is impaired, either by drinking, drugs, illness or other causes; business corporations; bankrupts; North American Indians living on a reservation; and enemy aliens.

Unit 7.1
Minors

A minor is in an enviable position as far as the law is concerned. As a general rule a minor can insist on every contract which he or she enters into being performed, providing it is legal. However, the other party cannot always hold the minor to the contract if the latter does not wish to go through with it.

Minors' contracts are regarded not as true contracts but as *quasi* contracts. This means that they look like contracts and are almost contracts. However, the difference from a normal contract is that the minor must get value for his money and can never be required to pay more than a fair and reasonable price. In a true contract, the terms, however fair or unfair, will be enforceable so long as all the requirements of a valid contract have been met.

The law with regard to minors' contracts is by no means clear-cut. However, certain basic rules have emerged from court decisions, although they are not always consistently applied.

One useful approach, when trying to determine a minor's legal position with regard to a conract that he or she has entered into, is to decide first of all whether the contract is executory, partly executed, or fully executed. *Executory* means that the contract is totally unperformed and all action must take place in the future; *partly executed* means that one party or both parties have performed but something remains to be done; and *fully executed* means that both parties have carried out all their obligations under the contract.

EXECUTORY CONTRACTS

If the contract is *executory* (that is, neither party has carried out any of the obligations under the contract), the minor generally is not bound by the contract. However, the adult party involved in the contract must be prepared to carry out his or her part of the bargain. In the event of disputes, minors cannot bring actions to court by themselves since they do not have legal capacity. However, the courts permit them to take cases to court through a "next friend"—either a parent, guardian, or specially appointed lawyer. The interests of minors without parents are supervised by an Official Guardian until a normal guardian has been appointed by the court. In some provinces, it should be noted, provincial legislation confers on minors the same right to sue for wages as adults.

PARTLY EXECUTED CONTRACTS

If the contract is *partly executed* (that is, something remains to be done by one or both parties), it is necessary to decide whether the minor's contract is for a necessity or a non-necessity.

The courts have in the past decided that contracts involving education, a necessary item of clothing, necessary food, essential lodging, a favourable employment contract, loans to pay for necessary goods and services, and even a car to travel to and from work, constitute necessities. Consequently, the minor is required to pay for them if the contract is partly executed. However, the courts have also ruled that an item that would normally be classed as a necessity, such as a suit of clothes, will not be considered a necessity if the minor already has an adequate supply of it.

Canadian courts generally do not regard a car as a necessity but look at the "use to which the vehicle will be put" (*Coull v. Kolbue* (1968), 68 W.W.R. 76). On the other hand, the purchase of a house by an infant married couple with a child was held to be necessary (*Soon v. Watson* (1962), 33 D.L.R. (2d) 428). In a case where money was borrowed by an infant to purchase different items, the court held that the lender could recover only that portion of the loan which had clearly been spent on necessaries—school transfer fee, school books, and a jacket—not money spent for car repairs and a life insurance policy (*Wong v. Kim Yee* (1961), 34 W.W.R. 506).

Student loans are governed by specific statutes in most provinces and are binding on the infant borrower by legislation. However, these Acts only cover courses at certain types of public educational institutions so that not all courses would be covered.

With respect to minors' contracts other than for necessary goods or services, the law has generally regarded such contracts as voidable, as opposed to void, at the option of the minor. Such a contract is valid until some act of repudiation is taken by the minor thereby rendering it void.

The following are some cases dealing with partly executed contracts involving minors.

Roberts v. Gray, [1913] 1 K.B. 520. A contract was entered into in May 1910, for eighteen months from April 1911, whereby the defendant (Gray), accompanied by his father, agreed to play exhibition billiards with a professional, John Roberts. Roberts was to receive the income and pay and deduct the expenses, the balance to be shared equally. John Roberts paid out several months' expense money and then after an argument over the size of the billiard balls, Gray, still a minor, repudiated the contract. The trial judge found that the contract was beneficial to the infant and awarded judgment for Roberts. On appeal it was held that an infant's contract for necessaries is binding. "This doctrine also applies not merely to bread and cheese and clothes, but to education and instruction. Since this contract involved playing billiards with a celebrated expert . . . the agreement was in effect for teaching, instruction and employment, and was reasonable and was for the benefit of the infant." Thus the infant, Gray, was required to repay expense money which had been advanced by Roberts.

Mercantile Union Guarantee Corp. v. Ball, [1937] 2 K.B. 498. In this case an infant, who carried on a business as a haulage contractor, entered into a conditional agreement to purchase a motor lorry (or truck) to be used in his business. When sued for arrears of instalments due, he pleaded the defence of infancy. The trial judge found that the contract was not for the benefit of the infant and the defence of infancy succeeded. On appeal, it was held that the contract must not only be within the class of contracts by which an infant may be bound; but it must also be one beneficial to the infant to be decided on the particular facts of each particular case. It was found to be quite impossible to differ from the trial judge's view that a contract for a large expensive lorry on hire purchase terms (conditional sale) was not a contract for the benefit of the infant. Thus the courts never regard being in business as a necessity for a minor and all contracts of trade or business are voidable.

Nash v. Inman, [1908] 2 K.B. 1. The plaintiff, a tailor, sued a freshman at Trinity College, for a bill of 145 pounds sterling for clothing supplied over eight months, including eleven fancy waistcoats. It was held on appeal that:

> Necessaries . . . mean goods suitable to the condition of life of such infant or minor or other person and to his actual requirements at the time of sale or delivery. . . . The trial judge came to the conclusion . . . that there was no evidence on which the jury might properly find that these goods were necessary to the actual requirements of the infant at the time of sale and delivery.

Suing a Minor in Tort for Negligence, Instead of in Contract

Because an infant cannot normally be held liable on a contract if the item is a non-necessity, the courts will not allow a person suing a minor for breach of contract to change the cause of an action in tort. This is the general rule. However, in the case of *Burnand v. Haggis* (1863), 14 C.B. (N.S.) 44, the defendant, a minor, hired a horse that he intended to let his friend ride and was told that under no circumstances must the horse be used to jump fences. This instruction was ignored and the horse became impaled on a stake and had to be destroyed. The jury at the original trial found that the defendant was an infant but also that this hiring was a necessary suitable to his station in life. On appeal, the judges found that what was done by the defendant was not an abuse of contract, but was the commitment of an act with the animal expressly forbidden by the owner. The judges stated:

> This is the case of a horse hired for one purpose and used for another; and more than that, it was let out to be used by one person and it was used by another person . . . it was let for riding on the road, and it was used for jumping over fences in a field. Therefore, it was an independent tort, for which the infant was liable, and it was wholly unnecessary to consider any question about what are necessaries.

What the judges did was to ignore whether the item was a necessary or not and held the infant liable on another ground entirely—namely, that of an independent tort. However, this is an exception. Normally the plaintiff is unable to change the court suit from contract to tort, if a contract is involved.

Cheating. Another point to be noted with regard to partly executed contracts is that while the minor is protected from the results of improvident contracts, providing they involve a non-necessary, there is a reluctance to allow the minor to cheat other persons.

In the case of *R. Leslie Limited v. Shiell*, [1914] 3 K.B. 607, money lenders lent money to a minor and sued to recover payment when the minor was just coming of age. At the trial the jury found that the defendant minor obtained the money by misrepresentation, alleging that he was an adult and the judge ordered him to make repayment. On appeal it was held, referring to the case of *Zurch v. Parsons* (1765), 3 Burr. 1804:

> This protection was to be used as a *shield not a sword*; therefore if an infant commits or utters slander, God forbid that he should not be answerable for it in a court of justice. But where an infant has made an improvident contract with a person who has been weak enough to contract with him, such person cannot resort to a court of law to enforce such contracts.

The appeal was allowed.

Sales of Goods Act. Finally it should be noted that, in the case of partly executed contracts, the provincial Sale of Goods Acts now specify that an infant or minor must pay a reasonable price for necessaries sold and delivered to him. "Necessaries" are defined in those Acts just as they were in England in 1893 in the first Sale of Goods Act—namely, as goods suitable to the condition in life of the minor and to the minor's actual requirements at the time of sale and delivery. Since the Sale of Goods Act specifies delivery as well as sale, a minor can legally repudiate a contract for necessaries at any time up to their delivery. Some provinces also have special Infants Acts conferring other rights, privileges, and immunities, on minors.

One can appreciate the public policy behind the law obligating a minor to perform his or her obligation under a contract for necessities—that is, to encourage merchants to sell necessities to minors with the assurance that the law will uphold the validity of such contracts.

EXECUTED CONTRACTS

The third and last type of contract in which a minor may be involved is a fully executed one (that is, one in which both parties have fulfilled their contractual obligations). While the court will not normally set the executed contract aside, the court may order that the minor be refunded any monies paid which exceed a reasonable charge.

CONTRACTS OF SERVICE

It has been established that, in addition to contracts for necessaries, a minor may be bound by contracts of service—that is, ones which enable him to earn a livelihood or be trained for some trade or profession. However, they must be shown to be beneficial to the minor—beneficial in the sense of offering some monetary advantage. Thus in the case of *Chaplin v. Leslie Frewin Ltd.*, [1966] Ch. 71, the son of Charlie Chaplin, together with his wife, agreed with a publishing company in return for a considerable advance payment to have his life story "ghost written" for later publication. However, he later changed his mind and tried to prevent publication on the grounds that the contract by which he had assigned copyright to the publisher was voidable because of his infancy. However, the judge held that the contract was binding because it enabled him "to make a start as an author and thus earn money to keep himself and his wife."

ON REACHING THE AGE OF MAJORITY

It is possible that a person may become involved, while still a minor, in contracts which continue after he or she reaches majority. Of course, minors are always bound for contracts involving necessities. However, in the case of partly executed contracts for non-necessities, it is necessary to distinguish whether the contracts are "one-shot" transactions or of continuing benefit.

The one-shot transaction is a contract in which the minor agrees to buy an item (for example, a canoe which is on sale at a special price), makes a down payment on it, and requests delivery in the spring—by which time the person has become an adult. Because the minor is not enjoying the benefit of the item from the time the contract is made until delivery is received, the court considers this to be a one-shot transaction and imposes no liability on the minor if he or she decides not to go through with the contract. In fact, the minor can demand repayment of the deposit at any time.

The other type of partly executed contract for non-necessities is what is termed a continuing-benefit transaction. It may involve an item such as land, a stock transaction, a partnership agreement, or a marriage settlement. It may also involve a non-necessity such as a car that a minor purchases on instalment terms at the age of, say, $17\frac{1}{2}$ and continues paying for, and enjoying the benefits of, past his or her 18th birthday. With this type of contract, the minor may repudiate the agreement, if he so desires, on reaching the age of majority. However, if he fails to repudiate within a short time afterwards, the court will assume that he wishes to be bound by the contract. In Ontario, there is now a statutory rule which requires that any contract involving a minor must be ratified by that person in writing when he or she reaches the age of majority. Otherwise, it is impossible to sue that person in court for breach of contract, except for continuing-benefit transactions.

RECOVERY OF DEPOSITS PAID BY MINORS

The effect of repudiation is, first of all, to relieve the person of any future liabilities—for example, from having to pay rent during the remainder of a lease. However, the infant is not able to recover money already paid if the other party has already performed his or her part of the contract. Thus in the case of *Short v. Field* (1914), 32 O.L.R. 395, the infant plaintiff had agreed to buy a house and lot from the defendant for $1,400, making a deposit of $200 towards the purchase. However, before he repudiated the contract, the infant installed a new tenant in the house at a higher rent and had a real estate agent view the house with the purpose of a resale. This was sufficient evidence in the eyes of the court that the other party had fulfilled his part of the agreement. Consequently, the infant was not permitted to recover his $200. A similar, more recent case is *Fannon v. Dobranski* (1970), 73 W.W.R. 371, in which an infant paid $300 cash for a secondhand car, which he then drove seventy miles until the transmission failed. He then returned the car and asked for his money back. However, the judge held that, since he had enjoyed ownership and possession of the car even for such a short time, he could not recover his money.

PARENTS' LIABILITY FOR INFANTS' CONTRACTS

Parents are only bound by contracts made by their children: (a) when they expressly authorize them to enter into such contracts; and (b) when they have previously honoured such contracts—whereby they implicitly agree that any time the minor enters into a contract they will pay the bill.

Interesting questions may arise in those provinces which have passed statutes that require parents to provide support for their dependent children. For example, Ontario's Family Law Reform Act requires parents, to the extent they are capable, to support a child, in accordance with the child's need, until the child reaches 18 years of age, so long as the child lives at home. The responsibility for support ceases if the child reaches 16 years of age and moves away from home. The question then arises as to whether a third party (such as a merchant) may avail himself or herself of the provisions of this statute to enforce payment against the parents.

REVIEW QUESTIONS

1. What is a minor? Why does the law afford such a person special treatment?

2. Why is it that minors' contracts are not regarded as true contracts but as "*quasi* contracts"?

3. Contracts involving a minor are usefully divided into three classes: executory, partly executed, and fully executed. Explain, with examples.

4. What is a minor's legal position with regard to an executory contract?

5. What is a minor's legal position with regard to a partly executed contract? Distinguish between contracts for necessities and for non-necessities.

6. "The protection afforded to a minor should be used as a shield not a sword." Explain and comment.

7. Usually a person suing a minor for breach of contract in the case of a non-necessity cannot change his cause of action to a tort or injury one. Why not? Give an exception to this general rule.

8. What is a minor's legal position with regard to an executed contract?

9. What is a person's legal responsibility, after reaching the age of majority, with regard to contracts for necessities made as a minor, but which still continue in force?

10. What is an adult person's legal responsibility with regard to partly executed contracts for non-necessities made when a minor? Distinguish between one-shot transactions and continuing-benefit transactions.

11. Parents are always bound by contracts made by their children. Comment.

PROBLEMS

1. A, a minor, is engaged in a partnership business with B. One year after A attains his majority, the firm is petitioned into bankruptcy. What is A's liability for partnership debts incurred before he became 18 years of age?

2. Harry, aged 17, went into the delivery business using a new pick-up truck. He undertook to deliver 500 gallons of ice-cream to a club picnic being held some distance out of town. On the way, in 35-degree temperature, the truck broke down. By the time the truck was repaired, the ice-cream had melted and the picnic was over. Explain and discuss Harry's legal responsibility.

3. Mr. Bullock, a young man under 18 years of age, whose father was a successful clothing merchant and who had worked in his father's store, decided to open a special store for teenagers. To help him get started in business he persuaded one of his father's major suppliers, a well known manufacturer of jeans, to give him a $10,000 advance of stock payable in six months. He leased premises from a landlord who had a large family. At the end of six months, when business failed to pick up, the young retail sales operator could not meet the monthly rental payments of $500. The young merchant offered to pay one month's rent to his landlord in stock instead of cash. All of the landlord's teenaged family were fitted for three pairs of jeans each up to a total of $500 in stock. In the meantime the jean manufacturer and supplier sued for his $10,000, and learning of the

payment of rent with $500 worth of jeans, the manufacturer also sued to recover this stock.

   (a) Comment on the amount of liability of the teenaged merchant for the $10,000 bill.

   (b) Give several reasons which might prevent the jean merchant from recovering the stock in trade paid to the landlord in lieu of rent.

4. A college student approaching her 18th birthday browsed around a major shopping mall. She came from a well-to-do family, which, in addition to providing her with normal college clothes, had provided her with one knee-length and one floor-length evening dress. She was in the process of deciding which dress she would wear to the senior's autumn ball. About this time she noticed a beautifully sequinned silk full-length evening dress, which she had always dreamed of owning, reduced from $300 to $150. As she was expecting money from an inheritance on her 18th birthday, she persuaded the department store to grant her credit and bought the dress. She was the belle of the ball in this dress, but the day after the ball she noticed that the material had pulled at the seams, most probably from her energetic dancing. Consider the following questions in relation to this situation.

   (a) She decided to return the dress, claiming she was not liable because of her minority, although she admitted that the stretching had probably been caused by her dancing. The department store objected that their policy was not to allow the return of worn clothing and they demanded $150. Discuss who won and why.

   (b) Suppose the dress was never worn, but the teenager forgot to return the dress until two weeks after her 18th birthday. Could she be forced to pay? Suppose she did not pay, but did not return the item until her 19th birthday.

   (c) Suppose it was proved in evidence that these sequinned dresses had sold everywhere else for $100, but our teenager had paid $150 cash. Could she receive a refund of her payment?

5. A young man met and wooed a young woman who had recently arrived in the city. They wanted to get married and, in discussing the question of funds, she revealed that she had joined a health club in her home town and paid $300, but had then decided to leave for her present location before she had the chance to participate in the recreational program. In the course of the discussion it was realized that as her 18th birthday was coming up, the $300 payment had been made while she was a minor. They wrote to the health club requesting a refund. The health club wrote back quoting a case in which the court had allowed a health club to keep a pre-payment. In the case cited, a doctor had prescribed exercise at a health centre as remedial treatment for a teenager who had then paid a year's subscription but decided to discontinue after only one month and sued to get her money back. Indicate and explain the factors which may be cited either for or against recovey by the young couple in this case.

6. Walton Warner, aged 17 years, purchased an automobile for $2,500 and

agreed to pay for it at the rate of $100 per month plus interest at 6% a year. He paid this amount faithfully for eighteen months. Then, when the car ceased to run, he told the seller that, as he had purchased this non-necessity while he was a minor and used it strictly for pleasure, he would not pay the outstanding balance, equal to seven monthly payments. Was he legally correct? Discuss.

READING

Toronto Marlboro Major Junior "A" Hockey Club v. Tonelli (1979), 96 D.L.R.(3d) 135 (Ont. C.A.).

Facts: In 1973, at age 16 Tonelli was drafted by the Toronto Marlboros and signed a two-year contract. In the autumn of 1974, the Marlboros unilaterally terminated it and required Tonelli: (1) to play for them for a period of three years; (2) to pay the club 20% of his gross remuneration for the first three years after signing a professional hockey contract (to compensate the club for the "time, effort and money" expended in his development as a player); (3) not to seek employment with any other team while the contract was in force. His salary was increased to $25 per week in addition to the club paying for his room, board, and tuition (while playing for the Marlboros). There was no realistic option except to sign the contract. The set of standardized conditions of employment and drastic changes, as described, were made in complete disregard of the rights of Tonelli and others under existing contracts. Any players who did not accept the conditions and sign the contract could not play in the League. These changes in the rules were made because the World Hockey Association had started to draft young players and since it was not compensating the Canadian Amateur Hockey Association for the development of young players, the CAHA was making the junior drafted players liable to pay these development fees over three years at 20% of their gross salaries (after turning professional). Tonelli repudiated the contract on his 18th birthday, and signed with Houston of the WHA. An application for an interim injunction to stop him from playing, made by the Marlboro Club, was refused by the court. The trial judge held that the contract was unenforceable.

Held (on appeal) per Blair J.A.:

This contract, signed by Tonelli when he was an infant, falls into the category of a contract of service. It can be enforced . . . only if it was for his benefit. . . .
 . . . [I]n *Chaplin v. Leslie Frewin (Publishers) Ltd.*, [1966] Ch. 71 . . . the son of a famous actor, while still a minor, contracted with a publishing company for the publication of his ghost-written memoirs describing his Bohemian life-style. . . . [Later] he sought an injunction to prohibit its publication on the ground that it contained scandalous material which was damaging to his reputation. The English Court of Appeal . . . [held] that the economic benefits to the author outweighed the harm the book might cause

to his reputation. . . . [P]ecuniary or economic considerations outweigh other factors. . . .

. . . I adopt Mr. Justice Morden's [trial judge] view of these disadvantages: "The theory underlying the validity of infants' service contracts, where beneficial, is that they afford the means to the infant of earning a living or provide to him necessary instruction to this end. . . . The present contract is difficult to justify. . . . The contract in question renders this impossible. Tonelli is prevented for a four-year period . . . from realizing his full potential in earnings and from developing his personal skills to their maximum effect [by professional hockey competition]." . . . [Tonelli's] principal objection was to the three-year term. . . .

From the pecuniary or economic standpoint, therefore, this contract was clearly disadvantageous . . . [N]ow consider whether its obvious disadvantages are counterbalanced. . . .

The benefit which must be demonstrated by the Marlboros is that the contract would make a contribution to his development as a hockey player which was a necessary condition of his advancement in the game. . . . [W]hen he signed his second contract, he did not require a further three years of apprenticeship in the Junior League. . . . Instead of contributing . . . the three year prolongation of his junior status could have hindered it.

. . . [W]here, as here, the bargaining position of the parties is manifestly unequal . . . courts are increasingly vigilant to protect the weaker party. . . .

. . . [In] *A. Schroeder Music Publishing Co. Ltd. v. Macaulay*, [1974] 3 All E.R. 616 . . . Lord Diplock, at p. 623 [stated]: ". . . in refusing to enforce provisions of a contract whereby one party agrees for the benefit of the other party to exploit or refrain from exploiting his own earning-power, the public policy which the Court is implementing is . . . the protection of those whose bargaining power is weak against being forced by those whose bargaining power is stronger to enter into bargains that are unconscionable."

These general rules . . . apply with particular force to infants' contracts where it must be demonstrated that the contract is beneficial to the infant. This is a higher test than whether the contract is reasonable and fair. . . . I cannot agree that the contract was for his benefit.

[The balance of the case dealt with the question of whether Tonelli should turn over $64,000 which the Houston Club had paid him in case he would ever become liable to pay 20% of his salary for 3 years to the Marlboro Club, which the latter club claimd he held as a constructive trustee. The Court threw out this contention.]

Appeal dismissed.

Unit 7.2
Other Persons

In this unit, we look at the contractual capacity of mentally impaired persons, corporations, bankrupts, North American Indians, and enemy aliens.

MENTALLY IMPAIRED PERSONS

A person who is confined to a mental institution may not enter into a contract unless it is done on his or her behalf by the Public Trustee under the Mental Health Act.

A person who wishes to have a contract set aside on the grounds that he or she was "mentally impaired" (drunk, drugged, or insane) must satisfy certain requirements. First, such a person must be so incapacitated that he or she did not realize what he or she was doing. Second, the person doing business with the person claiming to be mentally impaired must have been aware of this disability. Third, the contract must have been repudiated as soon as the mental impairment disappeared. Fourth, the party claiming release must be in a position to return all the benefit obtained under the contract. Such a possible release refers solely to contracts for items which are classified as non-necessities; even a drunken person will be responsible for items such as necessaries of life, purchased when he or she was intoxicated. As well as pleading "incapacity," a person who claims to have been mentally impaired at the time he signed a contract can enter a plea of *non est factum* ("it is not his deed") because he or she did not know what he or she was doing at the time. An example of the successful use of this defence plea is given on p. 164 of the book. As a practical matter these defences are difficult to substantiate in court.

Power of Attorney. Under the common law, once a person becomes mentally impaired, any powers of attorney previously made (such as appointment of an agent) ceases to be enforceable. However, statute law in Ontario now permits a person who anticipates mental impairment (such as Alzheimer's disease) to grant a permanent power of attorney to another person (a spouse, for instance). This power of attorney would be for the duration of the mentally impaired person's period of incapacity.

CORPORATIONS

A business corporation's capacity to contract varies according to whether the corporation was established under the registration system which is in force in Alberta, British Columbia, Manitoba, Newfoundland, Nova Scotia, Saskatchewan, the Northwest Territories, and the Yukon; or under the letters patent system which exists in New Brunswick, Prince Edward Island and Quebec. In Ontario, for many years, business corporations were established under the letters patent system. However, they are now established under a system of incorporation by articles, similar to the registration (or memorandum) system.

Those Incorporated by Registration.   If a corporation established under the registration system exceeds the powers conferred on it under the relevant federal or provincial Corporations Act, the courts will declare any such action *ultra vires*, or beyond its powers, and therefore legally unenforceable. This would include any contract entered into by the corporation that exceeds it powers. Furthermore, these powers, as set out in writing in the corporation's memorandum or articles of association and in the relevant Corporations Act, are interpreted very strictly by the courts. Consequently such a corporation must ensure that any contractual agreement or other act that it undertakes is *intra vires*, or within its powers. One way to help ensure that this is so, is by having its powers defined as widely as possible at the time of incorporation. However, in Ontario the present Business Corporations Act provides that all contracts are *intra vires*. The same is also true for most other provinces, as well as for the Canada Business Corporations Act.

   A classic case with regard to a corporation's capacity to contract is that of *Ashbury Railway & Carriage Co. v. Riche* (1875), L.R. 7 H.L. 653, which involved, as defendant, a company that was established to carry on the business of building contractors and to construct railways and railway equipment. The company then agreed to purchase an interest in a railway, that is, according to the House of Lords, "to invest in and operate a railway." Later, however, it refused to proceed with the purchase. When the vendor sued the company for breach of contract, the court held that, "the contract for that purpose was a complete nullity, that the corporation did not exist for that purpose, and that the contract created no rights and liabilities for the company or against it." Consequently, the vendor, as plaintiff, failed in his action.

Those Incorporated by Letters Patent.   The situation with regard to corporations established under the provincial letters patent system or under the federal Corporations Act is very different from that just outlined. Because such corporations are considered to be established by royal prerogative, which was accepted as part of the common law of England, the courts have adopted a more liberal view of their powers. This principle was firmly established in 1916 by the case of *Bonanza Creek v. R.* (1916), 26 D.L.R. 273, in which it was held that companies established by letters patent were in fact legitimate descendants of the old royal charter companies and consequently had very broad powers. In other words, the principle of strict interpretation established by the *Ashbury* case does not apply to companies incorporated by letters patent. Consequently, if such a corporation enters into a contract that exceeds the powers set out in its letters patent, the corporation's action will not be declared *ultra vires* by the courts and the contract will be legally enforceable. It should be mentioned, however, that a shareholder has the right to sue the directors of the corporation for breach of duty if the corporation does exceed its stated activities.

BANKRUPT PERSONS

Once a person declares bankruptcy all his or her previous contracts and debts are taken into consideration at the bankruptcy proceedings. After any secured and/or preferred creditors have been paid in full and the other creditors have been paid a pro rata, or proportionate, share of the claim, the judge may declare that the bankrupt is discharged. If so, all outstanding contracts (but not necessarily judgments such as alimony) are automatically cancelled as from that moment. While undischarged, the bankrupt is prohibited from entering any contract which exceeds $500 without revealing his or her legal status of bankruptcy. A bankrupt is discharged by the court upon application and only after the court is satisfied that it is appropriate to do so. It should be noted that a bankrupt person is not discharged from certain debts—for example, support payments, debts incurred to obtain necessities, and for goods obtained by fraud.

NORTH AMERICAN INDIANS

The legal status of Canada's Indians is constantly under review and steps are being taken to bring the Indians into complete parity with all other citizens of Canada. However, at the present time, Indians living on a reservation are not bound by any contracts made by them unless those contracts are approved by the Indian agent.

ENEMY ALIENS

Contracts with citizens of countries with which Canada is at war are either supsended or cancelled. Under the Frustrated Contracts Act and the common law dealing with frustrated contracts, a person can escape the consequences of his or her contract if that contract is terminated by an act of the Queen's enemies. In other cases, such contracts may be merely suspended until hostilities cease.

REVIEW QUESTIONS

1. A person in a mental institution may not enter into a contract. Comment.
2. If a person wishes to have a contract set aside on the grounds that he or she was drunk, drugged, or under a temporary delusion at the time of agreement, this person must satisfy the court as to certain requirements. What are they?
3. A business corporation has unlimited power to enter into contracts. Comment.

4. Does an undischarged bankrupt have the right to enter into contracts? What happens to a bankrupt's outstanding contracts when he or she is legally discharged by a judge?
5. What is the legal position of Canada's Indians with regard to the making of contracts?
6. If Canada goes to war with another country, what happens to contracts between residents of the two countries?

8

Requirement of Consent
(or Involuntary Contracts)

An additional requirement of a legally enforceable contract is that each person genuinely consents to the agreement. In practice, there have been many examples of contracts which have not met this requirement and whose validity has been successfully challenged in the courts. Depending on the circumstances, such lack of genuine consent may make a contract void, voidable, or illegal.

CONTRACTS THAT ARE VOID

In the case of a contract involving an illegality, such as a promise to pay one-third of the value for $100,000 worth of stolen diamonds, or to pay a ransom to kidnappers, the courts will not consider an action brought by either party against the other. All such contracts are *void* because of the possible suppression of a crime or other subversion of justice.

CONTRACTS THAT ARE VOIDABLE

There are other contracts which are merely *voidable*. One type would be those in which a *dominant* party has persuaded a *dominated* party to enter into a contract against the latter's will or better judgment—for example, a father influencing his daughter to pay twice the market value for his old used car. Another type would be those in which a minor has entered into a business transaction and then decided to abandon it. In these cases, the *dominated* party or the minor may receive court assistance in avoiding the contract—that is, by having the contract rescinded. This is because such contracts are voidable at their option, subject to their being able to return any benefit received.

The grounds on which the court may declare a contract voidable include duress, undue influence, certain types of mistake, misrepresentation, and lack of "utmost good faith."

Duress

This is the compulsion under which a person acts through fear of personal suffering—for example, being physically or mentally tortured, held a prisoner, or threatened with the publication of unfavourable information. This threat may relate not only to the individual who enters into a contract but also to his or her immediate family. This is an example of a voidable

contract in which the threatened party may move to have the court set the
contract aside. However, should the contract prove to be beneficial for
for the person who entered it under duress and if rescission is not sought, the
courts will hold that it is enforceable.

Undue Influence

This may be defined as the exertion by one person, often because of personal
relationship, of excessive control over the mind of another person, thereby
preventing that person from exercising the necessary independence of judgment to enter into a contract of his or her own free will.

At common law, a person alleging "undue influence," termed the *dominated party*, must normally prove to the court that he or she was under the
influence of the other party, the *dominating party*, and that such influence
was of such a nature as to rob him or her of free choice.

There are, however, situations in which, because of the relationship
between the persons involved, the onus of proof is reversed. There is, in legal
terms, a "rebuttable presumption of undue influence." Such relationships
include a parent and child, doctor and patient, lawyer and client, and
housekeeper and elderly employer. If such undue influence is alleged, it is
up to the stronger party to rebut the presumption by contrary evidence,
proving that the influence was fair, just, and reasonable and that no undue
influence was exerted with regard to the contract entered into. Perhaps the
best defence is to prove that the weaker party had competent, outside advice
in the matter.

This presumption of undue influence will arise in cases of obvious
unfairness or inequality of the parties. In, for example, *O'Rorke v. Boling-
broke* (1877), 2 App. Cas. 823, the judge stated that:

> In ordinary cases each party to a bargain must take care of his own
> interest, and it will not be presumed that undue advantage or contriv-
> ance has been resorted to on either side, but in the case of the "expectant
> heir" or of persons under pressure without adequate protection, and in
> the case of dealings with uneducated ignorant persons, the burden of
> showing the fairness of the transactions is thrown on the person who
> seeks to obtain the benefit of the transaction.

There are also persons who may claim undue influence but who do not
fall into the previous category—for example, the person who has full legal
capacity, has been able to obtain good advice, and is not suffering from
want. Undue influence will then only arise in the case of a filial relationship
(parent and child, for instance) or a fiduciary relationship (as with solicitor
and client). Even in such cases the court will not necessarily set aside gifts
made, for example, by children to parents, clients to solicitors, or penitents
to clergymen. *Wright v. Carter*, [1903] 1 Ch. 27, establishes that to maintain
a valid gift or sale from a client to solicitor, the relationship must have
already ceased, or the client must have had independent advice on all
material aspects of the transaction.

Where there is no relationship which raises the presumption of undue influence, the promisor or donor must prove that the alleged undue influence was in fact exercised. In the case of *Smith v. Kay* (1859), 7 H.L. Cas. 779, the plaintiff alleged that he had incurred liabilities to the defendant while under the influence of another older person who was introducing him to a life of extravagance and dissipation. Such influence was held to entitle the plaintiff to the protection of the court.

Lastly, since transactions occurring as the result of undue influence are *voidable* only, not *void*, the dominated party must exercise the right to have the contract rescinded as soon as the undue influence is withdrawn. Thus a plaintiff, who made gifts to a religious sisterhood from which she withdrew and who allowed five years to elapse before asserting a claim of undue influence, did not succeed in her claim because her lack of action amounted to affirmation of the gift (*Allcard v. Skinner* (1887), 36 Ch. D. 145).

In *Inche Noriah v. Sheik Ali Bin Omar*, [1929] A.C. 127, an aged and wholly illiterate woman made a gift of land to her nephew who managed her affairs. The court ruled out the gift, even though a lawyer had given her independent and honest advice prior to the execution of the deed. This was so because he did not know that the gift included practically all of her property and he did not explain that a will would be a wiser method of benefiting her nephew.

For many years, husband and wife were considered to fall within this category of relationships. Thus in the case of *Bank of Montreal v. Stuart*, [1911] A.C. 120, a wife, under the prompting of her husband's solicitor, mortgaged her entire property to the extent of $250,000 to clear up her husband's indebtedness. She then claimed undue influence and won. On appeal to the House of Lords, the court held as follows:

> Mr. Bruce [the husband's and bank's solicitor] undertook a duty towards Mrs. Stuart but he left her in a worse position than she would have been if she had not interfered at all. His course was plain. He ought to have endeavoured to advise the wife, and to place her position and the consequences of what she was doing fully and plainly before her. Probably, if not certainly, she would have rejected his intervention. And then he ought to have gone to the husband and insisted on the wife being separately advised . . . and if that was an impossibility . . . he ought to have retired from the business altogether and told the bank why he did so.

Accordingly the appeal was dismissed and Mrs. Stuart was refunded her $250,000.

MISTAKE

A person who enters into a contract must normally be prepared to accept the consequences of this action, however undesirable they may turn out to be. This principle is reflected in the oft-quoted Latin maxim *caveat emptor*, or "let the buyer beware." It is illustrated by the Canadian case of *Lindsay v. Heron* (1921), 50 D.L.R. 1. Here "Eastern Cafeterias Ltd." was being reorganized into the "Eastern Cafeterias of Canada Ltd." The plaintiff had seventy-five shares to sell of the new company. He offered them to the defendant, who, having obtained a quotation on "Eastern Cafeterias Ltd.," issued a cheque for $787.50 but later, discovering his mistake, stopped payment. The plaintiff won the original trial. On appeal, the judge held that:

> A plea of not "ad idem" from the mouths of those who admit that at the time they purchased they did not even know of the existence of the thing it is now contended they really meant to buy, seems to me a plea of nonsense. The most they can say, that, owing to their own want of care and that of others to whom they sought information as to value, they paid too much for the thing they bought; but even that "ad misericordiam" appeal comes ill from those . . . one who buys a "pig in a poke" has only himself to blame if it proves to be a kind quite different from which he needed and got.

Another illustration of this principle is the situation which occurs when an individual trades in his used car for a new one. How many would-be buyers tell the car dealer what is wrong with their used car while it is being appraised? In fact, there is no obligation in law to do so. The dealer will be bound by his appraisal figure. The same applies to the sale of a house. The contract of sale will be binding, so long as no false answers are given to specific questions such as, does the basement flood during storms? Or, does the well ever run dry?

A *mistake of value*, which is not induced by the seller, does not permit the buyer to get out of the contract. Thus, suppose that person A sees that person B has a watch containing many attractive features, such as being waterproof for scuba diving, having a stopwatch effect for racing, an alarm feature, and an extra hand which can remain on the home country time, while travelling in other time zones. A convinces B to sell the watch to A for $50, believing it to be worth much more. It turns out that it is a new imported watch which soon floods the market at a price of $25 and less. This is a mistake of value and, if not induced by the seller, the contract which is governed by the caveat emptor principle remains binding on both A and B.

A *mistake as to the law*, on the part of one of the parties to a contract, is also not a legally valid reason for a person to walk away from a contract. Suppose, for example, an ambitious business-minded student who has accumulated some savings through various jobs decides that she can make money by purchasing a large older house, near a university, and turning it into roomettes for single students. After she signs the agreement of purchase, she learns to her dismay that the area is zoned for single families only. Can she get out of the contract on the grounds of her mistake? The answer is "no," as the rule of caveat emptor would apply. This would be so even if the student told the seller of her intention to turn the building into roomettes for single students, as there is no duty on the seller to correct the buyer's knowledge of the zoning bylaws.

The law does, however, permit some contracts to be exempted from the caveat emptor rule. These are contracts in which there has been a common mistake, a mutual mistake, or a unilateral mistake. All of these exceptions are explained below.

Common Mistake

If two persons enter into a contract about something which has ceased to exist (for example, a house that has just burned down) there is no meeting of the minds and therefore no contract. This is said to be a situation of common mistake in that both parties were assuming that the subject matter existed, when, in fact, it did not.

In the case of *Couturier v. Hastie* (1852), 8 Ex. 40, the plaintiff chartered a vessel to load corn in Salonica and sent a bill of lading to the defendant in London. The defendant, the plaintiff's broker, sold the cargo of corn to a third party. En route to London, the corn fermented and had to be sold by the ship's master before delivery. The court rejected the action to recover the agreed price on the grounds that the cargo had ceased to exist at the time the sale was made in London, making the contract void.

Another example of a common mistake might be if in February I insured my summer cottage, which is snowbound during the winter. In the spring I discover that it has been destroyed by an avalanche, and on further investigation I discover that it was destroyed before the policy took effect. Both parties, insurer and insured, made the same mistake about an object which did not exist when the contract was made. Therefore the contract is void.

The common law rule with regard to common mistake has now been incorporated in the Sale of Goods Act. Thus, for example, the Ontario Sale of Goods Act, R.S.O), 1980, c. 462, s. 7, provides "Where there is a contract for the sale of specific goods and the goods without the knowledge of the seller have perished at the time the contract is made, the contract is void."

Rectification

In some situations involving what appears to be a common mistake, the court, while not setting aside the contract, will allow the written document to be altered to express the true intentions of the parties. This is accomplished by an equitable remedy called *rectification*. Rectification requires that: (1) the original agreement was complete in itself; (2) there was no change in the agreement between the time of its formation and that of its preparation in written form; and (3) the party seeking rectification can prove to the satisfaction of the court that the final document did not embody the terms of the original agreement. This is an exception to the *parol evidence rule* which states that parol evidence cannot be admitted to vary the terms of a written contract.

Mutual Mistake

This refers to a situation in which both parties made different mistakes rather than a common one.

The classic case on mutual mistake is that of *Raffles v. Wichelhaus* (1865), 159 E.R. 375. In this case, the plaintiff sold the defendant the complete cargo of cotton of a loaded ship called the S.S. Peerless. The defendant was interested in buying the cargo of the ship because he believed that the ship would arrive in October, whereas in fact it did not arrive until December. The court stated:

> There is nothing on the face of the contract to show that any particular ship called the "Peerless" was meant; but at the moment it appears that two ships called the "Peerless" were about to sail from Bombay, there is a latent ambiguity and evidence may be given for the purpose of showing that the defendant meant one "Peerless" and the plaintiff another. That being so, there was no consensus "ad idem" [meeting of the minds] and therefore no binding contract.

The plea of mutual mistake has been successfully raised where credit has been granted to the wrong person through: (a) a mistake in identity; (b) where there has been unclear writing: (c) where there has been a genuine misunderstanding about the units of measure (such as American gallons for Imperial gallons); and (d) where a mistake has occurred as a result of the intervention of a third party.

The case of *Henkel v. Pape* (1870), L.R. 6 Ex. 7, illustrates this last type of mistake. In this case, the judge held that a person is not bound by an offer wrongly transmitted by a telegraph clerk and accepted by the offeree. The post or telegraph office has no authority to convey the message except in the form presented to it.

Unilateral Mistake

This is a mistake by only one party to the contract. Normally the rule is *caveat emptor*, or "buyer beware." The only circumstances in which a person would be excluded from the caveat emptor rule in this respect is where there has been a case of mistaken identity, a genuine clerical error, or a situation in which a person has deliberately been misled and thought he was agreeing to something else (the "non est factum" rule).

Mistaken Identity.   For the plea of *mistaken identity* to succeed, the courts have ruled that:

1. there must have been an intention to deal with someone other than the actual contracting party;
2. that the other party was aware of this mistake;
3. that the correct identity of the contracting party was of crucial importance;
4. that reasonable steps were taken to establish the identity of that party; and
5. if the contract is void *ab initio* ("from the beginning"), no title passes and the goods may be recovered as soon as the mistake is discovered. If the contract is merely voidable, and if it is desired to get the goods back,

rather than money compensation, action must be taken to recover the goods before they pass into the hands of a third party purchaser for value—as opposed to a gratuitous donee (someone who receives the item as a gift).

This can be explained by the following: If the innocent or misled party was prepared to deal with the party who represented himself to be someone else, then the contract is merely voidable. Therefore action must be taken by the misled party to have the contract rescinded and the goods returned before the subject matter of the contract passes into the hands of a third party. If, however, the goods are in the hands of a third party, it would only be possible to sue for the price with little chance of recovery from the original buyer.

Suppose, that the court finds that the seller (the innocent party) took steps to establish the true identity of the other party and only intended to deal with the party being so represented and not necessarily with the individual carrying out the misrepresentation. Then the court would hold that there was never any passing of ownership of the goods because the contract was void. In such case, the seller may seek out and recover the goods.

It should be remembered, however, that no mistake of value or mistake of law is grounds for having a contract set aside.

A classic case involving mistaken identity is *Cundy v. Lindsay* (1878), 3 App. Cas. 459. In this case, a company which had had many dealings with a reputable firm by the name of Blenkiron & Co., 123 Wood Street, received an order from Blenkarn, 37 Wood Street, but the letter appeared to be from Blenkiron. The goods were shipped to the Blenkarn Company at 37 Wood Street and sold to a third party. It was held that an innocent purchaser could acquire no right to the goods because between the seller (the company) and Blenkarn, there was no contract. Lord Cairns said:

> Of him [Blenkarn] they knew nothing and of him they never thought. With him they never intended to deal. Their minds never even for an instant of time rested upon him, and as between him and them there was no consensus of mind which could lead to any agreement or contract whatever. As between him and them there was merely one side to the contract where, in order to produce a contract, two sides would be required.

The shippers then sued for conversion. The House of Lords held that the contract was only intended with Blenkiron & Co. Therefore, the contract was void from the beginning and no title had passed.

In another case, *Phillips v. Brooks Ltd.*, [1919] 2 K.B. 243, an individual bought pearls for 2,550 pounds sterling and a ring for 450 pounds sterling by passing himself off as Sir George Bullough, St. James Square. He gave a cheque for the total, and the plaintiff having checked the directory, allowed him to take the ring, as he stated it was for his wife's birthday. The ring was pawned to the defendants. The plaintiff sued the defendants for the return of the goods alleging that in the circumstances, he, the jeweller, had never parted with the title in them. The judge held that the jeweller intended to contract with the person who made the purchase and the contract though voidable was valid until disaffirmed and a valid title had passed. Thus, according to Chief Justice Morton:

> The minds of the parties met and agreed on all the terms of the sale, the thing sold, the price, and term of payment, the person selling and the person buying. . . . He [the plaintiff] could not have supposed that he was selling to any other person; his intention was to sell to the person present and identified by sight and hearing; it does not affect the sale because the buyer assumed a false name or practised any other deceit to induce the vendor to sell.

Genuine Clerical Error.   This refers to the situation in which there has been a genuine clerical error. Thus in *Webster v. Cecil* (1861), 54 E.R. 812, the parties were negotiating the sale of some plots of land belonging to Cecil. Webster offered 2,000 pounds sterling through his agent. Cecil refused, but after thinking it over, dispatched a letter to Webster offering to sell the land for 2,100 pounds, but either the figures were inserted wrongly or a clerical error was committed and the amount appeared as 1,200 pounds. Of course, Webster accepted by return of post. This was later described as an example of "palpable clerical mistake." It was held by the Master of the Rolls (Sir John Ronilly):

> The mistake has been clearly proved and the defendant had immediately given notice of it . . . in that state of case the court could not grant specific performance and compel a person to sell property for much less than its real value . . . 1,000 pounds less than he intended.

Non Est Factum ("It Was Not My Deed").   This is a situation in which a person has been deliberately misled into making an agreement but believing that, in doing so, he or she is in fact entering into an agreement about something else. Cases of this sort normally involve situations where there is some physical (sometimes mental) infirmity such as blindness or senility.

Another possible set of circumstances is illustrated by *Marks v. Imperial Life Assurance Co.*, [1949] 1 D.L.R. 613. In this case, an insured person's wife, named as beneficiary in certain insurance policies, signed with the insured a borrowing agreement in respect of each policy. It was found:

> that, acting on the advice of the insurance company's agent, the insured misrepresented to his wife the nature of the documents telling her that they were merely for the purpose of changing to her advantage the scheme of payment of the insurance monies.

It was held that the wife was entitled to succeed on a plea of *non est factum* since it was clear that the two documents signed by her were no relation in class or character to the documents described to her by her husband when she signed them. Quoting Chief Justice McRuer:

It would appear to be clear from these authorities that where a person signing a document is misled by the representation of another as to its true nature and character as distinct from the purport and effect of the contents it is invalid and the plea of 'non est factum' is a good plea. There is no evidence here which in any way involves the deceased in the carrying out of the work for which the promised subscription was made, other than the signing of the subscription paper itself.

MISREPRESENTATION

A contract may also be set aside when there has been innocent or fraudulent misrepresentation.

Innocent Misrepresentation

For such a claim to succeed, four elements must be present: (a) there must have been a false statement; (b) the misrepresentation must have been of fact not opinion; (c) the misrepresentation must have been material; and (d) the material point must have been the inducing factor in the contract.

Example. An actual situation involving innocent misrepresentation concerned a young man who applied for an insurance policy at the age of 20. During his youth he had been subject to rheumatic fever and had recovered. During the period from five to fifteen years of age, his parents, without telling him why they were sending him to a doctor, required him to attend an annual medical check-up. At the age of fifteen, the doctor decided that he was in excellent condition and told him not to bother returning for further examinations. The young man, who had neither knowledge of his previous serious illness, nor any idea of why he was required to undertake annual physical examinations, applied for an insurance policy. The insurance application contained a question asking whether he had had certain serious illnesses such as rheumatic fever, to which he, in all honesty, answered "no." As he thought his examinations with the doctor were merely annual checkups, he also innocently answered that he had not attended the doctor for any particular serious illnesses, and that he had had no serious past illness. The application form was received by the company and in due course the policy was issued. As is the custom with all insurance applications, the file was eventually referred to a retail credit agency for an investigation through neighbours, friends, and employers. This investigation finally revealed the true circumstances of the case, that the applicant had in fact had rheumatic fever at an early age and had attended a doctor for annual medical examinations from five to fifteen years of age.

There were four elements of innocent misrepresentation present in this case, namely:

1. The false statement: the applicant denied that he had had rheumatic fever, which was false;
2. Fact, not opinion: the applicant had in fact had rheumatic fever;

3. Material: a cold would possibly be immaterial but rheumatic fever can have such a damaging effect on the heart and other serious consequences that it is a material point;
4. The inducing factor in the contract: undoubtedly, if the insurance company had known of his previous illness, they would have been more reluctant to issue the policy, or would have required a higher premium.

As a result of the investigation, the company informed the applicant that the insurance policy was being cancelled and the reason therefor. It also advised him that if he re-submitted an application and undertook a medical examination, they would be happy to reconsider the matter. He did this, was found perfectly physically fit, and a new policy was issued at the normal premium rate.

Rescission.   In cases of innocent misrepresentation, the court will order rescission of the contract and insist that both parties be returned to their original position, so long as the victim is in a position to return the goods.

Fraud.   In distinguishing innocent misrepresentation from fraud, Cotten, L.J., in *Awkwright v. Newbold* (1881), 17 Ch. D. 301 at p. 320, stated:

> It must be borne in mind that in an action for setting aside a contract which has been obtained by misrepresentation, the plaintiff may succeed though the misrepresentation was innocent; but in an action for *deceit*, the representation to found the action must not be innocent, that is to say, it must be made either with a knowledge of its being false or with a reckless disregard as to whether it is or is not true.

Repudiation.   In the case of *Behn v. Burness* (1863), 3 B. & S. 751, a charter party was made, on October 19, in which it was agreed that Behn's ship "now in the port of Amsterdam" should proceed to Newport and there load a cargo of coals which she should carry to Hong Kong. In fact the ship was not in the port of Amsterdam and did not arrive there until October 23. When it subsequently arrived at Newport, Burness refused to load the coal and repudiated the contract. The question then arose: was this a condition which entitled the contract to be repudiated, or was it merely a representation which entitled Burness to damages after carrying out the contract? The court found this to be a condition which entitled the contract to be repudiated and stated:

> Properly speaking, a representation is a statement or assertion, made by one party to another, before or at the time of the contract, or some matter or circumstances relating to it. Though it is sometimes contained in the written instrument, it is not an integral part of the contract; and, consequently, the contract is not broken, though the representation proves to be untrue; nor is such untruth any cause of action nor has it any efficacy whatever unless the representation was made fraudulently either by reason of its being made with a knowledge of its untruth or by reason of its being made dishonestly with reckless

ignorance whether it was true or untrue. . . . Though representations are not usually contained in the written instrument of contract, yet they sometimes are. But it is plain that their insertion therein cannot alter their nature. A question, however, may arise whether a descriptive statement in a written instrument is a mere representation, or whether it is a substantive part of the contract. This is a question of construction which the court and not the jury must determine. If the court should come to the conclusion that such a statement by one party was intended to be a substantive part of his contract and not a mere representation, the often discussed question may, of course, be raised, whether this part of the contract is a condition precedent, or only an independent agreement, a breach of which will not justify repudiation of the contract, but will only be a cause of action for a compensation in damages.

Thus:

(a) *Representations* made at the time of entering into a contract, but not intended to form part of it, or to affect its validity (therefore, neither a condition nor a warranty) have no effect unless fraudulent in which case they make the contract voidable, at the discretion of the innocent party.

(b) *Conditions*, such as a statement or a promise which are of the essence of the contract, if untrue, but not intentionally so, entitle the innocent party to be discharged from the contract—for example, the charter party case of *Behn v. Burness, supra*.

(c) *Warranties*, i.e., incidental points or promises not going to the heart of the contract, such as the promise as part of a house-building agreement that extra insulation will lower my heating bill by 30%. A breach of a warranty (for instance, my heating bill drops by 28% instead of 30%) does not entitle either party to avoid the contract but may give rise to a claim for compensation.

(d) A condition may be treated as a warranty by the contracting parties, in which case the contract would be honoured.

In the case of *Bannerman v. White* (1861), 10 C.B. (N.S.) 844, Bannerman offered to sell hops to White, who agreed to purchase the year's crops on the understanding that no sulphur had been used in their growth. White, later learning that sulphur had been used, repudiated the contract. It turned out that Bannerman had forgotten he had used sulphur on five acres out of 300 acres to test a new machine, but had mixed the entire crop together. The court found that the affirmation "that no sulphur was used" became part of the contract, a true condition, so White was relieved of any liability, Erie C.J., stated:

> We avoid the term warranty because it is used in two senses, and the term condition because the question is whether that term is applicable. Then, the effect is that the defendants required and that the plaintiff gave his undertaking that no sulphur had been used. This undertaking was a preliminary stipulation, and if it had not been given, the defen-

dants would not have gone on with the treaty which resulted in the sale. In this sense it was the condition upon which the defendants contracted; and it would be contrary to the intention expressed by this stipulation that the contract should remain valid if sulphur had been used.

The intention of the parties governs in the making and in the construction of all contracts. If the parties so intend, the sale may be absolute, with a warranty super added, or the sale may be conditional, to be null if the warranty is broken. And upon this statement of facts, we think that the intention appears that the contract should be null if sulphur had been used; and upon this ground we agree that the rule should be discharged.

Fraudulent Misrepresentation

A person claiming fraudulent misrepresentation should be able to prove the existence of all the previous elements, as well as: the fact that the misrepresentation is made either deliberately or knowingly; or with reckless disregard for the truth; or as the intentional statement of a misleading half-truth.

In *Derry v. Peek* (1889), 14 App. Cas. 337, a leading case on this subject, the court stated at p. 374 that the false statement must be "made knowingly or without belief in its truth, or recklessly, careless whether it be true or false." In this case a prospectus had been issued by company directors who had succeeded in obtaining an Act of Parliament which authorized them to run trains in Plymouth. The Act authorized animal or steam power subject to the approval of local authorities. The prospectus mentioned only steam power which the directors believed the local board of trade would approve. The plaintiff bought shares on the strength of the prospectus. Eventually the authorities refused to authorize steam power.

The trial judge found that the defendants had reasonable grounds for the belief expressed in the prospectus and that they were innocent of fraud. The Court of Appeal held that although the prospectus expressed the honest belief of the directors it was a belief for which no reasonable grounds existed and the directors were therefore liable. The House of Lords held, as expressed by Lord Herschell:

> In my opinion making a false statement through want of care falls far short of, and is a very different thing from fraud, and the same may be said of a false representation honestly believed, though on innocent grounds. At the same time, I desire to say distinctly that when a false statement has been made, the questions whether there were reasonable grounds for believing it, and what were the means of knowledge in the possession of the person making it, are most weighty matters for consideration. The ground upon which an alleged belief was founded is a most important test of its reality. I can conceive many cases where the fact that an alleged belief was destitute of all reasonable foundation would suffice in itself to convince the court that it was not really entertained and that the representation was a fraudulent one.

Sometimes constructive fraud exists from the very relationship of the parties themselves. These are the special situations of undue influence mentioned earlier where the dominant party has to disprove any influence. Thus in the case of *Tate v. Williamson* (1866), 2 Ch. App. 55, an Oxford undergraduate, needing money, was counselled by a trusted advisor to sell his estate. The latter undertook to buy it himself without revealing the existence of valuable minerals in the soil. The court, giving its decision, stated:

> Whenever two persons stand in such a relation[ship] that, while it continues, confidence is necessarily reposed by one, and the influence which naturally grows out of that confidence is possessed by the other and this confidence is abused or the influence is exerted to obtain an advantage at the expense of the confiding party, the person so availing himself of this position will not be permitted to retain the advantage, although the transaction could not have been impeached if no such confidential relation had existed.

Normally, in cases of fraudulent misrepresentation, the court, in addition to returning the parties to their original position, will award damages for the deceit which has been practised on the injured party. This deceit, as well as being a tort, may be a criminal offence and the perpetrator, consequently, be subject to prosecution in the criminal court. If it is impossible to return the goods, if a third party had acquired them, if an offeree has confirmed acceptance, or if a completed conveyance, formal lease, or sale has occurred, the contract cannot be set aside for misrepresentation and money damages are the only remedy in common law.

In the case of *O'Flaherty v. McKinley*, [1953] 2 D.L.R. 514, the plaintiff bought for $1,325 a car which the defendant affirmed was a 1952 Hillman. After driving it for 7,000 miles the plaintiff discovered when he took it to another garage for tuning that it was a 1949 car. The court ruled that all the elements of fraudulent misrepresentation were present and the plaintiff obtained rescission of the contract, plus money damages, because the false representation was a vital condition of the contract. If the purchaser had resold the car to an innocent purchaser for value, the remedy of rescission would no longer have been available. However, the original purchaser could still have claimed damages for deceit.

To reduce the amount of fraudulent misrepresentation, most Canadian provinces have enacted legislation with respect to door-to-door sales, referral sales, pyramid sales, unsolicited telephone solicitation of shares, and "unfair business practices."

Misrepresentation sometimes arises in connection with business loans. The bank or other lender will rely heavily on the borrowing firm's financial statements in assessing its net worth and earnings prospects and deciding how much, if at all, to lend. If these statements are inaccurate, having been negligently or fraudulently prepared, the lender may suffer loss. If they were prepared by the borrower, and the errors were made innocently, the lender can void the contract. If they were prepared fraudulently, the lender can also sue for deceit. Suppose, however, they were prepared by a third party, such as a firm of public accountants. Then there may be no remedy in contract because of lack of privity between the lender and this third party. The courts may, however, follow the rule spelled out in *Hedley Byrne & Co. v. Heller & Partners Ltd.*, [1964] A.C. 465, and allow a claim in tort on the grounds that a person making up a statement of accounts, in circumstances where it is likely that a third party may rely on such accounts, has a *duty to be diligent and careful*—that is, a duty in tort. Such duty extends for the protection of third parties who may come to rely on statements made.

Finally, as a general rule, in the case of misrepresentation, the plaintiff must sue for both rescission and damages because, if damages alone are claimed and not awarded, the court will not grant rescission as an alternative. However, if fraudulent misrepresentation is claimed but is not proved to the court's satisfaction, the contract may be rescinded for innocent misrepresentation without the plaintiffs asking for this alternative remedy.

CONTRACTS OF UTMOST GOOD FAITH

Some contracts require more than the absence of innocent misrepresentation or fraud. These are contracts in which there is a dependency by one party on the other by virtue of a trust relationship and in which one of the parties has knowledge which is not accessible to the other and is therefore bound to tell him everything which may be supposed likely to affect his judgment. In other words, although all contracts may be invalidated by material misrepresentation, some contracts (those of *uberrimae fidei*—that is, of utmost good faith) may also be invalidated by the non-disclosure of a material fact.

For example, in the case of *London Assurance v. Mansel* (1879), 11 Ch. D. 363, the insured had truthfully answered questions as to whether he had policies of insurance on his life by stating he had two policies, but neglected to state that he had applied for other coverage and other policies which had been refused. In an application by the insurance company to have the contract set aside, Jessel M.R. stated:

> I am not prepared to lay down the law as making any difference in substance between one contract of assurance and another. . . . Whether it is life, or fire, or marine insurance, I take it *good faith* is required in all cases, and though there may be certain circumstances from the peculiar nature of marine insurance which require to be disclosed and which do not apply to other contracts of insurance, that is rather, in my opinion, an illustration of the application of the principle than a distinction in principle.

Contracts for the purchase of shares in companies are also contracts of utmost good faith. As stated by Kindersley, V.C. (Vice Chancellor), in *New Brunswick & Canada Railway & Land Co. v. Muggeridge* (1859), 1 Dr. & Sm. 381:

Those who issue a prospectus holding out to the public the great advantages which will accrue to persons who will take shares in a proposed undertaking and inviting them to take shares on the faith of the representations therein contained, are bound to state everything with strict and scrupulous accuracy, and not only to abstain from stating as fact that which is not so, but to omit not one fact within their knowledge the existence of which might in any degree affect the nature, or extent or quality of the privileges and advantages which the prospectus holds out as inducements to take shares.

Applications for licences granted pursuant to statutory authority also fall within this category. As far as suretyship and partnership are concerned, full disclosure becomes a requirement once the relationship of contract is established. Therefore a person who is a surety (one who guarantees another's performance—for example, repayment of a loan) is entitled to be informed by the other party (the lender) of anything which might affect the contract of guarantee—for example, that the borrower had been slow in repayment of a previous loan.

REVIEW QUESTIONS

1. Distinguish between void and voidable contracts.
2. What is meant by duress? Give three examples.
3. If a person is to claim undue influence, what must be proved in court?
4. What are typical relationships in which undue influence can arise?
5. The dominant party in certain personal relationships must disprove undue influence in transactions between those persons. What are the relationships?
6. A contract may sometimes be set aside on grounds of: (a) a common mistake; or (b) a mutual mistake. Explain.
7. What is meant by the equitable remedy of "rectification"?
8. A contract may sometimes be set aside on grounds of unilateral mistake. Explain the sets of circumstances (palpable clerical mistake and *non est factum*) in which this may occur.
9. What is innocent misrepresentation? What four elements must be present?
10. What is the legal remedy of "rescission"? Under what circumstances is it not available?
11. What is fraudulent misrepresentation? Give an example of your own.
12. What are the legal remedies for innocent and fraudulent misrepresentation?
13. What is meant by a contract of "utmost good faith"? Give three examples. What obligation is imposed by law on the more knowledgeable party in the contract?

PROBLEMS

1. A, who fancies himself as a diamond appraiser, bought from a jeweller

for $500 a diamond which he believed was worth $2,000. The jeweller believed it was worth only $200. It has now been independently valued by a gem appraiser at $1,200. Since both parties made different mistakes, it would appear that this contract is voidable by either party. Discuss.

2. A travelling salesman, carried away by a poker game, misappropriated $5,000 of his employer's funds. The following day, seized by fright and remorse, he ran away to another province. The employer's accountant called at the salesman's residence and, learning that the wife had a paid-up insurance policy with a $5,000 cash surrender value, threatened to have her husband arrested and imprisoned if she did not assign the policy to her husband's employer. She did so, but later sued to recover the policy. Could she succeed?

3. While a major highway was in the process of construction, the owner of a successful service station discovered that the new highway would probably run one half mile south of his site. He decided to sell and his service station was quickly sold to an eager buyer. Later, the new owner discovered to his chagrin that the major flow of traffic would be diverted south of his location and probably cause a substantial drop in business. What is his legal position?

4. Consider the facts in the case of *Sherwood v. Walker* (1887), 33 N.W. 919 (Mich. S.C.). In the spring of 1886 the plaintiff heard that the defendants had some Angus cattle for sale. Desirous of purchasing some, the plaintiff met the defendants at Walkerville where he was informed that there were a few head of Angus cattle left at the defendants' Greenfield farm. They asked the plaintiff to view them and stated that in all probability they were barren and would not breed. In accordance with this request, the plaintiff went out and looked at the cattle on May 5 and found one called Rose 2nd of Aberlone which he was desirous of purchasing. Terms were finally agreed on at 5½ cents per pound live weight, allowing fifty pounds for shrinkage. The sale was confirmed in writing on May 15, on which day the defendants gave an order to the plaintiff directing the man in charge of the farm, Mr. Graham, to deliver the cow to the plaintiff. On May 21, the plaintiff went to pick up the cow, delivering to Graham the order. Graham refused to hand over the cow, informing the plaintiff that in the meantime it had been discovered that Rose 2nd was with calf. Shortly thereafter, the plaintiff tendered $80 to the defendant Walker and demanded the cow again, but Walker refused to accept the money or to deliver the cow. The plaintiff then sued.

The defendants claimed that no contract had been made on the basis of mutual mistake; that is, the parties had contracted for the sale of a barren cow (whose value was $80) whereas in fact Rose 2nd was not only fertile but with calf. (She calved in October.) Her value as a breeder was estimated at from $750 to $1,000. Two lower courts found in favour of the plaintiff. Should the Supreme Court affirm or reverse these findings?

5. Mr. Shaw had been petitioned into bankruptcy by one of his creditors and as a result had lost his travel agency. His general creditors had only

collected fifty cents on the dollar from his assets but under Canadian bankruptcy law could not bring court actions to collect the balance of their accounts. He then incorporated a new travel agency with his wife as president. The local bank, which had only collected $5,000 on a $10,000 loan, sent its loan manager to call on him and tell him that unless he signed a promissory note for the $5,000 unpaid balance, they would give him a bad credit rating in case of any enquiries received. He signed the note but later refused to pay when it became due. Discuss Mr. Shaw's legal liability in this case.

6. A famous pianist was giving a concert in Canada and let it be known that he was interested in looking at antique pianos. Mr. Brookes called the concert office advising that he had a piano in his house which he had inherited from his mother who had been a concert pianist. The pianist arranged to take time off to visit the Brookes residence and immediately recognized the piano as an original Dusendorf, conservatively worth $100,000. He offered Brookes $20,000 which he gratefully accepted. Both were extremely satisfied with their bargain until Brookes realized he had lost a possible $80,000.

   Discuss the legal liability of the pianist, if any, in this case. Would the situation be any different if someone with no particular interest in music but interested in the art designs on the piano had offered $5,000 for the piano and resold it within a year to an art museum for $150,000?

7. A middle-aged secretary lost her father and mother just about the time she became acquainted with a used car salesman for whom she took a liking. As her parents left her some $20,000 cash, she decided to purchase a farm in sole ownership with this money, and operate a partnership, with the boy friend contributing his work in supervising the operation of the farm, such as the cultivating of crops. At this time he was contacted by the local bank and requested to make repayments of $17,000 on personal loans. He wrongly informed the bank that he was joint owner of the farm, agreed to surrender the receipts from the crops, and even gave a chattel mortgage on a new automobile which the secretary had purchased in her own name. The bank took the chattel and upon investigation realized that it belonged to the girl friend. Still they had a bailiff seize the car when the boy friend continued to be in arrears on his loan. The girl friend was called in by the bank, and made to sign a farm mortgage covering her partner's personal debts plus $2,000 in cash before the bank would release her car.

   Discuss all the legal implications arising out of this case which you feel are relevant. Refer to *McKenzie v. Bank of Montreal* (1975), 7 O.R. (2d) 521.

READINGS

W.W. Distributors & Co. Ltd. v. Thorsteinson (1960), 26 D.L.R. (2d) 365 (Man. C.A.).

Facts: Following the announcement in a local newspaper of her pending wedding, one of the defendants, a minor, received a call from a stranger who said he would like to call to present her with a gift. An appointment was arranged, and two salesmen called who before they left had pressured the infant bride-to-be and her mother into signing a purchase order for a set of cookware, a set of flatware, and an electric skillet for a total price of $239.50. As soon as the salesmen had left, the infant purchaser and her mother who had countersigned the financing document tried to cancel the contract, finally ordering the bank to stop payment on the down-payment cheque lent by the mother. They are now being sued for a total of $342.99. A fair price for the goods purchased was estimated at $145.95 by an independent expert.

Held per Freedman J.A.:

Where the defence of misrepresentation has been raised, and where the evidence indicates a specific warranty by the salesman that the defendants "were getting good value in exchange for their money," the court must examine the circumstances . . . whether what occurred was mere puffery . . . or . . . a deliberate act of deception which could vitiate the contract. If . . . the representation was part of an entire pattern of improper conduct—consisting of material mis-statements on the one hand and of wilful non-disclosure on the other—the Court is more easily led to a conclusion against the validity of the contract.

. . . Here it is clear that the representatives of the plaintiff not only did not provide an opportunity to the defendants to read and understand the contract, but by their tactics of pressure and speed deliberately sought to deny and succeeded in denying such opportunity to them [such as a $22.35 service charge, reading fee $2, 10% interest after maturity, 20% solicitor's fees if placed in hands of solicitor for non-payment]. In such circumstances the Court may grant protection on the grounds of equity. . . .

. . . The infant plaintiff stated that she entered into the contract only as a result of high pressure tactics of the two men. . . . As for the mother . . . she was not a purchaser or intending to become a purchaser [she had given a cheque for $50 by way of loan to her daughter], yet they asked her to sign the contract. . . . [T]he salesmen said ". . . It doesn't really mean anything except we would like to have your name on it with your daughter's." . . . His statement was a deliberate act of deception designed to procure the mother's signature to the document. . . .

Misrepresentation was raised as a defence, and the evidence amply confirms it. I think it would be unjust and inequitable to hold these ladies to a contract procured in the manner in which this one was.

Appeal dismissed.

Longley v. Barbrick (1962), 36 D.L.R. (2d) 672 (N.S. S.C.).

Facts: In 1946 Beatrice Barbrick purchased a property and gave back a mortgage to a Mrs. Drysdale. In 1958, as Mrs. Drysdale wanted the balance of

the mortgage (some $2,500), Mrs. Barbrick arranged with Town and Coun-
try Real Estate Company to get the money to pay Mrs. Drysdale. On January
23, 1959, she went to a lawyer's office in the Roy Building, Halifax, and
signed two documents which she claimed were not explained to her. The
first was the mortgage document for $2,500, the other was a collateral
agreement for the same amount which was a bonus for granting the said
mortgage. The $4,924 commitment was then assigned for value in April
1959 to a Mr. Longley, who is now suing for foreclosure because the
mortgage is in arrears.

Held per Coffin J.:

I find as a fact that Town and Country Real Estate undertook to arrange for
her a mortgage of $2,500 at 8% for 96 months and that she understood it was
for such a mortgage that she signed the application of January 16, 1959.

I also find that the mortgage and the collateral agreement were not fully
read and explained to her by the solicitor who drew up the documents. . . .
[I]f Town and Country Real Estate Ltd. had . . . instructed the defendant to
have independent advice before the documents were signed, the whole
unfortunate situation could have been avoided.

. . . [I]t is my view that the bonus of $2,500 is . . . void under the plea of *non
est factum* because she was so misled as the the contents of the documents
that her "mind did not go with her signature."

Mr. Longley . . . has his remedies against the original mortgagee under the
terms of the assignment of mortgage. . . .

The mortgage will be amended and the principal sum reduced from
$5,000 to $2,500 . . . and interest at 8%.

The defendant is entitled to a rectification of the said mortgage and an
accounting. . . .

The defendant will have costs and as she has succeeded substantially on
her counterclaim, the costs of the counterclaim.

Royal Bank of Canada v. Hale (1961), 30 D.L.R. (2d) 138 (B.C. S.C.).

Facts: In 1955, following a previous satisfactory transaction in 1955, the
Royal Bank at Kitimat loaned ABC Sheet Metal and Plumbing Limited
$25,000, taking as security: (a) five notes for $5,000 each; (b) an assignment of
ABC's book debts; and (c) personal guarantees from four ABC officers for
$25,000. The standard bank form was used and when the direct debt was
repaid, the bank claimed repayment under guarantee of all the indirect debts
since the bank guarantee form referred to all "direct and indirect debts
owing to the bank." Since the bank had returned the guarantee form when a
previous direct bank loan had been repaid, the ABC officers offered against
the bank's suit that they were misled by the document, pleading either
mutual or unilateral mistake.

Held per Munroe J.:

The intention of the plaintiff corporation . . . must be determined from the terms of the document [and since the form referred to both direct and indirect debts] . . . I cannot hold that the plaintiff was mistaken as to its legal effect, and the defence of mutual mistake therefore fails.

There remains . . . the major defence . . . that the guarantees ought not to be enforced *vis-à-vis* the indirect debt because of a unilateral mistake . . . as to the legal effect of the guarantee . . . induced by the (innocent) misrepresentation of the plaintiff. . . .

. . . [T]he defendants . . . were mistaken in their belief that they were thereby guaranteeing only the bank loans, and not the indirect debt. . . . [A] review of the business dealings between the parties in 1955 [shows that] . . . a loan was obtained from the plaintiff for $250,000 . . . and interlocking guarantees . . . for $500,000. . . . [W]hen the current loans were being negotiated, none of the plaintiff's officials nor any of the defendants ever thought about such indirect liability. . . . [T]he persons concerned intended . . . guarantees . . . to provide adequate security only for the loans . . . not to secure any obligation arising out of the assignment of book debts. . . . [G]uarantees contain no . . . reference to . . . pre-existing indirect liability . . . guarantees are for amounts identical to the bank loans . . . [T]he covering letter . . . enclosing the guarantee in which the defendant A.W. Hale showed defendants' understanding or misunderstanding, when he said, in part: "It was our understanding that we were personally guaranteeing the loan only." . . . [A]ll of these circumstances . . . lead to the irresistible inference and I find that, if the plaintiff's present interpretation of the guarantees is correct, it (the plaintiff) induced the defendants to think otherwise and thereby misled them. . . .

. . . [A]ll the plaintiff's officials . . . and the defendants, knew and understood that the real purpose of the guarantees was to guarantee only the bank loans. . . .

. . . [There is] need of the Courts, to restrict the pleas of mistake within narrow limits . . . [T]here is ample authority . . . that the Courts will relieve a person of his contract where a misunderstanding as to its true effect was induced, even though innocently, by the other party and where injustice would be done if performance were to be enforced. . . .

. . . [I]t would not only be inequitable but unconscionable not to relieve them from liability for the indirect obligations sued upon herein, which liability arose by reason of unilateral mistake on the part of the defendants, induced by the plaintiff, to be inferred from their previous dealings.

[The judge also found that since a printed form was used, the rule stated by Denning L.J. in *Neuchatal Asphalte Co. v. Barnett*, [1957] 1 All E.R. 362 at p. 365, applied: "We do not allow printed forms to be made a trap for the unwary." Plaintiffs there paid the balance owing on direct debts.]

Ron Engineering & Construction Eastern Ltd. v. R. (1979), 24 O.R. (2d) 332 (C.A.).

Facts: Tenders, to be submitted by June 28, 1972, were called by the

Ontario Water Resources Commission for work to be done in the City of North Bay. The plaintiff and appellant construction company obtained an extension of five days to submit its tender. The officer manager of the construction company went from Ottawa to Toronto, to which place the president of the construction company relayed a bid figure of $2,748,000 which she (the office manager) was to enter on the tender document for the total construction based on figures which he had just received from sub-contractors. The office manager then submitted the tender on her employer's behalf. In the meantime, the construction company president realized that he had omitted the cost of his own company's work, calculated at $750,058. The tender included a $150,000 deposit. This mistake was communicated to the Commission shortly after they had opened the tenders. The construction company's tender was some $630,000 lower than the next lowest tender. The Commission refused to consider the question of mistake but without signifying its acceptance, sent the appellant (the construction company) contract documents to execute. The Commission declared the deposit forfeited when the appellant refused to execute the contract.

Held per Arnup J.A.:

The judgment of this court in *Belle River Community Arena Inc. v. W.J.C. Kaufmann Co. Ltd.* (1978), 20 O.R. (2d) 447 . . . [was] that an offeree cannot accept an offer which he knows has been made by mistake which affects a fundamental term of the contract. . . . The error in question has been found to be, as it obviously was, material and important. . . .

. . . In our view, the Commission cannot utilize the contract document respecting the making of a deposit to forfeit that deposit in a case where the Commission has express knowledge of an error in the making of a tender, which error is substantial, material and important. . . .

. . . [A] commission or other owner calling for tenders is entitled to be sceptical when a bidder who is the low tenderer by a very substantial amount attempts to say, after the opening of tenders, that a mistake has been made. However, when that mistake is proven by the production of reasonable evidence, the person to whom the tender is made is not in a position to accept the tender or to seek to forfeit the bid deposit. . . .

. . . [J]udgment for the plaintiff [appellant] for $150,000 with costs of the action. The plaintiff will also be entitled to interest from September 26, 1972, to date of the trial judgment.

Appeal allowed.

9

Legality of Purpose

Another requirement of a valid contract is legality of purpose. Thus, for example, an agreement to commit a fraud, although it may meet all the other requirements of a valid contract, is illegal. Also, because of its illegal purpose, it is unenforceable in a court of law. The criterion is whether the purpose of the agreement is to do something that violates either common law or statute law (for example, the Criminal Code). As soon as a judge realizes that a contract has an illegal purpose, he or she will refuse to deal with it. This principle is expressed in the legal maxims: "the courts will not taint their hands with illegality" and "he who comes to court, must come with clean hands." However, the law will help an innocent party in an illegal contract. Thus, for example, if A and B conspired to defraud C, then C, as an innocent party, could sue A and B to get C's property back.

A distinction can be made between a *common law illegality* and a *statutory illegality*. The former would involve a criminal or civil wrong including matters that are *contrary to the public policy* of the country (such as contracts in restraint of trade or marriage). A statutory illegality would involve a contract whose purpose has been made illegal by Act of the federal Parliament or of a provincial legislature.

In the case of *Albert E. Daniels Ltd. v. Sangster* (1976), 12 O.R. (2d) 512 (C. Ct.) dealing with a claim by an unregistered company, the following quotation was made from the judgment in *St. John Shipping Corp. v. Joseph Rank Ltd* (1956) 3. All E.R. 683:

> There are two general principles. . . . The first is that a contract which is entered into with the object of committing an illegal act is unenforceable . . . If the intent is mutual [that is, to break the law] the contract is not enforceable and, if unilateral, it is unenforceable at the suit of the party involved [in the illegal act] . . . The second principle is that the Courts will not enforce a contract expressly or impliedly prohibited by Statute. . . . Thus in the former, one looks at the acts prohibited by statute, in the latter case the contracts which are prohibited. . . .
>
> In *Kocotis v. D'Angelo* [1958] O.R. 104, the true rule is that the Court should carefully consider in each case the terms of the statute or enactment that prohibits an act under a penalty, its object, the evil it was enacted to remedy, and the effect of holding contracts in relation to it void . . . and, if from all these considerations such an intention does not manifestly appear, the contracts should be sustained and enforced, otherwise they should be held void.

Sometimes, as we saw in the last chapter, a contract may also be void but not illegal.

TYPES OF ILLEGAL CONTRACTS

The following are examples of criminal and civil (tort) wrongs that deal with agreements which the courts will not enforce.

Agreement to Commit a Crime

An agreement to commit a crime is illegal. Thus if, for example, A promises B $1,000 to injure C, then B cannot take A to court to enforce payment of the money.

Agreement to Commit a Tort

A contract to commit a tort is also illegal. Thus if, for example, A agrees to pay B $1,000 to make false allegations about C's business practices, B cannot enlist the help of the courts to collect the money.

Agreement to Commit an Immoral Act

An agreement to commit an immoral act is another type of illegal contract— one that is contrary to public policy. Thus if A promises $500 to B in exchange for sexual favours but later refuses to pay, B could not sue A in court. A classic case involving this common law principle is *Pearce v. Brooks* (1866), L.R. 1 Ex. 213. In this case, a known prostitute made arrangements to buy a horse-carriage on a hire purchase agreement. One provision was that if she did not return the carriage before the second payment was due she would forfeit her deposit and pay for repairs, if any. The manufacturer sued for damages to the carriage, but the defendant (the prostitute) objected that the plaintiff knew the purpose of the carriage—that is, "so that she could solicit business"—and therefore the contract was tainted with illegality. The court ruled that to a contract for an illegal or an immoral purpose, the principle *ex turpi causa non oritur actio* ("from an illegal cause no legal action can arise") applied and whether it was an immoral or an illegal purpose it came equally within the terms of the maxim and the effect was the same: no cause of action could arise out of either one or the other.

Where a contract may be performed legally or illegally, the courts will presume that the parties intended the contract to be performed legally, unless there is evidence to show that both parties knew of the illegal purpose as in *Pearce v. Brooks*.

Obstruction of Justice

An agreement that interferes with the administration of justice is contrary to public policy and therefore illegal. Basically these are agreements which are most commonly intended to stifle prosecution. Thus in the case of *Lound v. Grimwade* (1888), 39 Ch. D. 605, the plaintiff was required to give a written bond to secure 3,000 pounds sterling and a mortgage as collateral security for the bond by the defendant because he had introduced the defendant to C, "a known swindler," who had robbed the defendant of considerable sums and was then on trial for the offence. In other words, the defendant, having received the bond, agreed not to take any legal action or other consequences against the plaintiff for this introduction. It was held, following the decision in *Egerton v. Earl Brownlow* (1853), 4 H.L. Cas. 1, "that any contract having a tendency, no matter how slight, to affect the administration of justice, is illegal. The present contract contemplated the prevention of criminal proceedings, which had been threatened against the plaintiff and must be set aside."

Another case involving this principle is *Symington v. Vancouver Breweries and Riefel*, [1931] 1 D.L.R. 935. In this case, the plaintiff had obtained information about an individual by the name of Ball who was illegally manufacturing alcoholic beverages and had been arrested by the police. Officials of the defendant breweries had then offered him $5,000 plus $1,000 for each month of imprisonment to which Ball would be sentenced following the plaintiff's testimony. Ball received twelve months' imprisonment and when all the promised money was not forthcoming, the plaintiff, Symington, sued the breweries.

In dismissing the action, the judge said:

> There is a peculiar and sinister element in this case which distinguishes it from all others that have been cited to us, viz., that it provides for remuneration upon a sliding scale corresponding in amount to the amount of the sentence secured by the informer's evidence. This is so direct and inevitable an incentive to perjury and other concomitant nefarious conduct that it cannot be in the public interest to countenance a transaction which is dangerous to such an exceptional degree to the administration of criminal justice.

Where both civil and criminal remedies exist, a compromise is permissible. This exception is stated in the case of *Keir v. Leeman* (1846), 6 Q.B. 321:

> We shall probably be safe in laying it down that the law will permit a compromise of all offences though made the subject of a criminal prosecution, for which offences the injured party might sue and recover damages in an [civil or private] action. it is often the only manner in which he can obtain redress. But, if the offence is of a public nature, no agreement can be valid, that is, founded on the consideration of stifling a prosecution for it.

Along this line would be an agreement by the Attorney General's branch to go easy on a police informer—that is, substitute a lesser charge for a more serious one. Such an agreement could of course not be enforced in a court of law.

At one time even agreements to refer matters in dispute to arbitration were regarded as an attempt "to oust the jurisdiction of the courts," but the obvious convenience of this method of settling disputes has long been recognized by the legislatures in enacting the various arbitration statutes.

Contracts with Enemy Aliens

It is illegal, as being against public policy, for a person to have contract dealings with enemy aliens, and existing contracts are immediately suspended when war breaks out. The courts also will not help Canadian subjects who "set about to raise loans or contract to supply arms for subjects of a friendly state to enable them to prosecute a war against the sovereign [or the legitimate government]."

On the other hand, it is doubtful whether the foregoing prohibition covers a contract to break the law of a foreign state, since our courts are not bound to enforce foreign law.

Injury to the Public Service

In the case of *Osborne v. Amalgamated Society of Railway Servants*, [1910] A.C. 87, public policy grounds made illegal an agreement whereby a member of Parliament in consideration of a salary paid to him by a political association agreed to vote on every subject in accordance with the directions of the association.

Restraint of Marriage

Any contract that imposes an unreasonable restraint on a person's right to marry is considered against the public interest and therefore illegal and unenforceable. Thus in the case of *Lowe v. Peers* (1768), 4 Burr. 2225 the following contract made under seal was held to be contrary to public policy: "I do truly promise Mrs. Catherine Lowe that I will not marry any person besides herself; if I do, I agree to pay to the said Catherine Lowe 2,000 pounds within three months next after I shall marry somebody else." This promise was held illegal because there was no promise of marriage on either side, and the agreement was purely restrictive.

This common law principle did not, however, prevent the RCMP from stipulating for many years in its employment contract for new constables that they should not marry for five years which was illegal.

Marriage brokerage contracts are also illegal under common law on the grounds that reckless or unsuitable marriages may be encouraged if third parties are free to reap financial profit therefrom (*Cole v. Gibson* (1750), 1 Ves. Sen. 503).

The breach of a promise to marry after his wife's death, made by a married man to a woman who knows him to be married, is not actionable because it is both inconsistent with the normal affection between spouses and may contribute to immorality (*Wilson v. Carnley*, [1908] 1 K.B. 740).

Abuse of the Legal Process

Suppose that A gives B several hundred dollars to help pay for B's lawsuit against C—a lawsuit in which A is not involved. A's action in this case is held to be illegal and termed "maintenance," unless it is supported by either of the following reasons: (a) A contemplates bringing an action himself against C on similar grounds as those used by B; or (b) A is acting out of charity and has a bona fide opinon that B's lawsuit is a just and proper one; or (c) A is helping, according to past court cases, a "poor relative," a "servant," or a "poor co-religionist." If the above circumstances do not apply, then the contract of maintenance is illegal and therefore unenforceable.

Maintenance was the basis of an action in *Neville v. London Express*, [1919] A.C. 368 at p. 390, where Lord Haldane said, "It is unlawful for a stranger to render officious assistance by money or otherwise to another person in which the third person has himself no legal interest, for its prosecution or defence."

In the case of *Dann v. Curzon* (1910), 104 L.T. 66, the advertising manager of a theatre chain had hired his wife and a friend to wear wide-brim hats to a performance. They were arrested when he staged a disturbance objecting to their hats as obscuring his view. When he later sued for wages for this advertising gimmick, the courts ruled that such a suit causing unnecessary litigation was against "public policy" and therefore unenforceable.

Champerty, which is the maintenance of a quarrel for a share in the proceeds, is something which most courts in Canada have repeatedly declared makes an agreement unenforceable. Champerty agreements are well known and allowed in the United States where lawyers will often sue on behalf of a client on the understanding that the fee will consist of a percentage of the award, but little or nothing if the case is dismissed. There is a tendency to reconsider the legality of contracts involving champerty in connection with lawyers' fees, and Alberta and Manitoba, by statute, now allow such contracts. However, maintenance and champerty are regarded as unlawful in most provinces because they tend to encourage litigation which is not bona fide but speculative.

UNDUE RESTRAINT OF TRADE

There are some business contracts that are illegal because they may injure the public interest. They include certain types of contracts between: (a) employer and employee; (b) the seller and buyer of a business; and (c) partners in a business.

Employer and Employee
The courts feel that, because of the superior bargaining position of the employer, every attempt should be made to safeguard the interests of the employee. The general rule is that, while the courts will not enforce a contract that prohibits an individual from earning a living, they will enforce restraints placed on the employee not to reveal trade secrets or a knowledge of secret processes or to engage in a business either for him- or herself or for a competitor to canvass the same customers.

The case of *Reliable Toy Co. v. Collins*, [1950] 4 D.L.R. 499, dealt with a chemist who was employed by a company of toy manufacturers. He had signed an agreement not to reveal secrets of the company process for colouring toys to competitors if he left the plaintiff's employ. When he left and went to work for a competitor, the plaintiff sued him for breaches of trade secrets. It was found that, on one point, the manufacture of cheap masks to colour toys, he was probably liable for having given out information. The court held, quoting the case of *Morris v. Soxelby*, [1916] 1 A.C. 688:

> Prima facie, of course, contracts such as the secrecy agreement are void as being against public policy and restraint of trade. To the general rule there are certain exceptions arising out of the general confidential relationship of master and servant, and there is also an exception to be made where a specific contract with respect to secrecy is entered into; but in all cases the court will decide whether such restrictions go beyond affording reasonable protection. . . . The case in which the court interferes for the purpose of protection is where use is made, not of the skills which a man may have acquired, but the secrets of the trade or profession he had no right to reveal to anyone else.

The court held in this case that Collins had committed a secrecy infraction and awarded $2,500 damages in favour of the Reliable Toy Co.

The case of *Gordon v. Ferguson*, included in the Readings at the end of this chapter, illustrates the law relating to restrictive competition agreements between partners. It points out that such agreements must always (a) allow an individual to earn a living and (b) be reasonable both in extent of geographical area and length of time.

Seller and Buyer of a Business

The courts look with favour on a contract in which the purchaser of a going business requires the vendor not to set up a competing business within a certain clearly defined geographical area and within a certain period of time. The only tests that will be applied to this are whether such restraint is reasonable and whether it prevents the vendor from earning a living. If, for example, the requirement is not to set up a similar business in Canada, the courts will probably rule that the provision is prohibitive, preventing the individual from earning a living, and therefore unreasonable. As a general rule, the courts will not reduce the geographical scope or number of years of such a provision to bring it into line with what they consider reasonable. In other words, the courts will not attempt to alter the terms of the contract. They will merely decide on its reasonableness or unreasonableness.

The classic case involving this type of contract in restraint of trade is *Nordenfelt v. Maxim Nordenfelt Guns Ltd.*, [1894] A.C. 535. In this case a Mr. Nordenfelt, who had built up a worldwide business in the manufacture of guns, sold out to a company formed by a number of his employees. He signed two covenants (or personal promises). One stated that he would not engage in the manufacture of guns anywhere else in the world for 25 years; the other stated that he would not work for competitors during this period. The court, after deciding that gun manufacturing was a worldwide business, considered it reasonable that Nordenfelt should enter into a contract not to manufacture guns anywhere else in the world. However, the court ruled that the second covenant was unreasonable because it would prevent Nordenfelt from earning a living. The court also went a step further in this case and held that the two covenants were divisible and that it could enforce the first one and declare the second illegal and therefore unenforceable.

The present situation in law is that interferences with individual liberty of action in trading, and restraints of trade are contrary to public policy and therefore void. However, there are exceptions to the general rule. Thus restraints of trade may be justified by the special circumstances of a particular case. However, any restriction must be "reasonable"—reasonable, that is, with regard to the interests of the parties concerned and to the interests of the public.

STATUTORY ILLEGALITIES

Combines Investigation Act

The Combines Investigation Act was first passed in Canada in 1892 to prevent business combinations, mergers, or monopolies that could amount to a restraint of trade. This occurred about the same time as the Sherman Act was being passed in the United States for a similar purpose. The Canadian government made it a criminal offence to participate in restraint of competition between businesses. Enforcement has been difficult due to the necessity of proving beyond a reasonable doubt that a merger or monopoly is detrimental to the "public interest," by proving a criminal offence.

In the U.S.A., the Sherman Act and its amending Acts are enforced by civil actions which only require a "preponderance of proof" (which is a lesser degree of proof). Even so, the United States authorities did not succeed in convicting a company president or vice-president personally for restraint of trade practices until the 1960s. The first Canadian convictions against individuals were only obtained in the Hamilton dredging scandal for bid rigging as a restraint of trade in 1980.

The Combines Investigation Act is continually being revised. The following is a summary of the present restraint of trade offences under this Act which are discussed in greater detail in Chapter 26.

(a) Merger—two or more companies combining to control a sector of business (s. 32).
(b) Monopoly—one company controlling prices because of a sole manufacturing and distribution position, e.g., *R. v. Eddy Match Co.* (1951), 104 C.C.C. 39.
(c) Any criminal restraint of trade such as bid rigging or following the leader's pricing guide (s. 32).
(d) Predatory pricing—i.e., price cutting a competitor out of business (s. 34).
(e) Discriminatory discounts—in the case of purchases of similar quantity and quality (s. 35).

(f) Misleading advertising (s. 36).

(g) Resale price maintenance—i.e., a manufacturer setting a minimum price at which products are to be sold (s. 38).

(h) A Canadian subsidiary of an American company following American rather than Canadian law.

This Act also contains provisions which allow the Restrictive Trade Practices Commission to review practices which may be against the public interest such as *refusal to deal, consignment sales, tied sales,* and *exclusive dealing*, which are practices which have been employed to keep prices up against the public interest.

There is one recent innovation in the combines legislation—namely, that the individual who suffers damages as a result of an offence under the Combines Investigation Act is provided with a *civil right of action* arising out of the offence. The trend of decided cases to date has provided that no right of action is created by the breach of other criminal statutes. It remains to be seen whether this remedy will be used and upheld since it seems to infringe on the provincial sphere of legislation, property and civil rights.

Consumer Protection Acts

There are also some provincial statutes that render certain transactions unenforceable or "voidable." For example, the Ontario Consumer Protection Act provides that a consumer must be given a written memorandum of any credit sales transaction over $50; otherwise he or she is not bound by its terms. As another example, the Ontario Landlord and Tenant Act provides that in the case of residential leases of a year or more, tenants not given a copy of the lease within twenty-one days are not bound by its provisions.

Some statutes place prohibitions on the contracting parties. Thus, for example, under the Ontario Consumer Protection Act, the consumer purchaser may not legally agree to give up the implied conditions and warranties of the Ontario Sales of Goods Act. Under the Ontario Family Law Reform Act, any disposition of the matrimonial home without the consent of both parties to a marriage is not binding. Under the Workers' Compensation Act, any agreement by an employee to waive his or her benefits is invalid.

The main Act in Ontario that permits individuals to withdraw from contracts is the *Business Practices Act*. This Act, discussed in Chapter 28, specifies over twenty different types of deceptive practices or unfair representations that allow a customer to void a contract.

Interest Act

At the federal level, the Interest Act provides that if no interest is stipulated in a loan agreement, no interest may be charged, and, if interest is mentioned but the rate is omitted, the maximum allowed per annum is 5%. The Lord's Day Act restricts activities on a Sunday to acts of mercy (such as an ambulance) or of necessity (such as a restaurant), but the provinces have been allowed to relax these restrictions, so that in most of Ontario, for example, according to the polled wishes of the residents of each county, liquor outlets, theatres, sports, and commodity stores with a restricted floor space and a number of employees are also allowed to open.

Partnerships Registration Act

The Ontario Partnerships Registration Act provides that an unregistered partnership may not sue in court—for example, to recover moneys owed to it by customers.

Unlicensed Work

According to various judgments (e.g., *Calax Construction Inc. v. Lepofsky* (1974), 5 O.R. (2d) 259 (H.C.)), the courts will refuse to allow an unlicensed tradesperson in those trades which require a licence, to pursue in contract law a claim for services. Thus, for example, in the case of *Kocotis v. D'Angelo* (1958), 13 D.L.R. (2d) 69, an unlicensed maintenance electrician performed work as an electrical contractor on behalf of the defendant, who had started doing the job personally but sought assistance when an inspector refused to pass the work. The (unlicensed electrician) plaintiff, although not being licensed for such work, sued for the balance of the contract price. However, a municipal bylaw, duly authorized under provincial legislation, provided that no person, not properly licensed thereunder, should contract for or do electrical work in the municipality and also forbade the hiring or employment of any person not so licensed. On appeal the court held that the contract was illegal and the court would not enforce it. The purpose of the bylaw was to protect the public against mistakes and loss that might arise from work done by unqualified electricians. The fact that it did not expressly exclude contract suits made by an unlicensed person was immaterial. It was clear that a person who entered into a contract in disobedience of the bylaw was making a forbidden contract and it could not be enforced.

Usury

The term usury is used to describe money-lending contracts in which the rate of interest is exorbitantly high. At one time, the "fair" rate of interest was based on a common law precedent that said that 48% per annum was not unfair. However, courts in Canada have not hesitated in the past to state that much lower rates of interest might be ruled "unconscionable." The maximum rate is controlled in Ontario by the Unconscionable Transactions Relief Act, while the federal government, by the Criminal Code, makes "loan sharking" (charging an interest rate of 60% or more per annum) a criminal offence.

Bets and Wagers

Betting is not illegal in Canada. However, an unpaid winner cannot obtain the court's help to collect the winnings. Indeed, if the wager involves a sport or pastime and the loser has already paid the debt, which amounts to over

$50, the Ontario Gaming Act, as one provincial example, allows the bettor to go to court within three months and reclaim the money.

The case of *Shaw v. Carter* (186), 26 L.C.J. 57, involved a contract that was considered illegal because of its gambling nature. In this case a contract was made by the defendant with a broker for the purchase of certain amounts of grain on the Chicago Grain Exchange. When the price of grain dropped, the purchaser refused to remit an amount equivalent to the loss to the broker. Accordingly, the broker sued for the amount outstanding. The court held that:

> A sale of goods to be delivered at a future period, admittedly made without any intention on the part of the seller to deliver or on the part of the purchaser to receive delivery of the goods, and on the understanding that the parties should settle with each other, at the period fixed for delivery by one party paying to the other the difference between the price of the sale and that which might prevail at the period fixed for delivery, is a mere gambling transaction and therefore, illegal, null and void.

The common law recognized a "wager" or "bet" as a type of contract that was not always enforceable but that was not necessarily illegal. A *wager* was described as follows in *Thacker v. Hardy* (1878), 4 Q.B.D. 685 at p. 695: "The essence of gaming and wagering is that one party is to win and the other to lose upon a future event, which at the time of the contract is of an uncertain nature—that is to say, if an event turns out one way, A will lose, but if it turns out the other way, he will win."

Generally, at common law, wagers which depended on the happening or ascertaining of an uncertain event made entirely for sport or pastime were enforceable. For example, in the famous case of *March v. Pigot* (1771), 5 Burr. 2802, two young men bet on the duration of their fathers' lives.

Eventually the courts ruled, as unenforceable, wagers that dealt with an indecent matter or that caused pain and injury to a third person, or tempted someone to break the law. Statutes were then passed that established the present rule that wagers are unenforceable; except that in Ontario, for example, in the case of a bet on a sport or pastime, if the loser has paid, the courts will assist in getting his or her money back.

Marine insurance, which is a type of wager, was unenforceable at common law unless the party taking out the insurance had an insurable interest. Although both marine insurance on cargoes today proceeding by sea, rail, road, or air, and life insurance require an insurable interest, the marine or fire insurance is to be paid only in the case of an event that may or may not happen; while in the case of life insurance, the event (death) must happen sooner or later.

REVIEW QUESTIONS

1. What is the attitude of the courts towards contracts formed for an illegal purpose?

2. Differentiate between "void" and "illegal" contracts.
3. Give an example of your own of an illegal contract involving: (a) a crime; (b) a tort.
4. Explain and discuss the legal effect of immorality when it is the subject matter of a contract.
5. Give two everyday examples of *obstruction of justice situations* in contracts.
6. In some societies, it is traditional to seek the services of a marriage broker to arrange suitable marriages. Discuss whether such contracts should be made legally enforceable in Canada? How enforceable are dating bureau contracts?
7. Do you believe there is any need for prohibiting contracts that involve a *maintenance* situation?
8. Illustrate with examples your understanding of the three main common law restraint of trade situations.
9. What is the basic difference between the criminal law requirement of proof—that is, "beyond a reasonable doubt" and the civil law requirement of "a preponderance of proof"? Discuss situations that might serve to illustrate this difference.
10. Give some examples of what you understand by misleading advertising under the Combines Investigation Act.
11. Give examples illustrating five different ways of avoiding a consumer contract under the Ontario Business Practices Act.
12. What attitude would the courts take towards an unlicensed lawyer or other professional who entered into contracts with customers who later failed to pay for the services received?
13. What statutes exist to regulate interest in Canada?
14. What is the Lord's Day Act? How does it operate in your province?
15. Why do the courts allow insurance claims yet not enforce betting contracts?

PROBLEMS

1. A person who had a claim for damages in tort did not have the financial means to pursue his claim. For this reason, and because he did not wish to incur legal fees if the action were unsuccessful, he made a special arrangement with his lawyer. This was that the lawyer should conduct the case on the basis that, if the claimant won, the lawyer should receive one-half of the recovered damages as his fee; if the claimant lost, the lawyer was to receive nothing. The lawyer won the case. What are the legal complications, if any, resulting from this situation?
2. A agreed to buy 1,000 shares from B, a stock promoter. The price of the shares on the day of the contract was $10 each. It was agreed that the price of the shares for the purpose of the sale would be calculated according to their market value on the fourteenth day after the contract was signed. If the price were to go up, A would receive the increase. If the price were to

go down, A would make up the loss, with no shares changing hands. The shares went up to $13 each. A consequently claimed $3,000. B objected that this amounted to gambling. Could A sue for the difference?

3. Mr. Maxwell was employed as a salesman of farming implements. He met a Mrs. T who told him that she would give him a $1,000 bonus for the loan of $4,000 for a month. He loaned her the money and was duly repaid. Thereafter he entered into many such loan ventures with Mrs. T, always at approximately the same rate of return. He then met a Mr. Dempster, who was a successful farmer and interested in making investments, about the time that Mrs. T asked him for a $15,000 loan. Maxwell asked Dempster whether he would like to lend him $15,000 to be given to Mrs. T and promised to return $21,000 in two days. Dempster then provided the money, and was repaid two days later by Maxwell, Mrs. T having repaid $25,000 (for a two-day loan of $15,000), of which $21,000 was given to Mr. Dempster, leaving Mr. Maxwell with a profit of $4,000. Later Mr. Maxwell asked Mr. Dempster for a loan of $40,000. Dempster tried to find out the purpose of the $40,000 advance, but Maxwell could tell him only that he was borrowing for Mrs. T. Maxwell offered a $20,000 bonus this time, but Dempster insisted on $30,000 which was finally agreed on. Mr. Maxwell is now bringing this action to reopen a transaction under the Unconscionable Transactions Relief Act, R.S.O. 1970, c. 472, s. 2: "Where, in respect of money lent, the court finds that, having regard to the risk and to all the circumstances, the cost of the loan is excessive and that a transaction is harsh and unconscionable, the Court may:

(a) reopen the transaction . . .

(b) notwithstanding any . . . agreement . . . reopen any account . . . and relieve the debtor from payment of any sum in excess . . .

(c) order the creditor to repay any such excess . . .

(d) set aside either wholly or in part or revise or alter any security given or agreement made in respect of money lent. . . ."

Courts of equity have for many years set aside transactions which were unconscionable. Material ingredients are proof of inequality in the position of the parties arising out of ignorance, need or distress of the weaker.

In three Ontario cases the view has been expressed that excessive interest alone may be sufficient to render the bargain harsh and unconscionable. In such cases the rate of interest was exacted from the borrower who was in dire need of the money and in none of such cases was the borrower in a position to make his own bargain on terms of equality.

In *All Canadian Peoples Finance Ltd. v. Marcjan* (1970), 10 D.L.R. (3d) 352, the court refused to set aside four short-term mortgages with rates from 60% to 74% where the borrower, a land speculator, stood to earn high profits.

Discuss who should win this case, giving legal reasons which support (a) Mr. Maxwell; (b) Mr. Dempster.

4. B is a partner in a partnership of real estate developers. Learning that his

firm is looking for a property identical to one that he already owns, he arranges for its sale to the firm without the other partners being aware that the property was his. Can his partners cancel the agreement of purchase when they learn the true facts, even if the property were the best obtainable at the time? Explain your answer.

READINGS

Scott v. Brown, Doering, McNab & Co., [1982] 2 Q.B. 724 (C.A.).

Facts: In this case the plaintiff brought an action against some stock-brokers, through whom he had purchased shares in a projected company, to obtain rescission of the purchase contract and repayment of the purchase money on the ground that the defendants, while acting as the plaintiff's brokers, had delivered their own shares to him instead of purchasing them on the stock exchange. At the trial it appeared from the plaintiff's own evidence that the money sought to be recovered had been paid by the plaintiff in pursuance of an agreement between him and one of the defendants by which such defendant was, with the money, to purchase on the stock exchange a number of shares in the company at a premium with the sole object of inducing the public to believe that there was a real market for the shares and that they were at a real premium. The object, in other words, was "to rig the market." The court applied the principle of *ex turpi causa non oritur actio.* Since the action was based on an illegal contract, the money could not be recovered. It was the transaction of purchase on the market at a particular price, and not the thing purchased, of which an illegal use was to be made.

Held per Lindley L.J. at p. 729:

The plaintiff's purchase was an actual purchase, not a sham purchase; that is true, but it is also true that the sole object of the purchase was to cheat and mislead the public. Under these circumstances the plaintiff must look elsewhere than to a court of justice for such assistance as he may require against the persons he employed to assist him in his fraud, if the claim to such assistance is based on his illegal contract. Any right which he may have irrespective of his illegal contract will, of course, be recognized and enforced. But his illegal contract confers no right on him: see *Pearce v. Brooks.*

Albert E. Daniels Ltd. v. Sangster (1976), 12 O.R. (2d) 512 (Co. Ct.).

Facts: The defendants entered into two successive contracts to lease a Pinto motor vehicle from Hamilton Hertz, a car rental agency, for the period from May to December 1973. The defendants failed to pay $1,115.26 owing on these contracts, alleging that the plaintiff company was not registered under the Corporations Information Act, S.O. 1971, and that the contract was therefore an illegality and the plaintiff could not collect.

Held per Lazier Co. Ct. J.:

I refer to the Corporations Information Act, 1971 and in particular s. 2 . . .: "2(1) No corporation shall carry on business in Ontario or identify itself . . . by a name or style other than its corporate name unless the name or style is first registered with the Minister." [Under penalty of up to $20,000 if the offender is a corporation; with a limitation period of one year after facts come to the knowledge of the Minister of Consumer and Commercial Relations.]

[The judge cited the following decisions:] *Calax Construction Inc. v. Lepofsky* (1974), 5 O.R. (2d) 259 at p. 260 . . .: "The general principle, founded on public policy, is that any transaction that is tainted by illegality in which both parties are equally involved is beyond the pale of the law. No person can claim any right or remedy whatsoever under an illegal transaction in which he has participated."

. . . [In] *St. John Shipping Corp. v. Joseph Rank Ltd.*, [1956] 3 All E.R. 683 . . . there was a contract of carriage . . . the plaintiffs conveyed a cargo of wheat in their ship, which when bunkered with fuel submerged below the load-line contrary to the provisions of the Merchant Shipping (Safety and Load-Line Conventions) Act, 1932. The maximum fine of 1,200 pounds [sterling] was imposed . . . but the freight earned . . . was 2,295 pounds. The defendant . . . withheld 2,000 pounds . . . [contending] that the contract was unenforceable . . . by reason of the illegality. . . . "[O]n the true construction of the Act of 1932 the contract for the carriage of goods in the ship was not within the ambit of the prohibition against overloading . . . accordingly did not render the contract unenforceable for illegality." . . .

"There are two general principles. The first is that a contract which is entered into with the object of committing an illegal act is unenforceable. . . . [I]f the intent is mutual [i.e., to break the law] the contract is not enforceable at all, and, if unilateral, it is unenforceable at the suit of the party who is proved to have it. . . . The second principle is that the court will not enforce a contract which is expressly or impliedly prohibited by statute." [Thus, in the former, one looks at the Acts which are prohibited; in the latter case, the contracts which are prohibited.] . . .

. . . [T]he Corporations Information Act, 1971 does not prohibit contracts of any sort, either expressly or impliedly. . . .

Shaw v. Groom, [1970] 2 Q.B. 504 . . . was a case where the plaintiff let a room in her house to the defendant for residential purposes at a rent of 7s. 11d. a week. [Neither of two] rent books contained all the information required by the Landlord and Tenant Act, 1962. . . . [T]he landlord's failure . . . [was] punishable by a maximum fine of 50 pounds.

On a claim by plaintiff . . . for arrears of rent amounting to 103 pounds, the defendant . . . contended that . . . [failure] to provide her with a proper rent book [was] an offence. . . .

"Held, allowing the appeal, (1) that since the plaintiff did not have to rely on the rent book as an essential ingredient for her cause of action and since the obligation to provide a rent book formed no part of the contract of letting but was a statutory requirement collateral to it, there was no illegality committed in the performance of the contract, and. . . . (2) that, in any event, where an illegality was committed in the course of performing a legal contract, the test as to the enforceability of the contract was whether on a true consideration of the relevant legislation as a whole Parliament had intended to preclude the plaintiff from enforcing the contract. . . ."

. . . [I]n *Kocotis v. D'Angelo*, [1958] O.R. 104 . . .: "The true rule is that the Court should carefully consider in each case the terms of the statute or enactment which prohibits an act under a penalty, its object, the evil it was enacted to remedy and the effect of holding contracts in relation to it void . . . and, if from all these considerations such an intention does not manifestly appear, the contracts should be sustained and enforced, otherwise they should be held void."

[For example in the following Acts, there is a provision against recovering charges for services] "The Medical Act, R.S.O. 1950 c. 228, s. 52, declares that a person not registered under the Act is not entitled to recover charges for his services." [Similarly the Veterinary Science Practice Act, the Solicitors Act, the Dentistry Act, the Real Estate and Business Brokers Act, and the Pharmacy Act prohibit an unlicensed party from recovering fees for services.]

. . . [O]n a consideration of the provisions of the Corporations Information Act, 1971 . . . in addition to the penalty there is no deprivation of the right of a corporation to recover for services in the course of its daily business. . . .

Accordingly, I do not find that the contracts entered into by the plaintiff with the defendant . . . are illegal and unenforceable.

. . . [E]x. 3 sets forth on its face "Hamilton Hertz a division of A.E. Daniels Ltd." The defendant can hardly allege it did not know that A.E. Daniels was involved with Hamilton Hertz. . . .

The plaintiff is entitled to judgment in the amount of $1,115.26 and costs.

Gordon v. Ferguson (1961), 30 D.L.R. (2d) 420 (N.S. S.C.).

Facts: Dr. Gordon employed a younger doctor, Dr. Ferguson, in his practice of medicine in Dartmouth, with the following provision in his employment contract: "The employee shall not, on the termination for any cause whatever of his employment herein, engage in the practice of medicine and/or surgery similar to that now carried on by the employer, or engage to work for any person, firm, or association of medical practitioners in the vicinity within the Town of Dartmouth . . . and a radius of twenty miles from the boundaries thereof, for a period of five years from the time the employment under this agreement ceases." The agreement was legally terminated by notice on January 5, 1961. Thereupon Dr. Ferguson opened a practice in Dartmouth and Dr. Gordon sued for an injunction to stop him under the foregoing clause. The trial judge held the contract reasonable insofar as the parties were concerned but unreasonable in point of area.

Held (on appeal) per MacDonald J.:

The clause prohibits certain types of activity in a local area for a specified period of time. The clause involves a restraint of trade and is presumed to be void as contrary to public policy but will be upheld if found to be reasonable having regard to the legitimate interests of the parties and also of the public. . . . The employer is entitled to covenant against misuse of trade secrets of which knowledge will be acquired in his service and . . . to prevent customers, clients or patients from being enticed away from him by a servant who has acquired knowledge of them or influence over them in the course of his service (See *Cheshire & Fifoot on Contracts*, 5th ed., p. 316). . . .

. . . [T]he restriction (in so far as it prohibits the practice of medicine of the kind specified) has the effect of preventing the employee from professional dealings . . . in the area . . . [unconnected] with the practice of the employer. . . . This is a clear ground of invalidity. (See *New Method Cleaners & Launderers Ltd. v. Hartley*, [1939] 1 D.L.R. 711.) . . . The root idea which permits restriction of the future activities of an employee as reasonable [is expressed in *Routh v. Jones*, [1947] 1 All E.R. 179 at p. 181:] ". . . the master would be exposed to *unfair competition* on the part of his former servant— *competition flowing* not so much from the personal skill of his former servant as *from the intimacies and knowledge of the master's business acquired by the servant from the circumstances of his employment.*" . . .

This inclusiveness of the ban on subsequent practice . . . taken in conjunction with the width of the area . . . and the length of time . . . is a factor . . . which cannot be cured by the doctrine of severance. . . .

. . . It is my view . . . that once the question of the legality of cl. 8 was put in issue, the question fell to be considered on the basis of the clause as written; and that no voluntary contraction of its physical coverage [because the plaintiff was willing to restrict the ban to Dartmouth] can avail to save it if the clause is invalid, *cf. Mills v. Gill*, [1952] 3 D.L.R. 27. . . .

. . . [I]n my view . . . the covenant, properly construed, is invalid for the reason indicated above and because it purports to apply to an area excessive in extent.

10

Statute of Frauds and the Requirement of Writing

In the seventeenth century, the British Parliament decided that certain types of contracts should be put in writing to be enforceable in court. Accordingly, in 1677, an Act entitled the "Statute of Frauds" was passed. Later, in the nineteenth century, each provincial legislature in Canada enacted a similar statute. Today, furthermore, other provincial statutes, such as the Sale of Goods Act, the Consumer Protection Act, and the Residential Tenancies Act, require written evidence.

STATUTE OF FRAUDS

In Ontario, s. 4 of the Statute of Frauds states that:

> No action shall be brought:
> (1) Whereby to charge any executor or administrator upon any special promise to answer damages out of his own estate, or
> (2) Whereby to charge any person upon any special promise to answer for the debt, default or miscarriage of any other person, or
> (3) To charge any person upon any contract or sale of lands, tenements or hereditaments or any interest in or concerning them, or
> (4) Upon any agreement that is not to be performed within the space of one year from the making thereof, or
> (5) Unless the agreement upon which the action is brought, or some memorandum or note thereof, is in writing and signed by the party to be charged therewith or some person thereunto by him lawfully authorized.

It is now possible, therefore, for a contract to be valid but, because it is not in writing, to be unenforceable in our courts. An example of this would be a person going to work for someone else on an oral contract for a period of three years. Let us say that he works for six months at $500 a month but has not been paid the $3,000 in wages. Under the Statute of Frauds he could not take the employer to court because this particular type of contract must be in writing to be enforceable. However, such a contract, although unenforceable, is still legally valid and could serve as a legally valid defence in court— for example, as a "set off" against money owed for some other reason to the employer. Thus, in the previous example, suppose the employee had purchased a secondhand car from his employer on which there was still $3,000 owing. Then his entitlement to $3,000 in unpaid wages, although not enforceable as a court claim, could be used by him as a defence against his employer's claim for the balance owing on the used car.

In the case of a future purchase of land, any deposit paid would have to be returned should the owner refuse to sell.

There are, of course, various advantages to having a contract in writing: the terms of the agreement are clearly specified; and it is not necessary to resort to memory or to call witnesses to determine just what was agreed.

Written Memorandum

From the court's point of view, the memorandum or other written evidence of the contract must contain all the essentials of a contract. Therefore if no mention is made of consideration, or the terms are uncertain, the contract is void. However, the memorandum need not be signed by both parties to make the contract enforceable. So long as the party that is being sued has placed his signature on the document, that is sufficient.

Suppose, for example, that a senior employee in a large company has been hired on an oral basis only. If this employee receives a termination notice that recognizes the terms of her employment and is signed by a company officer, this may be sufficient written evidence for a claim in court for wages still owed according to the terms of the oral contract of hiring. The important requirement is that the signature on the writing containing the terms of the contract be that of the party being sued. The signature of the plaintiff is not necessary.

Documents made under seal (called *specialties*) must by their very nature be in writing. An example is a deed transferring ownership of land and buildings from one party to another.

Let us now consider, in turn, each type of contract specified in the provincial Statute of Frauds.

Executor's Promise

This refers to the possibility that a deceased person's creditors may claim that the executor or administrator of a deceased person's estate promised to pay a claim against the deceased from his own pocket. For example, suppose that A was named in a will as the executor of a friend and, while at the funeral parlour, a creditor approached A regarding an outstanding claim against the deceased. To prevent any embarrassment, A whispered to the creditor that he would take care of the debt. Such a promise being oral would not be enforceable against A personally under the provisions of the Statute of Frauds.

Of course, the executor's function is to pay all legitimate claims against the deceased out of the proceeds of the estate before distributing the balance to the beneficiaries or heirs. In fact, few cases have been taken to court under this provision.

Guarantee

Suppose that A goes to a bank for a loan and the bank manager asks him for a guarantor. When told that B will guarantee the request for a loan, the bank manager telephones B and asks if she will repay the loan if A does not. If B agrees, then she is assuming secondary liability and, according to the law, should make such an agreement in writing. However, suppose that B, on hearing that A wants to borrow money, tells the bank manager to let A have the money and that B will repay the loan whether or not A repays it. Then B is considered by the courts to have assumed primary liability, which is a contract of indemnity, not covered by the Statute of Frauds, and therefore not required to be in writing.

An illustration of a contract that involved the distinction between a guarantee and an indemnity is *Sutton & Company v. Grey*, [1894] 1 Q.B. 285. In this case, the defendant, Grey, agreed to arrange on behalf of the plaintiffs, contracts for the sale of stocks. The idea was that he would receive half the commission earned by the plaintiffs as a result of stock sold. However, if the plaintiffs suffered any loss in these transactions, Grey would reimburse them. They did in fact suffer losses and, because the defendant failed to reimburse them, they sued him. The court held that if the defendant had been wholly unconnected with the contract except by his promise to pay the loss, then it was a guarantee and must be in writing; that if it was mixed or combined with another transaction whereby the defendant could gain, then it was not a guarantee but an indemnity which was enforceable even though not in writing.

A similar situation exists in the case of a *del credere* agency. This is a situation where an agent undertakes to sell goods on behalf of a client, but also guarantees payment out of his own pocket should the purchasers fail to pay. While normal guarantees must be in writing to be enforceable, the *del credere* agency is an exception. This is because the guarantee or promise to repay does not stand by itself but is combined with another transaction: namely, making sales for commission as an agent, and therefore such an agreement is enforceable even if only oral.

A particular twist in this distinction between a guarantee and an indemnity arises when an oral guarantee is given for a minor's contract for a non-necessity. Since the minor is not liable personally, the guarantor's contract might be regarded as one of indemnity, or direct promise to pay or to assume the primary liability, therefore an indemnity. The opposite argument could also apply. For example, suppose A agreed to guarantee a friend's written contract to purchase a large livingroom divan. On delivery, it was realized that the divan could not be moved through the door of the apartment, so it was returned and replaced by two smaller sections, without any knowledge on the part of the co-signor. In this case, the guarantor might be relieved of liability because of a change in the terms of the contract, even though the requirements of the Statute of Frauds are met. Thus any change in the nature of the contract of guarantee, without the knowledge and concurrence of the guarantor, normally serves to relieve the guarantor of any further liability under the contract.

Land Contracts

A conveyance, deed, or mortgage, any one of which is required to transfer the legal title or ownership of land from A to B, must be in writing and under seal; so also must be a lease over three years. All other transactions dealing with land, although not necessarily required to be under seal, must always be in writing to be enforceable. Thus the listing of a property for sale with a real estate broker, the offer to purchase, the acceptance, the demand for requisitions (for example, to clear up defects of title), and all the documents that relate to land must be in writing. Oddly enough, agreements to build a house, execute repairs, or obtain board and lodging are not required to be in writing.

The requirement of writing for a land contract is illustrated by the case of *Pearce v. Gardner*, [1897] 1 Q.B. 688. In this case, the plaintiff desired to buy some gravel to be dug and carried away. The defendant objected and claimed that there was no memorandum as required for the sale of land.

The plaintiff produced a letter addressed "Dear Sir," containing all the necessary information except his name and he said he had received it in a letter addressed to himself. The judge held that the envelope was a necessary concomitant of the letter without which it would not have reached its destination. According to his words, "If the name of the plaintiff had appeared on the letter that would have been sufficient, and in my opinion the effect is the same where the name appears on the envelope in which it was sent."

It should also be pointed out that a contract may be determined from the contents of more than one letter if it can be shown that these letters are related to each other.

Many cases under the heading of land contracts involve family situations in which a grown son or daughter has stayed home on the promise that he or she alone will inherit the family home or farm when the parents die. Often, when the will is read, the property is divided among all the children, despite the oral promise. Other cases involve the claims of legitimate heirs who believe they have been cheated out of their rightful inheritance—for example, when a housekeeper has been able to produce a note from her employer stating that if she looked after him for the rest of his life the home would become hers when the employer died. An example of this is *Thomas v. Thomas*, [1924] 2 Q.B. 851 referred to on page 132 in Chapter 6 dealing with consideration.

Part Performance.   Sometimes, in the case of land, part performance may eliminate the requirement of writing. Thus in the case of *Rawlinson v. Ames*, [1925] Ch. 96, the landlord made certain alterations to a flat at the request and under the supervision of the defendant. The defendant then refused to go through with the contract and was sued by the landlord. The judge held:

The true ground of the doctrine [of part performance] in equity is that if the court found a man in occupation of land or doing such acts with regard to it as would, prima facie, make him liable at law to an action of trespass, the court would hold that there was strong evidence from the nature of the use of the land that a contract existed and would therefore allow verbal evidence to be given to show the real circumstances under which possession was taken.

It was pointed out that there are three conditions necessary for part performance: (a) the contract must refer to land; (b) the acts must be referable to the contract alleged; and (c) it must be a fraud to take advantage of the fact that the contract is not in writing; that is, the plaintiff must perform the acts and he must suffer a loss if the contract is not enforced.

The courts have also held that payment of rent itself is not sufficient part performance to remove the contract from the scope of the Statute of Frauds. Some additional overt act, such as leaving baggage or painting a wall, must also have taken place.

Contracts for One Year or More
According to the law, contracts that cannot be performed by either party within one year from the date of making, should be in writing.

Thus if I hire A to work for me at $1,000 a month for two years the contract must be in writing, since neither A nor myself can complete our terms of the contract before the expiry of the two-year period.

Suppose, however, I hire A to work for me at a salary of $1,000 a month for the rest of her life. Since A could very well die within a year, and thus complete her part of the contract, the contract would not need to be in writing (according to the interpretation which has been placed on the final provision of s. 4 of the Ontario Statute of Frauds).

Employment contracts are discussed in detail in Chapter 19 (Employing Other Persons).

Also, suppose that I hire A for $1,000 a month for a period of two years with the proviso that, if her work is satisfactory, I will deposit the full salary to her credit in the local bank within six months. This contract is not within the Statute because I have performed my portion of the contract within the year's time limit.

An illustrative case of a contract of indefinite hiring which it was alleged could not be fulfilled by either party within the year was that of *Adams v. Union Cinemas Ltd.*, [1939] 3 All E.R. 136.

In this case, a person named Adams became the controller of a theatre chain at a salary of 2,000 pounds a year. He was hired for at least two years, but the contract was never put into writing. Later, the control of the company changed and Adams was given one month's notice. He sued for the balance of his two years' salary, but the defendant objected that the contract was for over a year and could not be performed by either party within the year and therefore should have been in writing. In this case one of the judges made the following statement:

I must confess that I should be very sorry to have to explain the facts of this case and the importance of the legal issues in this case to a foreigner, because I cannot imagine him asking: "Why is it that counsel for the defendants was apparently much more anxious even than the counsel for the plaintiffs to show that his client had entered into an agreement to employ the plaintiff for a longer time and at a larger salary? Is it because of undue generosity? . . . I can imagine that when one had to tell him that the reason was that, if only the defendants could satisfy the court that they had given their word to the plaintiff that they would employ him for two years . . . they need not pay him a penny and they were not bound to employ him.

The court found that Adams had only a contract of indefinite hiring, which could be performed within the year (that is, death). Therefore, it was enforceable even though oral. The court went on to say that in this case the contract could not be put to an end at a moment's notice. There would have to be a reasonable notice on either side: "I do not think having regard to the importance of it [employment] that one can possibly say that six months' notice is too much."

OTHER STATUTES

Sale of Goods Act

Each province has a Sale of Goods Act that, except for British Columbia, stipulates that with regard to the sale of goods for more than $40 there must be some evidence, either in the form of a written note or memorandum, or in the form of part receipt or payment, of all contracts dealing with the sale of goods which are purely executory—that is, to be carried out in the future. (This requirement has been deleted in B.C.). Thus, according to s. 5(1) of the Ontario's Sale of Goods Act:

> A contract for the sale of goods of the value of $40 or more is not enforceable by action unless the buyer accepts part of the goods so sold and actually receives them, or gives something in earnest to bind the contract or in part payment, or unless some note or memorandum in writing of the contract is made and signed by the party to be charged or his agent in that behalf.

The principle with regard to the sale of goods is that there must be some evidence, either in the form of a written memorandum, or in the form of part performance, in all contracts dealing with the sale of goods which are purely executory, that is, to be carried out in the future.

It should be noted that the Sale of Goods Act does not apply to barter, to hire, to consignment sales, to contracts where goods and services are mixed—for example, the repair of an automobile—nor to contracts involving real property.

The provision requiring writing or part performance does not apply to a sale which only exceeds $40 when the sales tax is added. However, the Sale of Goods provisions would apply to several purchases, each under $40, which total more than $40.

Even inspection of the goods to determine whether the shipment consists of the goods ordered, may constitute sufficient acceptance and part performance to eliminate the necessity for writing.

Sometimes a contract may come under the provisions of both the Sale of Goods Act and the Statute of Frauds. For example, an oral contract to deliver goods by instalment every three months for two years. This contract would be unenforceable under the Statute of Frauds because it is for over a year and incapable of completion by either party within the year. But otherwise it would be enforceable under the Sale of Goods Act because of the partial delivery.

Consumer Protection Act

All common law provinces now have Consumer Protection Acts relating to consumer purchases of goods or services—that is, goods for consumption by individuals as opposed to a business. These statutes provide that executory contracts for such goods or services, where the delivery, performance or payment is not made immediately, must be in writing. Also, each party must have a copy of the contract, including the details of any credit terms involved. In one case, the lender in a credit transaction was denied a right to recovery because a copy of the credit terms had been given to only one of the co-signors of the promissory note—namely, the husband but not the wife (*Household Finance Corp. v. McEllim*, [1970] 5 W.W.R. 187).

Ontario's Consumer Protection Act applies to executory contracts of $50 or more.

REVIEW QUESTIONS

1. What is the Statute of Frauds? What are its purposes?
2. Which types of contract are regulated by the Statute of Frauds?
3. "It is possible for a contract to be valid but unenforceable." Explain.
4. What is a "specialty"? Does it need to be in writing to be legally enforceable?
5. Distinguish, with an example, between a contract of guarantee and a contract of indemnity. Do they need to be in writing to be enforceable? Explain.
6. Does a *del credere* agency agreement need to be in writing to be enforceable? Explain.
7. Do the following need to be in writing to be enforceable: (a) a contract for the sale of land; (b) a contract for the sale of land and buildings, (c) a one-year lease; (d) a three-year lease?
8. Explain, with an illustration, the rule that part performance, in the case of a real estate transaction, may eliminate the requirement of writing.
9. What three conditions are necessary if a plea of part performance is to succeed in a breach of contract dispute?

10. Explain, with an employment example, the legal rule that contracts that cannot be performed within one year from the date of making should be in writing.

11. The Sale of Goods Act for each province stipulates that certain contracts must be in writing to be enforceable. What are they? What is the purpose of this rule?

12. What do you understand by the content of the memorandum that is required to satisfy the requirements of the Statute of Frauds?

13. A water pump is used in connection with repairs to a motorcar done by a mechanic under an oral contract. The service-station bill shows $60 for the pump and $25 for the repairs. If you do not pay, how much can the service station sue for? Which Act is involved?

14. The reason why the Consumer Protection Act requires writing for credit transactions is to ensure that buyers are made aware of all the charges included—not only the interest but also all additional charges, such as setting up the credit account, insurance, delivery charges, yearly maintenance, and so on. Discuss the usefulness of this statutory requirement among today's educated consumers.

15. What is the reason for the present distinction in the written requirements between an indemnity and a guarantee?

16. If a minor reneges on a loan guaranteed orally by her father, would there be any grounds for arguing that the father is nevertheless bound to pay?

PROBLEMS

1. John entered into an oral contract with Frank whereby Frank was to receive a commission of 5% if he was successful in selling John's house for $40,000. After the sale, John refused to pay the commission and wrote the following letter to Frank, "I know that we discussed the question of your selling my house for $40,000, for a 5% commission, but you will recall that there were no witnesses and neither one of us signed an agreement," signed John. What action can Frank take to seek his commission, in view of the fact that there was only an oral contract dealing with the proposed sale?

2. Frank and Henry entered into a written contract whereby Henry was to pay $100,000 for a house which Frank was to build according to an architect's specifications. Later Frank and Henry orally agreed to simplify the house for a decrease in price of $20,000. At the completion of the building, Henry paid only $80,000. Could Frank successfully sue for the balance of the original price?

3. Two brothers, who were both doctors, married two sisters and set up their practice in a small town. Each appointed the other as his executor in case of death. One day brother A was involved in an accident while driving his Ferrari and died of injuries. A large department store, learning of his accidental death, telephoned brother B and asked who would pay for the mink coat the deceased had just purchased for $5,000 and was taking to his wife at the time of the accident. Brother B promised, over the tele-

phone, to pay; but when the estate was settled, there was no money left to meet his claim. What is B's personal liability in this case? Explain.

4. Consider the facts in the case of *Yeoman Credit Ltd. v. Lather*, [1961] 2 All E.R. 294. The defendants entered into a hire-purchase agreement for a car with the plaintiff. (This is a form of conditional sale contract common in England.) The first defendant was known by all parties to be an infant, and the second defendant signed a contract which was stated to be a "Hire-Purchase Indemnity and Undertaking." The infant defendant paid the deposit but defaulted on the monthly instalments. The plaintiff sued the adult defendant on the basis of the contract of indemnity.

The court held that as the first defendant was an infant, the hire-purchase agreement with him was itself null and void. The adult defendant claimed that because of this nullity, his own contract despite its title was in reality a guarantee. A guarantee must involve a promise "to answer for the debt of another person." Since the court had already held that there was no such debt (since the first defendant was an infant), the adult defendant argued that there was nothing to guarantee. Plaintiff argued that there was indeed a contract of indemnity for which the adult defendant was solely liable.

Ignoring the terms used by the parties (a court must decide the issue on the facts, not the words, used by the parties), would you find for the plaintiff or the defendant? What are the reasons for your decision?

5. Mr. Temple was successfully employed as the general manager of the ABC Pulp & Paper Co. In October 1974, he noticed an advertisement which indicated that a consulting company was searching for a general manager for a competitor company (the XYZ Company) with an opportunity to participate in a profit-sharing plan. From this date until November 18 serious negotiations were carried on between the XYZ chairman and vice-president and Mr. Temple, during which it was verbally agreed that the latter was to be employed on a five-year contract at $40,000 per year plus car allowance. Confirmation of this employment was written by the chairman of XYZ Company to Temple on November 12, at which time Temple was asked to have his solicitors draw a formal agreement incorporating the agreed terms. This was done by Mr. Temple but before it was signed, pressure had been brought to bear on the XYZ Company, presumably by the ABC Company, following Mr. Temple's resignation and although he was introduced to two clients as the new general manager on November 14, he was never allowed to take up his job. On December 5 he was advised in writing that his application for the position was no longer being considered and that the formal agreement prepared by his solicitors would not be required. After this, Temple could not find any suitable employment in the fine paper industry so he started his own company which, luckily, prospered. He then sued the XYZ Company for damages for one year's salary, in lieu of notice or alternatively damages for wrongful dismissal.

The problem in this case was whether the termination letter of

December 5 was a sufficient memorandum of the agreement, referring as it did to the "draft agreement prepared by your solicitors," to satisfy the Statute of Frauds which required a written memorandum as evidence of an agreement.

In *Tiverton Estates Ltd. v. Wearwell Ltd.*, [1974] 1 All E.R. 209, the Court of Appeal held in a land case that "a memorandum must contain not only the terms of the contract but also recognition that a contract had been entered into."

In *Martin v. Haubner* (1896), 26 S.C.R. 142, the Court held "that a writing containing a statement as to the terms of a contract is sufficient, although it repudiates the contract."

Give arguments for your decision in this case as to who should win. Refer to *Adam v. General Paper Co. Ltd.* (1978), 19 O.R. (2d) 574.

READINGS

Wauchope v. Maida, [1972] 1 O.R. 27 (C.A.).

Facts: The circumstances of this case involved the plaintiff (purchaser), Wauchope, who entered into a contract on December 24, 1969, to buy a property in Etobicoke, Ontario, for $75,000 with a $4,000 deposit, a further $16,000 on closing, and a $55,000 10% per annum first mortgage, closing date April 1, 1970. The agreement was made conditional upon the vendor arranging a first mortgage by January 15, 1970. The purchaser was advised on January 14 that a first mortgage had been arranged for $45,000 with the balance being carried as a second by the vendor—that is, $10,000 at 10% per annum, as previously agreed in the written offer to purchase, if the first mortgagee would not approve a loan for the full $55,000. On March 31, 1970, the purchaser and her lawyer were informed that the conventional first mortgage would be at 10½% instead of 10%. During that day, following negotiations between the parties and their solicitors, the appellant verbally agreed to the first mortgage at 10½%, on condition that the second mortgage was reduced to $9,000 (thereby reducing the sale price by $1,000), and the necessary documents were executed. When the appellant's solicitor attended for the closing, she advised the defendant's solicitor that the purchase would not be closed except on the original terms ($55,000 in mortgages at 10%), the purchaser having changed her mind. The trial judge awarded judgment to the plaintiff purchaser to recover her deposit.

Held (on appeal) per Schroeder J.A.:

There was clearly an [oral] agreement to vary the original contract by providing that the purchaser was to accept or assume a first mortgage calling for interest at the rate of 10½% in consideration of the vendor agreeing to accept a second mortgage for $9,000 instead of $10,000. . . . The contract was still in an executory state and it is, of course, elementary that a promise can be good [valuable] consideration for a promise. . . .

[While] the Statute of Frauds . . . prohibits actions on an oral contract [for]

sale of lands . . . a parol agreement . . . which has been mutually assented to
. . . may be offered as a valid defence to an action for a breach of the original
contract.

. . . [A]lthough the alteration as to the first mortgage terms assented to by
both parties did not comply with the statute, it can still operate as a defence
[i.e., a valid but unenforceable contract]. An agreement which is unenforceable under the Statute of Frauds is not invalid, and in a case of this kind will
constitute to the same extent as if it complied with the statute a defence to a
claim by the other contracting party to recover money paid or other property
the title of which has passed in pursuance of it. . . .

. . . The plaintiff was bound in equity by the doctrine of estoppel to give
the defendants reasonable notice that the concession [agreement to pay
$10\frac{1}{2}$% for the first mortgage] was to be withdrawn and the strict position
under the contract restored. This would have involved the granting of a
reasonable extension of the closing date to enable the defendants to carry out
the contract as originally framed. . . .

. . . [T]he appellants were ready, able and willing to close the transaction
on the basis of the contract as amended and . . . the plaintiff repudiated it at
the time fixed for completion. She thereby lost her right to recover the sale
deposit made by her and the action fails. . . .

Appeal allowed.

Huttges v Verner (1975), 64 D.L.R. (3d) 374 (N.B. C.A.).

Facts: On April 11, the plaintiff, aged 70 years, visited the defendant, aged
90 years, and although he had tried unsuccessfully previously to get the
defendant to sell his land, got him on this occasion to agree to sell and gave
him a cheque for $100 as a deposit, but the plaintiff wanted cash. The
following memorandum signed by the defendant was offered in evidence:

> April 11, 1974
> Lots 5 & 6
> Sold to Henry Huttges
> for 10,000 dollars
> Deposited 100 dollars
>   David T. Verner

It was also acknowledged that although the defendant was illiterate, he
had just learned to print his name shortly before this incident. It was offered
in evidence that the plaintiff had agreed that the defendant could live on the
premises, although this was not included in the original memorandum of
the transaction nor in a subsequent receipt also signed by the defendant
which was allegedly completed when the plaintiff returned with $100 cash
because the defendant did not want the $100 cheque.

The defendant refused the tender of $9,900 for his 400 acres of land; and
the trial judge, although he found that the defendant had understood all the
terms of the agreement, held that the memorandum did not satisfy the

requirements of the Statute of Frauds because it did not contain all the terms of the oral agreement of sale—namely, that the defendant could live in the house on the property as long as he lived. The plaintiff however stated he would agree to this condition but the defendant denied any contract of sale.

Held (on appeal) per Hughes C.J.N.B.:

[Quoting from Williams on *Vendor and Purchaser* at p. 4:] "It is essential . . . that the terms of the agreement sought to be proved thereby shall be sufficiently ascertained therein. The parties to the contract and the property to be sold must therefore be sufficiently described, and the price, or the means of ascertaining it, be stated; and any other terms of the bargain . . . must be defined."

[In *Scott v. Bradley*, [1971] 1 All E.R. 583, the plaintiff was allowed to obtain specific performance after he waived a provision specifically for his benefit, whilst here the plaintiff is agreeing to let the defendant live in the house on the premises, whether as a life estate or as a licensee is not known, but the defendant on his part denies any agreement of sale.] I would therefore hold that the memorandum in the present case fails to contain all material terms required to be included and so fails to satisfy the Statute of Frauds. . . .

In *McCorkell v. McFarlane*, [1952] O.W.N. 653, McLennan J. said at pp. 654-5: "I have come to the conclusion that specific performance . . . ought to be refused on grounds of unfairness in matters extrinsic to the terms of the contract itself. . . . As to what may constitute unfairness . . . all the surrounding circumstances,—such as intimidation and duress of the defendant, . . . mental incapacity, . . . age or poverty, . . . acting without a solicitor, or that the price was not the full value." . . .

The advanced age of the defendant, his total illiteracy, his lack of independent advice, his lack of knowledge of the value of the property he was selling, and the fact that the plaintiff obtained a snap bargain . . . are circumstances which appear to me to be sufficient to justify refusing specific performance. . . . The property was worth considerably more than the $10,000 which the plaintiff offered. . . .

[Appeal allowed in part only—that is, the return of the $100 cash allegedly paid by the plaintiff to the defendant.]

Wakeham v. Mackenzie, [1968] 2 All. E.R. 783 (Ch. Div.)

Facts: In December 1963, the plaintiff, a widow of 67, agreed to move in with a 72-year-old widower and look after his house on the condition that he would leave the house and contents to her when he died. After he had promised her to draw up legal documentation to this effect, she moved in and gave up the government-subsidized flat that she had been occupying. No documents were drawn up and, when the widower died some three years later, she sued to have the contract carried out. The executor objected.

Held per Stamp J.:

[Judge Stamp found that such an agreement had been made, that the plaintiff held to her part of the bargain including her contribution of 2 pounds weekly for food, but the agreement was never drawn up. The main argument of the defendant was based on s. 40 of the Law of Property Act, 1925, which replaced s. 4 of the Statute of Frauds—namely, that all contracts relating to land must be in writing.]

What is said on behalf of the defendant is that the acts of the plaintiff in performing the contract are not referable to a contract relating to any land or to a contract relating to 172, Wilton Road [the widower's house] and, therefore, are not acts of part performance on which the plaintiff can rely. . . .

[In *Kingwood Estate Co. Ltd. v. Anderson*, [1962] 3 All E.R. 593, where landlords who were anxious to develop a piece of land occupied by a statutory tenant for the rest of her life, bought another property, persuaded her to move and thereupon served her with a notice to quit, all being done orally] [a]ll the lord justices took the view that there was a sufficient act of part performance to take the case outside s. 40 of the Law of Property Act, 1925. . . .

I conclude from [the foregoing case] first that it is not the law that the acts of part performance relied on must be not only referable to a contract such as alleged, but referable to no other title, the doctrine to that effect laid down by Warrington L.J. in *Chaproniere v. Lambert*, [1916-17] All E.R. Rep. at p. 1092, having been exploded; and, secondly, that the true rule is that the operation of acts of part performance requires only that the acts in question be such as must be referred to some contract and may be referred to the alleged one. . . .

The acts of part performance in this case, the giving up of the plaintiff's home, . . . moving into a new home, . . . looking after the deceased and looking after that home and putting 2 pounds a week into the common pot, . . . were such as must be referred to some contract. . . .

[They] were acts of part performance relating to 172, Wilton Road.

It is . . . worth noting . . . the case of *Maxwell v. Lady Mountacute* (1720), Prec. Ch. 526 . . .: ". . . where, on a treaty for marriage, or any other treaty . . . never reduced into writing . . . unless this be executed in part, neither party can compel the other to a specific performance . . . the Statute of Frauds is directly in their way; but if there was any agreement for reducing the same into writing, and that is prevented by the fraud and practice of the other party, that this court will in such case give relief. . . ."

Plaintiff entitled to specific performance.

11

Third Persons

PRIVITY OF CONTRACT

When two persons enter into a contract, they undertake legal obligations towards each other and no one else. This is known as *privity of contract*. Normally, therefore, only these persons can sue or be sued for breach of the contract. Sometimes, however, some other person may be affected and wish to sue. Such a person, who is not a direct party to the agreement, is called in law a third person, third party, or "stranger to the contract."

Suppose, for example, that A requests B, the owner of a grass-cutting service, to mow A's lawn. However, B, finding herself overburdened with work, then subcontracts the work to C. A, dissatisfied with the work done, refuses to pay C. In order to get his money, C (who is a third person to the contract) must sue B, who in turn must sue A. Because of the rule of privity of contract, C is not permitted to sue A even though it was A's lawn that was mown.

Consumers

Let us consider the person who suffers in some way from a product that he or some other person has bought.

Suppose, for example, that a person buys in a retail store some hamburger which later, because of bacteria, harms the members of the buyer's family. Then, if the buyer can prove that the meat was contaminated at the time of purchase, he can obtain damages from the store that sold the item under an implied condition of fitness in the Sale of Goods Act. However, the other family members do not have this right since there was no privity of contract between them and the storekeeper. Unfortunately, they were third persons to the contract.

It may be that the buyer would prefer, for financial reasons, to sue the manufacturer who made the product rather than the retailer who sold it to him. However, because there is no privity of contract between the buyer and the manufacturer, such an action is impossible. The buyer, although party to a contract with the retailer, is only a third person with regard to any contract made between the retailer and the manufacturer. Fortunately, although the buyer has no remedy in contract because of the privity rule, he may have the right to sue the manufacturer under the law of tort. This principle was established by the British House of Lords in the classic case of *Donoghue v. Stevenson*, [1932] A.C. 562. This decision, popularly referred to as the "snail in the bottle" case, involved a young lady who while in a shop drank ginger beer poured from an opaque bottle purchased by her friend. After drinking one glassful, she began to pour the remainder of the bottle into her glass when a decomposed snail emerged, causing her to become violently sick. The problem in this situation was that the injured party had no contractual relationship with either the shopkeeper or the manufacturer of the ginger beer. How then could the injured person be compensated? The House of Lords concluded that where a manufacturer packages an item in a container which does not permit an inspection by the intended consumer, a manufacturer is liable in tort for any imperfection in the goods which might injure a consumer. Naturally if an inspection permits the noxious nature of the product to be discovered, the consumer cannot proceed to use the product and afterwards claim damages. In conclusion, the young lady was compensated for her illness. But the remedy was a tort remedy, for injury caused, not a contract remedy—because there was no privity of contract between the injured party and the manufacturer, that is to say, no direct contractual relationship.

Tenants

A tenant has a direct contractual relationship with his or her landlord. But suppose that the tenant's family, friends, or relatives are injured as a result of the landlord's failure to maintain the premises in a satisfactory state of repair. Then, because there is no privity of contract between the landlord and these other persons, they cannot sue for breach of contract. Furthermore, unlike the manufacturer, the landlord normally has no liability in tort for any injuries suffered by the tenant's family or guests within the leased premises. However, the landlord may be liable for injuries sustained while they are using the common areas such as elevators, hallways, and steps pursuant to the law of occupier's liability discussed in Chapter 4.

Exceptions to the Privity of Contract Rule

An exception to the privity of contract rule occurs in the case of an equitable trust. Equity developed, so it is believed, when a knight went off to the Crusades and left all of his property in the care of a friend with express instructions to administer his property and pay the income to the knight's wife and children. When the knight failed to return, the friend, by virtue of the common law rule that the owner is the only person who has title, refused to turn over the proceeds from the rentals to the widow and her children. She appealed to the King who, being above the law, decided to administer an equitable remedy by insisting that the friend held his property in trust for the widow and her children. This created what is known as the *equitable trust* and the so-called friend had to pay the income to the dependents, even though there was no privity of contract between the widow and himself.

Similar in principle is the trust concept between husband and wife that has been recognized in domestic relations since the *Murdoch* decision in Western Canada in 1978. In that case the court ruled that a woman who had been married to a rancher for over twenty years had no right to any of the family assets on the breakup of their marriage. However, during the 1970s, the courts recognized the existence of what is known as a *constructive* or *resulting trust*—holding that the husband in marriage held the family property in trust for himself and his wife because of: (a) the wife's financial contribution, such as her share of the mortgage payments and groceries; and/or (b) labour contribution in the way of housework, child rearing, permitting the husband to devote his time to earning money, and so on. Because of these trusts, the courts in Canada have now held that the wife, on breakup of the marriage, is entitled to half the family assets—residence, contents, car, recreational property and even, in some cases, half of the husband's business assets. Ontario has included this trust concept in its Family Law Reform Act and most provinces have followed suit.

Another exception to the privity of contract rule is the beneficiary in an insurance policy. Such a person has no connection with the insurance company other than that he or she has been named the beneficiary by the owner of the policy. However, provincial legislatures have legislated to permit the beneficiary to sue in his or her own name if the insurance money is not forthcoming.

A third exception is the undisclosed principal. Thus, if the person who enters into a contract with a third party is the agent for an undisclosed person (the principal), that other person will be able to sue and be sued, when that person's identity is disclosed, for any breach of contract.

ASSIGNMENT OF AN OBLIGATION OR LIABILITY

Suppose that a person enters into a contract to perform a service for the other party—for example, a lawyer agreeing to defend a client in court. However, the person who is to perform the service (the promisor) later decides to let someone take his place. Normally, in the eyes of the law, this is a breach of contract. Such a substitution may take place only with the consent of the other party to the contract (the promisee). This is the legal requirement of personal performance and, in the example of the lawyer, would hinge on the fact that he or she specifically was hired and that, in the mind of the client, no one else is a satisfactory substitute.

By law, a creditor is entitled to insist that a debt be repaid by the person to whom the money was originally loaned. Any assignment of a liability may be made only with the consent of the creditor. Thus it is not legally possible, for example, for a person to borrow from a bank and then assign the debt to someone with a poorer credit rating, without the consent of the creditor.

VICARIOUS PERFORMANCE

There are other circumstances, however, where it is accepted that a person engaged to perform a service (for example, build a house) will engage other persons (bricklayer, plumber, carpenter, electrician), to help complete the task. Where this is the case, there is said to be *vicarious performance*—that is, someone else has done part or all of the work on behalf of the promisor. Although as a matter of necessity, such performance is permitted by law, the promisor still remains liable to the promisee for satisfactory performance of the work.

EQUITABLE ASSIGNMENTS

Mention should be made of the distinction between a sale or transfer of tangible goods (called *choses in possession*) and the transfer or assignment of certain rights (called *choses in action*). The former is the transfer of title in an actual or tangible item, which is capable of possession; the latter, the transfer or assignment of claims to property such as the right to collect a debt, to pursue a claim in court, stocks, insurance claims, which although intangible can be of considerable value.

The common law courts, while recognizing that choses in possession could be transferred, refused to recognize the right to transfer or assign a chose in action—for example, A's right to collect a debt from C, being assigned to B. Naturally, to have an enforceable assignment from A to B, some consideration would have to be shown moving from B to A. And the transaction requires two contracts, the first between A and C, and the second the assignment contract between A and B.

In the common law situation, B could not sue C because of the lack of privity of contract, C being a third party to the original contract. However, the Courts of Equity stepped in to remedy this situation. Nevertheless, because of the need for the debtor to be sure of what to pay and to whom if there was only a partial assignment, it was decided that the assignor A and the assignee B in the foregoing situation must join together in enforcing their claim against C. Otherwise C would have to sue A and B as co-defendants to ensure that, when the debt was repaid, C could obtain a release of the entire debt from the two parties concerned.

STATUTORY ASSIGNMENTS

The situation with regard to assignments was not very satisfactory. Consequently, provincial legislatures have passed statutes to allow a new party to be introduced into a contract and to give this new party the right to come to court and sue on the contract.

This right to introduce a third party into the contract is provided by s. 53(1) of the Conveyancing and Law of Property Act, which reads as follows:

> Any absolute assignment, made on or after the 31st day of December, 1897, by writing under the hand of the assignor not purporting to be by way of charge only, of any debt or other legal chose in action of which express notice in writing has been given to the debtor, trustee, or other person from whom the assignor would have been entitled to receive or claim such debt or chose in action is effectual in law, subject to all equities that would have been entitled to priority over the right of the assignee if this section had not been enacted, to pass and transfer the

legal right to such debt or chose in action from the date of such notice, and all other remedies for the same, and the power to give a good discharge for the same without the concurrence of the assignor.

The Conveyancing and Law of Property Act therefore allows a "third party" (the assignee) to enforce the debt (or other subject matter of the assignment) without having to receive the co-operation of the assignor who was an original party to the contract.

In addition, this means that anyone who has the right to receive money or some other consideration from a debtor or a person in a debtor situation, may assign this right from oneself, the assignor, to a third party, the assignee, who has no previous connection whatsoever with the contract, by observing the following requirements:

1. The assignment must be in writing.
2. There must be no increased burden—for example, no additional interest charge.
3. The debtor, who must pay the obligation to the new party, the assignee, must be informed of his obligation in writing.

The effect of this statutory assignment is that, if the debtor chooses to ignore it, the courts may require him, even though he has already paid his original creditor, also to pay the new assignee. It would be left up to him to sue the original assignor for the return of his money. If an assignor fraudulently or negligently assigns the debt owing to more than one party, then the first assignee is the person whom the debtor must pay in order to get a valid discharge.

It is possible in this situation that the two assignees may come forward both claiming that they are entitled to payment. This could occur, for example, if a person died having named two different persons as beneficiaries of his insurance policy. In such cases, the debtor may fulfil his contractual obligation by tendering the money to the court. It would then be up to the two beneficiaries to apply to the court to prove which of the two had the right to receive the proceeds.

DEBTOR'S DEFENCES

Suppose that B owes me $500 and I owe B $400 in connection with another item. If I assign to C in writing my right to receive payment from B, with no increased burden and with written notification to B, then under the laws of assignment B must pay C. But what of the fact that I owe $400 to B for, say, the purchase of a secondhand car? Does this mean that she must pay to C the $500 and then take the chance that she will not recover her $400 from me? The answer is no. B could have subtracted the $400 from the $500 she owed me and satisfied her obligation by paying me only $100. She has this same defence against any assignee to whom I may try to transfer the credit. Thus a debtor, on receiving notification of an assignment, can validly object to payment on any grounds on which he or she might validly have objected to payment against the assignor. Other defences that may be used by a debtor include the claim that the contract was obtained under duress, under undue influence, or that the debtor is a minor, which gives him or her the right to have the contract set aside as voidable.

Finally, if the assignee is not paid by the debtor, the assignee can always claim the amount from the assignor, who remains obligated under the contract despite the assignment.

FRAUDULENT ASSIGNMENT OF BOOK DEBTS

Sometimes, a business owner will decide to sell the outstanding accounts receivable to, say, a collection agency. However, this practice gives an opportunity to unscrupulous persons to dispose of an asset for less than market value. Suppose, for example, a business owner is approaching bankruptcy. Hoping that he can get something out of his $5,000 accounts receivable, he turns them over to a friend for $500, with the understanding that the friend will pay him half of anything he collects. As well as committing possible income tax evasion, the business owner is defrauding his creditors, who reasonably expect that he should receive far more than $500 for accounts receivable worth $5,000.

To prevent the foregoing, provincial legislatures have passed statutes requiring that all sales of accounts receivable be registered, within a minimum number of days, in the local county or district court. In Ontario, such an Act has been repealed and replaced by the various provisions of the Personal Property Security Act, by which all persons are deemed to have constructive notice of any registered Sale of Book Debts.

BANKRUPTCY

In the case of bankruptcy (either personal, by voluntary assignment to a licensed trustee; or when petitioned into bankruptcy by creditors), the court makes a transfer of all the assets of the bankrupt to the licensed trustee in bankruptcy. These assets may then be sold and the proceeds distributed first to secured creditors, secondly to preferred creditors, and lastly to general creditors (pro rata—that is, shared equally in proportion to the amounts owed).

ADMINISTRATION OF ESTATES

A person may die *testate* (that is, leaving a valid will) or *intestate* (that is, without a valid will). If the person dies testate, the estate is administered by an executor or executors; if intestate, by an administrator appointed by the court. The law confers on such executors or administrators all the rights of ownership of the deceased with the right, where and when authorized, to transfer good title to both real property and chattels from the deceased's estate to the beneficiaries or to third parties. The relevant provincial Acts are usually called the Probate Act, Intestate Act, or, in Ontario, the Succession Law Reform Act.

COLLATERAL WARRANTIES

In law, a person may be liable for breach of a warranty notwithstanding the fact that he or she has no contractual relationship with the person to whom the warranty is given. *Shanklin Pier v. Detel Products Ltd.*, [1951] 2 K.B. 854, dealt with a situation in which a paint manufacturer made representations concerning the qualities of his paint to pier owners who then caused the paint to be specified in a contract for painting the pier. The painting contractor purchased the paint and applied it to the pier. However, the paint failed. The owners sued not the paint contractor but the manufacturer, with whom they had no privity of contract.

Defence counsel said (at p. 856) that "in law a warranty could give rise to no enforceable cause of action except between the same parties as the parties to the main contract in relation to which the warranty was given." However, McNair J. replied in his judgment at p. 856:

> In principle, his submission seems to me to be unsound. If, as is elementary, the consideration for the warranty in the usual case is the entering into of a main contract in relation to which the warranty is given, I see no reason why there may not be an enforceable warranty between A and B supported by the consideration that B should cause C to enter into a contract with A or that B should do some other act for the benefit of A.

In other words, the manufacturer would have been liable if he had supplied the paint directly to the owners and was equally liable in supplying the paint indirectly.

During recent years, the courts have been more willing to extend liability on the collateral contract principle. A recent Ontario case involved liability under this principle in favour of a farmer who, based on the manufacturer's representations, had purchased a harvester that failed to perform as advertised. In 1983, in a New Brunswick case, *Hallmark Pool Corp. v. Storey*, 144 D.L.R. (3rd) 56, a Hallmark swimming pool had been ordered through a local dealer by the plaintiffs because of a manufacturer's guarantee. This had been published in the Fall-Winter 1972-73 edition of *House Beautiful*'s *Home Decorating* magazine and guaranteed the installed pool for fifteen years. However, after the pool had been ordered and installed through the local dealer, it started to deteriorate immediately and within four years was useless—despite a guarantee that appeared to read that the pool would be satisfactory in places with both extreme cold and extreme heat. It was then discovered that the fine print of the guarantee, which had to be read with a magnifying glass, guaranteed only some of the component parts. The court held that, although there was a contract with the local dealer, there was also a collateral contract with the manufacturer, based on the guarantee that led to the selection of this particular pool. The Judges of the New Brunswick Appeal Court referred to the case of *Carlill v. Carbolic Smokeball* [1893] 1 Q.B. 256 as a precedent for this finding. The advertisement of the fifteen-year guarantee was considered to be more than mere puffery and in fact was more binding than the advertisement in the Smokeball case, which merely promised a reward.

OTHER SITUATIONS

Other situations involving third persons, discussed elsewhere in this book, include: liability of an agent to third persons (Chapter 23) and the rights of a holder in due course of a negotiable instrument (Chapter 31).

REVIEW QUESTIONS

1. The normal rule in all contracts is that only the contracting parties can sue or be sued. Explain.
2. Suppose that A, a tenant, sublets his apartment to B, with the consent of C, the owner. But B fails to pay the rent. Can C, the owner, sue A for the rent?
3. What is required to make a legal assignment of a liability?
4. What was the legal principle established in the case of *Donoghue v. Stevenson*? Give an everyday example of the application of the "snail in the bottle" principle.
5. An equitable trust is an exception to the privity of contract rule in cases of breach of contract. Explain. Why did the common law courts require both the assignor and the assignee to sue the debtor who refused to pay?
6. What do you understand by the expression "a resulting trust"?
7. What is meant by vicarious performance? Give an example.
8. By law, any assignment of a liability (such as a bank loan) may be made only with the consent of the creditor. Explain.
9. Any person who is owed money or some other consideration may assign this right to someone else, so long as three requirements are met. What are they?
10. What should a debtor do if a creditor fraudulently or negligently assigns the debt to more than one party?
11. Suppose that A owes B $500 for some electrical work already done and B owes A $400 for some bricklaying. If A assigns the $500 debt owing by B to C, what is B's legal obligation?
12. What do you understand by the rights of the assignee, if such assignee-debtor, or obligee, is, for example, a minor or a dominated person claiming undue influence?
13. What should a business owner do, if she decides to sell her bad debt accounts to a collection agency, in order that her debtors will know with whom to settle their unpaid bills?

14. What is required to allow a consumer to sue a manufacturer, rather than a dealer, on the basis of an unsatisfactory purchase made on the basis of the manufacturer's claims contained in an explanatory brochure?

PROBLEMS

1. Which of the following is incorrect? Why?
   (a) Only a right to receive money or goods may be assigned without consent of the obligated party.
   (b) A liability can sometimes be assigned, if no special skills are involved.
   (c) In a subcontract, the original contractor who is replaced is freed from liability.
   (d) A liability may always be assigned with consent of the creditor or beneficiary.
2. Suppose that A owes B $100, and B owes C $100. If B tells A, by a document in writing, to pay $100 to C, which of the following may be incorrect:
   (a) This is a valid assignment;
   (b) If A ignores this document and pays B, he may still have to pay C;
   (c) C may sue A directly to recover his money;
   (d) This type of transaction is legalized by statute;
   (e) A cannot be required by law to pay anyone but his actual creditor.
3. Only interested parties to a contract may bring an action for breach of contract. Which of the following are legal exceptions:
   (a) If C replaces A in a contract with B, with the consent of all parties;
   (b) If A agrees to paint B's picture and she substitutes her sister C because she herself has a dental appointment;
   (c) If C replaces B as the creditor, with the transaction recorded, no increased burden, and A, the debtor, notified;
   (d) If my newspaper is delivered by my paper-boy's mother while he is away at camp;
   (e) None of the foregoing is an exception.
4. A assigns to his friend C his right to collect a debt of $100 owing from B. When C notifies B of the assignment by letter, B informs C that he intends to set off a claim of $50, which he has against A against the $100 debt. Could C sue for the whole amount and win?
5. H, who is 17 years of age, is a debtor. He borrowed $500 from J to buy a special tape recorder/radio combination and agreed to pay back in full in six months. J assigns this credit in writing to K, to whom he owes $500. K notifies H in writing of the assignment, but H refuses to pay it back even at the end of six months. While this is a valid assignment, is H required to pay back the loan to J or K? Discuss.
6. Consider the facts relating to assignment in the case of *Kemp v. Baerselman*, [1906] 2 K.B. 604. The plaintiff and defendant had entered into an agreement for the supplying of eggs by the defendant, a wholesaler, to the plaintiff, a baker. By the terms of the contract, the defendant agreed to

supply the plaintiff with all the eggs he would require for a period of one year. It was further agreed upon that so long as the eggs were supplied as needed, the plaintiff would not purchase eggs elsewhere. A rough estimate of the eggs required had been arrived at, at the time the contract was signed. Four months after the signing of the contract, the plaintiff sold his establishment to another bakery. He purported to assign the benefit of his contract with the defendant to the buyer. The defendant refused to honour the contract any longer. Assuming the formalities of assignment were complied with, was the assignment valid? Must the defendant deliver eggs to the new owner?

7. A young woman bought a carton of chocolate milk in a cardboard container at a corner grocery which bore the name of a major dairy firm. When she attempted to suck up the liquid through a straw, her mouth was cut by broken glass fragments in the carton. The manufacturer proved that the processing plant was foolproof. Admitting that the customer has a claim against the owner of the corner grocery for selling "unfit food" under the Sale of Goods Act, has she also a claim against the manufacturer? Discuss.

8. A woman lived in common law with a farmer for over twenty years. She bore their children, raised them, worked on the farm, helped with the livestock, planting, and harvesting, cooked for the workers, and assisted in her husband's water-hauling business. When her common law spouse decided to separate, although everything was owned in his name, she sued for a share. Is there any possibility that her claim could be recognized at common law? Discuss.

12

Completion of a Contract and Rules of Interpretation

There are various ways in which a contract may be completed. Each of these ways is explained and discussed in Unit 1 of this chapter. In Unit 2 we consider what evidence a judge takes into account in interpreting a contract.

Unit 12.1
Completion of a Contract

COMPLETION BY PERFORMANCE

The usual way to complete a contract is by each party carrying out his or her obligations thereunder. This is known as *performance*. Thus, in the purchase of a car, the purchaser pays the price and the dealer delivers the car. In travelling by public transportation, a person pays the fee and the transportation company takes that person to his or her destination. Of the many thousands of contracts that are made every day, most are completed by both the parties in each contract fulfilling their obligations towards each other.

Payment

This is normally made according to the terms of the original agreement—for example, cash in exchange for an automobile. Sometimes, however, one party may agree later to accept some other form of payment. Sometimes, also, when the contract cannot be completed exactly as agreed, the parties will agree to alter their respective obligations by what is known as "accord and satisfaction." This occurs where one party has defaulted in performance of his part of the contract, and a right of action arises in favour of the other party. This is settled usually by a money payment made by the party against whom the right exists and accepted by the other party in discharge of his right of action. For example, assume that A has arranged to have his damaged automobile repaired by his local garage. However, suppose the garage owner decides to close during August and go on vacation. Then he would have to ask A to take his car elsewhere and might pay for any extra costs incurred by the change in plan and subsequent delay.

Tender

In any contract, the parties involved must attempt to carry out their obligations by a procedure that is legally termed "tender." Thus if, for example, an electrician has been called by a home owner to repair the kitchen stove, she may offer her services by arriving at the homeowner's residence, properly equipped with her tools, knowledge, and licence and prepared to do the work. If a person is buying a car, he or she may tender by offering cash to the value of the car to the dealer. The dealer in turn tenders by offering the car, subject to payment.

Tender is *attempted performance*. If the contract consists of a sale of goods, and the seller's attempt at delivery is refused by the buyer, then the seller is excused from further performance and may immediately sue for breach of contract, claiming money damages. Suppose, on the other hand, the buyer offers to pay, but the seller fails to deliver. Then the buyer may arrange for someone else to provide the goods or services required. In some cases (for example, the purchase of a rare painting), the buyer may ask the court for an order of *specific performance* requiring the seller specifically to perform his or her part of the contract—that is, to hand over the goods or be in contempt of court for which he or she can be penalized by imprisonment and/or a fine.

The courts have ruled that, if, by the day set out in the contract for completion, once a party has tendered (offered to perform), that party has met his or her legal obligation. The party does not need to continue tendering throughout the day. Furthermore, once a tender has been refused by the other party, the tendering party is freed from any obligations under the contract.

If the tender refers to payment of a debt, the debtor must seek out the creditor. If the creditor refuses to accept a tender of the exact amount due, the debtor must make payment into court.

Legal Tender

When payment of cash is required by a contract, the tender of cash must always be made in accordance with the terms provided for legal tender. *Legal tender*, as laid down by the Parliament of Canada, consists of any denomination of Bank of Canada notes, any United Kingdom, United States, or Canadian gold coins, $10 in silver, $5 in nickels, and 25¢ in coppers. Tender of cash can be legally refused if it does not meet these requirements.

Some exceptions to the requirement of payment in legal tender are: (a) where the contract specifically provides that payment may be made by certified cheque; and (b) where it is the accepted custom of the particular trade or occupation that a certified personal cheque or an uncertified cheque is acceptable.

DISCHARGE BY MUTUAL AGREEMENT

Sometimes the parties to a contract, realizing that they cannot carry out their obligations, agree either to cancel the contract (usually, by a mutual release or waiver) or to alter its terms to suit their new needs. In such cases, where both parties are agreed, no cause of action for breach of contract arises. As it is the agreement of the parties which binds them in contract, another later agreement will suffice to abolish the previous agreement. The consideration for the new agreement is the relinquishment by both of their rights under the original agreement. However, it would appear that a partly executed contract (one in which only one of the parties has performed) cannot be discharged by an oral agreement (or *parol waiver*). Thus, according to Parke J. in *Foster v. Dawber* (1851), 6 Exch. 839 at p. 851, "It is competent for both parties to an executory contract, by mutual agreement, without any satisfaction, to discharge the obligation of that contract; but an executed contract cannot be discharged except by release under seal, or by performance of the obigation as by payment where the obligation is to be performed by payment."

MERGER

This occurs whenever a higher security is accepted in place of a lower, or whenever two parties to a simple contract execute a formal deed. In both of these cases the original contract is merely transferred or "merged" into a higher form. In the latter case a deed is considered superior to a simple contract in that it is executed under seal. The same thing occurs when a purchasing agent telephones an order to a seller and follows it up by a written order which is also classified as a merger into a higher form. By mutual agreement, both parties are discharged from the original contract.

NEW TERMS OR NEW PARTIES

A contract may also be discharged by the introduction of new terms or new parties. This amounts to a rescission of the original contract and the formation of a new contract. For example, if a building was to be completed by a certain day or compensation made for late completion and the parties made a new agreement for additional work, the new agreement would cause the compensation provision in the previous agreement to be waived.

Another example is the partnership situation where the parties may be changed by the retirement of one partner or by the introduction of a new partner and a new partnership agreement will replace the old. If the creditors, the old firm, and the new firm all agree, the debts of the old firm will become those of the new.

NOVATION

This occurs where one of the original parties to a contract, with the consent of the other party, is replaced by someone else who has agreed to take over the original party's obligations, the terms of the original contract remaining the same.

An example of novation is as follows. Suppose I hire A to mow my lawn and he decides one day to substitute B who does a satisfactory job. This is what would be termed a *subcontract situation*, and providing B does not come to me for his pay, there is no problem. However, suppose that A is going away for a lengthy period of time and, foreseeing that he will not be able to carry on with the contract of mowing the lawn, asks B to take his place. If B agrees, then A could come and ask me to accept B in his place. If I agree, then B and I enter into the same contract and A is freed from his obligations. That is what is called a "novation." In this situation, B may now demand his salary from me (or sue me for non-payment) once he has completed the job. Of course I may insist, on the basis of privity of contract (as discussed in the previous chapter), that A fulfil the obligation himself if I do not agree to the change of parties.

DISCHARGE PROVISIONS

A contract may itself contain provisions for its discharge. There are various reasons for such cancellation or alteration, as follows.

Arrival of a Stipulated Date or Event

For example, "this agreement of partnership is valid until December 31, 19--", or "valid until completion of the transaction."

Arrival of a Pre-arranged Condition

For example, ". . . unless either partner become sick, incapacitated, or insane." Such *escape clauses* permit a party to withdraw from the contract if desired—for example, not being forced to purchase a house if the stipulated mortgage financing cannot be arranged where such a condition is included in the offer to purchase.

In the case of *Head v. Tattersall* (1871), L.R. 7 Ex. 7, a contract contained two provisions: one, that the horse, which was the subject matter of the contract, had hunted with the Bicester hounds; and the second, that it was to answer to its description. Otherwise the buyer could return it. Neither of these conditions was met. However, the buyer returned the horse in an injured state. The court said, "The effect of the contract was to vest the property in the buyer subject to a right of rescission in a particular event when it would revest in the seller [*condition precedent*]. I think in such a case that the person who is eventually entitled to the property in the chattel ought to bear any loss arising from any depreciation in its value caused by an accident for which nobody is in fault." Thus the vendor (the original owner) had to bear the loss.

In the case of *Turney and Turney v. Zhilka* (1959), 18 D.L.R. (2d) 447 (S.C.C.), the two contracting parties agreed that their contract of sale and purchase of land would be subject to the annexation of the said land by the Village of Streetsville. This did not occur, so the contract provided for its own termination by a true *condition precedent*.

Most carrier contracts provide for a *condition subsequent* which event shall discharge either one or both parties from further liabilities under the contract.

In *Nugent v. Smith* (1875), 1 C.P.D. 423, the plaintiff's mare was to be carried by sea carrier from London to Aberdeen. The ship met rough weather, and the mare, being frightened, struggled violently, causing injuries from which she died. The plaintiff argued that this was not a case of an act of God, or inherent vice on the part of the mare. The court, holding the defendant carrier not liable, stated:

> The "Act of God" is a mere short way of expressing this proposition. A common carrier is not liable for any accident as to which he can show is due to natural causes, directly and exclusively, without human intervention, and that it could not have been prevented by any amount of foresight and pain and care reasonably to have been expected of him. A carrier does not insure against acts of nature and does not insure against defects of the thing carried itself, but in order to make out a defence, he must be able to prove that either cause taken separately or both taken together, formed the sole and direct and irresistible cause of the loss.

Proper Notice

Certain contracts such as contracts of service or leases may provide that one of the parties may terminate the contract by "proper notice." In the case of employment, the common law rule of notice of dismissal, corresponding in length to the frequency of the payment period, has been changed by, for example, the Employment Standards Act of Ontario to a minimum period of notice (or severance pay in the alternative), depending on the length of time the employee has worked: it may be as long as sixteen weeks, if more than 500 employees are being given notice at once by a large firm.

DISCHARGE BY IMPOSSIBILITY OF PERFORMANCE (FRUSTRATION)

Sometimes it may become impossible for one of the parties to complete his or her part of a contract—for example, a manufacturer not being able to produce the goods required because of a shortage of materials. Such an impossibility may be foreseen and provided for in the contract, or it may exist unknown to the parties (for instance, a fire destroying the factory that was to manufacture the goods ordered), or it may even arise after the contract is made.

Escape Clauses

Earlier in the book, we said that impossible consideration voids a contract; so does a situation where the subject matter of the contract does not exist— that is, a common mistake by the contracting parties. In all other contracts the general rule is that the parties will be bound by their contract, unless there is what is termed an "escape clause" that covers any subsequent impossibility—for example, an escape clause in a construction contract, covering interruptions caused by labour strikes or an escalation in material costs. Nevertheless, there are certain circumstances in which impossibility of performance may serve as valid grounds for discharge of a contract.

Lord Loreburn explains the doctrine of impossibility of performance in the following judgment in *Tamplin v. Anglo-Mexican Co.*, [1916] 2 A.C. 397 at p. 403:

> A court can and ought to examine the contract and the circumstances in which it was made, not of course to vary, but only to explain it, in order to see whether or not from the nature of it the parties must have made their bargain on the footing that a particular thing or state of things would continue to exist. And if they must have done so, then a term to that effect will be implied, though it be not expressed in the contract. . . .
> (1) Sometimes it is put that *performance has become impossible, and that the party concerned did not promise to perform an impossibility.* (2) Sometimes it is put that the parties *contemplated a certain state of things which fell out otherwise.* (3) In most of the cases, it is said that there was an *implied condition in the contract which operated to release the parties from performing it,* and in all of them I think that was at the bottom the principle upon which the court proceeded.

Unforeseen Destruction of Subject Matter

The case of *Taylor v. Caldwell* (1863), 3 B.&S. 826, was the first of a group of cases involving impossibility of performance. In this case, also called the Surrey Music Hall case, Caldwell, the defendant, had agreed to give Taylor, the plaintiff, the use of a music hall for a concert. However, the hall was destroyed by fire on the day before the performance, thereby denying its use to Taylor. He then sued Caldwell for damages. It was held that such a contract must be regarded as containing an implied condition that the parties shall be excused from their obligations if, before any breach of the contract occurs, performance becomes impossible from the perishing of the thing without default of the contractor.

It should be noted that, in cases of fire, the contract is only frustrated if the destruction is so extensive as to render further performance impossible; otherwise the contract is enforceable.

Other Types of Contracts

Over the years, three other types of contract involving impossibility of performance have merited special treatment by the court. These types of contract are now governed by the terms of each province's Frustrated Contracts Act. The circumstances that give rise to "frustrated contracts" are as follows.

Change in Law Making Contract Illegal.   Suppose I live in a municipality where the bylaw requires a new house to have a minimum area of 2,000 square feet. I make my contract with the builder but, just before the start of construction, the bylaw is changed to require a minimum floor area of 2,500 square feet. The contract with the builder is terminated under the provisions of the Frustrated Contracts Act.

We should remember that a contract that involves an illegal act at the time the contract is made is automatically invalid. However the situation described above is one in which a contract that involved a perfectly legal act when entered into has later, because of a change in the law, been deemed illegal. This also reflects the difference between common mistake and frustration of a contract.

Disability or Death Making Personal Services Impossible. Suppose a famous singer is scheduled to appear at a theatre. The week before the performance she discovers that her voice is weakening and, on consulting a doctor, discovers that she has strained her voice and requires six months' rest. In this situation a substitute will not do. Therefore the contract is terminated under the Frustrated Contracts Act because of personal disability. Another example of this situation would be a prominent hockey player on contract to a team in the NHL discovering that his leg injuries are so extensive as to prevent him from ever again playing competitively. His player's contract would be terminated by impossibility of performance. Here again, the courts would be careful to distinguish between permanent impossibility of performance and temporary disability such as a singer's sore throat which might only require the cancellation of a few performances.

Failure of Event to Occur. The classic case of a mutually anticipated event which ceases to exist or fails to occur involved the coronation of King Edward VII. In *Krell v. Henry*, [1903] 2 K.B. 740, the defendant agreed to hire the plaintiff's flat, which overlooked the coronation route, for June 26 and 27, 1902, the scheduled dates of Edward VII's coronation. However, Edward's illness forced a postponement of the event and the rent had not become payable when the postponement occurred. The plaintiff sued for the unpaid rent and lost. Vaughn Williams L.J., said:

> I do not think that the principle . . . is limited to cases in which the event causing the impossibility of performance is the destruction or non-existence of some thing which is the subject matter of the contract, or of some condition or state of things expressly specified as a condition of it. I think that you first have to ascertain, not necessarily from the terms of the contract, but if required from necessary inferences drawn from the surrounding circumstances, recognized by both contracting parties, what is the substance of the contract, and then to ask the question whether that substantial contract needs for its foundation the assumption of the existence of a particular state of things.

The case of *Chandler v. Webster*, [1904] 1 K.B. 493, like the *Krell v. Henry* case, also involved the rental of a room to watch the coronation of King Edward VII, where the plaintiff had paid 100 pounds in advance out of a total rent payable of 141 pounds. The court held that, since the rent was *totally* payable in advance, the plaintiff forfeited not only his deposit, but was also bound to pay the balance of the amount that was due before the frustrating event occurred.

However, in *Fibrosa Spolka Akcyjna v. Fairbairn Lawson Combe Barbour Ltd.*, [1943] A.C. 32, where a contract was terminated by frustration and the purchaser had received no benefit, it was held that the seller had to return any depoist received even though the defendant had already spent time and money in partially manufacturing machinery under the contract. On the other hand, if any benefit had been received by the purchaser, he would lose all his deposit.

The Frustrated Contracts Act now provides that if something has been done to complete the contract, enough of the deposit may be retained to cover any expenses incurred prior to the frustrating event. If no money has been paid but is due, the performing party may recover enough to cover expenses. In any event, the party providing goods or services may claim for any valuable benefit received by the other party.

DISCHARGE BY STATUTORY RELEASE

A bankrupt person who has made every effort to repay his or her debts may eventually be discharged unconditionally from bankruptcy by the court. He or she is thereby released under the Bankruptcy Act from any further obligation relating to past debts, claims, and other liabilities, except support payments and fraudulent debts.

DISCHARGE BECAUSE OF ALTERATION

An alteration in a written document may be grounds for the discharge of the document or deed, providing the following occurs:

1. the alteration must be made intentionally by a party to the contract while in his possession or by a stranger on his behalf;
2. without the consent of the other party;
3. material alteration; for example, it is conceivable that the change of a word might not discharge the contract.

On the other hand, if a document is lost, its contents may still be proved by oral evidence—for example, the lost will of a famous drafter of wills, St. Leonards, was proven in court by his daughter from memory.

REVIEW QUESTIONS

1. How are most contracts completed?
2. Suppose that A, a householder, telephones B, an electrician, and asks him to come to A's house to repair a faulty stove. However, when B arrives, ready to do the work, A tells him that his services are no longer required as A has fixed the stove herself. What is B's legal position?
3. A is required by contract to pay $100 in cash to B. A brings along a bag of pennies which B refuses to accept. What is B's legal position?
4. Suppose a buyer of real estate tenders, on the due date, the purchase

price in cash in accordance with an agreement of purchase and sale. However, the seller refuses to accept the money. What is the legal position of (a) the buyer and (b) the seller?

5. In the purchase of real estate, could cash legally be substituted in a contract that calls for a certified cheque?

6. Sometimes a contract is terminated before completion by mutual agreement. What are the circumstances in which this can occur?

7. Give an example of a contract being "merged into higher form."

8. What is meant by "novation"? Answer, with an example.

9. Distinguish between a "subcontract" situation and "novation."

10. What do you understand to be the principle of law contained in the *Nugent v. Smith* case?

11. A contract may itself contain provisions for its discharge. Explain, with examples.

12. Suppose that a customer has booked your restaurant for a wedding banquet. However, last night your chef, in a fit of rage, set fire to the kitchen so that it is now unfit for cooking. What is your liability to your customer?

13. What are the other three basic types of frustrated contracts? Give an example of each.

14. Can you explain the "right of recovery" situation in the cases that resulted from the cancellation of King Edward VII's coronation?

15. Do you agree that the law should allow cancellation of contracts for the situations contained in the Frustrated Contracts Act? Discuss.

16. Under what circumstances may a person be statutorily discharged from a contract?

17. When is alteration of a written document sufficient grounds for discharge of a contract?

PROBLEMS

1. Mike, a past season ticket holder of the Argonauts, caused several disturbances during last year's regular season games. When the time came to renew his season ticket, the stadium management sold him a ticket for cash with the stipulation that he was to behave properly or his ticket would be subject to cancellation. The first regular game was against the Tiger Cats and the police had to eject Mike for fighting in the stands. As a result, his season ticket was cancelled and his money refunded. Mike sued the Argonauts' management for breach of contract. Discuss.

2. A is suing for $10,000 for breach of contract. After offering to settle for $8,500, B tenders $8,500 into court. The case continues to trial, and finally A is awarded only $8,000. How are the costs awarded if both parties incur $100 legal expenses prior to trial and $100 after trial?

3. Consider the facts in the case of *Isabella Hall v. George Wright* (1859), 120 E.R. 695. The plaintiff and defendant were engaged to be married. Prior to the date of marriage, defendant contracted an incurable lung

disease which he pleaded "has occasioned frequent and severe bleeding from his lungs, and by reason of which disease defendant then became and was and from thenceforth has been, and still is, incapable of marriage without great danger of his life, and therefore unfit for the marriage state."

The plaintiff sued for breach of promise and the defendant's defence was as given above. It was proven that the fatigue and excitement of the marriage ceremony itself, as well as the physical exertion of sexual intercourse would greatly endanger the defendant's life. The jury found for the defendant. On appeal to the Queen's Bench, the four judges were evenly divided on this issue. What would be your decision?

4. The Maple Leaf hockey team hired Jim to play for them at a regular contract of $20,000 per year, plus a bonus of $200 for every goal over twenty which he might score. During his first season, Jim scored only fifteen goals. Does this under-performance entitle the Maple Leaf management to cancel the contract?

5. A and B enter into a written contract whereby A sells a farm to B. Before the conveyance of title is executed, B runs into financial difficulties, and A learns that another buyer, C, will pay more. If both A and B agree orally, could the original contract be legally cancelled? Discuss.

6. Fontabello is a famous singing star, whose reputation is so outstanding that when he is booked for the municipal theatre, the seats are quickly sold for all performances, with receipts totalling over $250,000. The first performance is scheduled for Friday, February 13. The star advises the municipal theatre management on February 12 that he intends to appear at a rival theatre instead. Could the municipal theatre management get a court order to hold him to his contract? Does this contract come under the Frustrated Contracts Act? Could the performance at the rival theatre be stopped, and if so, how? How would damages be calculated in this case, and who would be liable?

7. Mrs. Wright, having heard favourable comments about a hairdresser by the name of Lorenzo, on the other side of town, booked an appointment to have her hair permed by him. Later, during her appointment, she found that he spent considerable time answering phone calls and talking to a sales representative, leaving a lady assistant to look after her. When her hair was finally combed out, she was chagrined to find that it had not properly set. What is her legal position?

Unit 12.2
Rules of Interpretation

The general rule with regard to the interpretation of contracts is that a person who voluntarily enters into a contract will be bound by its terms. Consequently, a person who is asked to sign a contract, particularly a standard-form one, should first read carefully what he or she is about to sign. Also the person should insist on having anything objectionable changed. This can be done either by rewording the contract or by the addition of new clauses. Thus, for example, in buying a used car, the purchaser might insist on the inclusion of a clause whereby the dealer "warrants that it has not been involved in a major accident" or "that the mileage indicated on the odometer is correct." Whatever the case, the changes should be initialled by both parties. If such a written provision is not added, the buyer is bound by the written agreement as is and will not be permitted to present oral evidence to indicate otherwise. Of course, it may be possible in some instances to produce evidence that the contract involves mistake, duress, or lack of capacity on the part of one of the contracting parties. But normally this is not the case.

One problem that faces a judge in the common law courts is what oral evidence, if any, should be heard with regard to a contract in dispute. Another problem is how the words used in a contract should be understood. However, certain rules have been devised to help the judge resolve these problems, particularly with regard to *parol evidence*—that is, evidence extrinsic to or outside of the written agreement. This may be *oral evidence*—for example, by witnesses to the negotiations that preceded the signing of the contract, or it may be *written evidence*—for example, letters sent by one or other of the parties.

PAROL EVIDENCE RULE

The most fundamental rule of parol evidence is that a judge may not admit parol evidence that attempts to add to, vary, or contradict a written contract that is otherwise complete. Thus, for example, in the case of *Henderson v. Arthur*, [1907] 1 K.B. 10, Arthur, the defendant, who was leasing a theatre from Henderson, the plaintiff, had agreed in writing to pay the rent each quarter in advance. Later, Henderson agreed to accept a three-month bill, or promise to pay, from Arthur for each quarter's rent. However, when Arthur tendered such a bill, Henderson, having changed his mind, refused to accept it and insisted on payment in cash. On Arthur's failure to pay, Henderson began a lawsuit he eventually won on the grounds that the parol agreement contradicted the terms of the lease and evidence of such an agreement could not therefore be admitted in court.

The purpose of this parol evidence rule is quite clear: to discourage persons who enter into a contract, then later change their minds, from claiming in court that a term favourable to them had been omitted. Without such a rule, few people would be willing to enter into a business or other agreement for fear that the court, at the request of the other party, might later repudiate it.

EXCEPTIONS TO PAROL EVIDENCE RULE

There are some exceptions to the parol evidence rule:

1. admission of collateral terms to complete a written contract;
2. certain contract terms which must be explained;
3. introducing usage and custom into a contract;
4. application of equitable remedies to cases of mistake.

Completing a Written Contract

Parol evidence may be admitted to complete a written contract but not to vary it. This applies to a situation in which the parties to a contract have failed to put all the terms in writing. However, such parol evidence is only admissible if such supplementary or collateral terms complete, but not vary or contradict, the written agreement. Thus in the case of *Erskine v. Adeane* (1873), 8 Ch. App. 766, a farmer executed a lease and then suffered damage to his crops because the lessor had failed to kill off the game on the property as promised. The court held that oral evidence of the collateral agreement could be admitted because the lease itself was dependent on the other party's promise.

Parol evidence is also admissible to show that the parties intended to delay implementation of an agreement until the occurrence of a certain date or event. Thus, for example, A agreed in writing that B, a professional photographer, should take A's wedding pictures subject to an oral understanding that the contract would be terminated if the wedding were cancelled or postponed. Or, as in an actual case, *Pym v. Campbell* (1856), 6 E. & B. 370, the defendant, Campbell, agreed to buy from Pym, the plaintiff, a share of an invention. A written memorandum was signed to this effect but with the express verbal understanding that neither would be bound until a third person, Abernethie, had given approval. As such approval was not forthcoming, Campbell refused to proceed with the purchase. Thereupon Pym sued him for breach of contract and argued that the parol evidence of the verbal understanding was an attempt by Campbell to vary the terms of a legally binding, written contract. The judge declared the parol evidence admissible in court and concluded that there was in fact no legally binding agreement.

Finally, parol evidence has more recently been admitted in court to prove that a document was not intended by the signing parties to be a comprehensive statement of a contract which in fact had oral as well as written terms. In such cases, the judge may permit the remedy of "rectification" (see page 140).

Explaining Certain Contract Terms

The court will allow oral evidence in explanation of terms of latent (hidden or unexplained) ambiguity—for example, persons with the same name, or the terms "seaworthy," "reasonable manner," or "workmanlike manner." Thus in the case of *Burges v. Wickham* (1863), 3 B. & S. 669, the vessel *Ganges*, sent from England to India and intended for river traffic, was described as "seaworthy" in the insurance documents. However, both the owners and the underwriters realized that, although the ship would be made as seaworthy as possible, it was not really fit for the high seas. In fact, the ship was lost and the insurers subsequently refused to pay. The court held:

> It is always permitted to give extrinsic evidence to apply a written contract, and shew what was the subject-matter to which it refers. . . . for example, in a demise [rental] of a house with a covenant to keep it in *tenantable repair*, it is legitimate to enquire whether the house be an old one in St. Giles' or a new palace in Grosvenor Square for the purpose of ascertaining whether the tenant has complied with his covenant, for that which would be repair in a house of the one class is not so when applied to a house of the other.

Showing Usage of Trade or Locality

Examples of this would be a "baker's dozen," meaning 13, or the 10% extra included in a contract for the printing of stationery. Explanation of such terms will not be admitted unless it conforms with the rules of law (for instance, a contract required to be in writing under the Statute of Frauds) and is consistent with the contract itself, although it may be said in a certain sense to vary it. This rule was stated in *Brown v. Byrne* (1854), 3 E. & B. 716:

> Words perfectly unambiguous in their ordinary meaning are used by the contractors in a different sense from that. . . . In such cases, the evidence neither adds to, or qualifies, nor contradicts the written contract, it only ascertains it by expanding the language.

Permitting Application of Equitable Remedies in Cases of Mistake

Sometimes a written contract may, through the use of wrong terms, have a meaning completely different from that intended by the two parties. If there was a mutual mistake and the oral evidence is uncontradicted, the court may allow the equitable remedy of *rectification*—that is, allow the contract to be changed by oral evidence to reflect the true intention of the parties. This was the decision in *Webster v. Cecil* (1861), 30 Beav. 62, where the seller made a mistake in calculating his price. This mistake was known to the purchaser, who tried to take advantage of the contract by accepting the offer at a price which was $1,000 less than intended. The court allowed the seller to insert the correct price. In a recent Canadian case where a university asked for bids on a construction contract and tried to hold the tenderer to an offer in which there had been an obvious mistake, the court allowed evidence to prove that the tenderer had made a mistake in omitting the page of the contract containing the escalation clauses and that this fact was known to the acceptor.

In summary, it appears that, when all the exceptions to the parol evidence rule are considered, not very much is left of the restrictions contained in the rule itself.

INTERPRETATION OF EXPRESS TERMS

The express terms of a contract are those that the contracting parties have expressly said, written, or done. In interpreting the wording of the contract, the judge will first try to determine the parties' intentions according to the plain or ordinary meaning of the words used. However, this is not as straightforward as it sounds, as even the ordinary meaning of words can vary considerably. Suppose, for example, that A has agreed to paint B's offices for a fixed dollar amount. A assumed that B's price would include the paint. But B insists that the paint is "extra." If the judge were to examine the literal meaning of the words "to paint," he or she would find nothing to indicate who should provide the paint. Consequently, in making the decision, the judge would have to consider the evidence of any witnesses, special usage of words in the trade, the usual practice in the painting trade, the custom of the area, the price charged in relation to work done, and what happened in any previous painting jobs involving the two parties.

The judge will also attempt to determine the intentions of the parties when they entered into the contract, taking into account any prior negotiations and the circumstances involved. However, the judge must consider the words used in the contract as the basic indication of both parties' intentions and must be careful not to stray into the realm of speculation.

Often a judge will have to choose between the contradictory testimony of the two parties to the contract. The judge will then have to decide, considering all the circumstances, which statement is more reasonable and make the judgment accordingly.

Very often it would appear to make more sense for a judge to declare that, because of the ambiguity or even lack of wording, a contract is unenforceable. However, this course would defeat the purposes for which the civil courts have been established—namely, to settle disputes between conflicting parties, however difficult such a judgment may be.

PERFORMANCE ON TIME

The inclusion of a specific date for performance in a contract was at one time taken seriously by the common law courts. Consequently, failure to perform on time was considered a breach of a condition, giving the other party the right to consider the contract as terminated and to sue for damages. Later, however, the common law courts, applying equity, took a more lenient view. Thus, if the parties intended nothing more than performance within a reasonable time, the contract was considered to remain intact even though performance was not made on exactly the day stipulated. However, this view was not extended to business contracts where performance on time has always been considered to be of vital importance. Nowadays, to avoid misunderstanding, most contracts in which the date of performance is vital contain a clause to the effect that "time is of the essence."

INTERPRETATION OF IMPLIED TERMS

As well as express terms, there may also be implied terms in a contract. These may be imparted from Statutes such as the Bills of Exchange Act, the Sale of Goods Act, and the Insurance Acts, which require that certain types of contracts contain certain terms. A judge may also impute a term to a contract on the basis of local custom or usage in the trade or profession so long as such a term does not conflict with the parties' expressed intentions. A term may also be implied in a contract as a result of the judge's interpretation of the reasonable expectations of each party.

The courts have ruled that implied terms will only be included in a contract if this can be proved either from trade custom or to facilitate business (see *Douglas Bros, and Jones Ltd. v. MacQueen* (1959), 42 M.P.R. 256).

OTHER EVIDENCE

We have explained above how a judge will attempt to interpret the terms of a contract. However, it is also sometimes necessary for a judge to hear evidence as to whether a written contract actually exists. In this case, the rules relating to each type of evidence vary according to whether the dispute involves a contract under seal or a simple contract.

Existence of the Document

The existence of a document purporting to be a contract under seal is proven by written or oral evidence of its sealing and delivery to the person being sued.

The existence of a document purporting to be a simple contract (that is, a contract not under seal), as long as it is in writing and complete in itself, needs no other written or oral evidence. However, a document purporting to be a simple contract that is only partly evidenced by writing will need to be supplemented by oral evidence. Thus if, for example, A agrees in writing to pay $4,000 for B's car so long as it is delivered the next day, it would be necessary to supplement the document with oral evidence that the car was actually delivered the next day. In other words, the courts recognize a contract which is partly written and partly oral.

Whether the Document is a Contract

In the case of a contract under seal, it is not necessary to prove that the document is a valid document. This is because, in the eyes of the law, the instrument and the contract are synonymous. Once the sealing and delivery of the instrument is proven, so also is the fact that the document is a contrct under seal.

The situation is different, however, with regard to a simple contract. Here the document is considered only to be evidence of a contract. Oral evidence may also be necessary to prove that the document is admissible in court to prove that a document is in fact a legally binding contract. Conversely, parol evidence is admissible in court to prove that a document is not a valid contract. Thus, for example, oral or written evidence might be produced in court to show that A, by use of duress, force B, his wife, to sign over all her property to him. Or, that B was under age when he signed a contract to purchase a yacht or some other non-necessity.

REVIEW QUESTIONS

1. What is parol evidence?
2. What evidence is required to prove the existence of the document in the case of: (a) a contract under seal; (b) a simple contract?
3. In the case of a simple contract, proof of the existence of a written agreement does not automatically imply the existence of a valid contract. Explain, with an example.
4. Parol evidence is admissible in court for various purposes. What are they?
5. Is parol evidence admissible in order to add to, vary, or contradict a written contract that is otherwise complete? Illustrate your answers with reference to the case of *Henderson v. Arthur*.
6. What exceptions, if any, exist with regard to the rule contained in question 5?
7. Explain, with an example of your own, how the equitable remedy of rectification would apply to a contract.
8. What is meant by "express terms" of a contract?
9. How does a judge interpret the wording of a contract?
10. How does a judge interpret the inclusion of a date for performance in a contract?
11. What evidence is permissible to help prove the existence of a contract?
12. What evidence is permissible to help prove that a document is a contract?

READING

Robinson v. Galt Chemical Products Ltd., [1933] O.W.N. 502 (C.A.).

Facts: In this case the plaintiff Robinson and the defendant Galt Chemical Products Ltd. entered into a written contract which authorized the plaintiff to act as a brokerage agent for the sale of a product called "Charm." The contract was signed on November 1, 1925, and was said to be effective until mutually dissolved. Both parties benefited from the association. The plaintiff did the promotion in the spring, but the benefits were not fully realized until the fall. On June 31, 1931, the plaintiff was notified of the termination of the contract effective August 30, 1931. At the trial, the judge decided that he would change the contract to read that it could be "terminated by either party on reasonable notice."

Held (on appeal):

[The court stated that] . . . when a written contract is produced it requires cogent and convincing evidence to justify the court in altering its terms. . . .

. . . It is contended that there was a mutual mistake . . . the plaintiff specifically says he thought "It could not be cancelled except by consent of either party." There was no . . . evidence here as to justify . . . an amendment contrary to the understanding of the plaintiff. . . .

. . . [A] business contract . . . must be interpreted in a business way; and it would be a palpable absurdity to consider such a contract as a perpetual claim on the defendant to oblige it for all time to continue the plaintiff in such work; the only reasonable way of interpreting it is to consider it as terminable on reasonable notice [7 Halisbury, 2nd ed., pp. 182 and 183]. . . . Was the notice given a reasonable notice?

. . . [H]ere it may be months before the value of his services appears—an increased sale may brought about which will not be apparent for a considerable time. . . .

The plaintiff accepted the termination of his contract in November. . . .

The appeal should be allowed to the extent of giving plaintiff pay until the time he acted upon the dismissal. . . . The costs of the appeal should be paid by the defendant. . . .

13

Breach of Contract
and Remedies Therefor

Unit 13.1
Breach of Contract

RENUNCIATION

If one of the parties indicates his or her intention to renounce (that is, not to complete) a contract, the other party is excused from further performance. Thus in the case of *General Billposting Co. v. Atkinson* [1909] A.C. 118, an employee had signed an agreement not to compete with his employer for a certain period after termination of employment. He was later wrongfully dismissed without notice. The court held that the employee was no longer bound by the contract not to compete with his former employer.

Another example of breach of contract might involve a student hired for the summer months of June, July, and August. Suppose, on May 15, the hirer tells the student his services will no longer be required. The student would have the right to sue immediately for breach of contract or he may wait until June 1. This is known as "anticipatory breach."

The courts have held that the renunciation must relate to the whole performance, rather than just part of it. They have also held that if renunciation is not accepted immediately by the innocent party, then this party may lose his or her right of action should the other party subsequently announce the intention to complete the contract. Thus, in *Avery v. Bowden* (1856), 5 E.&B. 714, A agreed to sail his ship to Odessa, and take a cargo from X's agent within a certain number of days. The agent refused to supply the cargo, but A decided to wait until the days ran out. In the meantime, however, war broke out and it would have been illegal to accept the cargo. Since A had not acted immediately on the renunciation by X's agent, X was able to plead successfully that the contract was discharged by action of the Queen's enemies.

The same principle applies if one party has made it impossible by his actions to perform as agreed. For example, suppose I hire A to build a house for me beginning in July of this year. However, when July arrives, A has already taken a permanent job with a construction company. In this situation, A has put himself into a position where he cannot perform, so I am excused from the contract of hiring, yet may sue for damages. In effect, A has renounced his contract with me.

COMPLETE OR PARTIAL DISCHARGE

Failure of performance may either result in complete discharge or may only create a right of action resulting from the breach. It will depend on whether the subject matter involved consists of: (a) independent versus concurrent promises; (b) substantial performance; or (c) conditions or warranties. Each of these is now discussed.

Independent versus Concurrent Promises

The courts have held that, unless it is clear that the promises of the contracting parties are clearly *independent*, they will be regarded as concurrent. Thus in dealing with a sale of goods, Bayley J., in *Bloxham v. Sanders* (1825), 4 B.&C. 941 at 948, stated:

> Where goods are sold and nothing is said as to the time of the delivery, or the time of payment, and every thing the seller has to do with them is complete, the property vests in the buyer, so as to subject him to the risk of any accident which may happen to the goods and the seller is liable to deliver them whenever they are demanded upon payment of the price, but the buyer has no right to have possession of the goods till he pays the prices.

Therefore the breach by one party of his promise, which promise is central to the performance of the contract, will relieve the other party of the obligation to perform his part of the contract.

Partial or Substantial Performance

There are circumstances which occur during the course of performing a contract which give rise to the right of one of the parties to renounce, without further liability, his obligation to perform his part of the contract. This was illustrated by the case of *Millar's Karri & Jarrah Co. v. Weddel, Turner & Co.* (1908), 100 L.T. 128, where the court held that:

> If the breach is of such a kind or takes place in such circumstances as may reasonably lead to the inference that similar breaches will be committed in relation to subsequent deliveries, the whole contract may there and then be regarded as repudiated and may be rescinded. If for instance a buyer fails to pay for one delivery in such circumstances as to lead to the inference that he will not be able to pay for subsequent deliveries, or if the seller delivers goods differing from the requirements of the contract, and does so in such circumstances as to lead to the inference that he cannot, or will not, deliver any other kinds of goods in the future, the other contrcting party will be under no obligation to wait to see what will happen: he can at once cancel the contract and rid himself of the difficulty.

However, where the contract has been substantially performed (a question of fact to be determined by the court), the innocent party will not be excused from performance. Of course, the innocent party may well make a claim to obtain compensation for the deficiency in performance by the other party.

Conditions and Warranties

Over the years the common law courts have established the rule that, if the vital subject matter (or condition) of a contract is not fulfilled, the contract may be set aside on the grounds of breach of contract. Consequently, the injured party may withdraw from the contract and usually also sue for damages. However, if only a minor item is omitted, the contract must be carried out with compensation to the injured party for the deficiency. Thus, if a person orders a car with a 300 horsepower engine but receives a 200 horsepower one, this is a vital matter and can be treated as a breach of condition. Consequently, the purchaser can have the contract rescinded. However, suppose the only fault is the omission of a thin gold line around the body of the car. Then, although performance of the contract is not perfect, no breach of condition is considered to have occurred. There has been only what is termed a breach of warranty. The most that the purchaser can therefore request from the courts is that he be compensated either in money, or by having the line painted on the car to bring it up to specifications. Whether failure to perform exactly according to the terms of the contract is considered a breach of condition or a breach of warranty will depend on the circumstances.

Suppose that performance under a contract has been carried on for a period of time and what might normally be considered a breach of condition occurs. Then the courts will rule that because performance has already substantially taken place, the breach must be treated as a breach of warranty instead. This means that the aggrieved party is only entitled to damages.

Illustrative Cases

In *Lightburn v. Belmont Sales Ltd.* (1969), 69 W.W.R. 734, the buyer asked the dealer to sell him a cheap, economical, reliable car and the dealer recommended a Ford Cortina, which developed seventeen faults in six months and never operated satisfactorily. Even after six months the court held that there had never been proper acceptance and decided that all the faults taken together constituted a fundamental breach of condition which allowed the buyer to repudiate the contract and get his money back.

In *Behn v. Burness* (1863), 3 B.&S. 751, a ship was stated in the contract of the charter party "to be now in the port of Amsterdam." The fact that the ship was not in that port, as stated, amounted to a condition and permitted the charterer to be discharged from the contract.

In *Gladholm v. Hays* (1841) 2 M.&G. 257, a charter provided that "the vessel [was] to sail from England on or before the 4th of February next." The vessel did not sail until later, and on its arrival at Trieste, the charterer refused to load a cargo, declaring that the promise to leave by the specified date was a condition of the charter. He won the case.

The implied conditions of ownership, description, fitness, and merchantability contained in the Sale of Goods Act are example of conditions where the contract may be treated as terminated if they are not met—for example, if the food served in a restaurant is not fit to eat.

The nature of a *warranty*, and when it will be regarded as such, is illustrated by the case of *Bettini v. Gye* (1876), 1 Q.B.D. 183. In this case, the signer signed a contract to appear exclusively for the director of an opera company in London in operas and concerts. The contract provided that the singer attend six days of rehearsals prior to his engagement, but he did not arrive until forty-eight hours before the first performance. The director repudiated the contract. The court, in deciding the case, stated:

> Parties may think some matter, apparently of very little importance, essential; and if they sufficiently express an intention to make the literal fulfilment of such a thing a condition precedent, it will be one; or they may think that the performance of some matter, apparently of essential importance and prima facie a condition precedent, is not really vital and may be compensated for in damages, and if they sufficiently expressed such an intention, it will not be a condition precedent.

Since there was no expression of intention in the contract, the court applied its own interpretation as to whether a condition existed. It held that the term as to the rehearsals was not vital, and was not therefore a condition; its breach did not operate as a discharge and could be compensated for by damages.

In the case of a railway company, any failure to carry goods, except because of an act of God or inherent vice (such as goods improperly packed), is a breach of a condition, according to common law. In the case of the railway timetable, the railway merely warrants that the train will arrive on time.

However, if a vital term of the contract has been broken, this becomes in fact a breach of condition and the innocent party may have the contract cancelled, claim damages, and look elsewhere for performance. But if the innocent party goes on with the contract, and takes a benefit from it, it is too late to claim a breach of condition and the breach must be treated as a breach of warranty.

In *Pust v. Dowie* (1864), 5 B. & S. 20, the case of a charter to Sydney, the charterer agreed to pay 1,550 pounds sterling for the use of a vessel, providing the vessel would carry not less than 1000 tons of cargo. It happened that the ship could not carry this weight but the charter was carried out and the charterer later pleaded breach of condition. Blackburn J., stated:

> If, when the matter was *still executory*, the charterer had refused to put any goods on board, on the ground that the vessel was not of the capacity for which he had stipulated, I will not say that he might not have been justified in repudiating the contract altogether; in that case the condition would have been a condition precedent in the full sense.

But, he added:

Is not this a case in which a substantial part of the consideration has been received? And to say that the failure of a single ton (which would be enough to support the plea) is to prevent the defendant from being compelled to pay anything at all, would be deciding contrary to the exception put in the case of *Behn v. Burness.*

REVIEW QUESTIONS

1. What is meant by renunication of a contract? What are the injured party's legal rights?
2. A person may sometimes be able to have a contract set aside, or "repudiated." What are the grounds for this?
3. What is the purpose of the distinction between independent and concurrent promises?
4. What is meant by "substantial performance"?
5. Distinguish between a breach of condition and a breach of warranty.
6. Give your own example of a situation involving substantial performance which would allow only the innocent party to sue for breach of warranty.
7. Distinguish between the breach of condition situation in *Lightburn v. Belmont Sales* and the breach of warranty situation in *Bettini v. Gye.*

PROBLEMS

1. The plaintiff and his wife entered into a written contract on September 27, 1972, agreeing to purchase a new house to be constructed on a developer's building site for $43,375. The original closing date was December 15. The agreement provided for an extension of the closing date "for reasons such as strikes . . . unavoidable casualties" and it was so extended to March 15 by mutual agreement. The agreement also mentioned that, providing the interior was completed to liveable standard, the closing could take place and outside work could be completed later. There was also another provision which stated that the vendor could terminate the contract if he could not complete by the extended closing date. Although the purchaser was prepared to close and tendered accordingly through his solicitor, *the defendant terminated the contract,* returned a cheque for the deposit, and alleged impossibility to complete. It was found at the trial that *no work was done during September, October and very little in January and February, although it took two and a half to three months to complete a house.* The evidence also showed that the *plaintiff repeatedly pressed for completion* to the annoyance of the site manager. The plaintiff sued for specific performance or alternatively for damages for breach of contract.
   (a) Was this a proper contract in its form, i.e., written?
   (b) List some of the conditions.
   (c) Did the contract allow the developer to terminate?
   (d) What is such a provision classified or termed in law?

(e) What is specific performance?

(f) How would damages be calculated?

(g) On the facts who won the case?

(h) What formalities surround the extension of closing date?

(i) How would the plaintiff tender?

(See *Cull v. Heritage Mills Development Ltd.* (1974), 49 D.L.R. (3d) 521).

2. A contractor submitted a bid on a contract involving sanitary sewers and pumping stations in Port Colborne on the shores of Lake Erie. The contract provisions were extensive and the *contractor was liable for making his own preliminary tests* and calculations for the job before tendering, while the Ontario Water Resources Commission excluded itself from any liability. Test borings made by an independent agency were made available to any tenderers. The contractor's tender was accepted. *The job took an extra six months to complete mainly because of extensive water seepage.* The contractor then submitted a bill for $100,000 over the agreed price because of this unforeseen problem. This case was referred to a Board of Arbitration, which allowed the contractor approximately 50% of his claim which alleged fundamental breach of contract and claimed that, because of this, the disclaimers of the Water Resources Commission were ineffective.

Discuss some legal implications involved in this case and indicate the likely decision. Refer to *Re Baldasaro & McGregor Ltd. and R.* (1974), 4 O.R. (2d) 557.

READING

Lightburn v. Belmont Sales Ltd. (1969), 69 W.W.R. 734 (B.C. S.C.).

Facts: On April 8, 1978, Mr. Lightburn purchased a new 1968 Cortina motor vehicle, white in colour, for $2,705. In making his purchase, Mr. Lightburn first of all heard advertisements about this car over the radio. He told the car salesman that he wanted an economical, reliable car, and he purchased the Cortina on the salesman's assurance that the car would meet his requirements.

During the next eight months the car developed an electrical-circuit breakdown, oil pump trouble, battery trouble, oil leaks, and brake troubles. Finally, when it broke down during a bad storm, he returned it to the dealer and demanded his money back.

The plaintiff based his case on s. 20(a) of the Sale of Goods Act, R.S.B.C. 1960, c. 344: "there is no implied condition as to the quality or fitness for any particular purpose of goods . . . except . . . (a) where the buyer, expressly or by implication, makes known to the seller the particular purpose for which the goods are required, so as to show that the buyer relies on the seller's skill or judgment, and the goods are of a description which it is in the course of the seller's business to supply . . . there is an implied condition that the goods are reasonably fit for such purpose."

The foregoing implied condition applies to this case unless negated by an express clause or unless reduced to a warranty by s. 17(1): ". . . the buyer may waive the condition or may elect to treat the breach of such condition as a breach of warranty. . . ." or s. 17(3): "Where . . . the buyer has accepted the goods . . . or where the contract is for specific goods, the property in which has passed to the buyer, the breach of any condition to be fulfilled by the seller can only be treated as a breach of warranty. . . ."

There was an exempting clause in the retail buyer's agreement, i.e., clause C. 2: ". . . The Vendor's obligation under this warranty is limited to replacing or otherwise making good at the Vendor's location such parts as shall be returned to the Vendor. . . . *This warranty is expressly in lieu of all other conditions and warranties expressed or implied. . . .*"

The plaintiff alleged fundamental breach which, as such, was not governed by any exempting clause limiting the liability of the defendant.

Held per Ruttan J.:

The particular principle which applies here . . . is that where the defects are so numerous, that, taken en masse, they destroy the workable character of the thing sold, this may amount to a fundamental and total breach of contract. . . . I quote from the judgment . . . *Yeoman Credit Ltd. v. Apps*, [1962] 2 Q.B. 508 . . . at p. 520: "Whether there has been a breach of a fundamental condition . . . is a question of degree. . . . It may be as in *Pollock & Co. v. Macrae*, [1922] S.C. (H.L.) 192 (and in the present case) an accumulation of defects which, taken singly, might well have been within the exemption clause, but, taken en masse, constitute such a non-performance or repudiation . . . going to the root of the contract as disentitles the owners to take refuge behind an exception clause. . . ."

. . . [I]n *Suisse Atlantique Société D'Armement Maritime S.A. v. N.V. Rotterdamsche Kolen Centrale*, [1967] 1 A.C. 361 [it was stated that:] " . . . in so many cases exceptions clauses are to be found in rather small print sometimes on the back of the main terms of the contract and . . . the doctrine of "contra proferentes" has been applied . . . [T]hey are strictly construed against the contracting party seeking protection. . . . But where there is a breach of a fundamental term the law has taken an even firmer line for there is a strong . . . presumption that in inserting a clause of exclusion or limitation . . . the parties are not contemplating breaches of fundamental terms and such clauses do not apply to relieve a party from the consequences of such a breach. . . ."

. . . In my judgment, clause C. 2 of the sale contract . . . was never intended to cover a situation of fundamental breach. . . . [T]he clause is confined to an undertaking to replace defective parts and warrants that each part is free from defects. . . .

I find that if there has been a fundamental breach there is no exempting clause that prevents that breach from operating to determine the contract. . . .

I conclude that the defendant was in breach of a fundamental term of the contract to purchase a motor car of workable character. . . . The defendants cannot rely on the exempting clauses . . . the plaintiff is entitled to declare the contract void for fundamental breach and to have rescission thereof. . . .

There will be judgment therefore for the plaintiff in the amount of $2,075 for rescision, $29.50 [taxi, three battery charges, and parking for a replacement] as special damages and costs.

Unit 13.2
Remedies for Breach of Contract

Normally, when one party fails to perform his or her obligations under a contract, a breach has occurred and the offended party has three rights:

1. to be excused from further performance;
2. to sue for *quantum meruit*—that is, payment of a fair price for work done under the original contract; or
3. to sue for damages for the breach of the contract, and/or request the court to issue an order of specific performance, an injunction, or other equitable remedy.

QUANTUM MERUIT

In *Mavor v. Pyne* (1825), 3 Bing. 288, Best C.J. stated, "If a man agrees to deliver me one hundred quarters of corn, and after I have received ten quarters, I decline taking any more, he is in all events entitled to recover against me the value of the ten I have received."

If a man sits down in a barber-shop chair, his action may be construed as an offer to have his hair cut. If no price is agreed on, then the price would be the barber's posted price. If the man changed his mind while his hair was being cut, and refused to let the barber continue, the original contract would have been broken. In this case, the barber could claim in quantum meruit for the work done, which could be equivalent to part or the full price unless the work done was of no value. The same reasoning would apply if A, a lawyer, starts working on a case at B's request. Then suppose, after a month or two, that B informs A that she no longer wishes him to proceed with the case. Obviously, A is entitled to be paid for the time he has already spent.

The work for which payment is claimed under quantum meruit must always be in accordance with the terms of the contract, which the defendant must have an opportunity to accept or reject. In *Farman v. Liddesdale*, [1900] A.C. 190, a ship repairer did not do the work in the manner agreed, but did more than the contract called for. In this case, neither the original contract was performed, nor had the shipowner agreed to the work done in excess of the original contract. Therefore the court held that the ship owner, in taking back his ship, did not have to compensate the ship repairer in any way. This case would be a good precedent for the person who leaves his car with an automobile dealer's service department or auto garage for a tune-up and returns to be faced with a bill of $500, including charges for, say, replacement of brakes, shocks, and a valve repair job, which are not normally included in the trade term "tune-up." The original contract has not been carried out as contemplated and the substituted contract has not been accepted by the car owner, and the latter could refuse to pay for any of the unanticipated repairs.

However, quantum meruit claims are not deemed to arise when, for example, a father asks his son to help him put up a fence, or a friendly neighbour agrees to mow the lawn during a homeowner's absence.

MEASURE OF DAMAGES

Parke B., in *Robinson v. Harman* (1848), 1 Ex. 855, stated, "The rule of the common law is that where a party sustains a loss by reason of a breach of contract, he is, so far as money can do it, to be placed in the same situation, with respect to damages, as if the contract had been performed."

However, in *Hadley v. Baxendale* (1854), 9 Ex. 354, the court said that if the breach resulted in losses which neither party contemplated or could reasonably foresee, that only the damages which a reasonable man might contemplate when the contract was made are recoverable. Thus in *Horne v. Midland Railway Co.* (1873), L.R. 8 C.P. 131, where the purchasers wanted shoes of a certain quality delivered by a certain day to ensure a high price, the seller who gave them to a carrier to be delivered but did not stipulate the need for delivery by a certain date, could not recover his damages from the carrier when because of late delivery the purchasers refused to accept them.

In *Addis v. Gramophone Co.*, [1909] A.C. 488 at p. 491, a man who had been hired in Calcutta at a salary plus commission, with provision for six months' notice in case of dismissal, was improperly dismissed. He sued his employer and the court held that while he was entitled to damages for breach of contract, no damages were recognized in contract for injured feelings or difficulty in obtaining another job, but "were in the nature of compensation, not punishment."

LIQUIDATED DAMAGES

The two main types of damages, special and general, were explained in Chapter 4. So also were nominal, punitive, and consequential damages. Here we consider what are called "liquidated damages."

Sometimes a contract will specify a sum of money that is to be paid to the injured party in the event of late or non-performance. The judge will have to decide whether this amount should be considered as a *penalty* or as liquidated damages. The distinction is important because, if the amount is considered a *penalty*, the injured party forfeits his entire claim because the agreed amount was excessive. However, if the sum is considered to be "liquidated damages," the amount named in the contract may be claimed, because it is equivalent to the damage which actually occurred.

Occasionally the parties themselves will estimate the damages to be paid in the event of unsatisfactory performance or breach of contract. For example, if a school building is to be finished by September 1, damages at the rate of the cost of hiring alternative accommodation at, say, $500, may be fixed for each day of delay. These damages are called liquidated damages, and will only be allowed if the judge finds that the parties attempted to make a genuine estimate of the damages that would be suffered. If the parties did not attempt to make a genuine fair estimate of the amount of money to be lost, the judge will rule the liquidated damages estimate to be illegal, and rule out any damages whatsoever.

For example, in *Shatilla v. Feinstein*, [1923] 2 W.W.R. 1474, the defendant who had sold a dry goods business undertook in his contract with the purchaser not to engage in a similar business for five years, and agreed to pay $10,000 as liquidated damages for any breach of this undertaking. However, before the five years were up, he became a director in a competing firm. The court held that it would allow a pre-estimate of damages when it is possible to foresee damages which may result from the breach, but here the contract could be broken in many different ways; that is, by becoming a salesman, a deliveryman, an entrepreneur, and in each case the damages would be different, therefore the court viewed the pre-estimate as a penalty and disallowed it.

The courts will also allow the plaintiff to recover damages for loss of profit, in the case of non-delivery or only partial delivery. In such a case where the contract calls for goods to be delivered and sold on resale, the damages must be calculated to be the difference between the contract price and the market price on the date when delivery should have occurred.

In determining the intentions of the parties, the judge will consider all the circumstances involved in a contract and will apply the following rules:

(a) If the contract is for an item of unknown value, and a given amount of money is to be paid for the breach of one or more of its conditions, the amount specified may be recovered as liquidated damages. However, the amount must not be unreasonably large for the circumstances. Otherwise, it will be considered a penalty, therefore illegal, and the court will not order any damages paid.

(b) If the contract is for an item of known value, and a greater sum is to be paid on breach of the contract, then this is a penalty and not liquidated damages.

(c) If the contract consists of various terms, some of known value and others of unknown value, or some of large value and others of nominal value, and a given amount of money is to be paid for a breach of the contract, then it is presumed that this is a penalty.

Irrespective of whether the parties actually refer to such compensation clauses in the contract as "liquidated damages," the court is not bound by such a description and may rule that the clause is a "penalty" and therefore strike it out as being invalid.

SPECIFIC PERFORMANCE

Occasionally, the common law remedy of money damages was insufficient to compensate an injured party in a breach of contract case. Consequently, the Equity Courts came up with other remedies. One of these was specific performance. For example, suppose A has contracted to buy a house with an outlook that is particularly attractive to him, and the other party, B, decides not to go through with the sale. Then the court may decide that A cannot be compensated merely by being given money damages for the purchase of another house. A is not, in fact, getting the house he particularly wanted and arranged to buy. The same would apply if A had made arrangements to buy an antique Model "A" Ford car in excellent condition. If the other party refused to go through with the contract, it would be extremely difficult for A to buy a similar car elsewhere because of their relative scarcity. Therefore, the court would grant him specific performance and force the other party to sell him the car as originally agreed.

In *Ryan v. Mutual Tontine Association*, [1893] 1 Ch. 126, the court stated that "the remedy of specific performance was invented, and has been cautiously applied in order to meet cases where the ordinary remedy by an action for damages is not an adequate compensation for breach of contract. The juridiction to compel specific performance has always been treated as discretionary and confined within well-known rules." Thus money compensation might be inadequate in a contract concerning the sale of land. In the case of chattels, however, the remedy of specific performance would be reserved for items such as a rare Renoir painting, an "antique" automobile, or a "Chippendale" table.

Specific performance is granted only in cases where it would be fair and just. For example, in *Webster v. Cecil* (1861), 30 Beav. 62, where the seller made a palpable clerical error in his final quotation, having already refused an offer of $1,000 pounds more, the court refused to award specific performance in favour of the plaintiff. In this situation it would have been unfair for one party to force the mistaken terms upon the other party.

Finally, in connection with specific performance, we should mention that such a remedy will never be granted to enforce personal services—for example, to force a singer to perform or an athlete to compete. This is because the court has no practical way to ensure good performance and the courts will never make an order which they cannot enforce. Damages could however be claimed for breach of contract.

INJUNCTION

An injunction is a court order that either enforces a promise made or prevents one party from breaking a promise, such as a promise not to set up a competitive business following the sale of one's retail store or a promise not to reveal "trade secrets" on changing one's job. As another example, suppose A enters into a contract with a manufacturer whereby she obtains an exclusive sales distributorship for a particular province. Then suppose A later discovers that the same manufacturer had granted a similar distributorship in the same area to another party. Obviously, there has been a breach of A's contract. If money damages are unsatisfactory, A can ask the court to grant an injunction prohibiting the manufacturer from supplying another outlet so long as the contract with A exists.

In *Clegg v. Hands* (1890), 44 Ch.D. 503, an injunction restrained an innkeeper from buying his beer from anyone but the brewer with whom he had a contract. In *Lumley v. Wagner* (1852), 1 D.M. & C. 604, while a singer was not forced by specific performance to carry out her singing contract, an injunction restrained her from singing elsewhere. Generally, restrictive employment contracts are regarded as anti-competitive and therefore against public policy unless considered reasonable insofar as geographical area and duration are concerned. They should not deprive a person of his opportunity to earn a living at his chosen calling.

DISCHARGE OF RIGHT OF ACTION

Following a breach of contract, both parties may agree, by means of a "release," to discharge one another from their obligations under the contract. Since the innocent party may not be receiving any consideration, such a release should be made under seal.

A modern-day method of settling contract disputes is to resort to arbitration, in which case both parties are agreeing to accept the award and thus both are receiving new considerations.

On the other hand, discharge may result in what is termed "accord and satisfaction." In such a case, the innocent party, in return for giving up his right to sue, or his *accord*, receives some *satisfaction* such as:

1. a new right—for example, a negotiable instrument as payment;
2. a composition of creditors; for example, a creditor agreeing to accept only part of his debt because other creditors are being paid "pro rata" (in proportion to their credit);
3. or some different acceptable performance.

When a court of competent jurisdiction pronounces a judgment upon a breach of contract dispute, further obligations under the contract are discharged; the contract is "merged" into the court judgment. That is, all reference to rights and obligations is determined by the judgment and no further reference is made to the contract.

PAYMENT INTO COURT

This procedure was devised to allow a defendant to admit part or all of a claim, pay into court a certain sum, and be freed from court costs if the plaintiff persisted with a court action and failed to recover more at trial than the amount paid into court.

Suppose, for example, that A is being sued by B for $10,000 damages for injuries, loss of salary, and so on arising from a car accident. A discusses the case with his insurance company and agrees that there is liability for $5,000. The insurance company, on A's behalf, then tenders this amount to B and, if it is refused, pays it into court against the claim. If B continues with her court action and the judge awards less than $5,000, then B, who (as the winner) would normally be entitled to court costs, must pay her own costs plus those incurred by A as from the time of payment of the $5,000 into court. If the judge's award is for $5,001 or more, the payment into court would have no effect and B would be entitled to court costs, in accordance with the appropriate court tariffs.

WITHOUT PREJUDICE

The term "without prejudice" is used when a party wishes to negotiate a settlement and desires to admit some liability. Heading a letter "Without Prejudice" ensures that a court will not later allow use of this admission by the other party in a court action. No letter bearing such words is ever admitted in court either for or against the party which has originated it.

Furthermore, in some cases it has been held that written communication between the parties which has as its objective the settlement of a pending or proposed lawsuit will not be permitted to be used as evidence in court even where the words "without prejudice" do not appear.

REVIEW QUESTIONS

1. What is meant by the legal principle of *quantum meruit*?
2. What is meant by the term "liquidated damages"?
3. Distinguish, from the point of view of their different legal implications, between a "penalty" and "liquidated damages."
4. Under what contract circumstances will a judge rule that: (a) a penalty or (b) liquidated damages is appropriate?
5. What is the equitable remedy of "specific performance"? Give an example.
6. What is an injunction? Give an example.
7. Sometimes the defendant in a court case may be advised to make payment into court before the case is decided. Explain.

PROBLEMS

1. A drug store flyer contained the following statement: "One drug store chain did almost *45 million dollars in sales* . . . Shopper's Drug Mart offers the *best possible dollar value and saving in every item*, every day." It was proved at the trial that four specific items were being sold at prices higher than at comparable competitive stores. It was objected that the "best possible value" referred only to the advertising store.
   (a) Who took this case to court?
   (b) What level of legislation applies?

(c) What section of the Act would govern the charge to be laid in this case?

(d) Do you think the charge deserves a conviction?

(e) Do you think the flyer was misleading?

(f) Suppose the flyer was made up by an advertising agency. Where would responsibility lie?

(g) Who won the case?

2. In 1975, the plaintiffs were charged and convicted by the defendant union of "ratting" and were expelled from the union. The court held that the plaintiffs were wrongfully suspended or expelled, that they did not receive a fair hearing, and that charges of "ratting" were unfounded. They are now seeking damages for loss of reputation, lost wages, and mental distress. In *Addis v. Gramophone Co. Ltd.*, [1909] A.C. 488, dealing with a claim of wrongful dismissal, the Court held that damages could not be given for the "harsh and humiliating way in which he was dismissed." In *McGregor on Damages* (13th ed.), 1972, p. 456, para. 67: "If however the contract is not primarily a commercial one in the sense that it affects not the plaintiff's business interests, but his personal, social and family interests, the door is not closed to awarding damages for mental suffering . . . parties to the contract had such damage in their contemplation." In *Jarvis v. Swan Tours Ltd.*, [1973] 1 All E.R. 71, it was held that in a proper case damages for mental distress can be recovered in contract, just as damages for shock can be recovered in tort. One such case is a contract for a holiday, or any other contract to provide entertainment and enjoyment. If the contracting party breaks the contract, damages can be given for the disappointment, the distress, the upset, and the frustration caused.

Give any arguments which may be either for or against the plaintiffs in their claim for damages. Refer to *Tippett v. International Typographical Union, Local 226* (1976), 71 D.L.R. (3d) 146.

3. The plaintiff was a passenger in a sail boat owned by the defendant James Swan and operated by the defendant Henry G. Swan. In the course of a sailing manoeuvre, the plaintiff's arm was caught in the mainsheet and as a result the arm was broken. The plaintiff was granted an extension of time to issue his writ of summons on January 3, 1978. This extension of time was granted by virtue of the Canada Shipping Act, R.S.C. 1970, c. S-9, s. 645(2) which allows the court jurisdiction to extend the time limitation under subsection (1) which is quoted as follows:

> (1) No action is maintainable to enforce any claim or lien against a vessel or its owners in respect of any damage or loss to another vessel, its cargo or freight, or any property on board that vessel, or for damages for loss of life or personal injuries suffered by any person on board that vessel, caused by the fault of the former vessel, whether such vessel is wholly or partly in fault, unless proceedings therein are commenced within two years from the date when the damage or loss or injury was caused. . . .

The judge ruled that the foregoing section had no application to the facts of this case! Indicate the judge's reason or reasons. What limitation period should have applied to this case, if any? Refer to *Hovey v. Swan* (1978), 19 O.R. (2d) 725 (H.C.).

Unit 13.3
Limitation of Actions

Because people forget, witnesses die, and evidence becomes lost, the courts have always taken the attitude that a person must not delay in proceeding with a claim. Accordingly, the courts have developed the maxim: "the law will not help him who sleeps on his rights." This means that, under common law, failure to take a case to court and seek justice within a reasonable period of time will result in the right of action being lost, even though the claim itself may still exist.

In the United Kingdom, statutes provided that infancy, coverture, insanity, imprisonment, and absence "beyond the seas" prevented the operation of the statutes. Thus, in the classic case of *Musurus Bey v. Gadban*, [1894] 2 Q.B. 352, the defendant attempted to counter-claim from the estate of one of his creditors, a Turkish ambassador, for a twenty-year-old debt. The court held that he was protected by diplomatic immunity while ambassador, but since he had returned to Turkey and was "beyond the seas," the time limitation pursuant to the statute had not commenced to run, and the claim was not barred. Thus a judgment in England could be executed against the deceased ambassador's estate in that country.

PERIOD OF LIMITATION

Nowadays in Canada, this principle of "limitation" has been established by provincial and federal statutes which specify the maximum time period within which various types of action must be commenced. The general rule with regard to contract debts is that if six complete years have passed, the claim can no longer be enforced in court. Thus if A owes B $500 and B does not collect his debt within six years, the courts would say that because of the Statute of Limitations (which bars contract debts over six years) the debt is no longer collectable through court action. In Quebec, the period of limitation for business debts is five years.

The period of limitation may be longer or shorter than six years, depending on the province and on the subject matter—for example: judgments by courts of record; personal actions on a mortgagor's covenant to pay; actions to recover money out of land; actions for possession, foreclosure or sale; recovery of estates in land or of rent; action on bonds and agreements under seal; chattel mortgages; devices of real property; legacies; and actions against professionals.

Below, as one provincial example, we summarize various sections of the Ontario Limitations Act:

(a) Section 3 provides that the Crown has sixty years to pursue interests respecting land, rents, and revenues;

(b) Section 4 provides that individuals are limited to ten years in pursuing a right of interest in land;

(c) Section 25 provides that a widow is limited to ten years after the death of her husband in suing for dower (that is, acquired before 1978).

(d) Section 33 provides that access to right of air or light may not be acquired by prescription, but this provision does not apply to rights acquired twenty years before March 5, 1880.

(d) Section 31 provides that acquiring rights of way by easement or prescription to water or any land or water of the Crown or being the property of any person must be enjoyed without consent or agreement for over twenty years;

(f) Under section 45, personal actions for rent are limited to twenty years either on a bond or a judgment.

(g) Actions for trespass or simple contract or debt are limited to six years.

(h) Actions for assault, battery, and wounding are limited to four years.

(i) An action for a mortgage is limited to ten years.

(j) Section 50 provides that an acknowledgment within ten years or a part payment renews an indenture, specialty, or judgment for a further ten years.

(k) A promise by word only in case of contract or debt will be evidence of a new or continuing contract unless this acknowledgment is made by writing signed by the party chargeable or agent.

It should be noted that, although a claim may be unenforceable in court because of the Statute of Limitations or other similar Act, it remains in most cases a valid claim. Consequently, it may be enforced in some other way— for example, by right of set off against money owed for some other reason to the person against whom the claim is made. This situation is similar to that of certain contracts which, although valid, may under the Statute of Frauds be unenforceable if not expressed in writing.

Nowadays, it should be noted, most federal and provincial statutes that create a new right or a new obligation also prescribe a period of limitation within which such right must be exercised, or within which such obligation is binding. For example, highway traffic accidents, two years; claims against members of most professional associations, one year; claims against hospitals, one year; and claims against municipalities may even be limited to six months.

The limitation of time starts to run from the moment a debt or right is due. Thus, if A lends B $500 this year and says that he will collect his debt in three years' time, the Statute of Limitations will not start to run until then; and it will not be until six more years that the claim will be outlawed. However, disabilities on the part of A, such as unconsciousness, insanity, or infancy, serve to stop the limitation period from running out. So also does the fact that B leaves the country and places himself out of reach of the

jurisdiction of the courts for six years. The limitation period would only
start to run once he returns to Canada and the jurisdiction of the courts.
However, suppose that A sleeps on his rights for two or three years after
which time B puts himself out of the court's jurisdiction. Then, as the
limitation period has already commenced, the courts may rule that it is too
late for A to enforce his claim.

Extension

The period of limitation may occasionally be extended beyond the six years.
This occurs if the debtor makes some written acknowledgement of his debt.
For example, suppose that A owes B $300, and five years have elapsed
without A's being taken to court. A may feel some remorse at not having paid
his debt and send a $50 payment in the mail. The effect of this payment, or
any other written acknowledgement, is to extend the claim for a further six
years.

Revival

It is also possible that, even after the full period of limitation has expired, a
claim (other than a land claim) may be revived. Thus, if A receives a written
acknowledgement from debtor B of B's debt, admitting her liability
and her intention to repay, the debt is revived. This is true even though
many years may have passed since the debt was originally due. Once a debt is
revived, the period of limitation must run for a further six years before the
claim is outlawed.

The type of acknowledgement period to revive a debt was explained by
Mellish L.J., in *Re River Steamer Co.* (1871), 6 Ch. App. 820 at p. 828:

> There must be one of . . . three things to take the case out of the Statute
> [of Limitations]. Either there must be an acknowledgment of the debt,
> from which a promise to pay is to be implied; or, secondly, there must
> be an unconditional promise to pay the debt; or, thirdly, there must be a
> conditional promise to pay the debt, and evidence that the condition
> has been performed.

APPLICATION OF PAYMENTS

It is not uncommon that the parties to a contract will have some dispute
about its terms whereupon one party pays less than the other party believes
is owing. Similarly, where there are several different debts owing between
the parties one party pays only part of the total debt. In both of these
circumstances, the payor may or may not designate the debt to which the
payment is to be applied. There are certain rules governing the application
of payments on outstanding debts:

1. A debtor, in sending a payment, may allocate it to the payment of any
   particular debt. This could be either an outlawed debt or a debt which has
   just fallen due.

2. If no allocation is made and the amount paid coincides exactly with one of the debts, such debt will be deemed to have been paid.
3. If an odd amount is sent without any allocation, the creditor has the discretion to allocate it, even to an outlawed debt.
4. If no allocation is made and an odd amount is sent, the court on application will apply the remittance to the earliest non-outlawed debt.

An illustrative case is that of *Petryk v. Petryk* (1966), 56 W.W.R. 120 (Man. Q.B.). This case dealt with an action for goods sold and delivered, up to June 8, 1963. The action was brought in May 1965. A large part of the goods were alleged to have been sold and delivered more than six years prior to the beginning of the action, and recovery for these goods would normally be barred by s. 3(1)(*f*) of the Limitations of Actions Act. *It was necessary for the plaintiff to establish a payment on account within the six year period to offset the provision of the statute.* The defendant had applied for a forestry licence, also sold through the services of the creditor, making the necessary deposit of $500. A refund of $435 was made and by agreement this was applied to the defendant's account in 1959. The court ruled that the plaintiff was successful in part, since by agreement the refund was applied as a part payment to the account. This was sufficient to bring the account out of the provisions of the Limitations of Actions Act.

REAL PROPERTY

With regard to limitation of actions, real property occupies a special position. Suppose a mortgage deed was made between lender and borrower ten years ago and no acknowledgement or payment has been made during that period of time. Then, under in the Land Registry System, the mortgage will have no effect. Thus land claims, if not acted on, are barred after ten years.

Note should also be made here of what is called *adverse possession*. This means that if a person goes on to another person's land, openly, without consent, and lives on it or uses the property as an owner would (for example, by occupying a cottage) with the knowledge of all concerned and treats the land as his or her own by, for example, erecting buildings, tilling the soil, putting up fences, paying taxes, and so on, and does so for a period of ten years, this person acquires "squatter's rights" (*adverse possession*). Consequently, he or she may not be put out by the original owner.

Another aspect of the principle of adverse possession is that a "squatter" may obtain a "prescriptive easement" after using a right-of-way or easement for a period of twenty years as if he or she were the owner.

It is important to note that the principle of adverse possession applies only to land registered under the Land Registry System and not to land registered under the Land Titles System. The difference between these two systems is explained in Chapter 16.

SPECIALTIES AND COURT JUDGMENTS

A claim arising from a specialty (a document under seal) is not barred until twenty years have elapsed. The same period also applies to court judgments ordering a defendant to pay a money claim.

REVIEW QUESTIONS

 1. What is meant by the limitation of action? What is the pertinent legal maxim?
 2. Under the statute of limitations, the courts will not help a person collect a debt if more than a certain number of years have passed. What is the purpose of such legislation? What can a creditor do once this time period has elapsed?
 3. When does the limitation of time discussed previously begin to run?
 4. What happens to the limitation of time if the plaintiff suffers from unconsciousness, insanity, infancy, or other disability?
 5. What happens to the limitation of time if the debtor leaves the country?
 6. How might the period of limitations be extended?
 7. How can the period of limitations be revived? And for how long?
 8. A debtor may, in sending a payment, allocate it to the payment of any particular debt. Explain.
 9. If no allocation of the payment is made by the debtor, the court on application by the creditor will apply the remittance to which debt?
10. A claim to land expires after how many years? Explain.
11. What is meant by: (a) "adverse possession"; (b) prescriptive easement?
12. What is a specialty? What time limit applies to claims arising from a specialty?

PROBLEMS

 1. B has owed C $1,000 for ten years. On January 1, this year, B meets C and says, "I have always felt badly about not paying you that money, but you know I helped you in your business for a long time." Can C now sue B because of revival of contract?
 2. Mike, aged 16 years, was involved in a car crash twenty years ago. He was sued in the courts and represented by his father. The judge found him liable and ordered him to pay $20,000 damages. No action has been taken since. If Mike won $15,000 in a lottery today, could the other party still garnishee this windfall money?
 3. X and Y, who live in Ontario, were involved in a motor vehicle accident in that province. As they are neighbours and reputable citizens, they have attempted to work out an amicable settlement. However, fourteen months later, X suddenly decided that friends or not, he will have to take his action for damages against Y to the courts. Is his action now effectively barred by a provision in the Ontario Highway Traffic Act?
 4. In 1963, A obtained a loan of $1,000 from B. As evidence of good faith, A

signed a promissory note payable January 1, 1964. A suffered financial reverses, and in 1980, he wrote B a letter in which he acknowledged the debt. If the debt remains unpaid in 1985, and B sues, will B win?

5. D gave E written title to a plot of land in 1965. No one has lived on this land since that time. Can E now safely register his title?

3

LEGAL FORMS OF BUSINESS OWNERSHIP

In this part of the book, we consider the legal forms of ownership that may be used in starting and operating a business firm. In Chapter 14 we look at the sole proprietorship and partnership forms. In Chapter 15 we examine the incorporated business.

14

Sole Proprietorship and Partnership

There are four basic legal forms of business ownership in Canada: the sole proprietorship, the partnership, the corporation, and the co-operative. In this chapter, we consider the first two of these— the simplest for business owners to use as a legal framework for their activities. In the next chapter, we consider the other two forms. Depending on the nature of the business, the stage of its growth, and the number of persons involved, one of these legal forms of ownership is usually more appropriate than the others. The actual choice will depend on an understanding of the characteristics, and advantages and disadvantages, of each.

Unit 14.1
Sole Proprietorship

A sole proprietorship is the legal form that a businessperson operating alone can most easily use. The only alternative is the private business corporation discussed in the next chapter.

The sole proprietorship is the form of ownership used by many small businesses such as restaurants, florists, and other retail stores, as well as by business, professional, and tradespeople such as hairdressers, medical doctors, accountants, plumbers, and carpenters offering a service to the public.

ADVANTAGES

The advantages offered by this form of business ownership include: simplicity, low cost, high personal motivation, quickness and freedom of action, privacy, and ease of termination.

Simplicity. It is relatively simple for someone to establish a sole proprietorship. A person need only obtain a municipal business licence where necessary. However, if the owner wishes to give the business a name other than his or her own or wishes to use the words "and Company," the owner must register the name at the provincial or local registry office where such records are kept and made available to the public. In Ontario, for example, the business owner must file a signed declaration showing: full name and residence address; the name of the business and the date on which he or she first started to use it; an assurance that the proprietor is over 18 years of age or, if a minor, a statement of date of birth. Should the name conflict with that of an existing business, the owner of the new business must choose another name. The sole proprietor always has the right to use his or her own name, even if it is the same as that of a competitor, so long as it is not used in a manner intended to deceive the public. However, a sole proprietor does not have the right to use the terms "Corporation," "Limited," or "Incorporated" or their abbreviations, "Corp.," Ltd.," or "Inc." as part of the business's name because they imply, among other things, that the owner has limited rather than unlimited liability for the debts and other obligations of the business.

Low Cost.   It does not cost much to establish a sole proprietorship. Thus, for example, the fee for a municipal business licence is relatively small, varying according to the nature and size of the business and the municipality in which it is located. Also, the fee for filing a declaration, if necessary, with the divisional registry office is a nominal amount. Furthermore, there is no need to incur legal fees in drawing up a written agreement, as with a partnership, because only one owner is involved. Of course, the non-legal expenses can vary from almost nothing to thousands of dollars, depending on whether the business is to be started out of the person's home or involves, for example, the leasing, stocking, and equipping of good-quality retail premises.

High Personal Motivation.   Because all the profits after tax (or all the losses) accrue to the sole proprietor alone means that such a person is highly motivated to ensure the success of the business. Also, of course, the sole ownership of a business, with complete responsibility for its affairs, and the fact of being one's own boss, is a source of great personal challenge and satisfaction. This is shown by the willingness of many sole proprietors to work extremely long days and six-day weeks, often with little or no annual vacation, in their businesses, particularly during its early years.

Quickness and Freedom of Action.   The sole proprietor, having no partners to consult, can make business decisions quickly should the need arise. The owner can decide to open or close shop, hire or fire employees, add new lines of goods or discontinue old ones promptly and without discussion. He or she has the freedom to make the decisions, good or bad. Of course, this freedom is restricted to some extent by various government controls. The owner must, for example, pay taxes, observe local closing hours, labour laws, and fire and sanitary regulations. To provide certain services—for example, serve alocoholic drinks—the owner must obtain a special licence. In general, however, the sole proprietorship form of business has fewer government restrictions than the other forms of business ownership.

Privacy.   The sole proprietor, unlike the public business corporation, is not required by law to publish financial statements. Success or failure in the business is a private matter, restricted only to the proprietor, his or her accountant, Revenue Canada, and perhaps the local bank manager. This privacy aspect of the sole proprietorship is an important consideration when secret recipes, formulae, processes, contracts, or other confidential information are involved.

Ease of Termination.   So long as there are no bills outstanding, a sole proprietor need not ask anyone's permission to terminate business activities. Furthermore, unlike a business corporation, the proprietor does not need to advertise the fact in advance. He or she merely stops doing business.

DISADVANTAGES

The disadvantages of the sole proprietorship form of business ownership include: unlimited liability, limited talent, limited capital, lack of continuity, and possibly high income tax.

Unlimited Liability.   In the eyes of the law, the sole owner is alone responsible for all the contractual and other legal obligations of the business. Thus, although the owner can arrange, if he or she wishes, to share the profits with a manager or other employees, the owner cannot arrange for them to share the losses. Otherwise the business will be considered to be a partnership rather than a sole proprietorship.

The sole proprietor's liability is unlimited. This means that most of the owner's personal assets (such as house, furniture, car, and stocks) may be seized, if necessary, to pay the outstanding debts of the business. Thus a person's life savings could be wiped out by a business failure. The actual risk varies with the type of business. According to statistics of business failures, there is a high mortality rate among housebuilders and retail stores. However, other businesses, such as doctors' and dentists' practices, incur practically no financial risk so long as they have adequate liability insurance.

Many sole proprietors reduce the risk that unlimited personal liability entails by giving part of their personal assets to their family. Thus it is quite usual for the house in which the sole proprietor lives to belong to the spouse. Since the spouse is an independent legal person who can hold assets in his or her own name, there is no danger that the house might have to be sold to pay the owner's creditors. The only exception, in the case of an impending bankruptcy, is if the house were put in the spouse's name fairly recently with the deliberate intention of defrauding the creditors. There is, of course, a limit beyond which the prudent business owner will not want to go in transferring assets to a spouse. This is the point at which the owner begins to worry about losing the spouse rather than the business.

Limited Talent.   Few people are good at everything. Yet the sole proprietor is responsible for every aspect of the business—buying, selling, manufacturing, financing, accounting, advertising, personnel, customer relations, and so on. Although other people can be employed to help, the ultimate responsibility is still the proprietor's. Also, particularly in the early stages of a business, little cash is available to hire top-notch employees. One way of overcoming this is by employing part-time help—for example, an accountant to keep the financial records, prepare financial statements, and file the income tax return. Nevertheless, even with a small business, the sole proprietor can be overwhelmed by details: his or her abilities, however great, cannot cope with every facet of the business. Being the sole owner can be a considerable disadvantage, particularly if the owner wants to expand the business.

Limited Capital.   The sole proprietor must raise all the funds required for the business. The owner's investment is limited to personal savings and to what he or she can persuade relatives, friends, and the local bank manager to lend. Obviously, the bank will lend less to one person than it would to several as, say, in a partnership. The sole proprietor who later needs additional funds, perhaps for expansion, may find that they are just not available in the amount required. Many sole proprietors try to finance expansion by using reinvested profit, but others are forced to consider taking in partners with cash to invest.

Lack of Continuity.   Another disadvantage associated with the sole proprietorship form of ownership is that, unlike a business corporation, the business legally terminates on the death of the owner. Also, the sole proprietor's absence through illness can quickly cause havoc.

It is possible, in the case of death, for the administrators of the estate to continue the business under letters of administration. But usually such persons have no knowledge, real interest, or time to run the business. Sometimes an employee can manage the business in the absence of the owner for reasons of illness or vacation. But the sole proprietor is lucky to find someone trustworthy and affordable.

Possibly High Income Tax.   The income that the sole proprietor earns from the business must be included, along with any other income, in the personal income tax return. After the various personal exemptions and deductions, this income is then subject to personal income tax at progressive rates. The greater the taxable income, the higher the marginal rate of income tax on each additional dollar. Consequently, once the sole proprietor's business starts to prosper, the government takes 30, 40, or 50% of any extra profit. Once this situation occurs, the sole proprietor will seriously start to consider the incorporation of the business as a means of reducing income tax.

Unit 14.2
Partnership

A partnership is a business firm that is not incorporated but that has two or more owners who pool their talents, funds, trade secrets, and even reputations for profit. Like the sole proprietorship, this form of business ownership is used by many small businesses, such as wholesalers, retailers, doctors, lawyers, accountants, and realtors. In many provinces, doctors and lawyers are still not permitted by their association or society to incorporate their practices. The advantages and disadvantages of the partnership form of business ownership are similar to those of the sole proprietor, except that more than one person is involved.

JURISDICTION

Partnerships in Canada come within the provisions of s. 92 of the Constitution Act, 1867, and are controlled by the provinces as a matter of "local and private interest and licensing." Each common law province has a Partnerships Act, which embodies all the relevant decisions of the common law up to 1890 relating to the association of two or more persons in business which had previously been codified in England by the British Parliament. In Ontario, two other provincial Acts relate to partnerships. The first is the Limited Partnerships Act, whereby limited investment and limited liability may be established by following the provisions of the Act without the creation of a corporation. The second is the Partnerships Registration Act, which requires that all partnerships engaged in trading, manufacturing, or mining in Ontario (except processors of butter and cheese) must be registered to carry on business (ss. 8, 13). Of course, many other Acts may or may not affect partnerships. For example, if there is at least one employee, the partnership must remit payments under the federal Unemployment Insurance Act and the Canada Pension Act. If there are 15 employees or more, the partnership must make group contributions on behalf of employees to the Ontario Hospital Insurance Plan. There may also be a compulsory requirement to participate in a Workers' Compensation Plan. Certain businesses may require a special licence, such as a tavern which must have a licence under the Ontario Liquor Licence Act. A taxi partnership, for example, would have to be registered under municipal licensing regulations. The list is almost endless and each individual or group of individuals would have to search out the local regulations that apply to the chosen business.

FORMATION

A partnership is defined in the Ontario Partnerships Act as the relationship between persons carrying on business in common with a view to profit but does not include an incorporated group (s. 2). Generally, under s. 3, the sharing of profits is prima facie evidence of a partnership. At first glance it would seem that it is necessary to express some intention of being in business together either orally or in writing to formalize the partnership relationship. However, this is not the case, as a partnership may be deemed to exist by implication.

Section 3 of the Act specifies certain situations that may resemble a partnership but are not—for example, payment of a debt out of profits, paying an agent out of profits, paying a partner's widow an annuity, paying off the purchased goodwill by an annuity, repaying a loan out of profits, or the sharing of gross profits. Most of the foregoing are just methods of repaying a legitimate debt of the partnership. The sharing of costs in a joint venture, either in connection with procurement or sales, as long as each individual carries on his or her own business, is another example that is not to be considered a partnership. Usually, however, any agreement to share losses is considered to be prima facie evidence of a partnership.

Section 24 of the Partnerships Act provides that, unless otherwise stipulated by the partners:

1. general partners share equally in profits and contribute equally to losses;
2. the partnership must compensate a partner who has incurred expenses on behalf of the partnership;
3. interest on capital cannot be paid until profits are ascertained;
4. all partners are entitled to engage in management (in one case in which two partners formed a corporation to take over their existing business, the court later ordered the new corporation to be wound up in the same manner as a partnership unless one of the former partners, now the minority shareholder, was allowed to participate in management);
5. remuneration for the partnership business is strictly out of profits—so, while a salary is not payable, each partner may make a draw on profits in anticipation of a share of the profits.

Section 24 also provides that admission of a new partner requires the consent of all existing parnters. A change in the nature of the firm's business requires unanimous consent. Section 29 requires full disclosure of private profits, and s. 30 requires every partner to reveal any interest in a competitive business. These sections reflect the *uberrimae fidei* ("utmost good faith") aspect of a partnership. That is, there must be a full, open, and scrupulously honest relationship.

PARTNERSHIP AGREEMENT

A partnership is usually established by express agreement between the parties. Although many such agreements are purely oral, it is more prudent to draw up and sign a written contract, as illustrated below. Such a contract should contain at least the following:

1. The name, address, and purpose of the firm.
2. The name and address of each partner.
3. The amount of each partner's investment.
4. The way in which profits and losses are to be shared.
5. The drawing privileges, if any, of the partners (for example, $400 per week for each partner).
6. The duties of each partner.
7. The limits to a partner's right to individual action (for example, a stipulation that a partner may not financially commit the partnership for more than $1,500 without the other partner's written consent, such as by co-signing a cheque).
8. The life of the partnership (for example, a given number of years, with an automatic annual renewal thereafter).

Example of an Agreement of Partnership
(no set form prescribed by law)

AGREEMENT OF PARTNERSHIP

AGREEMENT made this 10th day of January 198-

BETWEEN Ralph Crocker, of 7 Cronin Drive, Brampton, Ontario, and Wolfgang Ostler, of 3572 Maitland Road, Mississauga, Ontario.

IN CONSIDERATION of the sum of One Dollar paid by each party to the other (the receipt whereof is hereby acknowledged) the parties do hereby mutually covenant and agree as follows:

1. That the said parties will, as partners, engage in and conduct the business of a hardware store.
2. That the name of the firm shall be Brampton Hardware.
3. That the term of the partnership shall commence on the 1st day of February, 198-, and shall continue until one month after one partner has notified the other partner in writing of his intention to withdraw from the partnership.
4. That the place of business shall be Sherwood Mall, Brampton, Ontario.
5. (a) That the capital of the firm shall be $40,000, to be contributed in equal cash amounts of $20,000 each on the signing of the Agreement.
   (b) That neither party's contribution to the partnership shall bear him interest.
6. That the partnership capital and all other partnership monies shall be deposited in the Sherwood Mall branch of the Bank of Nova Scotia, from which all withdrawals shall be only by cheques signed jointly by both partners.
7. (a) That books of accounts shall be kept in accordance with standard accounting procedures.
   (b) That these books shall be kept on the premises and shall be open to the inspection of either partner.
8. That each partner shall be entitled to draw $500 per week from the funds of the partnership on account of his profits.
9. (a) That at the end of January of every year, an inventory shall be taken and the assets, liabilities, and gross and net income of the business ascertained.
   (b) That the net profit or net loss shall be divided equally between the partners, and the account of each shall be credited or debited accordingly.
10. That neither partner shall, without the written consent of the other, draw, accept, sign, or endorse any bill of exchange, promissory

note, or cheque, or contract any debt on account of, or in the name of the partnership, except in the normal course of business and up to the amount of $500.

11. That each partner shall devote his whole time and attention to the partnership business, and shall not, during the term of the partnership, engage in any other business.

12. That should one of the partners die, his executors shall be entitled to receive the value of his share of the partnership property at the time of his death, together with 1% per month interest in lieu of profit from that day until final settlement of the property.

13. That on termination or dissolution of the partnership, other than by death of a partner, an audit shall immediately be made of the firm's assets and liabilities and the balance be divided equally between the partners.

14. (a) That in the event of a disagreement between the partners as to the conduct of the business, as to its dissolution, or as to any other matter concerning the business, the same shall be referred to arbitration within 10 days of written notice being served by one partner on the other.

(b) That each partner shall appoint one arbitrator, who shall in turn appoint a third arbitrator.

(c) That the matter referred to arbitration shall be decided by simple majority of the arbitrators.

IN WITNESS THEREOF the parties hereto set their hands and seals, the day and year first above written.

Witnesses:

Ray Pilarski   Ralph Crocker

Henry Brown   Wolfgang Ostler

---

9. The way in which a retired, deceased, or expelled partner's share of the partnership must be settled.

10. The manner in which disputes between partners are to be settled (for example, by arbitration or court action).

11. The manner in which the partnership may be dissolved in the event of a disagreement or other cause.

TYPES OF PARTNERSHIP

A partnership can be either a general or limited. In a general partnership, each partner has the right to share in the management of the business and has unlimited personal liability for any partnership debts. This liability is both joint and several; that is, all the partners are together (or jointly) liable for the debts of the partnership as well as being individually (or severally) responsible for all the partnership debts if the other partners are unable or unwilling to pay their portion.

A limited partnership has both general and limited partners. According to law, there must be at least one general partner with unlimited liability, but there may also be any number of limited partners whose liability for the debts of the partnership business is limited to their investment. Thus, according to the Limited Partnerships Act:

> The partnership may consist of one or more persons, who shall be called general partners, and of one or more persons who contribute in actual cash payments a specific sum as capital to the common stock, who shall be called limited partners.
>
> General partners are jointly and severally responsible . . . , but limited partners are not liable for the debts of the partnership beyond the amounts by them contributed to the capital.
>
> The general partners only shall be authorized to transact business and sign for the partnership, and to bind it.
>
> A limited partner may from time to time examine into the state and progress of the partnership business, and may advise as to its management, and he only becomes liable as a general partner if, in addition to the foregoing, he takes part of the control of the business.

ELIGIBILITY

Any person of any age may become a partner in a business. However, minors (persons less than 18 years of age) are not liable for the debts of the partnership unless guilty of fraud. However, should a minor repudiate the liabilities of a partnership, he or she is also disqualified from any future share of profits. A minor also has the right to repudiate the partnership agreement at any time before he or she becomes 18 or within a reasonable time thereafter. A minor who does not repudiate the agreement within this time is considered in the eyes of the law to be a full partner with all the attendant rights and obligations, including joint and several liability for debts incurred by the business after the minor reached the age of majority.

A married woman has the same right as a married man to enter into a partnership agreement. Her liability for the debts of the business partnership is limited, of course, to her own business and personal assets. The creditors cannot take those of her husband. A married woman may also, if she wishes, enter into a business partnership contract with her husband.

NAME OF PARTNERSHIP

The partners in a general partnership may, if they wish, use some or all their own actual names for the name of the partnership. If they wish to use some other name or names, such names may not be the same as those of a firm that is already registered; nor may they be sufficiently similar as to cause confusion. A partnership must not use the words, "Corporation," "Limited," "Incorporated," or their abbreviations "Corp.," "Ltd.," or "Inc." as part of its name, as these indicate limited liability.

The name of a limited partnership must include the name of one or more of the general partners. Should the name of a limited partner be included in the firm's name, the partner's position as a limited partner must be clearly indicated in the firm's letterhead. If not, the court may hold that he or she acted as a general partner and consequently has unlimited, rather than limited, liability.

REGISTRATION

A general partnership for trading, manufacturing, or mining purposes must be registered within a certain number of days. In Ontario, according to the Partnerships Registration Act, a signed declaration must be filed with the Ministry of Consumer and Commercial Relations showing the names of the partners, their addresses, the name of the partnership business, and the birth dates of any partners under 18 years of age. The Act also requires that a new declaration be filed whenever changes in the membership or in the name of the partnership takes place, or if a partnership is dissolved.

In the case of a limited partnership, a certificate, signed by each partner, must be filed at the registry office before the partnership is legally considered to have come into existence. The certificate includes: the name of the business; the general nature of the business; the name and address of each partner, indicating who is a general partner and who is a limited one; the amount of capital contributed by each limited partner; the date when the partnership is to begin and end; and the principal place of business of the partnership.

RESOLVING DISPUTES

Sometimes, when a dispute arises between the partners in a partnership business, there is no oral or written agreement or provision covering the point in issue. Or, in the case of an oral agreement, each partner may have a different version. Then, should the dispute come to court, the judge will make his judgment in accordance with the terms of the provincial Partnerships Act—one of the terms of which states that the partners shall share equally in profits and contribute equally to losses.

LIABILITY OF PARTNERS

The partners are collectively a firm, and may be sued either as a group or individually. Under s. 6 of the Partnerships Act, a partner is an agent for the firm and all other partners in all dealings relating to the firm's business except where any other party contracting with her or him knows of limitations to that partner's authority. Generally anyone dealing for the first time with a partner (who is really an agent vis-à-vis the other partners) is required by agency law to enquire into the agent's authority. Of course, a person who purports to act as an agent, as discussed in Chapter 23, is always liable to a third party. However, but the principals (in this case the other partners and the partnership as a whole), would be liable only if the person carrying out the business transaction has been acknowledged as a partner. From this moment until such partner terminates his or her association, or a restriction is placed on this partner's authority to contract on behalf of the partnership (for example, a maximum monetary limit per transaction), which termination or restriction is made public or conveyed specifically to the other contracting party, the partners and the partnership will be bound by the *doctrine of estoppel* to answer for all contracts made by that partner on their behalf. Pledging credit for personal use does not bind other members of the partnership (s. 8). All persons informed of a restriction on a partner's authority are bound by such restriction (s. 10). Any injury or loss caused by a partner in the course of business (for example in a traffic accident) renders both partners and firm liable (s. 12). Where money received is misapplied, the firm is liable (s. 12).

Loss, injury, or misappropriation of funds renders each partner jointly and severally liable; that is, the injured third party may recover either from all the partners or from any individual partner (s. 13). By s. 14, any trust money misappropriated for the firm's business is recoverable from any partner with notice.

Individual Liability.   The following illustrates each partner's individual liability:

1. A person is liable as a partner to anyone who acts on the representation that he or she is a partner (s. 15)—for example, a person lending his name to a partnership desirous of obtaining credit from a bank is liable as a partner.
2. An admission by a partner in the course of business is binding on the firm (s. 16)—for example, admitting that payment has been received for an unpaid account.
3. Notice to a partner is notice to the firm (s. 16)—this is adopted from agency law.
4. Liability starts only from the time of admission as a partner (s. 18). Thus, if the partnership indebtedness was $10,000 before partner C's admission to the partnership and increased by $5,000 after her admission, the new partner's liability would be limited to her proportionate share of the latter $5,000.
5. A partner may be liable after retirement, unless there is a novation agreement between the remaining partners and the creditors which absolves him or her of further liability (s. 18). Anything short of this would not affect any creditor who granted credit in the belief that a person is still a partner and without notification that retirement has taken place. Legal

notices in newspapers are designed to notify everyone of changes in partnership.

Section 36 provides that creditors are entitled to regard partners as members of the firm until either notified personally of disassociation or given constructive notice through, for example, an official provincial legal publication such as the *Ontario Gazette*. A partner may also give notice of retirement (s. 37). Partners will still remain bound for unfinished business (s. 38). Section 36 provides, however, that the estate of a deceased partner is not liable for debts dating from the partner's death or insolvency, or after retirement, providing such a retired partner is not known as a partner by creditors.

DISSOLUTION

A partnership may be terminated for any of the following reasons:

1. end of a fixed term (s. 32);
2. completion of a business undertaking (s. 32);
3. notice, either from date indicated, or if no date, from moment of communication (s. 32);
4. death or insolvency unless there is a prior agreement providing for continuation in such a contingency for example a buy-sell agreement (s. 33);
5. if a creditor levies execution against one partner's share;
6. if the firm is involved in an illegality (s. 34).

Any partner may, under s. 35, individually apply to terminate the partnership if:

1. one partner becomes mentally incompetent;
2. a partner becomes incapable of performing;
3. there is prejudicial conduct by one partner;
4. there is a breach of the partnership agreement;
5. the business is producing a loss;
6. there is any other reason which indicates the partnership should be dissolved.

DISTRIBUTION OF PARTNERSHIP PROPERTY

Under s. 39, partnership property must first of all be applied to pay off the firm's debts and liabilities. The second priority is to pay off any debt due from the firm to a partner.

In case of fraud or misrepresentation by one partner, any partner seeking rescission is entitled to a lien for his share of any surplus assets and also to stand as a creditor for any payments made on partnership liabilities and to be indemnified by the defrauder for any liabilities incurred (s. 41).

Under s. 42, carrying on a partnership after the death or withdrawal of a partner without an accounting, entitles the partner who has died or with-drawn to a share in the profits or 5% interest per annum on such partner's assets. However, if an option to acquire such partner's assets exists and is acted on, the deceased partner's estate is not entitled to any further share.

Section 44 provides for the following distribution of assets on final settling of accounts. Losses are to be settled first out of profits, next out of capital, and last by partners individually according to their share in the partnership profits. If there are assets, they are to be applied first of all to pay the debts of the firm owing to non-members. Secondly, partners are paid in proportion to their advances. Then partners are to be paid any share due from capital. Finally, any balance is to be divided in the same ratio as profits.

REVIEW QUESTIONS

1. What are the principal characteristics of the sole proprietorship form of business ownership?
2. How can a sole proprietorship be established? What is the cost?
3. What legal restrictions are placed on the name used for a sole proprie-torship business?
4. To what extent can a sole proprietor share his or her rights and obli-gations with one or more employees?
5. What degree of freedom does a sole proprietor enjoy in making deci-sions about his business?
6. How can a person terminate a sole proprietorship business?
7. What advantages does a sole proprietor enjoy other than those already mentioned in the previous questions?
8. What is meant by the unlimited personal liability of a sole proprietor? How can he reduce the effect of such liability?
9. What handicaps does a sole proprietor face in obtaining capital for his or her business?
10. Explain why limited talent is considered a disadvantage for the sole proprietorship form of business.
11. For what types of sole proprietorship business is lack of continuity considered a serious disadvantage? A less serious disadvantage?
12. Explain the income tax situation that faces a sole proprietor. How advantageous or disadvantageous is it?
13. Why is the sole proprietorship such a popular form of business owner-ship?
14. How would you define a partnership business?
15. What steps are involved in establishing a business partnership?
16. How necessary is a written partnership agreement? What basic points should be covered in such an agreement?
17. How can a partnership arise by implication? What rules are laid down in the Partnerships Act for determining whether a partnership exists?
18. Distinguish between a general partnership and a limited partnership.
19. A general partner's liability is both joint and several. Explain.

20. Who may enter into a business partnership? Explain in your answer the position of minors and married people.
21. What legal restrictions, if any, are placed on the choice of a name for a partnership? In this regard, how does the situation of the limited partnership vary from that of the general partnership?
22. How must a partnership be registered in your province?
23. How can a partnership dispute be resolved when the oral or written agreement does not cover the point in dispute?
24. Compare the general partnership with the sole proprietorship with regard to: (a) capital; (b) talent; (c) liability; (d) legal restrictions; and (e) income tax.
25. Why are the sole proprietorship and partnership forms of business ownership rarely used for large businesses?

PROBLEMS

1. (a) X, Y, and Z entered into a written partnership agreement whereby X agreed to provide a going business, Y new managerial ability, and Z $25,000 in new capital. If the agreement did not provide for a distribution of profits ratio, how should the profits be distributed?
   (b) What tax liability, if any, would be incurred by X, Y, and Z if profits were retained in the partnership instead of being distributed to each partner?
   (c) Suppose X died and this situation was not covered in the agreement. What would have happened to the partnership according to the law?
2. Jack and Frank were partners in a successful trucking company. Both intended to draw up a buy-sell agreement, funded by life insurance, to provide for the continuation of the business should one of them die. However, they never found time to do it. Frank's wife, Jill, was employed as office manager. When Frank was killed in a traffic accident, Jack and Jill decided to carry on the partnership, splitting the profits equally. At that time, Jill's share of the assets was $100,000. Due to labour unrest, postal strikes, and lack of orders, the partnership business then went into a steady decline. On bankruptcy, all the assets of the partnership, plus the private homes of each of the two partners, for a total of $200,000 were taken by the creditors. Has Jack any further liability?
3. A, B, and C decide to set up a consulting business. C is busy with another business but wants to contribute money only. It is agreed that all should share equally in the profits and losses of the business.
   (a) List the formalities in order of priority which the provincial law prescribes for a partnership in your province.
   (b) If the partners wish to prevent the dissolution of the partnership should one of the partners die, how should they proceed?
   (c) Is it possible to let one of the partners have a regular weekly draw? If so, how would profits be allocated?
   (d) Suppose they wish to transfer to a corporate type of organization — how could this be done? What formalities would be required?

(e) Two of the partners, A and B, don't want to let C participate in any of the partnership decisions. What could be done to remedy this situation?

(f) What could be done to inject $50,000 cash into the partnership business if it is decided to open up more offices?

(g) What formalities are necessary to terminate a partnership business?

(h) Are there any partnerships which operate under federal law?

(i) Why, if your answer to the foregoing is "No," can a company be incorporated under federal law?

(j) Which partnerships are excluded from registration?

4. The ABC Partnership, which was registered as a limited partnership, included a fourth partner, D, who, although a limited partner, interfered with the management and control of the partnership. When the partnership was sued by creditors for outstanding debts, the A, B, C members of the firm sought to add D as a co-defendant, alleging that D was equally liable since his acts of interference were largely responsible for this increased indebtedness. Discuss D's possible liability in this case. Refer to *Bowes & Hall v. Holland* (1857), 14 U.C.Q.B. 316 (C.A.).

5. Smith and Jones had formed an intention to enter into a partnership for the purpose of acquiring real estate and selling same at a profit. Shortly thereafter Smith acquired a choice piece of property without Jones' knowledge and managed to sell it for a $50,000 profit. Jones learned of this transaction and sued for his $25,000 share. Discuss the likely decision of the court and the reasons therefor. Assume in this case that there was no written partnership agreement and that no registration had taken place. Refer to *Powell v. Maddock* (1915), 25 D.L.R. 748 (Man.).

15

The Incorporated Business

A corporation (formerly called a limited company) is a business that is a legal entity created by law, quite separate from its owners, the shareholders. As such, the corporation has its own name, address, capital, and life.

The landmark case which held that a corporation was separate and distinct from its owner is that of *Salomon v. Salomon & Co. Ltd.*, [1897] A.C. 22. Salomon, a successful shoe manufacturer, incorporated in 1892, held most of the shares himself. He eventually sold his company to a group of employees. He took back bonds as part payment for the purchase.

When strikes subsequently forced the corporation into insolvency and bankruptcy, he claimed money owing to him, citing his status as a secured creditor, being a bondholder. The trustee in bankruptcy refused to recognize his claim, asserting that he was in fact the true debtor as the owner of the business, not a creditor.

Although Salomon lost at the trial court, he won on appeal, and since then the courts have generally respected the distinction between the corporation itself and the persons who own it. This is sometimes called the "corporate veil."

Because of the corporation's separate legal existence, any debts incurred by a corporation can be repaid only out of its assets. There is no recourse to its shareholders, except for certain recently legislated exceptions. Thus, for example, if a corporation is rendered insolvent by repurchasing its own share capital, the shareholders whose shares have been so purchased must compensate any unpaid creditors to the extent of the money received. As another example, under the Income Tax Act, related corporations are regarded as one for income tax purposes.

Generally speaking however, a corporation is quite different, from the liability point of view, from the sole proprietorship and general partnership. In the latter two forms, the owners are legally responsible for all the obligations of the business, and must therefore satisfy any outstanding claims from their own personal funds if the business assets are insufficient.

FEDERAL OR PROVINCIAL INCORPORATION

A business corporation may be established on the authorization of either the federal or the provincial government. Provincial incorporation is adequate if business is to be transacted in that province alone. All laws of general application such as income, sales, and property taxes, business licences, and compulsory annual returns apply equally to both types of business corporation.

About 10% of all business corporations in Canada are federally incorporated and include most of the largest ones.

PUBLIC AND PRIVATE BUSINESS CORPORATIONS

A distinction is made between business corporations that "offer their securities to the public" and those that do not. In other words, between corporations whose shares are widely held and corporations whose shares are closely held. The former are called *public business corporations* and the latter *private business corporations*, or *close corporations*. In order to safeguard the public interest, the federal and provincial Corporation Acts set out much stricter rules for the operation of public business corporations—for example, with regard to the duties of directors.

This distinction is now referred to as *offering* (public) and *non-offering* (private) corporations.

JURISDICTION

Residence of a corporation may be a factor in deciding whether it comes under the application of certain statutes. For example, under the federal Income Tax Act, a corporation must pay both federal and provincial tax on its world income if control resides in Canada; a non-resident corporation would only pay tax on income earned in Canada. Usually the location of the head office or the province of incorporation will determine residence. However, it is possible that a company may reside outside Canada, yet be considered a resident because it is controlled by residents.

METHODS OF INCORPORATION

Depending on its nature and geographical scope, a business firm may be incorporated in one of several different ways:

1. Under a provincial Business Corporations Act. This is the procedure used by the vast majority of business corporations.
2. Under a special Act of a provincial legislature such as a Loan and Trust Corporations Act. Such Acts relate to firms which are members of industries whose activities necessitate particular safeguards for the public interest and are carried on within the province.
3. Under the Canada Business Corporations Act. This applies to firms which intend to operate in many provinces rather than just one. However, a provincially incorporated company may obtain, in another province, an extraprovincial licence that allows it to operate there, without the need to incorporate federally.
4. Under a special Act of the Canadian Parliament—for example, the chartered banks and the Canadian National Railways.
5. By direct royal charter—for example, the Hudson's Bay Company.

PROVINCIAL CORPORATIONS ACTS

Each province has its own Act permitting the establishment of business corporations. Depending on the province, applicants must use one of the three systems of incorporation: the *registration system* which is in force in Alberta, British Columbia, Newfoundland, Nova Scotia, Saskatchewan, the Northwest Territories, and the Yukon; the *letters patent system* which prevails in Manitoba, New Brunswick, Prince Edward Island, and Quebec; or *incorporation by articles*, as in Ontario, under its Business Corporations Act. It should be noted that a Provincial Corporations Act applies in Ontario to non-business corporations—for instance, a charitable or educational corporation.

Registration System

This system, based on the English Companies Act, enables a corporation to be established by authority of Parliament rather than by royal prerogative. Persons wishing to set up a corporation must register a document called a memorandum of association with the Registrar of Joint Stock Companies for the particular province and pay the required fee. The memorandum of association contains the names of the applicants, the amount of share capital, and so on, as specified.

Under the registration system, a provincially incorporated firm may be one of three kinds:

1. A company with share capital divided into shares of par value or no par value. In this company, the shareholder's liability is limited to the unpaid portion of the shares for which he or she subscribes, and the word "Limited" must be the last word of the firm's name.
2. A company in which the liability of each member is limited to the amount that he or she individually agrees, in the memorandum of association, to contribute to the assets of the company in the event of its insolvency. Such a company is considered "Limited by Guarantee," and these words must be included in its name.
3. A company in which no limit is placed on the liability of each member. For this class of company, the signature of each subscriber in the memorandum of association must be witnessed.

Letters Patent System

Under this system, a corporation is established by the issuance by the Provincial Secretary (under the authority of the Crown's representative, the Lieutenant Governor of the province) of an incorporating document, called the letters patent. This document, sometimes called the charter, is similar to the royal charters formerly issued directly by the Crown and based on royal prerogative.

The procedure and requirements for incorporating a company under the provincial letters patent system vary from province to province. Typical requirements are as follows:

1. A corporation may be established under the Act for any purpose except a railway or loan and trust company.
2. The applicant or applicants for incorporation of a company must file with the Provincial Secretary an application showing:

    (a) The name in full, the place of residence, and the occupation of each of the applicants. These may be unlimited in number; they must all be 18 or more years of age.

    (b) The name of the company to be incorporated. This must not be the same as or similar to the name of a known corporation, association, partnership, individual, or business, if its use would be likely to deceive, except where consent has been given by the party concerned. Also, the company must use the word "Limited" or "Incorporated," or "Corporation," or its corresponding abbreviation "Ltd.," "Inc.," or "Corp." as the last word of its name.

    (c) The purpose for which the company is to be incorporated.

    (d) The place where the head office of the company is to be situated.

    (e) The authorized capital; the classes of shares, if any, into which it is to be divided; the number of shares of each class; and the par value of each share, or, if the shares are to be without par value, their maximum issue price, if any.

    (f) Where there are to be preference shares, the preferences, rights, conditions, restrictions, limitations, or prohibitions attaching to them, or to each class of them.

    (g) If the company is to be a private company, a statement to that effect and the restrictions to be placed on the transfer of its shares.

    (h) The names of the applicants who are to be the first directors of the company.

    (i) The class and number of shares to be taken by each applicant, and the amount to be paid for them.

    (j) Any other matters that the applicants desire to have included in the letters patent.

Incorporation by Articles

In Ontario, one or more corporate or natural persons over 18 years of age may incorporate by delivering to the provincial Minister of Consumer and Commercial Relations "articles of incorporation," setting out the name, purpose, place of head office, capital to be authorized, manner of distribution of shares, preferences respecting shares, restrictions on shares, number and names and addresses of directors, shares to be taken by them, and other pertinent data. Once the articles have been scrutinized by Ministry officials and found satisfactory and the required fees have been paid, the Minister will endorse the articles as "filed" and issue a certificate of incorporation, together with the articles, to the incorporators. It is the responsibility of the incorporators to be sure that the name of the corporation is not deceptive or confusingly similar to another existing firm.

CANADA BUSINESS CORPORATIONS ACT

Eligibility

It is possible to incorporate a company federally for most business purposes under the Canada Business Corporations Act. The only exclusions are: a bank, including a bank to which the Quebec Savings Act applies; an insurance company within the meaning of the Canadian and British Insurance Companies Act; or a loan company within the meaning of the Loan Companies Act.

Articles

To establish a company under the Canada Business Corporations Act, articles of incorporation must be signed by one or more individuals, no one of whom: (a) is less than 18 years of age; (b) is of unsound mind and has been so found by a court in Canada or elsewhere; or (c) is an undischarged bankrupt. The articles of incorporation, to be submitted to a special Registrar, must include the following particulars:

1. the name of the corporation;
2. the place within Canada where the registered office is to be situated;
3. the classes and any maximum number of shares that the corporation is authorized to issue, and

   (a) if there will be two or more classes of shares, the rights, privileges, restrictions and conditions attaching to each class of shares, and

   (b) if a class of shares may be issued in series, the authority given to the directors to fix the number of shares in, and to determine the designation, rights, privileges, restrictions and conditions attaching to the shares of each series;

4. if the right to transfer shares of the corporation is to be restricted, a statement that the right to transfer shares is restricted and the nature of such restrictions;
5. the number of directors or, subject to para. 101(a), the minimum and maximum number of directors of the corporation;
6. any restrictions on the businesses that the corporation may carry on.

Once the required articles are received, the Registrar will issue a certificate of incorporation, which brings the corporation into existence as from the issue date.

Name

The proposed name of the corporation must not be the same as, or similar to, the name of any other business in Canada, whether incorporated or not. Also, the name must not be objectionable on public grounds. To warn anyone doing business with the firm of the shareholders' limited liability for business debts, the company must include the word "Corporation," "Limited," "Incorporated," or the abbreviation "Corp.," "Ltd.," or "Inc."

or their French equivalent, as the last word of the corporate name. Also, to avoid deceiving the public, the corporation must display its proper corporate name (as opposed to its trade name, which would not contain any designation indicating that it is a corporation) conspicuously outside its place of business and mention it in all its notices, advertisements, and other documents.

CONSIDERATIONS APPLICABLE TO ALL BUSINESS CORPORATIONS

An *intra vires* contract is one which is said to be within the powers of a corporation while an *ultra vires* contract is one which exceeds its powers. A classic case in this regard is *Ashbury Railway & Carriage Co. v. Riche* (1875), L.R. 7 H.L. 653. It dealt with a situation in which a company, incorporated as "railway and railway equipment building contractors," undertook to buy and operate a railway. The purchase fell through and, when the vendor sued, the court held that the corporation did not have the capacity to engage in this type of contract. This case dealt with a company incorporated by memorandum of association. Therefore corporations in Alberta, Nova Scotia, and Saskatchewan, where corporations may be formed in this way, may have contracts outside their memoranda ruled beyond their capacity. British Columbia, by statute, has abolished the ultra vires concept.

The capacity of corporations in provinces which have a system of incorporation by letters patent was declared to be an extension of the royal powers that granted the letters patent—that is, the Crown. Therefore such corporations are considered to have a relatively unlimited capacity to enter into contracts (see *Bonanza Creek v. R.*, [1916] 1 A.C. 566).

In Ontario, a provincially incorporated firm has the capacity to enter into all types of contracts and obligations because of the provision in s. 16 of Ontario's Business Corporations Act that "no act is invalid because of lack of capacity or power."

Of course a royal charter corporation created by the Crown, such as the Hudson's Bay Company, has no limitations on its capacity.

CAPITAL STOCK

The ownership of a corporation is represented by its capital stock. This consists of common shares and also, in many cases, preferred (or preference) shares. The holders of these shares are known as shareholders or stockholders. Authorization to issue shares is obtained from the government concerned in the charter that establishes the corporation. The shares are issued as and when funds are required. Most corporations now issue their common shares at no-par value. The term "par value" means that a corporation has attached a definite price to the share, usually stated on the stock certificate (the written evidence of ownership) at the time of issuance. *No-par value*, or without par value, means that no price is stated. Preferred shares, however, have a par value since it is usually the basis on which their fixed dividend is calculated. The actual price or value of any share is what it will fetch in the stock market. This is known as the *market price* or *market value*.

It cannot be sufficiently emphasized that the par value of a share (which is arbitrarily set by the incorporators) has no relationship whatsoever to the market value of the share. The confusion in the terms "par value" and "market value" has caused many unsuspecting investors to lose money as a result.

The *book value* of a share is the value, as shown in the company books or accounts, of each share's portion of the corporation's assets. It is calculated by dividing the net worth of the corporation (total assets minus total liabilities) by the number of shares issued.

COMMON SHARES

Each common share of a corporation's capital stock entitles the owner to certain benefits: to vote at shareholder's meetings; to share in the profits made by the corporation; and to share in the assets of the corporation should it be liquidated.

Voting Rights
Normally, each common share entitles the owner to one vote at the shareholders' meetings. In some companies, two classes of common stock, A and B, are issued with the A class carrying the voting rights. Any person or group owning a majority of the voting common shares, or even just a substantial percentage, can appoint the board of directors and thereby control the management of the corporation. In raising additional long-term capital by selling more common shares, the directors must therefore take into account how these new shares may affect voting control. Normally the pro rata holdings of common shares may not be altered by the directors without offering each shareholder, in a new issue, the proportionate number of shares as presently held.

The term *holding company* is used to describe a firm that exercises control over subsidiary companies by means of ownership of all, a majority, or, in some cases, just a substantial portion of the voting shares of these companies. The holding company and its subsidiaries are known as a *conglomerate* or *group*.

Share of Profits
The common shareholders of a corporation have the right to any profits that remain after preferred shareholders have received their fixed rate of dividend. This right does not mean, however, that the profits have to be paid out to them. One of the duties of the corporation's board of directors is to decide how much of the profits shall be distributed to shareholders in the form of dividends, and how much shall be kept in the business as retained earnings.

If the dividend policy is unsatisfactory, the shareholders can change it only by changing the board of directors.

One of the most important reasons why directors retain earnings in the business is to provide additional long-term equity capital. From the shareholder's point of view, a conservative dividend policy is not entirely unfavourable. In the first place, the corporation will be in a stronger financial position, and this should be reflected in increased earnings. Secondly, the extra assets usually cause the market price of the shares to rise in anticipation of a future increase in dividends. This can result, when the shares are sold, in a capital gain for the seller.

Share of Assets

Usually the least important benefit to a shareholder is the right to share in the assets of the corporation on its liquidation. Normally a corporation is wound up because it is unprofitable; as a result there tends to be little money left for shareholders from the sale of the company's assets, once the various tax collectors, bondholders, and other creditors have been paid. This is even more so when the corporation is forced into bankruptcy by its creditors.

PREFERRED SHARES

The capital stock of a corporation may consist of preferred, or preference, shares as well as common shares. Where this is the case, the preferred shares, as the name applies, enjoy a favoured or "preferred" position, with regard to profits and assets.

Voting Rights

The right to vote is normally withheld from preferred shares in exchange for the preference given. However, the right to vote for the directors may become effective if preferred dividends have not been paid for a certain number of months or years as specified in the charter of the corporation. In this way, the preferred shareholders are given the opportunity to influence management, usually by having a representative on the board of directors.

Share of Profits

Preferred shareholders are entitled to receive from the profits of the corporation a fixed dividend on their shares before anything is distributed to the common shareholders. This fixed annual rate of dividend is set as a percentage of the par value of the share or as a specific amount per share.

The right to a preference in receiving profits applies, it should be noted, only to profits that are distributed. There is no contractual obligation for a company to pay a preferred dividend each year; the profits may be retained as additional long-term capital. However, preferred shares are normally cumulative, unless otherwise specifically stated. This means that any dividend withheld in one year must be paid in subsequent years, before any dividend can be paid on the common shares. Where a preferred share does not have this right, it is described as non-cumulative.

Some corporations give a preference to dividends to one preferred share over another. Where this is done, the different types of preferred shares are ranked Preferred A, Preferred B, and so on.

Share of Assets

Should the assets of a corporation be sold—for example, on voluntary liquidation—preferred shareholders rank before common shareholders in their claim to a share of the proceeds. They are, however, only entitled to receive the sum stated on the preferred share certificate. The common shareholders are entitled to receive all the remainder. The Canadian view for many years has been that preferred shareholders may share with common shareholders in company assets on winding up. However, a United Kingdom judge has held the contrary.

CAPITALIZATION

Most business corporations in Canada are private corporations that do not sell shares to the public, but raise funds from their own shareholders. On the other hand, many large public business corporations do rely on the sale of shares to the various financial institutions and other investors large and small, to raise additional sums of money. One of the major advantages of incorporation is the firm's greater ability to raise capital.

The raising of funds, or by selling shares, is closely controlled by the federal and provincial governments. For example, a special procedure is prescribed for the notice of meetings held by corporations which sell common shares to the public, and a special prospectus must be filed with the provincial Securities Commission.

Most public business corporations are established with a large authorized capital stock but sell only sufficient common shares to finance their present ventures. More shares may be issued later, within the limits of the authorized share capital, to raise more capital. Sometimes an investor may not have to pay the full price of the shares right away. Nevertheless the investor is liable for the full amount. Eventually, all shares are required to be paid up. In case of the firm's insolvency, the shareholder's liability is limited to his or her investment.

Preferred shares may also be sold to raise capital.

Another method of raising capital funds is to borrow money by the issue of bonds, which are in fact a claim on the corporation's assets, with the bondholder getting a share of the ownership and the corporation retaining the equity or right to redeem by paying off the bondholder. This was the position of Salomon in the *Salomon* case, mentioned previously. These bonds may have specific security for repayment (a *mortgage bond*) or a general claim on company assets (a *debenture bond*).

The Securities Commission also controls the issue of bonds in the same manner as the sale of shares by a public corporation.

CONTROL OF THE SALE OF SECURITIES

The sale of shares of public corporations is controlled in all provinces by legislation designed to ensure the annual licensing of brokers, investment dealers, broker-dealers, securities issuers and salespeople, with the power to suspend or revoke licences for cause.

All companies selling shares to the public are required to file a *prospectus* with the provincial securities commission. This is a document containing a full description of the securities being sold, voting rights, conversion privileges, nature of business, names and addresses of directors, use of proceeds from sales, remuneration of the underwriter, and general details and expectations of the corporation itself, including its past record.

SHAREHOLDERS AND THEIR RIGHTS

The owners of a business corporation are called the shareholders or stockholders. The following is a list of their rights, in general terms:

1. A business corporation must have at least one shareholder.
2. Each shareholder has limited liability. The shareholders of a corporation are not, as shareholders, liable for any liability, act, or default of the corporation.
3. Each shareholder is entitled to attend an annual shareholders' meeting. "The directors of a corporation shall call an annual meeting of shareholders not later than eighteen months after the corporation comes into existence and subsequently not later than fifteen months after the preceding meeting."
4. At shareholders' meetings, each shareholder is entitled to cast one vote for each share held, unless the articles state otherwise.
5. A shareholder's vote may be given in person or by proxy. A proxy is a written statement, signed by a shareholder, authorizing another person to vote on his or her behalf.
6. Each shareholder must be sent copies of the company's annual financial statements, together with a copy of the auditor's report, not less than twenty-one days before the shareholders' annual meeting.
7. Unless otherwise provided for in the articles of incorporation, all questions considered at the shareholders' meetings are determined by a simple majority of votes, with the chairman holding the deciding vote in the event of an equality of votes. The business transacted at the annual meeting normally includes: the president's report; the auditor's report; confirmation of bylaws passed by the directors since the previous meeting; election of the directors for the next year; appointment of the company auditors; and any other business. More serious matters, such as

a proposal to reorganize the company's share capital, require more than a simple majority.

8. A shareholder is entitled to receive the dividends that the directors declare payable.

9. A shareholder of a public company is free to transfer his or her fully paid shares of ownership to anyone else.

At the provincial level, as one example, the Ontario Business Corporations Act protects the interest of shareholders in various ways. By s. 99 of the Act, a shareholder may apply to the court to authorize a representative action to be brought to enforce the corporation's rights where, for example, the directors refuse to act. By s. 100 of the Act, if the corporation by resolution decides to amalgamate, to sell its business, or to effect a change of shares, a dissenting shareholder may insist on his or her shares being purchased by the company. By s. 101, an individual shareholder with a 10% interest may require directors to hold a meeting to pass any bylaw or resolution. Also, shareholders with a total of 5% of voting rights may force directors to circulate details of a resolution to be proposed at the next meeting. By s. 109, shareholders may requisition a general meeting. Under s. 112, each shareholder is entitled to one vote per share.

The Ontario Act also provides for cumulative voting for directors (s. 127)—for example, if five directors are to be elected, a shareholder holding 100 shares may cast 500 votes for one director or 100 for each of the five.

By s. 162, a shareholder may inspect the corporate records, which must be kept at the head office and which must include, according to s. 157: (1) articles of incorporation; (2) all by-laws and resolutions; (3) alphabetical lists of security holdings including shareholders and creditors; (4) directors' register; (5) proper accounting records; and (6) minutes of all official meetings.

According to ss. 168-185, the shareholders must be provided with advance information of the financial statements and the auditor's report. By s. 186, a shareholder may apply to the court to appoint an inspector to run the corporation and audit the accounts.

Section 188, providing for amendment of the Articles of Incorporation and s. 193, providing for reorganization of the authorized capital, both require notice to shareholders and approval by a three-quarters majority.

By ss. 203-215, the majority of shareholders at a general meeting may vote for voluntary winding up.

The following documents must be included with the financial statements: an income statement showing financial operations for the year; the balance sheet showing assets and liabilities, including location of assets and any changes in share capital; an analysis of changes in working capital; statements of retained earnings and contributed surplus. These statements must compare results of the present fiscal year with those of the preceding year.

PROBLEM SITUATIONS

Shareholders may sometimes be confronted with the following types of situations:

1. Instances of poor corporate management;
2. Where there are only a few shareholders in a closely held company, a majority shareholder may act unfairly towards a minority shareholder by firing him or her, raising his or her own salary, and so on;
3. Directors may attempt to exercise a fraud either on the corporation of the minority shareholder, by buying an asset owned by themselves at a high profit, allocating high salaries to themselves, and so on.

There is little a minority shareholder can do in a corporation unfortunate enough to have poor management, except hope that eventually either the directors will be changed or the management team will improve. The shareholder can always attempt to sell his or her shares, but this may be a problem if there is no ready market.

There have been cases reported where two individuals, who were successful on their own, decided to join together in business and incorporate. Often in such cases one of the two, usually the contributor of capital, retains 51% of the shares, thus retaining the controlling interest. Eventually the other shareholder does less and less and merely benefits from the profits. Even if the corporation is well administered, this situation may not satisfy the minority shareholder. Some court decisions have drawn an analogy between such a corporation and a partnership, and have allowed the dissatisfied shareholder to force the purchase of his or her shares by the majority holder or else force the corporation to be wound up.

The present trend towards the protection of minority shareholders is sometimes reflected in the existence of a separate *shareholder agreement* or private contract between the members of a private corporation. Typical provisions in such a contract would be the right of a shareholder to be employed, to have a voice in the management of the firm, and to be entitled to a fair market valuation of shares on severing his or her relationship with the corporation. The Canada Business Corporations Act has formally recognized such shareholder agreements.

DIRECTORS

The directors are the persons elected by the shareholders of the corporation to be responsible for the management of the business. The role of the directors has, however, been the subject of controversy for many years. It is sometimes argued that the directors' first responsibility, morally and legally, is to the corporation rather than to its shareholders.

The Canada Business Corporations Act stipulates that if shares in a corporation are to be sold to the public, there must be at least three directors, two of whom are not officers or employees of the company or of its affiliates. After the certificate of incorporation has been issued, the first directors have the power to meet to make bylaws, authorize the issue of shares, appoint officers, and transact other business. To be a director one must be eighteen years of age or more. The majority of the first directors and a majority of the subsequent directors must be resident Canadians. The shareholders, at their first meeting and at subsequent meetings, elect the directors for a term of not more than three years. Directors' terms may be staggered.

Powers

The directors are given the power to manage the business and have authority to make bylaws (legally enforceable rules governing the conduct of the business) covering such matters as:

1. The allotment of shares; the making of calls thereon; the payment thereof; the issuance and registration of certificates for shares; the forfeiture of shares for non-payment; the disposal of forfeited shares and of the proceeds thereof; and the transfer of shares.
2. The declaration and payment of dividends.
3. The amount of the share qualifications of the directors and the remuneration of the directors.
4. The appointment, functions, duties, and removal of all agents, officers, and servants of the company; the security, if any, to be given by them to the company; and their remuneration.
5. The time and place for the holding of meetings of the shareholders; the calling of meetings of the shareholders and of the board of directors; the quorum at such meetings; the requirements as to proxies; and the procedure in all things at such meetings.
6. The conduct in all other particulars of the affairs of the company not otherwise provided for.

Any new bylaws passed by the directors are effective only until the next annual shareholder's meeting, when they must be approved or rejected. Certain bylaws must be approved by more than a simple majority.

Restrictions

To protect the shareholders and the creditors of the company, various restrictions are placed on the powers of the directors by the Canada Business Corporations Act. For example, if the directors pay a dividend out of the capital fund of the company, they then become jointly and severally liable to the company and its creditors for the amount, if the company subsequently becomes insolvent.

Also, at each annual shareholders' meeting, the directors are required to present: an income statement for the specified period; a statement of surplus for that period; a statement of source and application of funds for that period; a balance sheet for the end of the period; the report of the auditor to the shareholders; and any other financial information required by the articles of incorporation or bylaws.

In Ontario, ss. 132-150 of the Business Corporations Act contain the major provisions affecting directors. There must be at least one director, but this number usually increases with the size of the company. By s. 132 the directors must manage or supervise the management of the affairs and business. By s. 134, a director must disclose his or her personal interest in any transaction concerning the corporation where such interest is material but he or she may benefit after such disclosure. Directors are jointly and severally liable if shares are not properly redeemed (s. 135). If directors declare dividends which lead to bankruptcy, they become jointly and severally liable (s. 136). Directors may be liable for six months' wages and twelve months' vacation pay to employees if the corporation becomes bankrupt (s. 139). Directors must exercise the care, diligence, and skill of a reasonably prudent person (s. 144). Directors are only entitled to be indemnified if cleared of personal liability (s. 147). Insiders (that is, persons holding over 10% of the shares) must file reports on any changes in shareholdings (s. 148). Section 21 authorizes the directors to make general bylaws.

The courts have held that the directors' first duty is towards the corporation rather than to the shareholders, unless they purport to act as agents for the shareholders in which case the directors fall into a position of "utmost good faith" in their relationship with the shareholders as principals.

The Ontario Business Corporations Act provides that directors must exercise the care, diligence, and skill of a reasonably prudent person. Thus the directors are required to deal with the company's business as carefully as they would with their own.

Section 134 of the Act spells out the disclosure required on the part of a director in transactions in which the director has a personal interest which might be material; otherwise any contract involving such director's property is voidable.

If a director is appointed as an agent to acquire property on behalf of the corporation, the rules of agency apply. A director may sometimes acquire knowledge of a profitable venture through his capacity as director. Before he is free to seek his own gain, he must make full disclosure to the corporation.

The situation involving fraud by a company director is best illustrated by an Ontario case involving "windfall" mining stock in the late 1960s. A Toronto millionaire and company director wrote the prospectus for the corporation, alleging that the mine showed good prospects, whereas in fact the final geologist's report indicated the contrary. Many small investors who purchased company shares eventually lost everything when the shares plummeted. An investigation disclosed her deliberate misrepresentation and she was tried, convicted, and served a jail sentence in her capacity as president and director of this corporation.

PROTECTION OF CREDITORS

In Ontario, the Business Corporations Act provides that directors will be personally liable if the payment of dividends results in the insolvency of the corporation. The Act also provides that both the directors and shareholders concerned remain liable to any creditors to the extent of any losses suffered as a result of a corporation redeeming its own share capital out of profits. Other ways of draining company funds—namely, issue of shares at a discount and loans to company officers—are also generally restricted or controlled by legislation.

BYLAWS

The day-to-day activities of a corporation are regulated either by *articles of association*, if dealing with a memorandum of association type corporation, or by *bylaws*, if dealing with a letters patent or certificate of incorporation type.

Normally bylaws are proposed by directors and must be confirmed by a three-quarters majority of the shareholders at the next general shareholders' meeting. Memorandum company directors resort to ordinary resolutions if articles are not essential.

There are three basic types of bylaws:

General Operating Rules.   These bylaws, usually passed at the first directors' meeting, regulate such matters as the number, qualifications, term, meetings, and quorum of directors; proxy voting; share allotment; dividend considerations; right to borrow; and signing officers. These bylaws are effective until confirmed or rejected by the first meeting of the shareholders (s. 21 of the Ontario Business Corporations Act).

Changes in the Incorporating Document.   Any bylaws that involve a change of capital (s. 188 of the Ontario Business Corporations Act) must be voted on by the shareholders and then sent to the appropriate government authority for approval. In the case of a letters patent corporation, supplementary letters patent would be required for any change in the nature of the corporation. For example, adding a French version to the name of the corporation.

Special Transactions.   Bylaws may be passed to empower the carrying out of certain transactions—for example, using profits to repurchase shares, or the sale of the corporation. In such cases, the province may provide for a special procedure to be followed. (See s. 100 of the Ontario Corporations Act.)

JOINT VENTURES

In large projects, such as oil exploration, several big companies may undertake a major project with specified percentages of contribution. While these joint ventures resemble a partnership, in fact they are set up as corporations and the corporate rules apply, except that the shareholders are corporations themselves.

Generally a joint venture is for a specific project, with a definite time limit, providing for limited liability and timing the joint venture's authority to act as an agent on behalf of its corporate shareholders. This form of organization may also be desirable where the participants do not want to enter into a partnership with all its legal and practical ramifications.

AGENCY

A corporation may act as an agent (for example, for shipping purposes) for another firm that is organized as a sole proprietorship, partnership, or corporation. In the *Salomon* case, the licensed trustee tried to prove that the purchasing company was just an agent for the principal shareholder Salomon, a contention that was rejected by the appeal court. If the finding had been the opposite, then the licensed trustee could have rejected Salomon's claim as a secured bond holder and retained the assets for distribution to the general creditors.

HIGHLIGHTS OF THE ONTARIO BUSINESS CORPORATIONS ACT, 1982

The following are the highlights of the Ontario Business Corporations Act which came into force in 1982. Many of these changes have been adopted by the federal government and provincial governments.

1. The tendency of the Act is to do away with par value shares in favour of non-par value shares;
2. The terms "private" and "public" corporations have been replaced in the Act by the terms "offering" (public) and "non-offering" (private) corporations.
3. Shareholder voting by mail is now accepted.
4. The shareholders, by a *unanimous shareholder agreement*, may restrict the authority of the directors on the points included in such agreement, but the shareholders thereby become liable in any situation that the directors might have become liable.
5. If shares are redeemed out of capital to the detriment of creditors (that is, they cannot therefore collect debts), both the directors and shareholders who have received capital payments become liable to such creditors.
6. A corporation may now have a number name rather than a word name.
7. A corporation need not have a corporate seal.
8. Generally no legal act by a corporation may be considered invalid regardless of its charter.
9. All corporations resident in Ontario must have a majority of Canadian directors.
10. An absentee director may cast his or her vote either in writing or by telephone.
11. Directors may be jointly and severally liable for:

    (a) issuing shares for less than full monetary consideration;
    (b) extending loans or financial assistance to corporate officers except, for example, to purchase a residence;

    (c) redeeming shares unlawfully—that is, causing bankruptcy or not paying of legitimate debts;

    (d) paying unlawful commissions, unlawful dividends, or indemnity to shareholders;

    (e) up to six months arrears of wages to employees and vacation pay for twelve months, providing they are sued within six months after the debt is due.

In addition an "insider" (officer or director) making use of confidential information for his or her own benefit must compensate any person for direct loss and is accountable to the corporation for any advantage or benefit received.

Fundamental changes in the articles of a corporation—such as change of head office, altering the number of shares, reducing capital, changing rights or privileges of shares, changing the number of directors or conditions on transfer of ownership of shares—may be initiated by a special resolution. The changes in "articles" will then become effective as soon as a certificate of amendment is endorsed by the director supervising the administration of the Ontario Business Corporation Act. In such case, a dissenting share-holder is entitled to be paid a fair value for his or her shares.

Finally, the new Act provides special regulations with regard to the takeover and amalgamation of two or more corporations. In the case of a takeover for which shareholders owning 90% of the shares have given their approval, the offerors may force the owners of the remaining 10% to sell their shares.

REVIEW QUESTIONS

1. What are the outstanding legal characteristics of the business corporation?
2. Distinguish between a private business corporation and a public business corporation.
3. A business firm may be provincially or federally incorporated. Explain the reasons for this difference.
4. Explain the four different ways in which a business corporation may be established in Canada.
5. Explain how a firm is incorporated, in your own province.
6. Distinguish between the registration system and the letters patent system of incorporation.
7. What requirements are imposed on the name that a business corporation may use?
8. What basic types of information must be divulged by the persons wishing to incorporate a firm?
9. Explain, with regard to company shares, the terms: (a) no-par value, (b) market value, and (c) book value.
10. What privileges does a common share confer on its owner?
11. How does a preferred share differ from a common share?

12. What rights does a shareholder enjoy under the Canada Business Corporations Act?
13. What are the rights and duties of a corporation director?
14. What advantages does the corporate form of business ownership offer to the small business operator?
15. What are the principal disadvantages of the corporate form of ownership?
16. How has Ontario's present Business Corporations Act altered the law governing business corporations?

PROBLEMS

1. A, B, and C decide to set up a business to manufacture household appliances. List five reasons why they should incorporate rather than form a partnership. What advantages does federal incorporation have over provincial, if any? What are the formalities of incorporation in your province?

2. A, B and C, having formed their corporation, decide to borrow $1,000,000 to set up their business.
   (a) In what different ways could this be done?
   (b) They decide to hold a general meeting of shareholders. What formalities are required, assuming that the 100 common shareholders hold 100,000 shares having subscribed $500,000 and the 100 preferred shareholders hold 100,000 shares, i.e., shares worth $5?
   (c) What is a par value share? A non-par value share?
   (d) What do you understand by cumulative voting for directors?

3. The case of *Salomon v. Salomon* was the first law case to hold that a corporation is a separate legal entity. The tendency lately has been to look behind the corporate need in certain circumstances. Explain some of these.

4. A corporation pledged most of its holdings, including a $1,000 T. Eaton bond, 200 common shares in Noranda Mines, 99,151 shares of Zahavy Mines Ltd., plus $5,000 cash to the pledgees. The question was: could this be done in view of s. 15(2) of the Business Corporations Act, which provided that a corporation may by special resolution sell or lease all property, and of s. 53(1) "by special by-law charge, mortgage, [etc.] all property . . . to secure any debt" obligations. Under s. 1(1)27 "a special resolution" requires a two-third majority of votes cast at a general meeting. A special by-law of the company had been passed providing for borrowing generally and giving security, but no meeting of the shareholders was every held to confirm the company's action of pledging most of its holdings.

   Was this transaction legal? Justify your answer with references to the Business Corporations Act. Refer to *North Rock Explorations Ltd. v. Zahavy Mines Ltd.* (1974), 3 O.R. (2d) 163.

5. The plaintiff, a shareholder of a business corporation, agreed to offer his shares for sale to the directors and officers of that corporation prior to

offering them on the open market. Thinking the market price likely to decline, the plaintiff made such an offer which was accepted to prevent the sudden release of shares on the market. Shortly before completion of the sale, a possibility of a company takeover occurred which might increase the value of the shares. The plaintiff was so informed, but carried on with the sale. Subsequently, when the takeover was completed and the shares rose in price, the plaintiff sued the company under a section of the Ontario Securities Act, R.S.O. 1970, c. 426 which imposed a liability on an insider who makes use of specific confidential information for his own benefit (regulations provide that an insider such as a director or officer must reveal any changes in his share holdings within forty days).

What are the legal positions of the plaintiff and defendants (the insiders) in this situation? Who should win? Refer to *Green v. Charterhouse Group Ltd.*, [1973] 2 O.R. 677.

6. A student with exceptional leadership qualities entered into a contract to work for a nursery company during the summer season. After a month he was promoted to the position of district director under a special contract entitling him to wages, expenses, and commissions on sales made by his district team. He received his salary and expenses on a regular basis, but on September 14 there was a balance of $1,009.82 owing to him in commissions. At this time the company went bankrupt. The student plaintiff sued the two directors of the company which had employed him, under s. 73(1) of the Corporations Act, R.S.O. 1960, c. 71: "The directors of a company are jointly and severally liable to the clerks, labourers, servants and apprentices and other wage earners . . . for all debts due . . . not exceeding six months wages, and for the vacation pay accrued for not more than twelve months under the Hours of Work and Vacations with Pay Act. . . ."

(a) One of the arguments raised was that this statute is penal but not remedial in nature. However, s. 10 of the Interpretation Act, R.S.O. 1970, c. 225, provides ". . . such fair, large and liberal construction and interpretation as will best ensure the attainment of the object of the Act." Did the plaintiff have a claim?

(b) It was also objected that commissions were not "wages." Discuss this point.

(c) Was the plaintiff within the class of persons intended to benefit from the Act? (Note the original section referred only to "labourers, servants and apprentices," while in s. 139 of the federal Business Corporations Act the class of persons includes employees; the right to vacation pay includes every employee; and employee includes "a person who is in receipt or entitled to compensation for labour or services.") Finally all cases which have excluded compensation have referred to members of the executive class, while here the supervisor could not hire and fire, fix salaries, or decide policy. Who should win in this case? Refer to *Lavitz v. Brock* (1974), 3 O.R. (2d) 583.

APPENDIX 15-A: COMPARISON OF DIFFERENT FORMS OF BUSINESS OWNERSHIP

Characteristic	Sole Proprietorship	Corporations	Partnerships	
			General	Limited
1. Method of creation	Must register if using different or plural name		Created by agreement of the parties; joint venture for profit	Same, but must file statutory form in public office
2. Liability of members	Unlimited liability	Shareholders have limited liability	Partners have unlimited liability	General partners—unlimited liability; limited partners—limited liability
3. Duration	Life of owner	May be perpetual, except for bankruptcy or winding up of shareholders	Termination by death, agreement, bankruptcy or withdrawal of a partner	The term provided in the certificate
4. Transferability of interest	May be transferred	Generally freely transferable subject to limits of contract between shareholders	Not transferable without consent of all partners	General partner—not transferable: limited partner—transferable
5. Management	By owner or employee	Shareholders elect directors who set policy and appoint a president	All partners in absence of agreement have equal voice	General partners have equal voice; limited partners have no voice
6. Taxation	Net income taxed as personal income, whether distributed or not	Income taxed to corporation; dividends taxed to shareholders	Not a taxable entity—net income taxed to partners whether distributed or not	Same

7. Legal entity for purpose of: a) Sue in firm's name b) Owning property in firm's name c) Bankruptcy d) Limited liability	Is a legal entity in all provinces for all purposes	a) May sue in firm's own name b) May own property c) Personal bankruptcy d) Cannot limit liability	By modern law is an entity for: a) Yes, must be registered b) Yes c) Yes d) No	
8. Transact business in other provinces	Must qualify to do business and obtain certificate of authority	Treated as an individual	No limitation	Copy of certificate must be filed in all countries where doing business
9. Incorporation fee, annual license fee, and annual reports	All required	None required except on initial registration	Registration fee only	Registration fee only
10. Modification of or amendment of articles	Must obtain Provincial approval	No requirement	Must file change	Must file changes
11. Agency	A shareholder is not an agent of the corporation Represented by officers	Employees may be appointed as agents	Each partner is both a principal and an agent of the co-partners	Limited partners are not principals or agents; general partners are the same as in general partnership

APPENDIX 15-B: SYNOPSIS OF THE ONTARIO BUSINESS CORPORATIONS ACT, 1982

Part I: Definitions and Application

S. 2: The Act does not apply to a company within the meaning of the Corporations Act which has objects of a social nature, or to a co-operative, or to an insurer, or to a credit union.

Part II: Incorporation

S. 1: A corporation may only practise a profession if the Act governing such profession permits it to do so.

S. 4: One or more persons or bodies Corporate may incorporate by signing articles of incorporation and sending the articles to the Director administering the Ontario Business Corporations Act under section 6 and, if endorsed in accordance with section 272, such certificate will constitute the Certificate of Incorporation.

S. 8: Allows a corporation to have a number name.

S. 9: Contains provisions regarding the corporate name including the words either in English or French, corresponding with Limited, Incorporated, or Corporation or the abbreviations Ltd., Inc., or Corp.

S. 13: A corporation need not have a corporate seal.

S. 17(3): No act of a corporation, including a transfer of property to or by the corporation is invalid by reason that the act is contrary to its articles, by-laws, a unanimous shareholder agreement or this Act.

S. 21(2): A corporation may ratify a contract made on its behalf before it came into existence—e.g., a contract to rent office space or equipment.

Part III: Corporate Finance

S. 22(a): Shares shall be without nominal or par value.

S. 23(3): A share shall not be issued until the consideration for the share is fully paid in money, or in property, or in past service that is the fair equivalent of (value of share).

S. 23(4): Directors must decide on fair value or property or service.

S. 24(2): The corporation must add to its share capital the consideration fixed by the directors for the acquisition of property or services.

S. 32(1): Allows a corporation to purchase or redeem any shares issued by it, providing under (2) that such redemption does not place the corporation in a position in which it would become unable to meet its liabilities.

S. 34(5): Where there is improper reduction, a creditor has two years to apply for an order to reimburse the corporation equal to any liability either paid to or extinguished with respect to a shareholder.

S. 38(1): The directors may declare and the corporation may pay a dividend either in shares, in property, or in money.

S. 42(4): A corporation may limit the number of shares which may be owned by any person whose ownership would fail to maintain the level of Canadian ownership prescribed in its articles.

Part IV: Sale of Restricted Shares

Part V: Deals with Indenture Trustees

Part VI: Sections 53-91 deal with Investment Securities

Part VIII: Deals with Shareholders

S. 92: Shareholders of a Corporation are not liable for any act, default, obligation or liability of a corporation except under:
  S. 34(5), where there is a reduction in capital;
  S. 108(5), which refers to a *unanimous shareholder agreement* restricting the power of the directors making the shareholders liable;
  or S. 242, which makes the shareholders liable to creditors for up to five years for any benefits received.

S. 93: Meeting of shareholders normally to be held in or outside Ontario, as determined by the directors.

S. 94(a): Directors must call first meeting within 18 months and within 15 months thereafter;

S. 95(5): Record date for list of shareholders shall be not more than 50 days and not less than 21 days before meeting;

S. 96: Notice of shareholders' meeting shall be (if an offering corporation) not less than 21 days and for any other corporation not less than 10 days but not more than 50 days.

S. 97: Normally all questions posed for the consideration of shareholders shall be determined by the majority of votes cast.

S. 99(1): A shareholder may submit a proposal which must be circulated;
  (4): One or more holders of shares totalling at least 5 per cent of shares may include nominations for directors;

S. 100(1): A corporation shall prepare an alphabetical list of shareholders, with shares held by each;

S. 101: Holders of a majority of shares entitled to vote may constitute a quorum;

S. 104: Provides for a resolution in writing signed by all the shareholders to be as valid as if passed at a meeting of the shareholders.

S. 105(1): The holders of not less than 5 per cent of the shares may requisition the directors to call a meeting of shareholders;
  (6): Shareholders' expenses must be reimbursed;

S. 108(1): Shareholders may make an agreement between themselves insofar as exercising voting rights;
  (2): Shareholders may, by written agreement, restrict the powers of directors;

S. 108(3): Where a person who is the beneficial owner of all the issued shares of a corporation restricts the powers of directors to manage business, the declaration is termed a *unanimous shareholder agreement*;

(5): parties to a unanimous shareholder agreement assume the powers of directors insofar as the restrictions apply and the directors are relieved of liability;

Part VIII: Proxies

S. 109(d): "Proxy" is an executed form of proxy by which a shareholder appoints another person to act on his or her behalf at a meeting of shareholders.

S. 111: The management of an offering corporation (i.e. offering its securities to the public) when sending notice of a meeting of shareholders must also send a form of proxy to each shareholder entitled to receive notice.

S. 114(2): A proxy holder has the same rights as the shareholder who appointed him (or her) i.e.: (a) to speak; (b) to vote by ballot; or (c) by a show of hands;

Part IX: Directors and Officers

S. 115(1): A director shall manage and supervise the management of the business and affairs of a corporation;

(2): An offering corporation (i.e. one which offers shares to public) must have at least three directors, otherwise one is enough;

S. 116(2): By-laws made by directors must be confirmed by shareholders at the next general meeting or stand rejected;

S. 117(1): At the first meeting, the directors may:

(a) make by-laws;

(b) adopt form of securities and records;

(c) authorize the issue of securities;

(d) appoint officers;

(e) appoint auditors until first meeting;

(f) make banking arrangements;

(g) transact other business.

S. 118(3): All resident corporations must have a majority of Canadian directors;

S. 130: A shareholder may vote the number of shares held times the number of directors being elected either for one director or according to choice, which is termed cumulated voting;

S. 121: Directors cease to hold office on death, resignation, if removed by an ordinary resolution (S. 122(1)) or by disqualification under S. 118, if under 18 years, unsound mind or bankrupt;

S. 124(1): Provides that in some cases directors may fill a vacancy among directors; or the articles may provide that only shareholders may elect directors;

S. 126: A meeting of the Board of Directors may be held at place of the registered office and in the case of a resident corporation the majority of the meetings must be held in Canada;

    (6): business shall not be transacted by a resident corporation unless the majority of directors are Canada; unless (7)(a) an absentee Canadian director approves in writing or by phone
        (b) thereby making the required majority of Canadain directors.

   (12): where there is only one director, such director constitutes a meeting;

S. 127(2): Directors may appoint a managing director of a committee, but such appointees have no authority to

    (3): (a) submit a question for approval to shareholders;
        (b) fill a director vacancy;
        (c) issue securities;
        (d) declare dividends;
        (e) purchase issued shares;
        (f) pay a commission;
        (g) approve a management information circular;
        (h) approve a takeover bid circular or issue a bid circular;
        (i) approve any financial statement (see s. 153);
        (j) adopt, amend or repeal bylaws.

S. 129: a resolution in writing signed by all the directors is as valid as if passed at a meeting of directors.

S. 130: *Liability of Directors*

S. 130(1): Directors are jointly and severally liable for issuing shares for non-monetary consideration at less than equivalent value.

    (2): Directors are also jointly and severally liable for:
        (a) any financial assistance contrary to Section 20; (i.e. loan, guarantee except in few exceptions, such as loan to employee to purchase a residence);
        (b) to purchase or redeem shares unlawfully;
        (c) pay a commission unlawfully;
        (d) pay an unauthorized dividend;
        (e) pay an unauthorized indemnity;
        (f) pay a shareholder unlawfully.

S. 131: Directors are liable for up to six months of employees' arrears of wages and vacation pay for 12 months, if sued within six months after debt is due and while still a director or within six months of being a director.

S. 132: Directors must disclose their interest if a party to a contract or transaction with the corporation or have a material interest in same;

    (8): where such disclosure is made and the transaction is confirmed by the shareholders, such director is not accountable for gains realized;

Standard of Care—Directors

S. 134(1): each director and officer must act honestly, in good faith and "exercise care, diligence and skill of a reasonably prudent person."

S. 136(1): a director may be indemnified against all costs, charges, and expenses in any civil or criminal case if he acted honestly and in good faith and in criminal proceedings enforced by a monetary penalty if he believed his conduct was lawful.

S. 136(4): insurance may be maintained against any liability except where liability relates to failure to act honestly and in good faith.
Insider Liability

S. 138(5): an insider making use of confidential information for his own benefit must compensate any person for any direct loss and is accountable to the corporation for any advantage or benefit received.

Part XI: Books and Records

S. 140: The following records must be kept at its registered office;
  (a) Articles and bylaws and copy of an unanimous shareholder agreement;
  (b) Meeting minutes and resolutions of shareholders;
  (c) Register of directors;
  (d) A securities register;

S. 140(2): (a) adequate accounting records;
  (b) minutes of meetings and resolutions of directors;

S. 141(2): Register of transfers and securities;

S. 144(1): Director appointed under the Ontario Business Corporations Act may examine records;

S. 145(1): Shareholders, creditors and legal representatives may examine records during business hours;

S. 146(1): shareholders, creditors and, in the case of "an offering corporation," any person may request a list of shareholders;

Part XII: Auditors and Financial Statements

S. 148: a non-offering corporation where shareholders consent and assets are under $2,500,000, gross operating revenues under $5 million or, where exempted by Director, need not appoint auditors nor keep financial statements available on record.

Part XIII: Investigations

S. 160: Provides that a security holder or the Commission may apply for an investigation of a corporation.

Part XIV: Fundamental Changes

S. 167: Articles of a corporation may be amended to allow for, among other things:
  (a) Change name;
  (b) Change location of registered office;
  (c) Add or remove any restriction to carry on business;
  (d) Change maximum number of shares or maximum consideration for shares;
  (e) Create new class of shares;

(f) Increase or reduce stated capital;

(g) Change designation or rights of shares;

(h) Change shares of any class;

(i) Divide a class of shares;

(j) Authorize directors to issue unissued shares;

(k) Change rights or privileges of shares;

(l) Revoke authority under (j) or (k);

(m) Change number of directors;

(n) Change conditions on the transfer of ownership of shares.

(4): the above changes require a special resolution except that

(3): directors may change a number company to a name company.

S. 168: A directors or any shareholder may make a proposal to amend articles per section 99, and the notice of meeting to amend articles shall state that a dissenting shareholder is entitled to be paid the fair value of his shares;

S. 177: The Director appointed under the Ontario Business Corporations Act shall, upon receipt of amended articles, endorse in accordance with S. 272, a certificate of amendment.

S. 172: Provides that a corporation may restate its articles in the above manner;

S. 174: Sets out the requirements for amalgamating agreements;

S. 177(4): Upon receipt of the Articles of amalgamation, the Director shall endorse the articles, constituting a certificate of amalgamation.

S. 178: The effect of amalgamation is to make the rights and liabilities of the amalgamating companies identical.

S. 180: Provides that an Ontario Corporation may apply to another jurisdiction to be recognized as if incorporated in that other jurisdiction.

S. 181: Deals with an arrangement including reorganization of shares amalgamation, transfers of securities, to another corporation etc.

S. 183(1): Unless otherwise provided, articles must provide that directors of a corporation have borrowing powers;

(2): The same applies to delegation of powers;

(3): Sale, lease, etc. of most of property other than in course of business requires approval of shareholders.

S. 184(1): in foregoing situations, changing rules re ownership of shares, re change of business rules, amalgamation, right to be recognized in another jurisdiction or sell or lease property; a shareholder may register a dissenting vote;

(4): Dissenting shareholder has a right to be paid fair value for his shares;

Part XV: Compulsory Acquisitions

S. 187: If within 180 days from a take-over bid or an issuer bid, 90 per cent of the security holders have accepted, the offeror may force the remaining 10 per cent to sell their shares to himself;

S. 189: Deals with going private transaction covering an amalgamation, arrangement, etc. carried out under this Act which would cause the interest of a holder of a participating security to be terminated without the consent of the holder.

Part XVI: Liquidation and Dissolution

SS. 192-204(1): Provides that shareholders of a corporation may by a special resolution require the corporation to be wound up voluntarily;

SS. 206-217: apply to a Corporation (S206(1)) being wound up by, for example, a Court order

    (a) where business dealings are unfair as regards a security holder, creditor, etc.

or (b) (i) a unanimous shareholder agreement provides for winding-up after the occurrence of a specified event

    (iii) Corporation because of its liabilities cannot carry on;

or (c) where shareholders by a special resolution request winding up.

S. 236: Provides for dissolution by the authorization of:

    (a) a special resolution or in the case of a non-offering corporation by at least 50 per cent of the votes of all shareholders;

    (b) consent in writing of all shareholders entitled to vote;

    (c) or consent of incorporators within two years if business not commenced;

S. 238: Provides for certificate of dissolution by Director;

S. 241(1): Despite dissolution (a) civil and criminal actions may be continued up to 5 years after dissolution.

Part XVII: Remedies, Offences, and Penalties

S. 251: Appeals from rulings of the Director appointed under the Ontario Business Corporations Act shall be to the Divisional Court;

S. 255: Anyone who makes (a) false statement of facts to any directions or rulings may be liable, if an individual, to a fine of $2,000. or if a body corporate, to $25,000., subject to the defence of reasonable diligence.

S. 257: The following offences are listed:

    (a) 29(5) transferring shares except to qualify for Canadian ownership, ofr license, permits, grants, etc.;

    (b) using a list of creditors obtained under section 52(5) except in an effort to influence the voting of holders of debt obligations;

    (c) not sending a form of proxy per s. 111(1)

    (d) not sending information circular with proxy, s. 112(1)

    (e) not exercising proxy as directed, s. 114(1)

    (f) not allowing shareholders and creditors to examine records, s. 145(1)

    (g) a director failing to appoint an auditor, s. 149(1)

(h) an auditor failing to attend a meeting as requested and answer questions, s. 150(2)

(i) directors not presenting financial statements and/or auditors' report at annual shareholders' meeting, s. 153(1)

(j) failing to comply with the Act or Regulations;

S. 257(1): provides for $2,000 fine or one year in jail (if an individual) or $25,000 fine (if a corporation);

S. 258: limits proceedings under ss. 255 or 257 to two years after facts on which charges are based first come to the attention of the directors.

4

REAL ESTATE LAW

In this part of the book, we consider the law relating to real property—that is, land and the buildings thereon. In Chapter 16, we consider the pitfalls involved in buying and owning real estate. In Chapter 17, we examine the use of real estate mortgages as security for loans to help finance the purchase of real property. And, finally in Chapter 18, we discuss the leasing of commercial and residential properties as an alternative to purchasing.

16

Buying and Owning Real Property

REAL PROPERTY AND PERSONAL PROPERTY

The law of property recognizes two categories of property: real property and personal property. *Real property* refers to land and anything permanently attached to it such as buildings, trees and fences. Other legal terms used to describe real property are immovable property, real estate, and realty. The second type of property, *personal property*, consists of things not falling into the category of real property such as cars, boats and any other property that is not land or affixed to land. Other terms used to describe personal property are chattels, or movable property.

Historically, a landowner was presumed to own not only the surface of the land, with its soil, rocks and minerals, and the trees, shrubs and grass growing on it, but all the air up to the sky and the soil to the centre of the earth below. However, the freedom of a landowner is now qualified in many respects.

RESTRICTIONS ON THE USE OF REAL PROPERTY

Crown Patents
As all land was originally considered to be owned by the Crown, any individual or corporation would have to receive a grant from the Crown by way of a Crown Patent which would pass title to the patentee. Such patents often contained various restrictions and reservations. For example, the Crown would reserve all rights to timber and minerals whenever patents were issued in favour of a subject of the Crown. Therefore, such timber and mineral rights could not be disposed of freely by the landowner.

Aviation
It would obviously be against the public interest for a landowner to have the right to restrict the use of the air space above the property so as to prevent the passage of aircraft. However, this would not prevent a landowner from commencing a civil action for negligence in the event that the persons on his or her land were injured, or the buildings damaged as a result of an aviation disaster overhead.

Community Planning
In the interests of planning community development, municipal and provincial governments have passed various statutes. These bylaws also restrict the use of land by a landowner. Thus, it is quite common for local bylaws to

prescribe the use of land and buildings, both existing and new ones, and to regulate building heights, building materials, and standards. Local laws also dictate the location and carrying capacity of roads and the location of parks and schools.

In addition, local governments require a landowner to maintain property in a sanitary condition and to keep the premises in good repair. In fact, local municipalities have created a vast body of regulations that must be complied with in both the construction and maintenance of buildings. For example, bylaws may require a property owner to clear snow and ice from the sidewalk in front of his or her property; otherwise the municipality may clean it at the landowner's expense. However, this does not entitle any person who slips and falls to sue for injuries or damage, because a (municipal or provincial) quasi-criminal provision does not create a civil right to sue. Also, all reasonable Canadians realize the danger of slipping on snow and ice.

Expropriation

Perhaps the greatest restriction on the free use of a person's land is the right of a government body to forceably take it away from its owner. However, *expropriation*, as it is called, is often considered necessary to further the public interest—for example, expropriating land for the purposes of straightening roads, enlarging an airport, or constructing a hydro line. If the owner agrees to sell the land, then the transaction is an ordinary purchase and sale transaction rather than an expropriation. The latter occurs only when the person will not sell at the price offered. Both the federal Parliament and provincial legislatures have passed Expropriation Acts to provide for such situations.

Nuisance

Subject to the restrictions previously mentioned, the owner of real property may use it as he or she sees fit as long as the owner does not use it to create a *nuisance*—that is, interfere with the ordinary conduct and enjoyment of neighbours. For example, a landowner may not allow garbage to collect on the property: the resulting obnoxious smells would interfere with the use and enjoyment by neighbours of their own land.

This prohibition covers inteference by noise, smell, vibration, overhanging branches or leaves, or the pollution upstream of water that flows through a neighbour's property.

The case of *Rylands v. Fletcher* (1868), L.R. 3 H.L. 330, established the principle that a landowner can be held responsible for any damage caused by the escape of potentially dangerous things (such as water) kept on his or her land. In this case, the plaintiff operated a mine on land adjoining the defendant's reservoir. However, there were mine shafts under the plaintiff's land and under the defendant's adjoining land, and these mine shafts were joined by connecting corridors. Through no fault of the defendant, the reservoir leaked and the water went down through the shafts on his land, crossed to the plaintiff's land through the connecting corridors, and disrupted some mining that was being done there. The plaintiff brought an action for damages against the defendant. The court held that the defendant was responsible for the damage caused by the water held in the reservoir.

INTERESTS IN LAND

There are many different types of interests that a person may hold in real property. These derive from the feudal system of land tenure that was established in England following thc Norman conquest in 1066. Under this system, the king retained ownership of all the land but permitted the noblemen and clergy to have use of most of it in return for military and other services. Over the years the requirement of rendering these services in return for the tenure in land gradually disappeared. This left only the ownership in land, which may now be transferred (or *conveyed*) from one person to another usually for a money consideration.

Fee Simple

The most valuable and complete form of real property ownership is called an "estate in fee simple." While in feudal times all land was held "of the crown" (that is, in some manner subsidiary to the Crown), today the owner of such land is in effect regarded as the true owner. The owner of land in fee simple and heirs can keep such land permanently, can freely sell or give it to someone else, or can dispose of it in any other way that the owner desires (called "freedom of alienation"). When such land is sold, the seller is described as the *grantor* (or *transferor* in the land titles system); the buyer is described as the *grantee* (or *transferee* in the land titles system); and the sale itself as a *grant* (or *transfer* in the land titles system). The term "freehold estate" is the historical reference to an interest in land which may be a fee simple or a life estate. An estate in fee simple is, in effect, ownership of land in perpetuity such that the heirs, executors, administrators, and assigns of the landowner would take over the land on his or her death. In contrast, all other interests in land have a shorter duration of ownership, along with other restrictions. The document that transfers a fee simple is called a *deed* or *conveyance* and must be made under seal.

Life Estate

This is an interest in land which lasts for the duration of the life of the person who has been granted the estate, or, if so designated, lasts so long as a specified third party is alive. This latter form of life estate is known as an estate *pour autre vie* ("for the life of another"). When the holder of a life estate dies, the property usually reverts to the grantor or heirs who are known, in legal terminology, as "reversioners." However, if a fee simple has during the period of the life estate been transferred to a third party, the property would then go to such a person (called the "remainderman"). For example, A grants a life estate to B and on B's death to C in fee simple. B would then have the right to occupy the land during her life and C would receive the fee simple on B's death. C is called the "remainderman." If the fee simple were not granted to C, then the fee simple reverts to A and A is called the "reversioner."

In order to sell property in which two persons have an interest, for example, a life tenant and a remainderman or a life tenant and a reversioner, both must join in the grant (or transfer). To make any changes on the property (for example, to cut down trees or pull down buildings), the life tenant must have permission from the remainderman. Insofar as repairs are concerned, the remainderman is solely liable.

During the course of the life estate, the "life tenant" may erect buildings on the land, may live in the buildings, or even grant a leasehold interest to someone else. Of course, a life tenant cannot grant a greater interest than he or she has. In addition, a life tenant is not permitted to commit waste or allow the property to deteriorate.

Dower.   Another form of life estate is called "dower." In accordance with the English common law, a wife was entitled, on the death of her husband, to a one-third life interest in the lands owned by her husband during their married life unless his wife barred her dower interest. This dower interest continued even after the husband sold his real property. If the husband died before the wife, the wife could exercise her right of dower in all land her husband owned at any time during his married life, except the land conveyed to others with the wife's bar of dower. The wife would be entitled to receive possession of one-third of the property or a one-third life interest in the income from the property in which she did not bar her dower interest.

Homestead Rights.   In the western provinces, the right of dower has been replaced by homestead rights. This is the right to remain in the home that the married couple has established as their matrimonial home, which cannot be sold unless both husband and wife consent. Wives are protected in all provinces, but husbands as well only in Alberta and Manitoba.

Family Law Reform.   In most provinces, dower has now been abolished by a Family Law Reform Act. The intent of the legislation is to give both spouses equal rights in the matrimonial home. In place of dower, Ontario's Family Law Reform Act requires the consent even of a spouse who may not be recorded on the title document prior to selling or mortgaging the matrimonial home. In the event that a person sells or mortgages the matrimonial home without the consent of his or her spouse, the conveyance will not be recognized at law and no interest will be conveyed to the grantee. It should be noted that both husband and wife are intended to be protected by the principle of consent whereas the principle of dower only protected the wife. The court may, however, make an exception to the requirement of consent in various circumstances set out in the statute. It should also be noted that the principle of consent only applies to a "matrimonial home" and not to other real property, which is commonly business and investment property. It is doubtful whether the principle of consent works in a negative manner, creating a restriction on the conveyance or mortgage of the matrimonial home. However, Ontario's Family Law Reform Act does create a right of possession in each spouse to the matrimonial home.

Leasehold Estate

The essence of a leasehold estate is that the exclusive right of possession to certain real property is given to the tenant for a period of time. The person who grants the lease is known as the *landlord* or *lessor* and the person to whom it is granted is known as the *tenant* or *lessee*. Leasehold is a lesser interest than either a fee simple or life estate, even though a ninety nine year lease may easily exceed the duration of life estate. When the lease expires, the land and buildings revert to the landlord. In Chapter 18, on leasing real property, we discuss some of the intricacies of the landlord and tenant relationship.

Condominium Estate

In some provinces, for example, Ontario and British Columbia, a person may hold land in condominium. This is a relatively new form of land ownership approved by the various provincial legislatures. Contrary to popular belief, a detached house may be part of a condominium complex, although the more common forms of condominium ownership involve apartments and townhouses. It is not uncommon as well to find industrial or commercial facilities using the condominium concept. The condominium estate involves both a fee simple ownership of a particular property plus an interest in the land and all common areas of the building in common with all other owners.

LESSER INTERESTS IN LAND

The interests in land described above all involve ownership of land either permanently or for a fixed or determinable period of time. Together with such ownership is the concomitant right to possession. It is possible, however, to have an interest in land that does not involve such possession.

Easements

An *easement* is a right enjoyed by one landowner over the land of another for a special purpose. One way of obtaining an easement is by a specific grant. The easement requires the existence of a "dominant tenement," which is the land that is benefiting from the easement, and a "servient tenement," which is the land subject to the easement. For example, the local hydro utility may acquire a right to place wires over a certain portion of a person's land for the purposes of the hydro utility and not for the purpose of the person's own use and enjoyment of his land. One type of easement is a *right-of-way*, which permits one to travel back and forth over the property of another to gain access to one's own land. Such a right-of-way allows passage over another's property without obstructing or having continuous use of the property that is the subject of the right-of-way.

An easement may also be established by an Act of the provincial legislature—for example, the right to widen a highway or to erect electrical transmission lines, or access by service personnel to townhouse units as provided for under the Condominium Act.

Easements may also be acquired by *prescription*—which is not a grant but is the legal recognition of a user's right to continued enjoyment of an easement by virtue of continual use. This principle is the same as that of "adverse possession" discussed later. The acquisition of a prescriptive easement requires open, continuous and notorious use of the easement without acknowledging the right of the true owner of the land. Such prescriptive rights are acquired only after a period of ten years. The principle of prescriptive easements does not apply in areas governed by the land titles system of registration.

An easement may also arise by implication—for example, when a person sells a piece of land with no access to a public road, or sells a building but not the land on which it stands. In these situations, the courts have held that there is an implied right of access from the public road to the landlocked piece of land or to the building.

ADVERSE POSSESSION

This is a method of extinguishing the title of the former owner of real property by possession for a statutory period under certain conditions. It has become known as "squatter's rights." In Ontario, the statutory period is ten years. Thus, according to s. 4 of the Ontario Limitation Act:

> No person shall make an entry or distress, or bring an action to recover any land or rent, but within ten years next after the time at which the right to make such entry or distress or to bring such action, first accrued to some person through whom he claims, or if the right did not accrue to any person through which he claims, then within ten years next after the time at which the right to make such entry or distress, or to bring such action, first accrued to the person making or bringing it.

A prescriptive easement is similar to the principle of title by adverse possession but differs from it in that the adverse user acquires only an easement that is the right to use such property for a specific use, such as the right to cross a neighbour's property.

Each province has in fact passed a Statute of Limitations which effectively limits the right of an owner of land to take action against a trespasser after a number of years has expired. The result is that the trespasser becomes recognized as the legal owner of the land. Thus the title of an owner may be extinguished by the occupier of land if the owner does not object to this occupation.

Adverse possession requires that the occupier must treat the land as his or her own, the occupation must be open and notorious, and the occupation must be continuous for a period of at least ten years. If it is interrupted by the true owner, for example, by an order for eviction of the occupier, the period of adverse possession must run all over again.

According to the principle of "tacking," an occupier may give possession to a second occupier without "interrupting" the time period; thus the time occupied by the first person will be added to the time occupied by the second person in calculating whether a ten-year period has elapsed.

It is important to note that the principle of adverse possession applies only to land registered under the land registry system and does not apply to land registered under the land titles system.

Encroachments

The term "encroachment" is used to describe a situation in which the owner of a piece of land also makes use of part of his neighbour's land. Thus, for example, a person may build a fence or garage wall which extends a few inches onto the neighbour's side of the lot line. Another example occurs when a drainpipe or roof extends part way over the neighbour's land. Such encroachment may be permitted legally by express written agreement of the owner of the land, in the form of a *licence* (as described below), perhaps in exchange for some monetary consideration, or may even be acquired by prescription.

Licence

Sometimes the owner of a piece of land will give another person permission to make use of it in some way, other than by a lease which grants exclusive possession to the lessee. This may be by way of a "licence." This occurs, for example, when a person perhaps unwittingly builds part of a fence on land belonging to a neighbour or to the public. Instead of being forced to take down the fence, the fence builder can be asked to pay a regular fee for this encroachment. However, such licence is revocable at any time and will usually state quite clearly that it gives the encroaching party no right of adverse possession.

Profits à Prendre

This is the right normally granted in conjunction with oil and mineral leases to remove part of the real property—that is, the oil or other mineral wealth. The essence of the profits à prendre concept is the conveyance of a right to make a profit rather than the right of occupation of land. The right to profits à prendre may arise by deed or may arise by prescription.

Restrictive Covenants

In some situations, the seller of a piece of land may wish to retain some form of control over the use of the land he or she is selling, especially if he retains real property in the vicinity. For example, the vendor may wish to ensure that the surrounding area be used for residential purposes only. In order to ensure that such conditions are continued, the vendor of the land may require the purchaser to agree in the deed to use the property, for example, for residential purposes or not to carry on a noisy business or any business whatsoever. The contractual promise that is extracted is known as a *covenant* and is believed to have originated in England in the late nineteenth century in what was known as the "Fish and Chips" case. In that case, a landowner selling off a piece of his property restricted its use by prohibiting fish and chips operations, as the smell, he alleged, would devalue the rest of his property.

In the purchase and sale transaction, the purchaser and vendor are bound by virtue of the principle of privity of contract. However, where the purchaser resells to a third party, the original vendor is unable to enforce such covenant against the third party purchaser as there is no contractual relationship between them. In an attempt to perpetuate the continuing obligations of subsequent purchasers, the vendor may require that such restrictive covenants be registered on the title to the property so as to give all future purchasers notice of the restrictive requirements.

The courts have come to recognize two forms of restrictive covenants. First, covenants that require some positive act by a purchaser—for example, the requirement to construct a garage; and, second, a covenant that is negative in nature—for example, the prohibition against using the premises for business. In the case of *Tulk v. Moxhay* (1848), 41 E.R. 1143, the court held that it would be too onerous to require a third party purchaser, with no privity of contract with the original vendor, to act positively—that is, to keep the property in good repair. However, but restrictive covenants creating a negative restriction—for example, prohibiting business activity—would be enforced.

This means that, as long as a subsequent purchaser is not required to expend money or perform some activity, this purchaser may be bound by a restrictive covenant registered against the title. In the event that the covenant becomes unduly restrictive or obsolete by virtue of the passage of time, it may be terminated on application to the court. In addition, various restrictive covenants which are contrary to public policy—for example, a restriction prohibiting the transfer of land to a certain race, colour, or creed of people—would be unenforceable, as contrary to the public interest.

Since 1950 in Ontario, restrictive covenants that offend the provincial Human Rights Code are void. Other restrictive covenants may be altered by application to the court under the Conveyancing and Law of Property Act. Also, under Ontario law, restrictive covenants have a forty-year limit, unless a shorter period is specified in the deed.

Restrictive covenants are commonly found in a building scheme or a plan of subdivision. This occurs when a person or firm subdivides a large piece of land into a number of residential or industrial building lots. The subdivider may impose a variety of restrictions on all the lots so as to ensure a certain character for the subdivision or neighbourhood. Examples of such restrictions are minimum building setbacks from the road, prohibition of any radio or television antenna or tower, agreements not to erect a fence above a certain height, not to erect a garden shed, not to repair one's car in the driveway, and not to park a snowmobile, camper-trailer, or boat in front of the house. These restrictions are sometimes found in agreements entered into by a subdivider and the local municipality and are registered on title. To be legally binding, they must be for the benefit of the whole area and must be uniform in nature. Such uniformity does not prohibit minor variations—for example, in lot sizes, to take account of corner lots and other odd pieces of land. If a person becomes an owner of one of these lots and violates these restrictions, any other owner (as well as the original subdivider) has the right to take the violator to court. However, all adjoining owners must be given a chance to appear. The fact that the property owner was unaware of such restrictions when he made his purchase is no defence. The possible of court remedy could be an *injunction*—that is, a court order prohibiting the violation or continued violation of the building scheme. Another possible court remedy could be a *mandatory injunction*—for example, an order to force the defendant to demolish the fence or take some other positive act to remedy the violation. In practice, a violation notice from the developer or the developer's solicitor threatening court action is usually sufficient.

CONCURRENT INTERESTS IN LAND

As discussed earlier, it is possible to establish various interests in one piece of land. For example, the owner of a fee simple may grant a life estate or a lease to any other person. Similarly, the ownership of land and/or an interest in land may be enjoyed by two or more persons simultaneously. Such co-owners have individual rights in relation to each other but are considered as one legal person in their dealings with other persons. The two basic types of simultaneous ownership are tenancy in common and joint tenancy.

Tenancy in Common

Such an interest in land occurs when two or more individuals acquire common ownership in real property. Initially, unless otherwise specified in the deed, tenants in common have equal shares in an undivided whole. Later, however, they may agree to hold unequal shares. A tenant in common is free to dispose of his or her interest in the property by will or by sale or by any other arrangement. A tenancy in common is often characterized by the principle of "unit of possession," whereby each owner is entitled to equal possession of the real property. In other words, no single owner may, without a court order, designate a specific portion of the property as his or her own or restrict the use or possession of any particular portion of the real property. Tenancy in common is the type of ownership most often adopted by persons engaging in a business relationship as each party wishes to retain the right to dispose of the interest to his or her family or to some other third party. In Ontario, two or more persons owning the same parcel of land are automatically tenants in common, unless shown in the deed as joint tenants.

Joint Tenancy

Land may also be owned by two or more persons on a joint tenancy basis, but only where concurrent interests are acquired simultaneously in a common document. The essence of a joint tenancy is the fact that the survivor (or survivors) of a joint tenant who dies inherits the interest of the deceased joint tenant. This form of ownership is often adopted by a husband and wife when acquiring a matrimonial home or other property they wish to give (or *devise*) to the survivor on the death of either one of them. A joint tenant may sever a relationship of joint tenancy, so as to turn it into a relationship of tenancy in common, by destroying the right of survivorship. The severance is achieved by one of the joint tenants conveying his or her interest to a third party. The remaining joint tenants are then considered to be tenants in common with respect to the new owner, but still joint tenants between themselves.

A joint tenancy is characterized by the presence of what is known as the "four unities": (a) unity of possession—whereby each owner is entitled to equal possession of the land; (b) unity of interest—whereby each owner has an equal interest in the land, including the equal sharing of rents or profits; (c) unity of title—whereby each owner has established his claim against the land by the same document; and (d) unity of time—whereby each owner has acquired his or her interest at the same time.

Should any of these characteristics disappear (for example, by one joint tenant conveying his interest to a third party) such joint tenancy will become a tenancy in common. However, the relationship between the original joint tenants remains a joint tenancy.

AGREEMENT OF PURCHASE AND SALE

A person who wishes to buy real property must do so by a written agreement as required by the provincial Statute of Frauds. In accordance with the law of contract, it is common for a purchaser to submit a formal offer in writing to the vendor whereby the purchaser offers to purchase the land and buildings in question. This offer is normally prepared by a real estate agent, if the property has been listed for sale by a real estate broker.

Unfortunately, the purchaser does not always realize that the acceptance of the offer by the vendor will automatically create a legal and binding agreement, the terms of which will govern the entire transaction. It is therefore usually in the best interests of the purchaser to consult a solicitor prior to signing and submitting an offer to purchase. Similarly, a vendor may wish to have the advice of his solicitor prior to signing acceptance of the offer submitted by the purchaser. Certainly, whenever circumstances require special terms to be included in the offer, or where the purchase price of the property is substantial, it is only prudent for the purchaser and the seller to have a lawyer scrutinize, if not prepare, the written agreement. If no real estate agent is involved, the purchaser may draw up the agreement or, more usually, ask a lawyer to do so.

The agreement of purchase and sale identifies the parties involved, including the agent, if any; specifically describes theproperty; indicates the dollar amount of the deposit accompanying the offer, the balance of the purchase price due on closing, and the mortgages, if any; and specifies that the title be "good and free from any encumbrances" (that is, mortgages, leases, easements, or any other title defects) except as indicated in the agreement and except as to any registered restrictions or covenants that run with the land provided that such are complied with. An example of a restriction is the requirement that any building erected on the land be of a specified nature and a specified distance from the street line in front of the building or from a boundary line. The agreement of purchase and sale may also include various conditions. For example, a purchaser may wish to have the agreement of purchase and sale conditional on obtaining sufficient and satisfactory financing terms before being required to purchase the property. Similarly, a purchaser may wish to include as part of the agreement a condition that he or she be absolved of all liability in the event of inability to sell the current residence at or above a specified price.

Another condition already mentioned is that the title be good and free from any encumbrances. It is therefore important for the purchaser to consult a solicitor preferably before signing the agreement or as soon as possible thereafter as the purchaser is allowed only a specific number of days "to examine the title at his own expense," a task normally undertaken by a solicitor.

It should be understood that the agreement of purchase and sale is merely an agreement to, among other things, deliver a deed to the property at a future specified time ("the closing date"). The agreement of purchase and sale is not itself the transfer of the title documents; however, the purchaser does acquire an interest in the lands being purchased.

The agreement of purchase and sale also provides for the apportionment between the purchaser and vendor of fire insurance premiums, fuel oil, rentals, mortgage interest, taxes, and similar expenses. These items are normally referred to as "adjustments" and are merely arithmetical calculations made to allocate all of the expenses of the property to the vendor up until the date of closing and to allocate all expenses attributable and accruing subsequently, to the purchaser. These adjustments are often overlooked by the purchaser who may be somewhat surprised to discover that he (or she) is required to pay often as much as several hundred dollars on account of adjustments at the date of closing.

The unwary purchaser should also be concerned with expenses such as a land transfer tax which, depending on the province, may well be one of the largest expenditures of money aside from the actual purchase price of the property. In Ontario, for example, land transfer tax is levied on all purchases of real property at the rate of 0.4% of the first $45,000 of the purchase price and 0.8% of the remainder. Thus, for example, where the purchase price amounts to $100,000, the land transfer tax would be $620. Such matters may of course be discussed with a solicitor even before entering into an agreement of purchase and sale so as to give the purchaser a realistic view of the total cost of purchasing, including all incidental costs.

LAND REGISTRATION SYSTEMS

There are two systems of land registration in Canada: the older Registry System and the Torrens, or Land Titles System.

Registry System

Once an agreement of purchase and sale has been made, the lawyer acting for the purchaser will conduct a title search. Under the Registry System of recording interests in land that exists in the four Atlantic provinces, throughout most of southern Ontario and parts of Manitoba, the purchaser (or his or her lawyer) must search the title to the property being acquired by tracing the title back at least forty years to ensure that a clear "root of title" exists. In searching the title, the solicitor will ensure that the documents previously involved have been properly executed, contain the necessary covenants and affidavits in compliance with various statutes affecting the transfer of land, and that there are no apparent adverse claims. The purchaser may also personally search for evidence of adverse possession by actually visiting the land. In addition, the purchaser's lawyer will search for evidence of unpaid property taxes at the municipal tax office and inquire whether any judgments are outstanding against any of the previous vendors of the land at the Sheriff's office. The purchaser's lawyer will also examine the survey of the property and submit a copy to the local building and zoning bylaw officials for their approval to ensure compliance with the building and zoning bylaws. It should be noted that, although leases under three years are not required to be registered on title, they may still affect the purchaser. Each transfer of land is recorded in the county registry office.

Land Titles System

The more recent system of land registration, named after its originator, is called the Torrens, or Land Titles System. This system prevails in the three western provinces, most of Manitoba, throughout northern Ontario and in various areas of southern Ontario. In areas where new subdivisions are being build in Ontario, or where condominiums are being created, the province of Ontario now requires that an application be made to the Ministry of Consumer and Commercial Relations to have the subject land transferred from the Registry System to the Land Titles System. The Land Titles System is a more convenient and guaranteed form of title ownership. Each real estate transaction in a land titles area is approved for registration by an approval officer of the appropriate Ministry. The government (through the Master of Land Titles) guarantees the accuracy of title as shown on the abstract (public record), which is brought up to date with each transaction. In fact, the government maintains an assurance fund which is made available to persons who have relied on the public record guaranteed by the Master of Land Titles and have suffered economic loss as a result thereof.

In the future, most provinces are expected to switch to a computerized system of land registration based on the Land Titles System. The objective will be to make title searching much easier, faster, and more economical. It will also avoid the danger of the Registry System under which the transfer of a property may be invalidated by defects in the title that have not been detected.

After the accuracy of the title has been satisfactorily established, the transfer of real property is is effected by means of a document known as a deed of conveyance (a "transfer" in Land Titles).

In Ontario, a subdivider must first get the title to his land certified under the Certification of Titles Act or entered into the Land Titles System before he can proceed to register a plan of subdivision. The purpose of this requirement is to obtain a guarantee of the validity of the title and to clear any doubts about the ownership or encumbrances on the land.

LEGAL DESCRIPTIONS

It is very important in the buying and selling of real estate that there be no confusion between one piece of land and another. This is achieved by describing in very specific terms, each piece of land according to location (by province, county, town, village, concession, lot) and size (frontage and depth). This is known as a *legal description*. It is much more exact than the municipal address commonly used to describe a property for purposes of mailing, etc.

In Ontario, for example, all the land was first divided into counties or districts which were in turn divided into townships, usually rectangular in shape. Later, as the population grew, villages, towns, boroughs, and cities were formed on land formerly belonging to the townships.

The land within each township was divided into concessions, numbered in Roman numerals beginning with I. The concessions were then divided, in the opposite direction, into lots, numbered in Arabic numerals starting with 1. The concessions were separated from each other by a strip of public property, called a road allowance. So also were some of the lots.

As a result of this method of land division, any piece of land could be specifically described as being, say, "Lot 3, in Concession IV, in the Township, City, Borough or Village of _____, in the County or District of _____".

Eventually, land within each concession lot was divided, by means of a plan of subdivision, into a number of smaller lots. A copy of such subdivision plan (for example, Brown's Plan) had to be filed in the public registry office for the county where it would be numbered. Thus a piece of land could be described even more specifically than before as being, say, "in the City of Mississauga, in the County of Peel, and being composed of the whole of Lot 33, according to Plan filed in the Registry Office for the

Registry Division of the County of Peel as Number 672." A subdivision lot could itself be further subdivided into halves, quarters, and even smaller portions such as "west fifty feet of Lot 32."

If a piece of land is of an irregular shape, it is also usually described in terms of compass degrees and bearings—for example "commencing at an iron bar found planted in the Northwesterly limit of Lot Four, thence South 51 degrees 37 minutes 00 seconds," and so on until arriving back at the starting point. This is called a "metes and bounds" description.

Land was measured in Ontario on the basis of chains and links. One hundred links equal one chain (66 feet). Eighty chains equal one mile. Each concession was 100 chains ($1\frac{1}{4}$ miles, or 6,600 feet) in length. And each concession lot 20 chains ($\frac{1}{4}$ mile, or 1,320 feet) in width by 100 chains (6,600 feet) in depth. All road allowances were one chain (66 feet) in width.

CONDOMINIUMS

As land values continue to increase, the prospect of owning a family dwelling has become more of a dream than a reality for many people. In order to allow for the economic development and community ownership of property and to facilitate the division of property into parts that are to be owned individually and parts that are to be owned in common with others, various provincial legislatures have passed a Condominium Act that provides for the use of such property and its management.

Documents
In order to establish a condominium as permitted under the Condominium Act, a developer or builder must first register two documents: (a) a description; and (b) a declaration, at the land titles office. The *description* includes: (i) a plan of survey showing the location and position of the buildings now in existence or to be constructed; and (ii) the structural plans, showing the location and shape of the proposed condominium units within the buildings.

The other document required—the *declaration*—is a written statement by the owner that he or she wishes to make the property a condominium under the Act and a clear statement of the basic principles that will govern its operation. Very important among the latter is the allocation of the common elements on a percentage basis, to the various individually-owned units.

Common Elements
Typically, in a high rise condominium apartment complex, areas such as corridors, hallways, lobbies, furnace rooms, games rooms, laundry rooms, pipes, cables, wires, and so on that cannot be individually owned but that nevertheless must be present if the building is to function properly, are the "common elements" that are owned by all the individual unit owners together as tenants in common. Therefore the responsibility for the maintenance and repair of the common elements falls on the unit owners as a

whole. The percentage ownership of the common elements attributable to each unit owner is usually set by the developer according to the relative market value of the unit compared with that of the others. Thus the owner of a three-bedroom unit would have a larger percentage of the common elements allotted to her or him than to the owner of a two-bedroom unit.

Each unit owner is entitled to a single vote at a meeting to elect the board of directors, notwithstanding that the percentage of the common elements may exceed that of a neighbour's. Where co-owners of a particular unit in the condominium disagree with regard to the casting of their vote at the meeting of the unit owners, the vote cannot be counted.

The concept of a "limited common element" applies to such areas as parking spaces. The condominium corporation has responsibility for their maintenance and repair, but the specific unit owner has the right to use a particular parking spot.

Bylaws

These are regulations passed by the board of directors and form part of the rules governing the operation of the condominium corporation. Minimum requirements for such bylaws are set out in the Condominium Act. It is usual for the board of directors to pass bylaws regulating the use that may be made of the individual condominium units—for example, no carrying on of a business, no keeping of pets, no hanging of clothes from balconies, no cooking on balconies. One of the duties of the board of directors is to register each bylaw, as it is approved, at the Land Titles office. The bylaws are ineffective until a copy is registered. Initially, when the condominium is formed, the developer is responsible for preparing and registering a detailed first bylaw.

Normally, outside the sphere of condominium law, an owner of property in an area which is subject to a restrictive covenant would have a problem in enforcing a positive obligation (such as keeping a unit clean or properly painted) on any new owners within the area once the original unit owner sells and moves on. As we saw earlier with regard to restrictive covenants, only negative obigations (such as not permitting undue noise) will be enforced by the courts once the land has changed hands. To overcome this obstacle, the Condominium Act specifically states that each unit owner (original or subsequent) must comply with the Act, with the declaration, and with the bylaws.

If a unit owner fails to meet obligations, the board of directors of the condominium corporation or any one of its members may ask the provincial Supreme court for an order directing the delinquent person to do so. One of the purposes of this compulsory compliance is to prevent a unit owner from letting his or her property deteriorate to the detriment of the neighbours.

Board of Directors

The *declaration* of a condominium contains information on the manner in which the condominium is to be managed. Basically, each condominium is set up as a corporation without share capital. Such a corporation has members rather than shareholders. Each unit owner in the condominium is automatically a member. Like a business corporation, the condominium corporation has a board of directors that is responsible for ensuring that the condominium is properly managed in accordance with the declaration. Pursuant to the Condominium Act of Ontario, the board of directors must consist of at least three directors, who are to be elected for a term of not more than three years. These directors however are eligible for re-election. In some condominiums, there are annual elections for one-third of the directors so that there is at any one time a relatively experienced board and at the same time a continuing turnover.

A director may be removed before the expiration of his or her term by a vote of unit owners who together own a majority of the units. Unless otherwise indicated by the bylaws, a majority of directors constitutes a quorum for the purposes of conducting the business of the corporation.

To assist and facilitate in the management of the condominium corporation, it is not uncommon for the board of directors to form committees consisting of directors or a combination of directors and owners to assist the board of directors. For example, an audit committee is normally formed for the purpose of planning and guiding the financial affairs of the corporation by preparing budgets and reviewing the financial statements. There is often a property management committee formed for the purpose of recommending policies to be taken on repairs, security and renovations.

It is also the responsibility of the board of directors to ensure that the insurance coverage on the common elements is sufficiently maintained and that the management contract, if any, is in order.

Rights and Obligations of Unit Owners

In purchasing a condominium unit, a person acquires certain rights and obligations pursuant to the Condominium Act. These rights and obligations are conferred on the unit owners as a matter of law and cannot be changed by the condominium declaration or bylaws. Some of the more important rights conferred on a unit owner include the following:

1. The right to exclusive ownership and use of the unit.
2. The right to an undivided interest in the common elements.
3. The right to make reasonable use of the common elements.
4. The right to the performance of any duty of the corporation.
5. The right to call a meeting of owners when a quorum of directors is not in office.
6. The right to raise any matter at an annual meeting relating to the affairs and business of the condominium.
7. The right to acquire the support of at least 15% of the owners of the units so as to requisition a meeting of the unit owners.
8. The right to notice of every owners' meeting.
9. The right to inspect the records of the condominium corporation.
10. The right to one vote at the condominium owners' meeting.

11. The right to vote by proxy.
12. The right to compliance by the other owners with the Condominium Act, declaration, bylaws, and rules.
13. The right to receive a copy of the financial statements and auditor's report before each annual meeting.
14. The right to require the condominium corporation to purchase his or her unit after having dissented in a vote relating to substantial modifications to the common elements.
15. The right to a share of the proceeds of the sale of the property or part of the common elements.
16. The right to apply for an order terminating the applicability of the Condominium Act to the property.
17. The right to share in the remainder of the assets of the condominium corporation after all valid claims against the condominium corporation have been paid and the property has ceased to be governed by the Condominium Act.

It should be noted that certain actions taken by a particular condominium corporation must be supported by a specified majority of votes cast or in the alternative a specified majority of unit owners. The Condominium Act of Ontario provides that, unless otherwise indicated in the Act, all questions proposed for the consideration of the owners at a meeting of owners shall be determined by a majority of the votes which are cast. There are, however, specific situations requiring more than a 50% majority of votes. For example, an amendment to the condominium declaration requires the consent of all owners as well as all registered mortgagees.

More than a 50% majority is also required where authorization is required for additions, alterations, or improvements to the common elements and changes in the assets of the condominium corporation. In the latter case, a vote of owners owning 80% of the units is required if the changes are substantial; otherwise the majority of the votes cast is sufficient. Similarly an authorization for the sale of the condominium corporation's property or anypart of the common elements will require the supporting vote of at least 80% of the units. Similarly, authority for the termination of the government of the property by the Condominium Act will require a vote of owners who own at least 80% of the units.

The Condominium Act also imposes various obligations on the unit owners for the purpose of protecting and insuring the proper use and enjoyment by all unit owners as a whole. Some of the major obligations imposed on the unit owner include the following:

1. The obligation not to carry on any activity in his or her unit or the common elements which may damage the condominium property.
2. The obligation to bear a proportional share of the costs of administering and managing the condominium corporation.
3. The obligation to comply with the Condominium Act, the declaration, the bylaws and the rules.

4. The obligation to notify the condominium corporation when he or she has rented the unit and to provide the condominium corporation with the lessee's name and the address of the owner.

It is, of course, of utmost importance that the unit owner recognizes his or her obligation to maintain the quality of the condominium property and assist in its effective management. It has often been found that apathy and carelessness result in the depreciation of the condominium property to the detriment of all the unit owners.

Common Expenses

The cost of operating a condominium building includes, in addition to any management fee, the maintenance, repairs, insurance, snow removal, heating, superintendent's wages, electricity, and water. Sometimes, of course, the utilities may be separately metered for each unit. In the Condominium Act, all expenses that are not directly chargeable to an individual condominium unit are called *common expenses* (also known as "maintenance fees"). In order to cover these expenses, the board of directors prepares an annual budget based in part on the previous year's cost experience and on a reasonable estimate of how costs will increase in the coming year. Once the budget for the coming year has been drawn up and approved, the cost is apportioned among the unit owners according to their percentage share of ownership of the common elements in the condominium building as specified in the condominium declaration. Each unit owner is then required to pay his or her share in monthly instalments. If a unit owner fails to pay, the board of directors has the power and the duty under the Condominium Act to register a lien against that unit for the sum in arrears. The lien may then be enforced through the courts just like a mortgage claim—by foreclosure, by court sale, or by ordinary court action against a unit owner in default. There is, of course, a certain pressure on the unit owner to pay such common expenses: a mortgagee, on being notified that the common expense payments are in arrears, may pay such arrears of common expenses and add the sum paid to the mortgage debt.

History

Condominium ownership has been used mainly for apartment buildings and townhouses (or row housing). However, it also has been used for some industrial malls and professional office buildings. The concept is not a new one, having been used in Europe and South America for many years. However, it has only become popular in the United States since the 1950s and even more recently in Canada.

After the Condominium Act was passed in Ontario in 1967, most people were at first reluctant to buy such units, fearing problems with co-owners, possibly high maintenance costs, and low resale values. Also, compared with a detached or semi-detached dwelling, the unit owner's rights seemed severely restricted. However, as the price of detached and semi-detached houses continued to soar, house buyers became willing to give condominiums a try—with reasonably satisfactory results. Such a unit—for example, a townhouse—meant reasonable accommodation at a reasonable price. Condominium ownership also enables people who prefer apartment living to do so as owners rather than as tenants.

Complaints

Although condominium units are becoming more and more popular, owners nevertheless voice serious complaints. Buildings, it is alleged, are left in a poorly finished condition by developers who sell and move on. Purchasers are misled by the developers' advertising and are often left with unfulfilled promises. Property taxes are unreasonably high on condominium units when compared with those on detached and semi-detached homes. Such taxes are also high when compared with the municipal services received—inadequate garbage collection, and no municipally provided snow removal, street lighting, or road maintenance.

Safeguards

The following safeguards for prospective purchasers have been included in the Ontario Condominium Act:

1. Section 38 provides that, where 80% of unit owners vote in favour of substantial alterations to the premises or, under s. 44, vote for a sale of the premises, any dissenters may demand that the majority owners purchase their units and common elements at fair market value.
2. Section 52 provides that any purchaser who has signed an agreement of purchase and sale must receive a copy of the disclosure statement provided for in the Act, including a narrative of significant features and a budget statement. The purchaser has ten days after the receipt of the said dislosure statement to rescind the agreement of purchase and sale.
3. Section 51 provides that, where there is a valid agreement of purchase and sale but the seller cannot deliver a deed of ownership suitable for registration, the purchaser may not be required to pay more than the total of the interest of the mortgage for the unit being purchased, plus reasonable taxes and projected monthly expenses.
4. Section 53 provides that any additional money paid by the purchaser, before a registrable title is available, shall be held in trust.

CO-OPERATIVES

There are some apartment buildings in Canada, the ownership of which is held by a provincially incorporated co-operative corporation. A person wishing to own an apartment in such a building must purchase common shares of the corporation. Depending on its size and location, the apartment might be valued at, say, twenty, twenty-five, or thirty shares. With his or her share purchase, the new owner receives a long-term lease for that particular apartment. Together the shareholders are both the owners and the tenants of the building.

In order to manage the building, the shareholders elect a board of directors. This board is responsible for such matters as hiring a superintendent and other staff, ensuring that maintenance and repairs are carried out, and enforcing the terms of the leases.

Co-operative apartments came into existence in Canada many years ago. However, this form of home ownership never became widely accepted. In fact, the co-operative was restricted in practice to a few, mainly luxury, apartment buildings in the major cities.

The co-operative apartment does, it is true, offer several advantages: the opportunity of home ownership; a way of avoiding future increases in rent; a means of sharing the cost of basic home ownership services; and a more relaxed style of living for persons, particularly the elderly, wishing to spend winters abroad or to avoid such burdens of home ownership as shovelling snow. However, there are also significant disadvantages. First, there is the liability of each shareholder for the mortgage assumed by the corporation as a whole. If one shareholder fails to meet his or her part of the mortgage commitment, the others must meet it. If many owners default, the mortgagee might even take over the building. A second disadvantage of a co-operative apartment is that an owner is also responsible for any property taxes unpaid by the other owners. A third important disadvantage (this time from the developer's point of view) is that under the provincial Securities Act a prospectus must be approved by the provincial Securities Commission before any shares can be advertised or sold to the public. Such a prospectus must contain a detailed statement of the project, its history, goals, principals involved, and other matters. In practice, approval may take considerable time.

The condominium form of ownership discussed earlier was designed to secure the advantages of the co-operative form but without the disadvantages. Thus, in a condominium, a person can own his or her own apartment or townhouse, but ownership, mortgage obligations, and tax liabilities are all registered against each individual apartment or townhouse. That is why condominiums, although a relatively new phenomenon in Canada, are now prevalent, whereas co-operatives are still relatively insignificant in the home ownership field.

CONSTRUCTION LIEN ACT

A person who enters into a contract for the construction or renovation of a building is required by law to hold back 10% of the contract price for a fixed period of time (forty-five days in Ontario) after the work is completed or abandoned. The purpose of this retention is to have funds available to meet the claims, or liens, of persons who have not been paid by the general contractor. Such claims may relate to unpaid wages of workmen employed on the project, unpaid subcontractors such as carpenters, plumbers, painters, and electricians, or unpaid suppliers of materials.

Unless a lien is "preserved" (that is, kept legally alive), it expires forty-five days after construction has been substantially completed or abandoned. A lien may be preserved either by (a) registering it against title or (b) where it does not relate to premises, by delivering a copy to the owner. A preserved lien can then be "perfected" by launching a civil claim. A perfected lien expires if the case is not set down for tiral within two years.

Distribution of the holdback (10% of the contract price) may take place either if the lien is not perfected or when a perfected lien expires (after two years). Such distribution will be made according to the priorities set out in the Construction Lien Act.

REVIEW QUESTIONS

1. What is meant by the term "real property"? What restrictions may curtail its use?
2. What was the legal principle established in the case of *Rylands v. Fletcher*? Explain.
3. What is meant by the term "fee simple"? How did it originate.
4. What are the rights and duties of the holder of a life estate?
5. What is meant by (a) the "right of dower"; (b) homestead rights?
6. What principle of law in Ontario has replaced the law of dower? Is it a better method of dealing with the problem?
7. Distinguish between a life estate and a leasehold estate.
8. What is a condominium estate?
9. What is an "easement"? Give three examples. How can an easement be acquired? Explain what is meant by a "prescriptive easement."
10. What is an "encroachment" in real estate?
11. What is meant by a "licence" in real estate?
12. What is meant by the term "adverse possession"? How does such possession come about?
13. What is an oil and mineral lease? Explain the concept of "profits à prendre."
14. How is the term "restrictive covenant" used with regard to interests in land? Why is a building scheme cited as a special type of restrictive covenant?
15. Distinguish between "tenancy in common" and "joint tenancy."
16. What are the essentials of an agreement of purchase and sale?
17. How are interests in land officially recorded?
18. What is a "title search"? What is its purpose?
19. How is a parcel of land described for legal purposes?
20. What documents must be registered before a condominium can be established?
21. What are the "common elements" in a condominium building? Who owns them?
22. How is the management of a condominium building organized?
23. What are the major problems involved in condominium ownership?
24. Explain how a co-operative building is legally organized. Include in your answer a discussion of the rights and obligations of unit owners.

25. What is a "construction lien"? How does it arise? What obligations does it impose?
26. What is "expropriation"? Give two actual examples of its use.
27. What is the different between positive restrictive covenants and negative restrictive covenants as it relates to a third party purchaser of land?
28. What is the essential advantage of owning a condominium as opposed to a unit in a "co-op"?
29. Give an example of the application of the principle of "tacking" as it relates to adverse possession.

PROBLEMS

1. A died, leaving his real estate to his widow for life and, after her death, to B and C equally. During the lifetime of Mrs. A, C died, leaving a will under which all of his property was to pass to his son C Junior. On Mrs. A's death, what should happen to the property?

2. D bought a home on the bank of a stream. A mile upstream a pulp mill was situated. The mill used the water in its process and discharged waste matter along with water into the stream, discolouring it and, on some days, causing odour. This had been going on for fifteen years and D knew the facts when he bought the home. He promptly brought action for an injunction to restrain the mill from pulluting the water. He had no use for the water except as scenery. Could he succeed?

3. E bought a small farm as a country estate. It fronted on the main road and terminated at the rear some 300 feet from a back road. The 300 feet was owned by a neighbour F who did not till the strip as it was separated by a wood from the rest of his farm. E frequently crossed the 300 feet with his motor car, as he found the back road convenient for some trips. He constructed a rough gate in the road fence for egress and ingress. He used the short cut from 1925 to 1967. In 1967, the neighbour F sold his farm to G. G dismantled the gate and restored the solid fence, forbidding E to cross his land. Was G entitled to do so?

4. H bought a piece of vacant land in 1966. In 1976 he wanted to redevelop the land but learned that the local public utilities commission (PUC) had a watermain running six feet under his property and right down the middle. The previous owners had allowed the PUC to construct the watermain. There are no visible signs of the existence of the watermain. H brings an action for trespass. The PUC claims it acquired an easement by prescription. What is the probable result?

5. In 1938 Mr. J purchased an island in the Trent Valley Canal System. However, in 1935, the previous owner permitted Mr. K to install a houseboat on the island. From 1935 until 1962, Mr. K and his family and friends spent considerable time each summer on the island. Personal belongings were left all winter, part of the island was cleared, a dock built, and other improvements were made. Mr. J never used the island except occasionally for hunting. K now claims he owns the island by adverse possession. What should be the result?

6. In this case an offer to buy a rural property was accepted and time was made *of the essence*. The agreement was eventually negotiated at $10,000 down and the balance to be secured by a mortgage. The price was $47,500, closing on September 30. The plaintiff's solicitor made a number of requisitions on title which required time to answer and a new closing date was arranged mutually for October 15. In the meantime, no action was taken by the defendant or his solicitor to prepare replies to the requisitions or questions about the title. Since the original closing date was past and a cash offer had been received, the defendant returned the plaintiff's deposit and cancelled the agreement. The plaintiff sued for specific performance.

What is the remedy of specific performance? Why is it asked for in a land case? Why do the defendants consider they are free to treat the agreement as at an end? What arguments favour the plaintiffs? Explain the nature and purpose of requisitions. Who should have won this case? Refer to *Roman v. Visneskie* (1974), 3 O.R. (2d) 734.

7. An offer to buy was made by an option secured by a $1,000 deposit to form part of the purchase price of $41,000 for 2.893 acres in Niagara, closing on April 30, 1972. This original option was extended to April 30, 1973, with *time of the essence*. There were some objections to title: (1) title partly by adverse possession; (2) an undischarged mortgage; (3) an undischarged conditional sale; (4) a restrictive covenant providing solely for one-family dwellings. Eventually agreement was reached on the objections and time for closing was extended to May 15, 1973. The vendor's deed, prepared and signed, was ready on the closing date, but the purchaser *only* tendered on the following day because he could not raise the money beforehand and had not really made up his mind to go ahead with the purchase until the last minute. This was because there had been some difficulty in obtaining municipal approval to subdivide the property into building lots. Because of the delay, the vendor refused to sell.

The purchaser had also, after his original option, become a real estate salesman. The Real Estate Broker's Act provides in s. 42(1) that such interest must be revealed to a prospective seller, which had not been done. The plaintiff sued for specific performance.

What is adverse possession? What is a restrictive covenant? What type of purchase by conditional sale could be registered on a land title? Comment on the failure to disclose status as a real estate agent. What is an option? Who won this case and why? Refer to *Beckett v. Karklins* (1974), 5 O.R. (2d) 211.

8. In February 1971, the plaintiff, who had been shopping in the defendant's grocery store, tripped when her feet became entangled in a plastic band used to tie magazines delivered to the store. She was carrying a box of groceries on her way out when she tripped. She broke her hip which required surgery and the insertion of a pin while her hip was healing.

General damages of $4,700 and special damages of $1,182.52 were assessed by the judge.

Discuss the grounds for liability, if any, in this case and the law which is applicable to this case. Refer to *Mainy v. Canada Safeway Ltd.* (1975), 57 D.L.R. (2d) 152.

9. A husband and wife entered into a contract to have a house built in a subdivision. They paid a down payment of $3,000 and the balance was to be paid on closing. The completion date was set at six months away, i.e., September. When this date arrived, the house was not quite completed, but could have been lived in, because the builder had only started construction within the last three months. The builder refused to let the purchasers move in, and returned their deposit, claiming no contract because he could not complete on time. The house was later sold to another couple. The original buyers sued for damages. How would these damages be calculated? Would the original buyers win? Give reasons.

10. Does a municipal government have the right to pass a zoning by-law which prohibits persons not related by blood, marriage, or adoption from living together in the same dwelling unit? Refer to *Bell v. R.*, April 24, 1979 (S.C.C.).

17

Mortgages

In virtually all contracts relating to the purchase of real estate, the purchaser is unwilling or unable to pay cash for the entire purchase price and must therefore seek to borrow the necessary additional funds. Normally the lender will require as security for repayment a contractual promise to repay, or "personal covenant," from the borrower as well as a "mortgage interest" in the real estate purchased. This is the granting of an interest in land by means of a formal legal document (called a *mortgage*) to secure the repayment of a loan. The creation of such a mortgage interest is accompanied by certain legal rights and obligations. Many of the questions that arise in relation to these rights and obligations may be answered by referring, first, to the mortgage document creating the interest in land; second, to the particular Mortgages Act effective in the province where the land is located; and, third, to the general body of mortgage case law that has developed as a result of decisions made in the courts.

A mortgage creates two obligations on the part of the borrower or mortgagor. One is the giving up of his or her legal rights of ownership of the land (real estate) to the lender during the duration of the mortgage, as specified in the mortgage document. The second is the contract, covenant, or personal agreement to repay the debt—which is an independent promise to pay which binds the borrower. The mortgagee or lender, of course, may abandon a land claim and choose to pursue the borrower only on the contract debt or promise to pay, which would certainly occur if the value of the mortgaged property dropped below the outstanding amount of the debt.

MORTGAGE TERMS

In a mortgage transaction, the borrower is referred to as the "mortgagor" and the lender who receives the interest in the land is known as the "mortgagee." When the loan which has given rise to the creation of the mortgage has been repaid, the mortgagee should release all his or her interest in the land and grant a "discharge of mortgage" to the mortgagor. In fact, the mortgagor retains the legal right after granting the mortgage to require the mortgagee to sign a discharge of the mortgage once the loan has been repaid. This reconveys to the mortgagor any interest in the land that the mortgagee acquired by virtue of the mortgage transaction. This right of the mortgagor to require such reconveyance is known as the "equity of redemption." In other words, when the loan is repaid the mortgagor has the right to redeem the property from any interest created in favour of the mortgagee.

You will recall from Chapter 16 that there are two systems of land registration: the Registry System and the Land Titles (Torrens) System.

Under the latter system, the mortgage is referred to as the "charge"; the mortgagor is referred to as the "chargor" and the mortgagee is referred to as the "chargee."

By definition, all fixtures on the property are considered in law to be an integral part of the land and therefore part of the real estate which constitutes security for the repayment of the loan. The loan itself may be used by the borrower for any purpose whatsoever.

FIRST, SECOND, AND THIRD MORTGAGES

A real estate owner may wish to borrow additional money after he or she has already granted a mortgage in favour of a lender. However, the new lender may require that a mortgage interest also be granted to him. Such a mortgage interest can only take second place to the one that already exists. This second security interest is known as a *second mortgage*. In the event that the borrower defaults in the payment of the first mortgage, the first mortgagee can exercise his rights against the property notwithstanding any rights that the second mortgagee may have. Therefore, the second mortgage bears the risk that the mortgagor may be unable to pay the required payments under the first mortgage as well as under the second mortgage. In contrast, the first mortgagee is quite unconcerned about the second mortgagee as the position of the first mortgagee is not affected by the default of the mortgagor in his payments on the second mortgage.

The priority of the mortgages is determined by the time of registration, provided both mortgages are registered. In the event that neither of the mortgages are registered, priority is determined by the date of execution of the mortgages. If a mortgagee, unaware of prior unregistered mortgages, registers his mortgage, such mortgage will take priority over the other unregistered mortgages, notwithstanding that they may have been executed prior to the mortgage being registered. It is therefore common practice, when lending money on the security of a mortgage, to require that a title search be conducted to determine the number of other mortgages, if any, already registered on the title which, by virtue of their prior registration, would have priority over the mortgage being contemplated.

Since the risk of non-repayment being accepted by the second mortgagee is greater than the risk being accepted by the first mortgagee, the second mortgagee will require a higher rate of interest to compensate for such greater risk. Similarly, a third mortgagee will require a rate of interest greater than that exacted by the second mortgagee.

ASSUMPTION OF A MORTGAGE

As part of an agreement of purchase and sale of land, the purchaser will often agree to accept all the responsibilities associated with a mortgage that has already been granted to a lender by the vendor. For example, the purchaser may agree that he or she will make up a $100,000 purchase price by accepting the responsibility for making the payments under an existing first mortgage of $70,000 and for paying the balance of the purchase price of $30,000 by cash or certified cheque. The process of the purchaser accepting all the responsibilities of the existing first mortgage is known as the "assumption of the first mortgage" by the purchaser. The purchaser should of course check as to the actual balance owing on the mortgage loan that he or she is assuming responsibility for. The purchaser should also be satisfied that there have been no violations of the mortgage that might give rise to the various remedies available to the mortgagee.

Sometimes the mortgage instrument may prohibit the assumption of the mortgage by a third party unless the written consent of the mortgagee is first obtained.

Although a purchaser assumes the responsibility of a mortgage, the mortgagee may pursue the vendor (the original mortgagor) for payment pursuant to the personal promise (or "covenant") of the original mortgagor to pay the amount of money due under the mortgage. The original mortgagor (vendor) may avoid future liability by arranging for the new owner to execute an assumption agreement whereby the new owner gives a personal covenant to the mortgagee to repay the loan and the mortgagee accepts the new mortgagor in place of the original mortgagor. Often the mortgagee will not consent to releasing the original mortgagor from the obligations in the mortgage but will consent to the assumption.

DUTIES OF THE MORTGAGOR

A mortgage transaction involves not only the creation of an interest in land but also the performance of a contract. According to the mortgage agreement, the mortgagor is normally obligated as follows:

1. to pay the principal sum of the loan as well as the interest required by the terms of the mortgage;
2. to pay taxes on the property;
3. to keep the premises adequately insured;
4. to keep the lands and buildings, erections, and improvements in good condition and repair;
5. to prevent any act of waste.

STANDARD SHORT-FORM OF MORTGAGE

The contents of the typical short-form of mortgage, normally used in real estate transactions, are as follows:

1. The date of execution of the mortgage instrument.
2. The names of the morgagor and mortgagee.
3. A recital indicating legal consideration has passed between the parties.
4. The principal amount of the loan.

5. The legal description of the land that is the subject of the mortgage.
6. The rate of interest payable.
7. The monthly or other regular date of payment of principal and interest.
8. The maturity date of the loan.
9. The remedies of the lender.
10. The duties of the mortgagor as set out above.
11. The remedies available to the mortgagee in the event of default as discussed below.

Other clauses that may be added to the standard-form mortgage document include the following:

12. The right of the mortgagor to repay the loan in part or in full at a time prior to the maturity date set out in the mortgage including a penalty for such prepayment, if any.
13. The right of the mortgagor to renew the loan on the maturity date.
14. A postponement clause permitting a prior mortgage to be replaced without losing its priority.
15. A third party's guarantee to repay the loan if necessary.
16. Provision of additional assets as collateral security for repayment of the loan.
17. A clause requiring the mortgagor to pay to the mortgagee along with mortgage payments a sum of money to be applied to the payment of realty taxes.
18. A provision in the mortgage requiring the mortgagor to provide the mortgagee with a series of post-dated cheques for the term of the mortgage.
19. The right of a mortgagee of a condominium to exercise any voting rights that the mortgagor may have at condominium meetings.

The mortgage instrument is signed, sealed, and delivered by the mortgagor in the presence of a witness. The mortgagor is also required to affix to the mortgage instrument an affidavit containing information as to his or her age and marital status. The witness to the signature of the mortgagor must then swear an affidavit, which is to be attached to the mortgage instrument and state that the witness was present and saw the mortgage instrument executed by the mortgagor, thereby verifying that the witness believes that the person who signed the mortgage document is the same person who is described as the mortgagor. Of course, all affidavits must be sworn before a duly qualified Commissioner of Oaths. Normally, such mortgage documents are signed before a solicitor who by virtue of being a solicitor is authorized by law to act as a Commissioner of Oaths.

REPAYMENT

Like any other contract, the conditions relating to the repayment of the mortgage are limited only by the imagination of the parties. However, the two most common forms of repayment arrangements are: first, a fixed monthly blended payment of principal and interest; and second, fixed monthly, quarterly, or annual payments of principal together with interest calculated on the declining balance of principal outstanding.

The Mortgages Act of Ontario permits a mortgagor to pay off the principal sum outstanding under the mortgage after a period of five years, notwithstanding that the stipulated period (or *term*) contained in the mortgage may be longer than five years. However, such repayment when made pursuant to the Mortgages Act will require a penalty equivalent to three months' interest on the principal balance outstanding. It should be noted that these provisions do not apply to mortgages granted by corporations.

The term of the mortgage may be prematurely terminated where a clause in the mortgage permits a prepayment of the principal sum outstanding with or without a penalty for such prepayment. Such clauses in the mortgage are known as "open privileges" and mortgages that contain such clauses are commonly referred to as "open mortgages." Similarly, there are mortgages that are partly open—ones that contain a special clause permitting the prepayment of a portion only of the principal sum outstanding at any given time. For example, certain special prepayment clauses permit a mortgagor to prepay a sum in addition to the regular monthly payment in an amount equal to 10% of the principal sum outstanding, such payments to be made on the anniversary date of the mortgage. Again, the possibilities and arrangements are numerous. The lender and the borrower may devise any scheme they wish, subject to the requirements of the Mortgages Act. For example, some lenders permit the borrower to schedule payments in accordance with anticipated salary increases, with a lower payment in the early years and higher payments in later years. Also, mortgages have been devised in recent years to allow senior citizens to borrow on the security of their home, thereby receiving annual or monthly payments to be recovered plus interest from the sale of the real estate after the owner's demise.

Amortization.   The principle of *amortization* means that repayment of the amount borrowed plus interest is scheduled over a given period of time so that when the last monthly payment is made, the loan is fully repaid, or "dead." Books of amortization tables are available that indicate the fixed monthly payments that would be required to pay off a loan amount at a given rate of interest over a preselected period of time (the *amortization period*). These fixed monthly blended payments contain interest on the outstanding principal plus an element of principal so as to reduce the outstanding balance of the loan to nil at the end of the amortization period.

The most common periods of amortization used today are twenty-five and thirty years. Some years ago when interest rates were relatively stable, lenders (typically financial institutions) granted loans based on a repayment period for the duration of the amortization period. As inflation increased, lenders began to realize that it was not in their best interest to commit themselves to a fixed rate of interest for a long period of time. For example, a lender might extend a mortgage loan at a 6% rate of interest only to discover after a period of three years that because of inflation the going rate of interest had risen to 11%. This effectively resulted in lenders being unable to maximize the rate of return on their money invested in mortgages. Therefore, lenders began to require the renegotiation of the terms of the mortgage after a period of five years notwithstanding that the true amortization period might be twenty-five or thirty years. The length of time after which the mortgage terms had to be renegotiated is now referred to as the "term" of the mortgage. It is not uncommon now for mortgages to have a term of one, two, or three years with an amortization period of twenty-five or thirty years.

REMEDIES FOR THE MORTGAGEE

Legal remedies are possible if a mortgagor defaults on the required payments of interest and/or principal. The mortgagee may:

1. sue in order to obtain title (or ownership) of the mortgaged property. This is called *foreclosure*.
2. sue for payment on the basis of the mortgagor's personal covenant to pay.
3. sue for possession of the mortgaged property in order to rent or sell it.
4. ask the court to sell the property.
5. ask the court to appoint a receiver to collect rents on his or her behalf.
6. sell the property, without court action, pursuant to the power of sale clause contained in the mortgage instrument.
7. take possession of the property, without court action.
8. seize any rents, without a court receiver being appointed.
9. like a landlord at common law, exercise the right of distress on chattels.

Foreclosure

The remedy of foreclosure is designed to permit the mortgagee, by using the court process, to obtain title (ownership) to the mortgaged property. Normally, the writ of summons in the foreclosure action will combine a claim for foreclosure, payment on the personal covenant to pay, and possession of the premises. The mortgagor is given fifteen days after the date on which he or she is served with a writ of foreclosure to file with the court a "notice desiring opportunity to redeem" ("DOR"). This is a notice filed with the court and served on the mortgagee indicating that the mortgagor wishes an opportunity to pay off all amounts owing to redeem the property pursuant to the mortgage instrument. As a matter of law, the mortgagor is entitled to a period of six months to redeem the property. In situations where the fair market value of the property exceeds the amount of the mortgage, the mortgagor is wise to file a notice DOR as it would be to the benefit of the mortgagor to sell the property subject to the mortgage and keep the excess for himself.

If the mortgagor does not file a notice DOR, the court will grant an immediate judgment for foreclosure, payment and possession. The mortgagee can then have the mortgagor evicted, and register the final judgment of foreclosure on title in the public registry office.

If the mortgagor files a notice DOR the court will automatically grant a six-month period of redemption. However, the court will also grant an immediate judgment for payment on the personal covenant as well as grant possession to the mortgagee. Therefore, during the six-month period of redemption the mortgagee is free to rent or occupy the premises. In many situations, the mortgagee will not take possession of the premises for the following reasons:

1. The mortgagee will be responsible to account for any profits or losses from the property as if he or she were the owner.
2. Occupation of the premises would be for an uncertain period, as the mortgagor may redeem the premises at any time within the six-month period.
3. By not taking possession of the premises, the mortgagor would be encouraged to stay on the premises and make an effort to redeem the mortgaged property.

If, however, the mortgagor is unable after the six-month period of redemption to redeem the premises, the mortgagee may apply to the court for a final order of foreclosure ("FOF"). The granting of a final order of foreclosure is equivalent to a conveyance to the mortgagee of the title to the mortgaged property. In the event that the mortgagee sells the property after becoming the owner pursuant to a judgment of foreclosure or a final order of foreclosure, any profit that may be realized upon a subsequent sale will accrue to the mortgagee as owner of the premises.

The legal effect of the judgment for foreclosure or a final order for foreclosure on the second, third, or other mortgagees is to effectively terminate their interest in the mortgaged premises. However, a mortgagee who intends to claim priority and terminate the interest of any subsequent mortgagee must serve a copy of the writ of foreclosure on the subsequent mortgagee. The subsequent mortgagee may then file a notice DOR and also be granted a six-month period of redemption. If no notice DOR is filed or the property is not redeemed within the six-month period, the subsequent mortgagees are debarred and foreclosed of any interest in the property that they may have had. As a rough and ready rule, a mortgagee may foreclose all subsequent mortgages and redeem all mortgagees claiming priority (foreclose "down," redeem "up").

Suing on the Personal Covenant

As the mortgage instrument contains a personal promise by the mortgagor to repay the principal sum plus interest, a default by the mortgagor in carrying out obligations may result in a lawsuit whereby the mortgagee claims a breach of promise by the mortgagor to pay a debt outstanding. While the mortgagor may sell the property to a third party, the mortgagor remains liable to the mortgagee notwithstanding such sale. A mortgagee may therefore choose to take the normal course of court action without pursuing the foreclosure or power of sale remedy discussed below.

Suing for Possession

The mortgagee who takes court action for foreclosure or payment on the covenant will normally also seek to recover possession of the premises so that the opportunity is available to rent or otherwise dispose of the property. It is unlikely that the mortgagee will sue for possession only.

Court Sale

Another course of action for a mortgagee, instead of pursuing the ones noted above, is to sue for a judicial sale, payment, and possession. In this situation, the mortgaged property is sold under the supervision of the court and the proceeds are used in accordance with the following priorities:

1. Payment of all expenses incident to the sale.
2. Payment of all interest and costs then due in respect to the mortgage.
3. Payment of the principal money due under the mortgage.
4. Payment of amounts due to subsequent mortgagees and encumbrancers in accordance with their priorities.
5. Payment of the remainder to the mortgagor.

It is advantageous to a mortgagee to exercise the right of foreclosure if the value of the mortgage is less than the amount of the market value of the property. This is because the excess value is retained by the mortgagee, whereas, in a court sale, any money remaining must be returned to the mortgagor.

Court-Appointed Receiver

In the case of a large industrial or commercial mortgage, a mortgagee may ask the court to appoint a receiver to collect the rent and other income. This remedy would be employed where the mortgagee wishes to ensure that the tenants continue to pay rent and that the rental income is properly applied so that the value of the property is maintained. This remedy is seldom used but is appropriate if the mortgagee cannot easily take possession of the property because of its large size (for example, a manufacturing plant) or if the security is threatened (for example, by bankruptcy proceedings against the mortgagor by other creditors).

Power of Sale

Under the usual terms of a mortgage contained in the standard short-form mortgage that may be purchased from legal stationers, the mortgagee has the power to sell the property without a court order. Although it is uncommon for a mortgage to be drawn on a document other than the standard short-form mortgage, the various Mortgages Acts of the provinces imply that the mortgagee has the right to sell the mortgaged property after a period of default. As the mortgagee would require possession of the premises in order to sell them effectively, the mortgagee may seek a court order to obtain possession.

In accordance with the terms of the standard-form mortgage, a mortgagee must wait at least fifteen days after default in payment. After this time he or she may give notice to the mortgagor and all subsequent encumbrancers (persons with a legal claim against the property) of intention to sell the mortgaged property after at least thirty-five days from the date of service of the notice. If the debt has not been settled, the mortgagee may proceed with the sale in accordance with the notice served on the mortgagor and subsequent encumbrancers. The proceeds of the sale are used to pay the amount owing to the mortgagee. Any surplus must be given to subsequent encumbrancers and the remaining money, if any, is paid to the mortgagor.

One advantage of using the power of sale remedy is that it is faster than foreclosure, which may involve a six-month waiting period in the event that a party to the action files a notice DOR. A second advantage is that personal service of the notice of sale is not required as the law provides that the notice of sale may be served by sending it by registered mail to the last known address of the mortgagor. In contrast, a writ of foreclosure must be served personally on the mortgagor. Therefore, where the mortgagor has absconded or makes him- or herself unavailable, the power of sale proceedings will be more convenient.

Take Posession

A mortgagee has the right, if the mortgage is in default, to enter the mortgaged property and take possession—so long as the mortgagee does not use force. Otherwise, to obtain possession the mortgagee must obtain a writ of possession which is issued pursuant to a court order. Once in possession, the mortgagee can rent the premises to someone else and use the rent to pay off the mortgage. However, the mortgagee must take care of the premises, make any necessary repairs, and advise the mortgagor of the rent collected and applied to the mortgage debt.

Seize Rents

Another possible course of action for a mortgagee whose mortgage is in default is to send a notice (called a "notice of attornment") to the tenants, if any, of the mortgaged property (for example, an office or apartment building) advising them to pay their rents to him. No court order is required; however, the mortgagee must account to the mortgagor for any rents collected in this way.

Right of Distress

Another possible remedy is for the mortgagee to enter the mortgaged property and seize all movable property (chattels). These items can then be sold and the proceeds used to reduce the mortgage debt. However, statutory limits are imposed on this "right to distrain." For example, the Mortgages Act of Ontario limits the right of distress to an amount equal to the arrears of interest on the mortgage loan.

ASSIGNMENT OF MORTGAGE

The mortgage document is a valuable piece of paper to own as it gives the right to its owner, the mortgagee, to receive various periodic payments pursuant to the mortgage. Like any other commodity, there is market for the purchase and sale of mortgages. A person who is engaged in the trading of mortgages, or in the finding of lenders so as to accommodate borrowers, is known as a *mortgage broker*. Such a person naturally charges a fee for services. Therefore, it may be wise to approach a financial institution that does not charge a mortgage brokerage fee to arrange a mortgage. However, circumstances may arise where the larger financial institutions are unable to satisfy a borrower's needs and the borrower may therefore find it worthwhile to use the services of a mortgage broker.

The act of selling the rights to a mortgage is known as an "assignment of mortgage." As in any other transaction involving land, formal legal documents are prepared which are registered on title so as to note the transfer of the interest in the mortgage to a third party purchaser. The mortgagee does not require the mortgagor's consent to the assignment of the mortgage. However, the mortgagor must, by law, be given notice of the assignment if he is to be bound thereby—that is, to obligate the mortgagor to make his payments to the new mortgagee (the assignee of the mortgage).

Where the interest rate set out in the mortgage which is being sold (or *assigned*) is lower than the current rate for such mortgages, the mortgage is often sold at a *discount*—in other words, for a value less than the principal amount of the mortgage debt. Conversely, in the event that the interest rate in the mortgage is higher than the current rate for such mortgages, the mortgage may be sold at a *premium*.

Mortgage brokers must be registered under the various provincial mortgage brokers statutes. Such legislation requires that each borrower be given a statement of mortgage which specifies the details, including the interest cost of the loan, the mortgage broker's fees, and any other incidental costs of obtaining the mortgage. The borrower must sign the statement received and keep one copy as a personal record.

REVIEW QUESTIONS

1. Explain the nature and purpose of a real estate mortgage.
2. Distinguish between a mortgagor and a mortgagee.
3. What is meant by the "equity of redemption"?
4. What basic information is usually contained in the standard short form of mortgage? What other clauses may be added?
5. Compare the rights of a first mortgagee, a second mortgagee, and a third mortgagee.
6. A mortgage loan may have a five-year term and a thirty-year amortization. Explain.
7. Under what circumstances may a mortgage loan be repaid before expiry of the agreed term?

8. What are a mortgagor's obligations, if any, to the lender if the mortgagor sells a mortgaged property to a third party?
9. Distinguish between an "assignment of mortgage" and a "notice of assignment."
10. What services does a mortgage broker perform?
11. What is meant by "foreclosure" of a mortgage?
12. What other remedies are available to a mortgagee if the mortgagor defaults on his or her required payments of interest or principal?
13. Is the mortgagor entitled to the excess proceeds of the sale after a mortgagee has exercised the right to sell the property after default?
14. Does the assumption of a mortgage require the consent of the mortgagee?
15. Explain the right of a mortgagee to "foreclose down and redeem up."
16. In what situation would a court-appointed receiver be appropriate?

PROBLEMS

1. The mortgagor originally borrowed $10,000 for five years at 8% per annum on October 30, 1976. An extension of the original regular mortgage agreement was made at 9½% from September 30, 1981, to September 30, 1986. As part of this agreement the mortgagor agreed "to keep the said principal money until the expiration of the extended period." Payment was made by blended payment of principal and interest. The judge ruled out the arguments that the agreement was inequitable and that because of his agreement to keep the principal for the period of the extension, the mortgagor lost his right to prepay. The final argument centred on the effect of s. 17(1) of the Mortgages Act and s. 10(1) of the (Dominion) Interest Act, that after five years the mortgage became open and the mortgagor was entitled to satisfy it by paying it off at any time.

   A mortgage is said to become *open* at the end of five years in Ontario. Why would the legislature have enacted such a provision? Why are present-day mortgages limited to five-year terms even though they may be amortized over twenty-five to forty years? What did the law provide for this extension agreement entered into voluntarily by the borrower? Refer to *Re Hodgson and Raskin* (1974), 4 O.R. (2d) 234.

2. A granted a mortgage to B which was registered by B. A then borrowed money from C and granted a mortgage to C who chose not to register the mortgage. A then borrowed money from D to pay B and A thereby granted a mortgage to D who also chose not to register his mortgage. The mortgage in favour of B was discharged. A, finding the need for more money, granted a further mortgage to E who registered his mortgage. A failed to make his monthly payment to E. E commenced a foreclosure action. What are the priorities for redemption and foreclosure?

3. A registered his mortgage against B's property. One year later, C registered a second mortgage. Three years later A renegotiated the terms of his mortgage with B to extend the time of repayment and change the interest

rate. Who is the holder of a first mortgage? What is the result of the increased interest rate on A's mortgage? Refer to *Reynolds Extrusion Co. Ltd. v. Cooper* (1978), 21 O.R. (2d) 416 (H.C.).

4. A granted a closed mortgage to B. A won a large prize in a lottery and immediately paid the principal balance outstanding together with accrued interest. All along B insisted on six months' interest as a bonus for prepayment. A demanded that B sign a mortgage discharge. B refused to do so and A sued to force B to grant a discharge. Will A succeed? Refer to *Little v. Commerce Capital Trust Co.*, March 6, 1979 (Ont. H.C.).

18

Leasing Real Property

NATURE OF A LEASE

An alternative available to a person or corporation who wishes to use real property but who is unable or unwilling to raise sufficient funds for a down payment to own property is to obtain a lease. The terms "landlord" and "lessor" are used to describe the owner of the property and the terms "tenant" and "lessee' to describe the person who rents or "leases" it. By such an arrangement, the legal interest in the land is divided between the lessee, who gets a leasehold interest for the period of time specified, and the lessor, who has a *reversionary interest*—that is, the right to obtain possession of his or her property on expiry of the term of the lease.

Essential Aspects

As discussed in Chapter 16, the essential aspects of a lease are, first, that exclusive possession be granted to the lessee and, second, that the exclusive possession granted be for a specific or ascertainable period of time. With respect to exclusive possession, an interest in the land is taken from the fee simple and granted to the lessee so that the lessee may use the property as he or she sees fit. The landlord, by virtue of granting the leasehold interest, gives up any right to possesssion, unless certain rights of possession are reserved for the landlord in the lease. For example, the landlord may wish to reserve the right to enter the premises for the purposes of repair or to show the property to prospective tenants or purchasers. Otherwise, the tenant may go so far as to eject the landlord (as a trespasser) from the premises if the landlord is not authorized to be there.

Any proper analysis of a lease must be viewed in terms of the grant of an interest in land as well as a contractual agreement. However, many of the principles of contract law, such as the duty to mitigate damages and the law relating to the frustration of contracts, do not apply in every circumstance.

Residential Tenancies

Many of the provinces of Canada have recognized that residential tenancies (those premises used for the purposes of a residence for the tenant) deserve special consideration. This is because the ordinary rules relating to tenancies may work a hardship on a tenant who relies on his or her lease to provide shelter. In fact, the special legislation relating to residential tenancies offers a wider range of protections for the tenant. Some landlords now argue that the balance has swung in the tenant's favour, in that the laws relating to residential tenancies appear to grant too much protection for the tenant, thus making the position of the landlord less and less desirable.

Landlords also point out that various provinces enforce some form of rent control thereby limiting the income of landlords. This too, they argue, is causing a decrease in the availability of residential premises.

In this chapter, commercial tenancies are discussed separately from residential tenancies.

REQUIREMENT OF WRITING

Because a lease is an interest in land, the Statute of Frauds normally requires that it be in writing. This is always true for a lease of three or more years. In some provinces, such leases must also be made under seal; otherwise they are deemed to be void.

In the case of leases for less than three years, the requirement of writing also exists for executory leases—that is, leases that are to be performed in the future. However, the requirement of writing is waived if there has been some additional act or part performance, such as moving in luggage or painting the premises, in addition to the payment of rent. Such additional act of performance, however, must specifically relate to the performance of the lease rather than being an act that may be construed to be performed in relation to some other contract. Thus, for example, the payment of money to the landlord may not be sufficient to bring the situation within the doctrine of part performance, which excuses the requirement of writing.

TYPES OF TENANCIES

Fixed Term

The most common form of tenancy is one whereby the landlord and tenant agree that the tenant, in return for a fixed monthly payment, is to occupy the premises for a fixed or predetermined period of time (*term certain*). At the end of this time, the tenant is expected to vacate the premises. Often, a lease will contain a renewal option that permits the tenant to stay on, if he or she wishes, at a higher agreed rent. Practically, where a renewal option is contained in a lease, the usual condition attached to such option is that the parties will have to agree on a new rent, which is usually higher than the original rent. Therefore, while the tenants may be offered an option to renew, such option is in fact not enforceable if the landlord decides to raise the rent unreasonably so as to discourage the tenant from continuing to stay in the premises.

An example of a fixed-term tenancy would be one in which the landlord grants a lease to a tenant from July 8 of this year to July 7 of next year.

Periodic Tenancy

A periodic tenancy is created if the landlord and tenant agree that the term of the lease is to be a series of continuous time intervals to be terminated by one party giving notice to the other. For example, a periodic tenancy may be created from year to year, month to month, or week to week. Such tenancies can arise as a result of oral or written agreements or by implication—for example, when a fixed-term lease expires and the tenant continues to occupy the premises and pay rent which is accepted by the landlord. If the previous fixed-term lease was for one year or more, the periodic tenancy will be held by the courts to be from year to year. Similarly, where the prior fixed-term lease is for a period of one month, and the tenant remains on the premises and pays rent which the landlord accepts, the periodic tenancy will be held to be from month to month.

Tenancy at Will

A tenancy at will may be created in various situations: when a prospective purchaser has been given permission by the landlord to occupy the premises prior to the conveyance by way of deed to the purchaser; when an existing tenant has been given permission to stay on after the premises have been sold, even though the tenant's lease has expired pending the demolition of the premises for redevelopment; or when a housekeeper or other employee has been given rent-free accommodation at the place of work. Either party may terminate the tenancy at any time. By the same token, such tenancy at will may continue indefinitely. As the term of tenancy is uncertain, there is some question as to whether such an arrangement is a tenancy at all. If the landlord accepts rent, a periodic tenancy may be held to have arisen based on the period of time during which the tenant pays rent.

A tenancy at will is not an interest in land which may be assigned to a third party.

Tenancy at Sufferance

Unlike a tenancy at will, where the landlord agrees to allow the tenant to remain on the premises, a tenancy at sufferance arises where the premises are occupied by a person against the will or without the knowledge of the landlord. Such a tenancy would occur if a lawful tenant refused to vacate after the lease had expired. The only difference between such a tenant at sufferance (or "overholding tenant") and a trespasser is that a trespasser's entry on the land is illegal, while the initial entry on the premises of a tenant at sufferance is lawful. The "tenant," as well as being liable to prosecution for trespass, must also pay a "use and occupation rent."

Here again, the term "tenancy at sufferance" may be considered a misnomer, as the term of the tenancy is uncertain and it does not, strictly speaking, qualify as a tenancy.

COMMERCIAL TENANCIES

As indicated earlier, different provinces have for consumer protection reasons created different sets of rules for tenancies which are considered to be for residential purposes as compared with tenancies for business or commercial purposes. It is therefore important in determining the answer to a legal question concerning leases to determine whether the nature of the lease is commercial or residential.

Nature of a Commercial Lease

Where the lease of land is entered into by a tenant for the purposes of carrying on some kind of business activity, the lease is normally viewed as a commercial tenancy. The statutes of the various provinces will give a greater certainty to the definition of "residential premises" in the event that certain questions arise. For example, where a tenant occupies under the terms of a lease premises which are used partly for living accommodation and partly for business purposes pursuant to a single lease, the tenant will be considered a commercial tenant unless he or she occupies only the residential portion of the premises and another tenant occupies the commercial premises. This situation is specifically covered under the definition of "residential premises" in the Landlord and Tenant Act of Ontario, which has now been amended by the Residential Tenancies Act. This latter Act has been passed for the purposes of creating a distinct separate body of law relating to residential tenancies in contrast to the prior legislation which dealt with both residential and commercial premises.

It is interesting to note that what may appear to be a commercial tenancy may in fact only be a licence to occupy commercial premises. For example, large department stores may permit travel agencies to operate independently within the confines of the department store even though there is no intention by the landlord or the tenant that the tenant have any interest in the land or exclusive possession so as to exclude the landlord from entering the premises.

Size of the Premises

In order to create sufficient certainty relating to the terms of the lease, it is important to specify the size of the premises being conveyed. This is also of great practical importance. For example, a tenant may enter into a lease agreement whereby he or she agrees to pay a fixed monthly sum for rent based on a cost per square foot. Where the premises are new and partitions are drawn on the floor plans, it may be discovered later that the tenant has more or less space than originally intended. Therefore the rent will have to be revised in accordance with the cost per square foot. In addition, most commercial tenancies provide for the tenant to have access to "common areas"—for example, elevators, stairwells, washrooms, and more typically the concourse area of a shopping mall. A commercial lease will normally provide that the tenant is responsible for a proportionate share of the common area expenses calculated and based on the ratio of the size of the tenant's premises to the entire "leased" or "leasable" area. It is especially important to pay particular attention as to whether the ratio is based on the "leased" or the "leasable" area. If the entire premises are not fully occupied, it would certainly advantageous to the tenant to base the proportionate share of the common expenses on the "leasable" area rather than on the "leased" area.

The courts have held that in a situation where an office or room or part of a floor area is leased and such area is bounded in part by an outside wall, the leased premises will include both sides of the wall so that the area occupied by the width of the wall is included and charged to the tenant as rent unless the lease or lease agreement provides otherwise.

Occupier's Liability

Situations often arise where either the tenant or a customer of the tenant is injured on the premises leased to the tenant or on the common area. However, the landlord has no duty at common law to keep the premises leased to the tenant in good repair. In addition, liability is on the "occupant" of the premises on which the accident occurs. By the very nature of the lease, which grants exclusive possession to the tenant and excludes occupation by the landlord, the landlord cannot be held liable for accidents occurring on the leased premises. However, there is the exceptional case where the landlord has by some negligent act or omission created a situation that ultimately causes harm on the leased premises, and the courts may well find that the landlord is responsible under the normal rules of negligence. Similarly, the landlord may also be responsible for committing some act of nuisance or some act that falls within the principle of "dangerous possessions" as defined in the case of *Rylands v. Fletcher* (1866), L.R. 1 Ex. 265, where such dangerous possessions (water) escaped onto a neighbour's property. The court ruled that strict liability attached to the owner of the land from which the water escaped.

In regard to the common areas, it is the duty of the landlord in relation to the tenant to ensure that the common areas will remain safe. This duty is created by virtue of an implied term in the lease to which the landlord and tenant are parties. It is the tenant's duty to take reasonable care to inspect the common areas and notify the landlord in the event that there is some danger.

The *Occupier's Liability Act*, summarized in Chapter 4, details the statutory liability of an occupier of premises in Ontario. This Act applies to all categories of users and has replaced the common law allocation of liability covering invitees, licensees, and trespassers. The general responsibility is to ensure that premises are "reasonably safe" for all users.

Tenant's Fixtures

The term "tenant's fixtures" is an anomalous term, in that a fixture is defined as a chattel that has become part of the real property by virtue of being affixed to it to such an extent that its removal would cause significant damages to the real property. The law provides that any fixture becomes part of the real property and accrues to the landlord. Therefore, strictly speaking there can be no such thing as a tenant's fixture. However, the term "tenant's fixtures" is used to refer to chattels that are placed on the leased premises for the purposes of a tenant's business or occupation or merely for convenience or decoration and may therefore be removed by the tenant at the termination of the tenancy. Where the chattel (for example, shelving) has been installed by (a) the landlord, (b) prior tenants, or (c) the current tenants so as to constitute a fixture, the tenant is not at liberty to remove such fixtures at the termination of the tenancy. Normally, where significant or irreparable damage would be caused to the leased premises by the removal of the tenant's fixture, the chattel in question will be considered to be a fixture and will consequently accrue to the landlord.

The famous case of *Stack v. T. Eaton Co.* (1902), 4 O.L.R. 335, sets out the rules which determine whether or not a chattel (belonging to the tenant) becomes a fixture (belonging to the landlord). In short, the Ontario Court of Appeal held that:

1. Articles that are on the leased premises and not attached to the land except by their own weight are not to be considered fixtures unless there is some contrary intention.
2. Articles that are affixed to the land even slightly are to be considered part of the land unless evidence to the contrary indicates that they were intended only to be chattels.
3. The degree of affixation and the object affixed are important factors in determining whether the articles are not what they first appeared to be in accordance with the first two rules.
4. The intention of the person affixing the articles to the premises is material only in so far as it can be determined from the degree and object of the affixation.
5. Tenant's fixtures installed for the purpose of trade form part of the premises, thereby giving the tenant the right to take them back and convert them into chattels by taking the articles at the termination of the tenancy.

Property Taxes

It is common for the standard-form commercial lease to contain a covenant by the lessor to pay all taxes and rates, municipal or otherwise, including water rates for the normal supply of cold water to the premises, except for business taxes. In addition, the standard-form commercial lease contains a clause whereby any increase in taxes by virtue of the lessee being a separate-school supporter will be paid by the lessee. The standard-form lease provides that the lessee will be responsible for an increase in property taxes attributable to the leased premises (a tax escalation clause). Of course, the landlord and the tenant may agree that the tenant is to pay all realty taxes and amend the lease accordingly.

In the absence of any specific agreement to the contrary, the landlord will be held responsible for paying realty taxes.

In addition to property taxes, the local municipality will normally levy a business tax based on the category of business conducted by the lessee. The standard-form commercial lease will normally contain a clause requiring the lesee to pay all business taxes in respect to the business carried on by the lessee.

Covenant to Pay Rent

The tenant is expected to pay the agreed rent. Usually, this is a fixed amount payable in advance on the first of each month. In contrast, mortgage payments are made in arrears; that is, the first payment is due and payable at the end of the first month of the term of the mortgage.

As in all other debtor and creditor obligations, it is the duty of the tenant to seek out the landlord to be sure that the rent is paid at the required time.

It is not uncommon in commercial leases to find that the landlord and the tenant have agreed to determine the rent by setting a base rent plus a fixed percentage of the gross sales or receipts of the particular tenant. This arrangement often permits someone starting a business to pay a lower amount during the initial stage of the business and similarly allows the landlord to benefit by the progress of the tenant and collect a higher rent as time goes on.

A landlord may also require a "security deposit" from the tenant so as to secure the performance by the tenant of all covenants under the lease. At the end of the term, the landlord has a fund for the cost incurred for any necessary repairs to restore the premises to the same state of repair as at the commencement of the lease. Some provinces—for example, Ontario—have abolished the right to demand a security deposit from residential tenants.

Assignment and Subletting

An *assignment* of a lease by a tenant occurs when the tenant conveys to a third party the entire leased premises for the entire remainder of the term. Where a portion of the premises is not leased by the tenant to a third party and is reserved to the tenant or when less than the total amount of time remaining under the tenant's lease is demised to a third party, this is known as a *sublease*. A sublease does not create any privity of contract or landlord-tenant relationship between the head landlord and the subtenant. However, an assignment takes the effect of removing the original tenant from the picture and creating a landlord and tenant relationship between the original landlord and the new subtenant.

The standard-form commercial lease normally contains a restriction on the tenant prohibiting the assignment or sublease of the whole or any part of the demised premises without the consent of the lessor. However, the various provinces provide in their Landlord and Tenant Acts that the landlord may not unreasonably withhold consent unless an express provision to the contrary is contained in the lease. One can appreciate that a landlord may not be willing to consent to a sublease where a new tenant may carry on a business that could create a danger to the landlord's property—for example, if such a business might pose a serious fire hazard. By the same token, one can appreciate the position of the tenant who may be forced to cease business operations for one reason or another and therefore wish to assign the lease to a third party so that the covenant requiring the payment of rent may be satisfied.

Independence of Covenants

The courts have held that the covenants contained in a commercial lease are independent of one another. In other words, breach of a covenant by the lessor does not entitle the lessee to breach any of the lessee's covenants. For example, where the landlord fails to repair the electrical system, the tenant is still obligated to pay rent, notwithstanding that it might be the duty of the landlord to repair the electrical system. The tenant may, of course, sue the landlord for breach of promise to repair the electrical system and claim appropriate damages.

By contrast, in the case of residential leases, many provinces including Ontario have provided that the covenants are deemed to be interdependent. This latter situation is the normal rule of contract law. The result, therefore, is that a breach of a covenant by a party to a residential tenancy will relieve the other party to that residential tenancy of a corresponding covenant, subject to the specific provisions in the Landlord and Tenant Act or other applicable statute.

Implied Covenants

In order that a lease may be given full effect, it is often necessary for the courts to imply, by virtue of the circumstances or by statute, the existence of certain covenants by each party. That is not to say that a court will freely imply covenants where it is not obvious that such covenants were intended. For example, the courts will imply that the landlord has covenanted to give the tenant "quiet enjoyment" (to be discussed). Or, in the case of furnished premises, that the landlord has covenanted to put the premises into a condition fit for habitation at the commencement of the term.

The Conveyancing and Law of Property Act of Ontario now provides that every lease for valuable consideration has an implied term that the landlord covenants:

1. that the landlord has the right to convey the premises;
2. that the landlord will grant quiet enjoyment to the tenants;
3. that the premises are free from encumbrances; and
4. that the landlord agrees to do all that is necessary to give full effect to the lease.

Correspondingly, the courts will imply that there is an implied covenant by the tenant to use the property in a proper and tenant-like manner so as to avoid the wasting of the property. *Waste* is defined by the courts to be an act or omission by the tenant which results in lasting damage to the property.

Repairs

In a commercial tenancy the landlord has no implied obligation to repair the premises. Normally, the standard-form lease will specify who bears the obligation to repair. Normally, the tenant will be responsible to repair the premises, pursuant to such standard-form leases, save and except any damage that may be caused by unusual occurrences such as fire, lightning, and tempest. In addition, a landlord is normally given the right to enter the premises to view the state of repair, the lessee being obligated to repair the premises in accordance with written notice by the landlord of any disrepair. Finally the standard-form lease normally provides that a tenant will leave the premises in a good state of repair when the lease has terminated. It is, of course recognized that during the term of the lease the premises will deteriorate in accordance with normal wear and tear. In the event that substantial damage is caused to the premises by extraordinary circumstances such as fire, a commercial lease will normally provide for an abatement in rent for the period during which the premises cannot be used for the purposes for which they were intended. The commercial lease will also provide that, if the premises cannot be used for a certain period of time (for example, 120 days), the lease will terminate.

The law relating to residential tenancies is quite different and will be discussed later in this chapter.

Use of Premises

The landlord will often insist, by means of a provision in the lease, that the tenant use the leased premises only for the purpose set out in the lease. Such a provision is important to the landlord as a landlord may be obligated to other tenants to restrict the use of premises to a certain type of business activity. For example, in a shopping mall, a landlord may have agreed with another tenant not to lease further premises in the mall to another food store. In addition, a landlord is also concerned that the use of the premises does not increase the risk of fire damage so as to invalidate any insurance policies that the landlord may have on the premises.

The clause in the lease relating to the use of the premises is also of great importance to the tenant, who may wish to sublet the premises part-way through the term of the lease. This is because any restrictive use indicated in the lease will also be binding on the subtenant.

Covenant For Quiet Enjoyment

Every lease contains an implied covenant that the landlord will refrain from disturbing the tenant during occupancy of the rented premises—for example, by entering the premises in the tenant's absence or without permission. A breach of this covenant for quiet enjoyment necessarily involves an interference by the landlord in the normal use and occupation of the whole or part of the premises. It has been held that the landlord's failing to supply heat to the premises during the winter months was tantamount to a breach of the covenant for quiet enjoyment. By the same token, it is not necessary that the landlord exercise actual physical interference with the use or enjoyment of the premises in order to commit a breach of the covenant. The criterion is whether the landlord's action negates the very purpose for which the premises were rented. For example, a landlord making excessive and intolerable noise is a breach of the covenant. However, such activity by a neighbour would not constitute a breach by the landlord of the covenant of quiet enjoyment. This would merely allow the tenant to take such civil action as may be necessary against the neighbour pursuant to the law of nuisance. If the landlord does retain the adjoining premises, he or she may not carry on such activity there that would render the leased premises unfit or substantially unfit for the purpose specified in the lease.

Insurance

Neither party to a lease is bound to insure the premises if no such requirement is contained in the lease. Normally, the landlord will assume the responsibility for obtaining appropriate fire and public liability insurance. The tenant would also obtain insurance for hazards (such as burglary) occurring on the rented premises.

The tenant may of course be interested in obtaining business interruption insurance in the event that the premises are damaged by fire and the tenant is obligated either to move to another physical location or to wait until the premises have been repaired in accordance with the terms of the lease.

Of course, a landlord and tenant may make and specify in the lease any arrangement that suits them. For example, the tenant may agree to carry insurance on the premises in respect to fire loss or to repair damage by fire and deduct such expense from future rent.

Termination of Lease

A lease may be terminated in several different ways:

1. by the expiry of the fixed rental period;
2. by the expiry of a period of proper notice;
3. by breach of a covenant by the landlord (for example, failure to make repairs to the heating system in accordance with the terms of the lease) or by the tenant (for example, failure to pay rent);
4. by the accidental destruction of the premises.

Before the expiry of a fixed-term tenancy, proper notice of termination should be served by the landlord on the tenant so as to prevent any implication of the creation of a new tenancy.

Where a commercial tenancy is periodic, the Landlord and Tenant Act of Ontario provides that a week's notice to quit or a month's notice to quit, ending with the week or the month, is sufficient notice to terminate a weekly or monthly tenancy, respectively, In order to terminate a yearly periodic tenancy, six months' notice is required. Of course, the length of notice required may be varied in accordance with a specific term contained in the lease. Where a tenant fails to vacate the premises pursuant to a commercial lease after proper notice has been given, the Landlord and Tenant Act of Ontario provides that the tenant shall be responsible to pay double the rent that would otherwise have to be paid until possession is surrendered to the landlord.

The landlord must be careful not to accept the rent unless the intention of the parties is made quite clear that such acceptance of rent does not constitute a waiver of the notice to vacate.

It should be noted that the covenants contained in commercial leases are independent and the law relating to the frustration of contract does not apply. Therefore, damage or destruction of the premises may not relieve a tenant of the obligation to continue paying rent. The tenant will have to prove that the damage or destruction constitutes a breach of the covenant of quiet enjoyment in order to escape the obligation to continue paying rent. However, the tenant may protect him- or herself by specifically including a provision in the lease whereby the obligation to pay rent will cease in the event that damage to or destruction of the premises makes it impossible to continue carrying on business. It is of the utmost importance for a tenant when he or she executes a lease to know the provisions of the lease—for example, if there is damage to the premises, whether the lease will continue, and whether there will be a continuing obligation to pay rent. For instance, it may be quite impractical for a tenant to receive an abatement of rent for a period of ninety days while still being obligated to continue with the lease once the premises are repaired, as such a lengthy interruption may cause irreparable harm to the tenant's business. Therefore, it is not uncommon to find commercial leases containing extensive provisions dealing with the eventuality of damage and destruction to the premises.

As a final note, a tenancy may terminate by operation of the law—for example, because of expropriation by a government body. Of course, the expropriations legislation normally provides some form of compensation to the tenant for the value of the lease plus damages for any disturbance.

REMEDIES OF THE LANDLORD

We now consider what a landlord may do if the tenant commits a breach of the lease.

Right of Distress

One remedy available to a landlord in a commercial tenancy is the "right of distress." This permits a landlord to seize and sell the goods of the tenant so as to satisfy any arrears of rent. A landlord who exercises this "right to distrain," as this remedy is also called, may not terminate the lease. To exercise both remedies would be illegal.

The provisions of the Landlord and Tenant Act of Ontario require that the distress be reasonable. That is, the landlord may not seize goods in excess of the value of the rent in arrears. The landlord must also be careful not to seize goods that do not belong to the tenant. For example, a tenant may rent certain machinery to carry on business which would not be subject to the landlord's right to distrain.

The landlord's right of distress may be exercised only after the date on which the rent is due and during daylight hours on weekdays without exercising force. The Executions Act normally exempts from distress those goods that are necessities of life such as food, clothing, bedding, tools of trade, utensils, sewing machines, and furniture.

It is illegal for a tenant to remove goods from the premises in order to defeat the right of the landlord to distrain. Where goods are fraudulently taken away by the tenant to prevent the landlord from seizing them because of arrears of rent, the landlord may seize such goods by requesting the assistance of a police officer.

Having seized the goods, the landlord is then required to give five days' notice to the tenant to recover the goods by paying all of the rent in arrears plus the costs of carrying out the distress process. If the tenant does not pay the arears of rent plus the costs, the landlord must then obtain two sworn appraisals and may proceed to sell the goods for the best price possible. Any excess received for the goods must be paid to the tenant.

Damages, Rent, and Possession

On default by the tenant of the covenant to pay rent, the landlord may commence court proceedings to recover the rent arrears plus any costs, such as the tenant's portion of the maintenance costs and realty taxes. In addition, the landlord may sue to recover possession of the premises.

In addition to suing for the arrears of rent, the landlord must decide what remedy to take with regard to the rent that will become due in the future. In other words, the landlord must consider his or her position in regard to rent accruing from the date of default to the termination of the lease. In that regard, a landlord has basically four choices:

1. to consider the lease as continuing, notwithstanding the abandonment by the tenant and sue the tenant for rent as the rent falls due;
2. to choose to re-rent the premises on behalf of the tenant and sue the tenant for any deficiency as the result of a lower rent being obtained from the new tenant;
3. to accept the surrender of the lease and sue for such arrears of rent as have accumulated since the date of abandonment;
4. to accept the surrender of the lease and sue for damages to the extent that the landlord has lost the benefit of the lease for the balance of the term.

The fourth remedy may be useful to a landlord in situations where the landlord loses rent by way of a percentage of the gross receipts and also loses rent from other tenants that would otherwise be possible to collect if the defaulting tenant had not abandoned the premises. This situation normally occurs in the shopping plaza situation where a large tenant (for example, a large department store chain operation) abandons the premises thereby resulting in significantly less traffic in the plaza.

Injunction

A landlord may seek an injunction if a tenant carries on a particular type of business that is specifically prohibited in the lease. Nothwithstanding the absence of an express prohibition in the lease, a landlord may also seek the remedy of injunction if a tenant carries on an activity unsuitable to the normal and ordinary use of the premises. An order of the court will effectively bar the tenant from continuing such a breach.

REMEDIES OF THE TENANT

The tenant can sue the landlord for breach of contract if the latter violates any of the express or implied covenants of the lease. The tenant may not, however, legally withhold rent as a means of forcing the landlord to fulfill his obligations. This of course is a result of the independence of the covenants contained in a commercial lease. If the tenant fails to obtain satisfaction, he or she may ask the court for an order declaring the tenancy to be terminated or an order for abatement of rent.

RESIDENTIAL TENANCIES

Government consumer protection policy has recently been focused on the various means of protecting residential tenants. This is because, as the cost of owning a home becomes prohibitive, more and more people are resorting to the renting of premises and such a relatively large proportion of our population is able to exert strong political pressure to ensure that their interests are sufficiently protected. As a result, most provinces have enacted legislation altering the law of landlord and tenant in favour of residential tenants. For example, in Ontarion in 1979, the government passed the Residential Tenancies Act, which changed the name of the Landlord and Tenant Act to the "Commercial Tenancies Act" so as to make it applicable to commercial tenancies only and created a new body of law for residential tenancies. The previous Landlord and Tenant Act of Ontario contained provisions in Part IV of the Act which applied only to residential tenancies.

Security Deposits

For many years landlords required a security deposit from tenants. This was a sum of money that would be returned at the end of the lease minus the cost of any damages to the premises. Security deposits are now illegal in Ontario. However, a landlord may require a tenant to pay the last month's rent in advance at the commencement of the lease. The landlord must then pay to the tenant interest on the last month's rent based on an interest rate set out in the statute (in Ontario, 6% per annum).

Right to Distrain

In Ontario, the Residential Tenancies Act abolished the right of a landlord to exercise the right to distrain. Therefore, in the event that a landlord does seek to exercise such right, the tenant may sue the landlord for the recovery of damages.

Frustration of a Residential Lease

As discussed in Chapter 12, if the subject matter of a contract is destroyed, the doctrine of frustration would normally excuse the parties from performance. However, the common law cases held that the doctrine of frustration would not apply to leases. Subsequently, this position was changed by the enactment of legislation to make the doctrine of frustration applicable to residential leases. Therefore, the destruction of the premises would now bring into play the Frustrated Contracts Act. It should be noted that an event must occur which causes the basis of the agreement to be frustrated; a mere inconvenience would not fit into this category. Also, a party to the contract would not be permitted to bring about a series of events that would result in the impossibility of performance of the lease.

Tenant's Right to Sublet or Assign
Under the Ontario Residential Tenancies Act, a tenant has the right to assign, sublet, or otherwise part with possession of the rented premises. However, a tenancy agreement may provide that the right of a tenant to assign or sublet is subject to the consent of the landlord. If such a provision is contained in the lease, the consent is not to be arbitrarily or unreasonably withheld. In the event that a landlord does refuse to consent unreasonably or arbitrarily, the tenant may make an application to the court to have the matter determined. It is, of course, reasonable for a landlord to refuse to give consent where a prospective tenant is not as desirable as the current tenant or where the nature of the proposed use is contrary to its intended use.

Interdependent Covenants
The Ontario legislation provides that the common law rules of contract respecting the effect of the breach of a material covenant by one party on the obligation to perform by the other party apply to residential tenancy agreements. Therefore, breach of a residential tenancy agreement by one party may excuse the other party from performing his or her obligations. The interdependence of covenants relates only to the covenants contained in the contract and not those implied by statute or otherwise by law.

As in the case of contract law, only a breach of a material covenant by one party will excuse the performance by the other and not merely the breach of a minor term. It is questionable in many circumstances which covenant may be considered to be a *material one*—one that goes to the heart of the lease contract. Eventually, it will be for a judge to determine in view of the circumstances in each case.

The law in Ontario at this point is unclear on whether a tenant will have the right to withhold rent if a material covenant is breached by the landlord or whether such breach entitles the tenant only to apply for a termination of the tenancy or to sue for specific performance. The weight of authority appears to be in favour of allowing a tenant to withhold rent where there has been substantial breach of the covenant of quiet enjoyment. Once the landlord has remedied this breach, all rent arrears become due and payable. Should the tenant feel that his or her use and enjoyment of the premises has been decreased so as to decrease the value of the premises, the tenant may make an application to the appropriate court to seek an abatement of rent rather than withholding a portion of the rent permanently by his or her own decision.

Accelerated Rent
The provisions of the law relating to residential tenancies relieve the tenant of the obligation to pay rent which becomes accelerated pursuant to a term

in the lease as a result of default. On remedying the default, the tenant is relieved of the obligation to pay accelerated rent.

Duty to Repair

The common law implies no obligation on the part of the landlord to put the leased premises into a good state of repair. However, the legislation in Ontario relating to residential tenancies now places an obligation on the landlord to provide and maintain the rented premises in a good state of repair, fit for habitation during the tenancy and complying with health and safety standards, even though the tenant may have been aware, at the beginning of the lease, of the state of disrepair. This obligation has been interpreted so as to create a responsibility on the landlord to provide proper lighting, ventilation, heating, and plumbing facilities. Included in the responsibility to repair is the landlord's obligation to inspect the premises on a periodic basis to ensure the continued state of good repair.

A tenant, on the other hand, is responsible for damages caused by his or her own wilful or negligent conduct or that of invited guests. As well, good housekeeping and cleanliness is a responsibility of the tenant.

Termination of a Residential Lease

The scope and nature of a residential tenancy has been significantly altered by the current legislation affecting residential tenancies. The normal termination of a lease by virtue of the passage of time pursuant to the lease no longer is the determining factor in requiring a tenant to vacate the premises. The Residential Tenancies Act now allows a fixed-term tenancy to be extended as a periodic tenancy merely by virtue of the tenant remaining on the premises. There is therefore a serious question as to whether a "fixed-term" tenancy exists for residential premises. The landlord may not evict the tenant without serving proper notice pursuant to the Residential Tenancies Act and subsequently making an application to the appropriate court to have a Writ of Possession issued so as to authorize the eviction of the tenant. If the landlord cannot come within the statutory causes for eviction so as to obtain a Writ of Possession, the landlord will be unable to recover possession of the premises. The landlord may apply to the court for a Writ of Possession where:

1. the tenant fails to pay rent after notice;
2. the tenant causes undue damage to the premises;
3. the tenant carries on an illegal activity on the premises;
4. the tenant exhibits anti-social behaviour;
5. the tenant endangers other tenants;
6. the tenant causes overcrowding of the premises;
7. the tenant misrepresents his or her income in a public housing project;
8. a caretaker's employment is to be terminated.

These eventualities will allow a landlord to make an application for a Writ of Possession prior to the end of the period or the term of the tenancy.

At the end of the term or period of tenancy, the landlord may make an application for a Writ of Possession based on:

1. the landlord's desire to demolish or extensively repair the premises;
2. conversion of the premises to a non-residential use;
3. the landlord wishing to occuping the premises or to have his or her family occupy the premises;
4. the tenant persistently being late in paying rent;
5. a tenant in a public housing project no longer qualifying to be in occupancy;
6. an employer terminating the employment of an employee;
7. a prospective purchaser going into occupation of a condominium unit and the agreement of puchase and sale terminating.

It is therefore impossible to terminate a residential tenancy simply because the landlord does not "like" the tenant.

Part IV of the Residential Tenancies Act contains an overriding provision permitting a judge to refuse to grant a Writ of Possession notwithstanding any other provision in the Act, unless he or she is satisfied, having regard to all the circumstances, that it would be unfair not to do so.

In addition, the Act specifically prohibits a landlord from withholding essential services such as heat, fuel, electricity, gas, and water so as to create pressure on the tenant to leave the premises. The Residential Tenancies Act contains specific notice provisions that must be complied with; otherwise all proceedings taken pursuant to the Act will be null and void.

REVIEW QUESTIONS

1. Explain the following terms: lease, lessor, and lessee.
2. Must a lease be in writing to be leagally enforceable? Explain.
3. What are a tenant's obligations with regard to the payment of rent?
4. What are a tenant's obligations with regard to assignment and subletting of the leased premises?
5. What are a landlord's obligations with regard to "quiet enjoyment"?
6. Who is responsible for repairs to leased premises?
7. What fixtures, if any, may a tenant remove on expiry of the lease?
8. Who is responsible for payment of property taxes and insurance on the leased premises?
9. Distinguish among the following: (a) fixed-term tenancy; (b) periodic tenancy; (c) tenancy at will; (d) tenancy at sufferance.
10. What legal remedies are available to a tenant if the landlord fails to meet his or her obligations?
11. What legal remedies are available to a landlord if the tenant fails to meet his or her obligations.
12. What are the ways in which a residential lease may be legally terminated?
13. In what ways does a commercial lease differ from a residential one?

14. What is meant by a "tenant's fixtures"?
15. Distinguish between assignment of a lease and subletting.
16. What is meant by the "independence of covenants"?
17. In a commercial tenancy, who is responsible for repairs?
18. Explain the landlord's covenant for quiet enjoyment.

PROBLEMS

1. Mrs. F moved into an apartment building. Amost immediately she began to suffer headaches, nausea, and was absent from work several times. This condition continued for eight months until an investigation showed that carbon monoxide funes from the parking garage below her apartment were seeping into the apartment and causing her illness. She sues the landlord. What is the likely result?

2. Your family has decided to operate a fruit business during the summer and you decide to lease a small business flat in the neighbourhood. You recall that your law studies indicated that in the case of rental of commercial premises, the lessee-renter takes the premises as found, contrary to residential premises which must be fit at all times according to statute law. You notice that the ceiling plaster seems to be cracking, but the landlord assures you it is all right. After the business has been carried on successfully for one month, part of the ceiling falls, badly injuring a customer and causing $2,000 in special damages, plus $4,000 in general damages for facial disfigurement.

   Who would the plaintiff customer sue? How is the degree of liability of the defendant business owner towards the injured customer expressed in legal terms? Who should win the case? Has the owner of the business flat any liability in this case?

3. On May 28, 1963, the owners of Yonge Eglinton Building at 2000 Yonge St. leased store premises to K & L Higgins Ltd. Clause 8 stated ". . . for the purpose of office supply stationery store." Clause 24, prepared by the purchaser's solicitor, covered normal items sold in a stationery store including tobacco products and, by clause 25, the landlord agreed not to let premises in the building to a business similar to the tenant. In April 1972, Higgins became aware that premises were being let to Supersave Drug Mart with the added right to sell tobacco supplies in addition to drug products. The plaintiff objected immediately and by this action sought *an injunction* to restrain the latter lease since the plaintiff alleged that 65% of his business was from tobacco product sales.

   The judge found that the lease must speak for itself, and since clauses 24 and 25 were drafted by the plaintiff's solicitor, if they didn't confer exclusive right to sell tobacco they must be construed against him.

   In a 1933 case dealing with overlap between a grocery and meat business and a delicatessen, such leases did not constitute a breach of the covenant not to lease to someone in the same business, since the businesses were separate and distinct. "The covenant invoked in this action is a restrictive one and in restraint of trade, and as such should be strictly construed." (*Stop & Shop Ltd. v. Independent Builders Ltd.*, [1933] O.R. 150.)

What was the nature of the covenant in this case? Would an exclusive covenant have been against the provisions of the Anti-Combines legislation? Would an exclusive covenant have been enforceable by this court? If an injunction had been granted, what would have been the legal effect in this case? Why should the ambiguous clauses be construed against the original tenant? Refer to *K. & L. Higgins Ltd. v. Yonge Eglinton Building Ltd.* (1974), 5 O.R. (2d) 563.

4. On March 30, 1973, the tenant rented premises at 84 Yorkville Ave. to be used as a discothèque *covenanting not to create any nuisances*, but the lease specifically provided that a discothèque was not a nuisance. There were two options: one allowing rental of a patio, the other providing for a two-year renewal. The rent was $1,200 per month for two years. On May 17, 1974, the landlord complained that the tenant was carrying on a nuisance. On July 24, the tenant was given ten days to eliminate the nuisances alleged of: accosting passers-by; permitting loitering; fighting; and providing heavily amplified music as late as 5 and 6 a.m. The tenant replied to this complaint, paid his rent on August 1, and exercised the "patio option," paying a further rental of $100 per month. The landlord barred the premises on August 6 and removed chattels.

The judge found that most of the incidents complained of occurred near and not on the premises, that the tenant was not committing a nuisance and furthermore, s. 19 of the Landlord and Tenant Act required the landlord to state the breach complained of, give time to remedy it plus any money compensation required. The landlord's acceptance of rent satisfactorily settled this complaint. "Where it appears that the tenant in good faith did what he was supposed to do in performance of the covenant, it would be most unjust for any Court . . . to turn such tenant out of possession."

Give your explanation of the type of nuisance which would constitute a breach of a covenant not to commit a nuisance. Could the landlord have locked out a residential tenant under provincial laws in case of a nuisance? What effect did the acceptance of rent by the landlord on August 1 have in this case? Discuss the exclusion of the word discothèque from the meaning of nuisance. Discuss the operation of an option for renewal. Refer to *Re Clark and Mihailescu* (1974), 5 O.R. (2d) 201.

5. Discuss how you would deal with the following situations:
   (a) A sublet where the landlord refuses to let you sublet the apartment.
   (b) As landlord, you discover that one of your tenants has spread earth in one of the bedrooms and is growing vegetables.
   (c) The landlord has served you with a notice dated June 6 of this year that your apartment rent will be raised 12% for the next twelve months.

6. Would a hotel patron who has lived in the hotel for fifteen years be

subject to the provisions of the Landlord and Tenant legislation? Refer to *Re Canadian Pacific Hotels Ltd. and Hodges* (1978), 96 D.L.R. (3d) 313 (Ont. Co. Ct.).

7. A tenant of residential premises sued the landlord where the landlord assured the tenants that the premises were available for occupation but in fact were not fit for habitation. Would the tenant succeed? Could the tenant recover the moving costs as well as the cost of meals paid for in restaurants due to the lack of cooking facilities?

READINGS

Re Carter and Randall, 145 D.L.R. (3d) p. 572

Held per MacKinnon Co. Ct. J.:

This is a judicial review of an order made by the rentalsman on February 1, 1983, in which the tenants were ordered to pay some landscaping costs for pruning of trees.

The landlord and tenant entered into a written lease.

The provision in question reads as follows:

> (b) Pay and discharge as soon as due, all charges for telephone, electricity, water, gas, fuel, oil and garbage disposal supplied to the premises and any expenses in connection with the upkeep of the landscaping thereof.

In her reasons, the rentalsman states that:

> Although it is unusual for the tenant to be responsible for the professional pruning the trees [*sic*], I find no contravention of the Residential Tenancy Act in the tenants agreeing to such a responsibility, and I find this clause to be "reasonable" as defined in section 10 of the Residential Tenancy Act and therefore enforceable.

Section 25 of the *Residential Tenancy Act*, R.S.B.C. 1979, c. 365, provides:

> 25(1) A landlord shall provide and maintain residential premises and residential property in a state of decoration and repair that
>
> > (a) complies with health and safety standards, including housing standards, required by law; and
> >
> > (b) having regard to the age, character and locality of the residential property, would make it reasonably suitable for occupation by a reasonable tenant who would be willing to rent it.
>
> (2) A landlord's duty under subsection (a) applies notwithstanding that a tenant knew of a breach by the landlord of subsection (1) at the time the landlord an tenant entered the tenancy agreement.
>
> (3) subsection (1) does not apply to that part of residential premises owned by a tenant.
>
> (4) A tenant shall

(a) maintain ordinary health, cleanliness and sanitary standards throughout residential premises in respect of which he has entered a tenancy agreement; and

(b) repair damage caused to residential premises and residential property, in respect of which he has entered a tenancy agreement, by his wilful or negligent act or omission, or that of a person permitted on the residential premises or residential property by him.

The provision places a statutory obligation on the landlord to provide and maintain the residential premises and property in a proper state of repair and decoration. The tenant's only obligation of repair arises if he himself has caused the damage by a wiful or negligent act or omission. Other than that the tenant's only obligation is to use the premises in a "tenant-like manner."

In my view s. 25(1) provides a statutory duty on the landlord to maintain the premises and property in a proper state of repair. The tenant is responsible for any work necessitated by his negligent act.

I find that the clause in the lease attempting to avoid the duty imposed by statute is void and unenforceable by virute of ss. 7(1) and (5) of the *Residential Tenancy Act.*

The matter is therefore remitted to the rentalsman to consider further in light of this judgment.

Application granted.

Re Scoffield and Strata Corporation, B.C. Ct. of Appeal, 3 Mar. 83

Appeal from a judgment of Dohm J. holding that Strata Corporation had properly imposed a fine and lien on the appellant unit owner.

Held per Nemetz C.J.B.C.:

In this case a dispute arose with a group of people banded together under the *Condominium Act,* R.S.B.C. 1979, c. 61, wherein the council in this Strata Corporation had been told that Mrs. Schoffield illegally had a cat on her premises. Without in any way informing the lady of this complaint the council proceeded to hold a meeting and hold discussions apparently and came to a decision and imposed a fine under the authority of the *Condominium Act.* There are, as was stated by Chief Justice Laskin in *Re Nicholson and Haldimand-Norfolk Regional Board of Com'rs of Police* (1978), 88 D.L.R. (3d) 671, [1979] 1 S.C.R. 311, 23 N.R. 410, and Mr. Justice Dickson in *Martineau v. Matsqui Institution Disciplinary Board (No. 2)* (1979), 106 D.L.R. (3d) 385, 50 C.C.C. (2d) 353, [1980] 1 S.C.R. 602, certain rules of fairness which must be observed. The degree to which the courts will impose rules will of course be determined by the circumstances of the case.

In this case all I will say is that there is a minimal requirement that this lady receive some notice to know why the council was meeting and to know that she stood the risk of being fined. In such circumstances I think that the council acted without fairness and I would therefore discharge the lady from the onus of paying the fine and discharge the lien which was placed against her property.

Seaton J.A.:—May I add that I agree with the Chief Justice. I think that within s. 42 of the *Condominium Act*, R.S.B.C. 1979 c. 61, it is open to an owner to come before the court alleging that an act of the Strata Corporation has been done that is unfairly prejudicial to the owner. This case falls properly within that section and the appeal should be allowed.

MacFarlane J.A.:—I would agree.

Nemetz C.J.B.C.:—The appeal is allowed accordingly.

Appeal allowed.

5

EMPLOYMENT LAW

19

Employing Other Persons (Common Law)

The term *employment law* refers to the body of rules that governs the relations between employer and employee. The Canadian rules have been created through common law (except in Quebec, which uses civil law) and statute law.

The origin of the present common law rules relating to employment is the old English "master and servant" relationship. Statute law derives from legislation at the federal and provincial levels and governs both the unionized and non-unionized worker. If statute law does not specifically cover the matter in question, the common law principles apply.

In this chapter and the next, we will examine both the common and statutory rules and their effect on the employer-employee relationship in Canada.

HISTORICAL BACKGROUND

From the time of the Norman Conquest until the mid-fourteenth century, English society was basically feudal: the former peasant class had been reduced to a state of serfdom, supplying labour services to the lord of the manor in exchange for the use of land on which to grow their own food. In the towns, strong craft and merchant guilds closely regulated members and their journeymen and apprentices. Workers had few, if any, rights. After the bubonic plague, or Black Death, in England in the mid-fourteenth century, however, there was a shortage of workers and, to prevent the remaining workers from using this situation to their advantage, the King approved two statutes that tried to restore the dominant position of the employer. By such legislation, there was a duty to work according to defined minimum standards: wages were fixed and an employee accepting higher wages was severely punished. The labour contract was legally enforced by the courts, with stiff penalties for any violation. It was from this humble beginning that modern employment law evolved.

The common law courts developed rules governing employment and the labour contract, and referred to the arrangement as a "master-servant" relationship. In particular, judges established rules regarding the creation and termination of that relationship and the rights and obligations of both parties while it was in force. Some of these rules are still important today. For instance, to see whether an employer-employee relationship exists (as opposed to an agency or an independent contractor situation) we usually examine the common law definitions because (a) although some statutes define the terms "employer" and "employee," the definitions apply only to that specific legislation and not to any other (many statutes do not even make a legal definition); and (b) statute law does not usually infringe on common law principles.

CHARACTERISTICS OF THE EMPLOYMENT RELATIONSHIP

The common law judges believed that a "contract of service" was an essential characteristic of an employment relationship. Thus, in a true employment relationship, the employer has the power to select, pay wages to, and control the method of doing the work of the employee and the employer has the right to dismiss the employee.

The employment relationship is different from the *independent contractor* situation. In the latter, the contractor may work to complete a certain job; be paid at the end of the job or when it is completed to the contracting party's satisfaction (as opposed to receiving wages in an employment situation); supply the equipment or tools; and perform work without direct supervision. An example of this would be a householder hiring a landscaping firm. If the owner becomes unhappy with the work he or she can dismiss the firm, or sue or be sued for breach of contract. The landscaping firm is not considered to be an employee of the householder; therefore there is no need to give the firm advance notice that its services are no longer required.

The employment relationship also differs from that of an *agency*, which is a particular form of the independent contractor situation. An agency relationship occurs when a person is employed as an agent by a person, known as the principal, to enter into contracts with third parties on the principal's behalf—for example, a real estate agent employed to sell one's house. Agency is discussed in detail in Chapter 23 of this book.

The distinction between an employment relationship and that of an independent contractor or agent is sometimes crucial—for example, in wrongful dismissal actions claiming that an employee has been "fired" without good or "just" cause. If the person involved does not enjoy the status of "employee," he or she is not entitled to any advance notice of dismissal, nor any compensation in lieu of notice. This principle of notice, or compensation in lieu thereof, originated from the idea that an employment contract contains an implied term that the employer is to provide an opportunity for the employee to work; when the employer ends it abruptly, the employee suffers a loss for which he or she should be compensated. Normally, the employee should be given advance notice in order to be able to look for and, it is hoped, find alternative employment.

The tests that the common law courts used to determine the kind of relationship that existed were: (a) who had control? (b) who owned the tools or equipment? and (c) who ran the chance of profit or the risk of loss therefrom? Thus in an employment situation, the employer usually supplies the tools and equipment, pays the wages, supplies other necessary funds, has direct supervision over the method of work, and stands to gain therefrom. The whole agreement is examined to see if an employment relationship exists. Although the common law tests are not always conclusive, they are helpful for this purpose.

CREATION OF THE EMPLOYMENT RELATIONSHIP

The employment relationship may be created orally or by writing or may be implied from the behaviour of the parties towards each other. The Statute of Frauds (discussed in Chapter 10) that exists in all the common law provinces states that, to be legally enforceable, a contract which cannot be performed by either party within one year must be in writing. Thus, an oral contract whereby a person is hired "for the rest of his life," would be valid because theoretically the person could die at any time and thus the contract could be performed within a year. However, if the contract required the person to work for say, two years, it would have to be in writing to be legally enforceable.

TERM OF THE EMPLOYMENT CONTRACT

The employment contract may be for a definite or an indefinite period of time. A contract for a specified term endures until it expires; if it is terminated earlier, the employee is to be paid the salary or wages for the complete period. Most contracts, however, are for an indefinite period. In this case the employment contract can end only after reasonable notice has been given. In both cases the employee has a duty to mitigate his or her damages by seeking employment elsewhere.

COMMON LAW DUTIES OF THE EMPLOYEE

The common law specifies that an employee owes certain duties to the employer. These include:

1. obeying lawful orders;
2. exercising care and skill;
3. exercising good faith and avoiding any conflict of interest;
4. accounting to the employer with regard to any financial matters; and
5. not divulging confidential information.

The employee who does anything incompatible with the faithful discharge of duties may be dismissed by the employer. The courts seem to assess the duties required according to the position held—for example, the duty to act in "good faith" is much stricter for a company president than for a company clerk. An employee who "moonlights" on company time may be fired for just cause. Nor is an employee allowed to retain any profits acquired by working during the term of employment, without the employer's consent, in any business that gives the employee an interest that conflicts with the duties owed to the employer. Thus moonlighting in spare time may create a legal obligation to account for the profits if the interest is likely to conflict with that of the company.

Confidential information which the employee may receive is not to be divulged publicly; otherwise it is a breach of the fiduciary duty in the employment relationship and just grounds for dismissal. If such information is revealed to third parties after the employment relationship ceases, the employer can possibly sue for damages. In determining what is "confidential," or a trade secret, the onus is on the employer. Sometimes the employment contract will spell out just what is confidential; however, if it fails to do so, the circumstances of the job may be held by implication to create a confidential relationship.

COMMON LAW DUTIES OF THE EMPLOYER

Under common law, there are various duties that an employer must fulfil with regard to employees. Some of these duties are now legislated—for instance, the various Workers' Compensation and Occupational Health and Safety Acts protecting the health and safety of the worker. Specifically, an employer must:

1. strictly observe the terms of any express contract between the employer and the employee or the labour union that represents the employee.
2. provide a safe place of work for the employee.
3. provide competent fellow employees whenever an employee's safety depends on them.
4. honour any liabilities the employee has incurred in the course of employment.
5. reimburse the employee for any expenses legitimately incurred in the course of employment.
6. issue orders as to the work to be done and establish rules for their implementation.
7. permit an employee to hold a second job (that is, "moonlight") in his or her spare time so long as it does not interfere or conflict with the company's interest (see discussion earlier in the chapter).
8. in certain occupations, provide a reasonable amount of work so that, for example, a stenographer will not lose skills through lack of practice; a waiter or waitress will not lose the opportunity to earn tips; an actress will not lose her audience popularity; and an ice-hockey player will not lose his skill and dexterity.

TERMINATION OF THE EMPLOYMENT CONTRACT

In an employment situation, both parties continually review and assess the relationship. The employer requires the work to be performed and the employee expects the wages and working conditions to be in accordance with the employment contract. When either becomes dissatisfied, the contract may be terminated, subject of course to the terms of the contract regarding duration and notice.

Employment contracts may be terminated by frustration (or "impossibility of performance"), by mutual agreement, or unilaterally.

Frustration.   This means that, through no fault of his or her own, one of the parties can no longer fulfil obligations—for example, permanent illness, death of the employer or employee, or bankruptcy of the employer. When such a situation arises, the parties are freed from their obligations towards each other.

Mutual Agreement.   This occurs where both parties voluntarily agree to terminate the contract, foregoing any right to notice.

Unilateral Termination.   This occurs where one party, without the agreement of the other, decides to terminate the employment contract: "you're fired" or "I'm quitting."

The common law imposes an obligation to give notice or pay compensation in lieu thereof on the party wishing to terminate the employment contract unilaterally. This obligation will vary, however, according to the term of the contract (the length of time for which it is to run) and according to whether there was "just cause" for dismissal.

Set Period of Notice.   Some employment contracts may include a provision stating the period of notice to be given (for example, should X not perform her employment duties satisfactorily, the company may terminate the employment by giving three months' notice). The inclusion of such a provision in an employment contract will help lessen litigation; many contracts, however, include no such provision. Although various statutes have been passed which specify the period of notice to be given to a dismissed employee, they do not apply to all employees. Furthermore, they provide only minimum protection and do not alter the common law. For example, Ontario's Employment Standards Act provides for one week's notice for an employee working more than three months but less than two years and does not apply to all employees—for example, workers in the construction industry.

Constructive Dismissal.   Dismissal usually takes place by means of an oral or written notice ("unfortunately your services are no longer required"). However, there is also what is called "constructive" dismissal. This occurs when the nature of the job is changed so much by the employer that the employee may elect to treat it as equivalent to an actual "firing." Previous cases indicate this can occur when there is: a demotion in job position; a reduction in salary; a substantial change in fringe benefits; a unilateral change in job description or job location; an employer hiring another person to perform the job of the employee; an employer temporarily unable to pay wages; and misconduct by the employer.

In "constructive dismissal" cases, the employee must act quickly and refuse to continue providing his or her services so as to indicate that the employee considers the employer's conduct tantamount to dismissal; otherwise it may be said the employee accepted (or *condoned*) the changes and the employee would be "estopped" from making any claim. Thus, if a corporate vice-president were asked to perform full-time office cleaning chores at half his salary, he could assert that the change was equivalent to being "fired." He could say that he should have had notice of such "firing" and, as the company did not do this, he would like compensation in lieu of such notice. (The extent of the notice required or the compensation to be paid is discussed later in this chapter.)

Just Cause for Dismissal. If "just cause" for dismissal exists, the employer may fire the employee immediately, without giving any advance notice (or compensation in lieu of notice). If there is any dispute as to what is "just cause," the onus to prove it in court lies with the employer. Some examples from previous cases of what is considered "just cause" are:

1. *Dishonesty* (even if the employee does not benefit from the act). The employment contract presumes a fiduciary duty on the part of the employee—that is, he or she will act in a trustworthy manner. If the employee acts dishonestly or in any other manner prejudicial to the employer's business, it is grounds for immediate dismissal. If the employee has taken any profit from the relationship (from, say, selling trade secrets), there is a duty to account to the employer for the money or other benefit received.
2. *Disobedience* (failure to carry out reasonable and lawful orders) is also grounds for immediate dismissasl. However, the refusal to carry out orders must be intentional and deliberate. Disobedience would not be a just cause for dismissal in a situation where an employee has been asked to perform work not connected with the job for which the employee was hired, or if the order would endanger the life of the employee (or give apprehension of danger).
3. *Incompetence.* This may occur if an employee, when hired, professes skills that he or she does not possess. However, if the employer knowingly accepts such lower standards, it may indicate condonation of the incompetence.
4. *Insolence.* This involves speaking or gesticulating to a superior in a derogatory manner and justifies immediate dismissal. A single act of insolent conduct is not usually sufficient ground for dismissal. Sometimes the employee may succeed in pleading provocation as a defence.
5. *Physical abuse.* This would include physical abuse of a superior or other employee, including sexual advances or attacks.
6. *Conflict of interest.* An employee may not engage in any activity that would be in actual or potential conflict with the interests of the employer—for example, helping someone to set up a similar business to compete with that of the employer.
7. *Conduct outside of working hours.* Sometimes, depending on the circumstances, the courts may hold that conduct during an employee's own

time justifies dismissal—for example, a public school teacher who is caught robbing a bank.

Sometimes the term "gross misconduct" is used to embrace several of the previously mentioned grounds for dismissal.

The disagreeable personality or drugged or intoxicated state of an employee is just ground for immediate dismissal only if an employer can show that such employee behaviour is prejudicial to the employer's interests. Job redundancy and temporary illness are not just grounds. As explained earlier, permanent illness may cause the employment contract to end, but this is due to "frustration" of the contract, discussed more fully in Chapter 12.

If a worker is dismissed for "just cause" during the middle of a pay period and has actually worked up to that time, payment is to be made according to the work done (this is based on the "quantum meruit" principle).

There is no doubt that an employee covered by a union contract has greater job protection than one who is not. At common law, it would appear that, as long as the required period of notice is given, an employer may discharge an employee at will.

WRONGFUL DISMISSAL

A common area of dispute, called *wrongful dismissal*, occurs when an employer unilaterally and without just cause terminates an employee's job and does not give adequate notice or compensation in lieu of such notice.

If an employee is fired without "just cause," notice must be given of such dismissal. If notice is not given, the employee should receive compensation equal to the amount of money that would have been earned during the period of notice. The employee may also be entitled to additional compensation known as "special damages," because of breach of the employment contract. In some cases the employee has been able to claim successfully for the loss of fringe benefits, bonuses (if part of a direct or implied contract), and moving and related costs. However, the compensation will be reduced by the amount of money that the employee makes from a new job during the required period of notice. In one case, *Lawson v. Dominion Securities Corp.*, [1977] 2 A.C.W.S. 259, the Ontario Court of Appeal stated:

> The governing principle is that damages for wrongful dismissal are, prima facie, the amount that the plaintiff would have earned had the employment continued according to the contract, subject to a deduction in respect of any amount accruing from any other employment which the plaintiff, in minimizing his damages, had obtained.

For example, if the employee were entitled to four months' notice, the employer might ask the employee to leave immediately and pay the employee four months' salary. If the employee found a new job after two months, at the same salary, the employee would theoretically be entitled to only two months' salary or compensation from the previous employer. To prevent fired employees from sitting back and not genuinely searching for new employment, the courts have stressed that the situation is really a breach of contract and that the employee has a duty to "mitigate" losses— that is, to try and find alternative work as soon as possible. If there is any doubt about the issue, the onus lies with the employer to prove that the employee has "failed to mitigate." If this is proven, the employee is entitled only to minimal damages. This would be the case if a dismissed employee if offered similar work at a similar wage by some other employer immediately after being fired but refuses to accept the position.

Length of Notice

What is the length of notice the common law specifies? It seems that the courts look at the age of the employee, the character of the job, the length of the person's employment in that job, and the availability of alternative similar work. It seems that a longer period of notice is required for employees with more senior positions, older age, and greater length of service. Each case is unique.

Some examples of the notice periods that the courts have found appropriate in cases involving "wrongful dismissal" are as follows: in *Munana v. MacMillan Bloedel*, [1977] 2 A.C.W.S. 364, the Senior Vice-President, Special Consultant on European Development, who worked for the company for two years and four months, was held entitled to eight and a half months' notice; in *Campbell v. Business Fleets Ltd.*, [1954] O.W.N. 98, a General Manager who worked three years and three months, was held entitled to twelve months' notice; in *Blair v. Southam Farwest Printing Co.*, [1977] 1 A.C.W.S. 747, a salesman who worked seven years was held entitled to five months' notice; and in *Baker v. Burns Foods Ltd.* (1977), 74 D.L.R. (3d) 762, a foreman, 61 years old, who had worked for the company for forty-two years, was held entitled to twelve months' notice.

Handling Dismissals

Nowadays, more and more companies are helping employees, whose services are no longer required, to find other work. This may involve counselling, retraining, and placement—sometimes with government assistance. Financially, also, termination of employment is being made less distressful by longer notice periods, severance pay, and early retirement schemes.

REVIEW QUESTIONS

1. What are the basic characteristics of an employment contract?
2. How, in the eyes of the law, are an employee, an independent contractor, and an agent different, even though they may be working for the same person?
3. To what extent does the requirement of writing apply to contracts of employment?

4. What duties does an employee have towards his employer?

5. Why do we examine the common law definition of an "employee"? What is its importance today?

6. Name and explain two situations in which an employment contract may be terminated.

7. Name and explain three situations of "constructive dismissal."

8. Name and explain three situations of dismissal for just cause.

9. If an employee feels he has been "constructively dismissed" should he continue providing services? Why?

PROBLEMS

1. A, a key employee, is working for B on a five-year written contract. Six months before the end of the contract, A leaves his job without giving notice. As most of B's clientele are attracted by A's personality, B takes A to court to force him to carry out the balance of the contract. What do you think will be the outcome?

2. The ABC Co. had a Vice-President who had ceased to fit the progressive image of the company. He had been employed for ten years and was 60 years old when it was decided to dismiss him with notice. His yearly salary was $48,000 and he was given sixty days' notice.
   (a) What is the statutory period of notice required in your province?
   (b) What factors might be used by a judge in assessing his entitlement if he sued for more monetary compensation?

3. One day Alex came into work and was told that the company had decided on some internal reorganization including reorganizing Alex's job. Instead of being Manager of Accounts Receivable in the company's office, Alex was to be in charge of sanitation at the company's factory 800 miles north, where he was to move "as soon as possible." What action should Alex take and why?

4. Acme Co. hired Cathy less than a year ago and has found her truly an "obnoxious employee." The company would like to "get rid of her" although she does perform her work well. What can the company do?

READINGS

Addis v. Gramophone Co. Ltd., [1909] A.C. 488 (Eng. H.L.).

Facts: Here the plaintiff was employed in Calcutta at a salary of 15 pounds per week, plus a commission on trade done. The employment contract provided for six months' notice. In October 1905 he was given six months' notice but, at the same time, his employers appointed his successor, refusing to let him act as the manager during the period of notice.

The plaintiff returned to England and sued for breach of contract in 1906. The trial jury awarded 600 pounds in respect of wrongful dismissal and 340 pounds in respect of lost commission. At the first appeal court, the court ruled that the plaintiff had no course of action and found for the defendant. The case then went to the House of Lords.

Held per Lord Atkinson at p. 493:

My Lords, I entirely concur with the judgment of my noble and learned friend on the woolsack. Much of the difficulty which has arisen in this case is due to the unscientific form in which the pleadings, as amended, have been framed, and the loose manner in which the proceedings at the trial were conducted.

The rights of the plaintiff, disembarrassed of the confusing methods by which they were sought to be enforced, are, in my opinion, clear. He had been illegally dismissed from his employment. He could have been legally dismissed by the six months' notice, which he, in fact, received, but the defendants did not wait for the expiry of that period. The damages plaintiff sustained by this illegal dismissal were (1) the wages for the period of six months during which his formal notice would have been current; (2) the profits or commission which would, in all reasonable probability, have been earned by him during the six months had he continued in the employment; and possibly (3) damages in respect of the time which might reasonably elapse before he could obtain other employment. He has been awarded a sum possibly of some hundreds of pounds, not in respect of any of these heads of damage, but in respect of the harsh and humiliating way in which he was dismissed, including, presumably, the pain he experienced by reason, it is alleged, of the imputation upon him conveyed by the manner of his dismissal. This is the only circumstance which makes the case of general importance, and this is the only point I think it necessary to deal with.

I have been unable to find any case decided in this country in which any countenance is given to the notion that a dismissed employee can recover in the shape of exemplary damages for illegal dismissal, in effect damages for defamation, for it amounts to that, except the case of *Maw v. Jones* [(1890), 25 Q.B.D. 107].

In that case Matthew J., as he then was, during the argument, while counsel was urging . . . that the measure of damages for the improper dismissal of an ordinary domestic servant was a month's wages and nothing more, no doubt interjected in the shape of a question the remark. "Have you ever heard the principle applied to a case where a false charge of misconduct has been made?" But the decision was that the direction of the judge at the trial was right.

Now, what was the character of that direction? The defendant had power to dismiss his apprentice, the plaintiff, on a week's notice, and had also power to dismiss him summarily if he should show a want of interest in his work. He dismissed the apprentice summarily without notice, assigning as a reason that he had been guilty of frequent acts of insubordination and that he had gone out at night without leave.

The judge at the trial told the jury that they were not bound to limit the damages to the week's notice he had lost, but that they might take into consideration the time the plaintiff would require to get new employment—the difficulty he would have as a discharged apprentice in getting employment elsewhere—and it was on this precise ground the direction was upheld. I do not think that this case is any authority whatever for the general proposition that exemplary damages may be recovered for wrongful dismissal, still less, of course, for breach of contract generally; but, such as it is, it is the only authority in the shape of a decided case which can be found upon the first-mentioned point.

I have always understood that damages for breach of contract were in the nature of compensation, not punishment. . . .

There are three well-known exceptions to the general rule applicable to the measure of damages for breach of contract, namely, actions against a banker for refusing to pay a customer's cheque when he has in his hands funds of the customer's to meet it, actions for breach of promise of marriage, and actions like that in *Flureau v. Thornhill,* [(1776), 2 W. Bl, 1078] where the vendor of real estate, without any fault on his part, fails to make title. I know of none other.

The peculiar nature of the fist two of these exceptions justified their existence. Ancient practice upholds the last, though it has often been adversely criticized, as in *Bain v. Fothergill* [(1874), L.R. 7 H.L. 158]. If there be a tendency to create a fourth exception it ought, in my view, to be checked rather than stimulated; inasmuch as to apply in their entirety the principles on which damages are measured in tort to cases of damages for breaches of contract would lead to confusion and uncertainty in commercial affairs, while to apply them only in part and in particular cases would create anomalies, lead occasionally to injustice, and make the law a still more "lawless science" than it is said to be.

For instance, in actions of tort, motive, if it may be taken into account to aggregate damages, as it undoubtedly may be, may also be taken into account to mitigate them, as may also the conduct of the plaintiff himself who seeks redress. Is this rule to be applied to actions of breach of contract? There are few breaches of contract more common than those which arise where men omit or refuse to repay what they have borrowed, or to pay for what they have bought. Is the creditor or vendor who sues for one of such breaches to have the sum he recovers lessened if he should be shown to be harsh, grasping, or pitiless, or even insulting, in enforcing his demand, or lessened because the debtor has struggled to pay, has failed because of misfortune, and has been suave, gracious, and apologetic in his refusal? On the other hand, is that sum to be increased if it should be shown that the debtor could have paid readily without any embarrassment, but refused with expression of contempt and contumely, from a malicious desire to injure his creditor?

Few parties to contracts have more often to complain of ingratitude and baseness than sureties. Are they, because of this, to be entitled to recover from the principal, often a trusted friend, who has deceived and betrayed them, more than they paid on that principal's behalf? If circumstances of aggravation are rightly to be taken into account in actions of contract at all, why should they not be taken into account in the case of the surety, and the rules and principles applicable to cases of tort applied to the full extent?

In many other cases of breach of contract there may be circumstances of malice, fraud, defamation, or violence, which would sustain an action of tort as an alternative remedy to an action for breach of contract. If one should select the former mode of redress, he may, no doubt, recover exemplary damages, or what is sometimes styled vindictive damages; but if he should choose to seek redress in the form of an action for breach of contract, he lets in all the consequences of that form of action. . . . One of these consequences is, I think, this: that he is to be paid adequate compensation in money for the loss of that which he would have received had his contract been kept, and no more.

I can conceive nothing more objectionable and embarrassing in litigation than trying in effect an action of libel or slander as a matter of aggravation in an action for illegal dismissal, the defendant being permitted, as he must in justice be permitted, to traverse the defamatory sense, rely on privilege, or raise every point which he could raise in an independent action brought for the alleged libel or slander itself.

In my opinion, exemplary damages ought not to be, and are not according to any true principle of law, recoverable in such an action as the present, and the sums awarded to the plaintiff should therefore be decreased by the amount at which they have been estimated, and credit for that item should not be allowed in his account.

Burton v. MacMillan Bloedel Ltd., [1976] 4 W.W.R. 267 (B.C. S.C.)

Held per Munroe J. at p. 267:

In this action the plaintiff claims damages for alleged wrongful dismissal by the defendant, one of the largest corporations doing business in British Columbia.

By letter dated 9th December 1974 the plaintiff, then aged 47, was discharged, effective 31st December 1974, from his position with the defendant as manager of the Engineering Service Department (Pulp and Paper Division), a position which he had occupied for three years under an oral contract of employment of indefinite term. The plaintiff had worked for the defendant for ten years and had been promoted from time to time. His services were entirely satisfactory and his competency is admitted. The parties considered that the employment was to be of a permanent character.

At the time of his dismissal the plaintiff was being paid an annual salary of $34,500 and was in receipt of fringe benefits having a value equivalent to 22 per cent of his salary. The defendant paid to the plaintiff his salary to 31st December 1974.

Counsel for the defendant submits that the plaintiff was discharged for cause and thus was not entitled to any notice or salary in lieu thereof.

In *Port Arthur Shipbuilding Co. v. Arthurs*, [1967] 2 W.R. 49 at 55, 62 D.L.R. (2d) 342 (sub nom. *Regina v. Arthurs; Ex parte Port Arthur Shipbuilding Co.*), reversed [1969] S.C.R. 85, 70 D.L.R. (3d) 693, the right of an employer to terminate the employment of an employee for cause was expressed by Schroeder J.A. as follows:

"If an employee has been guilty of serious misconduct, habitual neglect of duty, incompetence, or conduct incompatible with his duties, or prejudicial to the employer's business, or if he has been guilty of wilful disobedience to the employer's orders in a matter of substance, the law recognizes the employer's right summarily to dismiss the delinquent employee."

Here, the defendant asserts that the plaintiff refused to continue to perform his duties as manager of the Engineering Service Department and thus was guilty of "wilful disobedience to the employer's orders in a matter of substance". The plaintiff asserts that his refusal on and after 12th September 1974 to remain as such manager was justified because the effect of the reorganization of the defendant's hierarchy as of that date amounted to an unjustified demotion for him—a breach of contract and dismissal by conduct—a unilateral essential alteration in the terms and conditions of his employment. . . . The plaintiff felt that the new organization meant in effect that [a new] vice-president was to become the real manager of the Engineering Service Department and that the plaintiff would become his second in command . . . a feeling supported by the evidence that is confirmed to some extent by subsequent events since the position occupied by the plaintiff has not since been filled and the duties of that position have since been performed by the vice-president in question. While the plaintiff would not have suffered any loss of income or benefits had he remained as manager of the Engineering Service Department, or accepted other positions offered to him, upon the evidence I find that his role in such event would have been substantially different and limited. The words of Anderson J. in *O'Grady v. Insur. Corpn. of B.C.*, 10th October 1975 (not yet reported), are relevant and apply to the facts of this case. Anderson J. said:

"He would have suffered a substantial loss of prestige with consequent embarrassment and humiliation and would have been required to work under a general manager with whom he had had a serious confrontation. The abolition of his former role and the completely different and subordinate role he was offered amounted to a fundamental breach of contract. On the issue of mitigation, it was not unreasonable for him to reject the new position offered."

As McCardie J. said in *Rubel Bronze and Metal Co. v. Vos*, [1918] 1 K.B. 315 at 323:

"Dismissal may be effected by conduct as well as words. A man may dismiss his servant if he refuses by word or conduct to allow the servant to fulfill his contract of employment. . . . If the conduct of the employer amounts to a basic refusal to continue the servant on the agreed terms of employment, then there is at once a wrongful dismissal and a repudiation of the contract."

In *Hill v. Peter Gorman Ltd.* (1957), 9 D.L.R. (2d) 124 at 132 (Ont. C.A.), Mackay J.A. said:

"Where an employer attempts to vary the contractual terms . . . the employee . . . may refuse to accept it and if the employer persists in the attempted variation the employee may treat this persistence as a breach of contract and sue the employer for damages. . . .

I cannot agree that an employer has any unilateral right to change a contract or that by attempting to make such a change he can force an employee to either accept it or quit.". . .

Upon the evidence I find that the defendant committed a breach of its contract of employment with the plaintiff in September 1974 and that the plaintiff was dismissed in December 1974 without proper cause or lawful excuse. . . .

I hold that the plaintiff is entitled to payment of 15 months' salary in lieu of reasonable notice of termination of his employment: *Bardal v. Globe and Mail Ltd.*, [1960] O.W.N. 253, 24 D.L.R. (2d) 140. The plaintiff, for his part, was under a legal duty to take all reasonable steps to mitigate the loss suffered by him: *Paziuk v. Ethelbert* (1963), 45 W.W.R. 216 (Man.), and he did so. On 3rd November 1975 he obtained permanent employment with B.C. Hydro & Power Authority at an annual starting salary of $27,279 plus fringe benefits having a value equivalent to 22 per cent of his salary.

The defendant attempted in September 1974 to vary the terms and conditions of the plaintiff's employment. The said variation was never accepted by the plaintiff. Until the contract of employment was terminated by proper notice, the plaintiff was entitled to insist on performance of the original contract where, as here, he did not relinquish his rights thereunder: *Hill v. Peter Gorman Ltd.* at p. 132. Prior to his dismissal in December he was offered a choice of dismissal, resignation or a subordinate job. Thus the only offer which was before the plaintiff was the offer of employment on terms that he abandoned such legal rights as he had for damages for breach of contract against the defendant. This he was not required to do: *Washer v. B.C. Toll Highways & Bridges Authority* (1965), 53 W.W.R. 225, 53 D.L.R. (2d) 620 (B.C.C.A.). Accordingly, I hold that the time for the giving of reasonable notice is to be computed from 9th December 1974 and not from 12th September 1974.

I assess the damages sustained by the plaintiff at the sum of $35,014.50, calculated as follows:

15 months' salary	$43,125.00	
Plus 22% thereof—fringe benefits	9,487.50	
		52,612.50
Less		
Received by the plaintiff from the defendant for the period 9th December to 31st December 1974—salary and fringe benefits	2,602.00	

Received by the plaintiff from new
employer for salary and fringe benefits
for the period 3rd November 1975 to 9th
March 1976   11,645.00

Unemployment insurance received by
the plaintiff   3,351.00
                                                        _____
                                                                    17,598.00
                                                                    _____
                                                                   $35,014.50

The claim of the plaintiff for aggravated or exemplary damages is not
supported by the evidence and is disallowed.

The claim of the plaintiff for loss of pension benefits is disallowed since
no damage in respect thereof has been proved. The fringe benefits of 22 per
cent of salary include pension benefits and the plaintiff's new employer has
a pension plan conferring benefits similar to those of the defendant's plan.

Judgment accordingly. Costs will follow the event.

20

Employing Other Persons (Statute Law)

LEGISLATIVE JURISDICTION

The authority of the provincial legislatures to enact labour legislation derives from the Constitution Act, 1867, which gave them the power to pass laws concerning employer-employee relations under the category of "property and civil rights" (see Chapter 2). The federal Parliament's power to pass labour laws originates in three ways from that Act:

1. under the *general* power to pass "laws for the peace, order and good government of Canada in relation to all matters" that are not specifically given to the provinces;
2. under powers *specifically* granted to the federal Parliament (such as shipping and navigational matters); and
3. under a *residual* clause which gives the federal Parliament power on any matter that has not been specially given to the provinces.

Case law has established that the federal government has power to regulate labour relations of employees working in industries which have undertakings of an interprovincial, national, or international nature and operations declared for the general advantage of Canada or of two or more provinces; and any work, undertaking, or business outside the province's exclusive jurisdiction. Thus employees in such industries as shipping, navigation, interprovincial railways, airports, air transportation, radio and television broadcasting, banking, grain elevators, and flour and feed companies, certain Crown corporations (such as the CBC, CNR, and Air Canada are all regulated by federal legislation. Workers involved in industries and undertakings mentioned above, workers within the federal government, and workers employed under federal government work contracts or on works partly financed by federal government funds are all governed by federal legislation. In addition, the provinces have surrendered certain powers to enable the federal government to legislate programs of unemployment insurance and old age pensions. The federal government's powers to legislate are expanded during wartime under its emergency powers under the "peace, order and good government" clause of the Constitution Act, 1867, s. 91, at which time it uses its own normal powers as well as most of the powers normally used by the provinces.

Although the Constitution Act, 1867, tried to define jurisdictions, the division of powers between the federal Parliament and the provincial legislatures to legislate in labour matters is not always clear-cut. For instance, during the 1930s, the federal Parliament ratified three international conventions adopted by the International Labour Organization of the League of Nations concerning minimum hours, minimum wages, and a weekly day of rest, then tried to legislate three federal statutes giving effect to the conventions. The courts ruled on the validity of such federal legislation in a case—*Attorney General of Canada v Attorney General of Ontario; Reference re Three Labour Acts*, [1937] 1 D.L.R. 673—and held that the federal Parliament had no authority to pass such statutes because the subject matter was within provincial jurisdiction. Despite this embarrassment, the federal Parliament has not withdrawn its ratification and Canada is still bound internationally, although the three statutes are virtually ineffective in Canada.

There have been numerous cases trying to determine the extent of the legislative powers of the federal Parliament and provincial legislatures, respectively, in labour matters. Some of these have involved interprovincial bus transportation. In one case, although less than 2% of an employer's bus transportation business extended into another province, the court ruled that the employer and employees were subject to federal legislation because the business was willing at any time to provide its customers with such interprovincial service. In another case, where an employer's extra-provincial business was casual and small, the court ruled it was not subject to federal labour laws. Perhaps the true test to determine whether a business comes under federal or provincial power is summed up in the *Desrosier Cartage* case in which the Chairman of the Canada Labour Relations Board said:

> The true test . . . is whether the company has so arranged its physical properties and its operations so that its operations are carried on outside the province with a certain regularity or in accordance with a certain pattern.

From the above, we can see that, although the framers of the Constitution Act, 1867, tried to define the labour legislative powers of the federal Parliament and the provincial legislatures, they were not sufficiently explicit to avoid disputes—often because in 1867 they could not foresee the technological changes that our society would undergo.

FEDERAL LABOUR LEGISLATION

The major labour statute at the federal level is the Canada Labour Code, which came into effect in July 1971. It consisted of five parts: fair employment practices; female employees' equal pay; labour standards; safety of employees; and industrial relations. However, Part I has been repealed and replaced since March 1, 1978, by the Canadian Human Rights Act. Part II, "Female Employees' Equal Pay," has also been repealed. The Code regulates conditions of employment in most industries under federal jurisdiction. However, civil servants in certain occupations are governed by other federal statutes such as the Public Service Staff Relations Act, the Canada Shipping Act, and the Railway Act.

Minimum Wages

According to the Minimum Hourly Wage Order, a minimum wage is set for employees 17 years of age or over. The only exception is where special permission is given by the Minister of Labour—for example, in cases involving recognized apprenticeship or training programs or handicapped employees. Situations where persons under 17 years of age can work are limited; if they do, they are to be paid a specified minimum wage.

Hours of Work and Overtime Pay

The hours of work of employees are limited to eight hours per day and forty hours per week. If Ministry authorization is given, employees may work up to forty-eight hours per week with overtime pay of one and a half times the regular salary for each hour over eight hours per day or forty hours per week. Similar provisions regarding salary exist for employees involved in contracts made with the government under the Fair Wages and Hours of Labour Act. Double time is to be paid for work during an employee's only day of rest or during the second day of rest in a standard work week. Overtime provisions are not applicable to all employees—for instance, employees in managerial or supervisory functions or certain professions. Persons under seventeen years of age are not permitted to work between 11 p.m. and 6 a.m.

Collecting Wages

The federal Bankruptcy Act provides that persons owed wages, salaries, and commission have a statutory claim against a bankrupt for services rendered during the three months immediately preceding the bankruptcy to an amount of $500 and for valid disbursements up to $500. Such claims rank after secured creditors such as mortgagees. Then come claims for funeral costs (if applicable), administration costs, the supervision levy, followed by any further claims for wages.

Vacations and Holidays

Employees are to receive two weeks' vacation time with pay after they have completed one year of employment—that is, 4% of annual wages. This is to be given not later than ten months following the year in which it was earned. After employees have worked six consecutive years, they are to receive three weeks' annual vacation—that is, 6% of annual wages. An employee who leaves during a year is to be paid the equivalent of vacation pay for work that year, at either the 4% or 6% level. For example, a worker leaving after working one and a half years without any vacation is entitled to two weeks' vacation pay for the first year and one week's vacation pay for the six months earned: a total of three weeks' vacation pay. In order to qualify initially, the employee must have worked at least six months.

Employees are entitled to a paid holiday on each of the general holidays: New Year's Day; Good Friday; Victoria Day; Dominion Day; Labour Day; Thanksgiving Day; Remembrance Day; Christmas Day and Boxing Day.

Fair Employment Practices

The Canadian Human Rights Act, which replaced Part I of the Canada Labour Code, prohibits discrimination in any matter on grounds of race, national or ethnic origin, colour, religion, age, sex, marital status, convictions for which a pardon has been granted, and, in matters related to employment, physical handicap. It is a discriminatory practice to refuse to employ or continue to employ workers based on any of the above grounds, or for employer or employee organizations to establish a policy depriving people of employment because of such discrimination. Section 13 prohibits harrassment in the provision of goods, services, facilities, and accommodation in connection with commercial or residential premises and employment.

The Act does provide exceptions, however. They are granted if the specifications for employment are really bona fide occupational requirements or if employment is terminated at normal retirement age.

The Act is administered by the Canadian Human Rights Commission, which may appoint a conciliator to assist in resolving the dispute. It also ensures that complaints are investigated through a Human Rights Tribunal, and, on appeal, a Review Tribunal. An order of the Tribunal may be made an order of the Federal Court of Canada. Fines for violation of the Act range from up to $500 for an individual and up to $50,000 for an employer or an employers' or employees' association. The legislation also prohibits pay differentials between male and females based on sex discrimination alone. Merit and/or seniority, rather than sex, is to be the criterion for wage differentials.

The Code provides for maternity leave of seventeen weeks for female employees who have completed twelve consecutive months of employment. Certain conditions are to be met—for example, the employee must submit a medical certificate and written application at least four weeks before the leave of absence is to take place. The employee is to be reinstated after her maternity leave in the same or a similar job with no decrease in wages or benefits. Similar provisions exist for public service employees.

Persons employed by federal government contractors are also protected against discrimination. Thus the Fair Wages Policy Order prohibits discrimination by an employer in federal government construction and supply contracts, and the Fair Wages and Hours of Labour Act applies to every contract for construction, remodelling repair, or demolition of any work in any contract made with the Canadian government.

Termination of Employment

The Code stipulates that the employer is to give two weeks' written notice of dismissal, or two weeks' regular salary in lieu of notice, to employees who have worked for at least three months and who have not been dismissed for "just cause." If a large group of employees is being dismissed within a four-week period, certain notice requirements are obligatory: if 50-100 employees are to be dismissed, eight weeks' notice; if 100-300 employees, twelve weeks' notice; and if more than 300 employees, sixteen weeks' notice. In addition, the Ministry of Labour, the Canada Employment and Immigration Commission, and any trade union or other bargaining agent concerned is to receive notice of such dismissal.

If an employee is fired without just cause and has worked five consecutive years with the same employer, severance pay is to be paid (it is the lesser of two days' regular salary for each completed year of employment or forty days' regular wages).

Unemployment Insurance

Through an amendment to the Constitution Act, 1867, the federal government has since 1940 been given exclusive jurisdiction in unemployment insurance legislation. Originally, the legislation was similar to Britain's. However, numerous amendments have since been made. The Unemployment Insurance Act applies to almost all persons employed in Canada.

Coverage.   The scheme provides income to employees who have an interruption in earnings. It applies to all "employees" unless the Unemployment Insurance Act specifically excludes them. In fact, about 95% of the Canadian work force is covered by the insurance, including federal public servants, police force members, and Canadian Forces employees. The self employed, workers over 65 years of age, and some part-time workers are the principal exceptions.

Administration.   Unemployment insurance is administered by the Canada Employment and Immigration Commission (CEIC), which was formed in 1977 when the Unemployment Insurance Commission and the Department of Manpower and Immigration began working together. The commission also deals with employment programs and immigration.

Funds.   The insurance fund money comes from premiums from all employees in insurable employment, employers, and the federal government. Employee's contributions are deducted by the employer and automatically sent to the fund.

Eligibility for Benefits.   To be eligible for benefits, workers must work for at least twenty hours a week or, if they are paid by commission or piecework, they must make at least a specified minimum amount per week.

In order to qualify for benefits, there must be an interruption in earnings and the employee must have worked a certain number of weeks in the qualifying period. The period varies from ten to fourteen weeks, depending on the economic region of unemployment. (Canada is divided into forty-eight such regions.) People who apply for unemployment insurance a second time in fifty-two weeks may have to wait up to six weeks longer than first-time claimants. Once a claim is accepted, there is a two-week waiting period. The benefit rate is 60% of average weekly earnings up to a fixed maximum. The maximum period for which benefits can be paid is fifty weeks on one claim.

Employees collecting unemployment insurance benefits may also work part-time and earn up to 25% of their weekly benefit rate before deductions. Any income above 25% of the regular weekly benefits and all earnings during the waiting period are deducted from the unemployment insurance cheque.

Employees who are fired for misconduct, quit their job voluntarily, or turn down a suitable job offer are disqualified from benefits for up to six weeks beyond the normal two-week waiting period. Employees who have lost their jobs due to a labour dispute may not be eligible for benefits until the dispute ends.

If a person has lost a job, a Record of Employment form must be given or sent by the employer within five calendar days after the interruption of earnings. This form, the employee's social insurance number, and the application for benefit must be submitted before benefits can begin. Employees may be asked to fill out a formal active job search form and record contacts with employers. They may also be asked to register for work at an employment centre. As benefits are paid, the employee is required to fill in a "claimant report card." Employees must be available for work and actively searching for a job. If the employee is not making a reasonable effort, he or she may be refused further benefits.

Special Benefits.   Unemployment insurance also provides special benefits for sick, injured, quarantined, and pregnant employees. Special benefits are available, provided the employee worked at least twenty weeks within the last fifty-two weeks or since the start of the last claim, whichever is shorter. A person who is sick, injured, or quarantined and has worked the necessary twenty weeks could be eligible for up to fifteen weeks of illness benefits (at the same 60% of average weekly insurable earnings). Maternity benefits for fifteen consecutive weeks are also available. There is also a one-time special benefit of three weeks of benefits for people reaching sixty-five years of age. (after that age they no longer pay premiums and are no longer covered by the Act.)

Alternative Work.   The CEIC tries to help employees find alternative work. If employees are unable to find work in their areas, they may be eligible for travel money to the nearest place where there are jobs, as well as for a relocation grant to help them move when work is found. Payment of training allowances may also be available.

Claims.   Approximately three million claims are made for unemployment insurance annually. There are claims investigators to help reduce abuse of the program. Those trying to cheat the Commission may be liable for an administration penalty, as well as prosecution under the Unemployment Insurance Act or the Criminal Code.

Those who disagree with a claim decision can appeal it at no cost. Appeals are heard by an independent Board of Referees (a three-person group composed of people who do not work for CEIC, made up of a neutral chairperson, an employers' representative, and an employees' representative). Hearings may be in French or English, whichever the employee prefers. Further appeals may be made to an Umpire, who is a judge of the trial division of the Federal Court of Canada. The Umpire's decision is usually final. It may be possible, however, to make further appeals to the Federal Court of Appeal or even to the Supreme Court of Canada.

Canada Pension Plan

The Canada Pension Plan, a federal statute, and the Quebec Pension Plan are parallel programs legislated into force on May 5, 1965, as earnings-related schemes to provide retirement pensions and supplementary benefits to the retired, the disabled, surviving spouses and children, and orphans. Both the federal and provincial governments can legislate in this regard (through an amendment to the Constitution Act, 1867,) and pension credits are portable and accounted for as if they were earned under one plan. Benefits are in addition to any money payable under the Old Age Security Act. This Act has national application.

Contributions.   From January 1, 1966, contributions to the plan must be paid by all except "exempted" employees, employers, and the self-employed between eighteen and sixty-five years of age (or seventy years of age if the person continues working and does not apply for the retirement pension). The employee and employer must make matching contributions of 1.8% of the portion of an employee's salary that falls between the year's Basic Exemption and the year's Maximum Pensionable Earnings. A self-employed person pays a rate of 3.6%.

Exempted Employees.   Employees exempted from coverage include: migratory workers (such as workers in agriculture, horticulture, fishing, hunting, trapping, forestry, logging, and lumbering who do not spend at least twenty-five working days per year with the same employer or who do not earn at least $250 per year from the same employer), casual workers, provincial government employees and employees of foreign governments or international organizations, workers in certain miscellaneous jobs such as an employer's spouse, exchange teachers from another country, members of certain religious orders, and members of the judicature.

Benefits.   Benefits fall into six groups: retirement pensions, disability benefits, disabled contributor's benefits, child's benefit, death benefit, surviving spouse's benefit, and orphan benefits. A formal application must be made for benefits. In order to obtain maximum coverage, employers need to have contributed for ten years and no wage earner can miss more than 15% of the total working years and still obtain maximum benefits. People contributing less receive less.

The retirement pension is calculated through a formula whereby a contributor receives basically one-quarter of average monthly pensionable earnings to a given maximum.

All payments made under the Canada Pension Plan are indexed to the cost of living.

PROVINCIAL LABOUR LEGISLATION

As discussed previously, the provinces obtain power to pass labour laws through the authority of the "property and civil rights" clause in the Constitution Act, 1867. Thus each province has specific legislation dealing with employment standards.

Employment Standards

In Ontario, the Employment Standards Act sets out minimum labour standards for persons employed in that province. However, the Act does not apply to certain secondary school students performing work under a work experience program authorized by their school board; workers in a program approved by a community college or university; prison inmates involved in a work project or rehabilitation program; or offenders performing work under an order or sentence of a court. In addition, various other people are excluded from certain specific provisions of the Act. For example, the provisions for maximum hours of work, minimum wage, overtime pay, public holidays and vacation pay do not apply to:

1. qualified practitioners of architecture, chiropody, dentistry, law, medicine, optometry, pharmacy, professional engineering, psychology, public accounting, surveying, veterinary science, or students training for any of these professions;
2. persons employed in commercial fishing;
3. domestic servants employed directly by the householder;
4. registered real estate salespersons;
5. salespersons receiving commission who sell at places other than the employer's establishment;
6. most teachers;
7. persons employed on a farm in the primary production of eggs, milk, cattle, and the like;
8. Crown employees.

In addition, there are other exemptions applying in specific areas.

Minimum Wage Rates

All the provinces have legislation under which a provincial government board sets minimum wage rates, usually for both sexes, for industries in the province. The legislation is intended to ensure that a minimum standard of living is enjoyed by all employees and their families. For a few types of industrial employment, a higher minimum wage may be set under industrial standards laws. Provincially set minimum wage rates now cover almost all employment except farm labour and domestic service.

Minimum Age

Every province has set a minimum age below which a person may not be employed. In Ontario, for example, this limit is fifteen years of age for factory work, sixteen years of age for logging, eighteen years of age for mining below ground or at the working face of a surface mine, and fourteen years of age for work in shops, hotels, or restaurants. Persons under sixteen years of age may not, however, work in Ontario during school hours (8 a.m. to 5 p.m.) unless they have been granted special permission, or unless they are on school holidays. No person under sixteen years of age is to be in any public place for performance or offering anything for sale or selling between 9 p.m. and 6 a.m., although licences may be given for certain public entertainment situations provided certain conditions are met in accordance with the Child Welfare Act.

Limited Working Hours
The number of hours an employer may demand from an employee are limited by provincial statute in most provinces. Many employees do, however, work more than this on a voluntary basis.

In Ontario, for example, hours of work may not exceed eight hours per day and forty-eight hours per week. Persons excluded include supervisory and managerial employees, domestic servants, construction workers, resident janitors or caretakers, full-time firefighters, fishing or hunting guides, persons engaged in landscape gardening and mushroom providing. Overtime pay at one and a half times the regular rate must be provided for hours worked in excess of forty-four hours per week. Where employers and employees agree, a regular workday of up to twelve hours may be permitted by the Ministry of Labour. This allows a four-day workweek.

Collecting Wages
In Ontario, Employment Standards officers can assist employees in collecting wages due up to the amount of $4,000 per employee. A penalty of 10% may be imposed on the employer for each collection.

Annual Vacations with Pay
All the provinces have legislation providing for compulsory paid vacations for employees in most industries. Employees not covered may include farm workers and domestic servants, depending on the province. Vacation pay stamps are used in some provinces. The vacation requirement, after a year of service, is two weeks in all provinces except Saskatchewan (three weeks). Manitoba and Saskatchewan stipulate an extra week of paid vacation after five or ten years of service, respectively.

In Ontario, two weeks' vacation with pay is to be granted to employees who have completed one year of employment. This must be granted within ten months after the year in which it was earned. The employer can determine the dates when the vacation must be taken and can specify whether it is to be one two-week block or two separate weeks. If a business is sold and the employees continue working, all their rights to vacation with pay remain. Similar to the federal provisions, an employee who leaves before completing the year is entitled to 4% of wages earned to that date, which must be paid within seven days of termination.

Public Holidays

All the provinces now have legislation governing public holidays. On these days, employees must receive the regular pay even though they do not work; if they do work, they must be paid special overtime rates. The number of holidays named varies from five to nine, depending on the province. The provisions for payment also vary slightly between provinces.

In Ontario, the holidays are Good Friday, Dominion Day, Labour Day, Christmas Day, New Year's Day, Victoria Day, and Thanksgiving Day. Employees working on such days are entitled to one and a half times the regular pay for each hour worked. To be eligible, the employee must have worked for his employer for at least three months. This section does not apply to certain employees (those listed at the beginning of this section of the chapter, as well as residential building superintendents who live in the building superintended, taxi drivers, and students supervising children employed at a children's camp or employed in a recreational program operated by a charitable organization).

Fair Employment Practices

The 1982 Ontario Human Rights Code (excerpted in Appendix 20-A) deals principally with rights to accommodation, employment, access to public services, and provision of services. The Code provides that, in these areas, there must be no discrimination on grounds of race, ancestry, place of origin, colour, ethnic origin, citizenship, creed, sex, age, marital status, family, or handicap. According to the Act:

1. There must be no harrassment by the employer or fellow employees in the workplace nor by landlords in the case of accommodation.
2. Age covers the range of eighteen to sixty-five years inclusive.
3. Family status includes living with a person outside of wedlock.
4. A record of offences should be held only against someone who has served a sentence and whose record would obviously disqualify the person from such employment as police or security work.
5. Religious organizations may restrict hiring to persons of the same persuasion; associations of the handicapped may restrict participation to persons with similar disabilities.
6. For the sake of public decency, some services may be restricted to one sex.
7. It is not discrimination to insist on Canadian citizenship for some jobs.
8. Residential accommodation may be restricted to one sex.

The Ontario Human Rights Commission employs three commissioners to enforce this Act. Section 28(g) allows the Commission to investigate problems concerning discrimination. Section 28(h) encourages public, municipal, and private organizations to try to alleviate tension relating to human rights problems.

Equal Pay

Provincial legislation throughout Canada tries to ensure equal pay for men and women. British Columbia, New Brunswick, Nova Scotia, Ontario, and Prince Edward Island prohibit any discrimination in rates of pay between men and women doing the same work. In Alberta and Manitoba the statutes refer to identical or substantially identical work in the same establishment. The Saskatchewan Act refers to work of comparable character.

In Ontario, the Employment Standards Act tries to minimize sexual discrimination through an "equal pay for equal work" clause. Pay differentials are only allowed if they are based on a seniority system, a merit system, a system of measuring earnings by quantity or quality of production, or a differential based on any factor other than sex. If an employer does not comply with the provisions, an employment standards officer can determine the amount owing as a result of the unpaid differential and the employer will be liable to the employee for that amount, as unpaid wages.

Termination of Employment

In many provinces, an employer is required by law to give written notice of termination of employment in cases of individual dismissal. In Ontario, the notice requirement also includes collective dismissal. In Quebec, notice must also be given in cases of mass layoff.

In Ontario, the Employment Standards Act provides certain minimum notice requirements for employees who have worked for at least three months. An employee who has worked between three months and two years is to be given one week's notice; if two or more years but less than five years, two weeks' notice; five or more years but less than ten, four weeks' notice; and ten or more years, eight weeks' notice. A layoff for a period longer than thirteen weeks is deemed a "termination."

If a large group of employees is being terminated over four consecutive weeks, the employer is obliged to give eight weeks' notice if there are fifty or more but less than 200 employees; twelve weeks' notice if 200 or more but less than 500 employees; and sixteen weeks' notice if 500 or more employees.

An employee's time of service cannot be lost because of the sale or change in ownership of the business in which he or she is employed. The employee's total seniority counts in determining holiday pay, vacation pay, pregnancy leave, and termination of employment.

Apprenticeship

Some provinces require that certain tradespeople—for example, plumbers, carpenters, electricians, and barbers—undergo a period of apprenticeship training and pass a test before being allowed to offer their services as qualified craftspeople.

Apprenticeship refers to the program through which a person may reach journeyman status in a designated trade. It is jointly operated by the federal and provincial Departments of Labour (except in Ontario where it is the Ministry of Colleges and Universities).

The Adult Occupational Training Act empowers the federal government to make a contract with any province or employer to help pay part of the costs of providing occupational training to adults, to provide training allowances, to contribute to provincial research projects involving occupational training, and to make loans to the provinces for the purchase or construction of occupational training facilities. All the provinces and territories have apprenticeship programs which are administered by a Director of Apprenticeship or the equivalent. Provincial committees may also be appointed to establish rules for the training program. (In Ontario, the Apprenticeship and Tradesmen's Qualifications Act and regulations govern the relationship). The apprenticeship agreement must be written in the prescribed form and signed by the employer and the apprentice (minor's contracts must be signed by a parent or guardian). In Ontario, it must be approved and registered with the Director of Apprenticeship (the other provinces provides similar requirements).

The qualifications required for a person to begin an apprenticeship program vary provincially: in Ontario the person must be sixteen years of age and have grade ten education or equivalent. The length of training also varies. In Ontario the program requires at least two years of reasonably continuous employment; overtime work does not reduce this time. Wages in Ontario are to be not less than a fixed percentage of the rate of wages or its equivalent for a journeyman employed by the employer in that trade. In Ontario, there are also regulations regarding specific requirements for certain designated trades.

Maternity Leave

All provinces have made statutory provision for leaves of absence for maternity purposes, varying from sixteen weeks in British Columbia to twenty-one weeks in Alberta. Ontario allows seventeen weeks under certain conditions. Afterwards, the employee is to be reinstated in the same or a similar position with no decrease in wages or benefits.

Benefit Plans

Section 34 of the Ontario Employment Standards Act provides that such plans must not discriminate among employees on grounds of age, sex, and marital status.

REVIEW QUESTIONS

1. What are the grounds on which discrimination is prohibited under the Canadian Human Rights Act? Under the Ontario Human Rights Code?
2. What is the number of hours of work per week employees are limited to under federal legislation? Under Ontario legislation? What are the relevant Acts?
3. If the Acme Cross Trucking Co. wanted to dismiss 300 employees in one week, how much notice, if any, should they be given? By what legislation is Acme governed and why?
4. George is earning $400 per week. How much is the maximum amount that can be deducted from his pay cheque for "UI dues"?

5. Diane, who is collecting unemployment insurance benefits, has found a part-time job (two hours per day). How much, if any, income can Diane earn at the part-time job before it will affect her unemployment insurance benefits?

6. Once a claim for unemployment insurance has been accepted, how long is the "waiting period" before payments are made?

7. Before being unemployed, Sandra earned $500 per week. Assuming her UI claim is accepted, what benefits could she expect to be paid and why?

8. The summer was approaching and Sunny was looking forward to life at the cottage. He quit the job at which he had worked for the last three years and applied for UI. How long would he have to wait before his benefits are paid and why?

9. Name three types of employees who are exempted from the Canada Pension Plan.

10. What types of benefits are paid under the above-mentioned Act?

11. Name three types of employees who are not covered by Ontario's Employment Standards legislation regarding minimum wage.

12. What is the minimum age in your province for a person to be working: (a) in an office; (b) in mining below ground; (c) in a factory?

13. What is the extent of the federal government's responsibility for labour legislation in Canada?

14. What is the Canada Labour Code?

15. Explain briefly the key features, in your province, of the following types of provincial labour legislation: (a) minimum wage; (b) limited working hours; (c) annual vacations with pay; (d) minimum age; (e) fair employment practices; (f) equal pay; (g) apprenticeship; (h) notice of dismissal; (i) accident prevention; (j) public holidays.

16. How does the Ontario Human Rights Code help protect an employee?

17. Explain and discuss the main provisions of the Unemployment Insurance Act.

18. Explain the following aspects of the Canada Pension Plan: (a) eligibility; (b) contributions; (c) benefits.

PROBLEMS

1. George has worked at Acme Plumbing Co. for twelve months and would like to take his paid summer vacation. How much vacation is he entitled to? Under what legislation? Can he take the vacation all at once? When is he to receive such vacation?

2. Frank, a worker on the factory line of XYZ Co. is being paid $8 per hour for his work. This past week Frank's supervisor asked him to work late and consequently Frank worked sixty hours. How much should Frank be paid for this week and why?

3. An Ontario company employing provincial employees had bid successfully on a tender for a federal dredging contract for Halifax Harbour. Suppose the Nova Scotia minimum wage is $3.65 an hour, the Ontario

minimum is \$3.85, and the federal minimum is \$4.00. Which scale of pay would probably be used on this job? Why?

4. Margaret has been working for the post office for eleven months and wonders when she can take her trip to Florida. How much paid vacation is she entitled to and when must this time be given to her? Would it make any difference if she had been working for a private company within provincial labour jurisdiction?

5. Mary, who has worked for AB Co., a provincially incorporated private company, for ten years has just told her boss that she is pregnant and would like to take six weeks off to have the baby. Her boss says that all he can give her is her three weeks' vacation period and if she wants longer he cannot take her back. What law is her supervisor violating? What can she do?

READING

Re Ottawa West End Villa Ltd. and Ontario Nurses' Association (1980), 25 L.A.C. (2d) 65 (Ont. Arb. Bd.).

Held:

The grievors—Gwen Waugh and Gail Liston—claim that they have been underpaid for work which they performed on Thanksgiving Day, 1978. The parties agree that the grievors who are both "seniority employees"—Waugh is a part-time and Liston a relief nurse—worked on that day, October 9th, and were paid their regular rate (monthly rate of full-time classification plus 12% and not the holiday rate)—time and one-half. The evidence establishes that in the past—from 1976 or before, until the day in question—the invariable practice of the employer was to pay part-time and relief nurses, including the grievors, at the rate of time and one-half for the statutory holidays they worked. Mr. E. Garneau, the home's administrator, testified that this practice, which has survived several collective agreements, ceased after the employer received a memorandum from head office—Cikent Corporation. Until that memorandum was received, Mr. Garneau was of the view that part-time and relief nurses were entitled to be paid at time and one-half for time worked on holidays as, in Mr. Garneau's view, they are still entitled to be paid for overtime work.

The relevant Provisions of the collective agreement are:

Article XVI—Paid Holidays

16.01 The following days shall be recognized as paid holidays for active seniority employees:

(1) New Year's Day;
(2) Good Friday;
(3) Easter Day;
(4) Victoria Day;
(5) Dominion Day;

   (6) Civic Holiday (first Monday in August);
   (7) Labour Day;
   (8) Thanksgiving Day;
   (9) Christmas Day;
(10) Boxing Day.
(11) On and after August 2, 1978, a floating holiday to be taken at a
      time mutually agreeable between the nurse and the Employer. . . .

16.05 All work performed on any of the designated holidays by a seniority employee shall be paid for at time and one half his regular rate of pay in addition to the holiday pay for a qualified employee or be given another day off with pay in lieu.

Schedule "A"

Part-Time and Relief Nurses

A.01 As part-time and relief nurses are not entitled to any of the monetary benefits provided in the collective agreement, they shall be paid for as follows:

$$\frac{\text{(monthly rate of full-time classification x 12) plus 6\%}}{260} \quad \text{(on and after August 2, 1978 12\%)}$$

A.02 In addition, they shall be entitled to vacation pay based on 4% of their gross earnings and on and after August 2, 1978, after 200 hours worked, vacation pay shall be 6% of their gross earnings, and they shall be entitled to three (3) weeks' vacation time.

    Vacation pay for part-time and relief nurses calculated in accordance with A.02 shall be paid on a separate cheque each year, the last pay day in June. . . .

Article IX—Salaries. . . .

9.04 *Workmen's Compensation*

    A full-time nurse who, as a result of lost time, accident or compensatory illness suffered in the Employer's employment, is entitled to receive compensation under the Workmen's Compensation Act may have that appropriate fraction of her sick leave credits applied to supplement the compensation received from the Compensation Board. In such a case, the amount of compensation received by him or her, when added to the supplementation by the Nursing Home through the use of his or her sick leave credits will equal one hundred per cent (100%) of the nurse's regular earnings. . . .

Article X—Hours of Work

10.02 The regular work day for all employees covered by this agreement shall consist of seven and one-half (7½) hours exclusive of meal periods which, except under emergency conditions, shall be continuous and uninterrupted for a period or periods of not less than one-half (½) hour each. . . .

10.12 *Overtime*

(a) Authorized work performed in excess of seven and one-half (½) hours a day or beyond seventy-five (75) hours in a two week pay period as determined by the Employer will be counted as overtime work and will be paid for at the rate of time and one-half (1½) the employee's regular rate of pay, computed on an hourly basis.

(b) Where a nurse is required to work on a paid holiday or on a day for which she receives time and one-half her regular straight time hourly rate and she is required to work additional hours following her full tour on that day, she shall receive two times her regular straight time hourly rate for such additional hours worked.

Article XIV—Leave of Absence. . . .

14.07 Pay for sick leave is for the sole and only purpose of protecting employees against loss of income and will be granted only to employees with at least three (3) months of seniority on the following terms and conditions.

(a) Absence for injury compensable under the provisions of the Workmen's Compensation Act of Ontario shall not be charged against sick leave credits.

(b) Employees who have completed the probationary period shall be credited with three (3) days of sick leave and shall then accumulate sick leave credits at the rate of one and one-quarter (1¼) days per month of service. Once these credits are earned, they may be used when sickness forces the employee to remain at home from work. Sick leave credits used up will be deducted from the total credits accumulated.

(c) All unused sick leave may be accumulated up to a maximum of one hundred (100) days.

(d) The Employer may require the employee to produce a medical certificate before the employee becomes entitled to sick leave benefits.

(e) A nurse who is absent on maternity leave shall not be entitled to the benefits of this article. . . .

Article XV—Benefits

15.01 The Employer agrees to pay one hundred per cent (100%) of the present cost of premiums to provide the benefits of the present group insurance plan (exclusive of weekly indemnity benefit therein contained) and the Ontario Health Insurance Plan (OHIP) for all seniority employees who are actively at work or who are absent during the first month of a bona fide absence from work on account of illness or injury supported by a doctor's certificate. . . .

Article XVII—Vacations . . .

17.05 Seniority employees with more than one (1) year of service shall receive three (3) weeks vacation. Vacation pay for such employees will be six per cent (6%) of the earned wages of the employee for the vacation year. Nurses with five (5) years or more of service on and after August 2, 1978 shall receive four (4) weeks vacation paid for at eight per cent (8%) of the earned wages of the nurse for the vacation year.

The issue in a nutshell is whether the premium rate for "designated" holidays is a monetary benefit within the meaning of sch. A.01. If it is not, as the grievors contend, then they were entitled to be paid at time and one-half, and the grievance succeeds.

In support of his contention that the grievors were not underpaid, counsel for the company points out that holiday pay is considered by the arbitral jurisprudence to be an earned benefit and is described as part of the total wage package (see for example, Re Galco Food Products Ltd. and Allied Food Workers (1978), 18 L.A.C. (2d) 220 (Beck) at p. 221, and Re. U.A.W., Local 252, and Canadian Trailmobile Ltd. (1966), 17 L.A.C. 189 (Arthurs) at p. 191). Provisions for holiday pay have, counsel says, a quantifiable monetary value and cannot be distinguished from any other kind of remuneration payable to employees. That holiday pay is a "monetary benefit" is clear, counsel says, from the wording of the agreement itself. The present of sch. A.02 providing that part-time and relief nurses shall "In addition [to the rate specified in sch. A.01] be entitled to vacation pay based on 4% of their gross earnings . . ." is evidence, counsel says, that such employees are not entitled to holiday pay which, unlike vacation pay, is not specifically provided for.

Counsel for the union, on the other hand, contends that the term "monetary benefits" does not include the holiday pay premium. In counsel's view, the "monetary benefits" provided in the collective agreement include the benefits set out in art. 15 entitled "Benefits", i.e., group insurance and OHIP as well as pay for sick-leave (art. 14.07) and "Workmen's Compensation" (art. 9.04). The term "monetary benefits" does not, counsel contends, include such things as overtime (arts. 10.02 and 10.12) or premium pay for holidays. These latter two payments which counsel describes as "rights independent of the collective agreement being guaranteed by the Employment Standards Act" are contingent payments in that they depend upon the employer's scheduling.

This interpretation of the term "monetary benefits" is, counsel says, consistent with s. 27(1) of the Employment Standards Act, 1974 (Ont.), c. 112, which requires payment at a premium rate of not less than time and one-half for each hour worked on certain specified holidays of which Thanksgiving Day is one. The employer's argument, if accepted, would, counsel says, render sch. A.01 null and void—to the extent that it conflicts with the Employment Standards Act, 1974. It would, moreover, be inconsistent with the practice of the parties in the past.

Counsel contends that nothing can be inferred—concerning what constitutes a monetary benefit—from the present in the agreement of sch. A.02. Schedule A.02 was inserted, counsel says, to deal with the vacation entitlement and relief nurses who could if art. 17.05 were applied work one week and receive three weeks' vacation. Counsel contends that had sch. A.02 not been present, vacation pay would be in the same class as premium pay for holidays and overtime, i.e., it would not be a "monetary benefit".

It is well established that although an arbitrator derives his authority from the collective agreement under which he is appointed, he may (indeed he is obligated) in the course of his duty to construe a statute which is involved in the issues that have been brought before him (see *Re U.S.W., Local 2894, and Galt Metal Industries Ltd.* (1974), 5 L.A.C. (2d) 336n, 46 D.L.R. (3d) 150, [1975] 1 S.C.R. 517, *sub nom. McLeod et al. v. Egan et al.*). Whatever the precise extent of his authority with respect to the voiding of collective agreement provisions which are prohibited (see in this regard Paul Weiler, "The Remedial Authority of the Labour Arbitrator: Revised Judicial Version", 52 Can. Bar Rev. 29 (1974) at p. 44), it is clear and beyond dispute that an arbitrator may have recourse to statutes as an aid to interpretation—where the collective agreement is unclear or ambiguous. In that situation the collective agreement should be construed, if possible, so as not to conflict with the statutory provisions in question, i.e., the arbitrator must presume that the parties intended to act in a matter not contrary to law (see *Canadian Labour Arbitration*, (1977), Brown and Beatty, para. 2:2100, pp. 65-6).

There is no question in this case that a statutory provision is involved, namely, s. 27(1) of the Employment Standards Act, 1974. That section imposing a general obligation on employers to pay employees a premium rate for public holidays provides:

> 27(1) Subject to subsection 5 of section 26, where an employee works on a public holiday, the employer shall pay to the employee for each hour worked a premium rate of not less than one and one-half times his regular rate and, where the employee is entitled to the holiday with pay, his regular wages in addition thereto.

An exception is provided for in s. 5(1) of the Act, which reads as follows:

> 5(1) Where terms or conditions of employment in a collective agreement as defined in *The Labour Relations Act* confer a higher remuneration in money or a greater right or benefit for an employee respecting holidays than the provisions of Part VII, the terms or conditions of employment shall prevail.

If, as the employer contends, the premium rate for holiday pay is a "monetary benefit" can it be said that the collective agreement falls within the

s. 5(1) exception, that it confers a higher remuneration in money or a greater right or benefit for an employee respecting holidays than the Employment Standards Act, 1974?

In support of his contention that it can (does), Mr. Kowalyk argues that because part-time and relief nurses get the regular rate plus 12% for each and every day they work, including statutory holidays, the benefits in the collective agreement are more than adequate to cover those provided by the Employment Standards Act, 1974 namely, time and one-half for the seven public holidays specified therein. Counsel says that the only situation where the collective agreement would not be superior would be the situation where the person worked only the statutory holidays which is not the situation of the grievors.

This argument, appealing as it may be in the abstract, is not supported by the evidence before us. Assuming, but without finding, that it is possible for the parties to a collective agreement to agree that a particular wage rate—in this case the monthly rate for the full-time classification plus 12%—has been allocated in such a way as to make it comply with the s. 5(1) exception, the evidence does not indicate that this has been done. On the contrary, the evidence indicates that at the time the agreement was negotiated—the parties considered the 12% to be in lieu of such not insubstantial benefits as group insurance, OHIP, sick-leave, etc., and not in lieu of the premium rate for holidays. As indicated, the evidence is that at the time the collective agreement was negotiated, and after, both parties were under the impression that the holiday premium was not a monetary benefit. That being the case, it can hardly be said that the agreement confers a "higher remuneration in money or a greater right or benefit respecting holidays." The agreement may be capable of such a construction, but that is clearly not the construction the parties have given it. Put another way, we find that an employer cannot by a unilateral and *ex post facto* deduction, pull himself within the ambit of s. 5(1). We find that if, on a proper construction of sch. A.02, the premium rate for holiday pay is a monetary benefit, then the collective agreement is in violation of the Employment Standards Act, 1974.

This brings us to the specific problem of contract interpretation at hand. While we agree with Mr. Kowalyk that holiday pay is part of the wage package that does not, in our view, necessarily entail the conclusion that the premium rate for holidays in art. 16.05 is a monetary benefit within the meaning of sch. A.01. In *Re Galco Food Products Ltd.*, *supra*, it is stated that [p. 221]: ". . . as an earned benefit [holiday pay] ought not to be taken away unless very clear wording of the collective agreement, along with the facts of the particular case, require it." In the arbitrator's view, "there may be said to be a presumption in favour of an employee with respect to an entitlement to holiday pay". In *Canadian Trailmobile Ltd.*, *supra*, the arbitrator in a similar vein says [p. 191]:

To deprive him of holiday pay is therefore not merely to withhold a gift; it is to inflict a real loss on the employee in exactly the same way as depriving him of the chance to earn an ordinary day's pay. The company must show justification equally in both cases.

The collective agreement before me states in art. 16.05 that "All work performed on any of the designated holidays by a seniority employee shall be paid for at time and one half his regular rate of pay. . . ." This requirement, which is identical to that provided by the Employment Standards Act, 1974, in respect of the public holidays specified therein, is not explicitly restricted to full-time nurses. (As stated, the grievors are both seniority employees.) Moreoever, a conclusion that it is implicitly so restricted would, as Mr. Sato noted, seem to entail the further conclusion, a rather unlikely one, that part-time and relief nurses are not to receive a premium for overtime—something which Mr. Garneau did not consider to be the case. We agree with Mr. Sato that if overtime is not a monetary benefit, it is difficult to reach a contrary conclusion in respect of holiday pay.

When these considerations are taken into account, we have no difficulty in concluding that the collective agreement is ambiguous in its requirements, i.e., that the question of whether the premium rate for holidays is a "monetary benefit" is unclear. It follows that sch. A.01 should be interpreted so as not to conflict with the Employment Standards Act, 1974. Accordingly, we find that the term "monetary benefits" in sch. A.01 does not include the premium rate for holidays.

We would add that this interpretation accords with the view of the parties at the time the agreement was negotiated and after. As stated, the evidence is that up to October 8, 1978, holiday pay was not considered to be included in the term "monetary benefits."

We direct that the grievors be paid the difference between time and one-half of their regular pay and what they were actually paid for working on Thanksgiving Day, 1978.

APPENDIX 20-A: ONTARIO HUMAN RIGHTS CODE, 1981 (EXCERPTS)

An Act to revise and extend Protection of Human Rights in Ontario

PART I
FREEDOM FROM DISCRIMINATION

1. Every person has a right to equal treatment with respect to services, goods and facilities, without discrimination because of race, ancestry, place of origin, colour, ethnic origin, citizenship, creed, sex, age, marital status, family status or handicap.

2.—(1) Every person has a right to equal treatment with respect to the occupancy of accommodation, without discrimination because of race, ancestry, place of origin, colour, ethnic origin, citizenship, creed, sex, age, marital status, family status, handicap or the receipt of public assistance.

(2) Every person who occupies accommodation has a right to freedom from harassment by the landlord or agent of the landlord or by an occupant of the same building because of race, ancestry, place of origin, colour, ethnic origin, citizenship, creed, age, marital status, family status, handicap or the receipt of public assistance.

3. Every person having legal capacity has a right to contract on equal terms without discrimination because of race, ancestry, place of origin, colour, ethnic origin, citizenship, creed, sex, age, marital status, family status, or handicap.

4.—(1) Every person has a right to equal treatment with respect to employment without discrimination because of race, ancestry, place of origin, colour, ethnic origin, citizenship, creed, sex, age, record of offences, marital status, family status, or handicap.

(2) Every person who is an employee has a right to freedom from harassment in the workplace by the employer or agent of the employer or by another employee because of race, ancestry, place of origin, colour, ethnic origin, citizenship, creed, sex, age, record of offences, marital status, family status, or handicap.

5. Every person has a right to equal treatment with respect to membership in any trade union, trade or occupational association or self-governing profession without discrimination because of race, ancestry, place of origin, colour, ethnic origin, citizenship, creed, sex, age, marital status, family status, or handicap.

6.—(1) Every person who occupies accommodation has a right to freedom from harassment because of sex by the landlord or agent of the landlord or by an occupant of the same building.

(2) Every person who is an employee has a right to freedom from harassment in the workplace because of sex by his or her employer or agent of the employer or by another employee.

(3) Every person has a right to be free from,

    (a) a sexual solicitation or advance made by a person in a position to confer, grant or deny a benefit or advancement to the person where the person making the solicitation or advance knows or ought reasonably to know that it is unwelcome; or

    (b) a reprisal or a threat of reprisal for the rejection of a sexual solicitation or advance where the reprisal is made or threatened by a person in a position to confer, grant or deny a benefit or advancement to the person.

7. Every person has a right to claim and enforce his or her rights under this Act, to institute and participate in proceedings under this Act and to refuse to infringe a right of another person under this Act, without reprisal or threat of reprisal for so doing.

8. No person shall infringe or do, directly or indirectly, anything that infringes a right under this Part.

PART II
INTERPRETATION AND APPLICATION

9. In Part I and in this Part,

(a) "age" means an age that is eighteen years or more, except in sub-section 4(1) where "age" means an age that is eighteen years or more and less than sixty five years;

(b) "because of handicap" means for the reason that the person has or has had, or is believed to have or have had,

   (i) any degree of physical disability, infirmity, malformation or disfigurement that is caused by bodily injury, birth defect or illness and without limiting the generality of the foregoing, including diabetes, amputation, lack of physical co-ordination, blindness or visual impediment, deafness or hearing impediment, muteness or speech impediment, or physical reliance on a dog guide or on a wheelchair or other remedial appliance or device,

   (ii) any condition of mental retardation or impairment,

   (iii) a learning disability, or a dysfunction in one or more of the processes involved in understanding or using symbols or spoken language, or

   (iv) a mental disorder;

(c) "equal means subject to all requirements, qualifications and considerations that are not a prohibited ground of discrimination;

(d) "family status" means the status of being in a parent and child relationship;

(e) "group insurance" means insurance whereby the lives or well-being or the lives and well-being of a number of persons are insured severally under a single contract between an insurer and an association or an employer or other person;

(f) "harassment" means engaging in a course of vexatious comment or conduct that is known or ought reasonably to be known to be unwelcome;

(g) "marital status" means the status of being married, single, widowed, divorced or separated and includes the status of living with a person of the opposite sex in a conjugal relationship outside marriage;

(h) "record of offences" means a conviction for,

   (i) an offence in respect of which a pardon has been granted under the *Criminal Records Act* (Canada) and has not been revoked, or

   (ii) an offence in respect of any provincial enactment;

(i) "services" does not include a levy, fee, tax or periodic payment imposed by law;

(*j*) "spouse" means the person to whom a person of the opposite sex is married or with whom the person is living in a conjugal relationship outside marriage.

10. A right of a person under Part I is infringed where a requirement, qualification or consideration is imposed that is not discrimination on a prohibited ground but that would result in the exclusion, qualification or preference of a group of persons who are identified by a prohibited ground of discrimination and of whom the person is a member, except where,

> (*a*) the requirement, qualification or consideration is a reasonable and *bona fide* one in the circumstances; or
>
> (*b*) it is declared in this Act that to discriminate because of such ground is not an infringement of a right.

11. A right under Part I is infringed where the discrimination is because of relationship, association or dealings with a person or persons identified by a prohibited ground of discrimination.

12.—(1) A right under Part I is infringed by a person who publishes or displays before the public or causes the publication or display before the public or any notice, sign, symbol, emblem, or other similar representation that indicates the intention of the person to infringe a right under Part I or that is intended by the person to incite the infringement of a right under Part I.

(2) Subsection (1) shall not interfere with freedom of expression of opinion.

13.—(1) A right under Part I is not infringed by the implementation of a special program designed to relieve hardship or economic disadvantage or to assist disadvantaged persons or groups to achieve or attempt to achieve equal opportunity or that is likely to contribute to the elimination of the infringement of rights under Part I.

(2) The Commission may,

> (*a*) upon its own initiative;
>
> (*b*) upon application by a person seeking to implement a special program under the protection of subsection (1); or
>
> (*c*) upon a complaint in respect of which the protection of subsection (1) is claimed,

inquire into the special program and, in the discretion of the Commission, may by order declare,

> (*d*) that the special program, as defined in the order, does not satisfy the requirements of subsection (1); or
>
> (*e*) that the special program as defined in the order, with such modifications, if any, as the Commission considers advisable, satisfies the requirements of subsection (1).

(3) A person aggrieved by the making of an order under subsection (2) may request the Commission to reconsider its order and section 36, with necessary modifications, applies.

(4) Subsection (1) does not apply to a special program where an order is

made under clause (2)(*d*) or where an order is made under clause (2)(*e*) with modifications of the special program that are not implemented.

(5) Subsection (2) does not apply to a special program implemented by the Crown or an agency of the Crown.

14. A right under Part I to non-discrimination because of age is not infringed where an age of sixty-five years or over is a requirement, qualification or consideration for preferential treatment.

15.—(1) A right under Part I to non-discrimination because of citizenship is not infringed where Canadian citizenship is a requirement, qualification or consideration imposed or authorized by law.

(2) A right under Part I to non-discrimination because of citizenship is not infringed where Canadian citizenship or lawful admission to Canada for permanent residence is a requirement, qualification or consideration adopted for the purpose of fostering and developing participation in cultural, educational, trade union or athletic activities by Canadian citizens or persons lawfully admitted to Canada for permanent residence.

(3) A right under Part I to non-discrimination because of citizenship is not infringed where Canadian citizenship or domicile in Canada with the intention to obtain Canadian citizenship is a requirement, qualification or consideration adopted by an organization or enterprise for the holder of chief or senior executive positions.

16.—(1) A right of a person under this Act is not infringed for the reason only,

    (*a*) that the person does not have access to premises, services, goods, facilities or accommodation because of handicap, or that the premises, services, goods, facilities or accommodation lack the amenities that are appropriate for the person because of handicap; or

    (*b*) that the person is incapable of performing or fulfilling the essential duties or requirements attending the exercise of the right because of handicap.

(2) Where, after the investigation of a complaint, the Commission determines that the evidence does not warrant the appointment of a board of inquiry because of the application of subsection (1), the Commission may nevertheless use its best endeavours to effect a settlement as to the provision of access or amenities or as to the duties or requirements.

17. The rights under Part I to equal treatment with respect to services and facilities, with or without accommodation, is not infringed where membership or participation in a religious, philanthropic, educational, fraternal or social institution or organization that is primarily engaged in serving the interests of persons identified by a prohibited ground of discrimination is restricted to persons who are similarly identified.

18.—(1) This Act shall not be construed to adversely affect any right ot privilege respecting separate schools enjoyed by separate school boards or their supporters under *The Constitution Act, 1867* and the *Education Act.*

(2) This Act does not apply to affect the application of the *Education Act* with respect to the duties of teachers.

19.—(1) The right under section 1 to equal treatment with respect to services and facilities without discrimination because of sex is not infringed where the use of the services or facilities is restricted to persons of the same sex on the ground of public decency.

(2) The right under section 1 to equal treatment with respect to services and facilities is not infringed where membership in an athletic organization or participation in an athletic activity is restricted to persons of the same sex.

(3) The right under section 1 to equal treatment with respect to services and facilities is not infringed where a recreational club restricts or qualifies access to its services or facilities or gives preferences with respect to membership dues and other fees because of age, marital status or family status.

20.—(1) The right under section 2 to equal treatment with respect to the occupancy of residential accommodation without discrimination is not infringed by discrimination where the residential accommodation is in a dwelling in which the owner or his or her family reside if the occupant or occupants of the residential accommodation are required to share a bathroom or kitchen facility with the owner or family of the owner.

(2) The right under section 2 to equal treatment with respect to the occupancy of residential accommodation without discrimination because of sex is not infringed by discrimination on the ground where the occupancy of all the residential accommodation in the building, other than the accommodation, if any, of the owner or family of the owner, is restricted to persons who are of the same sex.

(3) The right under section 2 to equal treatment with respect to the occupancy of residential accommodation without discrimination because of marital status is not infringed by discrimination on the ground where the occupancy is in a building that contains not more than four dwelling units, one of which is occupied by the owner or family of the owner.

(4) The right under section 2 to equal treatment with respect to the occupancy of residential accommodation without discrimination because of family status is not infringed by discrimination on that ground where the residential accommodation is in a building, or designated part of the building, that contains more than one dwelling unit served by a common entrance and the occupancy of all the residential accommodation in the building or in the designated part of the building is restricted because of family status.

21. The right under sections 1 and 3 to equal treatment with respect to services and to contract on equal terms, without discrimination because of age, sex, marital status, family status, or handicap, is not infringed where a contract of automobile, life, accident or sickness or disability insurance or a contract of group insurance between an insurer and an association or person other than an employer, or a life annuity, differentiates or makes a distinction, exclusion or preference on reasonable and *bona fide* grounds because of age, sex, marital status, family status or handicap.

22.—(1) The right under section 4 to equal treatment with respect to employment is infringed where an invitation to apply for employment or an advertisement in connection with employment is published or displayed that directly or indirectly classifies or indicates qualifications by a prohibited ground of discrimination.

(2) The right under section 4 to equal treatment with respect to employment is infringed where a form of application for employment is used or a written or oral inquiry is made of an applicant that directly or indirectly classifies or indicates qualifications by a prohibited ground of discrimination.

(3) Nothing in subsection (2) precludes the asking of questions at a personal employment interview concerning a prohibited ground of discrimination where discrimination on such ground is permitted under this Act.

(4) The right under section 4 to equal treatment with respect to employment is infringed where an employment agency discriminates against a person because of a prohibited ground of discrimination in receiving, classifying, disposing of or otherwise acting upon applications for its services or in referring an applicant or applicants to an employer or agent of an employer.

23. The right under section 4 to equal treatment with respect to employment is not infringed where,

(*a*) a religious, philanthropic, educational, fraternal or social institution or organization that is primarily engaged in serving the interests of persons identified by their race, ancestry, place of origin, colour, ethnic origin, creed, sex, age, marital status or handicap employs only, or gives preference in employment to, persons similarly identified if the qualification is a reasonable and *bona fide* qualification because of the nature of the employment;

(*b*) The discrimination in employment is for reasons of age, sex, record of offences or marital status if the age, sex, record of offences or marital status of the applicant is a reasonable and *bona fide* qualification because of the nature of the employment;

(*c*) an individual person refuses to employ another for reasons of any prohibited ground of discrimination in section 4, where the primary duty of the employment is attending to the medical or personal needs of the person or of an ill child or an aged, infirm or ill spouse or other relative of the person; or

(*d*) an employer grants or withholds employment or advancement in employment to a person who is the spouse, child or parent of the employer or an employee.

24.—(1) The right under section 4 to equal treatment with respect to employment is infringed where employment is denied or made conditional because a term or condition of employment requires enrolment in an employee benefit, pension or superannuation plan or fund or a contract of group insurance between an insurer and an employer, that makes a distinction, preference or exclusion on a prohibited ground of discrimination.

(2) The right under section 4 to equal treatment with respect to employment without discrimination because of age, sex, marital status or family status is not infringed by an employee superannuation or pension plan or fund or a contract of group insurance between an insurer and an employer that complies with the *Employment Standards Act* and the regulations thereunder.

(3) The right under section 4 to equal treatment with respect to employment without discrimination because of handicap is not infringed,

  (*a*) where a reasonable and *bona fide* distinction, exclusion or preference is made in an employee disability or life insurance plan or benefit because of a pre-existing handicap that substantially increases the risk;

  (*b*) where a reasonable and *bona fide* distinction, exclusion or preference is made on the ground of a pre-existing handicap in respect of an employee-pay-all or participant-pay-all benefit in an employee benefit, pension or superannuation plan or fund or a contract of group insurance between an insurer and an employer or in respect of a plan, fund or policy that is offered by an employer to his employees if they are fewer than twenty-five in number.

(4) An employer shall pay to an employee who is excluded because of a handicap from an employee benefit, pension or superannuation plan or fund or a contract of group insurance between an insurer and the employer compensation equivalent to the contribution that the employer would make thereto on behalf of an employee who does not have a handicap.

25.—(1) It shall be deemed to be a condition of every contract entered into by or on behalf of the Crown or any agency thereof and of every subcontract entered into in the performance thereof that no right under section 4 will be infringed in the course of performing the contract.

(2) It shall be deemed to be a condition of every grant, contribution, loan or guarantee made by or on behalf of the Crown or any agency thereof that no right under section 4 will be infringed in the course of carrying out the purposes for which the grant, contribution, loan or guarantee was made.

(3) Where an infringement of a right under section 4 is found by a board of inquiry upon a complaint and constitutes a breach of a condition under this section, the breach of condition is sufficient grounds for cancellation of the contract, grant, contribution, loan or guarantee and refusal to enter into any further contract with or make any further grant, contribution, loan or guarantee to the same person.

PART III
THE ONTARIO HUMAN RIGHTS COMMISSION

26.—(1) The Ontario Human Rights Commission is continued and shall be composed of such persons, being not fewer than seven, as are appointed by the Lieutenant Governor in Council.

(2) The Commission is responsible to the Minister for the administration of this Act.

(3) The Lieutenant Governor in Council shall designate a member of the Commission as chairman, and a member as vice-chairman.

(4) The Lieutenant Governor in Council may fix the remuneration and allowance for expenses of the chairman, vice-chairman and members of the Commission.

(5) The employees of the Commission shall be appointed under the *Public Service Act.*

(6) The Commission may authorize any function of the Commission to be performed by a division of the Commission composed of at least three members of the Commission.

27.—(1) The Lieutenant Governor in Council shall designate at least three members of the Commission to constitute a race relations division of the Commission and shall designate one member of the race relations division as Commissionr for Race Relations.

(2) It is the function of the race relations division of the Commission to perform any of the functions of the Commission under clause 28(*f*), (*g*) or (*h*) relating to race, ancestry, place of origin, colour, ethnic origin or creed that are referred to it by the Commission and any other function referred to it by the Commission.

28. It is the function of the Commission,

    (*a*) to forward the policy that the dignity and worth of every person be recognized and that equal rights and opportunities be provided without discrimination that is contrary to law;

    (*b*) to promote an understanding and acceptance of and compliance with this Act;

    (*c*) to recommend for consideration a special plan or program designed to meet the requirements of subsection 13(1), subject to the right of a person aggrieved by the implementation of the plan or program to request the Commission to reconsider its recommendation and section 36 applies with necessary modifications;

    (*d*) to develop and conduct programs of public information and education and undertake, direct and encourage research designed to eliminate discriminatory practices that infringe rights under this Act;

    (*e*) to examine and review any statute or regulation, and any program or policy made by or under a statute and make recommendations on any provision, program or policy, that in its opinion is inconsistent with the intent of this Act;

(*f*) to inquire into incidents of and conditions leading or tending to lead to tension or conflict based upon identification by a prohibited ground of discrimination and take appropriate action to eliminate the source of tension or conflict;

(*g*) to initiate investigations into problems based upon identification by a prohibited ground of discrimination that may arise in a community, and encourage and co-ordinate plans, programs and activities to reduce or prevent such problems;

(*h*) to promote, assist and encourage public, municipal or private agencies, organizations, groups or persons to engage in programs to alleviate tensions and conflicts based upon identification by a prohibited ground of discrimination;

(*i*) to enforce this Act and orders of boards of inquiry; and

(*j*) to perform the functions assigned to it by this or any other Act.

PART IV
ENFORCEMENT

31.—(1) Where a person believes that a right of his under this Act has been infringed, the person may file with the Commission a complaint in a form approved by the Commission.

(2) The Commission may initiate a complaint by itself or at the request of any person.

(3) Where two or more complaints,

(*a*) bring into question a practice of infringement engaged in by the same person; or

(*b*) have questions of law or fact in common,

the Commission may combine the complaints and deal with them in the same proceeding.

32.—(1) Subject to section 33, the Commission shall investigate a complaint and endeavour to effect a settlement.

* * *

50. The short title is the Human Rights Code 1981.

21

Collective Bargaining

"Collective bargaining" refers to the process whereby employees bargain, as with one voice, through a trade union that has been recognized as the exclusive bargaining agent for them all. The process has not always been freely available to employees: for many years organized employee groups were viewed as conspiracies against the employer and were illegal. Gradually, however, and often through violent means, trade unions grew in number and membership, as did their legitimacy under the law. In Canada, the union movement has grown from a few small unions in the mid-nineteenth century to over three million members today, representing approximately one-third of the labour force.

THE COLLECTIVE BARGAINING PROCESS

Both the federal and provincial governments have laws that recognize the right of employees to join a union and participate in its lawful activities, and laws that regulate the actual collective bargaining process. The union that has been recognized as the exclusive bargaining agent negotiates and bargains with the employer to reach an employment agreement, the "collective agreement." The recognition of the union as exclusive bargaining agent usually occurs when the appropriate labour relations board "certifies" the union. The collective agreement, which is to be in writing for a minimum term specified by statute, sets out the rights and duties of both employer and employees. Both parties are to bargain in good faith to reach such agreement. Any problems regarding the agreement are to be settled by arbitration and before any strikes by employees or lockouts by employers can occur, certain conditions must be met.

FEDERAL LEGISLATION

At the federal level, Part V of the Canada Labour Code governs industrial relations of employees within federal jurisdiction (employees working on or in connection with any federal work, undertaking, or business). Specifically excluded are employees in managerial functions or employed in a confidential capacity in matters relating to industrial relations. The first federal legislation in this area was in 1900. Gradually, however, the government expanded its jurisdiction until a 1925 case (the *Snider* case) reminded it that it only had power to legislate in labour relation matters within its own federal jurisdiction.

The Canada Labour Code is administered by the federal Minister of Labour, who has delegated some authority to the Canada Labour Relations Board. The Board consists of a Chairman, one to four Vice-Chairmen, and between four to eight other members.

PROVINCIAL STATUTES

Provincial legislation generally parallels the federal Code. In Ontario, as one provincial example, there was some collective bargaining legislation in the nineteenth century (for example, the Trade Arbitration Act, 1873) but it was not until the 1930s that the provincial statutes became effective. The Ontario Labour Relations Act, enacted in 1948 and subsequently updated, governs industrial relations. Accomplishing the same basic principles as the federal Code, it is administered by a provincial labour relations board appointed by the Lieutenant Governor in Council and consisting of a Chairman, one or more Vice-Chairmen, and an equal number of employees and employers. The Ontario Rights of Labour Act is also important: it recognizes the legal status of trade unions and protects them from civil liability for lawful acts done in the course of a trade dispute, even if in restraint of trade.

APPLICATION OF THE LEGISLATION

The federal and provincial Acts apply to employees within their respective jurisdictions, and both specifically exclude: people employed in managerial functions or in a confidential capacity in matters relating to industrial relations; domestic servants; and people working in agriculture, horticulture, hunting and trapping. In Ontario, certain professional groups are also excluded (such as people in architecture, dentistry, land surveying, and members of the legal and medical professions entitled to practise in the province and employed in a professional capacity).

APPROPRIATE UNIT

A union that is a bargaining agent must represent a unit of employees that is an "appropriate" group. Appropriateness is determined exclusively by the relevant labour relations board. It tries to ensure that the group is homogeneous and tries not to intermingle groups in one union if they have greatly divergent interests. For instance, a union representing both retail clerks and steelworkers might not be "appropriate" because their interests are too diverse. The board at the same time tries to avoid unnecessarily fragmenting unions into too many smaller groups, which could result in none of them having an effective voice in bargaining with the employer. In deciding the appropriateness of industrial units, the Labour Relations Board considers: the desires of the employer and trade union; the community of interest among employees (the skills, conditions of employment, and nature of work); the organizational structure of the employer's firm; and the desire not to split the work force of an employer into too many bargaining units.

CERTIFICATION

Once the board determines that a unit is appropriate and a majority of the employees in it wish to be represented by a union, it has a duty to "certify" the union as the appropriate bargaining unit. To determine majority support, the board may consider conducting a representation vote: it is mandatory at the federal level for a group not yet represented by a union where evidence indicates 25% to 50% of the employees are members. At least 35% of employees eligible to vote must do so and the results are calculated on the basis of ballots cast.

In Ontario, the Board must order a representation vote if 45% to 55% of employees are members: if more than 55% are members, the vote is discretionary; if more than 35% of employees are members, the union may request a pre-hearing vote, which has the same effect as a representation vote. If less than 35% are members, the application is dismissed. The vote is judged on the basis of ballots cast.

When an employer is notified that a union is trying to be certified, no employment terms or conditions may be altered within certain time limits. Once certification has been obtained, the union has exclusive jurisdiction to represent all employees in the union (whether or not they are union members) and can insist that the employer bargain in good faith and bargain only with the certified union.

A union that is not certified as a bargaining agent may still represent the employees. At the federal level, this is possible if a majority of employees so agree; in Ontario, it is possible when an employer agrees in writing to recognize the union as the exclusive "bargaining agent" ("voluntary recognition").

TERMINATION OF BARGAINING RIGHTS

In both the federal and Ontario Acts, certification will not be given if the board is satisfied that a union is dominated or influenced by employers to the degree that its fitness to represent employees will be impaired or if a trade union discriminates as to the qualifications for membership.

Bargaining rights may be terminated in a number of ways and for various reasons. In Ontario, these reasons include: the certification of another union; a certification obtained by fraud; failure to give notice to bargain within the statutory time or, after giving notice, failure to bargain within certain time limits; the union fundamentally changing or ceasing to exist; an employees' application for a declaration at specified times during a collective agreement that the union does not represent them; and failure on the part of the union to make a first agreement within the first year of certification. In Ontario an employee may withdraw his or her support from a union after becoming a member and before the union is certified, by filing a "statement of desire" with the Board. This may be able to prevent his membership evidence from being counted. It must be signed and name the employer and union involved, although it need not follow a standard form. The employer and union do not see it but are informed that it has been submitted. At most it forces a representation vote rather than having a union certified outright.

NEGOTIATIONS

Once certification is achieved, the parties are required to begin negotiating a collective agreement. Once notice to bargain is given by the union to the employer, the parties must meet within fifteen days (or at such other time as they mutually agree). If the parties are unable to reach an agreement, they inform the Minister of Labour, who may, if it is considered advisable, direct the Labour Relations Board to investigate and settle the terms of the first agreement.

In Ontario, if an employer and union cannot agree on the terms of a collective agreement, either may ask the Minister of Labour to appoint a conciliation officer to try and help them reach some agreement. If the conciliator cannot, the Minister of Labour may then appoint a three-person conciliation board; usually this does not happen. Instead the conciliator issues a report stating the advisability of a conciliation board; this is called the "no-board report." The parties will be in a legal strike position fourteen days after the Minister mails the no-board report.

The parties may apply to the Minister of Labour before or during the strike for the appointment of a mediation officer to help them reach agreement: such appointment does not affect the period for a legal strike.

If the parties already have a collective agreement they wish to renew or renegotiate, they must give notice to this effect within ninety days before it is to expire (or such other time set out in the agreement). They must meet within a certain period after giving notice (twenty days for federal negotiations, fifteen days for Ontario). If they cannot agree on the terms, the procedures discussed above regarding conciliators, no-board report, legal strike position, and so on apply.

THE COLLECTIVE AGREEMENT

The collective agreement must be in writing and under both the federal and Ontairo Acts, its term must be for at least one year. If no time is specified in the agreement, its term is presumed to be for one year. It must provide for final settlement of any dispute by arbitration, which is to be binding and final. Disputes regarding alleged violation of the contract, its interpretation, application, and so on are initially to be solved through a grievance procedure whereby the parties try to reach a settlement themselves; failing this, the parties go to arbitration. The agreement sets out the conditions and terms of employment and usually makes provisions concerning wages, overtime, seniority, etc. The company retains "residual rights" to all terms of employment except those specified in the contract or dealt within the relevant labour standards laws.

UNION SECURITY

The union may demand a union security clause whereby all employees in the union must join the union or pay dues to the union as a condition of employment. The main types of union security clauses are as follows:

1. *Rand Formula* (or agency shop)—employees do not need to join the union, but non-members must pay the union an amount equal to dues.
2. *Closed Shop*—only union members can be hired.
3. *Union Shop*—all present and future employees must become and remain union members.
4. *Membership Maintenance*—no need to join a union, but those already members must maintain membership.
5. *Dues Checkoff*—no need to join the union but dues must be deducted.

In Ontario, the Labour Relations Act was amended in 1980 so that there is now a compulsory dues checkoff clause in every agreement; that is, the employer must deduct union dues from an employee's pay cheque. (The Board may, however, exempt employees from joining a union or paying dues if it is established that their objection is based on religious grounds; an equivalent amount is paid to a mutually agreed-on charity.)

UNFAIR LABOUR PRACTICES

Certain practices in collective bargaining have been deemed "unfair" and in violation of the relevant labour laws. These practices include an employer discriminating against employees who are union members or who are trying to form a union, or an employer dismissing an employee for union activity. Unfair practices listed in the Ontario Labour Relations Act include:

- failure to bargain in good faith;
- interference by an employer with a union or by a union with an employer;
- interference by an employer with employees because of union activity, by means of discharge, discrimination, or coercion;
- a union (where a collective agreement contains a union security provision) requiring an employer to discharge employees who have been denied union membership for legitimate union activity;
- a union breaching its duty of fair representation;
- an employer bargaining with a group other than the bargaining agent;
- a strike or lockout during the term of the collective agreement or before the conciliation process has been exhausted;
- reprisal by a union against members for refusing to engage in an unlawful strike;

- an employer altering working conditions without union consent, after notice to bargain has been given and no agreement is in operation, or after notice of certification application has been received by the employer;
- reprisal by either the employer or the trade union against employees because of their involvement in Board proceedings.

STRIKES AND LOCKOUTS

A strike is the withdrawal of services by the employees (and includes a slowdown or employees "booking off sick" in order to pressure their employer.) A lockout is the withdrawal of employment by the employer. Both these activities are prohibited during the currency of a collective agreement and until the prescribed conciliation process has been exhausted. Strikers are still considered employees. At the federal level, there may be no strike until the employer or union has served notice to begin collective bargaining, the bargaining fails to produce a new, or revise an existing contract, and the conciliation procedures prove unsuccessful. In Ontario a strike is illegal if it occurs: before a union has gained bargaining rights through certification; when a union is negotiating for a collective agreement but has not exhausted the conciliation procedures in the Labour Relations Act; or during the term of the collective agreement. It is an illegal strike whether or not the union supports the strikers' action. Now, in Ontario, striking employees are to vote on the employer's last offer. If an employee makes an unconditional application in writing to return to work within six months of the beginning of the strike, an employer is required to reinstate the employee to the former employment without discrimination, even though the employee has been on strike.

LIABILITY

Under the federal Code, an employer declaring or causing a lockout, or a union declaring or authorizing a strike in violation of the Code, is liable on summary conviction to a fine up to $1,000 per day of such activity. Every officer or representative of such employer or union who is guilty of a similar offence is liable to a fine up to $10,000. Violations of other provisions of the Code make the offender liable to smaller fines.

In Ontario every contravention of the Act, or any of the Board's orders or declarations, is punishable on summary conviction by a fine up to $1,000 for an individual and up to $10,000 for a company or trade union. Both the company and union are liable for authorized acts of their officers or agents and the latter may be prosecuted in their own name. In Ontario, before prosecution can begin, permission must be obtained by the Labour Relations Board. As mentioned earlier, unions were originally illegal on grounds of criminal conspiracy. Today, the Criminal Code states that intimidation and conspiracies are illegal; the Combines Investigation Act also contains anti-conspiracy provisions. To ensure that trade unions are not prosecuted under such legislation, statutes have been passed—for example, the federal Trade Unions Act and, in Ontario, the Rights of Labour Act—stating that unions are not unlawful just because they are in restraint of trade. The Combines Investigation Act also states that provisions relating to conspiracies do not apply to employees combining "for their own reasonable protection as ... employees." Statutes providing further protection have been passed in Saskatchewan, British Columbia and Ontario. In Ontario, the Rights of Labour Act, which legalizes unions by statute, protects them from civil liability for unlawful acts done in the course of a trade dispute, even if in restraint of trade.

REVIEW QUESTIONS

1. What is collective bargaining? Why is it favoured by employees?
2. Distinguish between federal and provincial labour relations statutes.
3. What criteria does the Ontario Labour Relations Board use in deciding the appropriateness of a unit of industrial workers?
4. A union wishes to become certified as the bargaining agent for the 100 employees in the clerical department of the Acme Co. What must it prove?
5. When may the bargaining rights of a union be terminated?
6. What is a "no-board report" and what is its effect?
7. What are the essentials of a collective agreement? What are usually the most contentious issues?
8. Is the settlement of a dispute by arbitration final?
9. What is the Rand Formula? What union security clause is new law in Ontario?
10. Explain three types of "unfair practice" by: (a) an employer; (b) a trade union.
11. Are strikers still employees?
12. John Hellman has been on strike with the Musicians Union Local XYZ for four months and is concerned about not being allowed to resume his job as Assistant Drummer of the ABC Symphony Orchestra. What should he do to ensure he can get his job back?
13. Must striking employees in Ontario be given an opportunity to vote on the company's latest offer? If so, why?

PROBLEMS

1. A union passed a resolution asking for an adjustment of pay due to inflation while a collective agreement was in force and proposed a work to rule plan. The plaintiff, Transport Labour Relations, is suing for an injunction to prohibit the slow-down as a form of strike. What is the federal and provincial law on this point? Refer to *Transport Labour Relations v. General Truck Drivers* (1975), 54 D.L.R. (3d) 457.
2. The owner of a western newspaper required his employees to work over-

time to publish his newspaper. They refused and he fired them. He then served them with a document for signature whereby they agreed to "normal work to publish the newspaper including overtime." The typographical union sought an injunction. The provisions of the relevant Saskatchewan Trade Unions Act are the same as the Ontario Act on this particular point. What provisions apply assuming there is a valid collective agreement? Refer to *Crozier v. Western Publishers Ltd.*, [1975] 2 W.W.R. 717 (Sask. C.A.).

3. A sweeper in a factory under a union contract was ordered to fill in for a worker on the line or pick up his pay from the office. He did neither but went home. What likely procedure must be followed to resolve this case?

4. A group of employees at Mr. Ricco's textile plant were trying to organize. The ringleader seemed to be Mr. Brant. Ricco arranged a meeting of all employees in the staff cafeteria one morning at 11 a.m. and told them that he would give them all a Christmas turkey if they did not organize. Later that day he told Brant that his services were no longer required due to his "absenteeism" (Brant was late for work that day; the first time in his four years with the company). What can Brant do? What is the likely result of this action?

5. On Monday, December 3, Joe Fraser, union steward of Local 9, Ironworkers, was suspended for fifteen days by his employer, Mr. X, after Fraser refused to work in an area he considered "a safety hazard." He told Mr. X that he should fix the area or he would be "given a free trip to explore the Harbour by Local 9." Mr. X suspended him on the spot. Fraser immediately informed his friends and within an hour all of Local 9 went on strike. The collective agreement between Local 9 and the employer expired November 30. Today, December 6, the employees are still on strike and as a result of the strike, Mr. X has lost $5,000 in direct expenses. What should Fraser have done? What can X do?

READING

Re Retail Store Employees Union, Local 832 and Canada Safeway Ltd. (1973), 41 D.L.R. (3d) 449 (Man. C.A.).

Facts: In this case a Mrs. Johannsen was discharged on September 5, 1972, by Safeway because she was in violation of the rules in working for another employer while on sick leave. A grievance was immediately processed on her behalf and the union sought arbitration. Unfortunately, by the time the arbitrators were selected, it was November 22 and, since the union representative was either out of the country or ill until early January, the decision reinstating Mrs. Johannsen was not given until January 20, 1973. The decision was to suspend Mrs. Johannsen for "six weeks only," but because the union appeared to have caused the delay, the union was ordered to pay one-half of her back wages after the six weeks' suspension.

At the trial, the Court of Queen's Bench held that it would be a breach of the "principles of natural justice" to penalize the union because of its representative's illness and ordered the award against the union quashed.

Held (on appeal):
[Section 24(d) of the union agreement provides that] In the event of termination, discharge or suspension of an employee, the Board of Arbitration shall have the right to sustain the employer's action or reinstate the employee with full, part or no back pay, with or without loss of seniority *or to settle the matter in any way it deems equitable....*

... After the first step in the grievance procedure [i.e., presenting the grievance] ... it could only have been the union who had the authority to carry matters forward. It was the union and the company who were parties to the settlement of the dispute....

... [T]he union, as a proper party to the arbitration, was subject to having an award made against it by the board as part of an equitable settlement....

In *Re Canadian Westinghouse Co. Ltd. and Local 164 Draftsmen's Association of Ontario*, [1962] O.R. 17, Aylesworth J.A. said at pp. 675-6: "... it is insufficient to defeat the application [of certiorari] if it can be said that the interpretation given to the agreement by the arbitrator is one which the language of the agreement reasonably will bear."...

... [T]he board, in this case, did not change the agreement but made an award which was authorized under the terms of the agreement and which was valid, in law.

... [T]here are no grounds for interference, by the Court, with the award.
                                                        Appeal allowed.

[Leave to appeal to the Supreme Court of Canada was dismissed with costs by the Manitoba Court of Appeal.]

22

Employee Health and Safety and Workers' Compensation

HEALTH AND SAFETY LEGISLATION

Most provinces now have a Factory or Industrial Health and Safety Act to help protect the health and safety of workers in factories and other workplaces. In Ontario, for example, this is the Occupational Health and Safety Act. Matters covered include sanitation, heating, lighting, ventilation, and the guarding of dangerous machinery. There are also provincial laws regulating the design, construction, installation, and operation of mechanical equipment such as boilers and pressure vessels, elevators and lifts and electrical installations; the use of gas- and oil-burning equipment and radiation-producing equipment such as laser sources; and the standards of qualification for workers who install, operate, or service such equipment. Nevertheless, despite this legislation, accidents do occur and employees are injured at their place of work.

Canada Labour Code

At the federal level, employees within federal labour jurisdiction (such as federal civil servants, interprovincial truckers, railroad and airline employees) are governed by either the Public Service Staff Relations Act or the Canada Labour Code.

Part IV of the Canada Labour Code tries to ensure safe working conditions for all employees in industries and undertakings under federal jurisdiction by: (a) specifying all the elements of a complete industrial safety program and the general obligation of employers and employees to perform their duties in a safe manner (also, an employee may legally refuse to work if conditions impose an imminent danger to his or her safety or health); (b) authorizing regulations to deal with problems of occupational safety; (c) authorizing the use of advisory committees and special task forces to assist in developing the industrial safety program, all to be accompanied by continuous consultation among federal and provincial government departments, industry, and organized labour; (d) providing for research into causes and prevention of accidents; (3) authorizing an extended program of safety education; (f) providing for regional safety officers and federally authorized provincial inspectors to enforce the Code; and (g) providing a procedure for complaints by employees about violations of the Code.

Occupational Health and Safety Act

Employees within provincial labour jurisdictions encounter health and safety standards of varying degrees. The Ontario Occupational Health and Safety Act, considered to be one of the most progressive provincial labour laws, gives the worker the right to refuse unhealthy or unsafe work; makes joint labour-management health and safety committees mandatory in many industries; extends the number of workers covered by the Act; and tries to control toxic substances in the workplace.

Although most workers are protected by the Act, it does not apply to all. The exceptions are owners of private residences and their employees; farming operations; teachers; faculty at a university or a related institution; and inmates working in a correctional institution or in work programs at a psychiatric, retardation or rehabilitation facility. Employers are to take reasonable precautions to protect workers and are to provide instruction to workers to protect them and to select health and safety representatives where required. Workers are to use all required protective equipment and work in compliance with the Act. If there is a union, it has the responsibility for selecting workers as health and safety representatives (or a committee) if required; if not required, it is to choose workers to represent co-workers who refuse to work for health and safety reasons. The government is to enforce the law by means of government appointed inspectors. However, at present there are less than 300 inspectors in Ontario, which has over 50,000 industrial establishments.

A worker who "has reason to believe" a job is unsafe or unhealthy, or who is aware of a contravention of the Act, can refuse to use any machinery. The right to refuse work is not extended to all workers (such as police and fire officers) and some have a modified right to refuse (such as ambulance and hospital workers). The worker must inform the supervisor, who then examines the situation in the presence of the worker and a health and safety representative or committee member (or, if a union exists, a worker selected by the union). If after the inspection the worker has "reasonable grounds" to refuse to work, a government inspector must be called in. The employer may assign the refusing worker another job until the situation is resolved. The law does not specifically state that a refusing worker must be paid, but it does state that the worker is not to be penalized for using these rights. If a worker feels he or she is being penalized, the worker may file a grievance and proceed to arbitration; after this a complaint may be filed with the Ontario Labour Relations Board. The burden of proof rests on the employer to show that it has not contravened the no-penalty clause.

Joint labour-management health and safety committees must be established in workplaces where there are twenty or more workers or where there is exposure to a toxic substance or physical agent regulated by a government order. There are exceptions to this rule (construction sites, offices, retail stores, restaurants). However, the Minister of Labour may still order the creation of a committee in any workplace. A committee need not be established if the Ministry is satisfied that there already exists a system for involving workers in health and safety in the workplace and that the system provides benefits equal to or greater than those granted by a committee under law. The committee can identify hazardous situations, make recommendations, and obtain information about health and safety from the employer. A worker-member of the committee has the right to inspect the workplace once a month. A similar function occurs at construction sites having over twenty workers; the contractor must select at least one health and safety representative.

Inspectors appointed under the Act have the power to enter any workplace at any time without a warrant or notice. They also have broad powers to inspect the work premises and to force the employer to provide information about the workplace. They can also order the employer to make necessary changes. Any worker, union, or employer unhappy with an inspector's order can appeal to the Director of the Occupational Health and Safety Division of the Ministry of Labour, whose decision is final.

COMMON LAW RIGHTS OF AN INJURED WORKER

To appreciate properly the present situation of the employee, one has to go back to the days of the industrial revolution in England. In those days, working conditions were harsh and the rights of an employee few.

The common law was not very generous to the employee. For example, if a worker died from injuries received at his occupation, the right to sue the employer died with the employee, thus leaving the employer free from any possibility of being pursued in the courts for negligence. The employer's defence in common law was that the person claiming injury was no longer alive and that the deceased person's right of action had died as well. Of course, the real losers were the employee's spouse and children, who were left without the benefit of a breadwinner. Later, legislation was passed to remedy this situation. It was known first as *Lord Campbell's Act* and subsequently as the *Fatal Accidents Act*. This legislation introduced a new rule: "If the deceased [employee] could have successfully entertained an action for his employer's negligence if he had lived, then the legislature provided that his estate could sue in his stead for the benefit of his wife and dependants." Apart from its humanitarian goals, the legislation was an attempt to ensure that the future support of the wife and children would not be thrust onto the public purse if the worker's death was caused by the negligence of the employer.

Another common law rule that worked hardship on the employee was that no damages would be awarded if the employee were in any way negligent. For example, suppose that an employee goes to work with his hard hat, proper working clothes, safety belt, but in his hurry puts on running shoes instead of safety boots. While at work he is injured by a falling beam which strikes him on the head, pierces his helmet, and kills him. At common law, if the employee (or his estate, under the Fatal Accidents Act) sued the employer, it would have been possible for the employer to plead that the employee was negligent in wearing running shoes instead of safety boots. Even though this fact had no influence whatsoever on the accident which caused the employee's death, the courts would have ruled that no action could be entertained—thus allowing the employer to escape liability.

Today, in Ontario, the *Negligence Act* provides that the degree of negligence must be apportioned. Thus, if a plaintiff were found 40% negligent, a claim for $10,000 would result in an award of $6,000.

A third common law defence available to an employer was that of *volenti non fit inuria* ("consent negates injury"). We have seen this principle applied before, in the chapter on torts. The examples given related to persons entering hospital who would be required to give their permission before undergoing an operation, and to persons participating in sports. With regard to employment, the maxim operated in this way: if a worker was injured in a particularly hazardous occupation, the employer would say that the worker consented to such injuries by applying for a position in that particular trade or occupation. Take, for example, the *Herd* case. This was a situation where workers employed in a mine proceeded on shift and, having reached the bottom of the mine shaft, decided that they would not work on that particular day because of a safety problem. They called the pit head and requested that the elevator be sent down the shaft to get them. However, the management delayed, with the result that their return to the surface was not achieved until about an hour and a half later. They brought an action against the owners of the mine and it was decided at the trial that miners, who work in the bottom of a mine some miles underground must expect delays in being returned to the surface and that, by the fact of being employed in this occupation, they consented to accept the hazards of this occupation. Accordingly, the miners lost their action for false imprisonment.

A fourth defence that an employer could use was that of the injury being caused by a fellow worker. Take, for example, a case in Massachusetts. Here the plaintiff, a railway maintenance worker, used his employer's commuter train to go to and from work. One day, after working at the end of the line, he boarded the train to return home. However, the train was then involved in an accident caused by the negligence of the engineer. All the other commuters successfully sued the railway company for negligence. But the railway maintenance worker lost his action because the railway was able to plead successfully that his accident was caused by a fellow worker.

WORKERS' COMPENSATION ACT

In 1906, the English Parliament passed a Workmen's Compensation Act. This Act was soon adopted by many other common law countries of the world, including Canada, where it is now known, depending on the province, as the Workmen's, or Workers' Compensation Act or Ordinance. The Ontario Act came into effect in 1915 and the British Columbia Act in the following year. All the Acts by the different provinces are similar.

The provincial Workers' Compensation Act established a system of government-run compulsory insurance to provide compensation and to provide medical aid to a worker who is injured by an accident in the course of work or who is disabled by a specified industrial disease. Most industries and occupations are now covered by the Acts. The exceptions are occupations where there is little or no risk of physical injury, and where the accident rate is minimal or where large employers provide similar coverage under government-approved plans, such as in banks or other financial institutions.

The Ontario Act (now called Workers' Compensation) provides compensation, medical aid, rehabilitation services, and pension for employees injured in on-the-job accidents. Some important provisions of the Act are:

1. The employer bears the full cost of payment into the fund and compensation assessments on approximately 150,000 Ontario business owners and industry employers. Employers are assessed at an amount based on the accident rate in the industry multiplied by the number of employees. Industries are classified according to their hazard (there are 108 classification groups in Schedule 1, where most employees are categorized). There is also a Schedule 2 where employers are individually liable for their employees' accident costs and pay their share of administrative costs. Workers employed by Schedule 2 employers receive compensation from the Board which charges the costs against the employers' deposits. Employers are assessed for each $100 or assessable payroll (up to a certain maximum per employee per annum). The employee pays nothing, either directly or indirectly. Compensation is paid by all the employers in a particular group of industries, not just by those whose employees sustain injury, thus the term "collective liability."

2. The employer benefits from this system because injured workers are effectively looked after; assessments are actuarially computed based on accident-cost records and payroll; accident costs are spread out because of the collective liability of the scheme; and employers avoid expensive lawsuits.

3. About 90% of Ontario's labour force are protected by the Act.

4. An employer's obligation, besides paying compensation costs, is to report any accident regarding lost time or medical aid within three days of learning about it. The employer is also supposed to provide a safe workplace.

5. The worker is assured of benefits simply by filing a claim through the employer. Any accident victim must immediately notify his employer who must in turn immediately notify the Workers' Compensation Board. A worker is still entitled to compensation despite the employer's neglect or refusal to furnish information or to pay the assessment or despite insolvency.

6. Compensation is paid even though the injury was the result of the

employee's own carelessness rather than the employer's. The only exceptions are where the injury is minor in nature; where the worker is disabled for less than a stated number of days; or where the injury is the result of the worker's own serious and wilful misconduct; and does not result in death or serious disablement. A Workers' Compensation Board receives and adjudicates all claims for compensation. Except in the Atlantic provinces, where appeals are allowed on points of law or on the jurisdiction of the Board, the Board's decision is final.

7. The employee loses the common law right to sue the employer for negligence and must accept the compensation provided under the Workers' Compensation Act.

8. Compensation comprises all *medical costs* (doctors, nurses, medicines, hospitals, X-rays); and *temporary total disability benefits* (75% of earnings up to a specified maximum per week). An injured worker who has received temporary disability benefits for the immediately preceding twelve weeks and is still not working but is still receiving such benefits may have the compensation adjusted by 10%. This adjustment can be made only once. Temporary partial disability benefits and permanent total disability benefits are also available. Fatal accident benefits include a burial allowance, a lump sum payment, and benefits for the dependent spouse, dependent children, dependent orphans, and other dependants. A clothing allowance is also available. The Board also provides vocational rehabilitation training to help employees return to the workplace.

9. The employee is assured of compensation for any accident (including deliberate injury by someone else), injury, or industrial disease (for example silicosis) that results from employment. However, no compensation is payable for other illnesses, such as a heart attack or appendicitis, even though occurring at work.

10. The coverage applies whether the injury was incurred during working hours or during break time, providing the lunch or coffee break occurred on the employer's premises.

11. It is conceivable that some employees who use their employer's transportation to and from work would also be covered by Workers' Compensation. However, the majority of workers are covered solely for injuries sustained at their place of work.

12. The Board may assist safety organizations by grants. The Act provides for the establishment of safety inspectors to inspect employment premises. Some Boards make use of television and other media to promote safe working practices.

13. Where an employer fails to meet safety standards or where the accident rate is too high in comparison with the remainder of the industry, the employer may be fined an amount equivalent to the annual assessment, depending on the circumstances.

14. Occupations not compulsorily assessed by the Workers' Compensation Board can apply to join the scheme voluntarily. So also can employers

in any occupation, as long as they pay a suitable additional premium.

15. In some provinces (for example, Alberta) there are periodic reviews of the working of the Workers' Compensation Act. In other provinces (for example, Ontario and British Columbia), Royal Commissions have conducted inquiries.

REVIEW QUESTIONS

1. What legislation has your province passed to help workers' health and safety?
2. To whom does the Occupational Health and Safety Act not apply?
3. What is meant by a "right to refuse" to work in an unsafe place? Who, if anyone, does not have this right?
4. What occurs after an employee has refused to work in the abovementioned situation?
5. When are joint labour management health and safety committees required to be formed?
6. If a worker is unhappy with a government health and safety inspector's order, what can he or she do?
7. Explain the nature and purpose of the Fatal Accidents Act.
8. Can an employer be excused from liability for an injury suffered by his employee, if the latter were in any way negligent?
9. To what extent does the doctrine of *volenti non fit injuria* apply to industrial accidents?
10. What was the legal position under common law of an employee injured by a fellow worker? Give an example.
11. What is the history of the Workers' Compensation Act in Canada?
12. Explain the purpose of the Workers' Compensation Act.
13. When is compensation payable to a worker, under the Act?
14. Which occupations are not covered by the Act?
15. Who pays for the benefits available under the Act?
16. How does a disabled employee arrange for benefits under the Act?
17. Under what circumstances can the Workers' Compensation Board refuse to pay benefits?
18. What types of benefits are available under the Act?
19. To what extent is the time and place of an injury important?
20. Would an employee be covered for injury while driving the employer's van while: (a) delivering goods; (b) driving to work?
21. What role does the Workers' Compensation Board play in promoting safe working conditions?
22. What control does the provincial government have over the operations of the Workers' Compensation Board?

PROBLEMS

1. Joe believes that the drill he is working on is unsafe. He informs his supervisor of this and is told that he had better continue working on it or

not to bother coming back to work. Joe refuses and is told that he is fired. What can he do?

2. A woman working in a company laboratory suffered an acid burn on her face which caused an under-the-skin burn and resulted in damage to her sinuses. Following medical treatment she discovered that she had become allergic to many different substances, causing respiratory inconvenience. Her expenses in treating this condition were considerable and the future prognosis is uncertain. What is her legal status?

3. A college student was hired to work for the summer as a houseman at a resort hotel in the Rockies. His job included moving carpets, polishing floors, emptying ash trays, fetching bedboards, and moving furniture. One day, the housekeeper of the hotel asked him to clean the windows, inside and out, in a suite on the eighth floor. As this would have involved standing on the window ledges with a safety strap attached to hooks on the window frame, and a 150-foot drop below, the student refused. Does the employer have the right to dismiss him without notice?

4. D works for E, an employer who has all of his employees covered under the Workers' Compensation Act. D is injured and permanently disabled at his place of work, as a result of the sheer negligence of his employer E and a fellow-worker F. D's regular salary is $12,500. D wants to sue E for negligence under common law in the hope that he can recover more than his maximum entitlement under the Workers' Compensation Act. What is your advice?

5. X, who works in a small manufacturing plant, slipped and broke his leg in the plant while he was going to lunch during his lunch break. How would his right to compensation vary, if at all, if the accident had occurred while X was crossing the road to visit a nearby restaurant?

READING

Re E.B. Eddy Forest Products Ltd. and Lumber and Sawmill Workers' Union, Local 2693 (1979), 24 L.A.C. (2d) 17 (Ont. Arb. Bd.).

Held:

This grievance involves a group of employees who claim that the employer violated art. 11.04 when it failed to pay them for eight hours on June 8, 1978. They seek compensation for that day. The relevant provisions of art. 11.04 read:

> 11.04
> (a) A day or shift worker, who is unable to work the full day or shift for reasons beyond his control, shall be paid for one-half day if he works less than four (4) hours, and for a full day if he works more than four (4) hours.
>
> (b) A day or shift worker who reports for work at his scheduled starting time and is unable to commence work due to reasons beyond his

control, shall receive four (4) hours' pay at his regular rate provided he remains available for two (2) hours from his scheduled starting time, accepts alternate work if so assigned and commences regular work when conditions permit.

If regular or alternate work commences in the first half of the shift on the first or subsequent days, the above payment shall not be made and the provisions of Section 11.04(a) will apply. Should the employee work any of the hours in the second half of the shift he shall receive four (4) hours pay for such hours. The Company will commence regular work as soon as conditions permit.

The parties acknowledge that when an employee is unable to commence work due to reasons beyond his control under art. 11.04 he is entitled to receive moneys as stipulated therein. Such moneys were referred to at the hearing as "stand-by" pay.

The grievors work in the woods cutting forest products, etc. They claim that it was raining at the commencement of their shift at 8:00 a.m. on June 8, 1978, and therefore it was hazardous to work in the woods. Accordingly, they were unable to work due to reasons beyond their control and are entitled to be paid under art. 11.04.

The facts surrounding the circumstances on June 8, 1978, are as follows. The grievors reside in Sultan, a distance of approximately 20 miles from the work site. They travel to and from work in a "school" type bus but which is supplied by the employer.

The bus is usually driven into the camp site by a garage mechanic. The garage is approximately one or one and one-half miles short of the actual work site. The bus is then driven the rest of the way by a member of the work crew (a Mr. Paul Coté).

It had rained during the early morning of June 8th. Indeed, union witnesses Norman Schouinard and Paul Fortin testified that it was still raining lightly at 8:00 a.m.

The men decided to proceed no further than the mechanic's garage that morning. They decided that it was too wet to work due to safety reasons.

Mr. Steve Garner, the foreman, had driven into the camp site in his truck behind the bus. His evidence was there was no rain falling at that time. He was informed upon entering the bus that the men considered it hazardous to work due to the weather and did not move on to the work site. Mr. Garner returned to his truck and contacted Mr. Godin, the superintendent, by radio and informed him of what was happening. Mr. Garner was directed to ask the men to proceed to the work site once more. After having done so he reported to Mr. Godin that he had received the same response. Mr. Godin then informed Mr. Garner that he would contact the Ministry of Labour to have inspectors come to the work site. Such action by the employer is required by the Employees' Health and Safety Act, 1976 (Ont.), c. 79 [since repealed by s. 42 and replaced by the Occupational Health and Safety Act, 1978 (Ont.), c. 83], s. 3(3).

The evidence is somewhat conflicting at this point. The union witnesses testified that Mr. Garner told them to stay on the bus to await the arrival of the Ministry of Labour inspectors. Mr. Garner denies having made such a statement.

In any event, Mr. Garner asked Mr. Schouinard if he planned to work to which he received an affirmative response. Mr. Schouinard is a union steward and a bulldozer operator. He was driven to the work site by Mr. Garner at approximately 8:15 or 8:20 a.m. While in Mr. Garner's truck Mr. Schouinard indicated that it was clearing up now and the men should be asked to go to work again. Mr. Schouinard testified that Mr. Garner indicated he did not want to "stick his neck out" and would not ask them again. By 9:00 or 9:30 a.m. the sun appeared and the rest of the day was sunny and clear. However, neither side made any overtures to the other. The Ministry of Labour inspectors did not arrive at the camp site until 2:00 or 2:30 p.m. Mr. Garner had been joined by Messrs. Charlesbois and Digby, two supervisors, around 10:00 a.m. and while they observed the men and bus they made no approach to them nor did the men approach the supervisors.

The Ministry of Labour inspectors met with the men (and Mr. Schouinard who had been returned from his work by Mr. Garner) until approximately 4:00 p.m. At that time the inspectors informed the supervisors that the men were prepared to go to work and they were taken to the work site where they worked for one-half hour (which was the end of their shift) and were paid for that one-half hour.

As stated earlier they seek payment for the full day pursuant to art. 11.04.

Article 11.04 has been the subject of two earlier arbitration decisions. One is dated November 1, 1978 (Brunner, Chairman) [unreported] wherein Yvon Fournier, the grievor refused to operate a defective overhead loader. The foreman was of the opinion that the machine was safe but the board found it to be unsafe and therefore the grievor had fallen within art. 11.04.

The board, however, made the following comments concerning art. 11.04 at pp. 11, 12 and 13 in its award:

> Before leaving this matter we wish to comment on the submission advanced by counsel for the union that the grievance would have been entitled to succeed even if it could not have been established that the machine was in fact unsafe. Proof of the grievor's belief, based on reasonable grounds, that the machine was unsafe to use or operate would have been sufficient, in his submission, to establish that the grievor was "unable to commence work due to reasons beyond his control" within the meaning of art. 11.04(b) of the collective agreement. To put his submission in a somewhat different way, a breach of art. 11.04(b) can be established by proof that the grievor had reasonable cause to believe that the machine that he was asked to operate was unsafe even if it is not proved, as a matter of fact, on a pre- ponderance of the credible evidence at the hearing, that the machine was in fact unsafe.
>
> With respect, we are unable to accept this submission.
>
> Whatever may be the result of a grievance which challenges the

imposition of discipline as a result of an employee's refusal to operate or use a machine which he on reasonable grounds believes to be unsafe, or the result of a grievance which calls into question compliance or noncompliance with the *Employees' Health and Safety Act, 1976*: when a grievor alleges that the company has violated art. 11.04(b) of the collective agreement between these parties, he must in order to succeed, satisfy the board of arbitration on a balance of probabilities, that the machine that he refused to operate or use, was in fact unsafe and unsafe to the extent that its use or operation would have exposed him to an unreasonable risk of harm. Unless he can satisfy that requirement, he does not, in our view, prove that he was "unable to commence work due to reasons beyond his control" within the meaning of the said article.

Another arbitration award between these parties (again Brunner, Chairman) dated May 24, 1979 [unreported], again considered art. 11.04. In that case the grievance was concerned with windy conditions allegedly making it hazardous to perform work. At pp. 9 and 10 of that award it was stated:

On this evidence we turn to what we see to be the essential issue in this matter, i.e., whether the work site on December 9, 1978, was safe as alleged by the company, or unsafe so that working would have exposed the employees to an unreasonable risk of harm, as contended for by the union. As stated in the award on the *Fournier* grievance, it is for the grievors who alleged that the company violated art. 11.04 of the collective agreement to satisfy the board of arbitration on a balance of probabilities that the work site was unsafe so that performance of work would in the prevailing circumstances, have exposed the employees in question, to an unreasonable risk of harm.

While a great deal of evidence was heard over whether or not the employees were told by Mr. Garner to wait in the bus until the inspectors from the Ministry of Labour arrived; as well as upon whom rested the responsibility to ask whether or not the grievors could go to work when it was apparent to everyone that the weather had cleared and the sun had shone, the issue remains whether or not art. 11.04 applies.

Some further general comments may be in order. It is agreed that when it rains or snows (heavily in the employer's judgment) the foremen stop work and place the men on "stand-by". Then art. 11.04 applies. The employer is concerned about safety conditions and recognizes the hazards that woodworking entails. However, very often the footing is wet due to dew, frost, snow, etc., and the employees must take necessary precautions to ensure good footing and have a firm grip on their power saws etc. Visibility is also an important factor. Poor visibility increases the hazardous nature of the work and is avoided when the foreman places the men on "stand-by".

In reviewing the evidence the board is not persuaded that the men were "unable to commence work due to reasons beyond [their] control". We agree, with respect, with the comments in the Brunner award in the *Fournier* decision that "in order to succeed the union must satisfy the board of arbitration on a balance of probabilities, that the . . . rain would have exposed them to an unreasonable risk of harm such that they were unable to commence work due to reasons beyond their control''. The evidence of Mr. Garner was that it was not raining at 8:00 a.m. Messrs. Schouinard and Fortin testified that it was raining, albeit lightly. Moreover, at 8:15 or 8:20 a.m. Mr. Schouinard suggested that they be asked again to proceed to the work site as the weather was clearing up. This was not done. Accordingly, we find that art. 11.04 was not applicable and cannot be relied on to support the grievance. Therefore, the grievance must be dismissed.

Finally, while a comment should be made concerning who should have contacted whom during the day in order to get the men to work we are of the opinion that a decision on it is not necessary to resolve the issue that is before us. We have found as a fact that the men were requested twice to proceed to the work site at 8:00 a.m. They refused, explaining that it was too wet, and relied on art. 11.04 in support of their action. We have found art. 11.04 to be inapplicable and therefore cannot sustain their claim.

During the evidence the union witnesses testified that Mr. Garner had instructed them to remain in the bus to await the arrival of the Ministry inspectors. He denied having made such a statement in his evidence. Initially, the union evidence indicated that Mr. Garner had invoked the ''stand-by'' provisions but this was later denied under cross-examination. In any event, the evidence establishes clearly that Mr. Garner left no doubt in the minds of the men on the bus that he wanted them to proceed directly to the work site and they refused. This board is persuaded that no ''stand-by'' was initiated by Mr. Garner and therefore does not assist the grievors.

We find that having refused to proceed to work when requested to do so by Mr. Garner, and, having failed to persuade the board, on a balance of probabilities, that art. 11.04 applies, the grievance must be and is hereby dismissed. We do not consider that further comments on this aspect of the matter will assist the parties and, not being necessary to resolve the dispute, we decline further comment. The grievance fails and is dismissed.

APPENDIX 22-A: SUMMARY OF THE WORKERS' COMPENSATION ACT, R.S.O. 1980, c. 539

S. 1(1)   (*a*) accident, includes wilful act, but not the act of the worker;
          (*b*) common-law wife—not legally married but cohabits and recognized as wife in the community.

S. 1(2)   Persons assisting in fire fighting deemed an employee of the township that called them out.

S. 3   Compensation covers any injury except one day's disablement or non-serious self-inflicted injury, but not death or serious injury.

S. 4   Employers under Schedule I contribute to the Accident Fund; those under Schedule II are liable individually.

S. 6   Coverage extends outside of Ontario, if employer and employee resident in Ontario, for up to six months' employment.

S. 6(4)	If employer outside of Ontario and benefits payable there, normally benefits to be only payable under this Act if employed in Ontario.
S. 6(6)	Steamer, railway, and transport workers are covered while out of Ontario.
S. 7	Sometimes worker may be required to elect to take benefits in Ontario or elsewhere.
S. 8	Worker may sue third party who caused injuries and if receives less than entitlement under this Act, the worker may be brought up to his Ontario entitlement.
S. 8(4)	Employer and the Board paying benefits are entitled to be subrogated to any claims favouring the employee.
S. 8(9)	This Act takes away injured employee's common law right of action against the employer or fellow employees.
S. 12	Cannot sue in Court for compensation, but must submit claims to Compensation Board.
S. 13	Moving out of Ontario disentitles the worker to compensation except when declared permanently disabled.
S. 14	Cuts out any right of action by employee against employer.
S. 16	Employee cannot waive benefits under Act.
S. 17	If employer liable individually, any private compensation agreement must be approved by Board.
S. 18(1)	Employer cannot deduct any part of compensation payable by employer from any of employees.
S. 18(2)	Penalty $50 fine and reimbursement.
S. 19	Compensation is not assignable or attachable.
S. 20	Claim must be made as soon as accident occurs and within six months from injury or death.
S. 20(5)	Allows exception if employer not prejudiced.
S. 21	Provides for compulsory medical examination.
S. 23	Provides for surgery, to avoid heavy compensation payment.
S. 24	Provides for review of compensation.
S. 27	Board may allow payments to be commuted after six months of receipt and disability is permanent, to allow purchase of annuity.
S. 36	Scale of compensation in case of death.
S. 36(2)	Common law wife of six years or one of two years with his child and no dependent widow is entitled to compensation.
S. 37	Widow remarrying is entitled to a lump sum of two years' payments.
S. 39	For total disability, entitled to 75% of average salary up to fixed maximum.
S. 52	Worker entitled to compensation is entitled to medical aid for the injury, plus choice of doctor.
S. 54	Rehabilitation expenses are authorized.
S. 55	Provides for Workers' Compensation Board.

S. 74(3)   Employees of certain designated associations for accident preventions are employees of the Board for superannuation fund purposes.

S. 75   The Board decides which employer is in Schedule I or II, and whether covered by this Act.

S. 87   The Accident Fund is provided by contributions made by employers.

S. 91   Board may increase employer assessment where injury record and accident cost is high.

S. 102   All Board information is privileged and confidential.

S. 104   Provides for yearly assessment on employers to meet compensation claims.

S. 113   Any surplus in the fund must be invested in securities under the Trustee Act.

S. 121   Accidents must be reported to the Board by the employer within three days.

S. 121(2)   Offence $200 fine.

S. 121(3)   Default in reporting, may have to pay amount of compensation awarded.

S. 122   Industrial disease to be treated as injury.

S. 123   Employers may form an association for safety prevention and Board may pay salary of any inspectors.

S. 125   Worker or legal representative in case of death may sue employer in Schedule I for defective machinery or negligence. (Refer to Family Law Reform Act.)

23

Using an Agent

Agency is an agreement between two persons, whereby one (the *principal*) appoints the other (the *agent*) to be a representative in a legally binding way, in transactions with other persons (or *third parties*)—notably, in the making of contracts. There is also another agreement involved in any agency situation—that between the principal and a third party. The law relating to each type of agreement creates different rights and obligations on the parties involved, as explained in this chapter.

There are many reasons why businesspersons find it necessary to appoint agents. First, geographical distance will require, for example, that a manufacturer appoint selling agents in other parts of the country. Second, the need for specialized knowledge will, for example, encourage a manufacturer to use the services of an import agent in a foreign country, or of an advertising firm at home. Third, the scale or complexity of a firm's operations may make imperative the delegation of part of the work to agents. Fourth, the principal's desire not to hire permanent employees but to arrange to have the work done as it arises on an agency basis will cause a property developer, for example, to use architects and realtors on a fee basis. Fifth, a principal's desire not to disclose his or her identity in a business transaction may, for example, cause a business firm planning a takeover of another firm to use several different stockbrokers as agents in acquiring a substantial number of shares.

Agency law has been developed mainly in the courts—that is, as part of the common law. It is only as the result of recent legislation relating to real estate, securities, partnerships, family law, and consumer protection in general, that some aspects of agency are now covered by statute law.

APPOINTMENT OF AN AGENT

Usually, in business, an agent is expressly appointed by means of a written contract setting out the duties and remuneration involved. It is desirable to have such a contract in writing: (a) in order to avoid disputes later on; and (b) to provide the agent with a written authorization that may be produced whenever the agent is required to provide identification and give evidence of appointment. Also, if the agent is required to execute agreements under seal on behalf of the principal, the courts have ruled that the agent must have been appointed under seal. An agent may also be expressly appointed by oral agreement.

A corporation, as a legal person rather than a natural one, must depend on its officers as agents to act on its behalf in all company dealings. Also, the

Partnership Acts of the various provinces specifically provide that all partners are agents of each other. In Ontario, the Family Law Reform Act makes each marriage partner automatically the agent of the other.

ESTABLISHING AN AGENT'S AUTHORITY

In order that an agent may make a binding contract under seal, it is necessary that the agent receive authority under seal. Such a formal authority is called a *power of attorney*, and this is the only case in which an agent's authority is required to be given in special form. The term is also loosely used to refer to an express written authorization of an agency relationship. Thus, for example, an export manager, who is leaving for visits abroad, might authorize his spouse to execute contracts on his behalf. Or, a shareholder who does not intend to be present at the annual general shareholders' meeting might give someone else power of attorney (by a written document called a *proxy*) to vote on her behalf. Or a person about to undergo a medical operation might sign a power of attorney authorizing someone to act on his behalf until he has fully recovered.

Sometimes there is a problem of deciding whether an agency actually exists. In this case, it is the responsibility of the third party dealing with the supposed agent to assure him- or herself of the agent's appointment and limits of authority. This assurance can result from previous dealings with the agent, by an examination of the agent's express authority, or by being told by the principal that the person is acting as an agent, or by contacting the principal to verify the agent's authority.

LEGAL COMPETENCE

Anybody, whether legally competent or not, can make use of an agent. However, the legal status of any contract entered into on the principal's behalf will be determined by the legal capacity of the principal. Thus, a principal who is legally competent will be bound by the contract. However, a principal who is legally incompetent—for example, a minor on whose behalf a contract for non-necessaries has been made—will not be bound by the contract. The key consideration is the legal competence of the principal, not of the agent. Thus a contract entered into by an agent who is legally incompetent (for example, a person under 18 years of age) would still be binding on a principal who is legally competent.

The principal's insanity or death terminates an agent's authority to act for a principal. A problem therefore arises when a so-called power of attorney has been given to a spouse to act for the other spouse while the latter is incapacitated during, for example, an operation or illness. Technically speaking, the agency would be terminated or at least suspended during this period because the principal, while unconscious, would be in no position to authorize or approve the agent's actions. Persons with Alzheimer's disease have realized this. As a result, knowing that their oncoming senility may affect any power of attorney which they have granted, such persons have approached the Ontario Government to pass legislation to make permanent the powers of attorney in such situations. Otherwise, when lack of mental capacity occurs, the only solution is for the party responsible to ask the Court to appoint a Committee to administer the incompetent person's affairs. However, this can be complicated and costly but at the same time assure's the court's supervision, which might not exist in the case of a power of attorney.

TYPES OF AGENTS

Most agents (for example, real estate brokers, lawyers, stock brokers, export agents, insurance agents, debt collectors, credit agencies, and employment agencies) offer their services for a fee to a number of different principals at the same time. Normally they act on behalf of only one principal in any given transaction. There is, however, one example of an agent who acts for parties in the same transaction. This is an *escrow holder* (or stakeholder) who holds cash, real estate deeds, company shares, or other valuables on behalf of two or more parties until a particular act has been completed.

AUTHORITY OF AN AGENT

Often a question arises as to the authority of an agent. Basically such authority is explicitly stated in writing in the agency agreement. However, the authority may extend beyond this.

Apparent Authority

For example, a person who appoints an agent or employs a manager to run a store will probably give the agent explicit instructions on a number of points such as prices, credit, and wages. However, the instructions, even if written down in the form of an express agency agreement, will not cover every facet of the operation. Nevertheless, the agent or manager will have the authority to act in all other matters related to the store as part of the obvious authority as the appointed agent or manager. This is *apparent authority*.

Implied Authority

Suppose that I have a son who one day goes to the best hotel in town and throws a big party for his friends. My son instructs the hotel manager to send the bill to me; and on receipt, I pay it without comment. By my action, the hotel management would be right in assuming that I have ratified my son's conduct. In fact, I have implied that I will meet my son's bills at that hotel whenever he incurs them.

The situation in this case is called, in law, "estoppel." It applies when one person (A) has created a state of affairs that leads another party (B) to conclude that a third party (C) is acting as agent for the first party (A). In the above example, the obvious conclusion drawn was that my son was acting as my agent in running up a bill at the hotel, because I had come along and paid the bill.

If I do not inform them that in future I will not meet the bill or that my son is not my implied agent, the doctrine of estoppel applies.

In dealing with an agent for the first time, a person is required to check into that agent's authority. It cannot be assumed that the doctrine of estoppel automatically applies. However, after transactions with the agent have been honoured by the agent's principal, it is no longer necessary to check into the agent's professed authority.

The mere conduct of the parties may create the inference that the principal has conferred authority to act as an agent on another person. In *Pickering v. Busk* (1812), 15 East 38, the plaintiff asked a broker to purchase hemp and enter it in the broker's name. The broker sold the hemp and, when the plaintiff sued for an accounting, it was held that by placing the goods in the broker's name, the broker was authorized to sell them. The judge, Lord Ellenborough, stated:

> Strangers can only look to the acts of the parties and to the external indicia of property, and not to the private communications which may pass between a principal and his agent broker; and if a person authorizes another to assume the apparent right of disposing of property in the ordinary course of trade, it must be presumed that the apparent authority is the real authority.

This type of agency may be described as *agency by estoppel*, meaning that "a man is not permitted to resist an inference which a reasonable person would necessarily draw from his words or conduct."

Special Authority

Certain agents have special authority flowing from their occupation; for example, an auctioneer has authority to sell, actual possession of goods, and a lien on the goods for his or her services. A *factor* is authorized by common law to sell goods possessed in his or her own name and may give credit, receive payment, and give a discharge. The factor has a lien on the goods for services to the principal. The factor may even pledge the goods, even if this authority has been withheld by the principal. A *broker* ordinarily makes a contract between the principal and a third party. The broker is personally liable if he or she does not indicate that he or she contracts as an agent, but a third party who learns of the principal's identity is free to sue the broker or the principal (*Higgins v. Senior* (1841), 8 M.&W. 834). A *commission agent* is employed to purchase or sell goods at the best possible price, with the title passing directly from seller to the buyer or vice versa without being held by such agent at all. A *del credere* agent not only undertakes to make contracts on behalf of a principal but also to guarantee payment to the principal if the payment is not forthcoming from the third party. This is a secondary liability which, according to the Statute of Frauds, would appear to be required to be put in writing. However, the courts have held that writing is normally not required because the promise of guarantee is only incidental to the real contract of agency.

AGENT OF NECESSITY

Sometimes compelling circumstances may lead a person to act on someone else's behalf, without that person's authorization—for example, calling an ambulance to take an ill person to the hospital or calling a plumber to repair a leaking pipe in a vacationing neighbour's home. However, as a general rule, the common law does not recognize this "agency of necessity." Therefore the person who called the ambulance, plumber, or whatever, will be required to pay if the person on whose behalf the act was undertaken refuses to do so.

One exception to this general rule relates to a wife who, through no fault of her own, is living apart from her husband. Thus the ruling in *J.N. Nabarro & Sons v. Kennedy*, [1954] 2 All E.R. 606, was that "a wife who has been deserted is an agent of necessity for her husband." Such a ruling goes back in time to the husband's former right to take all the wife's property on marriage—thus leaving her with no means of self-support. Nowaways, the common law rule is that such a wife may, pending an order for maintenance, enter into contracts on her husband's behalf, for necessaries such as food, clothing, and shelter for herself and children, should the husband fail to provide for them. However, such necessaries must be suitable to the style of living normally maintained by the husband. Also, the wife must be without adequate means of her own. A husband may be able to escape liability for such purchases if he can show that he has provided his spouse with an ample allowance to run the home.

As mentioned previously, family law legislation in certain provinces has eliminated the "agent of necessity" character of the wife and made her an equal partner in the marriage; thereby she is an agent capable of binding her husband in family purchases, and vice versa.

Another exception recognized by the courts is the captain of a ship who may bind the ship's owners as an agent of necessity when he or she is required to sell a cargo in danger of spoiling, to order emergency repairs, or in salvage operations at sea. Most of the common law decisions on this question refer to incidents which happened before the days of almost instantaneous communication. Nowadays, a ship's captain is usually in constant radio contact with the vessel's owners.

These exceptions should not be confused with "good samaritan" or "rescue" cases, where the rescuer arranges medical assistance or ambulance services for an unconscious person. An agency can come into play only when there is a competent principal who has authorized the action; in this case the principal is not competent.

RATIFICATION

A person may profess to be an agent of a principal without any express authority to do so. This would be the case of my son's hotel bill. If I later honour his obligations, then I have ratified his act.

As another example, suppose that a friend, knowing that I am a part-time farmer, has the opportunity to buy some hay cheaply and orders 4,000 bales for me. This could be done without any express, implied, or apparent agency simply by stating that he was acting as my agent and hoping that I would subsequently ratify his act. If I ratify his act, the contract is said to date from the time my so-called agent originally entered into the contract.

If, in the meantime, the hay has been sold to a third party and I have not yet ratified the act, my subsequent ratification would be ineffective. This is a situation in which the law protects the least responsible of two innocent parties—namely, the other party. I lose the hay because my delay in ratification has permitted a new and completely innocent party to become involved.

The common law position on ratification was stated by Tindal C.J. in *Wilson v. Truman* (1843), 6 Man. & G. at page 242 as follows: "an act done for another by a person not assuming to act for himself, but for such other person, although, without any precedent, authority, whatsoever, becomes the act of the principal, if subsequently ratified by him."

Sometimes ratification is ineffective or cannot be made. For example, suppose my agent entered into a contract to insure a cottage I own. However, just before she did so, the cottage burned down. Obviously, the contract can no longer be ratified because I could not myself have entered into the contract at that time.

In the case of *Keighley, Maxted & Co. v. Durant*, [1901] A.C. 240, Roberts, a corn merchant, was authorized to buy corn on behalf of another company as well as on his own behalf at a certain price. He bought the corn, without disclosing the agency relationship, at a higher price. There was agreement between the joint buyers the next day on the purchase but, when they failed to take delivery, the wheat was sold at a loss and the seller sued both. The seller recovered against the agent but vis-à-vis the principal, "a contract made by a person intending to contract on behalf of a third party, but without his authority, cannot be ratified by the third party, so as to render him liable to sue or to be sued on the contract *where the person who made the contract did not profess at the time of making it to be acting on behalf of a principal.*"

In summary, the following are the prerequisites for ratification:

1. The agent must contract for a competent principal.
2. The agent must act on behalf of a principal.
3. The principal must be in existence. See, for example, *Kelner v. Baxter* (1866), L.R. 2 C.P. 174, where the promoters of an unformed company entered into a contract on its behalf. When the company went bankrupt, the creditors sued the promoters, who alleged that this contract had been ratified by the company on incorporation. Willes J., giving the court judgment, stated: "Could the company become liable by a mere ratification? Clearly not. Ratification can only be by a person ascertained at

the time of the act done—by a person in existence either actually or in contemplation of law; as in the case of the assignees of bankrupts and administrators, whose title, for the protection of the estate, vests by relation."

4. The agent's act must be capable of being lawfully done by the principal—not, for example, the agent acting for a minor.
5. The principal must be capable of doing the act when ratification occurs.

Ratification may take place by words or by conduct accepting the benefit of the contract.

BREACH OF IMPLIED WARRANTY OF AUTHORITY

If a person states to a third party that he is acting for a principal when, in fact, he has not been so authorized, or his agency relationship has ceased to exist, or if there never was a principal, no contract will come into existence. The law also provides that, because the person purporting to be an agent gave an implied warranty of authority, he can be sued for the tort of deceit. If necessary, the third party can ask the court to rescind the contract.

An agent who honestly believes that he or she has authority to bind an existing principal will also be liable to be sued for "breach of implied warranty of authority" if such authority does not in fact exist. This may be because the principal is no longer alive when the agent enters into a contract or the contract in which the agent enters is *ultra vires* (beyond the powers of) the corporation represented.

DUTIES OF A PRINCIPAL TO AN AGENT

Unless specifically provided otherwise in the agency contract, the principal must:

1. pay the agent the agreed fee;
2. reimburse the agent for all expenses incurred in carrying out the principal's business, and indemnify him or her for all lawful acts and liabilities incurred (It should be noted that the agent has a lien on all the principal's goods in the agent's possession and, in some circumstances, may sell those goods to recover expenses);
3. observe all other conditions of the agency contract;
4. credit the agent with all sales (as opposed to orders) in the agent's territory—in other words, pay a commission only on filled orders, which would depend on stock available, credit rating of the customer, delivery date required, and so on.

DUTIES OF AN AGENT TO A PRINCIPAL

The relationship of an agent to a principal is said to be that of a contract of "utmost good faith." Such a contract requires that the agent always inform the principal of anything that might possibly be to the principal's disadvantage or advantage and let the principal (rather than the agent on the principal's behalf) decide which course to follow.

The main duties of an agent are as follows:

1. *The agent must obey the contract.* The agent should fulfil the terms of the contract and may not exceed his or her authority. The principal may be bound by apparent authority if the agent exceeds the actual authority and the third party has not been notified of any restriction of authority. However, the principal will always be able to hold the agent liable for any excess of authority.

2. *The agent must exercise diligence and display all the skills professed.* For example, a person professing to be an experienced export agent.

3. *The agent must not act negligently.* Thus a lawyer may be sued for not acting properly in representing a client—for example, in failing to sue before a claim is barred by a Statute of Limitation. Chartered accountants who have prepared financial statements for their clients have even been held liable to third parties who relied on such statements.

4. *Notice to the agent is notice to the principal.* This applies, for example, in an apartment building where the superintendent is given a notice to quit by a tenant. This is deemed to be notice to the principal. Revocation of an offer made to the agent is as effective as if the revocation were communicated directly to the principal.

5. *The agent may not normally delegate authority.* This is because an agent is a delegate of the principal and a delegate may not delegate his or her powers—this in accordance with the legal maxim of *delegatus non potest delegare.* Thus the principal is not responsible for the actions of an agent's delegate. This could arise, for example, if the agent were assisted by a brother or friend in negotiating a contract with a third party. The third party's only recourse, if dissatisfied, would be to sue such agent or delegate for breach of the implied warranty of authority.

6. *The agent must make an accounting to the principal.* Nowadays some agents—such as lawyers, accountants, and real estate agents—are required to handle their principal's funds in the normal course of their business. Legislatures or governing societies have also passed laws that require these agents to keep separate trust accounts, which are subject to regular external auditing.

7. With regard to the fiduciary or "utmost good faith" provision of the agency contract, the agent:

    (a) *must make full disclosure of all material facts*, particularly if he is going to sell any of his own items to the principal. This applies even if his own items are the best available in the circumstances;

    (b) *must not make secret profits or secret commissions.* For example, by using the principal's business premises to carry on other transactions, by representing both buyer and seller in the same transaction, or by accepting gifts or sums of money as an inducement to do business. The agent is liable to account to the principal for any such profits received. Thus in an English case, *Andrews v. Ramsay & Co.*, [1903] 2 K.B. 635, an auctioneer who undertook to sell property for 50 pounds commission, but who also received 20 pounds from the purchaser, was held not only to forfeit the 20 pounds received but also to have disentitled himself to the promised 50 pounds commission;

   (c) *must not carry a competing line.* However, it is permissible for an agent (an equipment dealer or food broker) to represent two or more principals in non-competing lines, as long as the agency agreement does not specifically forbid it.

8. If the agent breaches the contract, the principal can at once terminate it; becomes entitled to any secret profit; may repudiate any contracts with third parties; and can refuse payment of commission to the agent. An innocent third party may also repudiate a contract with the principal.

9. *An agent may not become the principal party in the transaction.* This could occur as in the case of *Johnson v. Kearly*, [1908] 2 K.B. 514, where a broker acting as an agent bought goods, added a markup, and sold them to his principal. The judge stated:

> It is absolutely inconsistent with the duty of an agent for purchase, in as much as it is the essential idea of a purchase through a broker or any other agent of the kind that the whole benefit of the purchase should go to the principal and the sole interest of the agent should be in the commission allowed him by his principal. The office of the broker is to make privity of contract between two principals, and this is entirely incompatible with making a contract at one price with the one and a corresponding contract at another price with the other.

Officers of a corporation (for example, the company president or the town mayor) are in fact agents employed in a fiduciary capacity and bound by all the rules relating to agents. Thus, for example, the Business Corporations Act of Ontario expressly requires company officers to reveal any personal interests in contracts being negotiated by their corporation. Similarly, elected municipal officers must make full revelation of any personal involvement in contracts negotiated by the municipality or face civil suits and criminal charges under the Criminal Code.

LIABILITY OF A PRINCIPAL TO THIRD PERSONS

A third party dealing with an agent for the first time must normally enquire into the agent's authority. The only exception is if such authority can be deemed customary in the type of business of the agent—that is, held by all similar agents.

If a principal has appointed the agent to a particular job—for example, general manager of a store—the principal is customarily bound by all acts carried out by the agent in the performance of normal duties.

A principal, dealings with third persons, can have three different types of liability: in contract; in tort; and in criminal law.

Contract Liability

In contract law, there are three different possible liability situations: first, where the agent, acting on behalf of a named principal, enters into an agreement with a third person; second, where the agent acts on behalf of an undisclosed principal in entering into such an agreement; and third, where the agent acts on his own behalf, instead of his principal's, in entering into the agreement.

Named Principal.   So long as an agent describes him- or herself to third parties as an agent, identifies the principal, and acts according to the agency agreement, the principal alone will be responsible to third parties for any commitments entered into by the agent. The agent incurs no liability. This is so even if the agent acts outside his or her real authority but within his or her apparent authority. Of course, the principal could hold the agent liable for excesses of authority.

The following statement was made in the case of *Edmunds v. Bushell and Jones* (1865), L.R. 1 Q.B. 97, where the manager drew and accepted drafts (that is, negotiable instruments) binding his principal, although the principal had prohibited this practice. The court said: "If a man employs another as an agent in a character which involves a particular authority, he cannot by a secret reservation divest him of authority." This would apply, for example, in circumstances where the manager of a shoe store is told by his principal not to buy shoes retailing at more than $25 per pair, after the store had carried shoes up to $75 per pair. If the manager ordered $5,000 worth of $50 shoes, from a company which had not been notified of this restriction on the agent's authority, the principal would have to pay this account, even though the principal might decide to dismiss the manager or hold him or her accountable.

Undisclosed Principal.   If the agent identifies himself as an agent, but refuses to disclose the identity of his principal, the third party has a choice either to sign the contract or refuse to do so. No complaints can be made after the contract has been signed. An example of such a situation occurs when a real estate firm is assembling options to purchase land and buildings for a projected real estate development project for a client who wishes to remain unknown.

To protect himself from personal liability in the case of an unnamed principal, the agent should, before or at the time of the contract, describe himself specifically as an agent only, without personal liability. When an agent acts for an undisclosed principal, and either the third party or the principal discover the identity of the other, they may sue and be sued under the contract, since the contract in reality exists only between them.

Of course, the principal, who is bound by any contracts entered into with third parties, can sue the agent for any breach of the agency agreement, including the agent's acting outside of his or her real authority. Just as it is the principal who has assumes the liability to third parties, so also is it the principal who has any rights under the contract signed by his agent. It is consequently the principal, not the agent, who can if necessary sue to enforce the contract or sue for damages if a breach of contract occurs.

Agent Acting on Own Behalf.   In some cases an agent will contract on his or her own behalf without revealing the existence of the principal. Then the third party has the choice of suing either the agent or, if his or her existence is discovered, the principal. However, the third party will have no recourse to the principal if the agent has acted as the true principal by describing him- or herself, for example, as the owner rather than the charterer of a ship, or if the third party has already sued the agent before discovering the principal's identity, or finally if the principal has already settled with the agent and paid the price involved before the principal's identity is discovered (*Armstrong v. Stokes* (1872), L.R. 7 Q.B. 508).

Tort Liability

In tort law, a principal may vicariously be held liable for torts committed by the agent—for example, if an agent causes a car accident while on his principal's business. However, the principal will be vicariously liable only if it can be proven that the agent was acting in the course of the principal's business. It is easier to claim vicarious liability in the employer-employee situation, where the employer controls the actions of employees, than where the agent acts independently.

If the agent commits a fraud *in the course of his employment*, both the agent and the principal are liable. If the fraud is outside the scope of his or her authority, only the agent will be liable. This proposition was expressed as follows in *S. Pearson & Son Ltd. v. Dublin Corp.*, [1907] A.C. 351:

> It matters not in respect of principal and agent (who represent but one person) which of them possesses the guilty knowledge or which of them makes the incriminating statement. If between them the misrepresentation is made so as to induce the wrong, and thereby damages are caused, it matters not which is the person who makes the misrepresentation or which is the person who had the guilty knowledge.

Another way of stating this would be the situation which may arise in selling a house. The seller (principal) could deliberately hide a latent defect by telling the agent the structure is sound, or hire an agent whom the principal knows has a reputation for falsifying or withholding information to achieve a sale. In either case the principal is liable; the agent is liable only in the latter case.

For a comment on the professional liability of an insurance company for the actions of its agent, see the case of *Fine's Flowers Ltd. v. General Accident Insurance et al (1974)* 49 D.L.R. (3rd) 64, in Chapter 4 of this book.

Criminal Liability

In criminal law, a principal will only be held guilty of a criminal offence committed by an agent only if the principal is a co-conspirator. An exception occurs where the agent is driving a company car. The company as principal may be liable to pay parking and speeding tickets in the case of quasi-criminal (provincial) offences.

TERMINATION OF AN AGENT'S AUTHORITY

The usual ways in which an agent's authority is terminated are as follows:

1. *No time period specified.* In this case, there is usually a provision in the agency agreement for one party, either the principal or the agent, to give written notice to the other of intention to terminate. If there is no provision, the agency agreement may be terminated at any time.
2. *Time period specified.* Here, the agency would be terminated by the expiry of the stated time period.
3. *Special transactions.* If the agency had been established for a specific transaction or project, the agency would be terminated on completion of that task.
4. *Frustration.* For example, a house listed for sale by a real estate broker (the agent) suddenly being destroyed by fire.
5. *Legal incapacity of principal or agent.* For example, because of death, insanity, bankruptcy, or, in the case of a business corporation, dissolution and surrender of charter.

In the case of revocation of an agent's authority, the principal may still be held liable to third parties, it should be noted, on the basis of the *doctrine of estoppel*. This is the legal principle that a person can be held liable for contracts entered into by another person if he or she has previously approved such contracts. The only way that a person can avoid this liability is by communicating to third parties that he or she will not be responsible for any future contracts that the "agent" enters into.

The ultimate responsibility for termination of the agent's authority belongs to the principal. If the principal dismisses an agent or restricts the agent's authority in any way, then the principal is under an obligation to spread this information to all persons with whom the agent has carried out business on the principal's behalf, or who might be under the impression that the agent is still authorized to carry out such transactions. This can be done by means of telephone calls, written letters, or advertisements in newspapers and in the provincial gazettes (the official publications of provincial legislatures which contain all legal notices issued weekly by the provincial government).

If an advertisement (for example, that an agent has ceased to represent a certain company) is placed in the provincial gazette, this advertisement is said to be *constructive notice*; that is, the public is deemed to have been informed whether the notice has been read or not.

Usually an agency will be terminated in accordance with the agreement made between the principal and the agent. No period of notice is prescribed as in the case of employment.

Well drawn-up franchise agreements will usually provide that the agency cannot be terminated without refunding the agent's deposit. Many franchise companies retain the right by contract to buy out any franchisee who breaks any of the conditions of the contract.

By law, the principal will usually remain liable for any contract made by the agent involving third parties. Therefore, in the case of a retiring partner, in order to ensure that he, as a former principal, incurs no further liability towards lenders or suppliers who have dealt with the partnership, he must ensure that they are informed of his retirement. Otherwise, he may be bound if they extend further credit in the belief that he is still connected with the partnership.

The principal may not revoke the agent's authority at will where the agent has given valuable consideration for it—such as in a franchise agreement. This principle is illustrated in the case of *Read v. Anderson* (1884), 13 Q.B.D. 779. The court held that revocation of authority would have involved an injury to the agent which must have been in contemplation of the parties when the contract of employment was made. It stated:

> There is a contract of employment between the principal and the agent which expressly or by implication regulates their relations; and if as part of this contract the principal has expressly or impliedly bargained not to revoke the authority and to indemnify the agent for acting in the ordinary course of his trade or business, he cannot be allowed to break the contract.

Physical or financial death (bankruptcy) of the principal immediately terminates an agent's authority. Therefore, for any default on contracts made after such events, the third party's only remedy is against the agent for *breach of an implied warranty of authority*. Of course, in the case of physical death, the executors of the deceased's estate would be liable for any contracts legally made by the agent before the principal's death. It would appear that powers of attorney made under seal would not be affected by the principal's death but remain irrevocable for the purposes intended.

Insanity also terminates an agency. In the case of *Yonge v. Toynbee*, [1901] 1 K.B. 215, the defendant hired solicitors to defend a case and then became insane. When the plaintiff learned of this, he moved to have the case dismissed and sued the solicitors for *breach of warranty of authority*. The appeal court held the solicitor-agents liable. As soon as insanity occurs, it terminates an agent's authority for all purposes, whether the third party has notice of it or not.

REMEDIES OF THE PRINCIPAL

Because of the "utmost good faith" relationship that the agent bears to the principal, the latter may always repudiate the agency contract when a breach of trust occurs. In such circumstances, the principal does not have to pay any commission to the agent and may claim any secret profits made by him or her.

Insofar as a third party is concerned, a principal is bound by an agent acting with implied or apparent authority. However, as a remedy, he or she may recover from the agent on the grounds that the agent exceeded authority.

In all legal contracts entered into by the agent acting within the scope of his or her authority, so long as the agency relationship is revealed, the principal, not the agent, is liable.

REMEDIES OF THE AGENT

An agent has a lien for any expenses incurred in the course of employment against any of the principal's goods which are still in the agent's possession. Also, an agent can always sue for indemnification for any expenses incurred.

An agent ranks as a preferred creditor for three months' wages up to a total of $500 under the federal Bankruptcy Act.

REVIEW QUESTIONS

1. What is an agency? What are the reasons for its existence?
2. How can an agent be appointed?
3. What is a power of attorney? Provide three examples.
4. How does the legal competence of an agent affect contracts entered into on his principal's behalf?
5. Explain the following types of agent:
   (a) insurance agent
   (b) credit agency
   (c) escrow holder
   (d) stockbroker
   (e) factor
   (f) broker
   (g) commission agent
   (h) del credere agent.
6. What is meant by the apparent authority of an agent? Illustrate with examples of your own.
7. What is the doctrine of estoppel? Give an example of a situation to which it might apply.
8. What is an agent of necessity? What are the recognized exceptions?
9. What is meant by ratification with regard to agency? What conditions must exist? When can a contract not be ratified?
10. A contract made with D by B, who states falsely that she is the agent for C, is binding on both C and D. Comment.
11. When is an agent liable to be sued for breach of implied warranty of authority?
12. What are the duties of a principal to the agent?
13. What are the duties of an agent to the principal?
14. If a principal revokes the contract with the agent, the agent should at once notify interested third parties. Comment.

15. What is constructive notice of agency? When might this occur?
16. In all contracts entered into by the agent, the principal not the agent is liable so long as the agency relationship has been revealed to the third party. Comment.
17. What is a principal's liability for torts committed by his or her agent? Give three examples of possible torts. In what way, if any, does this liability differ from that of an employer for torts committed by employees?
18. An agent may properly sell goods to the principal without disclosing that they belong to the agent, if the goods are exactly what the principal requires. Comment.
19. An agent is entitled to deduct legitimate overdue expenses from the proceeds of a sale before remitting the amount to his principal. Comment.
20. Genearlly, agents may "quit" without giving notice to their principal. Comment.

PROBLEMS

(*Note:* In problems 1 to 4, A = agent, P = principal, and T = third party.)

1. A was mayor of Edmonton. Before his election he acquired for $8,000 a 40% interest in undeveloped lands which lay in the path of future development. As mayor, A actually participated in the city council's deliberations for replotting the said lands. As a result of such deliberations, a scheme was devised which significantly enhanced the value of the lands as a result of which A enjoyed a windfall profit of $80,000. The City of Edmonton claimed as a principal the amount as profit for which A was accountable due to his fiduciary position with the city as its mayor. What should be the result?
2. P listed his property with A, a real estate agent. P agreed to pay A a commission if A procured an offer to purchase. Such an offer was procured, but it contained an ambiguous term which A failed to draw to the attention of P. As a result of the ambiguity the sale fell through. A brought an action to recover his commission according to the terms of the agreement and lost. A appealed. What is your decision? Refer to *Starr & Co. v. Watson*, [1973] 1 O.R. 148 (C.A.).
3. One EG had granted a gratuitious power of attorney to A. Subsequently EG became mentally incompetent. While in that state EG purported to grant a power of attorney to B and in that grant expressly revoked the first power of attorney granted to A. A sought a declaration that the grant to B was a nullity, and an injunction restraining B from acting under the power of attorney and damages. Should A succeed? Discuss this case in the light of mental incompetency and insanity. Refer to *Wilkinson v. Young*, [1972] 2 O.R. 239.
4. T entered into a contract with A, an agent of D Co., for the purchase of a trailer home. P Co. held out A generally as having authority to sell its

trailers and conduct its business in Whitehorse. But A's authority was limited in that he was not permitted to conclude any transaction until it had been approved by the Edmonton head office. Also the contract itself stated "Not valid unless signed and accepted by an officer of the Co." T knew of the limitation on A's authority as A had told him of it. After oral agreement had been reached, A was unable to obtain approval from the head office for the deal. Finally A told T that he had received approval by telephone and he signed the contract himself on behalf of P Co. P Co. refused to honour the contract. T sued on it and won at trial on the basis that A held out as possessing authority to act as he did. P Co. appealed. What is your decision? Refer to *Jensen v. South Trail Mobile Ltd.*, [1972] 5 W.W.R. 7 (Alta. C.A.).

5. Pratt, a real estate salesman for the plaintiff, realizing that Vacca Brothers had properties in which Ronvic was interested, obtained from the latter a $99,000 offer for two properties, and got the Vacca Brothers to accept this offer. It appeared that the Brothers did not read or write English, but they agreed to the purchase providing they had to pay only the salesman's fee of 5%, the form showing Pratt as the vendor's agent. The offer to purchase also included a provision whereby the seller agreed to service the lots, the cost of which was eventually calculated at $19,500. Pratt was paid $2,000 at the moment of acceptance and later tried to get the Vacca Brothers to sign a direction to pay the balance of the commission on closing. The Vacca Brothers are objecting to paying any commission explaining that their agent did not explain that they would have to pay the $19,000 to service the lots. Discuss this situation only with respect to the possible liability of the Vacca Brothers towards Pratt. Refer to *Leng Pugh Real Estate Ltd. v. Ronvic Construction Co Ltd.* (1974), 1 O.R. (2d) 539.

6. In this case, one solicitor made an offer of settlement to the claimant's solicitor who had knowledge that the claimant, his principal, had just died. The claimant's solicitor accepted the offer. The original solicitor/offeror, on learning of the claimant's death, repudiated the contract. What is the law covering this situation, assuming the solicitors were acting as agents? Refer to *MacKenzie v. Carrol* (1975), 53 D.L.R. (3d) 699.

7. This is a claim for purchase made by the defendant's wife both before and after separation. It was discovered that some of the purchases were made by the defendant himself, that although he claimed not to know of the accounts opened after the separation, he paid some money on account, and that the purchases were not extravagant. What law may determine the defendant's liability, if any, in this case? Refer to *Robert Simpson Co. Ltd. v. Twible* (1973), 1 O.R. (2d) 629.

READINGS

Hadikin Brothers Lumbering Ltd. v. Canadian Surety Co. (1975), 57 D.L.R. (3d) 632 (B.C. S.C.).

Facts: The owners of a lumber company, Hadikin Brothers, insured a motor vehicle consisting of a 1971 chip trailer which they acquired in April 1973 to haul up to twenty-five tons of wood chips at a time from their mill to buyers. In December, while the driver was proceeding out of the mill yard, the trailer became slightly stuck and applying more power, he experienced the sensation of the truck hitting a stone wall. On examining the trailer he observed that the main beam of the trailer had collapsed. The owners sued and eventually several adjusters successively examined the damage, the last appraiser estimating the total loss at $10,039.77 after deducting $2,000 from approximately $12,000 estimated to be the depreciated loss—that is, by deducting the scrap value of the damaged trailer which was kept by the mill. The insurers refused to pay, claiming that:

1. The adjuster had merely recommended a settlement.
2. The mill owners had given no consideration for the settlement.
3. The adjuster had no authority to bind the insurers.
4. Both parties were mistaken about coverage because this was an excluded risk—that is, loss not caused by a collission.

Held: In reviewing the evidence of the experts (witnesses) called to examine the breakage it was obvious that the breakage was not caused by a structural defect of the main beam but by a break caused by the wheels becoming stuck in the mud of the mill yard.

All the adjusters proceeded on the basis that the loss was covered. By allowing the plaintiffs to keep the damaged trailer as salvage and because of the fact that the plaintiffs immediately ordered a new trailer, it was established as a fact that both parties believed the adjusters were settling the loss. The fact that the brothers gave up their right to sue by accepting the settlement is valuable consideration (*Haigh v. Brooks* (1839), 10 Ad. & E. 309).

Did the adjuster Paling act within his authority? If he did not have actual authority, did he have ostensible (apparent) authority?

Per Andrews J.:

. . . In my opinion the law [whether an insurance adjuster has the authority to bind his company, as principal, to a settlement within the provisions of the policy] was correctly stated by Diplock L. J. in *Freeman & Lockyer v. Buckhurst Park Properties (Mangal) Ltd.*, [1964] 2 Q.B. 480 at pp. 503-4: "By so doing [putting the agent in a position carrying with it a usual authority] the principal represents to anyone who becomes aware that the agent is so acting that the agent has authority to enter on behalf of the principal into contracts with other persons of the kind which an agent so acting in the conduct of his principal's business has usually 'actual' authority to enter into.". . .

[As to the argument that there was a mutual mistake because the loss was not covered by a peril insured against,] . . . I have already found that the loss occurred as a result of a collision rather than a structural defect in the trailer. Consequently the loss was an insured risk. . . . Paling [the adjuster], on

behalf of the defendant company, took the risk that the chip trailer could not
be repaired economically. If on the true construction of the contract one of
the parties has assumed the risk in question the doctrine of mutual mistake
[i.e., that both made different mistakes about the condition of the trailer] has
no application: *Chitty on Contracts*, 23rd ed., para. 198. . . .

Judgment for plaintiff.

General Motors Acceptance Corp. of Canada Ltd. v. Weisman (1979), 96
D.L.R. (3d) 159 (Ont. Co. Ct.).

Facts: On August 2, 1975, Dan Kane Chev Olds Cadillac sold a Chevrolet
van to Weisman, the defendant, an officer of Universal Sports Newfoundland Ltd. It was disclosed that Anson, who was also an officer of the latter
company, previously tried to buy this van through the salesman Maini, but
since his credit standing was not satisfactory, it was arranged that the
purchase order should be signed by Weisman, a Toronto lawyer, who had
agreed to become a director of the Newfoundland company in whose name
the van was eventually purchased. There was some discussion about Weisman paying cash in this case, but when his credit card was investigated and
found satisfactory the purchase order was made out to Universal Sports etc.
and signed "Universal Sports (Newfoundland) Ltd. per S. J. Weisman," as a
credit transaction. It transpired that the Company had not yet been incorporated, but it had been planned to do so. Weisman had been asked to be a
director and he stated that he intended to sign only in that capacity. This
suit is against Weisman because, since the company did not exist and he
signed as an agent, he is personally liable.

Held per Macnab Co. Ct. J.:

The court [in *Black v. Smallwood* (1966), 39 A.L.J. 405 said:] ". . . the
fundamental question in every case [where a director has signed on behalf of
a non-existent corporation] must be what the parties intended or must be
fairly understood to have intended. If they have expressed themselves in
writing, the writing must be construed by the court. . . . [I]n the present case
[*Black v. Smallwood*] the respondents did not contract, or purport to contract on behalf of the non-existent company. They simply subscribed the
name of the non-existent company and added their own signatures as
directors in the belief that the company had been formed and that they were
directors. The fact that their signatures appeared as part of the company's
signature did not make them parties to the contract. . . ."
   . . . [I]n the case of *Newborne v. Sensolid (Great Britain) Ltd.*, [1954] 1 Q.B.
45 [where a writ was issued against the company buyers for failure to accept
goods] . . . "it was discovered that at the time when the contract was signed
the company . . . was not registered, and steps were taken to substitute for the
name of the company, as plaintiff, that of [the person whose signature had
authenticated the company contract.] . . . This contract purports to be a
contract by the company; it does not purport to be a contract by Mr.

Newborne [the signatory]. . . . The only person who had an contract here was the company, and Mr. Newborne's signature merely confirmed the company's signature. . . . [A]s the company was not in existence when the contract was signed there was never a contract. . . ."

[In *Wickberg v. Shatsky* (1969), 4 **D.L.R.** (3d) 540,] the headnote states: "Although one who signs purportedly as an agent for an unformed corporation or other non-existent principal may become personally liable for the performance of the contract on the ground that it must have been intended to bind someone, where the one with whom the agent so purports to contract is unaware that the principal is an unformed corporation, the parties do not share the same presumed intention and the agent is not liable in the absence of some warranty to authority or fraud.". . .

. . . In the result, the contract is a nullity, except . . . as against Anson who signed as co-purchaser. . . .

It might well be argued that Weisman warranted that the Company he purported to sign for was in existence, but since there is no claim for damages for breach of warranty of authority, or for fraud, I make no findings as to either of these possible heads of damages.

Action dismissed.

APPENDIX 23-A: TABLE OF COMPARISON: EMPLOYMENT, INDEPENDENT CONTRACTOR, AND AGENCY

Employer/Employee	Independent Contractor	Agency
1. two people employer/employee	generally two people principal contractor	three people involved, principal/agent and third party
2. paid by salary	paid by contract price	remuneration by commission
3. employer provides tools and supervises job	not supervised	allotted territory, works un-unsupervised
4. except for purchasing agents, sales clerks, etc., normally does not bring about contracts with third parties	contracts for independent contrator do not bind the person on whose behalf the work is done	main occupation is to bring about contracts between the principal and a third party
5. an employee who commits a crime is fully liable	an independent contractor who commits a crime is fully liable	an agent committing a crime is fully liable
6. generally employer not bound for contracts entered into by employees, except where expressly authorized or where in nature of employment, i.e., sales staff	person for whom work being done has generally no contractual liability for contracts entered into by independent contractors, except where a construction lien is registered by unpaid workers or suppliers	if agent acts and states he is acting as an agent for an existing principal then principal is liable. However, if agent's principal non-existent or agency not disclosed, then agent is fully liable
7. in torts, if employee is acting in scope of employment, then employer is liable. If employee is on "frolic of his own," then employer is not liable	in torts, except where person for whom work is being done is aware that work is of injurious nature, the principal is not responsible for independent contractor's torts	the liability of an employer for his agent's torts are quite similar to those of the employer/employee relationship
8. the employment relationship is terminated either by the arrival of a condition terminating the contract or is governed by the common law or statutory rules of notice unless grounds for firing without notice exists	the relationship is legally terminated only when the contract conditions are completed	this relationship may be terminated without notice unless a special contract exists— for example, where special consideration has been given in the case of an exclusive distributorship, etc.

6

MARKETING LAW

In this part of the book, we examine first of all the various provincial and federal laws that a business firm must respect in marketing its goods and services. Many of these laws, designed to protect the consumer, are of relatively recent origin. All are constantly being revised. We then consider the law relating to patents, trademarks, copyrights, and bailment.

24

Sale of Goods

A sale is a transaction in which the ownership of a good is transferred from one person to another in exchange for a monetary consideration. Over the years, such transactions have been one of the most fertile sources of legal dispute, for it is very easy for one of the parties involved to imagine, rightly or wrongly, that he or she has in some way been cheated. These disputes were taken to the common law courts for adjudication. From the decisions of these courts over many hundreds of years were established the principles of law governing transactions involving the sale of goods.

In 1893, the British Parliament passed a law called the Sale of Goods Act which codified all these common law principles. Subsequently, all the common law provinces of Canada adopted this Act in almost its original form.

DEFINITIONS

Under s. 1 of the Sale of Goods Act, a buyer is defined as a person agreeing to buy, or buying, goods which are defined as any "chattel personal" except choses in action (legal claims) and money.

A contract for the sale of goods is one whereby a seller transfers or agrees to transfer ownership (or title) to goods to a purchaser for a price or some other consideration. The Act provides that a sale transfers title immediately while an agreement to sell provides for a transfer in the future.

JURISDICTION

Often a contract is made between residents of two different legal jurisdictions—for example, a sale of goods contract between a wholesaler in Manitoba and a manufacturer in Ontario. In the event of a dispute, it may be important to decide in which jurisdiction the contract was made so that the courts may apply the appropriate provincial statutory laws. Usually, the contract will contain a clause stating which law will apply—for example, "this contract is subject to the Ontario Sale of Goods Act."

Sometimes the court may be called on to decide which law should be applied. Generally, this is the law most closely connected with the contract, as determined by an examination of the circumstances.

SCOPE OF THE SALE OF GOODS ACT

The Sale of Goods Act applies only to the sale of tangible moveable goods (called *chattels*). It does not cover the following transactions:

1. *real property sales*—namely, land and buildings;
2. *barter*—which consists of the exchange of one non-monetary item for another;
3. *consignment sales*—that is, the sale of goods stocked by a retailer who receives a commission for effecting a sale while title passes directly from owner to buyer;
4. *mortgages and pledges*—which are not sales of goods because they have no intrinsic value;
5. *bailment*—a contract by which an owner of goods temporarily entrusts custody of them to someone else (for example, a suit to be dry cleaned);
6. *paper money, shares, bonds, and other securities*—items considered to have no intrinsic value;
7. *materials supplied incidentally in carrying out a labour contract*—for example, repairing a boat or manufacturing furniture by contract, as the final value of the goods results more from the contribution of the skilled labour than the materials used;
8. *conditional sales*—goods sold on credit, whereby ownership passes to the purchaser only when the last payment has been made.

Also, the Sale of Goods Act applies only to *those transactions not specifically covered by the terms of a sales contract and transactions governed by a contract in which there are no provisions covering the particular issue.* All terms in a sales contract are respected by the courts. The courts will not interfere with parties who desire to set their own terms and arrive at them through a "meeting of the minds.".

The Sale of Goods Act applies not only to actual sales but also to agreements to sell. In a sale, ownership passes from the seller to the buyer according to the rules set out in this chapter, unless something is specifically stated to the contrary. However, in an agreement to sell, title is to pass at a later time, as stipulated in the agreement.

THE CONTRACT OF SALE

The requirements of contract law apply to all contracts of sale. Although a minor cannot be bound by a contract for non-necessities, under s. 3, minors and mentally incompetent persons are liable to pay for necessaries such as food, lodging, and clothing.

The sale contract may be oral or in writing, or both, or may be implied from the conduct of the parties themselves, such as a person picking boxes of strawberries in a "pick-your-own" field. The provisions of the Statute of Frauds relating to the requirement of part performance or a memorandum in writing for all sales of goods over $40 have been included in s. 5(1).

Section 7 provides that if specific goods are being sold and perish without the knowledge of the seller, the contract is rendered "void." The same applies to an agreement to sell specific goods.

The price of goods may be agreed to in the contract or determined in the course of business, such as the market price or a fair price, decided by a mutually acceptable third party such as an appraiser. In any event, the buyer must pay a reasonable price (s. 9). If the determination of the price is left up to a third party who does not act, the buyer must pay a reasonable price.

The Sale of Goods Act provisions apply both to existing goods and future goods—that is, those which are still to be grown or manufactured (s. 6).

TITLE

The difference between *title* (or legal ownership) and possession should be emphasized. According to the Sale of Goods Act, a sale occurs only when title passes from a seller to a buyer. The mere fact of possession does not mean that a sale has taken place.

Obviously, in any proposed sale, it is important to determine whether the seller really has title, or only possession, for only the owner can transfer ownership to someone else. Consequently, if I buy a car that has been stolen, I risk losing the money that I have paid if the true owner comes along or the police seize the stolen car. The only exception to the above rule, that only the true owner can pass title, is a situation in which the true owner has conferred apparent ownership on another person—for example, when goods are placed in the custody of an agent or factor.

F.O.B., C.I.F., AND C.O.D. QUOTATIONS

In a normal sale of goods, title passes from seller to buyer either at the time specified in the contract of sale, if there is one or, alternatively, according to the rules described in the Sale of Goods Act under the heading "Risk of Loss." However, when the buyer and seller are located some distance away from each other, the matter is not so simple. Over the years, rules dealing with various methods of shipment have established when title passes if not otherwise provided. Thus, in an F.O.B. (or "free on board") contract, the title is said to pass only at the time and place stated in the quotation. Thus if, for example, the quotation is "F.O.B. port of origin" then the title (and risk) passes at the moment when the goods are loaded onto a "public carrier" (boat, truck, rail, airplane, etc.) at the point of origin. If the quotation reads "F.O.B. port of destination," then the title passes only when the goods have reached the destination and the purchaser is notified.

In a C.I.F. (or "cost, insurance, and freight") quotation, title passes to the buyer at the seller's freight depot. However, the seller pays the insurance and freight charges involved in shipping the goods to the buyer, and the "C.I.F. price" quoted to the buyer will have included these costs. Sometimes the price quoted is a "C. & F." price—which means that the buyer will have to arrange the insurance.

In a C.O.D. ("cash on delivery") quotation, the seller or his agent have both possession and risk of loss of the goods until the cash has been paid and the goods delivered, even if title has already passed to the buyer.

RISK OF LOSS

Any risk of loss from theft or damage of goods in transit lies with the owner of the goods who must in turn seek redress from the carrier and insurance company involved. In the quotations just mentioned, the time and the place at which title passes from seller to buyer are clearly stated. However, in some instances, the parties to a sales transaction fail to indicate exactly when and where title will pass. So a dispute can arise over who is responsible for any loss.

Ascertained Goods

If it is not clear as to when title passed from one party to the other, any dispute will be judged according to the rules set out in s. 19 of the Sale of Goods Act, R.S.O. 1970, c. 421, which deals with the passing of title of *specific (or ascertained) goods in a deliverable state*. These are goods that, as well as being ready for delivery, are clearly identifiable.

The first rule set out in s. 19 of the Act is that the title passes at the time the offer is accepted. For example, suppose I go into a store and see a TV set with a "for sale" sign on it, and enquire whether I can take it away immediately, since the TV set would be a specific item, ready for immediate delivery. In this case, I become the owner as soon as my offer to buy has been accepted— even before payment terms or conditions of delivery have been arranged. I thus assume the risk of loss from, say, damage, even though the TV set is still in the store.

The second rule is that, if the specific goods are not in deliverable condition at the time of purchase but merely require some work to be done, such as replacing a picture tube in a used TV set, title passes to the buyer as soon as the necessary work has been done and he is notified that they are ready to be delivered or collected. Another example of such a sale is the purchase of a suit which requires some minor alterations before it can be worn.

The third rule in the case of specific identifiable goods is that, if some action is required on the part of the seller, such as weighing, measuring, counting, or appraising before the price of the goods can be determined, the title passes to the buyer only when this has been done and the buyer is notified therof. An example would be fruit or vegetables, taken from a store's display counter, which need to be weighed to determine their price.

The fourth rule is that, if specific identifiable goods are sold on approval, ownership does not pass to the buyer until he or she has done something to indicate approval. Such approval can be expressed—for example, by making payment, writing a letter of approval, or just telling the seller that the goods are going to be kept. It can also be implied—for example, by using, eating, selling, keeping, giving away, or even destroying the item. Keeping goods beyond a given number of days is an implied approval only if the buyer has previously agreed to accept goods on this basis (for example, through a record or book club membership). There is no implied approval if goods, sent on an unsolicited basis, are not returned to the seller. Under the common law rule, silence is never considered to be acceptance of an offer. This principle has been incorporated into modern consumer law statutes.

Unascertained Goods

We have just looked at the rules governing the loss of specific goods in a deliverable condition. We now look at the rules governing *non-specific (or unascertained) goods*—in other words, goods that are not readily identifiable and that may not even have been in existence at the time the contract was made.

First, there is the situation in which goods are bought by description (for example, from a catalogue) or by sample (for example, on the basis of a display model in a department store). When do the title and the risk pass to the buyer? It is not sufficient that the goods (for example, a refrigerator in the warehouse) be tagged with the buyer's name if it is left with all the others. This is because the tag can be easily removed. What is required is that the goods be wrapped and addressed to the buyer and removed to the shipping area and thus separated from the bulk (that is, from other similar goods).

As an example, suppose that a person takes a truck to a garage to have new tires installed. The mechanic, on leaving that night, merely chalks the person's name on the four new tires to be put onto the truck the following morning. Then, if the garage burns down during the night, the customer is not responsible for the tires. However, if the mechanic had installed the new tires and they are on the customer's truck when the fire occurs, the mechanic has done something definite to earmark the tires as the customer's. The customer can therefore be properly billed for their cost, even though the truck may no longer be serviceable.

In summary, title to an "unascertained" good passes to the buyer: (a) when the good has been separated from the bulk; and (b) when either the buyer has picked out the item and asked to have it set aside for delivery or the seller has done something to the goods at the buyer's request in acknowledgment of the sale—for example, setting it aside or despatching it to the customer.

Second, there is the situation in which the goods are not yet in existence, which applies only in an agreement to sell. The goods must still be grown or manufactured—for example, a field of tomatoes or a carload of television sets. In this case, ownership will pass to the buyer when the goods become specific or ascertained—that is, when the tomatoes can be harvested, or when the televisions are manufactured. It is not necessary that the buyer be notified that the crop is ready or the television sets have been manufactured. Title passes to the buyer as soon as the goods are produced or ready and appropriated to the contract. Goods are definitely appropriated to the contract when delivered to a public or common carrier pursuant to an F.O.B. or C.I.F. shipment, if the passing of title is not otherwise provided for in the sales contract.

Bills of Lading

A *bill of lading* is a document that entitles the holder or consignee to request delivery of the goods from the common carrier. A *straight bill of lading* entitles the holder to possession; while an *order bill of lading* restricts the right of possession to the party to whose order the bill of lading has been made out. In addition, a bill of lading serves as a receipt that the goods are in the hands of the common carrier and as evidence of the terms governing the shipment. The document is normally prepared by the carrier.

TERMS IN THE SALE OF GOODS CONTRACT

The contents of the contract of sale must be examined to decide what conditions or warranties exist. A vital matter of the contract, called a *condition,* results in a right to have the contract rescinded or cancelled if such condition is not met. A minor or incidental matter, called a *warranty,* although important to the perfection of the contract, merely gives rise to a claim for damages if missing (s. 12). This section also provides that if a contract is not severable and either the buyer has accepted goods or title has passed, a breach of condition must be treated as a breach of warranty only. By virtue of s. 33 the buyer has a right to examine goods before he or she is deemed to have accepted them, and the seller must allow time for acceptance. Acceptance is made known on the part of the buyer either by saying so, keeping the goods, or by treating them as his or her own. In *Lightburn v. Belmont Sales Ltd.* (1969), 69 W.W.R. 734, dealing with a Ford Cortina sale, the court held that there was no acceptance even after six months because the buyer had kept returning the car for repairs. In another case dealing with a computer purchased by the Municipality of Waterloo, Ontario, the court held that there had been no acceptance even after a year because the computer programmers were still trying during this whole period to make it work satisfactorily.

Express Conditions and Warranties

These conditions and warranties (popularly called "guarantees") are ones that are expressly declared by the seller when a good is sold to the buyer. Normally, they are stated in writing on the sales contract or on a special manufacturer's certificate that accompanies the good. However, a warranty given orally can also be legally binding if the sales contract is an oral one. Any warranty given after a good is sold is not binding on the seller unless it is made under seal or unless some new consideration is given in exchange.

Implied Conditions and Warranties

There are certain conditions and warranties implied on the part of a seller under the Sale of Goods Act.

True Owner.   First, it is an implied condition that the seller is the true owner of the goods and has therefore the right to sell them. Consequently, if the goods turn out to have been stolen and the buyer is required to hand them back to the true owner, the buyer can sue the seller for breach of this implied condition.

Free From Encumbrance.   Second, there is an implied warranty that no claims are outstanding on the goods sold—in other words, that the goods are free from encumbrance.

Quiet Enjoyment.   Third, there is an implied warranty that the buyer will have quiet enjoyment and possession—for example, that the seller of a car will not request the use of it for the following weekend.

Fitness.   Fourth, it is an implied condition, in certain circumstances, that the goods sold for a particular purpose are fit for that purpose.

Merchantability.   Fifth, there is an implied condition of merchantability—that the product sold is basically worth the money that was paid for it.

Description.   Finally, sixth, there is an implied condition of description that the goods will conform exactly to a sample or description in a catalogue.

Implied Condition of Fitness

Normally, the rule of *caveat emptor* applies to a buyer. However, this is not so if the buyer indicates to the seller what goods he needs, the exact purpose for which he needs them, and the fact that he is placing reliance on the seller's judgment in choosing them. In such a case, there is an implied *condition of fitness*—that is, that the seller will supply goods that are in satisfactory cndition and suitable for the purpose intended. However, the sale must be in the "ordinary course of business"—not a private sale. In *Lightburn v. Belmont Sales Ltd., supra*, the buyer asked the seller for a cheap, reliable car, and the dealer sold him a Ford Cortina which proved utterly unsuitable. The court held that by relying on the dealer's recommendation, the implied condition of fitness applied to this contract. Therefore, the buyer was entitled to have the sale rescinded. As another example, if I order a meal from a restaurant menu, there is an impied condition that the food will match the description. If, later, I am violently ill because of substandard food, I have the right to sue the restaurant owner for breach of the implied condition of fitness of the food served.

Prerequisites.   The following factors must exist before the implied condition of fitness will apply to a sale of goods contract:

1. the sale must be made in the course of the seller's business;
2. the seller must have knowledge of the purpose of the goods;
3. the buyer must rely on the seller's skill or judgment.

For example, it is readily appreciated that all of these factors apply in the provision of food in a restaurant, since this is a sale in the course of the restauranteur's business; and both parties are aware that the food served must be fit to eat.

In some cases this condition applies even if the buyer does not state the purpose for which he or she buys; for example, a bottle of cola is purchased for the purpose of drinking as decided in *Yedland v. National Café*, [1955] 5 D.L.R. 560 (Sask. C.A.). In the purchase of a hot-water bottle in *Preist v. Last*, [1903] 2 K.B. 148, the court held that the purpose of the purchase was obvious and, if the bottle burst, the seller was liable for injuries or damage caused.

The question of the buyer's reliance on the seller's judgment may be illustrated by the case of a person who buys coal to operate the boilers of a certain steamship. If it turns out that the coal is unsatisfactory, the court will hold that the seller knew the purpose for which the coal was required, so the implied condition of fitness applies. This implied condition has also covered cases where a noisy propellor was unfit for a particular ship; where a tractor could not be used for road construction; where a cow could not give milk; where ground nuts possessing an unknown toxin proved unfit as poultry feed; and even where a cola bottle exploded. On the other hand, a secondhand car "is reasonably fit for the purpose" if it is in roadworthy condition even if it is not as good as a new car (*Bartlett v. Sidney Marcus Ltd.*, [1965] 1 W.L.R. 1013 at p. 1017).

This liability, however, does not cover the situation where the goods are to be used by the buyer in an abnormal or unusual manner—for example, a Harris Tweed coat which caused a person with a very sensitive skin to develop dermatitis, or sausages which were uncooked in *Yachetti v. John Duff & Sons Ltd.*, [1943] 1 D.L.R. 194, thereby causing Mrs. Yachetti and her children to develop trichinosis while the husband who ate later, after the meat had been more thoroughly cooked, did not become ill. In other words, this was an abnormal use of the sausage meat and the buyer was liable for her own illness.

The same provision of the Sale of Goods Act contains an exclusionary clause to the effect that, if a person buys goods sold under a trade name, he or she is in fact not relying on the seller's selection of the goods. Therefore the implied condition of fitness does not apply insofar as the retailer is concerned. However, the manufacturer will still be liable on the grounds of negligence for failing to warn the user of the safe manner of dealing with the product—for example a hair dye (*O'Fallon v. Inecto Rapid (Can.) Ltd.*, [1940] 4 D.L.R. 276 (B.C. C.A.).

Implied Condition of Merchantability

The implied condition of merchantability also applies to contracts for the sale of goods. In one case, a person undertook to buy an automobile that was in good condition. Later, when he returned to pick it up, he found that the car had been stripped of chrome trim, the tires had been replaced by bald ones, and the car was no longer in running condition. The court held that to fulfil the condition of merchantability, the product must be such that a willing buyer, aware of its present condition, would be willing to pay the full price for it (refer to *Karsales (Harrow) Ltd. v. Wallis*, [1956] 1 W.L.R. 936).

Under s. 53 of the Sale of Goods Act, a buyer may waive these implied conditions or warranties. However, under the Ontario Consumer Protection Act, for example, this is no longer possible in the case of sales of consumer goods.

One of the most recent decisions on the question of merchantability was given in the case of *B. S. Brown & Sons Ltd. v. Craiks Ltd.*, [1970] 1 All E.R. 823, dealing with the purchase of cloth to be manufactured to detailed specifications which the buyers intended to use to make dresses. The cloth proved unsuitable to make dresses but proved suitable for other industrial purposes. Was the cloth of merchantable quality? Since the cloth was saleable for other purposes at a slightly reduced price, it was held to have been of merchantable quality, so the buyers lost their claim for damages for breach of the implied condition of merchantability. However, if there had been no resale value, the result would have been different.

Goods that contain a "hidden" defect are also not considered to be of merchantable quality, even though the buyer has examined them. thus, in *Wren v. Holt*, [1903] 1 K.B. 610, beer was contaminated by arsenic. However, since the defect was latent and no examination would have revealed it, the beer was held not to be of merchantable quality.

The main difference between the implied condition of fitness and the implied condition of merchantability seems to be that in sales under a trade or patent name, while fitness may be excluded, merchantability still applies; whereas in contracts where the seller has picked out and recommended goods at the buyer's request, merchantability may not apply, but the condition of fitness still applies.

In the United States, an attempt has been made to give a clearer meaning to the condition of merchantability by including in the Uniform Commercial Code a requirement that goods must:

1. comply with the contract description;
2. be of fair average quality (in the case of fungible goods);
3. be fit for ordinary use;
4. be of even kind, quality, and quantity;
5. conform with agreement regarding container, packaging, and labelling;
6. conform with affirmations of fact on the container or label.

DELIVERY AND PAYMENT

Once a good has been sold, the seller has a legal obligation to hand it over or "deliver" it and the buyer has a legal obligation to pay for it. If there is an express contract of sale, the terms of delivery and payment will be specified. If there is no such contract, the parties are bound by the rules set out in the Sale of Goods Act. The rules concern: (a) place of delivery; (b) time of delivery; (c) right of disposal; and (d) payment.

Place of Delivery

Under the Sale of Goods Act, a buyer must pick up the goods at the seller's place of business, making his own arrangements for transportation and insurance. Today, however, because of competitive pressure, many sellers, using their own vans or private carriers, will deliver the goods free of charge to the buyer's address. According to s. 28 of the Act, delivery is deemed to take place at the seller's place of business at a reasonable hour and when the goods are prepared for delivery by the seller. If goods are to be held by a third party, there is no delivery until such third party acknowledges receipt of the goods. By s. 31, delivery of goods to a public carrier is prima facie evidence of delivery to the buyer. In such a case, the seller must make a reasonable contract with the carrier, otherwise the buyer is entitled to reject the shipment.

Time of Delivery

Under the Act, the seller must "deliver" the goods, and the buyer accept them, within a reasonable period of time. The time of delivery is normally considered a warranty (which does not permit the contract to be set aside) unless stated to be a condition of the contract. An example of time of delivery being made a condition would be if I specify to a florist that I want a box of flowers delivered to an airplane before departure time. Any failure to deliver on time would amount to a breach of condition, entitling me to have the contract set aside and to receive compensation. Section 11 of the Sale of Goods Act provides that time is not "of the essence" unless so stipulated.

If there is a delay in delivery or acceptance, any damage to the goods is the responsibility of the party causing the delay, even though he may not be the owner at the time.

Delivery and acceptance of the goods should be of the whole order at one time unless shipment by instalments has been specifically agreed beforehand.

Right of Disposal

Some sellers, uncertain as to the solvency of their buyers, will retain ownership and possession of their goods until payment has been made. This can be done in various ways. *First*, by shipping the goods by the seller's own truck or van. Once the goods have been handed over for delivery to a public carrier, possession has passed out of the seller's hands and, except in the case of stoppage in transit, the seller will never be able to exercise his right of lien if the goods are not paid for. *Second*, the seller can send the goods C.O.D. (cash on delivery). *Third*, the seller can ship the goods to his own agent at the buyer's town with the understanding that the agent is to hand the goods over only upon receipt of payment. In this case, the goods are shipped under a bill of lading made out to the order of the seller himself or of his agent, usually a branch or a correspondent of the seller's own bank. The *bill of lading* (which is a document of title to the goods, as well as a shipping contract) is not handed over to the buyer until he or she has made satisfactory payment arrangements—for example, paying cash or signing a time draft. In all of these situations, the seller retains possession and can return the goods to his own warehouse if need be. If the buyer does not carry out his or her part of the sales contract, the goods may be re-sold and the buyer sued for any difference between the normal selling price and the price obtained on resale.

Payment

The normal requirement in common law and now under the Sale of Goods Act is that the seller should be paid for his goods when he delivers them. One exception, for which express agreement should be made between the parties, is the requirement of prepayment by the buyer—for example, "10% down and the remainder on completion delivery." Another exception, for which express agreement should also be made, is the granting of credit, or time to pay, by the seller to the buyer. Under the Act, the customary or a reasonable price must be paid for the goods if, for some reason, no price has been expressly stated in the sales contract. According to s. 37, the seller is unpaid if the whole price has not been paid, or if any negotiable instrument given in payment has not been honoured.

The unpaid seller may retain goods if still in his possession, under s. 38, and similarly under s. 39, if credit was not mentioned, or if credit has expired or the buyer is insolvent. Section 40 allows the seller to retain possession in the foregoing circumstances, where only partial delivery has occurred. The seller must pay for return delivery (s. 44). Goods are considered to be in transit unless the buyer or his agent takes possession or is notified of arrival unless the buyer rejects the goods (s. 43). Section 41 provides that the unpaid seller will forfeit his lien if the goods are delivered to the carrier or bailee for delivery to the buyer without reservation of disposal. Normally, however, the seller's lien is not defeated by any sale by the buyer to a third party unless the buyer is in possession of documents of title (s. 45).

STOPPAGE IN TRANSIT

If the seller learns that the buyer has become insolvent while the goods are in the hands of the public carrier for shipment, the seller may exercise the right of "stoppage in transit," whereby the carrier is requested not to deliver to the buyer or his agent nor notify the latter of the arrival of goods, but return them to the shipper at his or her expense (ss. 38, 42).

An example which serves to illustrate the foregoing might occur if I received an order to ship a carload of refrigerators from my refrigerator manufacturing plant in Toronto to the ABC Retail Co. in Vancouver, B.C., "F.O.B. station of origin, term 30 days, shipped CNR." Since, under the terms of the contract, the goods are unascertained, ownership would not pass until the goods are manufactured, picked out and loaded for shipment to the buyer at the Barrie railhead. Shipping by public carrier, i.e., C.N.R., would amount to giving up the seller's lien. Suppose, while the goods are in transit, the seller, learning of the ABC Co.'s insolvency, requests the CNR to return the shipment. Then the ABC Co.'s carload of refrigerators would be returned to the shipper's warehouse and probably sold to a new buyer by exercising the lien under s. 38. In this case the maximum loss to the seller could be 10% or 20%, while if the shipment reached the insolvent purchaser company, the seller would be lucky to realize 10% to 20% in all as a general creditor.

DISCLAIMER OR EXCULPATORY CLAUSES

Under the rules established in the case of *Hadley v. Baxendale* (1854), 9 Ex. 341, a buyer is entitled not only to recover direct damages, but also all consequential damages that were reasonably foreseeable at the time the contract was formed—which may run into many thousands of dollars. This possibility has caused manufacturers and other sellers to attempt to protect themselves against liability suits, by disclaimer or exclusion of liability clauses in their sales contracts.

The simplest way of excluding the conditions and warranties of the Sale of Goods Act is to provide a written contract that the contract "specifically excludes any implied warranties or conditions and the only product warranty is that expressed in the contract itself."

Another way of achieving this result is to state simply that the "sole warranty between the seller and the buyer is the warranty set out in the contract." Another form of disclaimer clause used by, for example, second-hand car dealers, is to state that the good is sold "as is." Very few suppliers of services fail to use some form of disclaimer clause. Thus, for example, dry cleaners state that they are "responsible for damages resulting from the dry cleaning process only and not for any damage resulting from the fabric, cloth or material itself." Car park operators disclaim "any liability for damages caused to automobiles while parked at the owner's risk." Restaurant owners disclaim liability for the "personal possessions" of guests taken from coat racks provided for the use of patrons. Hotels limit their liability for theft of a guest's belongings by signs placed at reception desks and in the rooms. Transportation companies limit their liability in various ways in the bill of lading.

There are also statutory limitations of liability, such as those imposed on the interprovincial transportation of household effects which, in Canada, for example, is set at so many cents per pound; or the statutory limitations for death or injury set out in agreements relating to international air transportation applicable to all member nations of the International Air Transportation Association.

Generally, the seller is in the position to impose the terms in the contract. Thus, for example, every purchaser of an automobile in Canada and the United States, particularly if bought on credit, must make the offer to buy on a standard form used by the dealers of the "Big Three" (Ford, General Motors and Chrysler). This form expressly negates all "implied" warranties and substitutes "express" warranties or promises which limit the buyer's rights under the Sale of Goods Act, for example, by reserving to the seller the option of repairing any so-called defects while the car is under warranty. A similar situations exists for major electrical goods, such as refrigerators, cookers, television sets, kitchen equipment and so on. "Guarantees offered with sales of these goods . . . generally offer short-term protection for buyers, frequently of a single year's duration, in exchange for the more extensive protection rights the customer would otherwise have."

Sometimes the customer will be required to sign a contract which runs into two or three pages, written in a strictly legal terminology, which eliminates liability on the part of the seller. Once this contract is signed the courts will not normally allow evidence to show misunderstanding on the part of the buyer.

It must be emphasized that in Canada since the 1960s, sellers are generally prohibited, under consumer protection legislation, from excluding the implied conditions of the Sale of Goods Act from a consumer sales contract. However, in other sales, the seller may be in a position to impose the terms in the sales contract.

Most customers are subjected to some "sales talk" and, in many cases, this sales talk helps decide which product to buy. Unfortunately for the buyer, if the product is not satisfactory, no evidence will be allowed to show misunderstanding, short of fraudulent misrepresentation, because oral evidence is not normally allowed to alter a written contract.

This situation was remedied in the United Kingdom by the Misrepresentation Act, 1967, which protects the buyer who has been led into a contract even by an innocent misrepresentation. Similarly, in Ontario and other provinces, the Business Practices Act (Appendix 28-A) provides twenty-three different ways for the unsuspecting owner to avoid a contract which has been induced by fraud, unfair advantage, trickery or misunderstanding.

The Ontario Law Reform Commission Report lists the following six grounds that have been used by the courts to avoid disclaimer clauses:

1. The disclaimer clause was not brought to the attention of the buyer at the time the contract was made; or
2. The disclaimer was only brought to the attention of the buyer after the contract was formed; or
3. Where the contract excludes implied warranties, the courts have found express warranties either in the contract or in the promises made.
4. Manufacturers have been prohibited from hiding behind the seller's exclusion of liability clauses;
5. Some courts have refused to accept the buyer acknowledged receipt that goods were received in good condition, because of lack of consideration;
6. The remaining cases fall under three main categories of construction, namely that stating an express warranty does not exclude implied warranties; and lastly, the Fundamental Breach provision, that a disclaimer clause is ineffective, if the contract has not, in fact, been performed.

Fundamental Breach

The *Albion Case*, [1953] 1 W.L.R. 1027, supports the proposition that there are limits to the application of exculpatory clauses. This would occur, for example, when such a clause in one part of the contract negates an essential obligation in the contract binding one of the parties to do something. In this case, the exculpatory clause would be repugnant and have to give way.

The law places no obligation on the seller to inform the buyer of his or her rights under the implied conditions relating to sales of goods. The courts, however, have consistently sought a way to help the buyer of defective merchandise who finds that the contract excludes any liability on the part of the seller.

In *Karsales (Harrow) Limited v. Wallis*, [1956] 1 W.L.R. 936, the court dealt with the situation of a Mr. Wallis who, in 1956, wanted to buy a second-hand Buick. He gave the automobile a trial run, found it satisfactory, and offered to buy it. It was then sold to a finance company from whom Mr. Wallis purchased it on an instalment basis. The contract included a clause stating that "no condition or warranty that the vehicle is roadworthy or as to its age, condition, fitness for any purpose, is given by the owner or implied herein." The car was delivered to Mr. Wallis after the agreement had been signed. By this time, the tires had been replaced by used ones, chrome strips were missing, valves were burnt out, and two pistons were broken. To repair it completely would have cost 150 pounds sterling. The court found that Mr. Wallis could reject the car despite the exclusion of liability provision because the car eventually delivered was fundamentally different from the car contracted for. "A car that will not go, is no car at all." In other words, there was a breach of the implied condition of merchantability.

In summary, the doctrine of "fundamental breach" will be applied so as to strike out an exculpatory clause which tends to negate the very essence of the contract. Of course, the court's discretion will be invoked as to when this principale will apply after considering the surrounding facts and circumstances.

The American courts have always maintained the right to strike down an exculpatory clause as against "public policy" unless it is reasonable.

REMEDIES OF BUYER FOR BREACH OF CONTRACT

Let us consider the remedies available to the buyer for three different types of breach of contract.

Non-Delivery of Goods.   The obvious remedy is that the buyer need not pay for non-delivered goods. If the non-delivered goods are unique (for example, a rare painting), the buyer's remedy is to ask for specific performance which, if it is ordered by the court, will force the seller to hand over the goods to the buyer. Otherwise the buyer's remedy is damages, the difference between the agreed price and the price of the same item elsewhere.

If the buyer planned to resell the goods, and the market has now disappeared, then he or she is entitled to his probable profit.

Breach of Condition.   Failure to deliver the goods, or delivery of goods that are extremely defective, or delivering too few of the ordered goods, entitles the buyer to treat the breach of contract as a breach of condition. In such circumstances, the breach goes right to the heart of the contract and the buyer may refuse to accept the goods altogether and look elsewhere for the supply. If, however, the buyer has used the goods, resold them, or kept them beyond a reasonable time, then it is no longer possible to treat the deficiency as a breach of condition. The remedy for breach of warranty is the only remedy available.

Breach of Warranty.   Here the buyer's remedy is to be put in the same position as if the contract had been wholly fulfilled. Thus, where the breach of warranty amounts to the seller's having failed, for example, to supply all the agreed accessories for a new car, the buyer, although bound to accept the goods, can insist on the balance of the contract being carried out.

REMEDIES OF SELLER FOR BREACH OF CONTRACT

We can look at the remedies available to the seller for breach of contract in five different sets of circumstances.

Seller Has Both Title and Possession.   In this situation, if the buyer refuses to pay for the goods, the seller can keep them and sue the buyer for damages. Alternatively, under the Sale of Goods Act, they can be sold to someone else, giving good title to that third party, so long as the seller notifies the original buyer of this intention. The same applies if the original buyer refused delivery or if the goods were retained by the seller following a stoppage in transit.

Seller has Neither Title Nor Possession.   In this situation, the remedy available to the seller is to sue the buyer for the value of the goods sold. The seller has no right to recover the goods since he or she is no longer the owner—unless the right of recovery is expressly included in the sales contract.

Stoppage in Transit.   Suppose the goods have been despatched by public carrier and the seller learns of the buyer's insolvency before the goods have reached the buyer's place of business. Then the common law allows him to dispatch a message immediately to the public carrier requesting that the goods be returned because of the buyer's insolvency. However, this ancient remedy is only available when: (a) the seller has given title to the buyer; (b) the seller has given up possession; (c) the goods are still in the hands of the common carrier; (d) the buyer has not been notified that the goods have arrived at his or her place of business; and (e) the buyer is insolvent—that is, unable to pay his or her debts. The seller who makes a mistake as to the existence of any of these pre-conditions is responsible for all damages caused to the buyer as a result.

Seller has Possession but No Title. This is a situation we have previously described, where, for example, the seller has sold ascertainable deliverable goods for later delivery and payment and title passes to the buyer upon offer and acceptance. If the buyer refuses to accept the goods or make satisfactory payment, the seller has the right of resale. Perishable goods may be sold at once; otherwise notice of intention to sell must be given to the buyer and the best possible price obtained. The defaulting first buyer is responsible for any loss suffered by the seller. If the buyer wishes to take the goods without paying for them, the seller has the right of lien on the goods to prevent this. However, this right of lien exists only if the contract specified payment on delivery, or the agreed period of credit has elapsed, or the buyer, although having previously been granted credit terms, has now become insolvent.

Seller has Title but No Possession. Suppose a firm has sold goods on approval to a buyer. Suppose also that the buyer has indicated approval by keeping the goods beyond a reasonable time, by using them, selling them, or otherwise disposing of them. However, he has not paid for them. The seller's remedy then is to sue for the value at which the goods were sold.

OTHER LEGISLATION

Other provincial statutes governing the sale of goods are the various Consumer Protection Acts described in Chapter 28 of this book.

At the federal level, an extremely important statute governing the sale of goods is the Combines Investigation Act, discussed in Chapter 26. Another is the Consumer Packaging and Labelling Act described in Chapter 27.

REVIEW QUESTIONS

1. Give examples of the types of goods covered under the Sale of Goods Act.
2. Jurisdiction in Sale of Goods contracts between different legal jurisdictions, called private international law, may be established by determining where the contract was "accepted." Give several illustrative examples covering sales by manufacturers and dealers in different provinces in Canada.
3. What transactions are specifically excluded from the Sale of Goods Act?
4. If the terms of a sales contract differ in any way from the principles set out in the Sale of Goods Act, they will be overruled in a court of law. Comment.
5. Does the Sale of Goods Act apply to actual sales, agreements to sell, or both? Give examples from your own experience.
6. A sale takes place when the seller gives possession of the goods to the buyer. Comment.
7. Discuss the requirement of "writing" in Sale of Goods Contracts.
8. Distinguish between "title" and "possession" of goods. Give examples.
9. What are the different Sale of Goods Act rules relating to the passing of ownership in sales of specific goods?

10. When are goods "ascertained" in the case of the sale of non-specific goods under the Sale of Goods Act?

11. If I enter a fruit market and fill a bag with cherries and take them to the counter to be weighed, when does title pass to me?

12. Suppose that I agree to buy a record player on approval but, after playing some records, am dissatisfied and return it to the store. The owner of the store then refuses to refund my money on the grounds that I have made use of the record player. What is my legal position?

13. Suppose that I enter into a contract to buy a farmer's crop of tomatoes for use in my canning factory. However, three months later, because of disease, the crop is wiped out. The farmer claims that he grew the tomatoes specifically for me and that I must pay for them. What would my legal position be if the contract did not specify when title was to pass? Is there a specific Sales of Goods provision that might apply here?

14. Give examples of F.O.B., C.I.F., and C.O.D. quotations.

15. Explain the principle of law contained in *Lightburn v. Belmont Sales Ltd.* (See page 453–54.)

16. Comment on "express conditions," relating to the sale of goods, which you may have encountered in your purchasing experience.

17. Certain conditions and warranties are implied on the part of a seller under the Sale of Goods Act. What are they? Give examples, illustrating each one.

18. Give examples illustrating the difference between a condition and a warranty in a sale of goods.

19. Give examples that distinguish between the application of the implied condition of fitness and that of merchantability to (a) new goods and (b) used goods.

20. Comment on the following in relation to the sale of an automobile for pleasure: (a) place of delivery; (b) time of delivery; (c) payment; and (d) right of disposal.

21. Discuss the effect of the common law right of "stoppage in transit," which has been incorporated into the Sale of Goods Act.

22. Consider the various reasons given by judges when disallowing "disclaimer or exculpatory" clauses. Do you consider such reasons to be acceptable in a society governed by the Rule of Law?

23. What are the remedies of the buyer for: (a) non-delivery of the goods; (b) breach of condition; and (c) breach of warranty?

24. What are the remedies of the seller for breach of contract: (a) when the seller has both title and possession; (b) when the seller has neither title nor possession; (c) when the seller has possession but no title; and (d) when the seller has title but no possession?

PROBLEMS

1. A brought her car to a service station operated by the lessee of a major tire manufacturer. She picked out four tires from the bulk stock and agreed

to leave her car overnight, during which time the tires could be changed. After the job had been done, but before the car was picked up, the garage burnt down! Who bears the tire loss?

2. Recently in Canada, the ex-mayor of one of the largest cities bought as a secondhand car the municipal limousine, which he had used while in office. He was over seventy years of age at the time and for the next two or three months he used this automobile which gave him good service. Then one day after he had just had the brakes adjusted by his mechanic, the brakes failed and he was involved in an accident injuring his wife and himself and damaging the car. He sued the makers of the automobile.

(a) Give reasons for your decision as to whether he should win or lose.

(b) If you were in his shoes, how would you proceed with your claim?

3. In a recent case involving the sale of a knitting machine, the purchaser was assured that any knitted product she made would be purchased by the seller and payment credited against her account. She had signed a promissory note attached to the conditional sale agreement and she was told to make her payments to a finance company. She dispatched several lots of knitted goods to the seller, but there was no reduction of the payments due the finance company.

(a) What would be the equitable way to deal with this situation?

(b) What is the present law covering this type of sale?

4. The Public Utilities Commission of Waterloo asked in 1967 for tenders for a computer capable of performing specified functions. Burroughs studied the requirement of the Commission by enquiring about the various tasks to be performed and by consulting Guelph Utilities, which was doing the bill and other functions for Waterloo. They finally recommended a specific machine, tendered, and won the contract. The deal provided for the machine to be sold to a Commercial Leasing Co. which in turn leased it to the Waterloo Utilities. Burroughs trained a Waterloo Commission operator, but after a year of adjusting the recommended machine could not get it to fulfil its job. Another machine was therefore recommended. Waterloo claimed rescision of the first contract, but Burroughs objected that it was too late because more than a reasonable time had elapsed since delivery and acceptance and that this machine had been selected because of its brand name, Burroughs, which excused the seller under a warranty of fitness. Finally the Commission continued to use the computer until the new one was received.

What provisions of the Sale of Goods Act are applicable here? Discuss acceptance under the Sale of Goods Act. Discuss warranty or condition of fitness. Discuss the defence of keeping the machine while Burroughs attempted to make it fulfil its job. Who won this case and why?

5. The plaintiff, a farm labourer, contacted the agent of a truck sales firm and told him that he wanted to buy a truck to haul gravel and asphalt in the country. The salesman stated that the truck selected had a good transmission, that the rebuilt motor had only driven fifty miles, that it

had "lots of power" and that it would keep its resale value as a future trade-in. The purchaser bought the truck for a total selling price of $9,180, including an old truck which he traded in, and undertook to do minor repairs to the lights, frame, brakes, and so on to pass the safety check. The contract contained a provision that the buyer was accepting the truck "as is" in the form of an exclusionary or disclaimer clause. The truck operated in all, five and a half days, during which the transmission leaked and "clunked," the water system and power steering leaked, and finally the motor, which had 25 less horsepower than alleged, quit running. Repairs would have totalled $7,000.

What are the arguments for and against the purchaser in this case? Refer to *Neilsen v. Maclin Motors Ltd.* (1976), 71 D.L.R. (3d) 744.

READINGS

Pullman Trailmobile Canada Ltd. v. Hamilton Transport Refrigeration Ltd. (1979), 96 D.L.R. (3d) 322 (Ont. H.C.).

Facts: In this case the plaintiff, a subsidiary of C.P.R., entered into a contract with Hamilton Transport Refrigeration Co. Ltd. for the supply and installation of seven transport refrigeration units at $7,266.90 each. The directors and officers of Hamilton Transport Refrigeration Co. Ltd. were also officers of the Southern Ontario Truck Sales & Service Inc. which had been borrowing and doing banking business with the Unity Bank, now the Provincial Bank of Canada, for some time. Some six personal demand guarantees had been taken from these companies and the four principal officers, in particular the president, Hamilton Morris. On January 3, 1975, Hamilton Morris had given the bank a floating debenture of $100,000, which allowed the defendant Hamilton to carry on his business, until the company fell into default on the principal and interest secured.

Following preliminary negotiations, the plaintiff had ordered the refrigeration units which were to be obtained from Thermo King U.S.A. On March 25, 1976, the order was accepted and a copy returned on March 29. Payment was to be made thirty days from date of invoice. On May 17, the plaintiff received an invoice stating the refrigeration units were ready for installation at the defendant's premises as agreed. The plaintiff forwarded a cheque for $72,669 which was certified at Hamilton's request and deposited in his account at the Provincial Bank, which refused to give him a draft to pay the supplier, Thermo King U.S.A.

In the meantime, the bank prepared a demand letter on each of the six debtors (two companies and four officers) and at the same time prepared a letter appointing a chartered accountant to act as receiver. On June 29, 1976, the characted accountant served the demand on Hamilton on behalf of the Southern Co. in the amount of $304,000 plus $73,900 interest. When Hamilton could not pay immediately, the chartered accountant showed him his appointment as receiver and obtained Hamilton's consent to his appointment as receiver. When the plaintiff was advised of the receivership, he tried to get the refrigeration units on July 14, 1976, but the receiver advised that they were under seizure. The plaintiff finally obtained an order for replevin by depositing three times the value of the units. This action was brought to resolve two questions:

1. Had the property passed to the plaintiff before the bank purported to seize the goods?
2. If the property had not passed, was the receiver validly appointed on June 19, 1976, in which case the goods became the property of the plaintiff when he claimed on July 16?

Held per Griffiths J.:

Rule 5 of s. 19 of the Sale of Goods Act governs . . .

"19. Unless a different intention appears . . .

Rule 5(i) Where there is a contract for the sale of unascertained or future goods by description or future goods by description and goods of that description and in a deliverable state are unconditionally appropriated to the contract, either by the seller with the assent of the buyer, or by the buyer with the assent of the seller, the property in the goods thereupon passes to the buyer, and such assent may be expressed or implied and may be given either before or after the appropriation is made."

. . . The identification and assignment of the goods to the contract . . . amounted to an unconditional appropriation to the contract. . . .

[The defendant Bank objected that] the provisions of s. 33 of the Sale of Goods Act, that where goods are delivered to the buyer not previously examined by him, then he is entitled to a reasonable opportunity to examine those goods . . . before he is obliged to accept them. . . .

. . . The reasonable inference from the evidence is that the plaintiff did not intend to inspect the refrigeration units, but was content to rely on the defendant Hamilton to see that the units were up to specification. . . .

. . . In my opinion when the parties appropriated the goods to the contract about June 16, 1976, property in the goods then passed to the plaintiff, subject to the condition that they revest [title returns to original owner] if upon examination the plaintiff found they were defective or did not comply with specifications. . . .

[In *Kwei Tek Chao v. British Traders & Shippers Ltd.*, [1954] 2 O.B. 459] involving the sale of goods under a c.i.f. contract, Devlin J., said at p. 487: "I think that the true view is that what the buyer obtains, when the title under the documents is given to him, is the property in the goods, subject to the condition that they revest if upon examination he finds them to be not in accordance with the contract. . . .

If the property passes conditionally the only ownership left in the seller is the reversionary interest in the property in the event of the condition subsequent operating to restore it to him [which reversionary interest would not entitle the receiver to claim ownership of the goods]." . . .

Was the receiver properly appointed? . . .

In the case of *Ronald Elwyn Lister Ltd. v. Dunlop Canada Ltd.* (1978), 19 O.R. (2d) 380, . . . Rutherford J. . . . at p. 402 said: "I accept Mr. Chappell's contention on behalf of the plaintiffs that the *West City Motors Case* is correct in stating that where money is payable on demand, the debtor is entitled to a reasonable time to meet the demand, the question of what is reasonable being a question of fact to be determined by the circumstances of the particular case." . . .

. . . [T]here is no evidence that the Southern company or the defendant Hamilton *given some time* could not have met the demand. . . . [T]he defendant Hamilton's [personal] liability under the debenture was limited to $100,000. . . . The defendant Hamilton had to its credit $92,000, so that the amount required . . . to stave off receivership was not as enormous as the claim against the Southern Company.

[Plaintiff entitled to declaration that it was, on July 20, 1976, the lawful owner. The replevin bond may be forthwith cancelled.]

Judgment for plaintiff.

Feed-Rite Mills (1962) Ltd. v. East-West Packers (1969) Ltd. (1975), 65 D.L.R. (3d) 175 (Man. Q.B.).

Facts: The defendant sold animal bones to the plaintiff for the purpose (known to the defendant) of processing and reselling them as an animal feed supplement. The defendant cooked the bones before supplying them in order to destroy the bacteria. Some of the bones supplied by the defendant to the plaintiff were improperly cooked and contaminated with bacteria. The bones were subsequently processed into animal feed by the plaintiff and caused the death of cattle belonging to the plaintiff's customers. The plaintiff, having paid damages to these customers, brought an action against the defendant for indemnity; $25,752.95 for dead animals plus costs of $10,904.97.

Held per Solomon J.:

Plaintiff maintained that on many occasions the defendant delivered jaw bones and skulls not properly cooked which had to be returned for further cooking [both to destroy bacteria inside the skulls, and to soften these bones so that the plaintiff's machine could crush them]. . . .

Defendant knew plaintiff was using bones purchased from it from manufacturing bone-meal for consumption by farm animals as feed supplement. . . .

I am satisfied the most probable source of the Salmonella Newport [poisoning] was the contaminated bones of dead animals delivered by defendant to plaintiff in the ordinary course of business. . . .

. . . [D]efendant was obliged to supply plaintiff with merchantable quality bones, and bones containing Salmonella Newport bacteria were not of merchantable quality. . . .

. . . Does defendant owe a duty to plaintiff to deliver to it quality bones which can be safely used in the manufacture of bone-meal? Section 16 of the [Manitoba] Sale of Goods Act provides: ". . . there is no implied warranty or condition as to the quality or fitness for any particular purpose of goods supplied under a contract of sale, except as follows: (a) Where the buyer . . . makes known . . . the particular purpose . . . so as to show that the buyer relies on the seller's skill or judgment, and the goods are of a description which it is . . . the seller's business to supply, . . . there is an implied condition that the goods shall be reasonably fit for the purposes. . . . (b) Where goods are bought by description from the seller who deals in goods of that description, . . . there is an implied condition that the goods shall be of merchantable quality: Provided that if the buyer has examined the goods, there shall be no implied condition as regards defects which the examination ought to have revealed." . . .

. . . No matter how closely plaintiff examined the bones, it could not have discovered they were contaminated with Salmonella Newport. . . . Surely . . . merchantable quality includes that they shall be free of infectious diseases. . . . I am satisfied that "merchantable quality" means that goods being consumed by humans or by farm animals are free from diseases harmful to the health of humans or animals. . . . I find that the bones were contaminated before they came to plaintiff's plant and the processing in plaintiff's plant did not contribute to the contamination of the product made from infected bones.

Judgment for plaintiff.

Yachetti v. John Duff & Sons Ltd., [1943] 1 D.L.R. 194 (Ont. H.C.).

Facts: Anna Yachetti bought sausages from a meat pedlar, Perigio Paolini, who had himself purchased and ground up the fresh pork from John Duff & Sons Ltd., a meat packing company. She cooked the sausages for approximately half an hour and then she and her children ate some of the sausages. The balance, after continued cooking, was eaten by her husband when he arrived home an hour later. She and her children took ill with trichinosis. She is suing Paolini for breach of the implied condition of fitness and John Duff & Sons Ltd. in tort for selling meat in such a form that the consumer could not be aware that it was dangerous until the product was consumed. The husband also sued for damages, which were loss of his wife's services while she was ill.

Held per Greene J.:

[Judge Greene dealt with the following arguments of the plaintiffs:]

[*First: the meat was diseased in that it contained an unknown deleterious substance, namely "trichinae larvae".*] All the meat produced . . . was inspected . . . under the provisions of the Meat and Canned Foods Act. The fresh pork . . . was . . . stamped "Canada approved". . . . The evidence established that . . . a test [for trichinae] is not commercially feasible. . . .

. . . In the light of the inspection by the Dominion Government inspectors, and the nonfeasibility of testing for the parasite, it is hard to conceive as to what other precaution the Duff Company could have taken in regard to the sale of fresh pork. . . . [F]resh pork has been sold from time immemorial without such warning [that it is unsafe to eat fresh pork without thorough cooking]. . . .

[*Second: the plaintiffs impute negligence against the Duff Company on the basis of a manufacturer's duty to the ultimate consumer.* A manufacturer who] "intends the article or chattel to reach the ultimate consumer in the form in which it left him with no reasonable possibility of intermediate examination, owes a duty to such consumer to take reasonable care in the manufacture, preparation, or putting up of the article or chattel so that it will not result in an injury to the consumer's life or property." . . .

It will be remembered that the *Donoghue* case dealt with a snail in ginger beer in an opaque bottle. . . . In all these cases negligence was found against the manufacturer on the principle of *res ipsa loquitur* . . . [i.e.] negligence in the manufacture was inferred. . . . [Here] the defendant meat packing company did not manufacture the hog or hogs [and no inspection would have discovered it because it was encysted in the hog's muscles].

[*Third: whether an absolute liability is imposed upon the meat producer by either the Public Health Act or the Animal Contagious Diseases Act.*] It is frequently a difficult matter to decide as to whether the violation of a penal statute founds an action for negligence. . . . It would be very harsh legislation . . . when it is impossible . . . for the vendor to find out whether the pork is infested. . . . Trichinae in fresh pork can be destroyed by heating to 131°F or by freezing for 20 days at a temperature of 5F° above zero. . . .

. . . [Evidence of experts] may be stated shortly to the effect that a hog with trichinae in it in the encysted form is not an unhealthy or diseased animal, nor is it unfit for food after being properly cooked. . . .

The pork was marked "Approved" by the Government inspectors under the [Meat and Canned Foods] Act and consequently was found by them to be "healthy and fit for food.". . .

. . . [T]here was no breach by Paolini of the implied warranty that the sausage meat was reasonably fit for the purpose for which it was sold, and was of merchantable quality.

The normal use of fresh pork is to eat it after cooking. . . .

The plaintiffs here did not notify the defendant Paolini that they desired to make an abnormal use of the fresh pork sausages purchased from him, and consequently they cannot invoke the provisions of the Sale of Goods Act.

[The actions against the defendants were dismissed. The damages of the husband assessed at $1,500; the wife at $7,500.]

APPENDIX 24-A: SYNOPSIS OF THE SALE OF GOODS ACT

S. 1(1)   Definitions:
            Buyer: person agreeing to buy or buying;

Document of Title: any warrant or order used for delivery of goods;

Goods: all chattels personal except those in action and money;

Specific goods: goods identified and agreed on at the time the contract of sale is made;

Warranty: an agreement relating to goods but collateral to main purpose of contract and giving rise to a claim for damages only.

S. 1(3)   Ceasing to pay debt indicates insolvency.

S. 2(1)   Contract for sale of goods is one whereby seller transfers or agrees to transfer property in goods to buyer for price or money consideration.

S. 2(3)   Sale transfers property to seller, agreement to sell relates to transfer at a future date.

S. 3(1)   Capacity is regulated by general law, but minor and mentally incompetent must pay for necessaries which are determined by station in life and requirements.

S. 4   Contract of sale may be in writing, oral, or mixture of both, or result from conduct of parties.

S. 5(1)   If over $40, contract of sale not enforceable without some part performance or memorandum in writing.

S. 5(3)   There is acceptance when buyer does anything which recognizes pre-existing contract of sale.

S. 6(1)   Goods may be existing or to be produced or manufactured, the latter being called future goods.

S. 6(2)   Goods may be bought on a contingency.

S. 7   In sale of specific goods, if goods have perished without knowledge of seller, contract is void.

S. 8   In agreement to sell if goods perish without fault, agreement is avoided.

S. 9   Price may be determined either by contract, by a third party, or by course of business.

S. 9(2)   If not determined as above, then buyer must pay a reasonable price.

S. 10   If third party does not fix price, agreement to sell is avoided except for goods the buyer has accepted and for which the reasonable price must be paid.

S. 11   Time not of essence of contract unless stipulated.

S. 12(1)   Buyer may treat breach of condition as a warranty.

S. 12(2)   Condition or warranty in a contract depends upon the construction of the contract, i.e. damages only, or rejection of goods for a condition.

S. 12(3)   If contract is not severable, and either buyer has accepted goods or property has passed, breach of any condition must be treated as a warranty *only*.

S. 13   In every contract of sale, there are normally the following implied conditions and/or warranties:

(a) that seller is owner and has right to sell;

(b) that buyer is to enjoy quiet possession;

(c) that there will be freedom from encumbrances or liens.

S. 14   Sale by description has implied condition that goods correspond with description or sample.

S. 15(1)   Where buyer lets seller know why he requires goods and relies on seller's skill there is an implied condition that goods will be reasonably *fit* for such purpose, but does not apply to goods sold under trade name only.

S. 15(2)   Implied condition of *merchantability* in goods bought by description from seller dealing in such goods except defects obvious on inspection.

S. 15(3)   Implied condition of *fitness* may be implied by trade.

S. 15(4)   Express warranty does not negate implied warranty unless inconsistent (N.B. has no effect now under Consumer Protection Act with regard to consumer goods).

S. 16   If contract so provides, a contract may be a sale by sample and then by implied condition:

(a) bulk must be same quality;

(b) buyer must have time to compare;

(c) goods must be free of any defect not obvious on examination.

S. 17   Unascertained goods, no property passes to buyer until ascertained.

S. 18(1)   Specific goods, property is transferred at time parties intended.

S. 18(1)   Intention is determined from terms of contract, conduct of parties, circumstances.

S. 19   Following rules help ascertain intention as to passing of property:

Rule 1—unconditional contract, specific goods, deliverable state, property passes when contract is made, regardless of payment or delivery;

Rule 2—in sale of specific goods (e.g. used TV) if seller required to do something (e.g. repair) to put in deliverable state, no property passes until work done and buyer notified;

Rule 3—sale of specific goods requiring weighing, measuring, testing, property only passes when this is done and buyer notified;

Rule 4—sales on approval, property passes:

(i) when buyer signifies acceptance,

(ii) when buyer keeps goods beyond approval period;

Rule 5— (i) sale of unascertained goods by description, property passes when goods in a deliverable state are unconditionally appropriated by either party with consent of the other, either before or after appropriation. Goods delivered to a carrier or bailee are deemed unconditionally appropriated if no right of disposal retained by seller.

S. 20(1)   Seller may sell goods subject to condition in which case property does not pass until condition fulfilled.

S. 20(2)	Goods shipped to order of seller or his agent indicates reservation of disposal.
S. 20(3)	Shipping subject to bill of lading and draft drawn on buyer, property does not pass until draft accepted.
S. 21	Goods at seller's risk until property in goods transferred to buyer, excepting goods at risk of party causing delay in delivery.
S. 22	Normally buyer does not get better title than seller, if seller not the owner unless owner prevented from denying right of seller to sell.
S. 23	Market overt such as in U.K. does not apply in Canada.
S. 24	Buyer buying from seller who has voidable title, gets good title if buying without notice (of defect).
S. 25(1)	Seller in possession of goods after sale may transfer good title to a third party buyer without notice (of defect).
S. 25(2)	Buyer in possession with consent of seller may transfer good title to third party buyer.
S. 25(3)	Foregoing section does not apply to property covered by a security document under the Personal Property Security Act.
S. 26	Seller must deliver goods and buyer accept and pay.
S. 27	Foregoing are concurrent conditions unless otherwise provided.
S. 28(1)	If nothing is said in contract buyer must pick up goods at seller's place of business or residence.
S. 28(2)	If seller is to send goods must do so in reasonable time.
S. 28(3)	If goods held by third party, i.e. bailee, no delivery to buyer until third party acknowledges he holds for buyer.
S. 28(4)	Delivery must be made as requested at reasonable hour.
S. 28(5)	Normally seller must put goods in a deliverable state.
S. 29(1)	If seller delivers less than contract, buyer may reject but must pay for any he keeps.
S. 29(2)	If larger quantity delivered, seller may reject all, or accept whole or part.
S. 29(3)	If seller delivers mixed goods, buyer may reject, accept part or whole.
S. 29(4)	Foregoing may be altered by trade or custom.
S. 30(1)	Unless agreed, buyer not required to accept by instalments.
S. 30(2)	In case of delivery and payment by instalments, facts of case will determine whether failure to deliver or accept is repudiation or damages situation.
S. 31(1)	Delivery of goods to carrier is *prima facie* delivery to buyer.
S. 31(2)	Seller must make reasonable contract with carrier or buyer entitled to repudiate delivery.
S. 32	If seller agrees to delivery other than at his business, risk of deterioration falls on buyer unless otherwise provided.
S. 33(1)	Buyer has a right to examine goods before he is deemed to have accepted them.
S. 33(2)	Seller must allow buyer time to examine prior to acceptance.
S. 34	Buyer deemed to have accepted goods if he says so, keeps them or treats them as his own.

S. 35   A buyer who refuses to accept goods with a legitimate excuse is *not* bound to return goods.

S. 36   Buyer is at least liable for loss resulting from refusal to take delivery within a reasonable time, if breach does not amount to repudiation.

S. 37   Seller is unpaid if whole price not paid, or when negotiable instrument given in payment not honoured.

S. 38(1)   Unpaid seller of goods, where property has passed:
(a) a lien on goods or right to retain goods while in possession;
(b) in case of insolvency a right of "stoppage *in transitu*";
(c) if property has not passed, seller may withhold delivery as above.

S. 39   If unpaid seller is in possession, he may retain goods if credit is not mentioned, credit has expired, or buyer is insolvent.

S. 39(2)   Seller may exercise lien even as bailee.

S. 40   If unpaid in case of part delivery, seller may withhold remainder unless agreed otherwise.

S. 41   Unpaid seller loses lien by delivery to carrier or bailee for delivery to buyer without reservation of disposal or where buyer lawfully obtains possession by waiver.

S. 42   Provides for "stoppage *in transitu*."

S. 43(1)   Goods are in transit until buyer or agent, takes possession, or

S. 43(3)   notified of arrival, unless

S. 43(4)   buyer rejects goods.

S. 43(5)   Where goods delivered by ship, facts determine whether master is carrier or buyer's agent.

S. 43(7)   Even part delivery may be stopped.

S. 44(1)   Unpaid seller may exercise lien by taking goods or notifying carrier to withhold delivery.

S. 44(2)   Seller must pay for return delivery.

S. 45   Normally seller's lien not defeated by buyer's disposition but if buyer lawfully has documents of title he may defeat lien and give good title to third party.

S. 46(1)   Contract of sale not rescinded by exercise of lien.

S. 46(2)   If seller sells goods under lien, third party buyer gets title against original buyer.

S. 46(3)   If seller sells perishables held on lien, buyer may be liable for loss occasioned.

S. 46(4)   If seller reserves right to resell on buyer's default, contract is cancelled; buyer may be liable for loss.

S. 47   If buyer has property in goods and refuses to pay, seller may sue for price.

S. 47(2)   If sale provides for payment regardless of delivery, seller may sue for payment.

S. 48(1)   If buyer wrongfully refuses to accept delivery, seller may sue for damages.

S. 48(2)   Damages are those resulting from breach.

S. 48(3)   If there is available market, loss is difference between contract price and current price.

S. 49   If seller refuses to deliver, buyer may claim damages (same rules as in s. 48 above).

S. 50   In case of specific goods, court may order specific performance.

S. 51   In case of breach of warranty, the buyer may claim a reduction in price or damages.

S. 52   Act does not affect rights to interest or return of consideration.

S. 53   Act provides that either buyer or seller may alter provisions of Act regarding implied conditions, etc. (now outlawed for consumer contracts).

S. 56   Lays down rules for sale by auction; normally seller cannot bid unless he has reserved a right to bid.

S. 57(1)   Rules of common law—i.e. fraud, misrepresentation, duress, mistake—continue to apply to sale of goods contracts.

S. 57(2)   Act does not apply to security documents or mortgages.

25

Product Liability and Consumer Warranties

DONOGHUE v. STEVENSON

The law of product liability in Canada gained attention after an English case decision, *Donoghue v. Stevenson* (1932) A.C. 562 in which the plaintiff alleged that she had suffered injury and damages as the result of drinking ginger beer from an opaque bottle which also contained a partly decomposed snail. The court held that, since there was no privity of contract between the injured girl and either the restauranteur or the manufacturer, because the bottle had been bought by her friend, the plaintiff could not sue in contract but possibly in negligence. Thus, according to the court:

> a manufacturer of products, which he sells in such a form as to show that he intends them to reach the ultimate consumer in the form in which they left him with no reasonable possibility of intermediate examination, and with the knowledge that the absence of reasonable care in the preparation or putting up of the products will result in injury to the consumer's life or property, owes a duty to the consumer to take that reasonable care.

This liability has not been confined to manufacturers in the narrow sense, because assemblers of component parts have subsequently been held liable under this principle of law, as well as manufacturers of the defective component itself. Liability has also been extended under the "snail in the bottle" principle to a retailer who, for example, fails in the reasonable duty of inspecting a car before its sale, and even to repairers and installers of certain products. Occasionally, rather than basing liability according to *Donoghue v. Stevenson*, the plaintiff will make the plea of "res ipsa loquitur." This principle can apply to a situation in which goods have been lost or damaged while under the control of the defendant who may thus only escape liability by proving that someone outside of his employ was negligent.

The decision in the "snail in the bottle" case used the word "consumer" as the class of persons afforded protection under the principle of liability enunciated in this case. In practice, the principle has even been extended to cover an innocent bystander (see *Martin v. T.W. Hand Fireworks Co. Ltd.*) who was injured by an errant firecracker while watching a fireworks display. The firecracker had been bought in a bulk package by a retailer from a fireworks manufacturer at the request of an association that was putting on a fireworks demonstration. The firecracker failed to operate as a rocket when lighted and ran along the ground instead, causing the personal injury to the bystander. Unfortunately there was no way that it could have been examined to reveal its defects

In the case of *Seaway Hotels Ltd. v. Consumers Gas Co.* (1959) C.R. 581, the court held that "if an actionable wrong has been done to the plaintiff he is entitled to recover all the damage resulting from it even if some part of the damage considered by itself would not be recoverable." In this case, lost wages and the cost of repairing damaged property was allowed. There has never been any doubt since the case of the "snail in the bottle case" that compensation for both life and property was recoverable. What was in question was the matter of pure economic loss. However, the case of *Hedley Byrne & Co. Ltd. v. Heller & Partners Ltd.* (1964) A.C. 465 (H.L.) provided that pure economic loss can be recovered for a negligent misstatement—for example, where there is reason to believe that some third party may act on the strength and believed veracity of such statements.

It would appear that liability for a defective product does not extend only to the product itself but also to any product in which the defective item has been incorporated—for example, a refrigeration unit in a commercial carrier truck or an air conditioner in a house (*Dutton v. Bognor Regis Urban District Council* (1972) 1 Q.B. 373 (C.A.)).

There is no doubt that liability may be imposed on a negligent manufacturer for damages arising from a defective product acquired by sale. However, another situation is where the product is obtained gratuitously such as the distribution of sample drugs and other products by a manufacturer. It would seem logical to extend tort liability at least to products distributed gratuitously for business-promotion purposes.

There is no satisfactory answer to the question of when the manufacturer begins to be liable for a non-apparent defect in any of its products. This could depend on the state of the art. For example, some twenty years ago no drug manufacturer had designed bottle caps that were safe against handling by small children. Today the situation is different, with safety caps available. Yet there must certainly be some products that were bottled earlier in an unsafe manner that are still on household shelves today. It is doubtful if the manufacturer would still be held liable if such bottles got into the wrong hands and caused injury. Today Federal American Law calls for the manufacturer to alert the users of its product as soon as a defect is discovered in the design of its product, or else such manufacturer must assume strict liability for all injuries and damages suffered by such users. Canadian law has not yet developed to this extent and each case is dealt with on its own merits. There may, however, be an obligation to warn in the case of inherently dangerous products.

Where there is a possibility of intermediate examination, the manufacturer may not be liable. For example, if a consumer was found to have drunk from a bottle of soda water containing a dead mouse, such person would probably not have as good a claim as the person who drank from a beer bottle where the liquid is coloured and encountered the same experience.

There are at least three defences open to the manufacturer against claims resulting from defects in manufactured products that have caused harm to a consumer. The first is that the product was tampered with by a third party. The second is that the product was permitted to deteriorate. The third is that the plaintiff, knowing of the danger, incurred the risk—for example, an individual opening a bottle of beer, drinking from the bottle, and realizing from the burning sensation in the mouth that the bottle had not been satisfactorily cleaned. The obvious thing to do is to spit out the contents before injury results.

As a general rule, where injury is suffered by a plaintiff from the use of a defectively manufactured product, the courts will be reluctant to excuse the manufacturer either on the principle of consent or remoteness of damage.

Strict Liability

In the case of *Rylands v. Fletcher* (1868) L.C. 3 H.L. 330, the owner of property erected a reservoir on his land which caused damage to his neighbour's mining operation when the water leaked down through mine shafts and crossed onto the neighbour's property causing damage thereby. The legal rule contained in this case was expressed as "the person who, for hisown purposes, brings on to his lands and collects and keeps there anything likely to do mischief if it escapes, must keep it at his peril; and if he does not do so, is prima facie answerable for all the damage which is the natural consequence of its escape." This amounts to strict liability and has been applied in the case of damage—for example, from an explosion. In one case the defendants erected a flagpole in a public park and were held liable for injuries caused to persons attending a demonstration who were injured by the collapse of the flagpole. In the foregoing case, the principle of *Rylands v. Fletcher* was applied, even though the defendants were not the owners of the land onto which the potentially dangerous object had been brought.

Nuisance

The case of *Russell Transport Co. v. Ont. Malleable Iron Co. Ltd.* (1952) O.R. 621 (referred to in Chapter 3) shows how a foundry, which had been in operation without any complaints for over forty years, was forced to take action to discontinue the release of a smoke containing acid mist which was observed to destroy the paint work on new cars, when the plaintiff started the practice of parking his new cars on a lot adjacent to the factory. Thus strict liability was applied to a nuisance—which is the act of using one's land to cause injury or harm to a neighbour in the occupation of his land, by the release of water, smoke, noise or other nuisance.

Fitness and Merchantability

Section 15 of the Ontario Sale of Goods Act sets out two implied conditions which apply to all contracts for the sale of goods, except where excluded. This section reads as follows:

15. Subject to this Act and any statute in that behalf, there is no implied warranty or condition as to the quality or fitness for any particular purpose of goods supplied under a contract of sale, except as follows:

   1. Where the buyer, expressly or by implication, makes known to the seller the particular purpose for which the goods are required so as to show that the buyer relies on the seller's skill or judgment, and the goods are of a description that it is in the course of the seller's business to supply (whether he is the manufacturer or not), there is an implied condition that the goods will be reasonably fit for such purpose, but in the case of a contract for the sale of a specified article under its patent or other trade name there is no implied condition as to its fitness for any particular purpose.
   2. Where goods are bought by description from a seller who deals in goods of that description (whether he is the manufacturer or not), there is an implied condition that the goods will be of merchantable quality but if the buyer has examined the goods, there is no implied condition as regards defects that such examination ought to have revealed.
   3. An implied warranty or condition as to quality or fitness for a particular purpose may be annexed by the usage of trade.
   4. An express warranty or condition does not negate a warranty or condition implied by this Act, unless inconsistent therewith.

The courts have used the foregoing section to protect the buyer unless it would be unreasonable for the buyer to rely on the seller's skill or judgment; for example, the manager of a supermarket could not be expected to be familiar with the characteristics of all of the products sold in the supermarket. In *Australian Knitting Mills Ltd. v. Grant* (1933) 50 C.L.R. 387 (the underwear contained acid which caused a skin irritation), the court stated that a breach of the condition of merchantability arose when no other person, if fully aware of the defect, would pay the same price for the goods. In another decision the implied condition of merchantability was held to mean that the "article is of such quality and in such condition that a reasonable man acting reasonably would after a full examination accept it under the circumstances of the case in performance of his offer to buy that article." (See *Bristol Tramways & Carriage Co. Ltd. v. Fiat Motors, Ltd.* (1910) 2 K.B. 831 (C.A.) at p. 841.)

The liability for breaches of fitness or merchantability was expressed in *Henry Kendal & Sons v. William Lillico & Sons Ltd.* (1969) A.C. 31 at p. 84:

If the law were always logical one would suppose that a buyer, who has obtained a right to rely on the seller's skill and judgment, would only obtain thereby an assurance that proper skill and judgment has been exercised, and would only be entitled to a remedy if a defect in the goods was due to failure to exercise such skill and judgment. But the law has always gone farther than that. By getting the seller to undertake to use his skill and judgment the buyer gets under (this section) an assurance that the goods will be reasonably fit for his purpose and that covers not only defects which the seller ought to have detected but also defects which are latent in the sense that even the utmost skill and judgment on the part of the seller would not have detected them.

In the Ontario case of *Buckley v. Lever Bros. Ltd.* (1953) O.R. 704, the plaintiff was injured by the shattering of one of the clothespins that she had purchased. The plaintiff recovered compensation in the way of damages for personal injuries, which considerably enlarged the rule of *Hadley v. Baxendale* (1854) 9 Exch 341, which provides that the seller would only be liable for all natural and foreseeable damages resulting from the breach of contract.

Privity of Contract

The common law does not provide for a right of action by anyone who is not a party to the contract. For example, a parent who buys a hair dryer and gives it to one of his children, who then suffers injury through its use. While such child could possibly sue in tort under the principle of the "snail in the bottle" case, any action to recover damages must be taken by the parent. This would however be ruled out insofar as harm or injury flowing from the use of the defective hairdryer because the parent has not suffered any injury. The most that the parent could sue for in contract is a return of the purchase price, or a replacement for the hairdryer.

The courts have even been prepared to extend the protection afforded by the implied conditions of the Sale of Goods Act to contracts of service, bailment and real estate transactions. For example, in *Miller v. Cannon Hill Estates, Ltd.* (1931) 2 K.B. 113, the court found that there is an implied warranty in the sale of an unfinished house that it will be properly built.

Civil Right of Action

With respect to liability arising from a breach of a criminal statute, it should be noted that section 31.1(1) of the Combines Investigation Act provides for a civil right of recovery for persons who suffer loss or damage as a result of conduct which is contrary to the Act or as the result of failure to comply with an order of the Restrictive Trade Practices Commission concerning refusal to deal, misuse of consignment selling practices, exclusive dealing, tied selling, anti-competitive behaviour, following extra-Canadian influence or orders, and Court orders generally pertaining to the Act. The only case which has been taken to Court on the basis of this decision has been dismissed because it was alleged that only the Provincial Government has the authority to create a civil right of action under the Constitution Act, 1867. In another case, *Heimler v. Calvert Caterers* (1974) 49 D.L.R. (3rd) 36, involving a wedding breakfast guest who became ill after eating food negligently handled by a food handler who was an undetected typhoid carrier, it was held that the Food and Drugs Act did not create a civil right of action. This decision included the following quotation from *Wasney v. Jurazsky* (1933) 1. D.L.R. 616 at 627:

> If a man who has or professes to have special knowledge or skill makes a representation by virtue thereof to another—be it advice, information or opinion—with the intention of inducing him to enter into a contract with him, he is under a duty to use reasonable care to see that the representation is correct, and that the advice, information or opinion is reliable. If he negligently gives unsound advice or misleading information or expresses an erroneous opinion, and thereby induces the other side to enter into a contract with him, he is liable in damages."

In Ontario, the Business Practices Act, now allows the innocent party in a contract which has been induced by misrepresentation, to rescind the contract, but no provision is made under this Act for an action for damages suffered.

COLLATERAL WARRANTIES

A recent development of contract law involves the question of collateral warranties. The case of *Shanklin Pier Ltd. v. Detel Products Ltd.* (1951) 2 K.B. 854, dealt with a situation where pier owners, having read about the qualities of a certain paint, contracted with a firm of paint contractors, to have their pier, which rested in salt water, painted using this particular brand of paint to be purchased by the contractors. The paint weathered within six months, although the advertisement stated that it should last four to five years. The plaintiff pier owners sued the paint manufacturers directly and the Court found the company liable under a collateral warranty—that is, the statements contained in their advertisement—even without privity of contract. The following statement by Lord Denning is quoted on this point:

> In English law an innocent misrepresentation may give rise to a right of rescission where that is possible, but not to a right of damages. That has never given us any difficulty in practice. Whenever a judge thinks that damages ought to be given, he finds that there was a collateral contract rather than an innocent misrepresentation. In practice when I get a representation prior to a contract which is broken and the man ought to pay damages I treat it as a collateral contract. I have never known any of my colleagues to do otherwise. [see Allan, "The Scope of the Contract" (1967) 41 Aust. L.J. 274 at 293.]

A recent decision, *Murray v. Sperry Rand Corp. et al* (1979) 5 B.L.R. 84 (Ont. H.C.J.), dealt with the question of a farmer who had read brochures about a certain type of harvesting and threshing machine which, so the brochures claimed, enable a job to be completed in one half of the time. He decided to buy such a machine and earn extra income by contract work in addition to farming. He approached a dealer, told him about the brochure, and decided to buy this particular harvester. This machine did not function properly, despite all the efforts of the company and the dealer's service people. As a matter of fact, the machine took twice as long to harvest a field rather than one half of the time. Finally the farmer became so indebted that he had to sell his farm and seek other employment. He brought an action against the manufacturers of the harvesting machine to rescind the contract. Of course, the obvious defence offered was the lack of privity of contract, because he had purchased the machine from the dealer, not from the manufacturers. but the court held that the manufacturer was liable on a *collateral warranty*, based on the fact that the buyer entered into a contract on the truth of the advertisements contained in the brochures, even though the harvester itself was purchased from a third party, and thus benefitted the manufacturer only indirectly.

CONCLUSIONS ON CONTRACT AND TORT LIABILITY

The preceding examination of the liability situation from the point of view of contract and tort, has disclosed the following facts: that at Common Law only a party with contractual privity may sue the other contracting party for a defective product. In such a case, under the *Hadley v. Baxendale* rule, only damages flowing naturally from the breach of contract are recoverable. Thus unless there is a contract of sale, and unless the plaintiff suffers damage or injury himself or herself, the law of contract offers no remedy— barring the exception provided by collateral warranties, which allow a person to sue a manufacturer on the basis of the statements contained in an advertisement or brochure.

The Sale of Goods Act, under the implied conditions of fitness, merchantability, description and sale by sample, also provides a remedy for breach of such conditions for the buyer of goods. The Consumer Protection Acts of most provinces also provide that the implied conditions of the Sale of Goods Act may not be negated in a Consumer Sale.

From a tort point of view, the plaintiff is allowed to sue the manufacturer under the "snail in the bottle" case for injuries caused by a product which does not allow any examination after the product leaves the factory and subsequently causes injury or harm to a user exercising reasonable care. Liability also exists on the part of the manufacturer, selling an inherently dangerous product which is either explosive or high inflammable, to take measures to advise any potential consumer of the dangerous hazards. There is also the principle of *Rylands v. Fletcher* for the escape of dangerous things which cause harm to the neighbour in the occupation of his land; however it may be difficult to apply the latter principle to the retailer or manufacturer of consumer goods.

CONSUMER WARRANTIES

Almost every major consumer appliance sold to Canadians today is accompanied by a "warranty." Thus most new television sets, for example, bear a warranty for at least twelve months. Most consumers understand that such a "warranty" is a promise or guarantee that the appliance or other product will be repaired or replaced if found to be unsatisfactory for the purpose for which it is intended during the length of time stipulated in the warranty. This is the popular meaning of the term "warranty."

In contract law, however, the word "warranty" has a different meaning— as, for example, in the Sale of Goods Act. In contract law, the term *condition* refers to a major provision of any contract. If such a provision does not exist, then, since it is fundamental to the contract, the contract is nullified. On the other hand, the term *warranty*, in its contract law sense, refers to a minor requirement of any contract. If such an item is non-existent or imperfect, the contract is not cancelled. The injured party is only allowed to collect damages, sufficient to return him to the position he would have been in, if the contract had been perfectly performed. An example of this legal meaning of condition and warranty would be a used car, sold as "in running condition." If it did not run after the sale, this would amount to a breach of condition and the buyer would be entitled to a refund of the purchase price. If, on the other hand, the muffler fell off as the car was being driven from the used-car lot, the buyer would still have a car in running condition. However, he might be able to claim compensation equivalent to the cost of repair of the muffler, as a breach of warranty.

In 1972, the Ontario Law Reform Commission published a study entitled a *"Report on Consumer Warranties and Guarantees in the Sale of Goods."* The report points out that because of the complexity of present-day goods, the consumer is no longer able to evaluate the goods purchased and must rely on brand names or highly coloured advertisements in making his selection. Also, the decline of quality control, lack of service facilities, manufacturers not honouring warranties and lack of standards of production all contribute to consumer dissatisfaction.

Some of the difficulties which now face the consumer, discussed in the report, are as follows:

1. The common law provides that unless both the seller and the conumer can be returned to their original positions before the sale, the Court will not rescind or cancel the contract.
2. The common law, following a decision laid down in 1625, does not consider an affirmation of fact sufficient as an express warranty unless it is intended to be promissory in character.
3. Most consumer goods contracts contain a provision that the contract alone embodies all the agreement between buyer and seller and specifically exclude any promises made by salespersons, with the result that the "parol evidence" rule does not permit a Court to enquire into any oral statements made at the time of the sale.
4. Many consumer complaints are related to the "durability" of a product which depends also, to a considerable extent, on the consumer's personal care and use of it. Used goods would appear to be covered by the implied

condition of "merchantability" set out in the Sale of Goods Act. The consumer should be satisfied if he or she gets reasonable value for his money. With regard to new items, even first-quality durable goods sometimes break down and reputable manufacturers should make provision for repairs beyond the warranty period, but there is no legal obligation to do so.

5. Normally, under section 51 of the Ontario Sale of Goods Act, and in accordance with the decision in *Hadley v. Baxendale* (1854) 9 Exch 341, a buyer may recover not only his direct damages, but also all consequential damages that were reasonably foreseeable. This provision alarms sellers so much that they invariably include a clause disclaiming responsibility for any matter other than that expressly stated in the contract.

The Ontario report considered several ways of dealing with the disclaimer problem. For example, the American legislation (article 2-302 of the Uniform Commercial Code and section 5.108 of the Uniform Consumer Credit Code) adopts the principle also found in the Ontario Unconscionable Transactions Relief Act which allows the court to interfere in unconscionable sales or other contracts. Other approaches include the Israeli legislation providing for prior government approval of contracts with disclaimer clauses; American legislation which permits only obvious express limitations; the statutory obligations imposed on manufacturers and retailers under the Farm Implements legislation in Canada; and the recent express prohibition by provincial consumer laws of disclaimer of the implied conditions of the Sale of Goods Act.

6. The Commission also studied problems relating to *vertical privity*, which under the common law prevents the consumer from suing the manufacturer for breach of contract where a purchase has been made through a retailer; and *horizontal privity* which prevents any person using the goods other than the original buyer from suing the seller for damages suffered.

The American law on the liability of the manufacturer to users was expressed in the case of *Randy Knitwear Inc. v. American Cyanamid Co.* (1962) 181 N.E. 2d 399 (N.Y.C.A.) where the New York Court of Appeals held a manufacturer of chemical resins liable for false representation that fabrics treated with resin were shrink-proof; privity was ignored; breach of warranty was said to "sound" both in contract and in tort.

In *Henningsen v. Bloomfield Motors* (1960) 161 A 2d 69, the wife of the buyer of a new car, which went off the road because of a defective steering arm, sued the manufacturer for injuries suffered. She was allowed to recover on the basis of implied warranties running with the vehicle from the manufacturer to the ultimate buyer or user, without any requirement of privity of contract.

The California Supreme Court abandoned implied warranties and held that manufacturer's liability was imposed as a rule of "public policy" and was tortious in character, *Greenman v. Yuba Power Products* (1963) 377 P. 2d 897.

The Ontario study also dealt with such warranty problems as the use of warranties as competitive devices (for example, those given by the Big Three automobile manufacturers); exaggerated warranties, such as ten-, twenty-, or fifty-year warranties; the restriction of warranties to the original purchaser; manufacturers imposing the obligation of service warranty problems on dealers; lemonproblems such as the non-repairable car; shortages of qualified mechanics and non-availability of spare parts.

The report also mentions the *Song-Beverly Consumer Warranty Act,* California, 1970, which imposes warranties of merchantability and fitness on all consumer goods except goods sold "as is," and provides that to do business the manufacturer must maintain service facilities and spare parts.

The study mentions that the Canadian Farm Implements legislation covers the warranty problem thoroughly by legislating warranty obligations, spelling out the buyer's rights against both dealer and manufacturer if the farm implement is not working, and covering the question of durability and spare parts. These Acts are enforced by penalties, licensing and, in some case, arbitration.

Some of the suggestions advanced for the enforcement of consumer rights include:

1. greater use of smaller claims courts;
2. provision of legal aid;
3. solicitor-client costs;
4. class actions;
5. Consumer Protection Bureaus to institute test cases;
6. industry-sponsored settlement procdures;
7. appointment of government officials to mediate consumer disputes similar to Swedish practices.

Present Canadian practices that ensure certain warranty standards include:

1. Federal Food and Drugs Act, section 5, which in respect of food states ". . . no person shall label, package, treat, process, sell or advertise any food in a manner that is false, misleading or deceptive or is likely to create an erroneous impression regarding its character, value, quantity, composition, merit or safety."
2. Similar provisions are contained in the Canadian Broadcasting Act, the Combines Investigations Act, the Consumer Protection Act, and the Textile Labelling and the Consumer Packaging and Labelling Acts.
3. Steps have been taken to promote consumer safety on the roads by, for example, the Federal Motor Vehicle Safety Act and, at the provincial level, by, for example, Ontario's Highway Traffic Act with its required Certificate of Mechanical Fitness for older cars. Canadian approved safety standards have also been established for certain products including hockey helmets, life preservers, and children's car seats.

The Report concludes by recommending that a new Act, to be known as the Consumer Products Warranties Act should be passed, consisting of:

1. A statement of the warranty obligations of the seller and maufacturer of a consumer product;
2. A code of basic guidelines for the contents of express performance warranties and their administration;
3. Machinery for the resolution of warranty disputes; and
4. General provisions for the administration of the Act.

Proposed Consumer Products Warranties Act

In August 1973, the Minister of Consumer and Commercial Relations circulated a Green Paper stating that it would appear that "the consumer currently must rely almost exclusively upon the conscience of the individual business man who has become the sole arbiter of what his warranty means and how it is applied." The principal shortcomings of the Sale of Goods Act were identified as follows:

> It proceeds from the fictitious premise that the parties are bargaining from positions of equal strength and sophistication and it uses concepts to describe and distinguish between different types of obligations that are now obsolete and difficult to apply. It supplies a framework of remedies for breaches of the seller's obligations that are unrelated to practical realities. Especially serious is the Act's preoccupation with the bilateral relationship between the seller and the buyer, which totally ignores the powerful position of the manufacturer in today's marketing structure. This results, at least in the Anglo-Canadian law, in shielding the manufacturer from contractual responsibility to the consumer. By the same token, the law has largely ignored the impact of manufacturers' express warranties and the defects in their contents and administration. Finally, our sales law is private law and it has failed to provide any meaningful machinery for the redress of consumer grievances. This last weakness is perhaps the most serious of all weaknesses, for as has been frequently observed, a right is only as strong as the remedy available to enforce it.

The Green Paper recommended a new warranty system with two basic components:

1. Basic Statutory Warranty—implied conditions of the Sale of Goods Act, somewhat revised;
2. Supplementary Warranties—includes statements made by a salesman, in an advertisement, or in another document.

The implied conditions of the Sale of Goods Act would now become part of the basic statutory warranty, plus a warranty or *reasonable durability* and a warranty of the *availability of spare parts and servicing facilities.*
Disclaimers against liability which would negate the basic statutory

warranties would be prohibited by a provision in the new Act similar to section 44a of the Ontario Consumer Protection Act.

The Ministry proposed formal guidelines for manufacturers' supplementary written warranties which would include:

1. name and address of warrantor;
2. legible warranty;
3. clearly worded;
4. words "warranty or guarantee" not to be used unless accompanied by a promise to reimburse or replace major components if defective;
5. duration must be stated;
6. claim processing must be indicated;
7. disputes must be settled by third party;
8. there must be no limitation or exclusion of existing statutory warranties.

On the question of horizontal and vertical privity, the Ministry accepts the principle that the manufacturer should be liable as well as the retailer under sales law and that remedies should be based on the concept of warranty, with the manufacturer, if sued, in some cases being entitled to claim subrogation or vouching-over from the retailer and vice versa.

The distinction in horizontal privity between the original buyer and user would be abolished.

Also, the Ministry stated, "The parol evidence rule should be abolished for consumer transactions and evidence of misrepresentation to the consumer which does not appear in the written agreement should be made admissible in Court".

The following recommendations were proposed relating to the consumer's remedies:

1. if defect fundamental: purchaser may reject product, claim refund of money and any foreseeable damages;
2. if defect not fundamental but not remedied: purchaser may also reject goods and claim a refund;
3. retailer may vouch over any part of claim paid by him which is attributable to manufacturer.

The redress procedure includes the following proposals:

1. The Consumer Protection Bureau would have the right to mediate, defend or sue on the consumer's behalf;
2. An arbitration system would be set up;
3. A warranty advisory council should be set up to advise the Consumer Protection Bureau and industry on all aspects of warranties and consumer protection;
4. The Consumer Registration Appeal Tribunal could be asked to assess loss to a complainant, order restitution, and also make a "cease and desist order";
5. The Consumer Protection Bureau should set up a testing program and publish more educational information.

To date, no further action has been taken with respect to the implementation of the proposed Consumer Products Warranties Act. However, in Ontario, for example, the Landlord and Tenant Act and the Business Practices Act now allow oral evidence to be heard to explain consumer contracts.

RECENT DEVELOPMENTS

In addition to the studies conducted in Ontario in an effort to produce a Consumer Warranties Act, which has been covered in the preceding pages, Saskatchewan, New Brunswick, and Quebec have also been active in legislating product liability legislation. In scope, the Saskatchewan Act greatly resembles the proposed Ontario Consumer Warranties Act, except that where the Ontario Act requires some contractual relationship, the Saskatchewan Act does not. Also, while the Ontario Act restricts liability to seller or manufacturer, the Saskatchewan Act also includes an importer from outside the province, where the manufacturer does not have a place of business in the province. It was intended to include a provision in the Act which would have made the manufacturer, seller, or employees responsible for any written or oral representations made as to the quality, quantity, condition, performance or efficiency of a consumer product. . . . operate as an express warranty if it was made to induce the sale of a product whether the consumer acted on it or not. However this last provision has not yet been promulgated. Finally while this act applies only to consumer products, the coverage in the matter of liability for defective products extends to a person reasonably expected to use, consume or be affected by a consumer product. The Act also implements the *Hadley v. Baxendale* rule that the defendant who is liable must assume responsibility for all personal injuries that were reasonably foreseeable as resulting from the breach of warranty.

HAZARDOUS PRODUCTS ACT

There are more and more products being sold to the consumer that are potentially dangerous—for example, household cleaning chemicals, plastic bags, children's toys, children's car seats, aerosol cans, electrical appliances and building adhesives. Consequently, in 1969, to help protect the consumer, the federal Parliament passed a Hazardous Products Act.

The most important provision of the Act is s. 3, which divides hazardous products into two main categories: banned products which cannot be advertised, sold or imported in Canada at all; and regulated products—those which cannot be advertised, sold or imported except as authorized and controlled by Regulations.

An example of a product falling into the first category is "jequirity beans." They were once imported from Mexico for use in children's necklaces, but were found to be highly poisonous. Another example is the banning of the use of cellulose nitrate for eye glass frames because of its high flammability risk. In the second category are, for example, household cleaners containing a great variety of chemical compounds. These must now indicate what remedial action is to be taken if a child or other person should accidentally swallow some of the product. Also, they must show on the label the symbols set out in the mandatory Hazardous Products Safety Coding, which has adopted the octagonal traffic sign for stop, meaning "danger," the diamond shape for "warning," and the upside down triangle for "caution." These are combined with the skull and cross bones for poison, the bursting bomb for explosive, the flame for inflammable, and the skeletal hand for corrosive. Furthermore, delivery of sample packages of household chemicals through mailboxes has now been prohibited. As another example, specific labelling requirements have now been laid down for children's chemistry sets.

REVIEW QUESTIONS

1. What is meant by the term "product liability"?
2. What is the basic principle in the law of torts with regard to product liability? Give an example of a defective product to which this rule might apply.
3. What is meant by the principle of "strict liability"? Why does this rule not apply in Canada? What is the situation here when a consumer suffers injury from a product?
4. What was the rule established in the case of *Donoghue v. Stevenson*?
5. How does the possibility of "intermediate examination" affect a manufacturer's product liability?
6. What is meant by the manufacturer's "duty to warn"? Explain with reference to *Lambert v. Lastoplex Chemicals*.

PROBLEMS

1. The plaintiff was injured when an extension ladder which he had purchased for his part-time painting business from Canadian Tire started to slide on the eaves-troughing of a house he was painting. He fell and injured his leg. The extension ladder fell under him, and after his accident it was observed that the left side of the ladder had buckled at the bottom. He was hospitalized off and on for over a year. When he had more or less fully recovered, one leg was one-half to one inch shorter and his regular employment as a factory hand was restricted to light jobs. He sued the manufacturers of the ladder, the distributors, and Canadian Tire, on the two counts of "res ipsa loquitur" and "product liability."

   The defendants explained their entire manufacturing process and the various tests conducted to try to determine how the bottom ladder could have possibly buckled. Tests showed that at least 800 pounds pressure was required to cause such a structural failure to one side of their ladder and that, out of thousands of similar ladders sold, no similar fault had occurred.

Discuss the application of "res ipsa loquitur" in this case. What is the liability of the manufacturers for their product in this case? What is the liability of the retailers, Canadian Tire? Who won the case? Refer to *McHugh v. Reynolds Extrusion Co. Ltd.* (1974), 7 O.R. (2d) 336.

2. The plaintiff was grinding rust on the paint work of his car when the grinding disc shattered. His lip was cut, requiring sixteen stitches. He fell to the ground, and his wrist was cut and teeth loosened by the shattering of the disc, or by the grinder itself. His total injuries were assessed at over $4,000 and he sued the grinder manufacturers for damages for selling defective products that caused him harm.

His claim was founded on the principle of the *Donoghue v. Stevenson* case (i.e., product made in such a way that its defective features or dangerous features are not apparent), "res ipsa loquitur," lack of warning of dangerous product, and breach of implied warranty of fitness.

The defendant explained the manufacturing process, explained the degree of care taken, and showed that the discs were not dangerous in the hands of competent users.

What is the duty established by *Donoghue v. Stevenson*? How does "res ipsa loquitur" affect this case? Differentiate between duty of care in Canada and "strict liability" in the United States. Who won the case and why? Refer to *Austin v. 3M Canada Ltd.* (1974), 7 O.R. (2d) 200.

3. One morning in 1969, the plaintiff, whose hot water heater, furnace, and stove had all been heated by natural gas since 1952, smelled gas when he got up to go to work. He checked the furnace and water heater, found no leaks, aired out the house, observed that the stove pilot light was out and, on relighting it, caused an explosion (the circulated air having created the proper mixture for an explosion). The house was completely ruined and had to be replaced. The plaintiff and his wife were badly injured. Despite 90% burns to his body, he recovered enough to return to work, but took an early retirement. His medical expenses were assessed at $13,000; his wife's at $1,020. His home replacement was fixed at $18,000, the contents at $8,000. His wife's claim for suffering, i.e. general damages, was $5,400 and his own were $40,000.

It was established that the explosion resulted from a defective flexible connection which joined the stove to the gas outlet. Since the plaintiff's stove had been connected, the gas company had realized that these flexible connections were not as good as double thickness connections and all new installations were made with different approved equipment. Inspections of all installed equipment is required by provincial law at least once every six years and evidence submitted at the trial revealed that these inspections were in fact made, but no attempt was made to pull the stove out and check the connection with the supply outlet.

What would have to be proved to establish the liability of the gas company? What is the general term given to the law which applies in such a case? Was there any evidence to support liability in this case? Who should win and why? Refer to *Lemesurier v. Union Gas Co. of Canada Ltd.* (1975), 8 O.R. (2d) 152.

4. A young Maritimer sat down to eat a bowl of fish chowder in a high-class restaurant. During his meal, a fish bone stuck in his throat. His life was saved only by the quick action of another patron with para-medical training. The Maritimer sued the owner of the restaurant to recover damages for the mental anguish he had suffered and the loss of wages resulting from a week spent recuperating. Discuss the arguments for and against recovery of damages in this case.

5. A major Canadian supermarket was charged under s. 7(2)(b) of the Consumer Packaging and Labelling Act, concerning "any expression, word figure, depiction or symbol that implies or may reasonably be regarded as implying that a pre-packaged product contains any matter not contained in it or does not contain any matter in fact contained in it." Here the facts were that the meat found to be "bottom round" was in fact labelled as "top sirloin." It was found as a matter of fact that one of the food packaging clerks had neglected to change the type of meat stamp being packaged despite the fact that the company had an elaborate system of employee training and education as to government regulations and requirements.

   Under s. 21(1) of the same Act, despite the fact that the offence was proved to have been committed by an employee, the accused supermarket may "establish that the offence was committed without his knowledge or consent and that he exercised *all due diligence* to prevent its commission." What would be your decision as to the liability of the supermarket in this case? Explain.

   An additional argument was raised concerning the right of the federal government to legislate *labelling regulations* which seem to deal with provincial concerns, such as the labelling of meat for consumption within the province. The test of the validity of the Consumer Packaging and Labelling Act, which is a criminal statute, is whether it is to prevent a deceptive practice (i.e., criminal) or to establish standards of labelling (regulation of a particular trade). Alternatively stated, is this type of labelling legislation affecting civil rights (i.e., *intra vires*, within the powers of the federal government) or legislation "in relation" to civil rights (i.e., *ultra vires*, exceeding the powers of the federal government). Outline in simple terms what you understand by the content of the foregoing paragraph.

READING

Shandloff v. City Dairy Ltd. and Moscoe, [1936] O.R. 579 (C.A.).

Facts: In this case a young woman dress finisher bought a bottle of chocolate milk from Moscoe which had been bottled by Dairy City Ltd. As she was sucking the chocolate milk through a straw, some particles of broken glass were sucked into her mouth. Broken glass was found in the chocolate milk.

An action was brought against Moscoe in contract and against the City Dair Ltd. in tort. At the trial, "negligence [was] found as a matter of inference from the existence of the broken glass in the bottle, taken in connection with all the known circumstances." The plaintiff lost her case against Moscoe but won against City Dairy Ltd. The Court awarded the plaintiff $240 damages.

Held (on appeal):

The whole subject was so exhaustively discussed in *M'Allister (or Donoghue) v. Stevenson*, [1932] A.C. 562, that a new starting point is there given. . . .

. . . Lord Atkin concludes, at p. 599: ". . . By Scots and English law alike a manufacturer of products, which he sells in such a form as to show that he intends them to reach the ultimate consumer in the form in which they left him with no reasonable possibility of intermediate examination, and with the knowledge that the absence of reasonable care in the preparation or putting up of the products will result in an injury to the consumer's life or property, owes a duty to the consumer to take that reasonable care.". . .

[In Lord Macmillan s view, at p. 611:] ". . . I rather regard this type of case as a special instance of negligence where the law exacts a degree of diligence so stringent as to amount practically to a guarantee of safety.". . .

The effect, as I take it, of these two cases [*Chapman v. Saddler & Co.*, [1929] A.C. 584, where a sling lent by a stevedore firm to a porterage company, broke and killed a porter and *Grant v. Australian Knitting Mills Ltd.*, [1936] A.C. 85, where underwear made of wool which contained a chemically irritant substance, which had been imperfectly removed and caused a rash to the wearer] is to establish that a manufacturer who prepares and puts upon the market food in a container which prevents examination by the ultimate consumer is liable to the ultimate consumer for any defects which exist in the goods so marketed which arise from negligence or lack of care. . . .

Has negligence been here established? . . .

Here, it was evidently clearly known to the defendant Dairy Company and appreciated by it that the breakage of glass was apt to occur in the process of bottling and marketing these containers and that the broken chips of glass were in themselves inherently dangerous. The utmost care was used but that care apparently was not sufficient. . . . Some employee did blunder.

The learned trial Judge himself inspecting the plant located the point in the course of manufacture where he thought sufficient care was not exercise, and I do not see my way to reverse him.

. . . The liability alleged against him [Moscoe] is upon contract. [Section 15 of the Sale of Goods Act, R.S.O. 1927, c. 163] provides that: ". . . there is no implied warranty or condition as to the quality or fitness . . . of goods supplied under a contract for sale, except as follows: (a) Where the buyer . . . makes known [his requirements] to the seller . . . and the goods are of a description which it is in the course of the seller's business to supply, . . . there is an implied condition that the goods shall be reasonably fit for such purpose.''

. . . The plaintiff [here] relied upon Moscoe's skill and judgment. . . . He is liable, although he is not the manufacturer, for there is an implied condition that the chocolate milk sold was of merchantable quality. [Section 63, which provides that this implied condition may be waived does not apply here because there was nothing in the conduct of the merchant and the customer from which such a negation might be inferred.] . . .

[In both *Grant v. Australian Knitting Mills Ltd. (supra)* and *Jackson v. Watson & Sons*, [1909] 2 K.B. 19, where the retailer was held liable for dangers resulting from the death of a wife who had consumed a tin of salmon which was unfit for human consumption, the retailers were held liable in contract for the breach of the implied conditions of the Sale of Goods Act.]

Appeal of City Dairy Ltd. dismissed with costs; cross-appeal of plaintiff [against Moscoe] allowed with costs.

26

Restrictive Trade Practices

In many types of manufacturing and retailing, the bulk of sales is now accounted for by a relatively small number of large firms. This trend towards industrial concentration has been accompanied by the growth of various types of restrictive trade practices designed to reduce competition and thereby increase profits. This situation has been detrimental to the consumer whose aim is to obtain high-quality goods at reasonable prices.

THE COMBINES INVESTIGATION ACT

To help protect the consumer, various types of legislation have been enacted. Thus, in 1889, the Canadian Parliament passed a *Combines Investigation Act* which now, following various amendments, prohibits three basic types of business activity:

1. Combinations that prevent or unduly lessen competition, purchase, sale, storage, rental, transportation, supply of commodities or price of insurance, and so on.
2. Mergers or monopolies that may operate to the detriment to the public.
3. Unfair trade practices, including price discrimination, predatory pricing, certain promotional allowances, resale price maintenance, and misleading advertising.

The Act now applies to trades, industries and professions, as well as to goods and services.

The federal Parliament has assumed jurisdiction in the "combines" field on the basis that conduct interfering with the rights of the consumer actually amounts to an offence against society, thus a crime. Such federal jurisdiction is authorized under s. 91(27) of the Constitution Act, 1867.

Combinations

Section 32.1. This section of the Act provides that it is an indictable offence which may result in up to five years imprisonment or a fine of up to $1 million or both, to conspire or combine to:

1. limit facilities for transporting, manufacturing, and so on;
2. prevent or lessen manufacture;
3. prevent or lessen competition in production;
4. otherwise restrain trade or commerce.

However, this section also provides that it is not an offence to make an agreement relating to the sharing of statistical or credit information, unless the agreement lessens competition in prices, quantity, and/or market distribution. This section does not apply to export agreements that do not injure domestic exports.

This section makes it an offence to institute a foreign directive application to a company doing business in Canada which, if entered into in Canada, would have been an offence under Section 32.

Section 32.2.   Under this Section, bid rigging, such as occurred in the Hamilton Dredging case, is an offence punishable as in Section 32(1).

Section 32.3.   Under this Section, conspiracies that may affect an individual athlete's chances to participate in professional sport or with a certain team are offences punishable as in Section 32(1).

Examples.   An investigation was made into the banding together of milk companies in Montreal in bidding for contracts for the supply of the requirements of several large users of milk products, one of which was The Queen Mary Veteran's Hospital. Under the mutually agreed system of bidding, the closest supplier would submit the lowest bid and thus normally get the contract award. In this particular province, prices of all milk products except skim milk were controlled by the Milk Board, so the only quotation that would be varied was the price of skim milk. It was found that this pre-agreed submission of bids was contrary to the Act.

As another example, seventeen companies that had been engaged in the manufacture and sale of paper containers were convicted and fined a total of $360,000 for participating in a conspiracy to lessen competition unduly contrary to s. 498(a)(d) of the Criminal Code, now s. 32(1)(c) of the Combines Investigation Act. In this case, the companies all used a common price manual to establish in each area across Canada common cost figures and common prices.

Finally, in 1979, the largest Canadian dredging companies and their senior officers were convicted of bid rigging, which consisted of pre-arranging who would submit the lowest bids at various federal government sites, thus eliminating competition. This was the first major case involving the imprisonment of company officers for anti-competition crimes in Canada.

Mergers

Section 33.   This section of the Act makes it an offence to participate in a merge that lessens competition or in a monopoly that is against the public interest. The punishment may be up to two years imprisonment on conviction for an indictable offence.

The following case summaries indicate some of the business agreements which have been prosecuted under this provision:

R. v. Staples.   This case dealt with the acquisition of 50% of the shares in a fruit sales agency by the largest fruit and grocer jobber in western Canada. The court found that there was "no detriment or likelihood of detriment to the public . . . and that ownership of one half of the shares in a company does not give control of the company . . . [or] any control of the Company's business."

The Eddy Match Company Case.   In this case, the defendant company was formed in 1927 by the merger of three match-producing companies then operating in Canada. By eliminating or absorbing competitors, by resale price maintenance, secret discounts and rebates, and so on, the defendants gained completed control over the wooden match industry. The Eddy Match Company was tried and convicted under the merger provisions for taking two steps in eliminating all its competition—namely, the waging of unfair, illegal, and unjust competition, and the purchasing and absorbing of the businesses of competitors, resulting in virtual impossibility for a new firm to establish itself in the same business in Canada.

The question of possible criminal mergers has also been considered by the Restrictive Trade Practices Commission in the following situations:

The Sugar Refining Case.   The court held that the sugar refineries were not guilty of forming a merger to the detriment of the public, because "there was no attempt to establish exorbitant profits."

The Zinc Oxide Case.   A report was prepared concerning the production, distribution and sale of zinc oxide by Zinc Oxide of Canada Ltd. (ZOCCO) which, in 1955, completed a merger which gave it control of 97% of production in Canada.

The Yeast Report.   This concerned Standard Brands which, in 1955, completed a merger that gave this company control of 85% of yeast production and sales in Canada.

The Meat Packers Case.   In 1955, the Commission reported that Canada Packers, which was already twice as large as any other meat packer in Canada, had acquired two other meat packaging companies. It was recommended that action should be taken either to dissolve the merger or prohibit further acquisitions.

The Electric Reduction Company Merger.   On January 12, 1970, a plea of guilty of having participated in a merger prohibited under s. 33 of the Combines Investigation Act was entered in the case of *R. v. Electric Reduction Co. of Canada.*

Unfair Trade Practices

Section 34.1.   This section makes it an offence to discriminate against competitors of a purchaser by means of varying discounts and rebates for like quality and quantity purchases; or selling at a lower price in one part of Canada to lessen competition, or predatory pricing (to eliminate a competitor). The offender may incur punishment of up to two years on conviction for an indictable offence.

Section 38.1.   Under this section it is an offence for a dealer to force a merchant or retailer to sell at a price less than a minimum, or at a certain mark-up. This is commonly referred to as resale price maintenance. There is, of course, an exception to this where the dealer may refuse to supply his product if his goods are being sold at cost or less than cost, as what is termed a "loss leader," to attract customers.

Investigations under this section of the Combines Investigation Act have resulted in convictions, for example, against a ski manufacturer for attempting to maintain fixed prices; against a ladies' wear manufacturer for refusing to supply a large retailer who refused to abide by the suggested resale price; and against an ovenware manufacturer for refusing to supply retailers who did not sell at its fixed prices. The rule is that a manufacturer may suggest a maximum price but may not set a minimum.

Enforcement

The enforcement of the Combines Investigation Act is shared by two agencies: (1) the Director of Investigation and Research and (2) the Restrictive Trade Practices Commission.

The Director of Investigation and Research may receive information about a breach of one of the statutory provisions either by a formal complaint signed by six citizens, directed to his office; or by a request from the Minister of Consumer and Corporate Affairs; or as the result of staff investigations. Enquiries are carried out subsequently and provide the Director with two possible avenues of procedure, if further action is warranted. He may process his report through the Restrictive Practices Commission, which will consider the report and forward its recommendations to the Minister. Alternatively, he may pass his report directly to the Minister when the case is one in which he considers immediate action is required—for example, misleading advertising or claims not based on an adequate and proper test.

Enforcement by the federal government is carried out as follows:

1. Where an offence has been disclosed, it will be normal procedure to proceed by indictment laid in the Federal Court of Canada or in the Supreme Court of the province in which the offence was committed. For example, following a direct reference to the Attorney General, twelve companies were charged and tried in the Supreme Court of Ontario, on April 17, 1972, under s. 32(1)(c), with having conspired to prevent or lessen unduly competition in the production, manufacture, sale or supply of ready-mix concrete in Metropolitan Toronto. Fines totalling $245,000 were imposed following unanimous pleas of "guilty."
2. In many cases investigated under this Act, the Director or the Restrictive Trade Practices Tribunal has found evidence of a practice that is contrary to the intent of the regulations, but there has been doubt as to whether a criminal offence has been committed. One recent case dealt with a complaint against a manufacturer of luggage who stopped selling his products to a luggage dealer who refused to sell at the suggested re-sale prices. Although the investigation did verify this allegation, the evidence

was not considered sufficient to support a criminal charge and the investigation was discontinued. Another case dealt with the lowering of cigarette prices by large chain stores in Montreal. Since this was only a secondary line product, and there was no evidence of predatory pricing, no action was taken.

3. In all cases where evidence of an offence is discovered and in some cases where no criminal charges are laid, but there is evidence of an illegal practice, the Director generally applies for an order of prohibition under s. 30 of the Act.

Two additional procedures are provided under the Combines Investigation Act, which depend more on government policy than on infractions disclosed as the result of investigations made under the Act. Under s. 29, the Federal Court of Canada may be asked by the Attorney General of Canada to correct the misuse of a patent or trademark where such right has been used to restrain trade or injure competition. Thus, in 1970, the Minister of Consumer and Corporate Affairs disclosed that the patent protection afforded to the tranquillizer drug "chlordiazepoxide hydrochloride," had been removed, to allow import by independent companies and a reduction in price to the consumer. Patent protection for some twenty-nine other drugs was removed at the same time.

Also, under s. 28, the Governor General in Council is empowered "to reduce or abolish the tariff on an article where it appears, as a result of an inquiry or from judicial proceedings taken pursuant to the Act, that a combination, merger or monopoly to promote unduly the advantage of manufacturers or dealers at the expense of the public, has existed and has been facilitated by the duties and customs imposed on the article."

The Office of the Director of Investigation and Research has also developed a program of compliance by which businesspeople are encouraged to discuss business policies that might cause some conflict with Canadian laws. An example of this procedure is the allowance by the Director of substantial discounts by manufacturers to a new store owner as opening day attractions, which otherwise would have been contrary to s. 34, the discriminatory discounts provision of the Act.

COMPETITION POLICY

The Economic Council of Canada Interim Report on Competition Policy of July, 1969, concluded with the following recommendations:

(a) The competition policy should ensure efficient resource use;
(b) Social control should be exerted;
(c) There should be government regulation only where monopolies have eliminated competitive market response;
(d) Canada's competition policy should be civil rather than criminal;
(e) A civil tribunal should be established to study mergers, business practices, export and specialization agreements;

(f) The competition policy should be extended to services;

(g) The duties of the Competitive Practices Tribunal would include:

    1. Determination of corporate mergers, to decide whether they are in the public interest;

    2. Examination of specialization agreements;

    3. Determination as to whether trade practices are in the public interest;

    4. Tribunal decisions would be subject to judicial review;

    5. The following business practices would continue to be criminal because they are never in the public interest: collusion, such as low-bid rigging; allocation of markets; collusion against new competitors; resale price maintenance; and misleading advertising.

OTHER COUNTRIES

In the United States, a basic anti-trust law, the Sherman Anti-Trust Act, was passed in 1890 with the purpose of controlling mergers and monopolies that could be to the detriment of the "public interest."

One example of a successful prosecution is as follows. For many years it had apparently been the practice for large electrical suppliers to get together unobtrusively and arrange collusive bidding, so that certain companies would be awarded pre-arranged contracts on the basis of the lowest pre-arranged bids. The conspiracy was finally brought out in the open in 1959, on complaints from officials of the Tennessee Valley Authority concerning identical bids they were receiving from manufacturers of highly technical electrical equipment, even though the bids were submitted in sealed envelopes. As many as forty-five individual defendants and twenty-nine corporations were involved. Fines of $9,924,500 were levied against the defendants, of which $137,000 was assessed against individuals. Jail terms of up to thirty days were imposed on seven persons, of whom four were vice-presidents.

It should be noted that the Canadian law is supported under the Criminal provisions of the Constitution, while the American anti-trust law has always been based on the Commerce clause of the American Constitution. This means that the U.S. government has a somewhat broader choice of sanctions which in turn has led to more flexibility in administration than in Canada. For instance, the Federal Trade Commission (FTC) has the power to regulate business by means of such administrative acts as "cease and desist orders," and so on. In Canada, the Restrictive Trade Practices Commission has only the power to recommend to the Minister that a charge be laid.

Canada has, in fact, been the beneficiary of a good deal of United States anti-trust activity. In an article in *The Canadian Bar Review*, D. G. Kilgour stated:

> Paradoxically a good case can be made for saying that the Sherman Act has had more effect on the Canadian economy than the Combines

Investigation Act has had . . . suffice it that American divestiture orders have resulted in restructuring several of our major industries in a way that no Canadian decree has ever done. For instance, American decrees have:

(a) caused ALCOA to divest itself of its Canadian subsidiary;
(b) caused F. I. Dupont de Nemours & Co. and Imperial Chemical Industries to split Canadian Industries Ltd. into two separate companies;
(c) severed Eddy Match Company from its international parents;
(d) caused the Canadian patent pool operated by General Electric, Westinghouse, and others to be loosened up to admit into Canada television sets made in the United States by competitors, etc.

Nothing comparable to this has happened by reason of our own legislation.

In the United Kingdom, the Restrictive Trade Practices Act, 1964, requires a wide range of restrictive agreements on prices and conditions of sale to be entered on a public register and "if found by the Restrictive Practices Court to be against 'public interest', such restrictions are void."

Numerous developments have taken place in Canada in the competitive field but the Canadian government has not yet proceeded to the stage of establishing a Competition Board advocated to replace the present Director of Investigation and Research. Some of these changes include:

1. All takeovers of existing Canadian companies by foreign firms are reviewed and only approved if found to be of significant benefit to Canada.
2. Section 31.2-31.4 allows the Restrictive Trade Practices Commission to review complaints in regard to refusal to deal, exclusive dealing, tied selling and consignment sales and prohibit such practices if found to be anti-competitive.
3. Section 31.5 makes it an offence for a foreign-owned subsidiary to follow the parent-country laws which may be contrary to the Canadian interest—for example, certain subsidiaries have attempted to comply with the United States Trading with the Enemy Act, which resulted in losing export contracts, which in turn caused Canadian workers to lose jobs.
4. Punishments have been increased so that convictions for the major offences may involve fines of up to one million dollars.

PROBLEMS

1. In *R. v. Sunbeam Corp. (Can.) Ltd.*, [1967] 1 O.R. 23, the Sunbeam Corporation sold its products to independent distributors who in turn sold them to retail dealers. The corporation sent to all dealers handling its products a circular setting out the "minimum profitable resale price of each article" and stating its intention to withhold supplies from persons who made a practice of "loss leading." The Sunbeam Corpora-

tion made the distributors visit retailers to induce them to keep to the stated retail prices. What section, if any, of the Combined Investigation Act may have been contravened in this case? Discuss the probable defences.

2. In the case of *R. v. B.C. Professional Pharmacists Society*, [1971] 1 W.W.R. 705, drugs were supplied to welfare recipients in accordance with a formula worked out between the Pharmaceutical Association of B.C. and the provincial government, but by 1968 this formula was no longer economically acceptable to the pharmacists. The B.C. Professional Pharmacists' Society, a body whose prime object was to improve the status of pharmacists, tried to persuade the government to agree to more favourable sale terms. The efforts having proved unsuccessful, the Society resolved by a large majority vote to impose a one dollar surcharge on every prescription until an acceptable contract was signed between the Society and the Minister of Welfare. The members of the Society were informed of this resolution and efforts were made to persuade all pharmacies to impose this surcharge. Discuss whether any criminal offence might be involved.

3. The accused were drain pipe manufacturing companies. Their main competitors were manufacturers of concrete pipe and their main customers were provincial roads departments, county boards, and municipalities. They were all members of the Canadian Steel Pipe Institute which, prior to 1962, was very competitive and suffered heavy price cutting. Realizing that it would be contrary to the provisions of the Combines Investigation Act for the members to get together and agree not to cut prices or to agree on prices, they decided on an "open pricing" policy whereby each firm would publish its price list. In 1963 one of the major producers published its price list and, from 1964 to 1967, all bidding on major contracts offered followed this price manual and was identical for all steel drain pipe components except where the tendering company was not a member of the institute. In fact prices quoted were identical down to the cents figure on some 160 different items quoted by different firms over this period. The institute member firms were charged under the Combines Investigation Act.

Has a criminal offence been committed in this case? How could the accused be taken to trial? What is the probable basis of the charge? Discuss some of the points which would have to be proved by the Crown to justify a conviction. Refer to *R. v. Armco Canada Ltd. and Nine Other Corporations* (1974), 6 O.R. (2d) 521.

4. You have been hired to re-organize the sales force of your new company which is a distribution type retail sales outlet similar to Consumers Distributing. The previous sales manager was an American and you find the following problems facing you:

(1) A request from the Director of Operations and Research under the Combines Investigation Act to explain the company policy of making a contract with one provincial retailer to sell "Super" radios at a

fixed price, and as a result withholding distribution to any retail outlets refusing to follow this pricing policy. Your predecessor, who has returned to the American headquarters of the company, said this was perfectly legal under the "Fair Trade" laws of the United States. What is the company's position and how would you deal with this problem?

(2) Your company carries a large line of English art, music, and other rare books. Correspondence on file indicates that these books are only sold at the publisher's list price in the U.K. Your retailers are refusing to carry these books, saying it is contrary to Canadian law to sell at fixed prices. How will you resolve this problem?

(3) The company has had a policy of standing by a twelve-month warranty for major durables and household appliances. This guarantee has been included on all advertising together with the words, "all other guarantees, warranties, etc., are excluded." The Better Business Bureau has written to the President complaining about this statement and also about the company policy of giving a rebate or credit for any successful sale following a referral from customers from door-to-door sales. The President wants your views on this point. What are they?

(4) The company pricing policy has always been prepared by consulting the catalogue of your closest competitor in the distribution field, namely Consumers Distributing. For similar goods the price has always been identical to the other company's retail prices; the company relies on special service to gain and retain customers. The catalogue producers want to consult with their catalogue counterparts at Consumers so that both companies will continue a similar pricing policy. What are your comments? Would you approve?

(5) Your company was incorporated under federal laws and has branch offices in several provinces. Part of the company operation includes a door-to-door sales force. Your top salesman, with an income over $40,000 a year and operating in a farming community, comes to you and says, "What is the Ontario Business Practices Act all about? I have been served with three writs, all of which say that I made oral statements about goods sold which later proved to be wrong, and also that I was selling without a licence. Does not *caveat emptor* and the parol evidence rule apply? How can I be charged under this Act? Aren't we a federal company?" What is your answer to these problems?

(6) Personnel has asked you for your comments on the company employment contract which contains a provision stating that every sales employee agrees not to work for a competitor company for ten years after leaving your company employ and a second clause providing that salespersons must agree not to use the firm's customer list for two years. What would your advice be?

APPENDIX 26-A: SUMMARY OF THE KEY SECTIONS OF THE COMBINES INVESTIGATION ACT, R.S.C. 1970, c. C-23 (as amended 1975)

S. 2   "Business" includes:
(a) manufacturing, producing, transporting, acquiring, supplying, storing and otherwise dealing in articles, and
(b) acquiring, supplying and otherwise dealing in services;
    "Article" means real and personal property of every description;
    "Merger" means acquisition by one or more persons, whether by purchase or lease of shares or assets or otherwise, of any control over or interest in the whole or part of the business of a competitor, supplier, customer or any other person, whereby competition
(a) in a trade, industry or profession,
(b) among the sources of supply of a trade, industry or profession,
(c) among the outlets for sales of a trade, industry or profession, or
(d) otherwise than in paragraphs (a), (b) and (c),
is or is likely to be lessened to the detriment or against the interest of the public, whether consumers, producers or others;
    "Monopoly" means a situation where one or more persons either substantially or completely control throughout Canada or any area thereof the class or species of business or are likely to operate it to the detriment or against the interest of the public, whether consumers, producers or others, but a situation shall not be deemed a monopoly within the meaning of this definition by reason only of the exercise of any right or enjoyment of any interest derived under the Patent Act, or any other Act of the Parliament of Canada.

S. 4   The Act does not prohibit associations of workers for reasonable collective bargaining activities.

S. 5   Appointment of Director of Investigation and Research.

S. 7   (1)Allows any six persons resident in Canada over 18 years of age to apply to the Director for an inquiry into an alleged offence or failure to carry out an order made under the Act.

S. 8   Inquiry by Director.

S. 9   Notice for Written Returns.

S. 10   (1) Entry of Premises.

S. 11   (1) Inspection of Documents.

S. 16   (1) Appointment of Restrictive Trade Practices Commission.

S. 17   (1) Oral examinations.

S. 28   Reduction or removal of customs duties to give the public the benefit of reasonable competition.

S. 29   Deals with use of copyright, trademark or patents to commit or facilitate the commission of an offence under the Combines Investigation Act. There is a provision for application to any competent Court by an Attorney General for an interim injunction (N.B.

the Court means Federal Court of Canada or a Superior Court of Criminal Jurisdiction).

S. 30 Regular appeals apply from the Provincial Supreme Court or Federal Court to the Supreme Court of Canada.

S. 31.1 (1) Provides for a *civil right of recovery* for persons who suffer loss or damage as a result of conduct which is contrary to the Act or failure to comply with an order of the Restrictive Trade Practices Commission such as refusal to deal, misuse of consignment selling practices, exclusive dealing, tied selling, anti-competitive behaviour, following extra-Canada influence or orders.

S. 31.1 (4) The *limitation period is two years* after the day when illegal conduct occurred or day when criminal proceedings disposed of, whichever is later.

Matters Reviewable By Commission

S. 31.2 *Refusal to Deal.* Authorizes the Commission, where a product is in ample supply and inadequate competition is the problem to recommend that duties, taxes, etc., be removed and order suppliers to supply retailer to put him on an equal footing with other business persons.

S. 31.3 *Consignment Sales.* Supplier may be ordered to abandon consignment sales where this is an attempt to control price or discriminate between consignees.

S. 31.4 *Exclusive Dealing* includes situations where suppliers will only supply product if customer agrees to deal only in product supplied or gets a better deal for agreeing to this situation.
Market Restriction means selling only to a defined segment of the market.
Tied Selling. Supplier agrees to supply only if the customer agrees to buy other products from supplier or nominee or gets a better deal for this agreement.

Where exclusive dealing, tied selling or market restriction may impede a firm in the market place, lessen competition, or impede sales of a product, the Commission first must hear the supplier's point of view. Then the Commission may make any order necessary to overcome such restriction and achieve true competition.

In certain cases the Commission will not make any order, e.g., allowing a reasonable time for entry of a new product, or where tied selling is related to securing a business loan or among affiliated business associations.

S. 31.5 *Foreign Decrees.* If the Commission finds that a foreign decree or order if implemented in Canada may adversely affect competition without any compensating benefits it may either prohibit the implementation of such judgment or order or alter it so that the negative effect is modified.

S. 31.6   Insofar as the possible effect of foreign laws or decrees being implemented in Canada which might adversely affect competition, without any compensating benefits, the Commission may either prohibit the implementation of such judgment or order or alter it so that the negative effect is modified.

In dealing with the alteration of the possible effect of foreign laws or decrees being implemented in Canada which might adversely affect competition, adversely affect Canada's foreign trade, adversely affect a trade or industry, or injure trade and commerce without any compensating benefits, the Commission after hearing arguments for this policy may either prohibit or modify the effect of such laws and directives.

Offences in Relation to Competition. The word "product" substituted for "article" and the words "trade, industry or profession" are substituted for "trade and industry". *Services are included in the classification of offences under this section.*

S. 32   (1) Every one who conspires, combines, agrees or arranges with another person

(a) to limit unduly the facilities for transporting, producing, manufacturing, supplying, storing, or dealing in any product,

(b) to prevent, limit or lessen, unduly, the manufacture or production of a product, or to enhance unreasonably the price thereof,

(c) to prevent, or lessen, unduly, competition in the production, manufature, purchase, barter, sale, storage, rental, transportation or supply of a product, or in the price of insurance upon persons or property, or

(d) to otherwise restrain or injure competition unduly, is guilty of an indictable offence and is liable to imprisonment for five years or a fine of one million dollars or to both.

Under this section it is not necessary to prove that the offending conspiracy could eliminate all competition.

Companies may share information on terminology, research, restriction of advertising, container size, adoption of metric system, environment protection, but not if the foregoing lessens competition in prices, quantity and quality of products, markets, methods of distribution.

S. 32.2   (1) "Bid-rigging" means:

(a) an agreement or arrangement between or among two or more persons whereby one or more of such persons agrees or undertakes not to submit a bid in response to a call or request for bids or tenders, and

(b) the submission, in response to a call or request for bids or tenders, of bids or tenders that are arrived at by agreement or arrangement between or among two or more bidders or tenderers, where the agreement or arrangement is not made known to the person calling for or requesting the bids or tenders at or before the time when any bid or tender is made by any person who is a party to the agreement or arrangement.

(2) Every one who is a party to bid-rigging is guilty of an indictable offence and is liable on conviction to a fine in the discretion of the court or to imprisonment for five years or to both.

S. 32.3   (1) *Professional Sport.* Agreements on conspiring to limit opportunities for players to participate in or to negotiate or to play for team of choice in professional or amateur sport is an offence punishable by a fine, 5 years' imprisonment, or both. However, consideration will be given to international agreements and keeping a proper balance between teams.

S. 33   This section of the Act makes it an offence to participate in a merger which lessens competition or in a monopoly which is against public interest. The punishment may be up to two years' imprisonment on conviction for an indictable offence.

S. 34   (1) Every one engaged in a business who:

(a) is a party or privy to, or assists in, any sale that discriminates to his knowledge, directly or indirectly, against competitors of a purchaser of articles from him in that any discount, rebate, allowance, price concession or other advantage is granted to the purchaser over and above any discount, rebate, allowance, price concession or other advantage that, at the time the articles are sold to such purchaser, is available to such competitors in respect of a sale of articles of like quality and quantity;

(b) engages in a policy of selling products in any area of Canada at prices lower than those exacted by him elsewhere in Canada, having the effect or tendency of substantially lessening competition or eliminating a competitor in such part of Canada, or designed to have such effect; or

(c) engages in a policy of selling products at prices unreasonably low, having the effect or tendency of substantially lessening competition or eliminating a competitor, or designed to have such effect,

is guilty of an indictable offence and is liable to imprisonment for two years.

Ss. 36&37 See Chapter 27.

S. 38   *Price Maintenance.* (1) Offence if supplying product, or having exclusive rights by patent, trademark, registered industrial design, to discourage by threat or any agreement reduction of price at which another person offers product or advertises product for sale or refuses to supply product or discriminate because of another person's pricing policy.

(2) Exception allowed by interrelated companies, partnerships or sole proprietorship.

(3) A suggestion as to a minimum resale price, unless explained that it is in no way binding, is proof of an attempt to influence.
(4) A publication of a price by a supplier may be an attempt to influence upwards a price unless explained.
(5) Above does not apply to price printed on package.
(6) It is an offence to attempt to influence supplier to withhold supplies from another person as a condition of doing business with the former.
(8) Punishment for offences in this section is imprisonment for two years.

S. 39   Civil rights are protected.

S. 44   (2) Only a superior court of criminal jurisdiction may try an offence under section 32, "conspiracy to reduce competition"; 32.1, "implementation of foreign conspiracies or agreements"; 32.2, bid-rigging; 32.3, interfering with athletic contracts; or 33.

S. 44.1   Prosecution under Part V may be lodged in accordance with review rules under Criminal Code and also if a company where head or branch office is located and otherwise wherever the accused resides or has his place of business.

S. 45   (1) Participant means anyone against whom proceedings have been instituted or who is alleged to have conspired.

S. 45.1   (1) Admits as evidence, reports of official statisticians or special studies made by the Director providing the other party is given advance notice.
             A certificate of such evidence is sufficient.

S. 46   (1) Confers on the Federal Court for the purposes of trials under the Combines Investigation Act the powers of a Superior Court of Criminal Jurisdiction.
             (2) Such trial shall be without jury.
             (3) Appeals lie to Federal Court of Appeal and Supreme Court of Canada.
             (4) In case of offences under Part V and sec. 46.1, accused cannot be tried in Federal Court without his consent.

S. 46.1   Failing to comply with an order of the Commission is an offence punishable by indictment to a fine, 5 years' imprisonment, or both; on summary conviction, 1 year, $25,000 fine, or both.

S. 47   (1) Authorizes the Director to enquire into any product where the trade or commerce situation may be monopolistic or in restraint of trade, or carry out enquiries as directed by the Minister to further the purposes of this Act.

27

False or Misleading Advertising

Whereas untold millions of dollars are spent each year informing the public about sports events and the stock markets, relatively little is spent informing consumers about the relative merits of various products and the possible dangers involved in their purchase. For many years, the legal principle of *caveat emptor*, or "buyer beware," has meant that once a person has examined a good and then purchased it, he or she has no legal remedy if the good proves unsatisfactory, except in the case of breaches of contract under the common law or breaches of the implied conditions of "merchantability" and "fitness" under the Sale of Goods Act.

In an attempt to remedy this situation, the federal and provincial governments have in recent years passed various types of consumer protection laws and established ministries to provide advice to the public and prosecute business firms which break the law. Also, privately published consumer magazines have found a ready market in a public aroused by Ralph Nader and other consumer protection proponents. Despite these efforts, the work of consumer protection is still in its infancy in Canada and the education of the consumer as to his or her rights remains an immense but necessary task.

COMMON LAW VERSUS STATUTE LAW

The common law provides remedies for some consumer problems. Suppose, for example, that a dangerous product is manufactured and sold and it causes injury to the purchaser. Then, if the purchaser can show that the manufacturer or supplier had a duty to take care, that a breach of this duty occurred and that injuries or other damages flowed from the breach, then the purchaser may be able to successfully sue such manufacturer or supplier in the civil courts.

Suppose a product turns out to be defective. If the breach of the sales contract is a minor one, only compensation is payable. However, if the product is so unsatisfactory as to be completely different in nature from the product bargained for, then, providing the product has not been used, the contract may be cancelled and the money refunded. However, except for stores with a policy of "goods satisfactory or money refunded," refunds for unsatisfactory goods are the exception rather than the rule, even under government-sponsored consumer protection. Consequently, despite the existence of common law remedies in cases involving torts (such as manufacturer's negligence) or contracts (for example, in the sale of goods), there is still a great need for government legislation to fill many important gaps. In this chapter and the next, we examine various types of consumer abuse and the legislation that has been passed, at both the federal and provincial levels, to help protect the consumer.

FALSE OR MISLEADING ADVERTISING

It is not always easy to determine whether a piece of advertising is false, misleading, merely a reasonable statement of opinion, or a "mere puffery" (for example, "the best headache remedy available"). Often it is a matter for a judge to decide. One of the first major judicial pronouncements on the nature of false or misleading advertising was made many years ago, in the case of *Carlill v. Carbolic Smokeball Company*, [1893] 1 Q.B. 269.

Carlill v. Carbolic Smokeball Company

In this case, a company desiring to promote its product advertised in a daily newspaper that if any person took its product, a pill, three times a day for a period of two weeks, and contracted influenza, it was prepared to pay one hundred pounds sterling reward. To show good faith, the firm deposited one thousand pounds sterling with the Alliance Bank, Regent Street, London. A Mrs. Carlill took the pill faithfully for two weeks, caught the "flu," then wrote to the company and demanded the reward. The company replied that its advertisement was merely "an invitation to do business." Therefore she should have first contacted the company and made an offer to take the pills. Then, following the firm's acceptance of her offer, an agreement would have been formed.

The judge ruled in these circumstances that anyone who makes a rash offer to the world at large, which can be accepted by performance, may be held accountable without direct communication of acceptance. In Judge Hawkins' words, which set a precedent in early consumer protection:

> Such advertisements do not appeal so much to the wise and thoughtful as to the credulous and weak portions of the community; and if the vendor of an article whether it be medicine, smoke, or anything else, with a view to increasing its sale and use, thinks fit publicly to promise to all who buy or use it, that, to those who shall not find it as surely efficacious as it is represented to him to be, he will pay a substantial sum of money, he most not be surprised if occasionally, he is held to his promise.

Combines Investigation Act

Statutory control of advertising in Canada is exercised chiefly under ss. 36 and 37 of the Combines Investigation Act.

Section 36.1. Under this section it is an offence to make material misrepresentations concerning prices at which articles are or have been sold. The most recent amendment to the Combines Investigation Act, s. 37, provides a punishment of up to five years for "a misleading statement to promote the sale of property, or business or commercial interest." The

majority of the convictions obtained, since the foregoing amendment became law, have occurred where the offender has either increased the normal
retail price to show a fictitious discount by really selling at the regular price,
or by advertising a fictitious regular price when, in fact, all of the other
merchants were selling at or near the special price advertised. For example, a
shampoo advertised at the special price of $1.49, when this was in fact the
regular price; or television sets advertised in Winnipeg at a regular price of
$1,025, which was in fact well above the regular price. Pianos were adver-
tised in Montreal at a regular price of $840, which was really $100 above the
other merchants' regular price. Electrically operated toy cars were advertised
in Ottawa at $39, reputedly reduced from the regular price of $59.98, when
the normal selling price was in fact $39.99.

Section 36.2.   This section makes it an offence punishable on indictment
by a fine or imprisonment or both and, on summary conviction, by a fine of
$25,000 or imprisonment for one year or both, for the purpose of promoting
or supplying any business interest:

(a) to make a misleading representation to the public;
(b) to make a representation that is not based on an adequate test;
(c) to make a misleading statement as to replacement;
(d) to make a misleading representation concerning the price at which the
      products have or will be sold.

The foregoing representations include statements on signs, wrappers,
store displays, and telephone selling. The general impression conveyed, as
well as the literal meaning, will apply in determining whether the representation is false.

This section also provides that representations relating to tests as to
performance, efficacy, and length of life of a product must be approved by
the party who made such test.

The provisions relating to "double ticketing" provide that any person
who charges more than the lowest price shown on products offered for sale is
guilty of an offence punishable by imprisonment for one year, or a fine of
$10,000, or both.

Section 36.3.   This section makes a scheme of pyramid selling, whereby
one person pays a fee to participate in a scheme and receives a fee or other
benefit from the recruitment of fees from other persons recruited into the
scheme, and on goods sold by such persons. Such an offence is punishable
on indictment by a fine, imprisonment for five years, or both or, on summary conviction, to a fine of $25,000, to imprisonment for one year, or both.

It should be noted that pyramid selling is not outlawed where permitted
by provincial law—for example, in Saskatchewan.

Section 36.4.   This section makes referral selling, whereby one person may
receive a rebate or other benefit for introducing other persons to buy a
product, an offence liable to the same punishments as "pyramid selling."
Again, provincial law may allow "referral selling."

Section 37. This section outlaws bargain prices with reference to regular prices without having sufficient supply on hand, subject to the defence of having taken steps to obtain a reasonable supply or of undertaking to supply the same within a reasonable time (such as "rainchecks"). It is an offence under s. 37(1) to sell a product above the advertised price.

Section 37.2. This section makes it an offence to use any lottery or game of chance to promote the sale of a product or business interest unless there is an adequate disclosure of the value of prizes or anything that affects a person's chances of winning, and the method of distribution of prizes. Also, the distribution of prizes must not be delayed.

It is a good defence in relation to misrepresentation to prove that such an offence resulted from an error and that adequate steps were taken to rectify such error.

In Canada, in 1970, a major tobacco company was fined $3,000 for false advertising in connection with an advertisement reading, "$5 in every pack of New Casino", under s. 33D91) (now s. 37) of the Combines Investigation Act. It was offered in defence that any reasonable man would realize that this meant a chance at a $5 prize only. Judge Sinclair of the Alberta Supreme Court, using almost identical words to those in the *Carlill v. Carbolic Smokeball Company* case, declared, "the protection of the section [of the Combines Investigation Act] is for 'the public', that vast multitude which includes the ignorant, the unthinking and the credulous." The judgment in this case is included as a Reading at the end of this chapter.

Administration. Responsibility for administering these and related provisions of the Act has been assigned to the Bureau of Competition Policy of the Federal Ministry of Consumer and Corporate Affairs.

False or Misleading Statements. The Director of Investigation and Research for the Combines Investigation Act has issued the following illustrative examples of false or misleading statements for which a firm may be prosecuted:

1. *Below our costs*: selling at a loss must be proved;
2. *No adequate test*: claims must be proved by tests;
3. *Lucky winner*: winners must be restricted—that is, not everybody;
4. *Bait and switch*: advertising a low-priced item as a "come-on" for a more expensive sale;
5. *Exorbitant prizes* which are advertised but never given;
6. *Stuffed apartment*: pretending that an apartment or house is being vacated and the furnishings are being sold at a discount;
7. *Free gift*: but to get it, must buy another item;
8. *Misrepresentation of origin*: enclosing a foreign-made article in a package marked "made in Canada."

Examples of False or Misleading Advertising. Other examples of prosecutions under the false or misleading advertising provisions of the Combines Investigation Act are as follows:

A large department store failed to reverse a conviction by a trial judge who had found the company guilty of having made materially misleading representations of the price at which a refrigerator model was regularly sold. For ten months out of a year, the price regularly charged by the company for this model was the price represented to be the sale price, and in the previous two years all sales were made at that price.

One of the largest department stores in Canada was charged for a materially misleading representation about the ordinary price of mink fur coats in an advertisement in the *Globe and Mail*, where the coats were shown as selling at $1,200 to $1,900 ordinarily. The court found that the sale went on for 114 days and therefore could not be a "sale," so the prices charged on the other days of the year could not be described as ordinary prices. The department store was fined $200 and further advertisements of this type were prohibited.

In June 1972, a leading Canadian supermarket chain was fined $8,000 in provincial court for misleading advertising in the sale of hockey helmets. An advertisement in the *Toronto Star* newspaper on November 18, 1972, described the helmets as having "approved safety design, completely adjustable head sizes, live action, moulded polyethylene lines for maximum comfort and protection." In fact, no authoritative body had approved the helmet's design and, at the time of the advertisement, no safety standards for helmets existed in Canada. Since January 1, 1974, helmets have required a seal of approval from the Canadian Standards Association. The company pleaded guilty to the charges by the federal Department of Consumer and Corporate Affairs that the statement describing the helmet was untrue, deceptive, or misleading as defined under the Combines Investigation Act.

The Criminal Code
The Criminal Code also deals with false or misleading advertising. Section 231(1) makes it an offence "for a person by deceit, falsehood or other fraudulent means, to cheat the public or any person, of any money, property, valuable security." This offence is punishable on conviction by a maximum of ten years in jail. Section 324 makes it an offence to use the mails to advertise schemes intended to deceive or defraud the public. The maximum penalty is two years imprisonment. Section 351 includes the offence of passing off wares or services as those ordered, or making false assertions regarding the kind, composition, origin, or manufacture of such wares or services. Section 354 deals with the sale of used, remade goods bearing the trademark or trade name of another person without disclosing these facts.

OTHER FEDERAL LEGISLATION

The following federal statutes also have provisions relating to false or misleading advertising: the Bank Act; the Broadcasting Act; the Food and Drugs Act; the Hazardous Products Act; the National Trade Mark and True Labelling Act; the Precious Metals Marking Act; and the Trade Marks Act.

A requirement intended to protect the health of consumers is the inclusion of a caption on all cigarette packages and advertisements—namely, "Danger to health increases with amount smoked."

The Consumer Packaging and Labelling Act

Consumers have constantly complained that goods are often packaged in a deceptive manner (for example, large boxes only partly full) and labelled incompletely (for example, not all ingredients listed or country of origin hidden). Consequently, in 1971, the federal Parliament passed a Consumer Packaging and Labelling Act, imposing, for example, labelling standards on imported goods and minimum information requirements on all "packaged products." The Act also authorizes the establishment of Regulation requirements as to the net quantity of goods that must be contained in a package, so enabling the Ministry of Consumer and Corporate Affairs to combat such defective practices as "slack fill." The Act also permits the Ministry to regulate the size and shape of containers of prepackaged goods when it considers that the consumer now tends to be confused. Regulations under the Act provide for the printing of French as well as English on labels; how a package is to be labelled (including size of label and position on the package); net quantity and how it must be declared on the label (for example, by weight or volume); and standardized container sizes for toothpaste, shampoo, and skin creams. Prepackaged goods sold for commercial use are exempt from the Regulations. The Act also makes provision for the labelling of prepackaged goods in metric units and the conversion program to be directed by a Metric Preparatory Commission.

The Textile Labelling Act

As the number of synthetic fibres has increased in recent years, so has the public confusion as to the washability, wearability, and relative cost of clothes and other textile products. As a result, in 1970 the federal Parliament passed a Textile Labelling Act.

One important provision of the Act requires that a label be attached to each product giving the generic name of each textile fibre comprising 5% or more of the total fibre weight of the article, and the identity of the manufacturer. The Act also indicates how the label is to be affixed. The sale or importation of consumer textiles in Canada, without the prescribed labelling, is prohibited. Also, false or misleading labelling is an offence.

The Regulations provided for in the Act specify in detail the products that must be labelled and the types of information that must be shown on the label. Instead of name and address, a manufacturer may show on the label a Manufacturing Number supplied by the Department of Consumer and Corporate Affairs. The Regulations also define and explain the permitted use of generic names. The products exempted from the Act are listed. And the use of such descriptive terms as "all" and "pure" when describing a textile and their implications, from the viewpoint of false or misleading representations, are spelled out. In announcing these new Regulations, the

Minister stated that consumers "will be better able to make confident textile purchases on the basis of quality, wear characteristics and cost."

PROVINCIAL LEGISLATION

Under the provisions of the Constitution Act, 1867, provincial control of advertising must be restricted to matters related to property and civil rights, local works and business undertakings, or matters of a local or private nature, as previously considered in Chapter 1. For example, s. 28 of the Ontario Mortgage Brokers Act, which covers false advertising, reads as follows:

> Where the Registrar believes on reasonable and probable grounds that a mortgage broker [collection agency, etc.] is making false, misleading or deceptive statements in any advertisement, circular . . . the Registrar may order the immediate cessation of the use of such material . . . the order of the Registrar shall take effect immediately, but the Tribunal may grant a stay until the Registrar's order becomes final.

The foregoing procedure provides for immediate control of misleading advertising and acts as a "brake" on the type of advertising which might be attempted, since the Registrar has absolute discretion to prohibit false or misleading advertising subject to Administrative Tribunal review. Similar provisions, covering false or misleading advertising, are included in all Acts administered by the Ontario Ministry of Consumer and Commercial Relations.

Some screening of advertisements is carried out by most provincial governments to prevent discrimination in advertisements under human rights legislation, such as age, sex, race, colour, creed and national origin. Some provinces, including Quebec, prohibit advertising directed at children which is intended to lead children to bring pressure to bear on their parents to buy certain products. Credit advertising is regulated by the provincial Consumer Protection Acts or by provincial credit disclosure laws

PRIVATE CONTROL

In addition to the control exercised over advertising by common and statute law, there is the self-regulation exercised by private advertisers themselves. Thus, the Canadian Advertising Advisory Board has prepared a Code of Ethics for Advertising to which members of the Canadian advertising industry are expected to adhere. The Code covers the following subjects: false or misleading advertising; price claims; testimonials; disparaging claims; guarantees; advertising to children; and bait and switch advertising. An Advertising Standards Council, composed of persons with outstanding advertising and business experience, arbitrate any alleged violations of the Code.

REVIEW QUESTIONS

1. What protection does the Common Law provide for the consumer? Explain the term "caveat emptor."
2. When is a commercial advertisement considered to be false? Misleading? Explain the legal principle established by the case of Carlill v. Carbolic Smokeball Company.
3. What protection does Section 36(1) of the Combines Investigation Act try to give the public from false or misleading advertising?
4. What is the scope and purpose of Section 37(1) of the Combines Investigation Act?
5. Give three examples of false or misleading statements.
6. False or misleading advertising may result in a criminal conviction. Explain.
7. What other federal statutes regulate commercial advertising?
8. Explain the nature and purpose of the Consumer Packaging and Labelling Act.
9. What are the main provisions of the Textile Labelling Act?
10. What role do the provincial governments play in preventing advertising abuse?
11. What steps has the advertising industry taken to regulate unethical advertising practices by its members?

PROBLEMS

1. What in your opinion is the basic difference between offences charged under ss. 36 and 37 of the Combines Investigation Act? Explain. Under what section would the following be charged?
   (a) A sale of mattresses, advertised as regularly priced at $99 but on sale at $39, if the regular price was closer to $49.
   (b) An apartment being used as a retail sales outlet by pretending that the contents are being sold because occupants are moving away.
   (c) Nylon rope being sold with the claim that it will withstand a 3,000-pound pull?
2. An American company advertised a special brand of refined oil for sale. it was later discovered that its product was refined from *used* oil. It was offered in defence, and quite rightly, that refined used oil is probably as good as new oil. Would this practice have been chargeable as an offence in Canada?
3. How would the following ads be dealt with in Canada?
   (a) The ad states that "used cars will be protected for the life of the car" and when a customer enquires, he learns that this merely means against defective title.
   (b) A muffler company advertises that replaced mufflers are guaranteed for the life of the car, but on enquiry one learns that this means only as long as the original customer owns the same car.
   (c) A soft drink company claims that its main product has a high vitamin content, which on testing is found to be false.

4. You are looking around in a specialty shop where you find and purchase a particularly good piece of soapstone carving, which bears a small sticker reading "made in Canada, price $50." You later notice that the sticker is slightly unstuck in the corner. You pull it off only to discover underneath a "made in Japan" insignia impressed in the product. What is your recourse? Which level of government would be interested in this case?

5. The liability of an offender under the Combines investigation provisions regarding "misleading statements to promote sales" is said to be one of "strict liability." What is the difference if any between this type of liability and your liability for an accident while driving a car?

READING

R. v. Imperial Tobacco Products Ltd. (1970), 16 D.L.R. (3d) 470 (Alta. S.C.).

Facts: In the fall of 1969, Imperial Tobacco conducted a contest to promote the sale of a new brand of cigarettes called "Casino." The advertisement read, "$5 in every pack of New Casino." In fact there was no $5 or coupon that could be exchanged for $5 but instead a game which, if played successfully, entitled the holder to qualify for a $5 prize. The company was charged under the Combines Investigation Act, R.S.C. 1952, c. 314, s. 33D(1) effective July 31, 1969.

Held per Sinclair J.:

The company says the entire Casino advertising program showed there was a game to be played before the money could be won. It says the average person—the "reasonable man" if you will, would not have been so incredulous as to believe that Imperial Tobacco was going to give $5 in cash in exchange for the purchase price of the package.

. . . It seems to me the protection afforded by the section [33D] is for "the public—that vast multitude which includes the ignorant, the unthinking and the credulous," to use an expression that appears in the Federal Trade Commission Prosecution cases in the United States. . . .

The plain fact of the matter is that the accused, to promote the sale of the Casino cigarettes, caused to be published an advertisement containing a statement purporting to be a statement of fact but which statement was untrue. [The Judge also held that "mens rea," i.e., a guilty mind or intention, on the part of the company was not an essential ingredient of this offence.] . . .

I am therefore satisfied beyond a reasonable doubt, and so find, that Imperial Tobacco Products Ltd. is guilty. . . .

[The Judge also decided that he could award the corporation a fine of $3,000 since this charge was laid as an indictable offence. Finally the Judge made an Order of Prohibition restraining the company from continuing or repeating the said offence.]

28

Consumer Protection

In the previous chapter, we considered how and to what extent consumers are protected from false or misleading advertising. In this chapter, we consider other types of consumer abuse and the statutory protection that exists.

HIGH-PRESSURE SELLING

Canadian consumers are often subjected to high-pressure selling, sometimes without even realizing it is taking place. This may occur, for example, when a door-to-door salesperson calls to sell ovenware, vacuum cleaners, brushes, books, records, and so on.

Most provincial governments have passed legislation regulating door-to-door sales. Thus, some provinces, including all the Maritime provinces, have Direct Sellers Acts, while others, such as Manitoba and British Columbia, have special provisions in their Consumer Protection Acts. One of the most important provisions is that sales contracts made on a door-to-door basis may be set aside within periods varying from two to ten days (the so-called cooling-off period). Another important provision is that the title or ownership of an item "traded in" does not pass from the customer within this waiting period.

Probably the most flagrant high-pressure selling has been by unregistered trades people selling services (such as chimneys, roofing and other building repairs and renovations, including insulation) to persons who, because of lack of knowledge, agree to contract prices far exceeding the true value of the services rendered. Provincial legislative controls have not been imposed on health or dancing contracts. In certain states of the United States, by contrast, such contracts have been restricted to periods of one year, to amounts of $500 and to prepaid amounts of not more than 5% of the services received. Some provinces now require that all door-to-door sales people be licensed and sometimes bonded. In some provinces this type of legislation applies only to contracts above a certain specified amount.

REFERRAL SELLING

This is a sales scheme whereby a seller asks a customer to supply names of other likely customers. In return, the seller promises to refund part of the price paid by this customer. This is usually conditional, however, on the seller actually selling a certain minimum amount of goods or services to these "referred" customers.

517

Usually, the first customer approached is only too willing to give other people's names in order to purchase the merchandise for next to nothing. The seller, on approaching the "referred" customers, then indicates that various neighbours have already bought the product and so instills confidence. In practice, such schemes have often been used to promote the door-to-door sales of high-priced, low-quality goods. Various provinces, in their Consumer Protection Acts, have now prohibited referral selling. The practice is also outlawed by the Combines Investigation Act, except where allowed under provincial laws.

UNSOLICITED GOODS

One of the problems that faces today's consumer is what to do with goods that, without any request by the recipient, are sent through the mail or left at the door. Such goods include books, records, and other merchandise, often misleadingly marked "C.O.D."; requests for donations from so-called charities; and even credit cards.

By common law, no legal obligation exists on the part of the consumer to pay for such goods or even to take care of them. Whatever the seller may suggest in any accompanying letters, the consumer has no obligation whatsoever. To reassure the public as to its legal position, some provincial governments have in fact passed legislation—for example, Ontario's Consumer Protection Act—which specifically denies any consumer liability for such goods.

So far as credit cards are concerned, their unsolicited distribution has been limited by provincial governments in two different ways. The first is to deny any liability on the part of the consumer for debts incurred by the use of a credit card unless that person has actually requested the card or it is a replacement for one previously requested. This method has been adopted by, for example, British Columbia and Nova Scotia in their Consumer Protection Acts. The second method used to restrict the unsolicited distribution of oil company, bank, and other credit cards is simply to prohibit the practice. Provinces in which it is now illegal to distribute unsolicited credit cards through the mail include Manitoba, New Brunswick, Ontario, Prince Edward Island, and Quebec.

SALES FRANCHISES

As yet, there is no Canadian law to control franchise selling. A *franchise* is the right to use a brand or name, trade secrets, even a standard form of display and retail premises, standard procedures, staff training, management aid, and so on. Such a franchise is usually given in exchange for an initial fee plus a percentage of gross revenue. Sometimes also the franchisee is contractually obliged to purchase all his supplies or goods for resale from the franchisor or his appointed suppliers. Examples of franchises are Canadian Tire, Kentucky Fried Chicken, Harvey's, and Howard Johnson.

One Canadian case involved a franchisor who was attemping to control not only the supply of the basic product but also all other supplies required by the franchisee. The court ruled that such control was excessive even though agreed to in the contract. Laws have now been proposed that would prevent such large distributors as the major oil companies from restricting the sale by gasoline service station lessees to one brand of parts and equipment. This would help to keep prices down and so benefit the public.

PYRAMID SALES

Pyramid selling is a marketing scheme whereby people are required to sell a product themselves and to recruit other persons to sell on their behalf and each level of management or distribution benefits from all the sales. What has brought such a scheme into disrepute is the fact that the people who are recruited are required to purchase several thousand dollars' worth of stock themselves, which, very often, they are unable to sell. As a result, many gullible individuals lose relatively large sums of money to unscrupulous promoters.

An example of a pyramid scheme was the promotion of a personality buildup or development program called "Dare To Be Great." Pyramid selling, originally regulated in Ontario because of the complaints that arose in the late 1960s about a major cosmetic distribution scheme, has now been prohibited.

Another province that has taken action is Saskatchewan, with its Pyramid Franchises Act, passed in 1972. This Act requires any pyramid scheme to be clearly defined, its promoters to be licensed and bonded, the forms of the pyramid franchise agreement to be filed and the franchisee to be allowed to cancel at any time any pyramid franchise agreement entered into and to receive back a prorated amount of the franchise fee. The Registrar is permitted, under the Act, to apply to the courts for compliance orders or restraining orders against anyone contravening the Act.

British Columbia has a Fair Sales Practices Act that also aims to restrict abuses involved in pyramid sales schemes. Although, unlike the other Acts, there is no licensing requirement, there are various provisions to protect the public. Thus, for example, a person is not allowed to solicit other people to join such a scheme until that person has genuinely sold goods and services equal in value to ten times or more his or her own investment.

MOTOR VEHICLE SAFETY

During the 1960s, Ralph Nader, the U.S. consumer protection advocate, drew the attention of the North American public to the safety defects of many American automobiles. In Canada in 1970, the federal Parliament, responding to public appeal, passed a Motor Vehicle Safety Act that: (a) sets required safety standards for motor vehicles of given classes and their components produced in Canada; and (b) prescribes safety standards for motor vehicles imported into Canada. The Act relates to most motor vehicles, including passenger cars, vans, trucks, motorcycles, snowmobiles, and trailers. The safety standards are intended "to protect persons against personal injury, impairment of health, or death." The Act also indicates the procedure for sending notice of defect and recall to consumers if required by the government.

Some of the major points covered by the many regulations that are continuously being issued under the Act are the use of the National Safety Mark; the issuance of information about defects, detailed technical instructions with regard to various motor vehicle components from the carburetor to the radiator; specifications and tolerance relating to the size and position of controls and outside equipment; and a variety of other safety specifications, for example, with regard to brakes.

Administration of the Act is the responsibility of the Road and Vehicle Traffic Safety Branch of the Ministry of Transport. Manufacturers, dealers and importers must all comply with the standards established by the Act, or risk penalties ranging up to $200,000 for a corporate violation. This includes such things as the failure to follow-up and correct a recommended modification.

EXORBITANT REPAIR COSTS

There are no laws in Canada controlling charges made for appliance and home repairs. A 1972 report on Consumer Warranties by the Ontario Law Reform Commission has revealed that, out of over half a million car sales, not one customer was refunded the purchase price and only fifteen cars were replaced. Once the manufacturer's guarantee expires, the rule of *caveat emptor* applies with a vengeance.

The complaint columns of many newspapers now handle thousands of consumer complaints yearly. Those that relate to repair costs often involve senior citizens who sometimes might be less knowledgeable and consequently more vulnerable than the average customer. The complaints were usually solved by coercion or publicity pressure. The Consumer Bureaus at both levels of government also try to mediate in exorbitant repair cost situations for which there are at present no statutory safeguards.

The province of Quebec now requires the seller of a used car to make any necessary repairs within ninety days of purchase. Metro Toronto also has passed a bylaw that requires motor vehicle repairers to guarantee their repairs.

LOAN REBATES

Very often, a consumer who wishes to repay a loan earlier than anticipated may be saddled with interest charges out of all proportion to those normally charged for a loan of such shorter duration. This occurs when the consumer has entered into a pre-calculated loan agreement, whereby he or she has agreed to pay a fixed monthly sum (say $150) for a given period of time. Eventually, if all the payments are made, the principal will be fully repaid and all interest charges met. However, each monthly payment contains an interest portion calculated on the assumption that the consumer borrows the principal for the full period of time. Consequently, if the loan is repaid earlier, interest charges on the amount borrowed will actually be much higher than the rate originally agreed to.

To overcome this problem, various provincial governments in their Consumer Protection Acts have specified how loan rebates are to be calculated and the amount of prepaid but unearned interest that a lender may retain. In British Columbia, the lender is permitted to keep the lesser of $15 or one-half of the prepaid interest.

LICENSING

One way of trying to ensure that consumers receive good value for their money is for provincial and municipal governments to license persons engaged in a particular trade or profession. Usually, a licence is not granted unless the person has followed a recognized course of instruction and passed qualifying examinations. Examples of persons regulated in this way are plumbers, electricians, denturists, lawyers, doctors, dentists, teachers, real estate brokers, travel agents, insurance agents, and door-to-door salespersons.

FOOD AND DRUGS

In Canada in the second half of the nineteenth century, the public health was considered to be in jeopardy because of the widespread adulteration of foodstuffs and drinks. In fact, when the first Canadian foodstuffs law was passed in 1875, more than 51% of foods sampled were adulterated. Today the situation is quite different, due in great part to federal legislation.

The Food and Drugs Act
The Food and Drugs Act classifies certain drugs, such as barbiturates, as controlled drugs, and other drugs, such as LSD, as restricted drugs. The Act prescribes how such drugs may be legally used. Narcotics come under the provisions of the Narcotics Control Act. Strict records must be kept by hospitals and pharmacists in dispensing any of the foregoing drugs.

The most important federal statute relating to this area is the Food and Drugs Act, passed in 1920 and subsequently revised. The general purpose of the Act is to protect consumers from injury to health and from fraud and other deceptive practices related to food and drugs.

Section 4 of the Act prohibits the sale of adulterated, unfit, putrid, or unsanitary food; s. 5 prohibits misleading advertising in the packaging of foods; s. 6 provides that, if food is advertised as meeting a prescribed standard, it must comply with this standard; and s. 7 deals with food prepared in unsanitary conditions.

With regard to drugs, s. 8 of the Act stipulates that these products must not be manufactured in an unsatisfactory manner or adulterated in any way, while s. 9 prohibits misleading advertising in drug products.

Enforcement of the Food and Drugs Act and its accompanying regulations is the responsibility of two federal government departments. Thus, the Ministry of Health and Welfare concerns itself mainly with potential health hazards of various products, the packaging and labelling of drugs, and sanitation. The Ministry of Consumer and Corporate Affairs looks after packaging and labelling requirements for food products as well as any misleading advertising used to promote their sale.

The Food and Drugs Act also allows federal government inspectors to enter manufacturing premises and, if necessary, seize goods and examine records. Penalties prescribed in s. 25 range from $500 or three months in jail for a summary conviction for a first offence, to $5,000 or three years, for a conviction by indictment.

The constitutional validity of the Food and Drug Act was confirmed by the case of *Standard Sausage Co. v. Lee*, [1934] 1 W.W.R. 81, which dealt with the addition of sodium sulphate to bring out the meat colour in sausages. The Court of Appeal held that, while the amount added in this instance was found not injurious to health, the Federal Food and Drug Act was constitutionally sound as "Parliament had authority to declare an apparently harmless act, a criminal act under s. 91(27) of the British North America Act."

Proprietary or Patent Medicine Act

Since 1909, with the passing of the Proprietary or Patent Medicine Act, all secret formulae must be registered if the medicine is to be taken internally. Control has now been extended to cover misleading advertising, contents of external preparations, and medicines proclaimed as cures—for example, for cancer.

Narcotics Control Act

Legitimate dispensing sources of narcotics are controlled under the Narcotics Control Act. The Royal Canadian Mounted Police tries to prevent illicit use, and Canada co-operates with the United Nations and the police forces of other countries in an effort to reduce trafficking. Drugs may be legally presribed only for medical use and strict records must be kept by doctors or pharmacists. Some drugs, such as LSD, are permitted to be used only for research purposes. The Narcotics Control Act permits the search of anyone and anything (except a dwelling house) if the police have reason to believe that drugs are to be found. In order to enter a dwelling without the permission of the owner or tenant, a search warrant or "writ of assistance" (both issued under the Narcotics Control Act) must first be obtained.

CONSUMER PROTECTION AGENCIES

There are various government agencies and private organizations that have been set up in Canada and elsewhere to help protect the consumer.

Federal Ministry of Consumer and Corporate Affairs
The federal government has established this Ministry to administer the whole field of consumer protection at the national level.

Standards Branch.   One important task of the Ministry, through its Standards Branch, is to protect the Canadian consumer against "economic fraud or hazards." This includes the development of standard specifications and test procedures for consumer products; technical and functional direction of field personnel who enforce the legislation or regulations; the approval of measuring devices; calibration, certification, and control of official reference standards.

The Standards Branch administers the following Acts:

1. The Weights and Measures Act, which permits the inspection of all weighing devices and measuring devices in Canada.
2. The Electrical Inspection Act to approve meters and periodical inspections to ensure statistical accuracy.
3. Commodities and Precious Metals Acts (the Precious Metals Marking Act and the National Trade Mark and True Labelling Act) to ensure the true labelling of furs, textiles, watch jewels, precious metals, and so on.

An important section of this Ministry is a Standards laboratory which carries out any research and testing required—for example, the flammability characteristics of materials used for children's clothing for the purpose of establishing standards for bedding and clothing; the dangerous aspects of toys, such as dolls' eyes attached by a sharp pin which may become hazardous if detached; the dangerous aspects of products with more than the maximum acid soluble lead in glaze allowed under the Hazardous Products Act; the hazardous aspects of children's car seats; and other unsafe aspects of modern automobile design.

Consumer Publications.   The Ministry also distributes various types of consumer publications.

Canadian Government Specifications Board (CGSB).   This organization was founded by the federal government in 1934 to prepare standards and specifications for commodities, equipment, materials, and processes in which government departments and agencies are interested as purchasers or users. Some specifications have become regarded as national standards, and over 1400 standards have been developed on such items as "mops," aluminum windows, and so on. Lately, the board has undertaken to produce standards on carpets, covering such points as durability, disclosure of ingredients, and colour retention. To date, at the federal government level, product testing appears to have been restricted to the development of improved purchasing decisions, the maintenance of responsive health and safety standards and the upgrading of industrial quality in products destined for export.

Provincial Ministry of Consumer and Commercial Relations

In Ontario, as one provincial example, government supervision of consumer protection is exercised through a separate Ministry of Consumer and Commercial Relations. Three key divisions of this Ministry are concerned with Business Practices, Property Rights, and Commercial Registration, respectively.

Enforcement of Statutes.   The responsibility for the enforcement of consumer protection statutes in Ontario lies with the Director of the Consumer Protection Division of the Ministry of Consumer and Commercial Relations, except for specialized areas, such as the Superintendent under the Insurance Act and the Chairman of the Securities Commission under the Securities Act. The main statutes under which supervision is exercised include:

1. The Credit Unions Act and Caisses Populaires Act;
2. The Bailiffs Act, the Collection Agencies Act, and the Mortgage Brokers Act;
3. The Motor Vehicles Dealers Act;
4. The Real Estate and Business Brokers Act;
5. The Cemeteries Act;
6. The Upholstered and Stuffed Articles Act;
7. The Consumer Reporting Act, Travel Industry Act, Consumer Protection Act, and Ontario Business Practices Act.

Most of the foregoing Acts provide for administration to be placed in the hands of a Registrar. Thus, the Real Estate Brokers Act, the Motor Vehicle Dealers Act and the Collection Agencies Act, all provide for registration. Salespeople employed by used car dealers, real estate salespeople, and itinerant salespeople must also be either registered or licensed. Separate trust funds must be set up for clients' money as deposits and bonding may be required in certain cases to ensure financial stability.

The Registrar may refuse to register an applicant or suspend or revoke a registration already granted. Enquiries may be ordered by the Registrar, Director, or Minister, where complaints are received or conduct is suspect.

A motor-car dealer or salesperson may request a hearing by the Commercial Registration Appeal Tribunal, if registration or licensing has been refused, revoked or suspended.

In case of non-compliance with a direction issued under these Acts, the Director may apply to the High Court of the province of Ontario for a restraining order.

Penalties provided for offences under these Acts range from $2,000 to imprisonment for not more than one year; except that in the case of a corporation, a fine of up to $25,000 may be imposed.

All of the Acts administered by the Ministry of Consumer and Commercial Relations in Ontario, are quite similar in operation; control and enforcement being maintained by registration, licensing, bonding, supervision of trust funds, and by mediation on behalf of dissatisfied customers. Criminal prosecutions are still rare.

Consumer Protection Bureaus.   Since, as a rule, these provincial offices have limited staff, most consumer problems are settled by mediation on a correspondence basis. Generally, a satisfactory compromise is reached between the dissatisfied customer and the merchant involved. Any flagrant abuse of the law is referred to the appropriate Registrar for decision as to whether any further action is required.

Where necessary, action is taken by the appropriate Registrar either to suspend or revoke a licence or to forfeit a bond, if such action seems warranted after a complete investigation. In Ontario, decisions may be appealed first to the Commercial Registration Appeal Tribunal and, from there, to the Supreme Court of Ontario.

Normally, the dissatisfied consumer must seek his or her own remedy through the courts under the provisions of, for example, the Ontario Business Practices Act. (See Appendix 28-A.)

Consumer Publications.   Most provinces are actively engaged in the preparation and distribution of consumer pamphlets and educational material. Ontario issues information bulletins and special pamphlets, such as "Helping the Consumer," "Before you buy," "Insurance," "Buying Real Estate," "Investments," "Buying a Used Car," "Questions About buying a Franchise," and so on.

Canadian Association of Consumers

Several private organizations in Canada aim to assist consumers. The Canadian Association of Consumers, as one example, started in 1941 as a women's consumer organization and developed into the Canadian Association of Consumers (CAC) in 1947. The association aims to "develop a more englightened opinion on economic affairs and consumer interests, and to express this opinion in such a way as to benefit the home, the community and the nation."

CAC has now been operating for many years. In 1970, the Association reached an agreement with the Consumer's Union (U.S.) whereby products purchased in Canada by CAC volunteers are tested in CU's independent testing laboratories and the results reported in the *Canadian Consumers* magazine.

The CAC reports that it has been influential in the following areas:

1. margarine—removal of ban (1948);
2. bacon—packaging made non-deceptive by removal of coloured wrapping-paper stripes (1965);
3. labelling—net contents must be shown on packages;

4. canned foods—weight shortages have resulted in a Government order, revising labels;
5. textiles—legislation has been implemented on standard sizes and labelling of fabrics, rugs, and the like;
6. other areas of influence—drugs, credit, housing, household chemicals, education, country of origin of products, and the like.

The CAC is best recognized today as a lobbying organization, attempting to protect the consumers' interest at public hearings of the Air Transport Board and other boards, which regulate radio, television, and telephone rates.

Consumer Council
Canada also has a Consumer Council, an independent, non-governmental group, appointed to advise the Federal Minister of Consumer and Corporate Affairs on any consumer matter. This organization has already issued reports on such topics as bankruptcy, consumer education in the future, etc.

Canadian Standards Association
Canada has its own independent Canadian Standards Association (CSA), a private testing organization, corresponding to Britain's British Standards Institute (BSI). As an example of the work of the CSA, one of its bulletins included information about the change to the metric system in Canada; highlighted the co-operation between the Federal Ministry of Consumer and Corporate Affairs and the Canadian Association of Consumers; reviewed recommended standards for all personal ski and tow equipment; and included a guide to the safe use of household appliances.

Better Business Bureau
The first Better Business Bureau, started in New York, was intended to deal with the question of advertising. Now, however, 85% of the enquiries deal with consumer protection in general. The Bureau has no statutory powers but relies on persuasion. For example, in dealing with a complaint regarding advertisements, the Better Business Bureau sends the complaint to the advertiser. The advertiser has ten days to answer. During this time the advertiser will either defend the ad or comply with the request of the Better Business Bureau. If the advertiser does not comply, the Bureau will then send a copy of the complaint to the advertising media, which may then rule the advertisement to be unacceptable. The Bureau has some 3,500 members in Toronto and is entirely supported by business.

The Better Business Bureau issues a variety of booklets to help protect consumers, and checks newspaper, radio, and television advertisements for unethical practices.

When a complaint is submitted by a consumer, he or she is asked to complete a Consumer Experience Record. The complaint is then investigated by the Bureau. A consumer may ask questions about trade practices by any member firm. Records are rated and indicate whether members follow the rules recommended by the Bureau.

The Better Business Bureau does not recommend firms, nor does it give legal advice. Members asking for information from the Bureau may get a written report, including the credit standing of the firm in question.

The Better Business Bureau has public relations programs for radio, television, and the schools. It also has an extensive library on consumer protection—for example, food freezer rackets, charter flights, paving, and life insurance.

Recently the Better Business Bureau has criticized the practices of many of Canada's charitable organizations because of the relatively small proportion of funds raised that is used for charitable purposes. In some charities, this proportion is as low as 25%.

REVIEW QUESTIONS

1. What is meant by "high-pressure selling?" Give some examples.
2. Explain the term "referral selling." Why can it be considered a consumer abuse? What protection exists?
3. What are "unsolicited goods"? Why does the public need protection from them? What protection exists?
4. Explain how sales franchising can harm the general public. How can abuse be prevented?
5. What are "pyramid sales"? Why have such sales schemes been regulated by some provincial governments?
6. "Motor vehicles are a constant source of consumer complaint." Discuss, with examples.
7. Why has a need for consumer protection arisen with regard to loan rebates?
8. To what extent has the licensing of trades and professions been successful in improving standards of service to the public? Discuss.
9. Explain the nature and purpose of the Food and Drugs Act.
10. Explain the scope and purpose of the Narcotics Control Act.
11. What functions does the Standards Branch of the Ministry of Consumer and Corporate Affairs perform in the area of consumer protection?
12. How does the Ministry of Consumer and Corporate Affairs publicize its consumer protection services?
13. How is provincial government supervision of consumer protection organized in your province?
14. Describe the history and role of the Canadian Association of Consumers.
15. What is the Canadian Standards Association? What are its functions?
16. Explain the origin, nature, and role of the Better Business Bureau.

PROBLEMS

1. A large tobacco company retailed a package of cigarettes at 50¢ a package with the following words printed on the package: "$5.00 in every pack of

New Casino." On investigation it was discovered that what was intended was to advertise that each person had a chance at a $5 prize with each package purchased. The Company was prosecuted under the Combines Investigation Act for misleading statements to promote the sale of goods under s. 37 of the Act. The judge found that the company was liable, that "mens rea" was not required to convict, and that the company was guilty regardless of intention. The punishment was a $3,000 fine. (In addition to this it was alleged that a syndicate broke the puzzle code, bought up packages so quickly the cigarettes could not be supplied to retail outlets, and in the end the company lost one-quarter of a million dollars to winners submitting correct solutions. At the trial the judge stated that the protection afforded by this section is for "the public — the vast multitude which includes the ignorant, the unthinking, the credulous."

Comment on the effect of "mens rea" in a criminal case. What was the basis of liability in this case in your opinion? Which organ of government is responsible for enforcing the law in the case of this and similar offences? Refer to *R. v. Imperial Tobacco Products Ltd.* (1970), 16 D.L.R. (3d) 470.

2. A drug company placed an advertisement prepared by an advertising agency which read as follows: "Shoppers Drug Mart offers the best possible dollar value of savings on every item, every day, whether drugs, vitamins, prescriptions or toiletries." Upon investigation it was discovered that nearly all items checked were being sold by other stores in the same area at prices less than in the store that had had this advertisement prepared. Discuss the probable charge which was laid in this case, the defences offered by the pharmacy owners, and the probable result. Refer to *R. v. Cunningham Drug Stores Ltd.* (1973), 17 C.C.C. (2d) 279.

3. On April 9, 1957, a written contract was completed between the plaintiff, a married woman, and the defendant, a motor car dealer, for the purchase of a new Dodge at the net price of $2,477, for which the plaintiff gave a cheque immediately. The contract read that the car was to be "grey with grey trim" and although no delivery date was fixed, the contract also contained the following terms: "I clearly understand that delivery of this car is contingent upon strikes, fires and other causes beyond our control and hereby agree to extend delivery date (as may be reasonably required accordingly), and it is mutually agreed that there are no warranties or representations except as stated herein and made in writing."

The trial judge found on the evidence submitted that the defendant agreed to deliver by the end of a week at the latest, and that as the result of a rush order the car was in fact ready for delivery ten days later, but the plaintiff refused to accept delivery. The trial judge found for the plaintiff ordering return of the purchase price, and the trial decision was appealed. This case involves the question of delivery under the Sale of Goods Act, and a conflict between the written contract and the understanding of the parties to the contract as to the date of delivery. Discuss any complications which you may see in this case and give your inter-pretation and decision. Refer to *Allen v. Danforth Motors Ltd.* (1958), 12 D.L.R. (2d) 572 (Ont. C.A.).

4. In 1968, a Mr. Thomas G. Lightburn asked his car dealer for a "cheap, economical, reliable car." The Ford Cortina was recommended by the dealer's salesman, which he purchased on April 8, 1968, for $2,705. The buyer relied on the seller's skill and judgment in providing a car fit for the stated purposes. The sales agreement also contained an express provision by the vendor agreeing to make good any defect, and provided that this express provision was in lieu of all other conditions and warranties. The purchaser used the car for eight months, during which time it developed the following faults: (a) failure to start; (b) electrical system trouble; (c) dead battery; (d) red generator light always on; (e) voltage regulator replaced three times; (f) crack in oil pump assembly; (g) oil leak; (h) brake trouble; (i) replaced master cylinder; (j) car hard to start in morning. Finally after 8,000 miles and eight months later the plaintiff repudiated the purchase. Give the arguments for the plaintiff and defendant in this case and the probable decision. Refer to *Lightburn v. Belmont Sales Ltd.* (1969), 69 W.W.R. 734.

5. The law on negotiable instruments in Canada provided that the holder in due course of a promissory note (i.e., the finance company buying up promissory notes used to finance consumer sales) is only affected by real defences (i.e., if the note was either given by an infant or forged) the holder would not be liable to personal or defect of title defences. This was the situation until 1953 in a case in which a promissory note was given by the purchaser covering the purchase of a truck plus a cash advance or $2,500 which was never advanced (*Traders Finance Corp. Ltd. v. Vanroboys*, [1955] O.R. 380). A second case involved the purchase of a knitting machine secured by a promissory note where the seller agreed to rebate part of the purchase price as payment for knitting submitted by the purchaser (*Federal Discount Corp. Ltd. v. St. Pierre*, [1962] O.R. 310). In 1970 the Negotiable Instruments Act was amended by adding ss. 188-192 providing that all negotiable paper involved in consumer sales must be so stamped and eliminating the defence against personal defences. Give your views on the need for and effect of this change in the law and the extent of the consumer protection provided.

READINGS

R. v. Steinberg's Ltd. (1977), 17 O.R. (2d) 559 (Prov. Ct.).

Facts: Between August 4, 1976, and September 9, 1976, Steinberg's in the District of York, Metropolitan Toronto was charged with two counts of falsely labelling cuts of beef, under s. 7(1) of the Consumer Packaging and Labelling Act, thereby committing offences under ss. 10(1)(a) and 20(1)(a) of this Act. Section 7 covers any label which contains any false or misleading representations. Section 10 covers the contents of the label which must contain a declaration of the net quantity. Section 20(1) provides the penalties: on summary conviction, a fine not exceeding $5,000; on indictment, a fine not exceeding $10,000. Section 21(1) provides that it is sufficient proof of the offence to establish that it was committed by an employee unless the accused can establish that he exercised "due diligence" to prevent the offence.

Held:

The court dealt with the question of the offences first and found that the accused, Steinberg's, had in fact mislabelled the meat—that is, bottom round as "sirloin tip" because the employee who had been labelling "sirloin tip" did not change the tab on the labelling machine when she started to label a new batch of meat. However, the judge also found that the employer exercised "due diligence" in an elaborate scheme of employee training and education as to governmental regulations and requirements and compliance therewith. This included manuals, oral expositions and direct discussion with affected personnel both as individuals and at group meetings on the job site inspection scheme. In the judge's opinion, the accused company exercised "due diligence" to prevent the occurrences which took place in the case at bar.

Per Harris Prov. Ct. J.:

I am, therefore, of the opinion that the Crown has failed to prove the charges against the accused beyond a reasonable doubt.

[Counsel for the accused argued that this Act was "ultra vires" Parliament because it did not state simply "label accurately or else" but went on to describe how the labelling should be done; thus it was designed not to prevent deceptive practices but to establish standards of labelling, which is regulation of a particular trade, i.e., under provincial jurisdiction, and is thus "ultra vires". It was shown in evidence that the Regulations published under the authority of the Act were as long as the Act itself.]

. . . [I]t seems to me clear and beyond dispute that a statute which in its entirety deals with honest labelling has a pith and substance which is the protection of the consumer, and is legislation "in relation to" criminal law. . . .

At p. 346 Freedman C.J.M., . . . said: ". . . we must look to the essential nature and purpose of the statute. If from such an examination we conclude the legislation falls within the domain of criminal law, its incidental effects on property and civil rights within the Province will not render it unconstitutional.". . .

In my opinion, the legislation in question in the case certainly affects property and civil rights, but is not an enactment "in relation to" that subject. . . .

. . . Lord Atkin [stated] in *A.-G.-B.C. v. A.-G. Can.* (1937), 67 C.C.C. 193: "The only limitation on the plenary power of the Dominion to determine what shall or shall not be criminal is the condition that Parliament shall not in the guise of enacting criminal legislation in truth and in substance encroach on any of the classes enumerated in s. 92. It is no objection that it does in fact affect them.". . .

The Consumer Packaging and Labelling Act has the public purpose of safeguarding the peace and security of consumers (i.e., their peace of mind and their security arising from the knowledge that they are not being fraudulently imposed upon by suppliers in cases where the consumer's means of knowledge is clearly inferior to that of the supplier) and of preventing the commercially immoral acts of false or intentionally misleading labelling and packaging. . . .

Once it is determined that the Act is within the federal criminal law power, then notwithstanding that it may incidentally affect property and civil rights in the Provinces [trading or selling meat in the Province] it is not possible . . . to suggest that the Act is *ultra vires* of Parliament.

Accused acquitted.

Heimler v. Calvert Caterers Ltd. (1974), 49 D.L.R. (3d) 36 (Ont. Co. Ct.).

Facts: The facts of this case disclose that the plaintiff partook of a wedding feast at the Balmy Beaches Club on March 20, 1971. He and seven other guests developed typhoid fever, and this action was brought over a year after the incident and the plaintiff had not yet fully recovered. His claim was for $1,533.33 out-of-pocket expenses and $1,750 general damages.

Held per Stortini Co. Ct. J.:

In dealing with the issue of liability on this case three matters must be considered:

1. Does the federal Food and Drugs Act, R.S.C. 1970, c. F-27, confer a cause of action on the plaintiff?
2. Is the defendant guilty of negligence?
3. If there is no negligence on the part of the defendant, then apart from the Food and Drugs Act, is there strict liability on the part of the defendant?

Question one: Does the federal Food and Drugs Act confer a civil cause of action? [Section 4 prohibits the sale of food which is poisonous, unfit, contains filthy, diseased substances, is adulterated, or packaged in unsanitary conditions.] . . .

In Canada . . . it appears that a federal statute cannot confer a civil right of action.

In . . . *Wasney v. Jurazsky*, [1933] 1 D.L.R. 616, the Manitoba Court of Appeal had this to say: ". . . although s. 119 of the Criminal Code regarding selling of ammunition to a minor can be referred to as setting up a standard of care which must be recognized in civil proceedings, [it] gives no right of action to a person injured through its breach . . . civil redress . . . must be determined by common law rules.". . .

... I find that the federal Food and Drugs Act does not confer a civil right of action to the plaintiff because of the inherent constitutional difficulties referred to, although, as it has been suggested, the provisions of the federal statute may be relevant in establishing a standard of care in the civil action.

It is clear that provincial statutes may create civil causes of action. . . .

In the case of *Lockett v. A. & M. Charles Ltd.*, [1938] 4 All E.R. 170, a restaurant had served food to the plaintiff who subsequently became ill. The Court found that the food was unfit for human consumption and held for the plaintiff on the basis there was a breach of an implied warranty that the food was so fit.

Question two: Is the defendant guilty of negligence?

... Mrs. I. [the food handler, whom it was established was an unknowing typhoid germ carrier] was a servant of the defendant. . . . Under the doctrine of *respondent superior* the defendant [caterers] is vicariously liable. . . .

... The duty of care resting upon [the food catering business] is similar to that imposed upon a restaurant. . . . [The] food prepared and served [must] be fit. . . . The standard of care is to use the same degree of care . . . as would be exercised by a reasonably prudent person skilled in the art of preparing food. . . .

A reasonably prudent restauranteur . . . ought to anticipate the presence of foreign and potentially dangerous substances in his food. . . . Defendant's servants were aware of the necessity of proper washing of hands after using the toilet. . . . The foreseeable risk of harm was transmission of germs. . . .

[As in the *Shandloff* case where glass chips were found in the chocolate milk container] . . . "The utmost care was used but that care apparently was not sufficient. . . . Some employee did blunder."

[Here] the defendant and its servants certainly appreciated the risk concerning the non-washing or improper washing of hands. [It was established at the trial that the typhoid germ is carried in the stool and it can only be communicated if the carrier handles food manually after having the bowel open without washing hands with soap and water.]

... [I]t can be reasonably inferred that on this particular occasion she failed to cleanse her hands and in the words of Middleton J.A., in the *Shandloff* case, "Some employee did blunder."

Question three: Strict liability. . . .

It appears that in the past 10 years a majority of the courts in the United States have imposed strict liability on the servers of food. . . .

... The Canadian jurisprudence has not yet developed to this extent and the law still proceeds on the basis of negligence, using the doctrine of *res ipsa loquitur* to assist the plaintiff in overcoming evidentiary burdens. . . .

Having found negligence on the part of the defendant, there will accordingly be judgment for the plaintiff against the defendant for $3,283.33 and costs.

Sandilands v. Guelph Datsun (1980) Ltd.

Action for rescision of a contract.

Held per Higgins Co. Ct. J.:

The plaintiff, James A. Sandlilands, contracted with the defendant, Guelph Datsun (1980) Ltd., a car dealer, for a passenger motor vehicle in his certain price range on the express stipulation, as seen from ex. 1, that it be fitted out for delivery at the price of $1,393, so that

1. it be "safety checked, and including
2. brakes, 4 tires (good used) replaced, full body job including rear quarter repainted, floor boards, trunk."

The plaintiff testified that he required these items because he was cautioned by the dealer's salesman during a road test of the car concerning the brakes, about safety check requirements and because he saw some rusting on a rocker panel.

The defendant delivered the car to the plaintiff on July 10, 1980, and supplied him with a Safety Standards Certificate on that date pursuant to the provisions of the *Highway Traffic Act*, R.S.O. 1980, c. 198, and he paid the purchase price in full. The contract between the parties confirmed that a Safety Standards Certificate was to be included and that there was to be no warranty. Nevertheless the plaintiff said in evidence that he relied that the defendant had fulfilled the specifications outlined under the heading of Optional Equipment in the contract and the president of the defendant, Gordon Dennis, acknowledged that he knew that the plaintiff was "relying on us."

Mr. Dennis further testified that the appraisal on the car in question here, when it was taken in trade by the defendant, was "it did not seem worth it to make it roadworthy". Those are his words.

Within four months, namely October 22, 1980, an inspector for the Ministry of Transportation and Communications, Peter Bond, a licensed mechanic for nine years, removed the licence plates from this car because he said it was not roadworthy. He said this was because

1. when he made a brake test that the right front brake line ruptured due to corrosion, and
2. there were perforations or holes in the chassis or frame and the floor pan part of which crumbled into a hole 9″ long and 2″ wide when he examined the car from below on a hoist. There were other similar holes.

Mr. Bond further stated that these rust locations must have been visible from underneath at the time the certificate was given in July, if a mechanic had looked, and that no repair work appeared to him to have ever been done in those areas, never mind as recently as July 1980. He submitted two photographs to show the holes. I accept his evidence.

The defendant argues that there was some duty on the plaintiff to mitigate his loss rather than invoke the provisions of the *Business Practices Act*, R.S.O 1980, c. 55, and claim rescission of the contract as he did by his letter to the defendant of November 6, 1980. It further contends that the plaintiff gave it no option or opportunity to repair the car or even to estimate such expense; at the same time the evidence is that the defendant denied the claim of the plaintiff with its responding letter of November 12, 1980, and did not seek any forbearance from the plaintiff nor make any effort to view the car until two days before the trial.

There is evidence that the cost of repair to the rust holes would be about $150. No testimony was given with reference to the defective brake problem other than that the cylinder in question was very high up under the car and hard to view. The fact that seeing the corrosiveness on this brake cylinder was difficult or impeded by its location or that the repair cost for the rust holes was small, if $150 is small, does not impel me to disregard the plaintiff's claim because he did not try to mitigate his loss.

The *Business Practices Act* is clear in providing a remedy to a consumer if an "unfair practice" has induced him to enter into an agreement: Section 4(1)(a) of the *Business Practices Act* reads:

> 4(1) Subject to subsection (2), any agreement, whether written, oral or implied, entered into by a consumer after a consumer representation that is an unfair practice and that induced the consumer to enter into the agreement,
>
> (a) may be rescinded by the consumer and the consumer is entitled to any remedy therefore that is at law available, including damages; . . .

Subsection (2) does not apply. One of the included remedies that a consumer may invoke is rescission, which is the one sought by this plaintiff.

I must then examine s. 2 of the Act to determine what shall be deemed an unfair practice. It reads in part:

> 2. For the purposes of this Act, the following shall be deemed to be unfair practices.
>
> (a) a false, misleading or deceptive consumer representation including, but without limiting the generality of the foregoing,
>
> > (i) a representation that the goods or services have sponsorship, approval, performance characteristics, accessories, uses, ingredients, benefits or quantities they do not have,
> >
> > .   .   .   .   .
> >
> > (iii) a representation that the goods are of a particular standard, quality, grade, style or model, if they are not,
> >
> > .   .   .   .   .
> >
> > (viii) a representation that the goods or services or any part thereof are available to the consumer when the person making the representation knows or ought to know they will not be supplied,

Both counsel advise me that there are no recorded cases as yet under this Act. I can find none either.

On the basis of any one of the following facts I find that this defendant has given a false or misleading consumer representation:

1. it supplied a car to the plaintiff which was equipped with brakes that would not stop it in an emergency and without adequate mechanical inspection to warrant the safety check given.
2. it supplied a car to the plaintiff which had not had its rust defects repaired although it had so contracted to do. The stipulation in the contract to provide a full body job was supplementary to the term requiring "safety checked."
3. it concerned itself with outfitting a car which it knew was not worth making roadworthy.

Any one of these representations amounted to an unfair practice designed to or resulting in this consumer being induced into the agreement or contract before me. Whether the condition of this car on the date of the signing of the agreement was such that an impossible burden was imposed on the defendant or not is not important. It accepted this contract and was either unable or unwilling to comply with it.

The defendant cannot now complain of the plaintiff's rigidity of attitude. His notice of remedy sought was received by the defendant within the time period specified in s. 4(6) of the *Business Practices Act*.

The plaintiff further puts forward his claim grounded on s. 15 of the *Sale of Goods Act*, R.S.O. 1980, c. 462. That he did not plead this statute may prejudice him only as regards costs. This argument is yet still open to him and I accept it as agreed by counsel for the defendant.

He contends that he made his particular purpose for which the car was required known to the defendant, that he relied on the defendant's skill and that the car is of a description within the defendant's course of business supply, namely roadworthy cars. Thus, he says, there is an implied warranty of fitness. I find that the car here was not transferred to the plaintiff in a condition capable of surviving four months' use and that the plaintiff should succeed on this ground as well.

By an erudite argument defendant's counsel has sought to persuade me that a new statute like this ought to be very strictly construed, that, in so many words, no remedy such as rescission should be available except in extreme cases, and that the remedy claimed by this plaintiff is an equitable one only to be allowed after examination of all the principles found in the various consumer statutes and the case law arising therefrom. I do not agree. The remedy sought by this plaintiff is not an equitable one, it is legal and open to him under this new statute—if he can prove the necessary ingredients—which I have held that he has. In any event what conduct could be more failing in equity—more fundamentally in breach of good faith—than to furnish a consumer who relied upon his advice and judgment with a used car which may not stop in an emergency or does not remain useful and roadworthy for even four months.

There will be judgment for the plaintiff for damages proven of $1,468 made up of:

(a) Damages proven,

	$1,393.00	cost of car
	30.00	storage
	45.00	expense for transport
	$1,468.00	

(b) a declaration that the contract has been rescinded,
(c) interest on the proven damages in accordance with the *Judicature Act*, R.S.O. 1980, c. 223.
(d) costs.

Judgment for plaintiff.

APPENDIX 28-A: SYNOPSIS OF THE BUSINESS PRACTICES ACT

S. 1   Definitions:

Consumer—excludes corporation and partnership carrying on a business.

Consumer representation—any offer, statement, proposal made in respect to supplying goods or services or for consideration for goods and services.

S. 2   (*a*) Unfair practices include false, misleading, or deceptive representations:

      (i) that goods or services are sponsored, approved, or have benefits or qualities not present

      (ii) as to sponsorship

      (iii) as to standard, quality, quantity

      (iv) as to new or unused goods which are not as specified

      (v) misrepresentation as to use

      (vi) misrepresentation as to why goods are available

      (vii) misrepresentation that goods previously supplied

      (viii) misrepresentation that goods will be available which is untrue

      (ix) that repairs are needed

      (x) as to price advantage

      (xi) that salesperson, employee, or agent has authority to finalize contract

      (xii) as to rights, remedies or obligations

      (xiii) exaggeration, innuendo or ambiguity or failing to state a material fact

      (xiv) as to reason for solicitation or communication

     (*b*) or the making of a representation by the supplier when

      (i) consumer is unable to understand the nature of the agreement because of language, physical or mental incapacity

      (ii) price is grossly excessive

      (iii) consumer cannot benefit from the transaction

    (iv) when consumer unable to pay

    (v) when transaction favors some one other than consumer

    (vi) when terms are inequitable to consumer

    (vii) when consumer will suffer if he relies on statement

    (viii) when undue pressure is put on consumer

  (c) other practices outlawed by the Lieutenant Governor in Council.

S. 3 Any of the foregoing are unfair practices which must not be engaged in.

S. 4 (1) Consumer may void any contract involving an unfair practice and supplier must return money and compensate for damages.

(2) Court may award exemplary and punitive damages.

(3) Assignee of a voided contract is limited to money received.

(4) A contract involving a misleading representation as in s. 2(a) may be voided up to six months after notice.

S. 5 Duties of Director include mediation, and keeping records of assurances of compliance and cease and desist orders.

S. 6 Provides for a notice of Director re order to cease a misleading practice or appear before the Commercial Registration Appeal Tribunal for a hearing. The Tribunal may either cancel the Director's order, vary it, or enforce it.

S. 7 Director may make an order effective immediately until hearing is held.

S. 8 Even though Tribunal's order may be appealed, the order may be effective immediately.

S. 9 Provides for an *assurance of voluntary compliance* which has the same effect as an order by the Director and such order may include a bond and compensation for injured consumers.

S. 10 Provides for investigations by persons appointed by the Minister with authority of an enquiry under Part II of the Public Inquiries Act, 1971.

S. 11 If the Director is led to believe by a statement under oath of an infraction against an order or assurance of voluntary compliance, he or she may order an investigation which must be conducted during reasonable hours and may even resort to obtaining a search warrant and seizing of records and the report shall be sent to the Minister.

S. 12 In case of an investigation, an order or an assurance of voluntary compliance, the Director may order third parties to hold any funds due persons involved until a release is given, with the objective of protecting consumers. In the foregoing situation, funds will not be frozen if a satisfactory bond or security is given. Alternatively a Court direction may be sought as to disposition. The Director may also advise the consumer of his or her rights under any unfair practice.

S. 16 Authorizes the Lieutenant Governor in Council to make regulations to enforce this Act including additional unfair practices.

S. 18   Maximum punishment of $2,000 or one year or both for false information, breaking a regulation, failing to observe order or voluntary compliance, or obstructing investigation. Same punishment for knowingly engaging in an unfair practice. Corporation may incur penalty of up to $25,000. Officers and directors responsible for conduct of business giving rise to offence may be a party to offence unless they can prove they had no knowledge of acts.

Time limitation of two years after offence for any prosecution. Act may be cited as the Business Practices Act.

29

Patents, Trademarks, Industrial Designs, and Copyrights

In Canada, a person who invents a new product, uses a special word, design or other symbol to identify a product, creates a new industrial design, or creates a literary or artistic work is usually granted the exclusive right to its use for a certain number of years. The federal statutes involved are the Patent Act, the Trademarks Act, the Industrial Design Act, and the Copyright Act. Responsibility for administering these laws is entrusted to the Bureau of Intellectual Property of the federal Department of Consumer and Corporate Affairs. The Bureau consists of the Patent Office, the Trademarks Office, the Copyright and Industrial Design Office, and other branches responsible for research, technical advice, and international aspects of intellectual property.

PATENTS

Letters patent, or "patent" for short, is a grant made by the federal government to an inventor, giving him the sole right to make, use, or sell his invention in Canada for a period of seventeen years from the date on which the patent was issued. The term "patentee" refers to the person who, for the time being, is entitled to the benefit of the patent.

An invention is defined in s. 2 of the Patent Act as "any new and useful art, process, machine, manufacture or composition of matter, or any new and useful improvement of any art, process, machine, manufacture or composition of matter."

Historically, letters patent were introduced in Tudor times in England as a means of attracting skilled craftsmen to that country by giving them a monopoly on the sale of their work. However, at the beginning of the seventeenth century, the English courts began to insist that such monopolies be only for useful inventions of benefit to society, and this principle was embodied in the Statute of Monopolies of 1624. A comprehensive statute relating to patents was enacted in Britain in 1852. The United States passed its first patent law in 1790. However, a patent law passed by the United States Congress in 1836 remains the basis for present patent legislation in that country.

In Canada, patent laws were passed by various provinces in the early nineteenth century but were superseded by the Patent Act passed in 1869 by the Dominion Parliament under the power conferred on it by s. 91(22) of the Constitution Act, 1867. The Canadian Act was modelled after the American rather than the British Act, but later amendments incorporated various features of the British system. However, the Canadian Act embodies the American principle that a patent is a reward for an invention rather than, as in the British Act, an exercise of a Crown prerogative, given as an inducement for a new trade or a new manufacture. The Canadian legislation also resembles that of the United States in that an inventor is not entitled to a patent if, before the invention, it was known or used by others in that country or if, before the invention, the invention was made in that country by another person who had not abandoned, suppressed, or concealed it.

By contrast, under the British statute, the patent is granted to the person who is first to file the invention.

In Canada another Patent Act was passed in 1872. This Act removed the controversial Canadian residence requirement of the previous Act and confirmed that the basis of the grant was "invention" rather than "discovery." In 1968, a new Patent Act was passed.

Purposes.   The principal purposes of the Canadian patent system, as set out by the Patent and Trademark Institute of Canada, are:

1. encouragement of investment in new production facilities and the manufacture of new products;
2. encouragement of industrial research and invention by individuals (by providing financial incentive);
3. provision of a marketplace for new technology;
4. provision of a medium for the dissemination of technical knowledge (achieved by requiring a propsective patentee to supply a detailed description of the invention at the time of patent application, which is then made public on expiry of the patent);
5. provision of the basis for the development of export markets and expansion of Canadian business into foreign countries.

Procedure.   The first step in obtaining a patent is for the inventor or agent to file an application with the Commissioner of Patents in Ottawa. This application, if it is to be approved, must meet all the requirements of the Patent Act and the Patent Rules. Thus the invention must not, for example, have been used publicly or sold in Canada for more than two years before the application is filed, or have been published anywhere in the world more than two years previously. The application consists of a petition (or request for a patent), a full description of the invention, the filing fee, and any drawings referred to in the description. If the invention can be graphically illustrated, drawings are usually required.

Patent Agent.   Often, an applicant will make use of the services of a registered patent agent to file an application for a patent. These are persons who are specially trained and qualified by examination to represent inventors. They will, for example, search the technical literature and patents to determine if the invention is already known and therefore unpatentable; prepare specifications and claims that meet the requirements of the Patent Act and provide sufficient protection for the invention; submit the application on behalf of their client and provide any necessary further information; and provide information and advice about the filing of patents in other countries—as a Canadian patent affords protection in Canada only. The description of the invention must be such that any person skilled in the subject can understand it and receive sufficient information to carry out the invention without recourse to the inventor.

Patent Examiner.   Once an application for a patent has been filed, a scientist or engineer employed by the Patent Office as a patent examiner will determine, after careful research into prior patents and the technical literature, whether the product is "new, useful, and a result of inventive ingenuity." The application is also checked to ensure that it complies with all the legal requirements and formalities. Should someone else have applied for a patent for the same invention, conflict proceedings must be conducted to determine who invented it first. Sometimes, the examination of an application may last several years, particularly if there are conflicting claims. If the application is not acceptable, the applicant is given the opportunity to amend it or to persuade the examiner to change his mind. Rejection of an application may be appealed to the Federal and Supreme Courts of Canada. Every year, about 29,000 applications are filed in Canada and about 24,000 patents granted; that is, they become public. Also, every year, more than 15,000 patents fall into the public domain. There is a filing fee for a patent application. However, unlike most European countries, no annual fee is required to keep a patent in force.

Patent Protection.   A person who has been granted a patent may sue in court anyone else who exploits the invention in Canada or imports the product from abroad. The court may award the patentee damages as compensation and issue an injunction ordering the infringing party to desist from manufacture or importation. There are also penalties under the Criminal Code for persons who deliberately violate patents. An inventor cannot prevent others from using his invention while his application for a patent is pending. However, if infringement does occur, the inventor may request faster consideration of his application by the Patent Office. The term "patent pending," seen on many products, has no legal significance. It merely serves to warn any other party who may be considering the manufacture of a similar good that an application for a patent has already been made. The inventor must police any infringement of his or her rights, as it would be impracticable for the Patent Office, in light of the vast number of patents granted each year, to attempt to do so.

   A foreign patent does not provide protection in Canada. Consequently, a foreign inventor must apply for a Canadian patent if he wishes such protection. Conversely, a Canadian inventor seeking protection abroad must obtain a patent in each foreign country.

Patent Licensing.   If a patentee does not wish to manufacture the product himself, he may sell the right to do so to someone else in return for a specific fee, called a royalty, on each unit manufactured and sold. The patentee may also sell the patent rights outright for a fixed sum.

The Commissioner of Patents may grant licences to use an invention to person other than the patentee, if the patentee:

1. does not work the invention in Canada or
2. hinders manufacture in Canada by importing from abroad or
3. refuses to grant a licence, contrary to public interest or
4. unfairly prejudices any industry in Canada.

In some cases, the Commissioner may even revoke a patent. Under recent legislation, licences may be granted to import medicines manufactured abroad. Licences may also be obtained as soon as a patent is issued, for all inventions intended for use in food and drugs. In such cases, the patentee receives licence fees as reimbursement.

Patent Office Record.   The Patent Office facilities are available to Canadian industry and the "Patent Office Record" is published weekly containing information about the 500 or 600 patents which were granted in the preceding week. The purpose of this publication is to keep industry informed of new inventions and to encourage it to investigate the possible relevance of such developments to their own business. Inventors wishing to sell or license issued Canadian patents may use the advertising services of the "Patent Office Record." The Department of Regional Industrial Expansion provides a service to bring principals together on an international basis.

Patent Costs.   The cost of preparing and filing a patent application varies from several hundred to several thousand dollars according to the complexity of the application, whether the inventor acts on his or her own behalf or employs a patent lawyer or other agent, and whether the applicant is a Canadian or foreign resident.

Costs of patent litigation in Canada are high. More than 90% of the cases, because of the large amount of damages claimed, are tried in the first instance at the Federal Court; the remainder in the provincial Supreme Courts. Appeals are heard in the Supreme Court of Canada.

TRADEMARKS

A trademark is a word, design, symbol, or combination thereof, that a person or firm uses to distinguish its goods or services from those of others. It may also be a "distinguishing guise"—that is, a distinctive way of shaping or packaging goods. As such, a trademark performs an important advertising and information function.

Once the right to a trademark has been established by use, an application for registration may be made to the Registrar of Trademarks. This is often done, on behalf of the applicant, by a registered trademark agent. The

Trademarks Office will then check the application to ensure that the mark does not resemble one registered earlier for the same type of goods or services; that it does not fall within one of the prohibited classes; and that it is not otherwise objectionable. Marks that are prohibited include royal, vice-regal, and government arms, crests, and flags; Red Cross emblems; national flags and emblems; scandalous or obscene matter; portraits or signatures of living individuals; marks used fraudulently or in a manner calculated to deceive the public; and marks that misrepresent the character, quality, or composition of the goods to which they are applied, or their place of origin. Also, a trademark should generally not be a word of the common English or French languages. Occasionally, a word initially invented as a trademark (for example, "aspirin") may be absorbed into the common language and lose its protected status. A more recent example of a product heading in that direction is "Kleenex."

After the Trademarks Office has completed its check, the trademark is advertised in the Trademarks Journal so that anyone who believes that his or her own trademark is being infringed may oppose registration. If no opposition is forthcoming within one month of the trademark being advertised, or if any such opposition is overruled by the Registrar, the mark is registered. The registration then remains in force for fifteen years, after which it may be renewed for further periods of fifteen years. Registration of the trademark gives the owner the exclusive right to its use throughout Canada with regard to the goods or services for which it was registered.

INDUSTRIAL DESIGNS

If a product has a particular shape, pattern, or ornamentation, it is possible to obtain exclusive right to that outward appearance for five years (renewable for a further period of five years) by registering it as an industrial design. Registration involves the filing of an application with the Commissioner of Patents and the payment of a fee. An industrial design may be registered in Canada if it is not identical with or similar to others already registered. If a design has already been made public in Canada, it can be registered any time up to one year from that date. Designs have been registered for a great variety of articles, including clothing, fabrics, wallpaper, furniture, jewelry, bottles, toys, electrical appliances, and office machines. Details or features of the construction, mode of operation or functioning of an article may be patentable as an invention, but cannot be part of what is registered as an industrial design under the Industrial Design Act.

COPYRIGHTS

Under the Copyright Act, every original literary, dramatic, musical, or artistic work is, as soon as it is created, automatically protected by copyright. Such works include paintings, drawings, sculptures, engravings, photographs, books, maps, charts, films, encyclopedias, newspapers, reviews, magazines, plays and architectural plans, as well as contrivances that mechanically reproduce sound, such as records, open-reel tapes, and cassettes.

The originator or author of any such work has the sole right to produce or reproduce it in any material form and to perform the work in public in Canada. However, the originator or author must have been a British subject or citizen of a country that adheres to the International Copyright Convention when he or she produced the work. Furthermore, in the case of a published work, it must have been first published within Her Majesty's Realms and Territories or in a Convention Country. The term of copyright for written works is the life of the author plus fifty years; for sound recordings and photographs, it is fifty years from the date of the original plate or negative.

The Copyright Act does not apply to designs that can be registered under the Industrial Design Act. Thus, if an artistic work is reproduced or expected to be reproduced by an industrial process in quantity exceeding fifty it loses its copyright protection. This applies, for example, to designs for printed paper hangings, textile goods, and figures.

On August 10, 1962, Canada ratified the Universal Copyright Convention (UCC) which affords automatic protection for unpublished works in UCC countries, including the United States. Under this convention, an original work published in Canada automatically receives copyright protection in the United States and other UCC countries provided all copies bear the symbol © accompanied by the name of the proprietor of the copyright and the year of publication.

While it is not a statutory requirement to register copyright, it is advantageous because it provides prima facie evidence of copyright ownership. To register copyright, a person must send an application to the Commissioner of Patents, with his or her name, title of the work, and registration fee. Copies of the work to be registered are not required. However, two copies of the first printing of every book printed in Canada must be sent to the National Library of Canada, Public Archives, Ottawa.

REGIONAL OFFICES

The Department of Consumer and Corporate Affairs maintains Regional Offices in Halifax, Montreal, Toronto, Winnipeg, and Vancouver. These offices will accept for onward transmission to Ottawa any documents required to be filed with the Commissioner of Patents or the Registrar of Trademarks in relation to patents, industrial designs, and copyrights. Enquiries may also be made directly to The Commissioner of Patents, Ottawa-Hull, Canada, K1A OE1, and to The Registrar of Trademarks, at the same address.

REVIEW QUESTIONS

1. What is a patent? What are its purposes? How long does it last?
2. What is an invention?
3. What is the procedure for obtaining a patent?
4. What is a patent agent? What services does he or she perform?
5. What does the Patent Office do once an application for a patent has been received?
6. What are A's legal rights if B exploits her invention or imports the product from abroad: (a) if A has a patent on her invention; (b) if the patent is pending?
7. Under what circumstances may the Commissioner of Patents grant a licence to use an invention to someone other than the patentee?
8. What protection does a person with a Canadian patent receive abroad? What protection does a person with a foreign patent receive in Canada? What other steps, if any, must be taken to ensure protection?
9. What is a trademark? What are its purposes?
10. What is the procedure for obtaining the exclusive right to use a trademark in Canada?
11. What marks may not be used, by law, as a trademark?
12. How long does registration of a trademark last?
13. What is an industrial design? Give examples.
14. What is the registration procedure for an industrial design?
15. What is a copyright? What products are eligible for copyright?
16. How does a copyright come about?
17. What requirements must be met by a person who wishes to receive the copyright to his or her work?
18. How long does a copyright last?
19. What is the Universal Copyright Convention? What benefits does it confer on persons in signatory countries?
20. What is the procedure for registering a copyright? If such registration is not compulsory, what then is its purpose?

30

Bailments

Bailment is the relationship created by a contract in which an owner of goods (called a bailor) temporarily entrusts custody of these items to another person (called the bailee) for some mutually acceptable reason. Ownership of the goods remains with the bailor.

In the case of *Coggs v. Bernard* (1704), 2 Ld. Raym. 909, 92 E.R. 107, the following bailment situations were listed: goods to be kept by the bailee for the use of the bailor; useful goods lent *gratis* to be resturned in kind; goods hired by the bailee for his or her own use; goods delivered as a pawn or pledge of security; goods to be carried; or something to be done for reward.

Normally, for a contract to be considered a bailment, the identical goods must later be returned to the bailor. However, this rule does not apply in the case of goods such as grain, oil, and sugar where one unit of the particular grade of the good is the same as any other.

Most bailments require only that the bailee exercise reasonable care of the goods involved. However, under common law, innkeepers and common carriers have for many centuries been held strictly liable for such goods. Nowadays, this liability is restricted by statute to a fixed maximum amount so long as the required notice is displayed. However, an innkeeper is still absolutely liable for items placed in the hotel safe.

RENTAL BAILMENT

One very important type of bailment is one in which a person rents or leases goods to another for a fee. Such bailments are now used extensively in business as a means of obtaining equipment, vehicles, and other capital items. They offer the advantages:

1. of reducing the amount of owners' capital required in the business;
2. of reducing corporate income taxes payable since the full rental amount can be shown as an operating expense; and
3. of assuring the bailee of satisfactory equipment, as the bailor is obliged to replace any defective item or carry out repairs at his or her own expense.

The responsibilities of the bailor, in a rental bailment, are:

1. to provide an item in satisfactory operating condition and remaining so during the term of hire;
2. to let the bailee have full use of the item for the agreed rental period (the only circumstance in which the bailor can legally take back the item sooner is if the bailee has committed a breach of the rental contract);
3. to warn the bailee of any possible dangers in the use of the article;

4. to carry out necessary repairs or replace a defective piece of equipment; and
5. to reimburse the bailee for any injury or damage caused by defects in the item rented where the bailor was aware of the defects or could reasonably be expected to be aware of them—even if the baillee was given the chance to examine the goods or actually did inspect them.

It should be noted that, because a rental of an item is a bailment and not a sale, the rule of *caveat emptor* (or "buyer beware") is not applicable.

The responsibilities of the bailee (or hirer) of the goods are:

1. to exercise reasonable care in the use of the goods (however, the bailee is not responsible for normal "wear and tear";
2. not to sublet the goods to any other party or the bailee becomes liable for any damage to them even through no fault of his or her own;
3. to surrender custody of the goods at the expiry of the lease (a bailee attempting to sell or pawn the goods could be found guilty of the crime of fraudulent conversion);
4. to pay the agreed rental (even though he or she may return the goods earlier than agreed) as the bailee remains bound by the terms of the original contract; and
5. to advise the bailor of any need for repairs. (A bailee who has any repairs undertaken without the bailor's express consent is not legally entitled to recover the cost and is liable for any damage caused by unskilled repair. The only exception might be if the bailee acted as an "agent of necessity" in ordering emergency repairs.)

Any of the provisions previously listed may be altered by mutual consent of the parties, so long as the rental agreement in its final form meets all the requirements of a valid contract.

GRATUITOUS BAILMENT

This type of bailment covers the situation in which, for example, a friend borrows an item such as a lawnmower for his own use without any intention of paying for it; or in which, for example, temporary custody of an item such as a car belonging to another person is accepted because the latter has no storage facilities and is going away on a business trip. In such situations, where there is no remuneration involved, the bailee's duty of care is less than where there is some form of consideration. The general rule is that the bailee is required to take as good care of these items as he or she would normally take of his or her own, with slightly greater care if the goods are being used for the bailee's own advantage.

The case of *Stevenson v. Toronto Board of Education* (1919), 46 O.L.R. 146, supports the rule that the bailee in a gratuitous situation is responsible for loss or injury only when caused by the bailee's negligence—that is, want of "reasonable care," namely the care which is ordinarily taken under such circumstances.

REPAIR, SERVICE, AND PROCESSING

A person may temporarily give some goods to another for:

1. repairs—for example, an automobile, a pair of shoes, or a watch;
2. service—for example, laundry and dry cleaning of clothes;
3. processing—for example, raw materials; or
4. to make temporary use of, for example, a water pump rented from a Rent-All Store.

The person giving is the bailor, and the person receiving is the bailee.

Bailor's Responsibilities

These are, first of all, to pay for the services as agreed. Thus, if I take my car to a garage, I should authorize only the repairs I feel are required. Then, if the bailee (the garage owner) carries out any additional repairs, I am not obliged to pay for them. However, if I signed a blanket authority, I must pay for all necessary repairs. If I request that work be stopped before completion, I am obliged to pay only for work so far done. If the charges were not specifically agreed beforehand, the bailor must pay the customary or reasonable charges for such work.

A second responsibility of the bailor is not to deliver noxious goods (ones that have some inherent danger such as fumes or explosive qualities) without informing the bailee of their nature.

Bailee's Responsibilities

These are:

1. to take "reasonable" care of the goods (if the bailee puts them to personal use, the bailee becomes absolutely liable for any damage to them);
2. to do the required work within a reasonable time;
3. not to charge for any unauthorized work (thus, if a mechanic unnecessarily puts in new spark plugs and points in a car, no charge can legally be made for this extra work, nor may the items be removed once they have become part of the repair job); and
4. to possess the skill claimed (the bailee may be sued if lack of skill has resulted in damage to the goods entrusted to the bailee).

QUANTUM MERUIT

Occasionally, for some reason a bailee may complete only part of the required work. In such a case, if the work done is of some value to the bailor, the bailee is entitled to be paid on a *quantum meruit* basis (meaning "payment for work done"). However, if the bailor had previously specified that he or she required a complete job or if such a complete job is obviously necessary, the bailee is not entitled to receive anything for incomplete work. Of course, if the owner orders the work stopped before the bailee has completed the repairs, the contract is breached. This means that the bailee is entitled to payment for the work done, plus possible damages for the breach of contract.

LIENS

A bailee is entitled to hold the goods until paid for services and has a lien (or claim) on them until such payment is made. A *lien* is the right to retain possession of a person's goods until money owing (for example, transportation or storage charges) has been paid. There are two types of lien. A *specific lien* is the right to retain a particular item, such as a car which has just been repaired by a garage owner. This right does not extend to other cars or other property owned by the debtor. Examples of persons who, by their occupation, have specific liens on goods left with them are: the repair person, the service person, the warehouser, the auctioneer, the carrier, and the unpaid seller. A *general lien* is the right to retain possession of any of the debtor's assets that happen to be in the creditor's possession. An example of such a lien is a bank's right to retain any securities which a firm may have in the bank. The bank may make use of its general lien to sell the most liquid of these securities. However, with both specific and general liens, the creditor must follow a definite procedure in selling any of the debtor's assets. Thus, for example, in Ontario an unpaid repair person may sell the repaired item at auction after three months if he or she has given the debtor notice and advertised the auction one week before it is held. The same provisions apply under the Innkeepers Act with regard to the goods of a guest, boarder, or lodger.

It should be pointed out that a lien is the right to retain only the goods already in the creditor's possession. It is not the right to go out and seize the debtor's assets—for example, a car from the driveway. Once a creditor has voluntarily given up possession of the debtor's goods, the right of lien is lost, and cannot be re-established. Normally, a creditor may not use the goods retained. An exception is trained animals, which may be exhibited and any admission fees used to reduce the amount of their owner's debt.

STORAGE OR WAREHOUSING

A person will sometimes need to place an article with someone else for storage or safekeeping—for example, furniture in a depository, grain in an elevator, goods in a warehouse, cars in a garage, boats in a marina, and jewellery and valuable documents in a bank safety deposit box. This is a special type of bailment with its own rules.

Bailor's Responsibilities. These are: (a) to pay the agreed rental or, in the absence of prior agreement, what is customary or reasonable; and (b) not to store noxious goods or to package goods in such a way (for example a leaky barrel) that they may later damage other goods in the warehouse.

In Ontario, s. 2 of the Warehouseman's Lien Act provides that a warehouser has a lien over goods in his or her possession to cover charges for storage, money advanced for transportation, and so on. This Act also provides the procedure to satisfy this lien—that is, first giving twenty-one days' notice to the interested owner, followed by notices in a daily newspaper two weeks apart, then public auction, with the balance exceeding the lien being paid to the owner or deposited in court. Each province in Canada, except Newfoundland, has a similar Act.

Bailee's Responsibilities. These are:

1. To exercise reasonable care. Thus in the case of *Herbert v. C.A. Ward Ltd.*, [1937] O.W.N. 139, a warehouser was held liable for damage to furniture and household goods left with him as he failed to show circumstances negating negligence on his part. In the case of an animal, such as a horse, requiring exercise, the bailee may exercise the animal. However, if he or she rents it out, the bailee becomes liable for any injury the animal sustains.
2. To ensure special care in the case of goods accepted on that basis—for example, furs stored for the summer, or apples in cold storage.
3. To surrender the goods on receipt of the proper authorization. Since goods are frequently assigned or sold while they are in the warehouse, the claimant may not be the same person as the one who placed the items in storage. The warehouser must give up possession of the goods to the holder of the warehouse receipt, on payment of the storage charges.
4. The restaurant owner who provides a checkroom, but clearly indicates by signs that he or she is assuming no responsibility, can escape responsibility for loss from, say, theft. The restaurant owner is also not responsible for loss if the guest chooses to retain control over the belongings by, for example, draping his or her coat over a chair. However, the restaurant owner would still remain liable for gross negligence—for example, if one of the kitchen staff set fire to the cloak room, or if one of the waitresses spilled food on the guest's clothing.

In Ontario, car parks are subject to the rules of warehousing. A few cases in this province have involved situations in which the car park owner has put up a sign stated that "charges are for parking space only." This has been interpreted as signifying a change in the nature of the contract from one of bailment to one in which the car owner by virtue of the licence has a right to use the space only and the car owner remains liable for any damage to the vehicle. However, it would be difficult to claim that the contract was not one of bailment if the car park owner insisted on holding the keys (*Bata v. City Parking Canada Ltd.* (1973), 2 O.R. (2d) 446).

SECURITIES AND VALUABLES

Another type of bailment is one in which a person leaves precious articles (called pawns) with a pawnbroker as security for repayment of a loan. By law, the pawnbroker (the bailee) must take reasonable care of the goods and must return them to the holder of the pawn ticket when full repayment of the loan and full repayment of the lawful interest is made. The pawnbroker who makes use of the goods becomes strictly liable for any damage.

A similar type of bailment is one in which a person borrows money from a bank or finance company and gives the lender stocks, bonds, or a life insurance policy with a cash surrender value as security, or collateral. Here also the lender (the bailee) must take reasonable care of the items. Section 178 of the Bank Act, allows a bank to lend money to a firm on the security of its inventory. In this case the borrower retains custody of the inventory.

If a borrower fails to repay a loan, the lender has the right to sell the asset pledged as security. The lender may do this at once, without notification to the borrower, if a definite time limit was set for repayment. Otherwise written notice should first be sent to the borrower to demand repayment and advise the borrower of the intended sale. Pawnbrokers usually wait a year from the last interest payment before selling "unredeemed pledges."

With regard to most items given as security (or *collateral*) for a loan, the borrower is normally entitled to receive what remains after payment of the principal, interest, and expenses. However, in the case of items pledged with a pawnbroker, the Pawnbrokers Act of Ontario provides that, after a final notice has been given to the borrower, title in the goods passes to the pawnbroker.

RES IPSA LOQUITUR

Normally, in the case of negligence, the burden of proof lies with the plaintiff. However, in bailment, where an item is damaged, the opposite is true. If negligence is alleged, then to escape liability under this maxim, the bailee must show that the damage or injury was caused by third party negligence.

The legal principle of *res ipsa loquitur* ("the thing speaks for itself") is applied whenever an item is placed in the control and exclusive custody of another party. Since the bailee alone knows what happens to the item while it is in his or her custody, it is only reasonable that the bailor should expect proper care of the item. If, when the bailor comes to collect the item, he or she notices that something has happened to it, he naturally assumes that the damage or defect has occurred while the item was in custody of the bailee. And he is entitled to say, "When I placed the item in custody it was intact; now when I take it out there is something wrong with it; and I don't know what caused it." Therefore he is entitled to ask the bailee either to give a satisfactory explanation or to assume liability for the damage. If the bailee can show that the damage was due to the negligence of a third party, then the plea of *res ipsa loquitur* fails, and the bailor must look elsewhere for remedy. This may be difficult (for example, in an air crash) when the causes of the accident may never be discovered.

CARRIAGE OF GOODS

Another type of bailment is one in which a person entrusts goods to a common or public carrier. This is a rail, air, or road transportation company (such as the CN or Air Canada) which has agreed to transport for a fee any freight offered for carriage so long as the company has sufficient transportation facilities.

The responsibilities of the bailor (called the shipper or consignor in contracts of carriage) are:

1. To pay the statutory schedule rates. These are usually prepaid, but goods may also be sent "freight collect." The contract of carriage (the bill of lading) always reserves for the bailee a right of lien on the goods as a safeguard against non-payment of the rates.
2. To describe the goods accurately on the bill of lading so that the correct freight rate may be charged.
3. To package the goods properly. The condition of the goods will be marked on the bill of lading; a "clean" bill of lading signifying that the goods have been received by the public carrier in "apparent good order and condition."
4. To ensure that the goods are not harmful. Unlike other types of bailment, the liability of the common carrier (the bailee) for damage to the goods extends beyond that caused by his or her own negligence. By tradition, it is expected the goods will be delivered safely to their destination. This means that the common carrier must insure the goods to avoid financial loss as a result of non-delivery. The only exceptions to this broad liability are when damage is caused by: acts of God, or *force majeure*, such as floods or earthquakes; war or riots; or inherent vice or defect in the goods (for example, improper packaging or diseased cattle).

The carrier's liability, it should be noted, is limited only to the actual value of the goods declared. Thus, if the bailor shipped gold under the description of lead and the gold disappeared, the carrier would be required to pay only for the cost of lead.

Some statutes, designed to enable public carriers to quote more competitive rates to the public, restrict a carrier's absolute liability to a fixed maximum amount.

The broad liability of public carriers for the safety of the goods carried was based on the fact that such carriers had complete, unsupervised control of them. However, with regard to any passengers carried, public carriers are liable for injuries only if negligence can be proved. Also public carriers are permitted by statute to insert a clause on special "cheap excursion tickets" to reduce their liability for injuries.

Once a consignee has been informed that the goods have arrived and has been given a reasonable amount of time (usually forty-eight hours) in which to collect them, the public carrier's absolute liability terminates. Instead, the carrier becomes liable as a warehouser for the care of stored goods. The consignee may be charged storage fees (called *demurrage*) once the forty-eight hours have expired.

So far we have considered the responsibilities of a public carrier. There are, however, two other types of carrier. A *gratuitous carrier* is a person who transports goods for nothing—for example, a person doing a favour for a friend. A *private carrier* is a person or firm that transports goods for a reward either occasionally or as a regular, specialized service—for example, furniture removals. Both these types of carrier are subject to the normal rules of bailment.

HOTELS

The innkeeper (as the hotel owner is called in law) has been liable since the Middle Ages for the safety of guests' belongings. The common law judges, realizing that a traveller might be beset by highwaymen all along the way, held that the innkeeper had a public duty to receive the traveller, together with belongings, as a guest. Once the inn was safely reached, the traveller could relax in the knowledge that the innkeeper was absolutely liable as an insurer for the safety of the goods.

Because of the innkeeper's ease of access to guests' belongings, the courts have held that this liability should be absolute—that is, the innkeeper is fully liable even though the fault is not his or her own, except where protection has been afforded by statute.

The only exceptions to the innkeeper's absolute liability are: (a) loss caused by the guest's own negligence—for example, if the guest entertains unreliable persons in his or her room and leaves them unsupervised; and (b) statutory protection—whereby, in some provinces, the innkeeper is allowed by statute to limit his liability to the amount set out in a sign if he displays this sign prominently in a public place. In Ontario, s. 4 of the Innkeepers Act limits an innkeeper's liability to $40 if he posts the relevant section of the Act in the bedrooms, the public rooms, and the office. Most provinces have the same statutory provisions as Ontario, except Newfoundland and Saskatchewan, where only one notice is required in the hotel entrance, and Manitoba, which has no similar provision. The amounts of liability also vary from province to province. Newfoundland requires registration of the guest before the innkeeper becomes liable. In other provinces, a person may become a guest even without registration. For example, in Alberta, a woman who was attending an oil wives' banquet in a hotel, at which her $1,000 mink coat was stolen, was held to be a hotel guest and entitled to recover her loss from the hotel keeper.

However, despite a sign an innkeeper is fully liable if:

1. the loss is caused by the acts of the servants;
2. the goods were offered to employees of the inn to be placed in safekeeping and were not accepted; or

3. the item lost is a car or a horse and was kept in a garage, lot, or stable run by the hotel.

In an English court case, *Olley v. Marlborough Court Ltd.*, [1949] 1 All E.R. 127, a guest registered at a hotel, picked up her room key, but was not made aware of the limitation of the hotel's liability until she had reached her room. She subsequently suffered a baggage loss as a guest of the hotel. The court held that because the conditions limiting the liability of the innkeeper were not prominently displayed, she was not bound by them, and therefore the innkeeper was liable for her total loss.

Of course, the tort rules regarding the owner's liability apply to the guest's person. Thus the guest is in the position of an invitee because of the commercial relationship and is therefore entitled to be notified of any unusual dangers that the innkeeper knows of or should know of. However, the guest is always required to exercise the care of a reasonable person. Now in Ontario, under the Occupier's Liability Act, the occupier must exercise "reasonable care" towards all users of the premises.

An innkeeper is distinct from and has greater legal responsibilities than rooming and boarding house operators and apartment owners.

SAFETY DEPOSIT BOXES

Very few cases have involved rental of safety deposit boxes. It would appear that this type of contract is one of storage or warehousing under the definition of a warehouser in, for example, the Warehouse Receipts Act of Ontario. Accordingly, a bank or trust company or other operator of a safety deposit box service should be able to dispose of unclaimed goods as provided in the Act.

REVIEW QUESTIONS

1. What is meant by the term "bailment"?
2. What are the responsibilities of the bailor in a rental bailment?
3. What are the responsibilities of the bailee in the rental bailment?
4. What is a gratuitous bailment? What is the bailee's duty of care in this type of arrangement?
5. When goods are given to another person for repair, service, or processing, what are the bailor's responsibilities?
6. When a person receives goods on a temporary basis for repair, service, or processing, what are the bailee's responsibilities?
7. Explain, with an example, the term *quantum meruit*.
8. In the case of a storage or warehousing agreement, what are the responsibilities of: (a) the bailor; (b) the bailee?
9. What is meant by the legal principle of *res ipsa loquitur*? Illustrate your answer with two bailment examples.
10. Distinguish among a common carrier, a gratuitous carrier, and a private carrier.

11. In the case of the common carrier, what are the duties of: (a) the bailor; (b) the bailee?
12. What is *demurrage*? When does it occur?
13. What is the liability of the owner of a hotel for the belongings of a guest?
14. What liability does the hotel owner have for the personal safety of his guests?
15. What is a lien? Distinguish between a specific lien and a general lien.
16. If there has been a gratutious bailment, the bailee cannot be held responsible:
    (a) unless he or she had been negligent;
    (b) unless he or she had been grossly negligent;
    (c) under any circumstances;
    (d) unless it can be shown that the goods had been stolen.
17. The operator of a restaurant checkroom is completely responsible for the safety of the goods left with him. Comment.
18. A repair person is entitled to make a reasonable charge for doing necessary, but unauthorized repairs to articles left with him. Comment.
19. A common carrier is always completely liable for his or her negligence. Comment.

PROBLEMS

1. Consider the facts in the case of *Lamont v. Canadian Transfer Co. Ltd.* (1909), 19 O.L.R. 291 (C.A.). The plaintiff arrived in port at Toronto. He handed his baggage checks to his father-in-law who was to arrange to have his trunks sent to his home. The father-in-law gave the checks to a customs officer with whom he was acquainted together with 25¢ and asked him to make the necessary arrangements to ship the trunks. The customs officer gave the checks and 25¢ to one Dunn, an agent of the defendant shipping company, with directions to send on the trunks. Dunn took the checks, located the trunks, then replaced the ship checks on the trunks with checks of the Canadian Transfer Co. Fifteen minutes later the customs officer returned and asked for a receipt which was given to him. He forwarded the receipt, which he had not read, to Lamont. Lamont did not read the receipt until ten days later. On the face of the receipt was a legible notice stating that the company was "not liable for any loss or damage of any trunk for over $50." One of Lamont's trunks, which was never located, was worth considerably more. Plaintiff sued the defendant for the value of his trunk. What is the defendant's liability on this contract for bailment?

2. Debbie brought her car into the local garage for specific repairs which were completed. Debbie refused to pay and the mechanic refused to surrender the car, claiming a mechanics' lien. Debbie then requested her boyfriend, Ronnie, to attend at the garage in the middle of the night to repossess the car. Ronnie did so. Has the garage owner lost his mechanic's lien? Give reasons. Would the position be any different if the

mechanic performed repairs which were unauthorized along with the work requested? How?

3. Jensen operated a warehouse which accepted some 230 crates of plywood from Kryt for storage. The crates were accepted over a period of three months, and after each delivery, Kryt, the owner of the plywood cases or units, was sent a warehouse receipt in which was contained a provision that the liability of the warehouseman for each case or unit was limited to $50 in case of loss unless a special contract was entered into at the time the warehouse contract was made. The cases were destroyed by fire, admittedly caused by the negligence of an employee of the warehouse-man who placed an electric heater too close to the cases, causing the fire. The bailor-owner recovered $85,000, the full value of the plywood at the first trial. The warehouseman appealed claiming that the $50 limitation applied reducing his liability to $11,000. Much of the argument turned on the interpretation of the following clause 3(4): "a warehouseman may insert in a receipt issued by him any other term or condition that does not impair his obligation to exercise such care and diligence in regard to the goods as a careful and vigilant owner of similar goods would exercise in the custody of them in similar circumstances." The warehouseman argued that the $50 limitation was not included under the above restriction, while the bailor-owner, now respondent, is claiming that the $50 limitation charge was ruled out by the above.

Assuming that the limitation clause was part of the bailment contract, give two arguments for and against full recovery in this case. Refer to *Evans Products Ltd. v. Crest Warehousing* (1977), 95 D.L.R. (3d) 631.

READINGS

Minichiello v. Devonshire Hotel (1967) Ltd. (1976), 66 D.L.R. (3d) 619 (B.C S.C.).

Facts: On Christmas eve a jeweller closed his shop, put his best jewellery in an attaché case, placed it in the trunk of his car, and drove with his fiancee to the Devonshire Hotel to deliver a ring. He parked in the hotel parking lot and was asked to leave the keys in the car, as he had done before. He was given a parking stub. He was reluctant to leave the keys and told the attendant that he had valuables in the car trunk and requested him to be especially careful with the keys. Thirty-seven minutes later when he returned to pick up his car, the car had been moved to another place. He turned in the parking ticket, paid 40¢, and drove home. Thirty minutes later he discovered his loss and returned to report the theft and inspect his parking ticket. He then learned that the ticket stated in small print that cars were to be picked up at the owner's risk and liability and that the parking company was not responsible for damage, loss of car, or contents due to theft, fire, and so on. The plaintiff claimed against the defendant for breach of its duty as an alleged bailee for reward, claiming that no one had pointed out the disclaimer provisions of the ticket, that when he went to pick up his keys they were in his car, instead of being in the attendant's office, and the doors of the car were unlocked.

Held per Rae J.:

In these circumstances, whatever else may be said, the conditions on the ticket do not operate to absolve the defendant of responsibility: see *Appleton v. Ritchie Taxi*, [1942] 3 D.L.R. 546 at p. 549 *et seq.*

. . . As hereinafter set out the defendant owed a duty of care. Indeed, one of the conditions on the ticket reads: "Reasonable care by our employees constitutes full discharge of our liability." The theft here arose from the negligence of the defendant's employee as hereinafter set out. The conditions on the ticket are to be construed strictly against the defendant. The conditions do not exempt the defendant from negligence even if the plaintiff is bound by them: see *Brown v. Toronto Auto Parks Ltd.*, [1955] 2 D.L.R. 525 at p. 527. . . .

The principal issues in the case at bar are whether the defendant became a bailee not only of the plaintiff's vehicle but also of the jewellery in the trunk, and if it did, whether it did so for reward. If the defendant was a bailee for reward it is responsible to take such care of the plaintiff's goods as a careful and vigilant man would exercise in the custody of his own chattels of a similar description and character in similar circumstances: see, e.g., 2 Hals., 3rd ed., p. 114, para. 225.

Further, if the defendant is a bailee for reward then the onus is upon it to show that the loss did not occur through its lack of proper care: see e.g., 2 Hals., 3rd ed., p. 117, para. 227.

. . . The keys, including the trunk key, were left in the ignition of the veicle by the attendant, with the door unlocked. Assuming the defendant was a bailee for reward of the jewellery in the trunk, the defendant did not take proper care in the circumstances.

I return to the principal issues. First, was the defendant a bailee of the jewellery? In the case of chattels which might reasonably be expected to be carried in an automobile there is a constructive bailment of the chattels as well as of the automobile: see *Heffron v. Imperial Parking Co.* (1974), 46 D.L.R. (3d) 642 at p. 653, 3 O.R. (2d) 722. . . . I have already stated what was said by the plaintiff to the defendant's attendant as to valuables being in the car when he left the vehicle with the attendant. The defendant's attendant has the ostensible authority to accept the chattels: see, e.g., *Mendelssohn v. Normand, Ltd.*, [1969] 2 All E.R. 1215 at p. 1218.

. . . The Mendelssohn case, supra, however, is of some assistance. There the vehicle being left had luggage on the back seat. One piece of luggage was a suitcase containing jewellery and other valuables. The driver of the vehicle was about to lock it when he was told by the attendant that he was not permitted to lock the vehicle. The driver then "explained to him that the luggage was rather valuable and that I would not be long." . . . [W]hen the driver returned he found the door of the car unlocked and the key in the ignition. The suitcase was missing and the defendant was held responsible in damages to the amount of 200 pounds. . . .

In the case at bar there was a sign requiring the plaintiff to leave the car keys. . . . The manager and president of the defendant said customers were required to leave their car keys, and to leave them in the ignition, and that customarily the customer was asked by the attendant to leave the keys. Here the keys were, in fact, left as already stated. . . .

These circumstances, in my view, constitute the defendant bailee not only of the vehicle but also of the valuables. The valuables in this case consisted of a considerable quantity of jewellery. . . . It was open to the defendant to limit or exclude its liability by a suitable condition or conditions made part of the contract either by appropriate sign or signs, or by conditions on the ticket or otherwise in such a way that the plaintiff might be deemed, in reason, to have had notice of the limitation or exclusion. It did not do that.

I have, of course considered the relatively high value of the articles involved here, but surely it is a matter of principle and not degree which one must consider. In the *Mendelssohn* case the valuables were of considerably less value than those in question here, but the notice given was substantially the same. When applying a precedent one is concerned with principle rather than with fact. . . .

So I conclude that there was a bailment of the jewellery. Then was it a bailment for reward? . . . [H]e was the guest of the defendant for a short period in its bar when he and his companion had a drink and he was charged for the parking of the vehicle after he gave notice that it contained valuables. . . .

In my view, in the circumstances, here, if one asked the question as I have done, "what was bailed?", the answer must be the vehicle and the valuables. If one next asked, "was there consideration given?", the answer must be that there was. That being so, it was not a gratuitous bailment. . . .

I turn next to the defendant's plea of contributory negligence. The defence says that the loss of the jewellery was, in part, the plaintiff's fault and that the *Contributory Negligence Act*, R.S.B.C. 1960, c. 74, should be applied, i.e., that the plaintiff failed to take reasonable care for the safety of his own jewellery. . . .

I have already indicated that a sign on the lot required those parking vehicles to leave the keys (plural). . . .

. . . The key was, in a manner of speaking, an indicium of control of possession, and it was appropriate that, since the plaintiff was entrusting the safekeeping of the jewellery to the defendant, he should entrust the key also. . . . [S]o the key to the trunk gives control over the valuables being placed in the defendant's care. The trunk key was part of the bailment. . . .

I have concluded that the sole effective cause of the theft was the negligence of the defendant's attendant as already referred to. The defendant is liable as a bailee for reward.

I turn next to the matter of damages. The claim as put forward at the trial approximates $17,000. . . . I express the hope that they may be able to agree on the quantum of damages. Having commenced an examination of the vouchers, I suggest that counsel should, themselves, or by solicitors, examine each item against the alleged relevant voucher with care. If counsel are unable to agree they may speak to the matter further.

Judgment for plaintiff.

Vic Priestly Landscaping Contracting Ltd. v. Elder (1978), 19 O.R. (2d) 591 (Co. Ct.).

Facts: Vic Priestly undertook by a verbal contract to erect a marquee tent for Marianne Elder for the purpose of a horse show being held on their farm and sponsored, unknown to the owner of the tent, by James D. Service and the Mustang Financial Corp. Ltd. The tent was to be used for displays and a private contractor George Dronoff was also hired by the sponsors to act as a caterer supplying drinks and operating a barbeque. The show went off as planned. However, on the Monday morning, when the caterer returned to pick up the barbeque, he placed the used coals in a cardboard box outside the west tent wall. A fire resulted and destroyed the tent. The bailor and owner of the tent who had been paid his rental fee then sued for the cost of the tent, $1,400.

Held:

The court made the following points relating to this case:

Bailment
In the case of *A. R. Williams Machinery Co. Ltd. v. Muttart Builders Supply (Winnipeg) Ltd.* (1961) 30 D.L.R. (2d) 339 it was stated "the borrower is not responsible for reasonable wear and tear . . . but he is liable for negligence . . . [which] depends upon the circumstances of each particular case, the nature of the chattel lent, and the character and occupation of the borrower."

A statement of the law as it is generally understood is contained in *Catalytic Construction Co. of Canada Ltd. v. Austin Co. Ltd.,* [1957] O.W.N. 290: "the onus was cast upon the defendant to satisfy the court that the damage caused to the plaintiff's property did not occur as the result of negligence properly attributable to the defendant."

Therefore the defendants are bailees and as such are obliged to produce the tent or explain how it disappeared without negligence on their part.

Agency
The defendants, the Elders, claim that they acted only as agents. Yet Victor Priestly was unaware of the principals, Service, et al. According to G.H.L. Fridman in the *Law of Agency*, 4th ed. (Butterworth, 1976, p. 202), "since the agent contracts personally where his principal is undisclosed, . . . the agent, as well as the undisclosed principal may sue and be sued upon the contract. . . . It is clear that once the third party knows that there is a principal, he may choose between which of the two parties who are liable to him."

In *McMillan v. Barton* (1890), 19 O.A.R. 603 at p. 613, it was held that agents may claim indemnification vis-à-vis their principal.

Negligence of the third party

To escape the liability the defendants must show that the fire was not an accident but caused *by the negligence of a third party.*

The judge found as a fact that it was more reasonable to conclude that the fire occurred by the negligence of a third party than to conclude that the fire occurred without negligence, i.e., barbecue coals left in a cardboard box.

Effect of finding negligence on the part of a third party

The defendants can argue that they have not the onus on them as bailees by showing that the loss occurred through the negligence of a third party, George Dronoff.

Vicarious liability for an independent contractor

In *Savage v. Wilby,* [1954] S.C.R. 376 at p. 378, it was stated (paraphrased) that a man who orders work that maybe injurious to his neighbour must personally ensure that no mischief occurs. (In this case an independent contractor damaged the premises by using an inflammable paint remover which caused a fire and the lessee of the premises and hirer was held liable.)

The use of fire in any situation where it is likely to spread and cause damage is an inherently dangerous activity such that there will be vicarious liability for the negligence of an independent contractor.

Indemnification from the third party

See *McFee v. Joss* (1924), 56 O.L.R. 578 at p. 284. Mr. Justice Morand stated: "This right of indemnity [by a negligent third party] is based on the principle that every one is responsible for his own negligence, and if another is, by a judgment of a court, compelled to pay damages which ought to have been paid by the wrongdoer, such damages may be recovered from the wrongdoer. . . ."

Conclusion

The Elders were not liable as bailees since the destruction occurred as the negligence of a third party. Service et al., as principals, are liable for the negligence of an independent contractor carrying out a hazardous activity, but are entitled to be indemnified by the independent contractor. The plaintiff gets judgment for $1,400 plus costs against the defendant Service et al.

7

FINANCIAL LAW

In this final part of the book, we consider the laws that a business firm must observe in the conduct of its financial affairs.

31

Negotiable Instruments

Business firms are constantly issuing cheques, drafts, promissory notes, and other financial instruments to other firms and individuals in payment of goods and services bought and/or in recognition of a debt incurred. Many of these financial instruments can be transferred, by endorsement (explained later), to third parties. When this right to transfer ownership and possession of the financial claim involved to a third party is recognized by law, the instrument then becomes a *negotiable instrument*. Unlike the usual assignment of contractual obligations, the transfer, or "negotiation," of such instruments is characterized by the absence of any need to give notice of the assignment to or obtain the consent of the drawer or promissor, even though he or she will be liable to any new assignee. Furthermore, the assignee has the right to sue any previous endorsers, as well as the drawer, if payment is not forthcoming.

The common law relating to negotiable instruments has developed slowly over the centuries, with its origins in the "law merchant," the commercial law that evolved in the mediaeval fairs of Britain and continental Europe. The common law now recognizes a great variety of negotiable instruments: cheques, drafts, promissory notes, bonds, interest coupons, dividend warrants, bank notes, post office money orders, express money orders, bills of lading, warehouse receipts, letters of credit, and share certificates.

BILLS OF EXCHANGE ACT

In 1882, the British Parliament passed a statute, the Bills of Exchange Act, that codified much of the common law relating to negotiable instruments. In 1890, Canada followed suit with its own Bills of Exchange Act, an almost exact replica of the British statute. However, these Acts relate only to certain types of negotiable instruments: cheques, drafts, and promissory notes. Consequently, any legal dispute involving any other type of negotiable instrument is revolved by reference to the common law.

Negotiability
Section 17 of the Bills of Exchange Act sets out certain criteria that a financial instrument must fulfil if it is to be legally negotiable. These are as follows:

1. The instrument must be in writing and signed by the drawer (if a cheque or draft) or maker (if a promissory note). Writing includes printing,

typing, tracing, while the signing may be done by using a stamp. The signature may even appear in the body of the note.

2. It must be an order or promise to pay an exact amount of money (a "sum certain"). A request is not sufficient.

3. The order or promise must be unconditional—for example, not a promise to pay on completion of a building now under construction.

According to s. 18, "an instrument expressed to be payable on a contingency is not a bill." Thus, a note payable "when I marry" is said to be payable on a contingency because it may never occur; but if the note reads "when I die," the payment date is fixed because the condition must eventually be met.

4. The sum of money involved must be payable either on demand or at a fixed or determinable time in the future. For example, it might even be three months after a person's death, an event which must eventually occur.

5. The complete instrument, not just a part, must be negotiated.

6. It must be made out to the order of a specified person or to bearer.

TYPES OF NEGOTIABLE INSTRUMENTS

There are two main types of negotiable instruments: drafts, and promissory notes.

Drafts

This is a written order, signed by the drawer, addressed to another party (the drawee), instructing him or her to pay a certain sum of money to a third party (the payee), either on demand, at sight, or any specified number of days or months after sight or after date.

The drawer is the person who writes out the draft. The drawee is the person or firm to whom the drawer has sold goods or services, often on credit, and who is being called upon to pay. The payee is usually the drawer's bank. Normally there are three parties to a draft, but s. 19 provides that either the drawer or the drawee may also be the payee.

A draft is defined in s. 17 of the bills of Exchange Act as:

> an unconditional order in writing addressed by one person to another, signed by the person giving it, requiring the person to whom it is addressed to pay, on demand or at a fixed or determinable time, a sum certain in money to or to the order of a specified person or to bearer.

Drafts, or bills of exchange, have been in use since the earliest days of commerce. This is because they provide an effective and relatively safe method of transferring funds from one person to another. By using a bank draft, for example, to pay for goods purchased, a merchant can avoid the dangers involved in carrying cash over long distances. Thus if A in Paris owed money to B in Lisbon and C in Lisbon owed money to A in Paris, the debt could be paid merely by A's instructing C to pay B. Of course, it would be unusual for C to owe A exactly the same amount as A owed B, or to owe it at the same time. Consequently, banks undertook this type of financial transaction, matching the obligations of one merchant with those of another. Eventually, if A wished to pay a debt in Lisbon, Rotterdam, or elsewhere, he would merely go to his bank in Paris. The bank would then provide him with a draft drawn on its branch or correspondent bank in the required city. The bank draft would instruct the bank in the other city to make the necessary payment. Conversely, business firms in Lisbon would go to their bank to arrange payments in Paris. As a result, financial obligations in all cities would be met with a transfer of little or no cash, as payments in one place would tend to offset payments in another.

The most common form of draft is a *cheque*. This is a written order to one's bank to pay from one's account a stated sum to the person named on the cheque when that person asks for it. According to s. 162(2) of the Bills of Exchange Act, a cheque is "a bill of exchange drawn on a bank and payable on demand." The person who writes the cheque is called the drawer. The bank on which the cheque is drawn is known as the drawee—in this case acting as the drawer's agent in paying the cheque out of the drawer's account. And the person to whom the money is to be paid is called the payee. Payment on demand means that payment must be made as soon as the cheque is presented for payment either by the payee or agent (usually the bank). Unlike other bills of exchange, there are no additional three days of grace before payment need be made.

Instead of using cash to make a payment, most people nowadays will use a cheque, particularly if large sums are involved. In fact, most creditors and employees now expect to be paid by cheque. Also, many business firms now prefer to receive cheques from customers rather than send out sight or time drafts to them for acceptance. Cheques have the virtue of being an extremely simple and safe method of making payment by mail, particularly for business transactions within a country. Because of the importance of maintaining a good credit rating, the firms that issue them are usually careful to ensure that there are sufficient funds in their bank account. Despite its popularity, a cheque—even though certified by a bank—is still not legal tender but may be acceptable as cash either because of trade usage or because of agreement between the parties. A creditor still has the legal right to insist on payment in Bank of Canada notes and in coins up to designated amounts for each denomination.

Delivery is the act of transferring a cheque from the drawer to the payee. Until this is done, the drawer has no liability and may in fact tear up the cheque. Delivery may be made in one of two ways: (a) it may be given to the payee in person (called "actual delivery"); or (b) it may be given to the payee's agent or notice be sent to the payee that the instrument is complete and ready for him or her (called "constructive delivery").

In practice, many people avoid giving a cheque or other negotiable instrument dated on a Sunday. Legally, however, a negotiable instrument dated on a Sunday or other legal holiday is perfectly valid, providing it is for payment of a debt contracted on a day other than Sunday or a statutory holiday unless permitted by statute.

Promissory Notes

The second type of negotiable instrument is a promissory note. According to s. 176 of the Bills of Exchange Act, this is:

> an unconditional promise in writing made by one person to another, signed by the maker, engaging to pay, on demand or at a fixed or determinable future time, a sum certain in money to or to the order of a specified person or to bearer.

There are several different types of promissory note:

Fixed Date Note.   With this note, a person obligates him- or herself to pay a lump sum of money at a specific date in the future.

Demand Note.   With this type of note, the sum owing is payable at any time, on demand of the lender, rather than at a fixed future date.

Joint Note.   This is the same as the one previously illustrated, except that two or more makers sign it rather than just one. Such a note reads "We" promise to pay. Each joint maker is liable for the full amount owing on the promissory note. If default does occur, the lender should sue all the joint makers together, because only one judgment may be obtained in court on a joint note. Therefore, if only one maker were sued and the judgment was not satisfied (paid), no further action could be taken through the courts. Of course, if one maker has to pay the full amount of the note, he or she may sue the other makers to recover the portions that they should have paid, under the principle of subrogation for each maker's share (s. 179).

Joint and Several Note.   This is a promissory note also signed by two or more persons. However, the note reads "I" promise to pay, rather than "We" promise to pay, as the words "I promise" represent the promise of each person. Each maker is also separately liable for the full amount of the note. The lender has the right, even though a judgment has been obtained against one of the makers, to sue the other makers for any amount still unpaid.

ISSUE OF A NEGOTIABLE INSTRUMENT

Cheques

A cheque is considered to have been issued when it has been written (that is, completed by the drawer) and delivered. Most cheques are now issued on the standard forms supplied by each bank or trust company. All that the drawer has to do is fill in the date, the name of the payee, the sum to be paid, and the drawer's signature of authorization, as shown in Figure 31.1.

According to the Bills of Exchange Act, the writing on a cheque may be "printed, painted, engraved, lithographed, or otherwise traced or copied." This legal interpretation of writing applies to the figures and signature as well as to the words. Thus a person need not write anything on a cheque in his or her own handwriting. Even the signature may be a printed facsimile one.

If a completed cheque is lost or stolen before delivery has taken place, then it is not valid in the hands of whoever takes the instrument unless such person takes it as a holder in due course, as will be explained later. Thus the finder or the thief could not claim against the maker or the drawee.

Certification of a Cheque.   Sometimes a person selling goods or services, or a government agency collecting fees, may ask to be paid by cash or certified cheque. The latter is a cheque, certified by the branch of the bank on which it is drawn, that the bank will make payment when it is presented. Certification takes the form of the bank's stamping "Certified" or "Accepted" across the face of the cheque, together with the name and branch of the bank and the date. Such certification may be made at the request of either the drawer or the holder.

Before certifying a cheque, a bank will ascertain that there are sufficient funds in the drawer's account and deduct the required amount. Once a cheque has been certified, the bank assumes liability for making payment and the holder may have recourse to either the drawer or the drawee. Also, very important, the drawer cannot stop payment unless he or she can return the cheque or provide the bank with some security to indemnify it against loss should the cheque (if, for example, lost or stolen) be deposited with another bank.

Certification, in the case of the holder of a cheque, may be requested for one of several different reasons: to avoid carrying a large amount of cash; to deposit the cheque at his or her own bank; to negotiate the cheque to someone else; or to prevent the drawer from stopping payment on the cheque before the date on which the holder wishes to cash it.

Figure 31.1: Personal Cheque

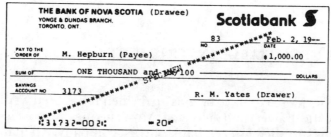

Courtesy The Bank of Nova Scotia

Postdating of a Cheque.   Sometimes, the drawer of a cheque will "post-date" it—that is, write on the cheque a date so many days or even weeks later than the day on which the cheque is written and signed. This is done, for example, with regard to mortgage and other loan repayments whereby the borrower saves the trouble of writing and mailing a cheque each month. It is also done when, for example, a person is away for some time from his or her regular place of abode and wishes to pay utility and other bills on time, without having to pay in advance.

The bank on which the cheque is drawn is legally bound to obey the instructions given by the drawer. This means, of course, that the bank may not make payment on the cheque before the due date. Thus the cheque is payable "on demand" only when that due date arrives. the drawer has the right to stop payment on (or "countermand") the postdated cheque at any time before the due date.

Drafts
Although not legally required to do so, most firms issue their drafts on the blank forms provided by the chartered banks. (See Figure 31.2.)

Promissory Notes
These may be drawn up by either the person who owes a sum of money or the one to whom it is owed. However, for convenience, many people use the standard blank form available at each bank. An example is shown in Figure 31.3.

PAYMENT OF A NEGOTIABLE INSTRUMENT

According to the Bills of Exchange Act, a cheque is payable on demand. Thus, as soon as the date shown on the cheque arrives, the payee has the right to present the cheque at the drawer's bank for payment. The drawer has the legal responsibility for making sure that sufficient funds are available in his or her bank account to make payment. In fact, a person who draws a cheque while knowing that there are insufficient funds in the bank account (an "NSF cheque") is committing a criminal offence.

While a cheque is payable on demand, all other negotiable instruments must be expressed as payable on demand or at a fixed or determinable future time (ss. 23 and 24). A note payable at sight, in Canada, automatically invokes a period three days' grace, while a cheque does not. (In this case sight is not regarded as "on demand.")

In computing time in negotiable instruments:

1. By s. 42, any bill not payable on demand adds three days of grace. (If the last day of grace falls on a holiday or non-juridical day, the date of payment is extended to the next business day.)
2. Section 43 lays down Sundays and major holidays as juridical days, plus any other days proclaimed by the provinces or municipalities.

Figure 31.2: Time Draft

			FORWARDING BANK'S NUMBER
SPACE BELOW FOR ACCEPTANCE STAMP	DUE August 17, 19--		
	June 17, 19 --		73256
Sixty days AFTER DATE, FOR VALUE RECEIVED.			
PAY TO THE ORDER OF The Bank of Nova Scotia (Payee) THE SUM OF			
Four Thousand and xx/100 DOLLARS $ 4,000.00			RECEIVING BANK'S NUMBER
To M. T. Corbett Ltd. (Drawee)			14987
215 Industrial Drive			
Oshawa, Ontario	Ace Heating Supplies Ltd. per: D.C. Sherk (Drawer)		
No. 773a			

Courtesy The Bank of Nova Scotia

Figure 31.3: Promissory Note Drawn at a Future Date

Due March 11, 19-- $ 2,500.00

Date December 11, 19--

Three months after date I promise to pay

to the order of J. J. Alexander (Payee)

at the Yonge and Dundas Branch of THE BANK OF NOVA SCOTIA.

the sum of Two Thousand Five Hundred and xx/100 Dollars

Value received

S. T. MacKenzie (Maker)

Form No 232 Printed in Canada

Courtesy The Bank of Nova Scotia

3. In counting by days, exclude the day when time begins and include the day of payment (s. 44).

4. In counting by months, use the same day in each month. If there is no such day, use the last day of the next month. Add three days' grace in all cases. Thus, a bill payable a month from January 31 becomes payable on February 28 plus three days of grace, March 3; if the third day is a Sunday, then the date for payment is March 4 (s. 46).

5. Not specifying the place where payable, antedating, postdating, or even dating on a Sunday does not invalidate a bill (s. 27). Section 30 authorizes the holder of an undated bill to insert the correct date of issue or acceptance.

ENDORSEMENT

The Bills of Exchange Act requires that an order instrument (one in which the payee is specifically named) be endorsed by the payee before it can be legally transferred to a third party. However, a bearer instrument may be legally transferred merely by delivery by the bearer to someone else. In practice, however, a bank will usually ask the payee to endorse bearer instruments as well as order instruments as a means of identification.

Endorsement occurs when the payee's signature, either by itself or with some written instruction, is written on the back of a cheque or other negotiable instrument.

If several persons have endorsed the cheque or other instrument, the holder has the choice of which one to turn to for payment if the drawee fails to pay. However, the holder must have given each of them notice of dishonour when the drawee defaulted. The endorser who is forced to pay may in turn have recourse for reimbursement to any prior endorser. In practice, relatively few cheques, notes, and the like are endorsed by more than one person.

If the signature of the drawer or endorser of the instrument has been forged, the person who stands to lose is the one who immediately acquires it after the forgery has occurred. If this person should endorse the instrument and pass it on to another party, he or she will eventually be held liable for payment.

A person who endorses a negotiable instrument and gives it to another party also gives an implied warranty that he or she is the proper owner. Should this not be the case, the endorser can be sued for breach of implied warranty of title. In practice, banks are reluctant to cash even a doubly endorsed cheque.

Types of Endorsement

There are many different types of endorsement, for cheques, drafts, and promissory notes.

Blank Endorsement. With this type of endorsement, used for an order cheque, the payee, R.M. Stoddart, merely writes her signature on the back of the instrument. The result is that it becomes a bearer instrument and is negotiable by the person to whom it has been given—say, N. Benson. It may now be legally transferred from person to person any number of times without further endorsement, or it may be converted to a special endorsement merely by writing a direction above the endorser's signature. In practice, it is normal for each holder to endorse his or her name when negotiating the instrument.

Special Endorsement. Here the payee, R.M. Stoddart, writes "pay to the order of N. Benson," followed by her (the payee's) signature. This means that N. Benson, the third party, must endorse the instrument before it can be transferred to another person. Benson may in turn endorse it in blank or specially, so making the instrument either a bearer or an order instrument.

Restrictive Endorsement. Here the payee, R.M. Stoddart, restricts any further transfer of the instrument by writing, for example, "for deposit only to the account of R.M. Stoddart" on the back of it, along with her (the payee's) signature. This type of endorsement, used by most business firms on cheques received from customers, means that such cheques may only be deposited in the firm's bank account. No employee or other person may cash such an instrument. Another type of restrictive endorsement is for the payee to write, say, "pay N. Benson only," followed by his (the payee's signature. This has the effect that only N. Benson can cash the instrument; he cannot transfer it to someone else (s. 68).

Identification Endorsement.   This occurs when another party identifies the payee by writing on the back of the instrument a statement such as "N. Benson is hereby identified by me," followed by the identifying party's signature. This incurs liability only if the identification proves to be false.

Waiver of Protest.   In this case, a payee or drawee may avoid the costs involved in formally protesting the instrument, if it is unpaid, by writing on the back of it, "protest waived," followed by his signature.

Qualified Endorsement.   Here the payee transfers an instrument in such a way as to avoid any liability should the drawer fail to make payment. This is done by writing, say, "R.M. Stoddart, *without recourse*" on the back of the instrument.

Conditional Endorsement.   This is an endorsement that contains a condition that must be fulfilled if payment is to be made. Since the original promise is unconditional, this type of endorsement does not invalidate the negotiability of the instrument.

Accommodation Endorsement.   Sometimes the party about to receive a promissory note (for example, a bank or other short-term lender) will require that the maker obtain a guarantee of payment from a suitable third party. Such a guarantee would usually take the form of an accommodation endorsement—whereby the other person, the guarantor, writes on the back of the note such words as "I hereby guarantee payment on this note," followed by the signature. If the maker of the promissory note fails to make payment on the due date, the guarantor is liable for payment. If such an event occurs, the guarantor can then seek to recover his or her money by suing the maker of the note for breach of implied contract to indemnify the guarantor for having to meet payment on the note.

Liability of the Endorser

Under the Bills of Exchange Act, the person who endorses an instrument is liable to any other person who later holds or endorses it should the drawer fail to make payment. Thus if, for example, B deposits at his bank a cheque endorsed by A (the original payee) only to be informed later than payment has been refused, B can recover the money from A, who in turn must try to recover the money from the drawer of the cheque. The only exceptions to this rule are persons who make an identification endorsement (unless wrongly made) or a qualified one.

  If the instrument had been endorsed by not only A, but B to C, C to D, and

D to E, then if E sued the maker and the instrument was dishonoured, E could sue any of the endorsers preceding her. So E could recover from D, then D could sue C, and so on. However, if E chose to sue B, and recovered, B, C, and D would be excused from further liability and B could sue only A.

HOLDER IN DUE COURSE

This is the name given in law to a person to whom a valid negotiable instrument has been negotiated. Strictly defined, this person is "a party to whom there was duly transferred, for value, in good faith, without notice of any defect, an instrument that was complete and regular on the face of it, that is not overdue or dishonoured."

Duly transferred means that the cheque, draft, or promissory note, with the required endorsement, was physically transferred to this person.

For value means that the person paid something of value ("consideration") for it.

In good faith means that he or she acquired it honestly.

Without notice of defect means that the recipient was unaware that the person from whom he or she received it was not the rightful owner.

Complete and regular on the face of it means that the instrument was properly filled out with the names of the drawer, drawee, and payee; the drawee's signature and subsequent endorsements; the maturity date; the correct amount in both words and numbers; alterations duly initialled; and absence of erasure marks or missing pieces.

Not overdue means, in the case of a date instrument, that the maturity date plus the three days of grace have not passed; and, in the case of a demand instrument (such as a cheque), that no more than a reasonable time has gone by since it was issued.

Not dishonoured means that the instrument was accepted by the drawee.

The significance of the concept of a holder in due course is that such a person acquires a privileged position in the eyes of the law. Normally, when a debt is assigned by a creditor to another party, the debtor retains any personal defences that he might have had against the original creditor. Thus a debtor may be justified in refusing further payment to the original creditor, for any one of a variety of reasons: for example, fraud, duress, undue influence, infancy, insanity, illegality, or breach of contract. And the debtor retains this right even though the debt (for example, for raw materials for a manufacturing plant) has been assigned to someone else, such as a finance company.

In the case of negotiable instruments, by contrast, the debtor does not always retain against a new creditor the defences that he or she might have used against the original creditor. One exception, as we saw earlier, was with regard to consumer bills and notes. Another is if the holder in due course was aware of the debtor's claims. A business firm, having accepted a draft or promissory note for goods that later turn out to be defective, can easily find itself therefore having to pay for such goods in full to a bank or finance company. It cannot legally refuse such payment. It can sue the original creditor only on such grounds as breach of implied warranty of merchantability, or misrepresentation, in the hope of recovering its money.

The reason why negotiable instruments have been treated differently from other assigned debts for so long is a practical one. Only if a debtor were required by law to repay the debt as agreed would the banks be willing to discount drafts without prolonged and exhaustive enquiries. And, if the wheels of commerce were to turn smoothly, the discounting of commercial drafts (to say nothing of the cashing of cheques drawn on other banks), had to be fairly quick. For only by letting the banks assume the financing of a business firm's short-term trade credit to its customers could a firm maintain its necessary cash flow and liquidity. Unfortunately, in the case of consumer goods sold on credit, some unscrupulous business firms have abused the privileged position of negotiable instruments transferred to a third party, to avoid their warranty and other liabilities. Hence the 1970 amendment to the Bills of Exchange Act relating to consumer purchases involving negotiable instruments.

DEFENCES

Sometimes the person who is liable to pay on a negotiable instrument may refuse to do so for some justifiable reason. These reasons, which the person may use in court when sued by the holder of the instrument, are called, in legal terminology, defences. They are of two main types: (a) real defences and (b) personal defences, including defect of title defences. Which of these defences may be used will depend on the legal relationship of the defendant to the plaintiff.

If the two parties involved have a direct relationship (for example, the drawer of a draft and its acceptor), they are termed *immediate parties* and the defendant may use both types of defences. If the two parties have an indirect relationship (for example, the drawer of a cheque and the endorsee—that is, the person to whom it has been endorsed by the payee), they are called *remote parties* and may not use the personal defences. However, if such a remote party legally qualifies as a holder in due course, the defendant may use real defences. If the remote party does not qualify, the defendant may use both real defences and defect of title defences.

Real Defences

These are defences that a person owing money on a negotiable instrument may use to support his refusal to pay—either to an immediate party or a remote party. They include:

1. the defendant being an infant when he or she signed the instrument;
2. the defendant not being the principal of a self-styled agent;
3. the defendant's signature having been forged on the instrument;
4. the instrument having been altered subsequent to the defendant's signature;
5. the instrument having been cancelled subsequent to the defendant's signature;
6. the instrument having been misrepresented to the defendant prior to or at the time of signing; and
7. the instrument being incomplete and undelivered when it fell into the wrong hands.

Infancy of the Defendant.   A person who was under eighteen years of age when he or she signed a negotiable instrument, cannot be held liable for it. This is true even if the reason for signing it was to pay for necessities. Of course, the infant can by law be required to pay a reasonable amount for them to their supplier. But this would be the result of a lawsuit for breach of sales contract, not the result of an action based on the negotiable instrument itself.

Not the True Principal.   If someone purporting to be an agent signs a negotiable instrument on behalf of another person, then the latter person (the alleged principal) is not bound thereby. He or she would be bound only if the so-called **agent** had real authority (that is, had been given express authorization by him or her to act as agent) or had apparent authority (that is, could be presumed by third parties, as a result of their past experience, to have authority to act as agent).

Forgery of the Defendant's Signature.   A person can refuse to honour a negotiable instrument on the grounds that his or her signature has been forged. This may be someone who the holder of the instrument claims is its drawer or endorser. However, there is a legal obligation on such a person, as soon as he or she learns of the forgery, to notify any present or likely future holder of the instrument of this fact. Failure to do so may, by the doctrine of promissory estoppel, prevent using forgery as a defence for non-payment. This is because he or she lets another party go on believing that he will honour the commitment.

Alteration of the Instrument.   If a negotiable instrument has been altered (usually to increase the amount payable), the drawer or endorser prior to the alteration can use this fact as a defence for non-payment. However, to be a valid defence, such an alteration must be visible to the naked eye. A person who endorses such an instrument, subsequent to the visible alteration, is fully liable for the amount by which the value of the instrument has been increased by the alteration.

Cancellation of the Instrument.   A person who cancels an instrument that he or she has signed (for example, a cheque) may use this as a defence for non-payment of the sum involved.

Misrepresentation of the Instrument. If the person who has signed a negotiable instrument can show that the nature of the instrument was misrepresented to him or her, misrepresentation can be used as a defence for non-payment. This would be the case if a person, without negligence, signed a promissory note on another party's assurance that it was a loan application. The traditional name for this defence is *non est factum*.

Non-delivery of an Incomplete Instrument. Suppose that an instrument is incomplete (for example, a person's signature on a blank piece of paper) and undelivered (that is, not given to the proper party in the normal way). Then if it is wrongfully taken by someone else, the person whose signature is involved may plead the non-delivery of an incomplete instrument as a defence for non-payment when the instrument is eventually presented for payment.

Personal Defences

These defences, which can be used only if the defendant has an immediate relationship to the holder of the instrument, are (a) lack of consideration and (b) right to set-off.

Lack of Consideration. If the defendant can prove that nothing of value was given by the holder or a prior party (for example, the person who endorsed it to the holder) in exchange for the instrument, he or she cannot be held liable. As with any contract, consideration must be present to make it legally enforceable. Thus a person, who accepted a draft in payment of goods received but subsequently discovered that the goods had not been sent, could plead lack of consideration for the draft.

Right of Set-Off. If the holder of a negotiable instrument owes money to the defendant as a result of another or related transaction, the defendant may claim to have the amount set off against the amount owed on the instrument. Suppose, for example, a firm buys goods on credit and accepts a time draft in acknowledgement. Shortly thereafter, it discovers that a substantial proportion of the goods are defective and refuses to make payment on the draft when it falls due. Then the firm could ask in court, using the defence of set-off, to have the value of the defective goods subtracted from the amount owing on the instrument. This defence would not, however, be valid if the draft had been negotiated to a third party—for example, a finance company. Such negotiation would mean that the two parties involved are now remote parties rather than immediate parties.

Defect of Title Defences

These are defences that a person owing money on a negotiable instrument may use to defend non-payment—either to an immediate party or to a remote party who does not qualify as a holder in due course.

A negotiable instrument may be legally defective for any one of the following reasons:

1. lack of true consent of the person who signed it;
2. illegality of the underlying contract;
3. incapacity to enter into a contract of the person who signed it;
4. non-delivery of the completed instrument;
5. prior discharge of the instrument; or
6. lack of authority by a so-called agent to complete a signed instrument.

Each of these reasons constitutes a valid defence for non-payment so long as the holder of the instrument is an immediate party.

If a holder in due course of a negotiable instrument received it "with out notice of any defect," then the right to payment would not be affected by such defects. However, if the holder was aware of any of these defects in title, then the person is not, in the eyes of the law, a holder in due course. This means that the person who signed the instrument can use any one of the above defects of title as a defence for non-payment. Let us now consider these defences.

Lack of Consent. A person may be persuaded against his will to sign a negotiable instrument. This may be as a result of: (a) undue influence—for example, doctor and patient or lawyer and client; (b) duress—for example, threat of violence or public ridicule; or (c) fraud—for example, a promissory note being represented to the signer as some other document. This is a valid defence for non-payment.

Illegality. A cheque or other negotiable instrument may be given in payment of an illegal act—for example, committing an assault on a third party. Consequently, the courts would not enforce payment.

Legal Incapacity. A person may sign a negotiable instrument while drunk or insane. However, for a valid defence, the person must prove that this was his or her condition at the time of signing, that the other party was aware of it, and that as soon as the person returned to normal and realized of what had happened, he or she took steps to cancel the instrument. Depending on the circumstances, insanity may occasionally be held to be a real defence. Regardless of the circumstances, infancy (as we saw earlier) constitutes a real defence.

Non-delivery of a Completed Instrument. If a person is to be liable on a negotiable instrument, he or she must deliver the instrument to the other party as well as sign it. If, consequently, a completed cheque, draft, or note falls into the wrong hands, the person who has signed the instrument may claim absence of delivery as a legitimate defence.

Prior Discharge. A negotiable instrument such as a time draft or promissory note may be discharged before its due date by payment of the sum of money owing. However, it is conceivable that this same instrument may later be presented for payment a second time. In such a case, the acceptor of the draft or maker of the promissory note can plead prior discharge as a defence for non-payment. But to succeed, the defendant must have ensured that the instrument was properly cancelled at the time of discharge. This is usually done by stamping or writing the word "paid," together with the date and signature of the payee, across the face of the instrument.

Lack of Authority.   A person who signs and delivers an incomplete negotiable instrument runs the risk that the other party will not complete the instrument as directed—for example, if a customer sends a supplier a signed, blank cheque to be completed with the amount owing once that amount is determined. If the drawer's trust is abused, he or she can refuse payment using the defence of lack of authority in the so-called agent to complete the instrument in such a way. This is another defect of little valid against an immediate party or a remote party who does not qualify as a holder in due course. Since the cheque or other instrument might be negotiated to a holder in due course, against whom this defence would not stand, it is obviously foolhardy to sign and deliver an incomplete instrument.

CONSUMER BILLS AND NOTES

In 1970, the Bills of Exchange Act was amended to include a new part (Part V) entitled Consumer Bills and Notes. In the amendment, a consumer bill is defined as a bill of exchange which has been issued with regard to a consumer purchase. A consumer note is defined as a promissory note issued with regard to such a purchase. In both cases, the purchaser, or anybody signing on the purchaser's behalf, is liable to pay the amount specified. Included within the definition of a consumer bill is a cheque that has been postdated more than thirty days. Also in the amendment to the Act, a consumer purchase is defined as a purchase of goods or services, other than a cash purchase, from a person who is in the business of selling or providing such goods or services. Excluded from the definition are goods that are to be resold or used in the purchaser's own business or profession.

Under the amendment, in s. 190, every consumer bill or note is required to have the words "Consumer Purchase" marked prominently and legibly on its face. This must be done before or at the time of the signing of the instrument by the purchaser or anyone acting on his or her behalf. If a consumer bill or note is not marked as required, it is legally void. The only exception to this rule is if the bill or note falls into the hands of a "holder in due course" without the holder's being given notice that the bill or note is a consumer one. Anybody who persuades a consumer to sign an unmarked consumer bill or note is subject to a heavy fine.

The purpose of the amendment to the Act was to remedy hardships that had arisen as the result of the strict application to modern retail credit transactions of the existing law of negotiable instruments. Such a hardship was as follows: a person would buy goods on credit and sign a conditional sale contract together with a bill of exchange or promissory note. In the bill or note, he or she would undertake to pay the seller, by instalments, the amount owing plus interest. The seller would then discount this bill or note with a finance company in order to obtain ready cash. The finance company would then start to collect the purchaser's payments.

The case that led to the change in the Bills of Exchange Act concerning consumer purchases involved a housewife in the province of Quebec. She was persuaded to buy a knitting machine when she was told by the salesman that she would be credited, against payments due, for all the knitted products she sent in to the seller. The note that she signed was assigned to a finance company. Although she knitted enough to keep up her payments, the finance company sued for the balance outstanding. The judge decided that the seller's tactics were known to the finance company, that they were not dealing at "arm's length," and that the finance company could not plead the status of a "holder in due course" but was subject to any defences available against immediate parties—in this case, the misrepresentation.

As an extreme case, a purchaser might have become, through no fault of his or her own, the owner of some worthless goods for which he would have had to continue to pay in the months and even years ahead.

A purchaser may now use, against a holder in due course of a consumer bill or note, the same defences that he could use against the seller. Furthermore, despite any agreement to the contrary, this right of the purchaser may not be waived. Today, consequently, a person who has bought goods on credit which have been misrepresented or are otherwise defective, can withhold payment against the finance company to whom the conditional sales contract has been "sold" until the matter is resolved.

An unscrupulous seller might have been tempted to evade the regulations by requiring a prospective purchaser to go to an affiliated finance company or other lender to borrow the money required for the purchase, rather than sign a conditional sale contract. To prevent this, the amendment contains a clause whereby any credit purchase in which the seller and the lender are guilty of collusion (a relationship that is less than arm's length) is automatically considered a consumer purchase. This means, consequently, that the promissory note issued to cover the loan must be marked "Consumer Purchase" and treated accordingly. Some provinces (for example, Ontario) also provide in consumer protection legislation that an assignee of a credit sale is subject to the same defences that a debtor would have against the assignor.

REVIEW QUESTIONS

1. What is a negotiable instrument? What are the main types in use in Canada?
2. How does the negotiation of such an instrument differ from the usual assignment of a contractual obligation?

3. What are the statutory requirements for the negotiability of an instrument?
4. What is a cheque? Distinguish among the drawer, drawee, and payee.
5. What are the advantages and disadvantages of using cheques as a means of payment?
6. What are the statutory requirements for the drawing of a cheque?
7. How does a bank try to ensure that payments by cheque are properly authorized?
8. Should a cheque or other negotiable instrument be given the date of a Sunday or other legal holiday?
9. What is meant by the endorsement of a cheque?
10. Explain the following types of endorsement: (a) blank; (b) special; and (c) restrictive.
11. What are the other types of endorsement? Explain each.
12. Explain, with regard to a cheque, the legal liability of: (a) its drawer; (b) its endorser. How is this liability affected by a delay in presenting the cheque for payment?
13. Under what circumstances may a bank refuse to honour a cheque?
14. What should the holder of a cheque do if, on presenting for payment, it is dishonoured?
15. How and why is a cheque sometimes certified? What is a bank's liability on a cheque that it has certified?
16. Why is a cheque sometimes postdated? What is the bank's liability in such a case?
17. What is a draft? Distinguish among the drawer, the drawee, and the payee.
18. What is meant by the "acceptance" of a draft? How soon must this be done? What legal obligation does it impose?
19. When and where should a draft be presented for payment?
20. Distinguish between a sight draft and a time draft.
21. What is meant by the "discounting" of a draft? What is its purpose?
22. Explain the nature and purpose of a bank draft.
23. What are promissory notes? Why are they used so much?
24. What is: (a) a demand note; (b) a joint note? Explain the makers' liability.
25. Explain: (a) an instalment note; (b) a lien note.
26. What is an accommodation endorsement?
27. When and where must a promissory note be presented for payment?
28. What are consumer bills and notes? What is the significance of this distinction?
29. Why was it considered necessary to amend the Bills of Exchange Act with regard to bills and notes issued in connection with a consumer purchase?
30. How does a draft differ from a cheque?
31. What is meant by a "holder in due course"?

32. Why is the holder in due course of a negotiable instrument considered to occupy a privileged position in the eyes of the law?

33. Distinguish between the immediate parties and the remote parties with regard to a negotiable instrument.

34. What are "personal defences"? For what purpose can they be used? Against whom?

35. What are the various types of "real defence"? Against whom can they be used?

36. Explain the following defences: (a) lack of consent; (b) illegality; (c) incapacity.

37. What are the other defect of title defences? Against whom can they be used?

38. How and why did negotiable instruments come into being?

PROBLEMS

1. In *Interprovincial Building Credits Ltd. v. Soltys* (1967), 64 D.L.R. (2d) 194, the defendant, a farmer, contracted for the sale to him and erection of a prefabricated steel farm building by C, a builder, and gave a promissory note for the balance of the purchase price. The building was so badly put together as to be worthless for some purposes. The plaintiff was informed that C was responsible for erecting the building and that this process had barely commenced. The note was negotiated through a third party to the plaintiff, who had carried through similar transactions with C. The plaintiff claimed to be a holder in due course. Discuss the defence available against the plaintiff in 1967 and today.

2. In *Sniderman v. McGarry*, [1967] 1 O.R. 321, M was the manager of a hotel owned by an estate, the executors of which, M's brother and sister, were the defendants. M privately gave two cheques to the plaintiff as security for a cash loan made to him through an intermediary. The cheques were on a form with the printed name of the hotel at the top, but signed by M personally. The plaintiff sued the defendants on the ground that M had signed for the defendants, and if not with actual authority, then within the scope of an implied or ostensible authority to do so. Should the plaintiff recover from the defendants in this case?

3. In *Algonquin Building Credits Ltd. v. Scholz* (1966), 56 W.W.R. 331, the defendants gave a promissory note to the vendors for goods which were never delivered. The vendors negotiated the note to the plaintiff which paid the discount value for it without notice that the goods had not been delivered. Are the defendants liable to pay?

4. In the case of *Neptune Acceptance Ltd. v. Williams* (1975), 49 D.L.R. (3d) 663, an entrepreneur induced Williams to buy a cigarette vending machine by explaining that he could earn good money simply by keeping the machine replenished at a good location. Williams agreed to buy by conditional sale a machine for $1,777.75 which was financed by

the plaintiff finance company secured by a promissory note marked "consumer purchase." Williams was really sold a used vending machine at an undesirable location. The plaintiff finance company sued as the holder of a promissory note made out to the entrepreneur J. & S. Enterprises. (The note was supplied by the plaintiff company Neptune and by its terms the payments were to be made at Neptune's offices.) The plaintiff could not deny that its own stamped form was not a consumer purchase. Consequently the Bills of Exchange Act, R.S.C. 1970, c. B-5, s. 191 [en. R.S.C. 1970, c. 4 (1st Supp.), s. 1] was applicable, whereby Neptune was subject to the defences available by the defendant against the entrepreneur. Further the close connection between Neptune and the entrepreneur was sufficient to deprive the plaintiff finance company of the status of a holder in due course. Explain the judge's line of reasoning. What would have been the probable outcome of the case if the plaintiff had not been deprived of his status as a holder in due course?

5. X was the maker of a promissory note. S had endorsed the note. When the note became due, payment was not made, so the bank to whom the note had been negotiated as holder in due course, protested the note for non-payment. Notice of protest was sent to S in accordance with the Bills of Exchange Act. Unknown to the bank, S had died prior to the note having matured. Notice was thus served on the respondent who was the executor of the S estate. Appellant, knowing of the death of S, took up the note from the bank and sued respondent on it. At trial the action was dismissed. What should be the outcome on appeal?

32

Consumer Credit

Over the years, members of the public have borrowed heavily from banks and other lenders. Also, particularly in recent years, they have purchased more and more goods on credit, paying only a small portion of the price at the time of purchase. In both cases, the public has agreed to pay interest on the loan or credit involved. However, experience has shown that many consumers have been charged an exorbitant rate of interest and kept ignorant of the actual borrowing cost. As a result, the need for government protection in this area has been very great.

PROMISSORY NOTE

A consumer who borrows money from a bank, finance company, or credit union is normally required to sign a promissory note. This is a document in which the consumer promises either to repay the sum borrowed "on demand" or at a given time, plus interest, or to make a given number of monthly payments of principal and interest until the loan has been fully repaid. Sometimes, a person's spouse or another person in good financial standing may be asked to co-sign the promissory note. This means that such a person will be liable for repayment of the loan should the actual borrower default on the obligations. In order to give greater protection to the consumer, the federal Bills of Exchange Act was amended in 1970 to require that a promissory note signed in connection with a sales agreement, such as a conditional sales contract, be marked "consumer purchase." This has the legal effect that the creditor cannot sue the consumer on the basis of the promissory note if the seller has not met its obligations under the sales contract—for example, has sold defective goods.

CHATTEL MORTGAGE

If the consumer is well known or the loan amount is relatively small, the lender may only require the borrower's signature on the promissory note as security for repayment of the loan. This promise to make repayment is called a "personal covenant." However, very often, the lender may require some other security. Usually this will take the form of a legal claim such as a chattel mortgage or other financing agreement, whereby the lender can sell the asset to obtain the necessary money if the borrower fails to make the required payments. Such mortgage must be registered pursuant to Ontario's Personal Property Security Act to be valid against a would-be purchaser of this secured asset.

At the provincial level, Consumer Protection Acts (which apply to consumer sales only) now provide that:

1. the implied conditions of the Sale of Goods Act may not be negated in a Sale, and
2. any assignee collecting payment (such as a finance company of the seller) is subject to the same defences as the seller if the buyer has a legal claim against defective goods.

In other words, the Consumer Protection prohibits "disclaimer clauses" whereby a seller, finance company, or other creditor could isolate itself from any consumer complaint about the goods sold. By means of a disclaimer, the consumer usually had to agree that the company would not be responsible for any defects in goods or service and that the consumer waived the right of claim. Now such a clause is illegal.

MAXIMUM RATES OF INTEREST

One way to protect the consumer from exorbitant credit costs has been to pass legislation imposing maximum rates of interest. However, the United Kingdom repeal of usury laws in 1858 extended its effect to Canada and the provinces. Consequently, there was no legislative control of lending in Canada during the period of 1858 to 1906, except the Dominion Interest Act, which merely fixed the maximum interest rate at 5% where interest was provided for, but no rate was included.

The Money Lenders Act was in force from 1906 to 1956, but it was apparently ineffective because of the conflict between s. 6, which provided for interest alone, and s. 7, which referred to both interest and expenses, and because there was no licensing requirement or enforcement supervision.

The Small Loans Act, abolished in 1981, provided for uniform all-inclusive credit charge ceilings for all loans of $1,500 or less. However, most finance companies in Canada preferred to lend more than $1,500, which escaped the low interest rates set by the Small Loans Act.

Until 1967, the maximum rate of interest charged by chartered banks was set by the Bank Act at 6% per annum. However, this ceiling was removed on July 8, 1967. The banks' present lending rates are much higher and tied to changes in the interest rate on treasury bills, which may vary weekly.

At the provincial level, Ontario, in 1912, passed the Money Lenders Act, which contained a provision providing for relief in "unconscionable transactions." Similar provisions are now contained in the Ontario Unconscionable Transactions Relief Act, and similar legislation has been adopted by all of the Canadian provinces. The Ontario Unconscionable Transactions Relief Act provides that only a fair rate of interest may be charged by money lenders. It also gives extensive power to the courts to reduce the amount of interest charged.

DISCLOSURE OF BORROWING COSTS

Governments, judges and consumer protection agencies have long realized that the unscrupulous seller and/or the associated lender were in an advantageous position vis-à-vis the customer in transactions involving the sale of goods on credit. Many customers are encouraged or induced to buy a more expensive item or even additional items provided payments could be spread over a long period. A charge is added for the administrative time taken in setting up charge accounts, and possibly a hidden charge for a bad debt reserve account. The credit seller may sell goods at a higher markup than the cash seller, thus masking the true credit costs. Usually, when a third party financing agent is used, such as a finance company, the seller expects a "kickback" or "bonus" as a reward for handing over the financing to the finance company, which must then include this expense in the interest rate charged to the consumer.

ONTARIO CONSUMER PROTECTION ACT

The consumer protection legislation passed in 1966 in Ontario provided for the disclosure of borrowing costs in all credit transactions. The basic disclosure required is "the cost of borrowing expressed in dollars and cents and the percentage that the cost of borrowing bears to the purchase price, expressed as an annual rate applied to the unpaid balance. . . ."

This Act applies to all executory consumer contracts for goods and services where the purchase price exceeds $50. Provision is made for the registration of itinerant sellers. The buyer is allowed two days to rescind a contract negotiated or arranged other than at the seller's permanent place of business. In the case of credit transactions, s. 36 of the Ontario Act, also requires in writing, the following information:

1. dollar and cent cost of goods or services, plus other fees paid by the seller or credit provider;
2. amount of down payment or trade-in if the seller is also the lender;
3. amount by which the seller's price exceeds the deposit or trade-in;
4. cost of borrowing in dollars and cents;
5. percentage that the cost of borrowing bears either to the sum loaned by credit provider, or the balance to be paid to the seller, expressed as an annual rate according to a formula provided by the regulations;
6. additional amounts for insurance, official fees and possible additional charges on default.

All advertising for credit must show the full cost of the credit.

All Consumer Acts in Canada require disclosure of both the dollar cost and the effective annual rate of interest, thus permitting credit consumers to discover the terms of their borrowing before actually purchasing a good.

The provinces of Alberta, Manitoba, New Brunswick, and Prince Edward

Island do not require rate disclosure for small amounts, but the other provinces seem to comply with the provisions of the law despite protests that the annual percentage rate will be high because of administrative costs.

All of the Canadian Acts exclude variable or revolving credit accounts from the disclosure provisions, except for requiring disclosure at the inception of a credit contract of a scale of annual percentages that the buyer will be charged on unpaid balances, plus the dollar cost, to permit comparisons. Under this exception, the borrower/buyer is billed, for example, on April 1 on the outstanding balance on the first of the preceding month at a percentage rate of interest. Even a bill of $100 during the previous month will not incur a charge if the opening balance was nil. By paying off the $100 within a specified period of time, the customer has use of the money without interest charges. On the other hand, if payment is deferred beyond the due date, interest will be charged.

Control over the enforcement of credit disclosure provisions is exercised by:

1. provincial legislation providing that if the cost of credit is not disclosed, then the borrower is only required to pay the amount disclosed;
2. making non-disclosure a criminal offence, punishable in Ontario, for example, by imprisonment for up to one year, a $2,000 fine, or both;
3. some provinces exercising control by licensing similar to the techniques used in regulating consumer loan companies.

DEBT RECOVERY

A consumer who is unable to repay money borrowed may face various types of action by the creditor. Usually, the consumer will receive a firm reminder that a payment is overdue, then perhaps a telephone call, and finally one or more letters threatening legal action. If these are of no avail, the creditor (for example, a department store) may turn the overdue account over to a collection agency. Often a firm will wait three to six months before taking such action—one reason being the high percentage fee charged by the agency. Alternatively, the creditor may commence proceedings against the borrower in the Provincial Court, Small Claims Division, for small amounts or in the District Court for larger amounts. Or, if the loan is secured by a chattel mortgage, the creditor may decide instead to seize and sell the good involved. In some provinces, the creditor can either seize or sue—but in any event, only the amount owing may be recovered.

If the matter is taken to court, the creditor will initiate the action by a statement of claim for moneys against the person concerned. if the debtor rebuts the claim and answers either in person or by submitting a statement of defence, the judge will make a decision based on the facts involved—usually that the debtor does indeed owe the money. The debtor who fails to show up in court loses by default and a judgment is entered against him or her.

Once the creditor has the judgment (the legal basis for enforcing the claim) he or she can:

1. continue to demand payment from the debtor, using the judgment as additional persuasion;
2. garnishee the wages of the debtor;
3. have some of the debtor's assets seized;
4. have a judgment (or show-cause) summons issued, requiring the consumer to appear in court to explain why the debt is not being paid; or
5. turn over the claim to a collection agency.

A *collection agency* is a firm that specializes in the collection of outstanding debts. It charges the creditor, as the principal, a fee calculated as a percentage of the money actually collected. If the creditor has not yet taken the debtor to court, the agency will probably do this in order to aid collection of the debt.

A *"direction of garnishee"* is a court order requiring an employer to pay over a certain portion of an employee's wages to the creditor, to meet the employee's debt. However, this may mean taking money needed for basic family needs. Some provinces have consequently passed legislation to help the debtor in this regard. Thus, in Ontario for example, the Wages Act now provides that 80% of wages are exempt from seizure; that assignment of wages to secure a debt is invalid except in the case of a credit union; and that dismissal from employment because of garnishee proceedings is illegal.

Under the Constitution Act, 1867, legislation governing debt consolidation and debt relief is the responsibility of the federal Parliament. Thus Part X of the federal Bankruptcy Act provides that a debtor may apply to the court for relief by declaring debts, names of creditors, income, and basic needs. Following this, an arrangement is made whereby these debts are gradually paid by the court from weekly payments made out of the debtor's wages at a rate which he can afford. Similar provincial legislation is now in effect in Prince Edward Island, Nova Scotia, Manitoba, Alberta, Saskatchewan, and Quebec (in which province the "Lacombe Law" has existed for some time). Finance companies also provide for debt consolidation by a single loan to cover all indebtedness, often with a combined lower monthly instalment payment but, of course, for a much longer period of time.

Mention should also be made that in Ontario, persons who are in receipt of government assistance, either through the Family Benefits Act, or the General Welfare Assistance Act, are assisted in family budgeting by the officers of the Provincial Social Welfare Department. Also the Provincial Court, Small Claims Division, of Ontario provides a procedure whereby debtors may apply for relief from the claims of their creditors by agreeing to make a monthly remittance to the Court Referee who, in turn, undertakes to see that all outstanding debts are consolidated and eventually settled.

FUNDS HELD IN TRUST

There is definitely a consumer interest to be protected in all funds or deposits which are held in trust. For many years now the (provincial) Superintendent of Insurance has been responsible for the supervision of the investments of provincial insurance companies and pension funds. This is achieved by yearly inspections to ensure that compulsory reserves, for insurance policies which have a cash surrender value, have been invested in the prescribed investments allowed under the Ontario Insurance Act. Similar supervision is also exercised over trust companies, which are required to submit yearly returns of funds on deposit; semi-annual returns reflecting any changes in investments and loans, and quarterly returns as to deposits as required under the Loan and Trust Corporations Act. In Ontario, individual trust investments with an approved trust company are guaranteed up to the amount of $60,000 for each investor.

Supervision is also exercised over the accounting for moneys held by credit unions.

How far should the government go in its supervision of moneys held in trust? Much adverse publicity has been given in all major countries to the operations of travel agencies which accept clients' deposits for future travel arrangements, to hotels demanding booking deposits, to companies or individuals who charter space on aircraft and ships, demanding payment in advance. Should every type of deposit held for clients be required to be reported to some government supervisory agency? If so, the accounting required would be incredible, especially if it were to include all consumer purchases where deposits are made but the goods are not picked up immediately.

Lawyers, as a professional group, have long been known to hold their client's money in trust. The Law Societies in Canada require each lawyer to operate a separate trust account for such funds and annually account for such funds. Audits are frequently carried out, subject to disciplinary action by the Barristers' Societies for improper accounting. The Ontario government has moved into the trust supervision area by requiring separate accounts on the part of all collection agencies; mortgage brokers; real estate and business brokers; motor vehicle dealers; cemetery owners and operators; travel agents; and so on. Consumers are being educated not to give advance deposits to door-to-door sales people, air charter agencies, home repair and home appliance and maintenance schemes, at least before a ticket has been received, goods have been delivered, or work has been done. All of these different types of businesses, even if not controlled by the provincial authorities, must generally have a municipal permit to operate legally. A great deal of control could be exercised by co-operation between municipalities and government by instituting licensing and bonding for all legitimate businesses accepting payments or deposits in advance of delivery of goods or services.

REVIEW QUESTIONS

1. What is meant by the term "consumer credit"?
2. What are the various sources of consumer credit?
3. Explain the advantages and disadvantages, including legal responsibilities, of credit cards.
4. What significance attaches to the fact that a promissory note signed in connection with a sales agreement must now be marked "consumer purchase"?
5. What is a chattel mortgage?
6. What is a "disclaimer clause"?
7. What statutory control exists over interest charged for consumer credit?
8. What has been done to make the suppliers of consumer credit disclose the cost of borrowing to the consumer?
9. What action may a consumer face from a creditor if he fails to repay a loan?
10. What protection exists for members of the public who leave funds in trust with others?

PROBLEM

1. In one recent case a buyer of a knitting machine on credit signed a promissory note for her purchase. Her agreement provided that if she submitted suitably knitted products, the seller would buy them from her and credit her account. No accounting was made despite the number of products submitted. Instead she was sued by the finance company which had financed the sale. (The law of negotiable instruments provides that the ony defence against such a claim is either "infancy or fraud" which did not exist here, at least on the part of the finance company.) The judge, however, disallowed the claim because of the close relationship between the seller and the finance company. Do you agree with the social justice of this decision? What is the present-day law in this situation?

APPENDIX 32-A: SYNOPSIS OF THE CONSUMER PROTECTION ACT, R.S.O. 1980, c. 87

S. 1(i)   Executory contract—delivery of goods, performance of services or payment in full of the consideration is not made at time contract is entered into.

S. 4(1)   Itinerant seller (*i.e.* seller not selling at own place of business) must be registered.

S. 18   Applies to executory contracts for goods and services where price or cost of borrowing exceeds $50.00.

S. 19   Every executory contract except variable credit (*i.e.*, revolving budget account) shall be in writing and include:

- name and addresses;
- description of goods or services;
- price of statement;
- type of security, *i.e.*, conditional sale;
- disclosure of costs of borrowing (refer to s. 24);
- warranty, if any must be stated.

(2) Not binding on buyer unless above complied with, signed by both and given a duplicate of original.

S. 21(3) Deposits or trade-ins must be returned if contract not made.

S. 21 Contracts not made at seller's place of business may be cancelled by notice within two days of making.

(3) Title on trade-ins does not pass until expiry of two-day period.

S. 23 No repossession after two-thirds paid except by judge's order.

S. 24 Except for variable credit transactions, the seller must give the buyer a written statement, including:

(a) amount borrowed or cash price of goods or services;

(b) amount of trade-in or deposit paid to seller;

(c) how (a) exceeds (b);

(d) cost of borrowing;

(e) percentage cost of borrowing bears to price as annual interest;

(f) additional charges for default.

S. 25 Where budget buying concerned, the seller must initially give the buyer a statement showing the cost of buying on credit and then every month (four to five weeks) provide him with an up-to-date statement; showing total debt at beginning, credits and purchases in period, cost of borrowing in dollars and cents, and outstanding balance.

S. 28 In case of prepayment, the borrower is entitled to a proportionate credit in respect to sum borrowed.

S. 29 All advertising, print, radio, TV, must show the cost of borrowing per ss. 24 and 25.

S. 30 Assignment of negotiable instruments must include the statement in s. 24 and if seller is assignor, a copy of the contract.

S. 31(1) Assignee of any rights of a lender has no greater rights than, and is subject to the same obligations, liabilities and duties as assignor.

S. 33 May not waive provisions of this Act.

S. 34(2) May not negate the implied conditions of the Sale of Goods Act in any consumer sale.

S. 35 Existing rights of borrower and buyer are preserved.

S. 36(3) No legal obligation on part of recipient of unsolicited goods, credit cards, notwithstanding use, misuse, loss, or damage.

S. 37(2) Outlaws referral selling.

S. 38 Registrar may order cessation of false misleading advertising.

S. 39 Punishments:

(1) Summary conviction: $2,000 fine, one year imprisonment, or both.

(2) Corporation—$25,000 fine.

(3) Limitation 3 years after offence.

S. 40   Regulations by Lieutenant Governor in Council:

Fees for registration;

Form and size of print on contracts;

Maintenance of trust accounts by sellers;

How to express cost of borrowing as a percentage;

Apportionment of borrowing costs on prepayment;

Exempting sellers from provision;

Prescribing forms and indicating information to be verified affidavit.

33

Credit Reporting and Invasion of Privacy

Business firms, to reduce their risk of financial loss from consumer loans and consumer credit, consider it essential to seek information about would-be borrowers, employees, insurance applicants, and others. But this has inevitably led to the invasion of the individual's privacy—an invasion of a right long held sacrosanct in our democratic society.

PRIVATE INFORMATION AGENCIES

There are three major types of private information agencies in Canada that collect data on the consumer. By definition, we exclude our three levels of government, which in fact collect a great deal of information about everyone.

Credit Bureau. This type of agency collects and stores data about every consumer, in a particular geographical area, who has, at one time or another, made use of credit. The data is primarily of a credit nature and is divulged only to firms which subscribe to the credit service. The agency derives its income from annual membership subscriptions plus a fee for each information report supplied.

There are about 150 credit bureaus in Canada, most of which are locally owned and operated. However, several major centre bureaus including Montreal, Calgary and London, Ontario, belong to one firm, the Retail Credit company of Canada—the Canadian subsidiary of Retail Credit of Atlanta. Information exchange between various bureaus is facilitated by common membership in an organization called the Associated Credit Bureaus of Canada. The Association also has a Code of Ethics which members agree to follow.

Personal Investigation Agency. Such an agency will undertake, through field work, telephone calls, and checks of government records, to investigate an individual's personal situation including drug and alcohol habits, education record, health record, employment record, personal assets, marital status, and so on. The information is obtained at the request of insurance companies, employers, and others who are greatly concerned about a person's background. The Retail Credit Company of Canada, as well as being a credit bureau, is the chief agency of this type in Canada. A second important agency is the Hopper-Holmes Bureau, also a subsidiary of a U.S. firm.

Information Exchange.   The third type of private information agency is the *information exchange*. Thus, for example, finance companies in Canada operate a Lenders Information Exchange to ensure, amongst other things, that a consumer does not borrow excessively by going to different companies. In fact, the aim is to restrict a borrower to a maximum of two and a half loans, that is, two loans in his own name and one co-signed. If a finance company knowingly exceeds this limit, it may be fined by the association and may be required to indemnify other members for losses incurred if the borrower defaults on loans made by them.

TYPES OF INFORMATION COLLECTED

Until the 1970s, the types of information being collected in Canada and elsewhere included: name, age, residence, marriage, divorce, inheritance, earnings, criminal record, bank account, debts assumed and paid, slow pay, fast pay, no pay. In a person's credit file could be found: his or her address, family status, place of employment, approximate salary, charge accounts, payment income, and, in the case of insurance company files, hospital records and "moral hazards"—extramarital affairs, homosexuality, heavy drinking, or other social observations that could affect the risk.

BUILDING UP OF CREDIT FILE

The credit bureau file about a person is built up in the following manner:

1. The Bureau receives a report for any of the purposes mentioned above.
2. An investigator is assigned to carry out a personal investigation by contacting employers, friends, school teachers, neighbours, corner grocery stores, debt collection agencies, police sources, and so on.
3. From the total information obtained, it is usually possible to assemble a more or less accurate report of the subject's background, character and credit record.
4. Each time a new request for information is received, the record is updated by a fresh investigation and, it is hoped, after several reports, a more or less true picture emerges.
5. For many years, all truly adverse reports have been reinvestigated to ensure that any adverse comments are in fact substantiated before being passed on to the enquirer.

There are, of course, local credit bureaus in each large city or town which are generally only concerned with the pure credit rating of the person. In this case, files are generally built up from records of previous failures to pay, garnishee proceedings or judgments recorded, and by telephone calls.

As a rule, these sources are restricted in their usefulness to credit background alone. There is reason to believe that once a poor record is established, it is difficult to change it for the better, which accentuates the need for protection.

USERS OF CREDIT INFORMATION

Every business firm that extends credit to its customers wishes to know the credit background and "credit rating" of its new customers and sometimes of its old ones.

All applications for life insurance and automobile coverage are automatically investigated, as well as applications for employment and bonding. Any bank, finance company, mortgage company, or other lending institution will want to know a would-be borrower's credit record. Property managers need to know the credit worthiness of persons wishing to rent apartments and houses.

DANGERS TO THE CONSUMER AND DEMOCRATIC SOCIETY

It is often argued that the average consumer must be willing to relinquish some privacy in exchange for the opportunity of borrowing money or receiving credit.

However, there exists a danger that this personal information, however necessary, may fall into the wrong hands. Also such information may be inaccurate and consequently unfairly penalize the person concerned when he applies for credit.

The wide scale use of computerized credit information will facilitate the collection and storage of more detailed data, with speedier access. However, the following problems may well result:

1. The information may be available and distributed to more persons than originally intended by the person providing the information.
2. The mechanical operation may be open to theft by time sharing, by wiretapping, by copying, and so on.
3. Unlike present-day credit bureau reports where the manager, who has had years of experience, makes a personal assessment of credit worthiness, the computer operator is required to make an assessment or recorded information without the experience or opportunity of a personal assessment.
4. There is a need to ensure that consumer reporting agencies exercise their grave responsibilities with fairness, impartiality, and a respect for the consumer's right to privacy.

All countries now recognize the need for accurate, factual information by credit reporting agencies for credit, employment, accommodation, and other similar purposes. At the same time, the problems arising from uncontrolled investigations, from uncorroborated sources, from outdated information, from lack of standardized assessments, from uncontrolled distribution, from storage in data banks accessible to any and all users, and from the lack of procedures for correcting wrongful or derogatory information have already prompted some legislatures to consider or implement laws along the general provisions of the United States Fair Credit Reporting Act.

ABSENCE OF COMMON LAW PROTECTION

The protection afforded to a person by the common law is summarized in the following principle, attributed to William Pitt, the Earl of Chatham: "A man's house is his castle . . . the poorest man may in his cottage bid defiance to all the forces of the Crown. It may be frail; its roof may shake; the wind may blow through it; the storm may enter; the rain may enter; but the King of England cannot enter. All his forces dare not cross the threshold of this ruined tenement."

However, while the courts have been strong in their protection of citizens against trespass to their lands, or goods, the only protection against invasions of privacy are those which concern a person's character and reputation. Such protection has been granted in the form of injunctions and damages, if there has been publication of a false statement or assertion, which has been shown to lower the reputation of the individual in the minds of friends or other "right-thinking" people. This assumes that the maker of the statement could not plead the defence of "privilege," which covers comments made by a newspaper critic, member of Parliament, judicial officer, teacher or employer.

At the present time there is no right of action either in Canadian or United Kingdom law, against invasion of privacy as represented by the contents of a credit report prepared by a credit agency in good faith and without malice. This is based on the decision in *London Association for the Protection of Trade and Another v. Greenlands*, concerning an untruthful report submitted by a reporting agency against the reputation of the plaintiff company which, it was alleged, constituted libel. The court held that the trader requesting the information could employ an agent to gather this information, and that this was a privileged situation which could only be attacked if the publication was maliciously made (which was not proved in this case). The relevant portion of Lord Buckmaster's decision reads as follows:

A trader is clearly entitled to make enquiries about the commercial credit of a person with whom he proposes to trade. He need not make those enquiries himself. He may constitute an agent on his behalf. He need not enquire of any person of whom he has personal knowledge or with whom he has had trade relations. If the enquiry by honestly and prudently made, it is impossible to fix exact limits within which the enquiry must be confined. The extended character of trade, the modern combinations of many businesses of a different nature under one control, the innumerable and far-reaching branches by which modern enterprise is extended are all considerations which must be borne in mind in considering how far enquiry as to a new customer can be properly made. This, of course, is not the only consideration; there is at the same time the essential need of safeguarding commercial credit against the most dangerous and insidious of all enemies—the dissemination of prejudicial rumour, the author of which cannot be easily identified nor its medium readily disclosed . . . that decision leaves untouched the wider question whether groups of people, however large, may not combine together in order to obtain for the benefit of each other the necessary information for carrying on their business. They can themselves control through their committee, the person by whom the enquires are made and the method by which such enquiries are conducted and they obviously have an interest in not receiving inaccurate and misleading statements.

Interference with privacy has also been classified into the four categories included hereunder:

1. Intrusion up the subject's seclusion, solitude or own private affairs; such as *Coles v. Smith*, where the plaintiff was being intimidated by the correspondent and his own wife into not offering a defence to divorce proceedings.
2. Public disclosure of embarrassing private facts about the plaintiff.
3. Publicity placing the plaintiff in a false light in the public eye.
4. Defendant appropriating for his own advantage the plaintiff's name or likeness.

CREDIT REPORTING LEGISLATION

In recent years, legislation has been passed to control the activities of credit reporting agencies. Thus a comprehensive Act, the Personal Investigations Act, was passed by Manitoba in 1971; a Credit Reporting Agencies Act by Saskatchewan in 1972; and similar Acts by Nova Scotia, British Columbia, and Ontario, in 1973.

In general, the various provincial credit reporting statutes require:

1. licensing for all agencies defined in the Act;
2. the establishment of procedures for application and refusal of licensing;
3. restrictions as to the persons who may have access to the information;
4. the listing of the types of information that may or may not be included in a person's file;
5. the right of a consumer to see his or her file;
6. rights and procedures to dispute a file;
7. that a consumer give consent for the preparation of a credit report;
8. that an agency take reasonable steps to ensure the accuracy of its reports.

Ontario Consumer Reporting Act

This Act limits the categories of persons, companies, and so on, which may request information from a consumer reporting agency, except on the written consent of the consumer, or on the authority of a court order, or for purposes of credit, tenancy application, employment, insurance, or business need. Government departments and the police can be provided with identification information, such as names, addresses, employment. Section 9 contains a list of thirteen types of information that must not be included in the consumer report, such as bankruptcies, non-payment of taxes, criminal convictions after a lapse of seven years, statute barred judgments and debts. The consumer must be informed beforehand of the credit provider's intention to procure a credit report. The customer must be notified of any refusal of credit resulting from information contained in the credit report, and the consumer reporting agency must advise the customer of the information held, and the sources of credit information. The agency must re-investigate any facts the customer alleges are incorrect and, if necessary, rectify the report. The Registrar of credit reporting agencies, which must all be registered under the Act, may also order correction.

PRIVACY GUIDELINES

As the result of government interest, the Associated Credit Bureaus of the United States and Canada have recommended a set of principles called the "Protection of Privacy Guidelines." According to these guidelines, each individual would be allowed to see his or her file; only identification information would be supplied to non-credit granting government agencies; information for credit granting would be supplied; personnel records would be kept separately from credit ones; records of bankruptcies and arrests would be maintained; and files would be destroyed after seven years.

REVIEW QUESTIONS

1. What is meant by credit reporting? Why is it considered necessary?
2. Who collects credit information in Canada?
3. What types of credit information are collected?
4. What steps are involved in building up a credit file?
5. Who makes use of the credit information collected?
6. Why is credit reporting considered dangerous for our society?
7. What protection does the common law provide against the invasion of a person's privacy by credit reporting agencies or others?
8. What legislation has been passed in your province to regulate the activities of credit reporting agencies?

APPENDIX 33-A: SYNOPSIS OF THE CONSUMER REPORTING ACT, R.S.O. 1980, c. 89

S. 1(1)   Definitions:
  (*a*) Consumer—natural person, except in course of business, trade, employment.
  (*d*) Credit information—such as name, age, occupation, resi-

dence, spouse, dependants, education, qualifications, employment, income, paying habits, assets, etc.

    (*k*) Personal information—other than credit information, about character, reputation, health, mode of living, etc.

S. 1(2)   May not waive provisions of Act.

S. 2   Provides for a Registrar of Consumer Reporting Agencies.

S. 3   Must be registered if a consumer reporting agency or a personal information investigation agency.

S. 4   Provides for entitlement to or renewal of registration except where (a) not financially responsible or (b) past conduct indicates lack of integrity and honesty.

S. 5   Registrar may refuse to register, to renew or may suspend or revoke a registration for any reason which would disentitle an applicant to registration.

S. 6(4)   Applicant refused registration may request a hearing.

S. 8   Information from consumer reporting agency files may only be revaled:

    (*a*) upon a court order;

    (*b*) upon consumer's written consent;

    (*c*) according to this Act;

    (*d*) in a consumer report for credit, tenancy agreement, employment, insurance, for a purpose authorized under an Act, for a direct business need, or to update previous information.

S. 8(3)   Government agencies may be provided information as to address, name, places of employment, present and past.

S. 8(4)   Files may only be sold to another registered agency.

S. 9   Consumer reports must be fair and information extracted only from files available in Canada and capable of being shown to consumer.

S. 9(5)   Excluded information:

    (*a*) Anything not the best information relating to credit;

    (*b*) Unfavourable information if uncorroborated unless indicated;

    (*c*) Seven-year-old judgment unless unpaid;

    (*d*) Judgment against consumer without name and address of creditor;

    (*e*) Bankruptcy seven years after date of discharge;

    (*f*) Statute barred judgments, collections, debts;

    (*g*) Non-payment of taxes if seven years old;

    (*h*) Criminal convictions after seven years or if offender pardoned;

    (*i*) Seven-year-old writs, not indicating present status;

    (*j*) Withdrawn criminal charges;

    (*k*) Seven-year-old adverse information;

    (*l*) Discriminatory information prohibited under Human Rights Code;

(*m*) Oral information unless recorded on file.

S. 10	Consumer who requests must be advised if a consumer report is being obtained in connection with transaction involving consumer.
S. 10(2)	Consumer must be advised of request for personal information report;
S. 10(3)	Consumer must be advised of request for a credit report;
S. 10(4)	Assignee of a credit transaction must also give information if procuring a credit report;
S. 10(5)	Content of credit information report cannot be passed on to other credit granting agencies without notifying the consumer;
S. 10(7)	The consumer must be advised of the source of information if credit being denied or charges increased.
S. 11	Consumer may obtain from consumer reporting agency, all information, sources of credit information, names of users of report, and copies of all oral information transmitted, and be informed of his right to protest.
	N.B. The consumer reporting agency may withhold medical reports provided by the consumer's own doctor, but consumer may appear in person with another person, and may make an abstract of all other information after proving identity.
S. 12	Consumer reporting agency must re-investigate disputed facts; and if the report is corrected shall immediately inform all interested parties.
S. 13	Registrar may order correction of inaccurage information, with distribution of correction, but any aggrieved party may apply to Commercial Registration Appeal Tribunal.
S. 14	Consumer reporting agency must advise any change of address, officers.
S. 15	The Registrar may also request a report in connection with any complaint.
S. 16	Minister may order an inquiry under this Act according to Part II of the Public Inquiries Act, 1971.
S. 17	Authorizes the Director to order an investigation if Act contravened or criminal offence relating to fitness for registration.
S. 17(2)	Powers of investigator;
S. 17(3)	Cannot obstruct investigator;
S. 17(4)	Justice of the Peace may issue a warrant authorizing a search and entry even of dwelling between sunrise and sunset.
S. 18	All matters investigated under this Act are confidential.
S. 18(2)	Administrators shall not be required to give evidence of an investigation under this Act, except for proceedings under Act.
S. 20	Director may apply to a judge of the High Court for a restraining Order for non-compliance under this Act.
	May appeal to the Divisional Court under this section.
S. 21	The penalty for furnishing false information under this Act or

failure to comply with the regulations incurs a penalty under summary conviction of $2,000 fine, imprisonment for one year, or both. Limitation for false information, one year after the Director is informed. Limitation for failure to comply with an order or the Act, is two years.

S. 24   Provides for regulations made by Lieutenant Governor in Council.

34

Insurance

It is impossible to prevent the occurrence of fire, theft, personal injury, and other hazards that may threaten a business firm with financial loss. However, it is possible to spread these *risks*, as they are called, over many firms rather than make them the burden of just one.

There is, of course, no way that a business firm can protect itself completely from the possibility of financial loss. As consumer demand changes, new laws are enacted, wage rates are increased, and new competitors emerge, a firm's revenue and expenses are invariably affected, either for better or for worse. Nevertheless business risk can be significantly reduced: (a) by insurance; and (b) by such other measures as diversification of products and investments, better market analysis, larger reserves of working capital, and more thorough plant safety precautions.

INSURABILITY

Not all business risk are insurable. The essential requirements for insurability are: (a) the loss must be entirely accidental; (b) the loss must be measurable; (c) the loss will be incurred by only a small percentage of the group at any time; and (d) there will be a relatively large number of firms seeking insurance for the same type of risk.

CONTRACT OF INSURANCE

If the business risk (such as financial loss from fire in the business premises) is insurable, a company may enter into a contract (called a *policy*) with an insurance company and in return for a periodic or lump sum payment (called a *premium*) have all or most of any loss met by that company. The insurance company is the *insurer* or *underwriter*. The firm that has contracted for the insurance protection is the *insured*. And the person or firm to whom any reimbursement for loss is to be paid, if other than the insured, is the *beneficiary*. In life insurance policies, whenever the life of someone other than the contracting party is insured, a distinction is made between the *insured* and the *life insured*.

The principal elements of an insurance policy, or contract, are the names of the insurer, the insured, and the beneficiary; the type of risk covered; the amount of money for which the risk is insured; the time period involved; the amount of the premium; and the various exemptions and other limitations of coverage.

In drawing up a contract, an insurance company will usually make use of its standard form policy. However, if the insured requires more extensive coverage, the insurer will add to the contract an attachment called a *rider*. Should the insurer and insured wish to alter the existing terms of the policy in any way, they can do this by means of an *endorsement*.

An insurance policy is a special type of business contract between the insurance company (the insurer) on the one hand and the business firm or private individual (the insured) on the other. To be a legally enforceable contract, it must possess all the various requirements of a contract such as offer and acceptance, consideration, and so on, as discussed earlier in this book. There is nothing to prevent an insurance policy being tailored to the needs of the person being insured. However, for convenience, most insurance companies have developed their own standard policies and standard clauses. To prevent the insurer from unduly limiting his or her insurance liability and from committing other undesirable practices, both the federal and provincial governments have passed insurance laws.

Utmost Good Faith Contract

A contract of insurance is a contract of "utmost good faith." Therefore the insured must in all cases reveal anything to his or her detriment as well as in his or her favour. For example, in the case of a warehouse in which explosives are to be stored, the insured would be required to state this in a fire insurance policy. If the insured applied for car insurance and required special hand controls, it would be necessary to declare this requirement. In the case of life insurance, any questions covering special health risks would have to be truthfully answered. The only time when health may not be a factor in taking out a life insurance policy occurs when a group term policy is initially taken out for all the employees by a firm or institution. In such a case, because statistics have shown that there is less likelihood of death among people actively at work as a group, the group term insurance policy covers everyone without the requirement for a medical examination. Employees joining the firm after the group insurance plan has commenced, however, will be required to submit to a medical examination.

Misrepresentation

The Uniform Insurance Acts do, however, provide that, in the case of *innocent misrepresentation*, if such misrepresentation has not been discovered by the Insurer within two years, that it will be too late to void the policy. On the other hand, in the case of *fraudulent misrepresentation*, the policy may always be voided, except insofar as age, in which case the face value of the policy will be adjusted to conform with the insurance purchased by the amount of premium paid.

Investigations

While insurance companies do not generally advertise this fact, all insurance policies are followed up by a routine investigation by an independent investigation company, which is bound to reveal any major differences from the replies submitted in the insurance application form. In addition, most life insurance companies belong to a central agency that retains files of all applicants who have been medically examined and either rejected as uninsurable or rated because of some medical problem.

Terms and Conditions

A standard insurance policy is prepared in advance by each insurance company. However, it must conform with the requirements specified in the provincial or federal Insurance Act, whichever is applicable. Thus, for example, s. 91(1) of Ontario's Insurance Act stipulates with regard to contracts other than accident and sickness, life, and marine:

> All the terms and conditions of the contract of insurance shall be set out in full in the policy or by writing securely attached to it when issued, and, unless so set out, no term of the contract or condition, stipulation, warranty or proviso modifying or impairing its effect is valid or admissible in evidence to the prejudice of the insured or beneficiary.

Furthermore, s. 94(1) states:

> Every policy shall contain the name of the insurer, the name of the insured, the name of the person or persons to whom the insurance money is payable, the amount, or the method of determining the amount of the premium for the insurance, the subject matter of the insurance, the indemnity for which the liability is to accrue, the date upon which the insurance takes effect and the date it terminates or the method by which the latter is fixed or to be fixed.

Other terms that must, by the provincial Insurance Act, be included in a contract of fire insurance relate to:

1. *Property of others.* The insurer is not normally liable for loss or damage to the property of persons other than the insured.
2. *Change of interest.* The insurer is liable for loss or damage occurring after an authorized assignment under the Bankruptcy Act or change of title by succession, by operation of law, or by death.
3. *Termination of insurance.* How the contract may be terminated.
4. *Requirements after loss.* The insured's responsibility for promptly notifying the insurer of the loss, making an inventory, and so on.
5. *Fraud.* How fraud can void any claim.
6. *Who may give notice and proof.* The insured, if absent or unable, may use an agent.
7. *Salvage.* The insured must take all reasonable steps to prevent further damage.
8. *Entry, control, abandonment.* The insurer has immediate right of access and entry to ascertain extent of loss or damage but may not take control or possession.
9. *Appraisal.* If there is a dispute as to the value of the property insured, the property saved, or the amount of the loss, two competent and disinterested appraisers are to be used.

10. *When loss payable.* Within sixty days, after completion of proof of loss.
11. *Replacement.* The insurer, instead of making payment, may repair, replace, or rebuild.
12. *Action.* Claims must be made within one year.
13. *Notice.* How notice is to be sent.

Material Change

One of the standard requirements of any insurance policy other than life is that the insured promptly notify the insurer of any change that the insured either knows of or can control which affects the insurance risk. Failure to provide prompt notice may free the insurer from liability under the policy. The statutory condition, under the heading "Material Change," that must be included in, for example, fire insurance policies issued in Ontario, reads in part:

> Any change material to the risk and within the control and knowledge of the insured avoids the contract as to the part affected thereby, unless the change is promptly notified in writing to the insurer or its local agent, and the insurer when so notified may return the unearned portion, if any, of the premium paid and cancel the contract.

Assignment

Property insurance may not be assigned by the insured to another party without the consent of the insurer. This is because the behaviour of the person involved can materially affect the risk. By contrast, life insurance may be assigned without the insurer's consent. However, the insurer should be notified of such assignment. In practice, many life insurance policies are conditionally assigned every day using the cash surrender value of them as collateral for a bank or other loan. Such an assignment does not in any way alter the risk of the person's death.

STATUTORY CONTROL

Various statutes regulate the activities of insurance companies in Canada.

Federal Legislation

At the federal level, there are the Canadian and British Insurance Companies Act and the Foreign Insurance Companies Act, both passed in 1952. These two Acts provide for:

1. The compulsory registration of all except provincial insurance companies.
2. Periodical financial returns.
3. Specification of the types of securities in which insurance companies may invest.
4. The amount of assets to be retained in Canada.
5. The frequency and types of reports to be submitted for inspection.
6. Minimum required reserves and their manner of computation.

Provincial Legislation

At the provincial level, each government has at least one statute regulating insurance activities within its jurisdiction. These statutes provide for:

1. The appointment of a superintendent of insurance to supervise the activities and financial status of provincially licensed insurance companies.
2. The establishment of licensing requirements for insurers, agents, brokers, and adjusters.
3. The description of the terms that must be contained in every insurance policy.
4. A clear statement of the types of risks not covered by an insurance policy unless expressly included.
5. The degree to which an insurance company may restrict its liability.
6. The way in which misrepresentation can affect an insurance policy.
7. The liability of a life insurer in the case of suicide.
8. The requirements for a person to have an insurable interest.
9. The rights of beneficiaries and assignees.
10. The type of proof that an insurer may require before payment of a claim.

The purpose of both the federal and provincial statutes is to make sure that insurance companies and the persons associated with them do not abuse the important position that they occupy in society—for example, by misusing the funds collected from the insured or failing to pay justifiable claims as they occur. The provincial governments have also tried to ensure, through their statutes, that the standard insurance policy is practically uniform throughout Canada.

GOVERNMENT INSURANCE

Traditionally, insurance in Canada has been provided by private insurance companies. However, the federal and provincial governments, as well as regulating the activities of the private companies by the various Insurance Acts, have also offered insurance of their own. Usually, this has been of three types:

1. insurance not offered by the private companies because of lack of profitability—for example, crop insurance;
2. insurance for which the private companies were charging too much—for example, automobile insurance; and
3. insurance that requires compulsory membership and government support to become financially viable—for example, unemployment insurance, hospital and medical insurance, and Workers' Compensation.

TYPES OF INSURANCE

A business firm faces four main types of insurable risk: (a) loss of property; (b) legal liability; (c) loss of earning power; and (d) employee death, sickness, injury, or unemployment. The first two kinds of risk are covered by the various types of property and "casualty" insurance (a casualty is an unfortunate accident or other event). The third type is covered by life insurance, and the fourth type by casualty and life insurance, government as well as private.

Fire Insurance

When a business firm acquires a building, it must make sure, even before title or ownership is transferred, that there is adequate fire insurance. Fire damage to property is in fact one of the most common business risks that face a business firm. Fortunately, any financial loss can be reduced by fire insurance of the building. The amount for which the building is insured should be periodically raised, as inflation continues, to conform with current replacement cost, minus an allowance for depreciation. Thus, if a ten-year-old building would now cost $80,000 to replace, then (assuming depreciation of 2% a year) it should be insured for $64,000. The amount relates, of course, only to the building, as the land on which it stands cannot be damaged by fire. Also, the building should not be overinsured, as the insurance company will not pay more than the present value of the building.

Type of Construction. The actual cost of fire insurance varies according to the type of construction (concrete, brick, or wood) of the building, its location in the municipality (with particular reference to fire hydrants), and the history of fire losses in the area. The cost, or premium, is then quoted at so many cents per $100 of insurance, either on an annual or three-year basis.

Co-insurance Clause. As very few buildings are completely destroyed by fire, business firms have a natural tendency to underinsure their property. To discourage this practice, fire insurance companies usually insert a co-insurance clause in their contracts. Such a clause requires the business firm to insure a property for at least 80% of its current market value (if the firm is to be fully reimbursed for its loss). Thus a building worth $200,000 must be insured for at least $160,000. If a business firm carries less insurance than required under a co-insurance clause, its indemnification for loss is adjusted rateably.

This co-insurance factor may be explained by the following equation, assuming 80% of the value of a $200,000 building is $160,000 in relation to a fire loss of $100,000:

$$\frac{\text{(amount of insurance purchased 60\%)}}{\text{(80\% of value of building for full coverage)}} \times \text{(amount of loss)} = \begin{array}{l}\text{amount} \\ \text{paid} \\ \text{by insurer}\end{array}$$

i.e. $\dfrac{\$120,000}{\$160,000} \times \$100,000 = \$75,000$

Consequential Losses. If a building is damaged by fire, a business firm may also suffer loss of rental income (if all or part has been rented to other firms or persons); loss of output in the case of a manufacturing plant; loss of sales in the case of retail establishment; or additional expenses from renting alternative accommodation. These losses, called consequential losses, are not normally included in the standard fire insurance policy. However, a consequential-loss clause can usually be included for an additional premium.

Duties of the Insured. There are certain duties imposed on the insured under the terms of the standard fire insurance policy. Thus the insured must:

1. pay the premium;
2. obtain permission from the insurer to leave the premises vacant or unsupervised for more than a specified number of days (say, four);
3. keep all furnaces, fireplaces, chimneys, and other heating equipment in safe condition;
4. must notify the insurer if the insured intends to store explosives or combustibles on the premises; and
5. advise the insurer of any additional risks—adding a fireplace or garage to the house.

Subrogation. The standard fire insurance policy contains the clause: "The Insurer, upon making any payment or assuming liability therefor under this Policy shall be subrogated to all rights of recovery of the Insured aganst any person, and may bring action in the name of the Insured to enforce such rights. . . ." This means that, if the insurer has to reimburse the insured for a fire loss caused by a third party, the insurer obtains the insured's right to sue the third party for damages for negligence or other tort. Thus the insurance company can actively seek to recover from the third party the money that it has paid to the insured.

Exclusions. In every fire insurance policy, the insurer specifically excludes certain types of losses from coverage. The only way that the insured can obtain protection against these risks is by payment of an additional premium. Some examples of exclusions are as follows:

Falling Object: "There is no liability under this Section for loss or damage caused (a) to glass constituting part of a building, (b) by snowslide, landslide or any other earth movement."

Lightning damaging electrical devices or appliances.

Riot.

Smoke: "There is no liability under this Section for loss or damage directly or indirectly caused by smoke from a fireplace."

Rupture of heating, plumbing, sprinkler, or air conditioning system or by escape of water from any such system or from a public watermain: "There is no liability under this Section for loss or damage directly or indirectly caused by freezing of any part of such a system which is not within a building in which heat is maintained during the usual heating season . . . to any such system directly or indirectly caused by rust or corrosion . . . etc."

Vandalism or Malicious Acts: "There is no liability under this Section for loss or damage occurring while a building insured is vacant . . . in course of construction . . . to glass constituting part of a building . . . directly or indirectly caused by theft . . . caused by the insured's spouse or any member of the same household."

Windstorm or hail: "There is no liability under this Section for loss or damage to an outdoor radio or television antenna or its appurtenances or to trees, lawns, plants, shrubs, or fences."

Automobile Insurance

The standard automobile insurance policy provides a car owner with protection against three major types of risk:

Bodily injury or death. This is to the operator of an automobile by an accident arising out of use or operation—benefits include medical, death, dismemberment, and total disability payments.

Loss of or damage to the insured automobile. That is, indemnification against direct and accidental loss of or damage to the automobile, including its equipment. This coverage may, at the insured's request, be loss or damage from all perils; from collision or upset; comprehensive—that is, from any peril other than by collision with another object or by upset; or specified perils—that is, caused by fire, lightning, theft or attempt thereat, windstorm, earthquake, hail, explosion, riot or civil commotion, falling or forced landing of aircraft or of parts thereof, rising water, or the stranding, sinking, burning, derailment or collision of any conveyance on which the automobile is being transported on land or water.

Third party liability. That is, legal liability for bodily injury to or death of any other person or damage to other property. By law, every car owner is required to possess this type of insurance, which may be purchased on its own.

The insurance policy specifies: (a) the risks covered; (b) the benefits payable; (c) general provisions, definitions, and exclusions; and (d) statutory conditions.

An automobile insurance policy is usually issued once, then renewed on an annual basis by means of a renewal certificate.

Business Automobile Insurance. There is a special basic automobile insurance policy for partnerships and corporations that own and operate their own passenger cars. It provides coverage for claims by third parties, for bodily injury, and property damage. However, its coverage usually excludes: (a) any injury caused by a fellow employee who is using the firm's car on his employer's business; (b) loss of or damage to property owned or transported by the firm; and (c) damage to property rented to the firm or in its care, except damage to a residence or private residence.

A much broader policy, called a comprehensive auto liability policy, is available to firms which own or rent passenger cars or trucks. Such a policy protects a firm from third party claims, related to bodily injury or property damage, that arise from the use of the firm's own or rented cars and trucks by its own personnel and from the employees' use of own cars on company business. There are also fleet liability and fleet physical damage policies available to firms which own five or more vehicles. The greater the number of vehicles, the larger the discount from standard insurance rates. There are also special insurance policies for auto dealers, garages and service stations, repairers, and parking lots.

No-Fault Auto Insurance.   Since January 1, 1972, every automobile liability policy sold in Ontario has by law contained limited no-fault accident coverage. Similar plans are in force in Alberta, British Columbia, and Saskatchewan.

The no-fault principle is that benefits are paid promptly no matter who is to blame for the accident. With ordinary insurance, a person might have to wait months and even years for compensation until the insurance companies involved had battled the matter out in court.

Under Ontario's limited no-fault accident plan, if the head of the household (defined as the member of the family earning the most income) is killed in an accident, the widow or primary dependant receives $10,000 and each additional dependant, $2,000. Funeral expenses of $500 are also paid. A person who cannot work because of the accident receives 80% of normal earnings up to a maximum of $140 per week. There is also reimbursement for certain housekeeping, medical, and hospital expenses.

The plan covers the person insured, the members of the family living at home, anyone else riding in the car, and any pedestrians who might be injured in the accident. The person insured, after making the claim under the accidents benefits coverage, also has the right to sue the other driver in court for further compensation.

A proposal has been made by the Insurance Bureau of Canada (an agency to which most insurance companies belong) for a somewhat different no-fault insurance scheme, called Vari-plan. Under this scheme, the insured person's own company would provide compensation in 90% of all accidents. This compensation would be more generous than under the present plan. However, the insured person would have to give up the right to go to court except in the most serious cases of damage or injury. Such a scheme, it is suggested, would unclog the courts of insurance claims. However, the proposal has met with considerable opposition on the grounds that it would mean the insured must accept the amount of compensation set out under the plan (except in serious cases) and give up the basic right of a Canadian citizen to use the courts to settle disputes.

Marine Insurance

A business firm involved in shipping goods from one part of Canada to another or to foreign countries faces the risk of financial loss from damage to these goods in transit. To protect itself from this danger, it can purchase marine insurance.

Ocean Marine Insurance.   Also called wet marine, this insurance covers goods shipped by sea (and the vessel in which they are shipped), while in port, on the high seas, and on inland waterways such as the St. Lawrence River. The hazards covered include sinking, capsizing, stranding, collision, burning, contact with sea water, improper navigation, and theft. The insurance contract is tailored to the individual firm's requirements and may be for a single voyage or for a given period of time, depending on the type of risk. There is no standard ocean marine policy because of the many different types of cargoes, ships, and routes. However, there are a number of standard clauses.

Inland Marine Insurance.   This is of two basic types: inland transportation insurance and personal property floaters. Inland transportation insurance covers goods that are shipped within a country by truck, rail, airplane, or boat and covers losses from a broad range of perils, including fire, theft, lightning, wind, hail, flood, and collision. Coverage may also be purchased for goods before and after transit and such goods as contractor's equipment and farm implements. Personal property floater policies provide insurance coverage against loss of personal property both at home and away from home.

Burglary, Robbery, and Theft Insurance

Every business firm faces the danger of financial loss from burglary, robbery, and theft. Burglary is forced entry into premises for purposes of stealing. Robbery is the taking of property from another person by actual or threatened violence. Theft is the act of stealing. Since it does not necessarily involve burglary or robbery, theft is the broadest risk to cover by insurance and is consequently the most expensive.

There are many different types of policies covering these risks—for example, a combined burglary and robbery policy for small retail stores. Hazards that may be covered under the various types of policies include burglary of safes and inventory; burglary damage to money, securities, merchandise, furniture, and equipment; and robbery inside and outside the premises. However, such policies usually restrict the insurer's liability to a relatively small amount for items such as cash, jewellery, and negotiable securities that can easily be stolen.

Plate Glass Insurance

Most retail stores have plate glass in their display windows. If the glass is broken as a result of a fire, the cost of replacement would be met under the terms of the owner's fire insurance policy. However, the glass may be broken from other causes: for example, a nearby explosion, burglary, or an automobile accident. Consequently, to protect against loss from these other types of breakage, the owner will take out plate glass insurance.

Fidelity Bonding

Another source of possible financial loss to a firm is the dishonest employee. This is particularly true of firms such as banks, finance and trust companies, and retail stores, whose employees may have access to large amounts of cash. To reduce the risk of this type of financial loss, known as the risk of defalcation, a business firm will usually arrange with a bonding company for a fidelity bond covering some (for example, bank tellers and supermarket cashiers) or all of its employees. In the latter case, the term schedule bond is sometimes used. In return for a periodic payment, the business firm receives reimbursement for any money misappropriated by its employees. Should a loss occur, the bonding company, through its right of subrogation, can sue the person or persons responsible for loss—if they can be found.

Surety Bonding

A firm may also suffer financial loss if a third party fails to meet its obligations—for example, the failure of a building contractor to complete a factory or office building on time. To guard against such a loss, a firm can take out a surety bond. The surety company will then assume responsibility for any loss and for ensuring completion of the contract.

Credit Insurance

Whenever a firm extends credit to its customers, there is bound to be some percentage of bad debt. It is not possible for a firm to protect itself completely against this type of financial loss other than by charging a higher price for goods sold to its customers. However, manufacturers, wholesalers, and some retailers can obtain credit insurance to cover abnormal losses. The cost of the insurance is determined by the insurer's appraisal of the creditworthiness of the firm's credit customers.

Canadian firms exporting abroad can insure themselves against risk of loss from bad debt by purchasing special export insurance from the Export Development Corporation, a federal government agency.

Public-Liability Insurance

Business firms, through ownership of property and various business activities, are in constant contact with the general public. Consequently, a business firm is liable to be sued for any personal injury or property damage to a third party caused by the firm's negligence—that is, failure to exercise due caution or prudence when involving others. Examples of such negligence are: a druggist's error in preparing prescriptions; food poisoning in a restaurant; medical malpractice; and personal injury caused by a slippery shop floor. To protect itself from any financial loss from this source, a business firm will usually purchase public-liability (or third party) insurance.

Public-liability insurance includes the following types: business liability, professional liability, product liability, and personal liability. *Business liability* insurance provides a broad, general coverage for business firms against claims by third parties for negligence and other torts. *Professional liability insurance* is coverage provided to persons engaged in medicine, law, and other professions against claims by clients. This is also known as malpractice insurance. *Product liability insurance* is provided to manufacturers against the risk that a new product may prove harmful to the public and give rise to claims for substantial monetary damages. *Personal liability insurance* is coverage provided to business owners and private individuals against losses arising from other persons' tort claims. In all types of liability policy, the usual agreement by the insurer is to reimburse the insured the full amount of the loss up to the face limit of the policy—for example, $100,000.

Business Interruption Insurance

If a fire or other insured peril occurs, a business firm should, with adequate fire insurance, receive enough money to rebuild the premises and buy new stocks of materials for manufacture or goods for resale. However, it would be faced with the problem of paying fixed expenses such as salaries and wages of essential employees, interest on bank and other loans, taxes, and rent.

With a business interruption insurance policy, a firm receives full compensation for such trading losses as: net income lost because of lost sales; continuing fixed expenses, or "overhead"; and extra expenses incurred in trying to keep the business operating after interruption by an insured peril. If records of accounts receivable are destroyed, the policy may also cover losses from additional bad debt caused thereby. If desired, all payroll (not just that of essential employees) may be insured. The cost of business interruption insurance varies according to the gross earnings of a business. Compensation commences as soon as damage from an insured peril has interrupted normal business operations and continues until the premises are repaired or rebuilt. As with fire insurance, there is a mandatory co-insurance clause requiring the insured to maintain the business interruption insurance at at least 50% of gross earnings. This figure may be 80% if, for example, more than one location is covered.

Contingent interruption insurance provides a business firm with protection from loss caused by business interruption of a different origin. This is damage to the premises of principal suppliers, rather than to its own. Such damage can cause a sharp decline in supplies of materials and the like to the customer firm and thereby cause an interruption in its business operations.

LIFE INSURANCE

Many business firms take out an insurance policy on the lives of their key personnel. These might include owners, a president or general manager, a treasurer, leading salespeople, a purchasing manager, or design engineer. Consequently, if such a person dies, the firm receives a substantial sum of cash to cover any loss that may be incurred in the operation of the business. Such loss may arise because the deceased person may have been responsible, for example, for most of the sales or for the good credit rating of the business.

Term Insurance. The type of life insurance purchased may be *term insurance*. In such a case, as with automobile insurance, the firm pays only for protection against loss. It pays the premium and is the beneficiary. There is no savings and investment element as there is with other types of life insurance policies such as straight-life or endowment. However, a firm may choose the latter types of policy in order to build up a cash reserve that may be paid to the key people on their retirement and used in the meantime as collateral for bank or other loans.

Since all insurance is based on the law of averages, the insurance company actuaries calculate, on the basis of their mortality tables, how many deaths will occur at a certain age per year and thus calculate on an average what their losses will be. Thus, for example, at age eleven, only one death normally occurs out of 2,000 children of this age (one-half death per 1,000), so the insurance company would be required to collect 50¢ each from two thousand families to meet the cost of each $1,000 of insurance coverage. If we add an administrative charge of $5 to each policy, this roughly equates what the insurance company must collect for each term insurance policy of $1,000 sold for a child eleven years of age. The cost of term insurance would thus vary for each age group and would increase in cost depending on age, so that at age ninety-nine, the cost of $1,000 of term insurance would be $1,000 since death is imminent: life expectancy is only six months.

Term insurance is useful because of its low cost and because it normally includes a feature that allows coverage to be renewed without a medical examination, thus protecting the insured's insurability. Term insurance may be purchased on a yearly basis, on a five-yearly basis, and so on.

Financially much more advantageous is *group term* insurance, which is purchased on a group basis—for example for the employees of a certain firm or the members of an association. This type of insurance is purchased for a premium of a few cents per $1,000 of coverage because statistics have proven that persons actively at work rarely die.

Whole Life. The most popular type of insurance sold from the insurance company's point of view is called *whole life*. In addition to the death benefit which has been described in relation to the term policy, the whole life policy includes a savings element, which after three years allows the policy owner to either borrow against the savings portion while the policy is in effect, or is returnable, when terminating the policy, as a cash surrender benefit.

Governments supervise the type of investments permitted for such policy savings elements while in the hands of the insurance company. However, the insurance company returns only a portion of the earnings on such investments to the policy holder, the amount varying according to whether the holder pays an extra premium on return for yearly dividends, or whether the holder has purchased a whole life policy on a single-premium or a level premium throughout the duration of the policy, or on a premium which keeps pace with probable earnings.

An attractive feature of a whole life policy is that the holder may borrow against the cash surrender value at whatever rate of interest was in effect on the date when the policy was purchased. Another useful feature is the fact that if premiums are discontinued, the policy must continue in effect until the cash surrender value is used up.

An *endowment policy* is strictly a whole life policy which is usually used as a vehicle for saving money. For example, if I wish to save $10,000 as a down payment on a house, I can take out a ten-year endowment policy for $10,000. Each year the insurance company will collect a premium of $1,000 plus the cost of a term insurance benefit based on my age and an administrative charge. If I die during the ten-year period, my beneficiary will be entitled to $10,000. If I live, the insurance company will pay out $10,000 in savings to me at the end of the period. The company, of course, has had the use of this money for ten years and has earned a considerable amount in interest, part of which is kept by the insurer and part returned to the insured.

Offences under the Ontario Insurance Act

Section 361 of the Ontario Insurance Act makes "twisting" by an agent an offence. This refers to a situation whereby an insurance agent attempts to persuade the holder of a life insurance policy with either a cash value or paid-up value to cause such policy to lapse or to be surrendered or to for the purpose of effecting a policy with another insurer—for example, a term insurance policy with a larger amount of coverage, but without a savings element, for a smaller premium.

Section 361(a) includes the following offences which may be committed by an insurance agent: making false statement or representation; making an incomplete comparison; giving preference with respect to a policy of life insurance because of a special professional or business relationship.

Section 393 includes the following unfair and deceptive acts, which have the effect of making the person contravening them guilty of an offence punishable as if selling insurance without a licence: commission of a prohibited act; unfair discrimination between individuals of same class; unfair discrimination between rates in Ontario; misleading illustration or memorandum; misleading statements regarding policies; incomplete comparison; giving money or other gift as an inducement to buy an insurance policy; any unauthorized charge for premium; and unreasonable delay in settlement of claim.

Partnership Insurance

As seen in Chapter 14, if one of the partners in a partnership dies, then unless the partners have previously made a written agreement providing for the continuation of the partnership in this eventuality, the partnership must be dissolved and the assets distributed before the remaining members may continue as a new partnership. To avoid being forced into this situation, most partnership firms have a buy-sell agreement providing for the purchase of a deceased partner's share of the business by the surviving partners. They also have an insurance policy on the life of each partner. In the event of death, sufficient cash is thereby made available to finance the purchase of the deceased partner's share of the business.

Buy-Sell Agreement. Such an agreement usually covers the following main points:

1. how the ownership of the business is divided among the partners;
2. the agreement of the surviving partners to buy the deceased partner's share of the business;
3. the agreement of each partner to sell his or her share of the business on death;
4. the way in which the price is to be determined and provision for review of the price arrived at in this way, at the request of the surviving partners or the executors of the deceased partner's estate;
5. the insurance policies to be held to provide funds for the purchase of the deceased partner's share of the business;
6. each partner to own policies of the partner's lives and pay the premiums;
7. how any surplus funds are to be distributed; and
8. the duration of the buy-sell agreement.

Sole Proprietor. In the case of a sole proprietorship, life insurance can also play a useful role. If the business is to be discontinued, stock may have to be sold at a loss, outstanding debts paid, and some accounts receivable written off. Certainly, there will be a need for ready cash. If the business is to be sold, there may be considerable delay before any funds are received even if the price is a reasonable one. If the business is to be continued (for example, by a member of the deceased person's family) there may be some delay before this person can be freed from other obligations. Also, after the takeover, it will probably be some time before profits regain their previous level, if at all. As with a partnership, there can be a buy-sell agreement between the present owner and the person who would like to buy the business after the owner's death (for example, a relative, employee, or supplier who wishes to control a key outlet). In all these circumstances, sole proprietorship insurance can provide ready cash in time of need.

REVIEW QUESTIONS

1. Not all business risks are insurable. What are the essential requirements for insurability?
2. An insurance company can afford to offer insurance protection because of the law of averages. Explain.
3. Distinguish among: (a) an insurance agent; (b) an insurance broker; (c) an insurance adjuster.

4. What constitutes an offer in a contract of insurance?
5. A person who applies for insurance must act "in utmost good faith." Explain.
6. What is contingent interruption insurance?
7. What does the provincial Insurance Act stipulate with regard to the terms and conditions of a contract of insurance?
8. What is a "material change" in the case of an insurance policy? What are the insured's obligations in this regard?
9. What other statutory conditions must be included in a contract of insurance?
10. Normally, an insurer may refuse payment if a claim made under an insurance policy is the result of a crime or tort committed by the insured. What is the only exception to this rule?
11. An insurance contract may be declared void on grounds of an "absence of an insurable interest." Explain.
12. May an insurance policy be legally assigned without the insurer's consent?
13. What federal statutory control is exercised over insurance companies in Canada?
14. What provincial control is exercised over the insurance industry?
15. Since business is primarily carried on within each province, which level of government normally has jurisdiction in the business of insurance? Why?
16. Who normally makes the offer to buy insurance?
17. List the normal contents of a policy of insurance.
18. Discuss the requirement of "utmost good faith."
19. How do the courts view "standard form insurance contracts"?
20. How does material change affect a life insurance policy? a car insurance policy?
21. What do you understand by "statutory conditions" in a fire insurance policy?
22. Discuss whose consent is required to assign: (a) a life insurance policy? (b) a car insurance policy when the ownership has changed?
23. When and why does a government become involved in insurance? What is the main interest of governments in relation to insurance?
24. What are the main types of coverage provided by an automobile insurance policy?
25. Discuss the question of "no fault insurance." Does Ontario have any kind of "no fault" insurance? How far do you think that the concept of "no fault" insurance can be carried in our society?
26. Discuss the following terms:
    (a) group term policy:
    (b) insurer;
    (c) insurance broker;
    (d) agent;
    (e) insured;
    (f) life insured;

(g) rider;

(h) endorsement.

27. Suppose a bicycle is stolen from your parents' home, is there any insurance policy which might cover this type of loss? What about the loss of a pair of glasses inadvertently left on a trans-atlantic aircraft?

28. Discuss the purpose of:

(a) plate glass insurance;

(b) fidelity bonding;

(c) surety bonding;

(d) credit insurance;

(e) public liability insurance.

29. Explain the need for, and benefits of, business interruption insurance.

30. What types of insurance are offered by the government?

31. How does one decide how much fire insurance to take out on a commercial property?

32. How is the cost of fire insurance determined? How is it quoted?

33. What is meant by a co-insurance clause?

34. What is a consequential loss?

35. What are the chief features of a buy-sell agreement?

36. What are the duties of the insured under the terms of a standard fire insurance policy?

37. Give three examples of statutory conditions contained in every fire insurance policy.

38. What is meant by subrogation in the case of a fire insurance policy?

39. What is an "exclusion" in a fire insurance policy? Give three examples.

40. What are the three major types of risk covered by the standard automobile insurance policy?

41. What additional coverage is provided by business automobile insurance?

42. What is no-fault automobile insurance? Why has it been adopted in some provinces?

43. What are the basic types of marine insurance? Explain each.

44. Distinguish between: (a) burglary; (b) robbery; (c) theft.

45. What risks are covered by plate glass insurance?

46. Distinguish between fidelity bonding and surety bonding.

47. What is credit insurance? What special facilities are available to Canadian exporters?

48. What is partnership insurance?

49. What are the various types of public-liability insurance that a business firm may require?

50. Explain the need for key-personnel insurance.

PROBLEMS

1. The defendant company issued C with a comprehensive policy of insurance covering his truck. C sold the truck to P and handed him the insurance policy and an application form for a new policy. P then drove

the truck and struck and injured the plaintiff, who sued the defendant under the policy. Will the plaintiff recover damages?

2. The question in the case of *Myers v. Thompson*, [1967] 2 O.R. 335, dealt with liability either on the part of the agent or his company, the insurer, or both. An insurance agent undertook gratuitously to convert the insured's term insurance policy in order to minimize succession duties. The insured referred the agent to his solicitor for instructions which the agent received but which he did not carry out. Also, he failed to tell the insured that he had not done so and in consequence extra succession duty was levied against the insured's estate when he died. Plaintiff, the insured's executor, sued both the agent and the insurance company for the loss. Discuss the agent's liability in this case.

3. In the case of *G. A. Baert Construction (1966) Ltd. v. Canadian General Insurance Co.*, [1966] I.L.R. 1-177, a policy was issued by the appellant insurance company to the respondents, the owner and general contractor for a building under construction which covered "all the property . . . for which the insured is legally responsible." Materials placed on the property by subcontractors, but not yet incorporated in the building, were destroyed by fire. The appellant denied liability on the ground that it had not insured the property of the subcontractors and that the materials had not passed to the respondents. If the contractor was responsible for these building materials, irrespective of ownership, was the insurance company liable? Discuss.

4. In the case of *Aberdeen Paving Ltd. v. Guildhall Insurance of Canada* (1966), 51 M.P.R. 288, the plaintiff's tractor was insured with the defendant against "collision." For some unknown reason it slid into a lake, causing damage and expense in salvaging. Was there a collision in this case within the terms of the policy, thereby allowing the plaintiff paving company to recover its losses?

5. In the case of *Canadian Indemnity Co. v. Campbell* (1966), 56 W.W.R. 57, the plaintiff sued to recover sums it had been forced to pay to the claimants after an accident in which the insured defendant was solely to blame, basing its claim on the breach of a condition in the policy that the insured should not drive his car while under the influence of intoxicants " to such an extent as to be incapable of proper control" of the car. There was evidence to show impairment. Discuss the possible outcome of this case, particularly with regard to impairment and "under the influence."

35

Bankruptcy

Not every business firm finds that its endeavours are profitably rewarded. In fact, a good number of business firms fail in Canada every year. This is particularly true of new businesses whose foundation, from the start, is often blind enthusiasm rather than a cool-headed appraisal of the likely earning power and capital requirements of the business. Although a small-business venture may eventually be highly profitable, it may taken months (and in some cases even years) for the owner to build up a good clientele. If there is insufficient cash available in the business to pay for wages, materials, and supplies during this interim period before the firm breaks even, the owner may find that the business has become financially insolvent. Even though the owner may have started out with adequate cash, he or she may through unwise financial policy tie up far too much of it in fixed assets and slow-moving goods for resale. Furthermore, the owner's bank may not be willing to help the business out. It is essential therefore for businesses, large as well as small, to carefully watch their cash flow (through, for example, a daily or weekly cash budget) to ensure that they always have enough cash available to pay their bills; otherwise they may become insolvent and no longer able to operate. There are also many businesses which, despite the most careful cash-flow management, just cannot make a profit and will eventually be included among the annual statistics of Canadian business failures. According to Dun & Bradstreet of Canada Limited, the reasons for such failure may be: (a) neglect due to incompetence, lack of managerial experience, unbalanced experience, or lack of experience in the line evidenced by inability to avoid conditions which resulted in inadequate sales, competitive weakness, heavy operating expenses, inventory difficulties, receivables difficulties, excessive fixed assets, or poor location; (b) neglect due to poor health, bad habits, marital difficulties; (c) fraud on the part of the principals, reflected by irregular disposal of assets, premeditated overbuy, misleading name; or (d) disaster such as fire, flood, burglary, employees' fraud, strike, some of which could have been covered by insurance.

THE BANKRUPTCY ACT

Until 1919 in Canada, there was only scattered provincial government regulation of persons or business firms who were no longer able to pay their debts. However, in that year, a Bankruptcy Act was passed by the federal Parliament as specifically authorized by the Constitution Act, 1867. Later, in 1949, a new federal Bankruptcy Act was passed—one that was substantially revised in 1966.

Purposes.   The three main purposes of the Act are:

1. to protect creditors by establishing a method of handling a debtor's assets and sharing these on a fair and equitable basis;
2. to help the honest debtor by eventually providing him or her with a new start in life through formal discharge of his obligations; and
3. to establish uniform bankruptcy regulations and proceedings throughout Canada.

Bankrupt Defined.   The term "bankrupt" is commonly used to mean someone who cannot pay his or her bills. Legally, however, it has a special, restricted meaning. Thus a person may be financially insolvent without necessarily being bankrupt. Insolvency is a state of financial affairs that usually precedes bankruptcy. The Bankruptcy Act defines an *insolvent person* as:

> a person who is not bankrupt and who resides or carries on business in Canada, whose liabilities to creditors provable as claims under this Act amount to one thousand dollars, and
>
> (*a*) who is for any reason unable to meet his obligations as they generally become due, or
>
> (*b*) who has ceased paying his current obligations in the ordinary course of business as they generally become due, or
>
> (*c*) the aggregate of whose property is not, at fair valuation, sufficient, or, if disposed of at a fairly conducted sale under legal process, would not be sufficient to enable payment of all his obligations, due and accruing due.

By contrast, a *bankrupt* is defined as: "a person who has made an assignment or against whom a receiving order has been made."

Under the Act, a "person" includes not only individuals but also partnerships, unincorporated associations, corporations, co-operative societies, and others. Excluded from "corporations" for purposes of the Act are building societies having a capital stock, incorporated banks, savings banks, insurance companies, trust companies, loan companies and railway companies. These are governed by special statutes.

Superintendent of Bankruptcy
An official called the Superintendent of Bankruptcy is appointed to supervise the administration of all estates covered by the Act. The functions include: issuing licences to persons to act as trustees in bankruptcy; keeping a record of all licences and renewals issued; requiring, in certain circumstances, the deposit of guaranty bonds by trustees; keeping records of bankruptcy proceedings; inspecting or investigating, at his or her discretion, estates covered by the Act; receiving, recording, and investigating complaints by creditors and others; examining trustees' accounts of receipts and disbursements and final statements; and investigating the character and quali-

fications of persons applying for a licence to act as a trustee in bankruptcy.

To facilitate the administration of the Act, each province of Canada is designated as a bankruptcy district. Each district can then, on the advice of the Superintendent, be divided into two or more bankruptcy divisions.

Each bankruptcy division is placed in the hands of one or more official receivers. These bankruptcy officials (deemed to be officers of the court) must report to the Superintendent every bankruptcy that originates in their division.

RECEIVING ORDER

Under s. 25(1) of the Act, one or more of a person's creditors may file in court a petition for a receiving order against a debtor if: (a) the debts owing to these creditors amount to $1,000; and (b) the debtor has committed an act of bankruptcy (which generally includes either attempting to defraud creditors or give preference to one creditor over another) within the six months immediatelyp rior to the filing of the petition. A debtor is defined in the Act as an insolvent person or any person who, at the time an act of bankruptcy was committed by him or her, resided or carried on business in Canada.

By s. 25(7), if the court is dissatisfied with the proof of the facts alleged in the petition, or is satisfied by the debtor that he or she can repay the debts, or is shown some other good reason why a receiving order should not be made, it will dismiss the petition by the creditor or creditors.

Under s. 28(1), if it is shown necessary for the protection of the estate, the court may, at any time after the filing of a petition and before a receiving order is made, appoint a licensed trustee as interim receiver of part or all of the property of the debtor. Under s. 28(2), the interim receiver may, under the direction of the court, take conservatory measures and summarily dispose of property that is perishable or likely to depreciate rapidly in value and exercise such control over the debtor's business as the court deems advisable. However, the interim receiver must not interfere unduly with the debtor in the carrying on of the business.

If the court decides to issue a receiving order against a debtor, it must then appoint a licensed trustee as trustee of the property of the bankrupt.

Assignments

Under s. 31 of the Act, an insolvent person may assign all his property to an official receiver for the general benefit of his creditors. In the eyes of the law, it is considered irresponsible for a person to continue to trade once he knows that he is insolvent. In fact, such conduct may be held against him when he applies for a discharge from bankruptcy. Such an assignment should be accompanied by details of the property, of the creditors, and of the claims.

Proposals

Under s. 32, an insolvent person or a bankrupt is allowed to make a proposal to his creditors for the settlement of his debts. Such a proposal, containing a scheme of arrantement or composition, must be lodged with a licensed trustee who will examine the person's financial affairs and then call a meeting of the creditors at which the proposal may be accepted or rejected. If the proposal is accepted, the trustee must then ask the court for its approval. After hearing the trustee's report on the debtor's conduct and the views of the trustee, the debtor, and any creditors, the court will approve or reject the proposal. The acceptance of such a proposal constitutes an alternative to bankruptcy proceedings.

OBLIGATIONS OF THE BANKRUPT

The Bankruptcy Act tries to ensure that all the assets of a bankrupt person are made available to satisfy the claims of creditors. Some of the obligations of the bankrupt specifically mentioned in the Act are as follows: not to remove any property from the province and not to dispose of assets while aware of impending bankruptcy, such as a fraudulent assignment of book debts. Also, shareholders are required to pay the balance of any unpaid shares.

ADMINISTRATION OF A BANKRUPT'S ESTATE

Once a person has become bankrupt, either by petition or assignment, the trustee appointed to administer the estate must, under s. 80 of the Act, find out the names and addresses of the creditors. Then, within five days from the date of appointment, the trustee must notify them of the first meeting of creditors. Also, the trustee must arrange for notice of the bankruptcy and of the first meeting of creditors to be published in the *Canada Gazette* and in a local newspaper.

First Meeting of Creditors.   The purpose of the first meeting of creditors is to consider the affairs of the bankrupt, to affirm the appointment of the trustee or substitute another, to appoint inspectors and to give such directions to the trustee as the creditors may see fit with reference to the administration of the estate. Subsequent meetings may be called at the discretion of the trustee, when directed by court, and whenever requested by a majority of the inspectors or by 25% in number of the creditors holding 25% in value of the proved claims.

Inspectors.   At the first or a subsequent meeting, the creditors must appoint from one to five inspectors of the estate of the bankrupt. The duties of such inspectors are: from time to time to verify the bank balance, examine the trustee's accounts and inquire into the adequacy of the security filed by the trustee; and to approve the trustee's final statement of receipts and disbursements, dividend sheet and disposition of unrealized property. Before such approval is given, the inspectors must satisfy themselves that: all the property has been accounted for; the administration of the estate has been completed as far as can reasonably be done; the disbursements and expenses incurred are proper and have been duly authorized; and the fees and remuneration are just and reasonable in the circumstances.

Claims.   Under s. 95(1), all debts and liabilities, present or future, to which the bankrupt is subject at the date of the bankruptcy are considered to be claims provable. These also include debts and liablities to which the bankrupt may become subject before his discharge by reason of any obligation incurred before the date of the bankruptcy. Under s. 97(1), every creditor must prove his or her claim; a creditor who fails to do so is not entitled to share in any distribution that may be made. Under s. 106(1), the trustee has to examine every proof and the grounds of the claim, and may require further evidence in support of it.

Priority of Claims.   Under s. 107(1), the proceeds realized from the property of a bankrupt must, subject to the rights of secured creditors, be applied in the following priority payment:

1. in the case of a deceased bankrupt, the reasonable funeral and testamentary expenses;
2. the expenses and fees of the trustee, followed by legal costs involved in administration of the estate;
3. the special levy imposed under the Act to help defray the expenses of supervision by the Superintendent of Bankruptcy;
4. wages, salaries, commissions or compensation of any clerk, servant, travelling salesperson, labourer, or worker for services rendered during the three months immediately preceding the bankruptcy, up to $500 each; in the case of a travelling salesperson, for disbursements properly incurred in and about the bankrupt's business during those three months, an additional $300;
5. municipal taxes assessed or levied against the bankrupt within the two years immediately preceding the bankruptcy—so long as they do not constitute a preferential lien or charge against the real property of the bankrupt and not exceeding the value of the bankrupt's interest in the property;
6. rent owed to a landlord for the three months immediately preceding the bankruptcy and accelerated rent for up to three months following the bankruptcy;
7. one solicitor's bill of costs, including sheriff's fees and land registration fees;
8. all indebtedness of the bankrupt under any Workers' Compensation Act, any Unemployment Insurance Act, any provision of the Income Tax Act, or the Income War Tax Act;
9. claims resulting from injuries to employees of the bankrupt to which the provisions of any Workers' Compensation Act do not apply, but only to the extent of moneys received from persons or companies guaranteeing the bankrupt against damages resulting from such injuries;
10. claims of the Crown not previously mentioned in this section, in right of Canada or of any province.

A "secured creditor" means a person holding a mortgage, hypothec, pledge, charge, lien, or privilege on or against the property of the debtor or any part thereof as security for a debt due. It also means, under the Act, a person whose claim is based on or secured by a negotiable instrument held as collateral security and on which the debtor is only indirectly or secondarily liable. Such creditors are entitled to have their claims satisfied before the unsecured creditors are paid.

Dividends.   Under s. 119(1), the trustee must from time to time, as required by the inspectors, pay dividends to the unsecured creditors. However, the trustee must retain sufficient funds to cover the costs of administration.

Final Statement.   The trustee is required under s. 123 to prepare a final statement of receipts and disbursements containing a complete account of: all moneys received by the trustee out of the property of the bankrupt or otherwise; the amount of interest received by the trustee; all moneys disbursed and expenses incurred; the remuneration claimed by the trustee; and the full particulars, description, and value of all property of the bankrupt that has not been sold or realized and the reason therefor. This statement, after it has been approved by the inspectors, is then forwarded to the Superintendent of Bankruptcy for his scrutiny and comments. Finally, the trustee has to forward by registered mail to every creditor whose claim has been proved, to the registrar, to the Superintendent and to the bankrupt: a copy of the final statement of receipts and disbursements; a copy of the dividend sheet; and a notice in a prescribed form of the intention to pay a final dividend after the expiration of fifteen days from the mailing of these documents and to apply to the court for future discharge not less than thirty days after payment of the dividend.

Examination.   Under s. 132(1), the official receiver is required to examine the bankrupt under oath as to his or her conduct, the causes of the bankruptcy and the disposition of his property. The official receiver is also required to prepare a report of any facts or circumstances that in his or her opinion require special consideration or further explanation or investigation. A copy of the notes of the examination and of the report must be forwarded to the Superintendent, to the trustee, and to the court. The receiver must also inform the creditors, at their first meeting, of the contents of the notes and report.

Under s. 132(4), the official receiver may inquire into or investigate the conduct of the bankrupt, the causes of the bankruptcy, and the disposition of property. The receiver may also be directed to do so by the Superintendent. Also, the receiver must report his findings to the court, the trustee, and the Superintendent.

Discharge of Bankrupts.   Under s. 139(1), the making of a receiving order against or an assignment by any person except a corporation operates as an appliction for discharge—unless the bankrupt waives this right. However, under s. 139(4), a corporation may not apply for a discharge unless it has satisfied the creditors in full.

Under s. 141(1), the trustee must prepare for the Superintendent a report specifying:

(a) the name of the debtor and, where the debtor is a corporation, the names and addresses of the directors and officers of the corporation and, when applicable, the names of the persons who in the opinion of the trustee actively controlled the day-to-day operations of the corporation or the business of the debtor or who in the opinion of the trustee were responsible for the greater proportion of the debtor's liabilities or under whose directions in the opinion of the trustee the greater proportion of the debtor's liabilities were incurred;

(b) whether in the opinion of the trustee the deficiency between the assets and the liabilities of the debtor has been satisfactorily accounted for or if not whether there is evidence of a substantial disappearance of property that is not accounted for;

(c) a statement of opinion by the trustee with respect to the probable causes of the bankruptcy, arrived at after consultation with the inspectors and other person, which shall be expressed as resulting from one or more of the probable cuases in the following enumeration, namely:

    (i) misfortune;
    (ii) inexperience,
    (iii) incompetence,
    (iv) carelessness,
    (v) over-expansion,
    (vi) unwarranted speculation,
    (vii) gross negligence,
    (viii) fraud, and
    (ix) other probable cause (to be specified); and

(d) a statement of the facts and information on which the trustee relied in arriving at the opinion expressed pursuant to paragraphs (b) and (c).

Under s. 142(1), the court may: either grant or refuse an absolute order of discharge; suspend the operation of the order for a specified time; or grant an order of discharge subject to terms or conditions regarding any future earnings or income of the bankrupt.

In s. 143(1), the grounds on which a discharge may be refused, suspended, or granted conditionally are specified as follows:

(a) the assets of the bankrupt are not of a value equal to fifty cents in the dollar on the amount of his unsecured liabilities, unless he satisfies the court that the fact that the assets are not of value equal to fifty cents in the dollar on the amount of his unsecured liabilities has arisen from circumstances for which he cannot justly be held responsible;

(b) the bankrupt has omitted to keep such books of account as are usual and proper in the business carried on by him and as sufficiently disclose his business transactions and financial position within the three years immediately preceding his bankruptcy;

(c) the bankrupt has continued to trade after knowing himself to be insolvent;

(d) the bankrupt has failed to account satisfactorily for any loss of assets or for any deficiency of assets to meet his liabilities;

(e) the bankrupt has brought on, or contributed to, his bankruptcy by rash and hazardous speculations, or by unjustifiable extravagance in living, or by gambling or by culpable neglect of his business affairs;

(f) the bankrupt has put any of his creditors to unnecessary expense by a frivolous or vexatious defence to any action properly brought against him;

(g) the bankrupt has, within the three months preceding the date of his bankruptcy, incurred unjustifiable expense by bringing a frivolous or vexatious action;

(h) the bankrupt has, within the three months preceding the date of his bankruptcy, when unable to pay his debts as they became due, given an undue preference to any of his creditors;

(i) the bankrupt has, within the three months preceding the date of his bankruptcy, incurred liabilities with a view to making his assets equal to fifty cents in the dollar on the amount of his unsecured liabilities;

(j) the bankrupt has on any previous occasion been bankrupt or made a proposal to his creditors;

(k) the bankrupt has been guilty of any fraud or fraudulent breach of trust;

(l) the bankrupt has committed any offence under this Act or any other statute in connection with his property, his bankruptcy or the proceedings thereunder;

(m) the bankrupt has failed to perform the duties imposed on him under this Act or to comply with any order of the court.

A discharge, even unconditional, does not release a bankrupt from all financial obligations. Thus, as indicated in s. 148(1), he or she is still liable for:

(a) any fine or penalty imposed by a court or any debt arising out of a recognizance or bail bond;

(b) any debt or liability for alimony;

(c) any debt or liability under a maintenance or affiliation order or under an agreement for maintenance and support of a spouse or child living apart from the bankrupt;

(d) any debt or liability arising out of a fraud, embezzlement, misappropriation or defalcation while acting in a fiduciary capacity;

(e) any debt or liability for obtaining property by false pretences or fraudulent misrepresentation;

(f) liability for the dividend that a creditor would have been entitled to receive on any provable claim not disclosed to the trustee, unless such creditor had notice or knowledge of the bankrutpcy and failed to take reasonable action to prove his claim; or

(g) any debt or liability for goods supplied as necessaries of life and the court may make such order for payment thereof as it deems just or expedient.

COURTS AND PROCEDURE

Section 153(1) specifies the courts that are to have jurisdiction in bankruptcy proceedings: namely, the highest trial court in each province—usually the supreme court. Other sections deal with the authority of the courts, the powers of the court registrars, appeals, and legal costs.

BANKRUPTCY OFFENCES

Part VIII of the Act sets out the various types of bankruptcy offences and the penalties involved. Thus, according to s. 169, any bankrupt who generally does not co-operate with bankruptcy officials by failure to answer questions after or within the twelve months preceding bankruptcy and who fails to reveal a true statement of affairs, makes false representation, removes property worth more than $50, or disposes of property obtained on credit other than by way of regular trading business, is guilty of an offence and is liable on summary conviction to imprisonment for a term not exceeding one year or on conviction under indictment to imprisonment for a term not exceeding three years, and the provisions of the Criminal code authorizing the imposition of a fine in addition to or in lieu of imprisonment do not apply.

Also, according to s. 170, an undischarged bankrupt who:

(a) engages in any trade or business without disclosing to all persons with whom he enters into any business transaction that he is an undischarged bankrupt; or

(b) obtains credit for a purpose other than the supply of necessaries for himself and family to the extent of five hundred dollars or more from any person without informing that person that he is an undischarged bankrupt;

is guilty of an offence and is liable on summary conviction to imprisonment for a term not exceeding one year.

OTHER LEGISLATION

Several other federal and provincial laws help creditors to protect their interests against persons who can no longer meet their financial obligations or who wish to terminate their business activities and dispose of their assets for some other reason.

At the federal level, there are:

The Winding-up Act   indicates the procedure to be followed when a federally incorporated company wishes to surrender its charter and discontinue its activities.

The Company Creditors' Arrangement Act   regulates the claims of bondholders.

The Farmers' Creditors Act   provides a method by which a farmer may make a proposal to creditors for the settlement of debts. If the proposal is rejected, the creditors may then proceed against the farmer according to the terms of the federal Bankruptcy Act.

At the provincial level, there is the following legislation:

The Corporations Act   provides, among other things, for the winding up of provincially incorporated companies in a similar manner to the federal Winding Up Act.

The Bulk Sales Act.   The would-be purchasers of a business are required to inform all creditors of the business of the intended purchased and to follow a special procedure in paying the purchase price.

The Construction Lien Act.   Creditors who have provided work or materials for the improvement of land or buildings may obtain an interest therein as security for payment by registering a claim, or lien.

The Wages Act.   A creditor may apply to the court to have a person's wages garnisheed—that is, deducted at source, by the employer and paid to the creditor. However, only 20% of the wage earned may be garnisheed. Furthermore, an employer is now prohibited from using the fact of garnishment as grounds for dismissing an employee.

PROPOSED NEW BANKRUPTCY ACT

In May 1975, the federal government tabled in the House of Commons Bill C-60, a proposed new Bankruptcy and Insolvency Act. Although the bill had the praiseworthy aim of attempting to modernize the present Bankruptcy Act and related statutes, it was heavily criticized and suffered considerable modification. Since 1975, other attempts to amend the Bankruptcy Act have been made. The proposed amendments would include: (a) the opportunity for consumer and corporate debtors to make arrangements for rescheduling and reducing debt repayment as an alternative to bankruptcy; (b) imposition on directors and officers of a bankrupt firm of personal liability for corporate deficits if, in their own interest, they carried on business harmful to the corporation; (c) the proposed automatic suspension, once a bankruptcy petition has been filed, of legal proceedings launched against a debtor by the creditors; and (d) giving a wage earner priority over all creditors, including secured creditors, on all the property of his employer in trying to recover unpaid wages up to a maximum of $2,000 per person. At present, a wage earner ranks fourth in order of priority for unsecured creditors and may only file a claim for back pay up to a maximum of $500.

REVIEW QUESTIONS

1. Why is it that each year many firms are forced to cease operations?
2. What are the three main purposes of the federal Bankruptcy Act?
3. Distinguish among: (a) an insolvent person; (b) a bankrupt; (c) a debtor.
4. What federal legislation, apart from the Bankruptcy Act, has been passed with regard to creditors' rights?
5. Who is the Superintendent of Bankruptcy? What are his functions?
6. How is Canada divided geographically for purposes of administration of the Bankruptcy Act?
7. What is a receiving order? When may a person's creditors petition for such an order? What happens if it is granted?
8. What provincial legislation has been passed with regard to creditors' rights?
9. Explain the role of an interim receiver.
10. Explain the nature and purpose of an "assignment."
11. What is meant under the Act by a "proposal"? By whom must such a proposal be approved?
12. What property of a bankrupt may be divided, under the Act, among the creditors?
13. Give three examples of the obligations that are imposed on a bankrupt by the Bankruptcy Act.
14. What procedure must a trustee follow when first appointed to administer a bankrupt's estate?
15. What are the specific purposes of the first meeting of creditors?
16. What are the duties of the inspectors appointed for the bankrupt's estate?
17. What are "claims provable" under the Act?
18. What priority of payment applies to the debts of a bankrupt?
19. What is a secured creditor? What priority is attached to his or her claims on a bankrupt's estate?
20. What must the trustee supply to each creditor after the bankrupt's affairs have been settled?
21. What are the principal duties of a bankrupt?
22. Who is responsible for the conduct of a bankrupt corporation?
23. What is an official receiver? What are his or her duties?
24. Under what circumstances may a bankrupt be arrested and his or her property seized?
25. With regard to the discharge of a bankrupt, what report must the trustee prepare?

26. What are the grounds on which the discharge of a bankrupt may be refused, suspended, or granted conditionally?
27. Which courts are given jurisdiction over bankruptcy proceedings in Canada?
28. What are the principal types of bankruptcy offence and the penalties involved?

PROBLEMS

1. The lease between a landlord and his tenant provided for accelerated rent and repossession if a breach of contract occurred. The tenant, who went bankrupt, made an assignment for the benefit of his creditors. Discuss the amount of the landlord's claim as a preferred creditor and as a general creditor, assuming that the accelerated rent clause took effect before the effective date of bankruptcy. Refer to *Re Prairie Farm Power Ltd.* (1974), 49 D.L.R. (3d) 736 (Alta.).

2. A provincially incorporated company has been petitioned into bankruptcy by its creditors under the Bankruptcy Act. The trustee has reported the following situation:

Sale of Assets

Cash	$ 1,000
Accounts Receivable	2,000
Inventories.................................	25,000
Real Property	30,000
	$58,000

Liabilities

First Mortgage.............................	$15,000
Bank Loan on Inventory	10,000
(secured under s. 88 of the Bank Act)	
Municipal Taxes	1,000
Workers' Compensation	1,500
Unemployment Insurance	1,500
Canada Pension Contributions	1,000
Employee Wages Payable	7,500
(3 at $500 per month, including son for 5 months)	
Trade Accounts.............................	35,000
Bankruptcy Court Costs	1,000
Trustee's Fee	1,500

   (a) Show the balance after secured creditors have been paid.
   (b) Show the balance after preferred creditors have been paid.
   (c) Show which creditors rank *pro rata* and the dollar percentage received.
   (d) Are there any unprotected creditors?
   (e) What would be the situation if this were a corporation controlled by a

single individual who had transferred the real property asset to the spouse for $5,000 over five years ago while the company was solvent and who was now leasing the premises to the company?

(f) What would the judge require as evidence before granting a receiving order?

(g) Would it be possible for the owner of this business to start over again in the same occupation?

3. A trustee in bankruptcy disallowed a claim by an employee under s. 13(2) of the Employment Standards Act, R.S.O. 1970, c. 147, which required that an employer give notice in the manner and for the period prescribed by the regulations, and until the expiry of such notice the termination should not take effect. It was conceded that the employee was entitled to eight weeks' wages if this section applied. The Registrar allowed the claim, overruling the trustee. How do you think the Supreme Court in Bankruptcy would dispose of this claim? Which category of claim would it belong to under the Bankruptcy Act? Refer to *Re Malone Lynch Securities Ltd.*, [1972] 3 O.R. 725.

4. On January 18, Amanda, a creditor of Charisma, filed a writ against the latter and was granted leave to file judgment on two clear days to the debtor company. On January 22, judgment was signed when no one appeared for the debtor company, Charisma. On January 26, the sheriff, served with an execution order, seized from Charisma's bank, a cheque for $3,440 and paid it over to the claimant, Amanda, less expenses.

In the meantime, on January 22, the debtor company, Charisma, made a proposal to its creditors under s. 41(10), which provided that if a proposal was refused by the court, the insolvent debtor should be deemed to have made an assignment in bankruptcy on the day when the proposal was filed, i.e., January 22. The judge in bankruptcy refused to approve the proposal.

There was now a question as to whether the trustee was entitled to a return of the $3,440 seized by the sheriff, in which case Amanda would only be entitled to rank rateably since the object of the Bankruptcy Act was to ensure that the property of an insolvent person or corporation should be made available for the benefit of creditors rateably, subject only to the priorities established or recognized by the Act.

How would you resolve this dilemma? Refer to *Amanda Designs Boutique Ltd. v. Charisma Fashions Ltd.*, [1972] 3 O.R. 68.

5. In this case one of a bankrupt's creditors sold aluminum products valued at $9,330 to the bankrupt on May 27. Some seven weeks later the debtor/bankrupt signed a written agreement acknowledging the property in the aluminium would remain that of the creditor until paid for, i.e., a consignment sale agreement. (To constitute a consignment sale; that is, where no title passes until a third party buys the goods, separate accounts must be maintained, the inventory must be separated, and there must be a provision for payment of commission.) The debtor went bankrupt on December 6. The creditor repossessed the aluminium on the basis of the

consignment agreement. The trustee now wants the return of this asset. What is the law in this situation? Refer to *Re Krisandra Yachts* (1974), 18 C.B.R. (N.S.) 39.

READING

Mercure v. A. Marquette & Fils Inc. (1975), 65 D.L.R. (3d) 136 (S.C.C.).

Facts: In this case the debtor company borrowed $12,000 as a mortgage loan from the plaintiff and agreed to insure up to the total amount of its mortgages. In 1966, a first mortgage for $5,526 was held by a "Caisse Populaire" and a second mortgage of $8,064 was still held by the plaintiff. An insurance policy of $5,000 was payable to the Caisse Populaire, while another policy of $5,000 was payable to the debtor. An insurance clause in the plaintiff's mortgage provided that, while the policies would be kept up by the debtor, the benefit in case of fire would be paid to the mortgagees.

A trustee in bankruptcy was appointed on January 27, 1966, and while this trustee was notified that the policies would lapse, he did not reinstate them nor notify the mortgage holders to allow them to keep the policies in force. A fire occurred on April 28-29, 1966, and the mortgagee having lost his security sued the trustee in bankruptcy for his negligence in not preserving the insurance. The trustee objected that no action could be taken against him under s. 171 for an action taken, but the court held that this did not apply to inaction such as occurred in this case. The trustee also appealed on the grounds of absence of fault.

Held:

[Section 13(1) provides that the trustee must insure and keep insured all and any insurable property of the debtor while s. 13(2) provides that such insurance shall be payable to the trustee.]

. . . [T]he secured creditors [including mortgagees] receive the same protection as if the debtor had not gone bankrupt. . . . [T]he debtor's successor, trustee-appellant had a general obligation to respect the right of respondent [mortgagee (to keep the insurance in force)] as stipulated in the insurance clause. . . .

[The appellant objected that the secured creditor should have procured his own insurance.] The solution of the Court of Appeal is a much better one: appellant's fault makes him liable because respondent was entitled to preference with regard to insurance compensation. Furthermore, the Court of Appeal was also right in concluding the respondent [mortgagee] was also entitled to be notified of the situation by the trustee, which would have enabled it to protect its rights.

Appeal dismissed.

36

Secured Transactions

For many hundreds of years, the law has recognized the validity of secured transactions. These are transactions involving the lending of money or the sale, on credit, of goods that have some asset pledged as security for repayment. In ancient Rome, if a borrower defaulted on his debt, not only was his property seized but also he, his wife, and children were sold into slavery. As recently as the nineteenth century, Charles Dickens, for example, had to leave school and go to work to pay off his father's debts, so that his father might be released from debtors' prison. Nowadays, only the asset pledged as security can be taken from the debtor—not his or her liberty as well.

SECURITY INTEREST

It is easy for a consumer unwittingly to purchase goods that the seller, although the true owner, may have previously pledged as security for a loan. If default on the principal or interest payments occurs, the pledgee has the right to have the good sold and the proceeds used to repay the debt, interest, and other expenses. Such a charge or claim against a good, known as a *security interest*, has been defined as "goods, other than building materials, that have been affixed to the realty, fixtures, documents of title, instruments, securities, chattel papers or intangibles, that secures payment or performance of an obligation and includes an interest arising from an assignment of book debts." Or more simply, as "an interest in personal property or fixtures which secures payment or performance of an obligation."

In the past, the concept of a "security interest" has been looked at purely from the viewpoint of the lender and his desire for protection. However, security interests are also important from the consumer point of view in that would-be purchasers of secondhand goods should be informed of any prior secured interests or charges. In this chapter we confine our attention to this latter point of view.

Historical Development. Historically, the idea of reserving a security interest to ensure payment of a debt arose out of the practice of giving title and possession of land belonging to a borrower as security for repayment of a loan. However, there was an obvious disadvantage to this situation, particularly if the borrower was counting on the sale of the produce from the land to earn the money to pay off the debt. Eventually the lender was permitted to ensure his rights without going into possession by a security called a mortgage. When the practice of immediate foreclosure developed (whereby the property was seized when the borrower failed to repay the debt on the due date), the Court of Equity stepped in to enforce the borrower's equity of redemption, since the loan was usually only one-tenth of the total value of the land. Originally, redemption was allowed up to several years after the foreclosure by the mortgagee. Gradually, each legislative jurisdiction has fixed a limit for redemption by the mortgagor.

MORTGAGE OF REAL ESTATE

Possibly the best known way of giving security for a loan is a real estate mortgage whereby the owner of the real property (the borrower or *mortgagor*) gives up the fee simple title in the land to the lender, or *mortgagee*, retaining only, as evidence of right to ownership, the *equity of redemption*—which is his or her right above anyone else to pay off the debt, and obtain a discharge of the mortgage. Mortgages were discussed in detail in Chapter 17.

HIRE-PURCHASE AGREEMENTS

During the nineteenth century, the English common law courts gave recognition to the hire-purchase agreement, whereby the seller of a good retained ownership (or *title*) to it while the buyer paid a rental fee, and did not become the owner until the entire purchase price plus interest had been paid. Thus the buyer only had possession of the good which could be seized if the payments were not made. Under a hire-purchase agreement, the seller remains the owner unless the ownership is assigned to a finance company. Therefore the seller can always repossess the item if the conditions of hiring are not met. Thus in the case of *Helby v. Mathews*, [1895] A.C. 471, a buyer entered into a hire-purchase agreement at a monthly rental of ten shillings and sixpence which provided that the subject matter of the purchase, namely a piano, would not become his property before 18 pounds, 18 shillings had been paid. It also provided that the agreement could be terminated at any time. The buyer pawned the piano and the seller sued for recovery of the chattel as the agreed sum had not been paid. In its judgment, the House of Lords found that, since the buyer had not bound himself to pay the full purchase price, no property had passed to him, and the seller could recover possession from the pawnbroker.

Under a hire-purchase agreement, the seller-owner of goods has the same obligations as the lessor of goods under the rules of bailment. Thus the purchaser-lessee must be informed of any peculiarities, such as special details of maintenance, that the item possesses. The owner-lessor remains liable for product defects or injuries that may be caused by defective goods. The owner-lessor also remains liable for the upkeep of the goods during the currency of the hire-purchase unless contrary provisions are included in the contract.

If the purchase is a true hire-purchase agreement (whereby the buyer merely rents with an option to buy), then the buyer is free to return the goods at any time. If, however, there is an actual purchase, or agreement to purchase on hire-purchase terms, then the buyer may not return the goods without breach of contract. Also, an innocent third party who purchases the goods, without notice of the hire-purchase contract, acquires good title and need not return them to the seller-owner, even though the original purchaser has not paid for them. The only recourse for the original seller-owner is to sue the original purchaser on the basis of the hire-purchase agreement.

At the present time in Canada, Granada TV and some car leasing companies operate on the hire-purchase principle, in that the lessee of a television or car rents the good for a monthly fee with the right to purchase it at its depreciated value at the end of the lease. The hire-purchase agreement is used in the province of Manitoba. Elsewhere a conditional-sale agreement is more usual.

CONDITIONAL SALES

Many goods, particularly those involving relatively large sums of money, are no longer bought outright for cash. Instead, the buyer makes only a small down payment, equivalent to say 10 or 20% of the total price, and pays the balance in equal amounts over a number of months or even years. However, the buyer obtains immediate possession of the goods. To protect the seller, the buyer, who has received ownership of the goods, agrees in a *conditional sales contract* to give up this ownership to the seller as security until the last payment has been made. This type of sales transaction is called a *conditional sale*.

Standard Terms
The standard terms contained in a conditional sales contract are as follows:

1. A full description of the goods and the buyer's acknowledgement that he has received them.
2. The price of the goods and the buyer's promise to pay it in specified instalments at stated future dates. This promise is in the form of a promissory note called a lien note. Also, there is usually an acceleration clause that provides that the balance of the price must be paid at once if an instalment is not met. Since time is declared to be "of the essence," any failure to make a payment on the due date is considered by the courts to be a breach of condition of the contract. Consequently, the buyer can thereupon be sued for the full price of the goods purchased.
3. A statement that ownership of the goods is to remain with the seller until full payment has been made. If this clause were not included, title would pass to the buyer on delivery.
4. A statement that responsibility for taking "reasonable care" of the goods rests with the buyer. Often, the buyer is required to insure the goods with the seller named as beneficiary in the insurance policy.
5. The buyer's agreement that, in the event of non-payment, the buyer will return the goods to the seller.
6. A statement of the seller's right, in the event of non-payment, to enter the

buyer's premises and take back (or "repossess") the goods, without being liable to be sued for trespass. However, by common law, a seller may not use force in repossessing goods. If there is physical resistance by the buyer, the seller must request from the court a *replevin* (or recovery) order. If granted, the order can then be executed by the sheriff's officer or bailiff with any necessary amount of force. Some provinces provide that if the goods are repossessed, any unpaid balance is forfeited. Ontario, by consumer legislation, prohibits repossession if the goods are two-thirds paid for.

7. A statement of the seller's right, even after repossession of the goods, to keep all the payments made so far.

8. A statement of the seller's right to resell the repossessed goods. Usually, the seller is required by provincial law to wait a specified period before doing so. This is to give the buyer an opportunity to redeem the goods by paying all the money owing plus interest, as well as all reasonable expenses incurred by the seller in repossessing the goods.

9. A statement that the seller has the right to sue the buyer for any financial loss from the resale of the goods. However, the seller must make a reasonable attempt to obtain a good price for them. Also, in most provinces, the seller must provide the buyer (in the case of goods costing more than a certain amount) with a detailed statement of the money owed before the sale.

10. A statement prohibiting the buyer from removing the goods from the premises without first informing the seller or, in some instances, without first obtaining the seller's consent.

Apparent Ownership

At common law, a seller has the right to take back the goods sold on a conditional sale basis if the buyer fails to keep up his payments. However, if the buyer, in violation of his agreement, resells these goods to a genuinely innocent third party (that is, a person who is unaware of the conditional sale), title would normally pass to this third party. This is because the new seller, by the fact of possession, has apparent ownership. The only legal remedy then available to the original owner is to sue the new seller for the full price of the goods on grounds of breach of the conditional sales contract. To prevent the original seller from being put in this position, the Ontario Personal Property Security Act, and similar Acts in other provinces, specifically reserve ownership to him, so long as certain requirements are met. In Ontario, for example, these requirements are:

1. The conditional sales contract must be in writing and signed by the buyer. (The buyer must be given a copy of the contract within twenty days.)

2. A copy of the agreement must be registered in the provincial registry office. This must be done within a specified time limit. (Late registrations are permitted, if a valid reason exists.)

A person who buys a secondhand good can protect himself from buying goods that the seller does not really own by: checking with the Personal Property Security Registry; or asking the seller for evidence of ownership—for example, a receipt from the original seller, which can then be checked under the Act.

Summary of Rights and Duties

The following is a summary of the rights and duties of the buyer and seller in a conditional sale.

The Buyer.   As long as the buyer keeps up the payments, he or she has the right to full use of the goods. At the same time, reasonable care must be taken of them. Certainly, the buyer must not part with them (for example, by giving them away, selling, or pawning them) or convert them into any other form (for example, furniture into firewood). A buyer who does can be guilty not only of breach of contract but also of the criminal offence of fraudulent conversion—a type of theft.

Once he has made all the payments, the buyer becomes the owner of the goods and can then do as he likes with them. Also, he is entitled to obtain a release or discharge from the seller as well as the return of his promissory note. On request, the seller will cancel any registrations made against the buyer. Or the buyer can do this by showing the discharged contract at the registry office.

The Seller.   Until all the payments are made, the seller remains the owner of the goods. If the payments are not kept up, the seller has the right to repossess the goods and to retain all money so far received. He or she may not use force to take back his goods. However, even if they have been attached to a building (for example, air conditioning equipment) and thus become fixtures, the seller may remove them so long as he or she repairs any damage.

BILL OF SALE

A bill of sale is a formal document (always witnessed, and often under seal) issued by a seller that serves as official proof that a good has been sold and that right of ownership has passed from the seller to the buyer. It is quite different from the sales slip that is normally issued when a sale is made.

The reason for the requirement of a bill of sale is that if a person buys a good but cannot immediately take it away with him (for example, a couple buying used furniture from a household that is moving away, and not having a place to store the furniture immediately), he is exposed to a risk. This risk is that the seller, although no longer the true owner of the goods, has what is termed "apparent ownership." If he should sell the goods once more, this time to an innocent third party (one who is unaware of the previous sale), this second buyer would then obtain title to the goods. The first buyer could then only sue the seller for damages and have him charged with fraudulent conversion—a criminal offence.

To prevent a buyer from being exposed to this type of situation, each province provides for protection and notification to third parties by registration. However, for the non-possessing buyer (the true owner) to receive protection, various requirements must be met:

1. The bill of sale must be in writing and signed by the seller.
2. A copy of the bill of sale must be registered in the local registry within a limited number of days.

The protection afforded by registration, if these requirements are met, is that the buyer remains the true owner of the goods he purchased but did not take immediate possession of even though the seller resells them to a genuinely innocent third party. Such a party must return the goods to the true owner (the first buyer) and must sue the apparent owner (the seller) for damages for breach of the implied condition that he had the right to sell the goods.

CHATTEL MORTGAGE

A chattel mortgage is a document that a borrower (the mortgagor) gives to a lender (the mortgagee), by which ownership of goods offered by the borrower as security for repayment of the loan is temporarily transferred to the lender. Examples of goods that are often bought subject to a chattel mortgage are cars, major household appliances, furniture, and boats. Frequently, the chattel mortgage is extended to cover practically all of the debtor's moveable personal assets. Once the loan is fully repaid, ownership of the goods reverts to the former borrower. Although, during the period of the loan, ownership is with the lender, the borrower keeps the goods, can use them, and is, to anyone else, their apparent owner.

Basically, the provisions of a chattel mortgage are similar to those of the conditional sales contract—namely, the debtor's agreement to make regular, periodical payments; and the creditor's right, in the event of non-payment, to take the goods (but without force), re-sell them, retain any payments so far made, and if necessary sue the debtor for any shortage.

Registration in Provinces without a Personal Property Security Act. To protect the lender from the risk that the borrower may sell or otherwise dispose of the mortgaged goods to an unsuspecting third party, the provincial governments require that all mortgages be registered. Once this is done, the lender is protected from loss of ownership because of a borrower's sale to an innocent third party. However, the lender retains his rights against the borrower on the basis of the chattel mortgage, whether it is registered or not.

Assignment. One of the rights of a lender is to make over (or assign) a mortgage that he has received to another party without the borrower's consent. Thus the lender who wishes to receive the money earlier can sell the mortgage to a finance company or other financial institution. The borrower, similarly, has the right to assign the mortgaged goods. However, to remove the goods from the borrower's premises requires the lender's consent. Although the third party buying the mortgaged goods assumes the mortgage liability, the original borrower (the mortgagor) also still remains liable to the mortgagee under his personal covenant, or direct promise to the lender to repay the loan.

In provinces where an Act similar to Ontario's Personal Property Security Act is in effect, the seller's title or right of ownership is only protected by registration or possession.

BULK SALE

The term bulk sale refers to several possible situations: where a business sells part or all of its inventory other than in the normal course of its operations; where a retail firm sells its fixtures; where a manufacturing firm sells its machinery and equipment; and where a firm sells a major interest in its business (other than the sale by a partner of his share of a business).

Most provinces now have a Bulk Sales Act that governs transactions of this sort. The main purpose of the Acts is to protect unsecured creditors who might otherwise find that the business owners who owe them money have sold their goods, fixtures, equipment, or even the complete business, at unreasonably low prices and disappeared with the proceeds. The Acts provide that unless the creditors of a business are paid in full within a specified number of months of such a bulk sale, the sale may be annulled by the court on grounds of fraud.

A prospective buyer in a bulk sale transaction is faced with the risk that he or she may eventually have to pay the creditors as well as the present vendor, or alternatively, be forced to surrender the goods to the creditors. To avoid this situation, the prospective buyer should, in accordance with the provincial Bulk Sales Act, obtain from the seller a sworn list of all the seller's secured and unsecured creditors with the amounts owed. The prospective buyer can safely go ahead with the purchase if: the seller swears by affidavit that all his creditors have now been paid in fully; or the seller has made adequate provision to pay his creditors in full immediately after the sale; or all the creditors agree in writing to waive their rights; or in Ontario, if the statement of indebtedness shows that no more than $2,500 is owed to all the seller's unsecured creditors, that no more than the same amount is owed to all his secured creditors, and the buyer is unaware, from his own sources of information, of any larger amounts owing.

In some provinces, a buyer may make a deposit on the purchase price of the goods without observing the foregoing requirements. However, the amount is quite limited—10% in Ontario and 5% or less in other provinces. In Ontario, a buyer under a bulk sale must file an affidavit in the District Court within five days of the transaction, providing full details. In Ontario and Newfoundland a buyer may safely pay the full amount to the seller if the buyer first obtains a court order from a judge who believes that the sale is in the creditors' best interests.

THE REGISTRATION SYSTEM

We have seen that a conditional sales agreement allows the seller, by the registration of this document, to protect its interest against the whole world unless the secured item falls into the hands of an innkeeper.

The Bills of Sale Act protects the actual owner by registration even where the goods are in the possession of another party. The chattel mortgage provisions protect the lender who has granted credit on the security of an item or items retained in the possession of the borrower. The Sale of Book Debts Act ensures the bona fides of the transactions, in the interests of the creditors of the seller by specifying the registration of certain documentation. Finally, the Bulk Sales Act protects the creditors of the seller also by requiring certain formalities preceding the sale.

All of the foregoing require documents recording the transactions in question to be entered in the respective registers kept at the Provincial Court Registry or Personal Property Securities Act registry within certain prescribed time limits and accompanied by the prescribed supporting affidavits.

Any buyer of a secondhand item in Canada should, in theory, search the appropriate register for evidence of outstanding claims on goods being offered for sale.

However, the main weakness of the present registration system is that it is expensive; that is, a copy of the conditional sales agreement must itself be registered in a central location, which may involve transportation costs. It is complicated, because the documentation and affidavits required are not entirely suited to today's highly mobile way of life, since an item against which there is a registered claim may be offered for sale far away from the original place of registration.

It should also be noted that a security lien registered against a dealer, who is selling in the course of his business, does not affect the title of a bona fide purchaser who is buying as a customer.

In 1967, Ontario passed the Personal Property Securities Act, which replaced the previous system of registration for all security in chattels. This new Act has copied Article 9 of the United States Uniform Commercial Code which provides, generally, that security interest in goods may be "perfected" (meaning full protected) either by taking possession of the chattel itself or by registration. The Ontario legislation provides for a computerized province-wide registration system, and is now fully operative.

PERSONAL PROPERTY SECURITY ACT

Ontario, as well as most other provinces, now have a Personal Property Security Act that governs all credit contracts (called "security agreements") such as conditional sales contracts, chattel mortgages, hire-purchase agreements, and leases intended as securities. These agreements may continue to be used and the seller's claim is said to be *perfected* (protected) either by actual possession of the chattel or by registration under the Act. Under the Act, a debtor must sign the security agreement and be given a copy within ten days. Also, such contracts must be registered within thirty days at the local Registration Office if the creditor is to be protected against the sale of the goods to third parties. The registration of a chattel mortgage must be renewed every three years. The seller, under a conditional sales agreement, of manufactured goods with his or her name on them, or household goods, must also register his agreement to enjoy protection against third parties. The debtor who has fully paid the amount owing has the right to demand a Certificate of Discharge from the creditor. The creditor must supply this within ten days or face a penalty.

An unsatisfied creditor, under the Act, has the right to:

1. enter the debtor's premises and render the goods unusuable;
2. take possession of the goods by lawful means if more than one-third of the price is still owing;
3. dispose of the goods by any reasonable means, after giving the debtor fifteen days' notice (however, any surplus must be given to the other creditors, if any, and what is left to the debtor);
4. retain the goods, so long as he or she notifies the debtor and all other interested parties, and receives no objections within fifteen days.

At any time before the goods are disposed of, the debtor or any other interested party may redeem the item by paying the debt in full.

CORPORATE FINANCING

Corporations have different methods of financing their business undertakings. The most common method of raising capital is to sell common shares under the capitalization authorized for the corporation. If the certificate or other document of incorporation so provides, funds may also be raised by the sale of preferred shares. None of the foregoing is really secured, except that the preferred shares must be redeemed before the common shareholders may share in the net proceeds on dissolution.

A corporation may also raise money by issuing certificates of indebtedness called *bonds.* If repayment of the loan is secured by specific items of real estate, the bonds are known as *corporate mortgage bonds,* and the bondholders have a prior claim over other creditors on these assets. However, it is quite common for a bond issue to be secured by a *floating charge* on all the assets of the corporation including raw materials, inventory, equipment, land, buildings, in which case the bond is known as a *debenture.*

The issue of bonds must be made in accordance with the regulations of the Provincial Securities Commission (Ontario) or equivalent provincial laws. And the assets which are used as security must be identified and registered publicly. The financial statements must indicate the indebtedness of the company to its bondholders who rank as secured creditors in the event of the corporation's insolvency.

SECTION 178 OF THE BANK ACT

Should a corporation intend to borrow money from a bank under the provisions of s. 178 of the Bank Act as well as issue a bond, the trust deed for the bond must contain a provision specifying that the bank will have a prior claim to any bondholder on the corporation's assets.

The banks' practice of lending money to processors of raw materials, and to the farming, mining, and fishing industries, has long been a feature of the Canadian economy. The idea behind this type of secured loan which is also termed a floating charge is to enable the borrower to have sufficient working capital to finance his operations until the goods are sold and the revenue received. This type of loan not only covers the direct cost of making the product but also any incidental equipment such as industrial machinery, farm equipment, boats, or trucks. The security is the raw materials, crop, or other products, and the equipment needed to grow or process the same.

With such a loan, the borrower does not surrender his or her title, nor possession of the secured goods. However, s. 178 requires the holder/borrower to take care of the goods, account for the proceeds, and incur no further claims. It also contains a special provision entitling the bank to take possession of the goods in the event of the borrower's failure to repay the loan. Section 178 also prevents an innocent purchaser or creditor from obtaining a prior claim, by ensuring that such party has prior notice of the bank's claim by requiring the bank to file a statement of such claim in the nearest office of the Bank of Canada.

The following are additional forms of security which may be requested by a bank or other financial lending institution:

1. Assignment of a warehouse receipt or order bill of lading, both evidence of ownership of goods.
2. Real estate mortgages within the limitations prescribed by banking and government regulations.
3. Chattel mortgages covering chattels and actionable claims.
4. A guarantee, such as in the case of *Royal Bank of Canada v. Hale* (1961), 30 D.L.R. (2d) 138 (B.C. S.C.), where the directors were requested to personally guarantee direct loans.
5. Assignments, such as book debts, accounts receivable, and life insurance policies.
6. Assignment of stocks and bonds. One of the most popular forms of security offered by individual borrowers is Canada Savings Bonds.
7. Court decisions have also held that a bank may apply against the customer's indebtedness any bank drafts held for collection, as well as any credit in the customer's various general bank accounts.

Index of Cases

Federal Statutes

Provincial Statutes

Subject Index